FREUD

FREUD

IN HIS TIME AND OURS

Élisabeth Roudinesco

Translated by Catherine Porter

HARVARD UNIVERSITY PRESS

CAMBRIDGE, MASSACHUSETTS • LONDON, ENGLAND • 2016

First printing

First published as *Sigmund Freud en son temps et dans le nôtre*
© Editions du Seuil, 2014

Library of Congress Cataloging-in-Publication Data

Names: Roudinesco, Elisabeth, 1944– author. | Porter, Catherine,
 1941– translator.
Title: Freud in his time and ours / Élisabeth Roudinesco ;
 translated by Catherine Porter.
Other titles: Sigmund Freud en son temps et dans le nôtre.
 English
Description: Cambridge, Massachusetts : Harvard University
 Press, 2016. | "First published as Sigmund Freud en son temps et
 dans le nôtre"—Title page verso. | Includes bibliographical
 references and index.
Identifiers: LCCN 2016013065 | ISBN 9780674659568 (alk. paper)
Subjects: LCSH: Freud, Sigmund, 1856–1939. | Psychoanalysts—
 Austria—Biography. | Psychoanalysis—History. | Austria—
 History—19th century. | Austria—History—20th century.
Classification: LCC BF109.F74 R6813 | DDC 150.19/52092 [B]—dc23
 LC record available at https://lccn.loc.gov/2016013065

The secret of a human being is not his Oedipus complex. . . . It is the very limit of his freedom, his ability to resist torture and death.

Jean-Paul Sartre

Contents

Translator's Note

Wherever possible, I relied on published English-language translations of the works cited in this volume; translations of quoted material not otherwise attributed are my own. In addition to the conventional list of works cited, the author's account of the sources on which she drew and a history of French translations of Freud's work are included at the end of this volume in the bibliographical essay "Freud in French."

With the author's consent and assistance, I occasionally provided supplementary information in the text or the notes to make references more accessible to English-speaking readers. I owe many thanks to Élisabeth Roudinesco for her prompt and generous responses to my questions; to my colleague Susan Tarrow for her help with library research; and to my first and best reader, Philip Lewis, for his insights and contributions.

FREUD

Introduction

A MAN IS NOT REALLY dead, Jorge Luis Borges said, until the last man who knew him has also died. This is the case for Sigmund Freud today, although there are still a few rare individuals who may have encountered him when they were children. Freud spent his life writing, however, and even if he once destroyed some working documents and letters so as to complicate the task of his future biographers, he was so passionate about traces, archaeology, and memory that what was lost hardly matters in the face of what has been preserved. Despite the losses, the historian is confronted with an overabundance of archives, and consequently with a plurality of interpretations.

In addition to some twenty volumes and more than three hundred articles, Freud left a significant quantity of notes, drafts, diaries, dedications, and annotations in the immense library that is now housed in the Freud Museum in London. He wrote about twenty thousand letters, it seems, of which half are extant.[1] Most of these have now been published in English and/or French; others are being prepared for publication in German. To these must be added the rich collection of talks and interviews gathered in the 1950s by Kurt Robert Eissler, a psychoanalyst who emigrated from Vienna to New York, as well as texts concerning 170 patients, texts that have been identified but for the most part are very little known.

Translated into some fifty languages, Freud's works came into the public domain in 2010. His archives too are now largely accessible in the manuscript department of the Library of Congress (LoC) in Washington, DC, after thirty years of polemics and fierce battles.[2] Various documents can also be consulted in the Freud Museum in Vienna.

Several dozen biographies have been written about Freud, from the first one published during his lifetime (1934) by his disciple Fritz Wittels, who had become an American, to Peter Gay's, published in 1988. In between, there was the monumental three-volume edifice by Ernest Jones (1953–1957), contested by Henri F. Ellenberger in 1970 and by the more recent studies in scholarly historiography with which I associate my own work. The historiographic effort made by Emilio Rodrigué (1996) must also be mentioned: Freud's first Latin American biographer had the audacity to invent a mad Freud closer to one of Gabriel Garcia Márquez's characters than to a scholar from prewar Europe. Every psychoanalytic school has its own Freud—Freudians, post-Freudians, Kleinians, Lacanians, culturalists, independents—and every country, too, has created its own. Every moment of Freud's life has been discussed and every line of his work interpreted in multiple ways, to such an extent that one can draw up a Georges Perec–style list: Freud and Judaism, Freud and religion, Freud and women, Freud the clinician, Freud the family man, Freud with his cigars, Freud and neurons, Freud and dogs, Freud and Freemasons, and so on. Turning to the many practitioners of radical anti-Freudianism (or Freud-bashing), still more Freuds can be found: Freud the rapacious, Freud the organizer of a clinical gulag, the demoniacal, incestuous, lying, counterfeiting, fascist Freud. Views of Freud appear in every form of expression and narrative: caricatures, comic books, art books, portraits, drawings, photographs, classical novels, pornographic novels, detective stories, fictionalized narratives in films, documentary films, television series.

After decades of hagiography, hatred, scholarly studies, innovative interpretations, and abusive declarations, after multiple returns to his texts punctuating the history of the second half of the twentieth century, we have great difficulty knowing who Freud really was, so thoroughly have the commentaries, fantasies, legends, and rumors masked the reality of this thinker, in his time and in ours.

This is why, having spent a great deal of time with the texts and the sites of Freudian memory in my teaching, travels, and research, I have undertaken to set forth in a critical manner Freud's life, the genesis of his writings, the symbolic revolution he initiated at the dawn of the

Belle Époque, the pessimistic torments he suffered in the Golden Twenties, and the painful moments when his enterprises were destroyed by dictatorial regimes. The opening of the archives and access to the entire set of yet unmined documents made such an approach possible, and the task was encouraged by the fact that no French historian had yet ventured onto this terrain, which had long been dominated by first-rate research in English.

In this connection, I want to express thanks to the late Jacques Le Goff, who, during a long conversation, seeing my hesitation, strongly encouraged me to embark on the project and gave me precious advice on how best to observe Freud constructing his own era while he was being constructed by it.

This book, then, divided into four parts, offers the life story of an ambitious man who came from a long line of Jewish tradesmen from eastern Galicia, a man who allowed himself the luxury, throughout a long, troubled period—the unraveling of the Central European empires, the Great War, the economic crisis, the triumph of Nazism—of being, simultaneously, an enlightened conservative seeking to liberate sex the better to control it, a decipherer of enigmas, an attentive observer of the animal species, a friend of women, a stoic well versed in the classics, a "disillusionist" of the imaginary, an heir to German Romanticism, a debunker of myths regarding consciousness, but also and perhaps especially a Viennese Jew, a deconstructor of Judaism and of communitarian identities, just as attached to the tradition of the Greek tragedies (Oedipus) as to the heritage of Shakespeare's theater (Hamlet).

Even as he turned toward the most rigorous science of his day, physiology, he consumed cocaine to treat his neurasthenia, and he believed he had discovered, in 1884, its digestive benefits. He ventured into the world of the irrational and of dreams, seeing himself in the struggles between Faust and Mephisto and between Jacob and the angel; he then founded a circle of followers modeled on Plato's republic, bringing with him disciples obsessed with the quest for a revolution in consciousness. Claiming to apply his innovations to all realms of knowledge, he was mistaken about the literary innovations of his contemporaries, even though they were borrowing his models; he was ignorant of the art and painting of

his time; he adopted rather conservative ideological and political positions; but he imposed on modern subjectivity a staggering mythology of origins whose power seems more alive than ever, even as efforts to eradicate it continue. Around the edges of the story of the famous man, I have taken up, as a counterpoint, the stories of selected patients. Some led parallel lives that had nothing to do with the presentation of their "cases." Others reconstructed their own treatments as fiction. Still others, more anonymous, have been brought out of the shadows by the opening of the archives.

Freud always thought that what he was discovering in the unconscious foreshadowed what was happening to people in reality. I have chosen to reverse this proposition and show that what Freud thought he was discovering was at bottom nothing but the product of a society, a familial environment, and a political situation whose signification he interpreted masterfully so as to ascribe it to the work of the unconscious.

Here are the man and the work immersed in historical time, in the long duration of a narrative in which are intermingled small and large events, private and public life, madness, love, friendships, dialogues extended over time, exhaustion and melancholy, tragedies of death and war, and exile, and moving finally toward the kingdom of an always uncertain future, always to be reinvented.

PART ONE

The Life

Beginnings

IN THE MID-NINETEENTH CENTURY, the aspiration to self-government had caught fire among the peoples of Europe. Everywhere from east to west, at the heart of nations that were already democratic, within communities that remained archaic, and among minorities that had been integrated into the Central European empires, a new ideal of emancipation was taking hold in the public mind, illustrating the prophetic injunction formulated by Louis Antoine de Saint-Just in 1794: "Let Europe learn that you no longer want a single unhappy man on earth or any oppressor on French territory: let this example bear fruit on the earth. . . . Happiness is a new idea in Europe."[1]

The year 1848 was a turning point, inaugurating the springtime of peoples and revolutions, the springtime of liberalism and socialism, the dawn of communism. After years of wars, massacres, subjugations, and rebellions, people with different languages and customs demanded the abolition of the old monarchic regimes that had been restored in countries in which the Napoleonic epic had earlier contributed to the expansion of the ideals of 1789: "A spectre is haunting Europe—," Karl Marx and Friedrich Engels wrote in 1848, "the spectre of communism. All the powers of the old Europe have entered into a holy alliance to exorcise this spectre."[2]

While revolutions were being suppressed throughout Europe, the ideas they conveyed continued to spread in varying fashion, depending on whether they referred to the French *Lumières,* characterized by the search for an ideal universal civilization based on a political practice, or to the German *Aufklärung,* with its philosophical vocation rooted in the Reformation.[3]

However, in the mid-nineteenth century, both conceptions of Enlightenment (civilization and *Kultur*)—the first being universalist and the second more grounded in identities—fell into conflict with political regimes that sought to restore and give new forms to the old world order, which had been seriously shaken by the revolutionary springtime. Nationalism was born of this conflict.

To respond to the aspirations of the peoples of Europe and to combat the universalism of Enlightenment ideals, the rapidly expanding industrial bourgeoisie adopted the idea of nationhood as its own, so as to turn it against the opposing position. This bourgeoisie thus sought not to unify men among themselves but to serve the interests of hierarchical nations, conceived as entities distinct from one another, each construed as the sum of its particularisms. The French Enlightenment principle according to which man should be defined as a free subject, and the German ideal of culture rooted in identity, were succeeded by a doctrine obliging all human beings to belong to a community or a race: man in himself does not exist, it was said, but only *particular* men, bound to a territory, to a nation-state. Each person had an obligation to be French, Italian, or German, and so on, before being a subject under law in an abstract sense.

In this rapidly mutating European world, the Jews, too, subscribed to an ideal of emancipation. Having become full citizens in 1791, the French Jews had acquired the same rights as other citizens, on the condition that they renounce any claim of dual identity. The only thing that should count, they were advised, was access to the status of subject under the law, freed from the servitudes of religion and from the influence of their community. On these terms, they were authorized to practice the religion of their choice, in private. For the secular state, by the same token, Judaism became a religion like any other; it was no longer the religion that had been despised since the Middle Ages, no longer the religion of the chosen people that had given birth to Christianity. The idea that one could define oneself as a Jew in the sense of Jewish identity was contrary to the universal ideal of French secularism.

In Germany, the land of Luther's Reformation, the process of emancipation sought by Haskalah—the Jewish Enlightenment movement founded by Moses Mendelssohn—aimed not to integrate the Jews as full-

fledged citizens, but rather to allow them to be "Jews *and* Germans" simultaneously. Opposed to Hasidism (another component of the Enlightenment that tried to revalorize Jewish spirituality, especially in eastern Europe) the partisans of Haskalah asserted that modern Jews could live according to two positive forms of belonging, one stemming from faith, the other from the land—provided, however, that they shed the burdens of an overly constraining religious tradition.

Throughout the industrializing, German-speaking world, from northern Europe to *Mitteleuropa,* the Ashkenazi Jews had not acquired the same rights as the Jews in France. Spread among the four major provinces that had once made up the heart of the Germanic Holy Roman Empire—Galicia, Moravia, Bohemia, and Silesia—and subsequently attached to the Austro-Hungarian Empire, they in fact occupied a larger territory with uncertain boundaries (the famous *Yiddishland*), where they were grouped in communities that spoke the same language and circulated within a shifting zone encompassing Poland, Lithuania, Belorussia, Ukraine, Romania, and Hungary.

Not having access to all the professions, these Ashkenazi Jews, if they were to escape from the humiliation of being Jews, had few options; they could convert, engage in Jewish self-hatred, or seek intellectual success. The latter was often chosen in the mode of revenge: "It was a commonplace that Jews excelled at the university," William Johnston writes, "because their families exhorted them to study harder in order to overcome prejudice."[4]

The emancipated Jews of the nineteenth century thus thought they could escape from their ancestral persecution by integrating into industrial and intellectual society in various ways, depending on the country in which they lived: as full citizens in France, as individuals belonging to a community in England and later in the United States, as Jewish German subjects in the Germanic world, and as minorities in the Central European empires. Many of them modified their family names during the various migrations that affected them, producing Germanized or Frenchified versions of Polish, Russian, and Romanian names. A large number renounced circumcision or converted.

But as nationalism began to turn away from the old ideals of the springtime of peoples, these Jews were rejected, no longer for their religion but

for their "race." That is, they were identified by an invisible belonging that seemed to resist conversion and that by the same token condemned them to define themselves, like the other peoples, as originating from a nation. Such was the paradox of the birth of anti-Semitism, which took the place of the old anti-Judaism. Jews ceased to be ostracized for practicing the *other* religion—the first monotheism—but they were rejected as belonging to a race in search of a nation.

If for centuries the Europeans had had to deal only with Jews as a group—that is, as a people of pariahs who were aware of the rejection that they provoked and who conceived of their group's unity or its universality without reference to any borders—they were about to have to confront a people that, like themselves, was forced to define itself as a nation: the Jewish nation. But what is a nation without borders? What is a people without a territory? What are a nation and a people composed of subjects and individuals who are not citizens anywhere, since they originated in different nations?[5]

It was into this effervescent world, marked by the gradual urbanization and Germanization of the Habsburg Jews, that Jacob Kallamon (Kalman) Freud was born, in Tysmenitz, a village *(shtetl)* of eastern Galicia, on December 18, 1815, six months after the defeat of Napoleon's troops at Waterloo.[6] Like many Jews settled in that part of eastern Europe, henceforth part of the Habsburg Empire, Jacob's father, Schlomo Freud, born in Buczacz, was a tradesman. After the birth of her oldest son, Schlomo's wife, Peppi Hofmann-Freud, daughter of Abraham Siskind Hofmann, who traded in cloth and other staple merchandise, gave birth to two other sons—Abae and Josef—and a daughter. The name Freud was doubtless derived from the first name of Schlomo's great-grandmother, Freide.

A tradesman in wool in Breslau, Abae was unlucky with his children, a hydrocephalic, feeble-minded son and another who went mad. Decades later, Freud would reflect on his uncles and cousins during a trip to Paris in 1886. By that point a fervent admirer of Jean-Martin Charcot, he was convinced that neuroses were hereditary in origin, and did not hesitate to assert that his family was afflicted with a "neuro-pathological" flaw: "As a neurologist I am about as worried by such things as a sailor is by the sea." And he added, "These stories are very common in Jewish families."[7]

Around the middle of 1832, in Tysmenitz, when he was barely seventeen years old, Jacob married young Sally Kanner, a tradesman's daughter. According to the custom that prevailed at the time, the marriage was arranged between the two families. The couple lived initially in the Kanner family home, where Sally gave birth to two sons, Emanuel in 1833 and Philipp a year later. She had two more children who died very young.

Siskind Hofmann and Schlomo Freud got along famously. As was often the case in the extended families of the *shtetl,* governed by the law of the father and consanguine marriages, three generations lived under the same roof or in the same neighborhood. The women remained at home to bring up the children in the company of their mothers, sisters, mothers-in-law, servants, or governesses, while the men—fathers, sons, and sons-in-law—took care of business outside the home: on one side, feminine power reduced to the territory of intimacy and domestic tasks, on the other, masculine power in perpetual exile. At the heart of this familial order, where everyone occupied a well-defined place from birth to death, the relations between father-in-law and son-in-law proved as important as the relations between father and son, grandfather and grandson, or uncle and nephew. Married as an adolescent and already the father of two sons at nineteen, Jacob perpetuated that tradition. Like his father, he became accustomed to accompanying his maternal grandfather (Siskind) on his business trips to Moravia, where the Austrian policy of assimilation was more rigorous than in Galicia, and thus more oriented not only to the Germanization of the Jews, but also toward their integration into a more urban life.

The two men slept in Jewish inns, respected the ancestral rites, and in so doing bumped up against discriminatory laws, even as they discovered ways of life more modern than their own in the *shtetl*. The older man remained attached to the heritage of Hasidism, whereas Jacob, even though he remained pious and completely conversant with the sacred language, began to take an interest in the ideals of Haskalah.[8] At the age of twenty, Jacob became his grandfather's associate.

In July 1884, they carried out an administrative undertaking together through which they sought to be registered on the list of Jews "tolerated" in Freiberg. Reminding the authorities that he bought cloth in Moravia to be dyed in Galicia, and that he excelled as a trader in hemp,

honey, and suet, Siskind requested the extension of his own passport and that of his grandson. After many bureaucratic hassles, they were granted "tolerance."

Four years later, the popular revolution that upset Europe allowed the Jews of the Austro-Hungarian Empire to obtain civil and political rights. Urbanization was progressing while, under the influence of a demographic explosion, the Jewish populations of Galicia were emigrating toward the west and the south.[9] Jacob profited from that situation, which enabled him to ask to establish residency in Freiberg. Over the years, he gradually loosened the ties that still bound him to his father's Hasidic tradition, the better to pull away from the *shtetl* mentality and integrate into the new bourgeois society.

And to mark his evolution, he acquired a copy of Ludwig Philippson's translation of the Bible, the first translation from the Hebrew text into German. Published between 1838 and 1854 for use by Reformed Jews, the work respected the integrity of the Holy Scripture, but the text was accompanied by a sumptuous iconography borrowed from ancient Egypt. On the endpaper, Jacob wrote the date November 1, 1848, in this way celebrating the springtime of peoples.

Having become liberal in his thinking, even though he retained the habit of punctuating his remarks with countless anecdotes drawn from the long tradition of Jewish humor, Jacob came to neglect religious ceremonies. But he liked to celebrate Purim and Pesach as family festivals. The first commemorated the Jews' deliverance from the Persian Empire, the second their exodus from Egypt and the end of the subjugation of man by man: two celebrations of freedom that anchored Jacob's attachment to the ideals of popular rebellions.

Between 1848 and 1852, Jacob pursued his itinerant life. When Sally died, he married a certain Rebekka, daughter of a tradesman; they had no children together, but at age nineteen his oldest son married a young Jew, Maria Rokach, whose family had come from Russia. In 1855, Maria gave birth to her first child, Johann (John) Freud, a future playmate of his uncle Sigmund, who was born one year later. Next came Pauline, born November 20, 1856.[10]

Emanuel, Jacob's first son, became his father's associate, just as Jacob had been his father's and his grandfather's. As for the younger son Philipp,

he remained single and did not start a family until he had settled in Manchester, where he emigrated with his brother around 1858, when his father left Freiberg. Both of them made their fortunes in the cloth and jewelry trades. Historians have found traces of Jacob's second marriage, but Jacob never mentioned it. Had he repudiated Rebekka? There is no evidence of this. Some commentators invented a novel's worth of drama around this second wife, about whom we know virtually nothing; Sigmund Freud was unaware of her existence.[11]

The fact remains that on July 29, 1855, Jacob entered into a new marriage with a young woman, Amalia Nathanson, daughter of Jacob Nathanson, a tradesman from Odessa who had settled in Vienna. Born in Brody in 1835, Amalia was the only daughter among five children; she was of the same generation as her husband's two sons. The union was blessed according to Reform rites by Isaac Noah Mannheimer. The officiant recited the seven nuptial benedictions, and the new spouses broke a glass underfoot in memory of the destruction of the Jerusalem Temple.

Imperious, authoritarian, and probably suffering much more than her mother and grandmother had suffered from the absence of individual freedom that still limited the women of the time to being mothers and nothing else, Amalia refused to allow herself to be confined within a model for family life that was on its way to extinction. However, she lacked the means to rebel against her condition as a housewife. Slender, elegant, beautiful, vivacious, and capable of powerful physical, psychic, and moral resistance, she knew how to preserve her autonomy in a rapidly changing world. She gave her husband, who was old enough to be her father, eight children in ten years. They were three boys and five girls: Sigmund, Julius, Anna, Regine Debora (called Rosa), Maria (called Mitzi), Esther Adolfine (called Dolfi), Pauline Regine (called Paula), and Alexander. In other words, she was continually pregnant between the date of her marriage and the birth of her last son in 1866. No one knows why this woman who was so fertile had no more children after that.

On May 6, 1856, then, she gave birth to her first son, Sigmund (Sigismund), whose first name was Schlomo (Shelomoh), in honor of the patriarch of Tysmenitz. Jacob, who had noted in Hebrew in his famous Bible the date of his father's death, February 21, added that of this new Schlomo's birth; his son was "admitted into the Alliance" (circumcised) a week

later.[12] In 1891, Jacob offered his son the Bible as a birthday present, after having it rebound: "Son who is dear to me, Shelomoh. . . . I have presented it to you as a memorial and as a reminder of love from your father, who loves you with everlasting love. . . . In the capital city Vienna 29 Nisan [5]651 6 May [1]891."[13]

From the day he was born, Sigmund was a source of pride and satisfaction for Amalia. She called him "my golden Sigi," preferred to speak Yiddish to him, and favored him over her other children, convinced that he would become a great man. One day, in a bakery, she met an old woman who announced that Amalia's son was a genius. This reinforced her certainty, which Freud always found ridiculous: "Prophecies of this kind must be very common: there are so many mothers filled with happy expectations and so many old peasant-women and others of the kind who make up for the loss of their power to control things in the present world by concentrating on it in the future."[14]

Amalia got Jacob to share her conviction, and he began to admire his son, thinking that the boy would one day outshine his father. Whereas the men of the family, helped by their sons-in-law or supported by their fathers-in-law, had always seen each other as honest traders in wool and various other commodities, Jacob, who now subscribed fully to the Jewish Enlightenment, thought very early on that his son could achieve a different fate from that of his ancestors: no longer trade, but knowledge. Thus he initiated the boy into the biblical narrative as if it were a genealogical family novel, which gave the young Freud intense pleasure. Throughout his school days he continued to immerse himself in the biblical language, especially through his contact with Samuel Hammerschlag, his Hebrew professor, who also helped him finance his studies: "A spark from the same fire which animated the spirit of the great Jewish seers and prophets burned in him."[15]

Whatever he may have said on the subject, Freud thus became acquainted very early with the sacred text. Nothing appealed to him more, in his childhood, than the Egyptian saga of Moses, the adventures of Joseph and his brothers, or the multiple marriages of the hundred-year-old patriarchs, who produced numerous progeny with their wives, their concubines, or their servants. He adored Samson, Saul, David, and Jacob. In the Judaic texts, he found some of the structural features of his own family,

and he was to deduce from this later on that a large family was always a blessing even as it was also a source of worry. Happy to enjoy his fantasies and daydreams, he liked to imagine that his half brother Philipp, who lived under the same roof, was his mother's real husband, and that his father was actually his grandfather. So he manifested jealousy toward Philipp, who was unmarried, whereas he got along very well with his other half brother, Emanuel, who had married a woman of his own generation. Certain historians have imagined, without offering the slightest proof, that Philipp had really been Amalia's lover.

Attached to his seductive young mother, who loved him in an egocentric way, as a child Freud looked at her as a virile and sexually desirable woman. During one train trip between Freiberg and Leipzig, he was dazzled by her nudity, and later recounted the famous anxiety dream in which he saw her asleep, borne on her bed by human figures with birds' beaks that reminded him of the Egyptian divinities reproduced in the paternal Bible. Later on, he considered that children who had been preferred by their mothers carried with them, as adults, an unshakable optimism. Moreover, he drew from this conviction the idea that the love relations between mothers and sons were the most perfect and the most devoid of ambivalence. In reality, he was never able to elucidate the nature of his connection with his mother. For him, maternal love—and, even more, a mother's love for her son—was naturally self-evident.

With his "Nannie," he discovered another aspect of maternal love. Hired as a children's nursemaid, Resi Wittek (or Monika)[16] was elderly, ugly, and hardly desirable: just the opposite of Amalia. But she brought the boy affection and sensuality. In short, something physical that was lacking in his relation to his mother: as he wrote later, "She was my instructress in sexual matters. . . . She washed me in reddish water in which she had previously washed herself."[17] A devout Catholic, Monika spoke to Sigmund in Czech, told him stories of devils and saints, and took him into churches where the cult of Mary was celebrated. In this way he discovered the second monotheistic religion, one of the flesh, sin, confession, and guilt, with its pious images, its rosaries, its baroque iconography, and its representations of hell. When he got home, Sigmund preached and glorified the name of the Christian God. But when Anna was born, Philipp, the "bad" brother, had Monika put in prison for theft. Deprived both of

his mother, who was confined to her room after childbirth, and his nurse, Sigmund began to scream. He was absolutely convinced that Amalia had been locked away in a trunk.

In 1905, in his *Three Essays on Human Sexuality,* he asserted that nursemaids who are not very conscientious put children to sleep by caressing their genitals.[18] When they became aware of this remark, several commentators imagined later on that Monika had handled little Sigmund's penis and that this was undoubtedly the source of his passion for the study of human sexuality.[19] The idea of a Freud abused by his nursemaid thus made headway, like so many other rumors surrounding the private life of the founder of psychoanalysis.

As a child, Sigmund had Pauline and John as his playmates; they formed a trio. Thirty years later, in an essay titled "Screen Memories," he told how a thirty-eight-year-old man, whom he had cured of a phobia, had remembered a childhood incident that masked another, much more repressed memory.

In fact, in this text, Freud mobilized his own memories to illustrate his theory, and the man whose story he told was none other than himself. Three cousins, two boys and a girl, were playing in a meadow, he said, and each of the children gathered a bouquet. As the girl had collected the most flowers, the two boys, jealous, grabbed them away from her. When she complained to a country woman, who consoled her by giving her a piece of bread, the boys threw down the flowers so they could get their own share of the loaf: "In my memory the bread tastes quite delicious—and at that point the scene breaks off." Freud then explained that "taking flowers away from a girl means to deflower her."[20]

That was all it took for certain commentators, confusing unconscious fantasy with reality, to assert that Freud as a child had actually deflowered his niece with the complicity of his nephew.

The legend of a Freud who was the victim of abuse by his nurse and the rapist of his niece thus has its source, like all the other legends, in Freud's own work, which is continually reinterpreted in the light of speculations or unfounded constructions. What has been established with certainty, in contrast, is that Freud maintained relations of complicity and rivalry with the nephew who was older than he. Like all boys dealing with girls their own age, John and Sigmund sometimes treated Pauline "shock-

ingly."[21] They were inseparable, they loved each other, they attacked each other, or they argued. Comparing this childhood friendship to that of Brutus and Caesar, Freud made it the matrix of what would be his later relationships with the men around him—teachers, disciples, friends, adversaries, enemies: "My emotional life has always insisted that I should have an intimate friend and a hated enemy. I have always been able to provide myself afresh with both, and it has not infrequently happened that the ideal situation of childhood has been so completely reproduced that friend and enemy have come together in a single individual."[22]

In 1860, the Freud family moved to Leopoldstadt, a working-class suburb of Vienna inhabited by poor Jews, many of whom lived in unsanitary housing. Pregnant once again, Amalia contracted tuberculosis and had to spend several extended rest periods in the Carpathians. At that time, Jacob was still describing himself as a wool merchant. However, he was a victim of the mechanization of textile production, and he never managed to become a prosperous tradesman. With the help of his sons from his first marriage, he nevertheless succeeded in ensuring a decent life for his numerous offspring.

After having been the embodiment of strong paternal authority, Jacob now came across as a weak, humiliated man. Thus he cultivated with more intensity than ever the dream that his son would know a destiny more glorious than his own, but that he would nevertheless not forget to honor what his father had once been: "My Sigmund's little toe is cleverer than my head, but he would never dare to contradict me!"[23] Schlomo-Sigismund was the first of the long line of Freuds, out of the *shtetl* of eastern Europe, to become something other than a tradesman.[24]

Freud's identification with conquering figures—Hannibal, Alexander, Napoleon—dates from this period: first victors, then vanquished, but each always ready to avenge his father or surpass him. As evidence, there is the memory of a scene from childhood during which Sigmund had heard his father relate an old anecdote intended to convince him that the present was better than the past. One time, Jacob had told him, "a Christian came up to me and with a single blow knocked off my cap into the mud and shouted: 'Jew! get off the pavement!'" And when the boy asked what his father had done, Jacob replied, "I went into the roadway and picked up my cap."[25]

The young Sigmund countered this scene, which he disliked, with another more in keeping with his aspirations: the historic scene in which Hamilcar had made his son Hannibal swear that he would take vengeance against the Romans and that he would defend Carthage to the death.[26]

Thus the young man's imagination spawned a concern for restoring the memory of a patriarchal presence that was continually breaking down before his eyes. The anecdote of the cap accounted in effect not only for the story of a paternal weakness in the face of anti-Semitism, but also for the itinerary of a son who had very early on given himself the mission of symbolically revalidating the law of the father by an act of Hannibalian rebellion. Not only was it necessary to surpass the father, but it was also necessary for the son to change his culture without ever betraying the Jewish identity of his ancestors. By tracing out his destiny in this way, Freud reconnected with the story of the sons of the Jewish bourgeois tradesmen of the Austro-Hungarian Empire, obliged to de-Judaize themselves in order to become intellectuals or scholars. To exist as Jews, they had to adopt Greek, Latin, and German cultures.

Ernst Simon, an Israeli philosopher born in Berlin, asserted in 1980 that Freud had prepared for his bar mitzvah and had gone through the ceremony when he was thirteen. In support of this claim, he brought up something Freud himself had said. Freud related that one day, when he was fourteen, he had received as a gift the works of the German Jewish writer Ludwig Börne, an admirer of the French Revolution and an heir of the Enlightenment. Freud had reverently preserved these books as the only ones left from his youth. And Simon deduced from this that they had been offered on his thirteenth birthday, and that it was thus a gift offered on the occasion of his bar mitzvah. This interpretation is doubtless seductive, but there is no proof that the ceremony actually took place. In contrast, it is certain that Freud admired this writer, from whom he retained the following: "A shameful and cowardly fear of thinking holds every one of us back. More repressive than any governmental censorship is the censorship which public opinion exercises over the works of our intellect."[27]

During the summer of 1865, Josef Freud, Jacob's brother, was arrested for possession of counterfeit bank notes. A few months later he was condemned to ten years in prison. "My father, whose hair turned grey from

grief in a few days, used always to say that Uncle Josef was not a bad man but only a simpleton."[28] Nothing allows us to say, as certain commentators have done, that this affair was hidden from young Sigmund to the point of provoking a major existential "catastrophe" in his subjective experience as an adult.[29] In fact, Freud was sensitive to this further humiliation of his father, and he later recalled in that context that the uncle-nephew relationship had been a source of both hatred and friendship in his own childhood.

At age thirteen, Freud made friends with Eduard Silberstein, the son of a Romanian Jewish banker who had settled in Iasi, then in Braila on the Danube.[30] Brought up by a half-mad father and subjected to religious orthodoxy, Eduard aspired to free thought; that was how he became the fellow student and friend of Jacob's son at the Realgymnasium of Vienna and then at the Obergymnasium.

Bonds between the two boys' families developed over time. Anna Silberstein and Amalia Freud met at the thermal spa in Roznau to sample the baths and talk over their domestic problems, while the two boys, passionate about literature, played at being heroes of novels. The better to feed their daydreams, they founded an "Academia castellana," in homage to their favorite writer, Cervantes. At the heart of this band, of which they were the only members, their intellectual pleasures stemmed from their liberal use of speech accessible only to initiates. They exchanged missives in German and Spanish, larding both languages with words that functioned as codes. And to mark their veneration for the picaresque novel, they each took a name borrowed from the famous "Colloquy of the Dogs" in *The Exemplary Novels of Cervantes*.

In this story, Cervantes features the dog Berganza, an inveterate narrator, and the dog Scipio, a bitter, cynical philosopher, both sons of the sorceress Montiela, to whom they owe their astonishing ability to wax eloquent on the vagaries of the human soul. Through their colloquy, the writer engaged in a ferocious critique of the human perversions and injustices of his day.

It is hardly astonishing that Freud chose to call himself Scipio, asserting his own faith in the inability of human beings to control their passions. And yet, he said, "a thinking man" is the only one who can decide in these matters: "[He] is his own legislator, his confessor, and absolver."[31]

Imbued very early with such a conception of human freedom, when he reached the age of adolescence Freud had an ambivalent attitude toward his own sexuality. On the one hand, he suffered from the frustrations imposed by the society in which he lived, viewing them as the cause of the darkest subjective torments; on the other hand, he regarded the display of drives as a source of destruction. This ambivalence was doubtless a factor in his pronounced obsession with mastering disorders of the ego. Preferring unassuaged desire to bodily pleasures, he did not hesitate to recall a childhood scene during which he had urinated in his parents' bedroom, in their presence: "The boy will come to nothing," Jacob had said. Stung by this paternal pronouncement, for years afterward Freud kept count of all his intellectual successes, in order to prove to himself that he would never be a good-for-nothing.[32] A Jew without God, an emancipated puritan capable of controlling his impulses and of criticizing the damaging effects of puritanism, Freud provided a portrait of himself as a well-governed rebel, fascinated from childhood on by the mysteries and extravagances of human sexuality. He always defined himself as an "old-style liberal," drawing nourishment from the *Neue Freie Presse,* the principal daily newspaper of the Austro-Hungarian Empire,[33] founded in 1864; its collaborators included prominent Viennese intellectuals such as Hugo von Hofmannsthal, Stefan Zweig, Arthur Schnitzler, and Theodor Herzl.

During the summer of 1871, accompanied by Eduard, Freud spent some time in Freiberg in the family of Ignaz Fluss, a trader in textiles and a long-time friend of Jacob Freud. Made uneasy by Ignaz's twelve-year-old daughter Gisela, the sister of his comrade Emil Fluss, Sigmund gave her the name "Ichthyosaurus," and called himself "Prince of Lias and Lord of the Cretacian," alluding to a poem by Viktor von Scheffel on the end of the Saurians, animals who rebelled against the order of the world but were powerless to prevent the final catastrophe.

The following year, Freud saw Gisela again. Feigning indifference, he let her return to her boarding school and then began to wander in the forests of his childhood, imagining what his life might have been like if his parents had not left Freiberg and if, instead of taking on his new Viennese destiny, he had agreed to take up his father's business, marrying— at the same age as his father—a girl from his own milieu.

And, the better to put an end to the prehistoric era of impossible love between Saurians (the Lord of the Cretacian and Ichthyosaurus), he explained to Eduard that the true object of his desire was not Gisela but Eleonora, the girl's mother: "It would seem that I have transferred my esteem for the mother to friendship for the daughter. I am, or consider myself to be, a keen observer; my life in a large family circle, in which so many characters develop, has sharpened my eye, and I am full of admiration for this woman whom none of her children can fully match."[34]

Eleonora Fluss possessed qualities that Amalia lacked. Modern, liberal, cultivated, she had freed herself from the spirit of the ghetto. As for her husband, unlike Jacob Freud, Ignaz Fluss had proved able to surmount the crisis that had struck the textile industry. Having preserved his fortune, he had not left Freiberg for Vienna, a city Freud detested, for he loved nature—flowers, mushrooms, forests, animals, and life in the open air. On the occasion of this return to his birthplace, the young Freud thus created for himself a dual "family romance." While he imagined what his life could have been like if he had made his career in the textile business, he also aspired to a different set of parents, with a father exactly like Ignaz and a mother like Eleonora. That allowed him, of course, to sublimate his attraction to Gisela: it was one way to take his distance from his father, who had not been obliged, at Sigmund's age, to rein in his sexuality.

An anecdote shows to what extent the young Freud was capable of inventing a family romance that conformed to his desires while also passing harsh judgment on families that broke the rules of appropriate bourgeois behavior. And of course he believed that at the heart of this system Jewish families had the duty of being more exemplary than others. Thus he was horrified, in September 1872, to discover the banal crudeness of a couple of relatives on the train ride back from Freiberg to Vienna: "He was made of the stuff of which destiny makes scoundrels, when the time comes: crafty, dishonest, maintained by his devoted family in the conviction of being a man of talent, but without principles and without a conception of the world. A woman from Bohemia, a cook, the owner of the most perfect bulldog face I have ever seen, stitched over all that. I had had enough of that riffraff. During the conversation, I learned that the Jewish lady and all her family were from Meseritsch; that is just the dung-heap that suits that sort of product."[35] And, a few lines later, sensitive to

the suffering of neurotic mothers, he related to Emil Fluss his encounter, in the same train, with "a nervous, excited, trembling woman, accompanied by a twelve-year-old girl with a face like an angel." He hadn't stopped looking at her throughout the entire trip: "So I arrived in Vienna. Once again, I saw the nervous mother and the blond child, and I promised myself that I would note where, in the Viennese crowds, I shall meet them again. Thus ends my little novel."[36]

Educated in a liberal manner, within an endogamous family system still marked by the tradition of arranged marriages, Freud had a happy childhood, between a father who could have been his grandfather, a mother who could have married his half brother, and nephews who were his own age. If his five sisters worshipped their brother, they also judged him tyrannical. He supervised their reading; he could not tolerate the sound of the piano, which disturbed him in his own cherished studies; and he found it normal that they were relegated to a common bedroom lit by candles, while he had a room to himself and the enjoyment of an oil lamp.

Like most of the women of their generation, Freud's sisters were destined only to become wives, mothers, or domestic servants. They received no intellectual training that might have allowed them to escape from their condition. Only Anna pursued further studies, training to become a schoolteacher. When she was about sixteen, she was courted by an old uncle of the Nathanson family who had set out to seek a new wife and claimed he would take her to Odessa. Horrified by the idea of a consanguineous union between an adolescent and an old man, Freud opposed it vigorously.[37] Anna later had the opportunity to make an excellent marriage with Eli Bernays, Freud's future brother-in-law, then to emigrate to the United States, where her five children led prosperous lives.[38]

Rosa, Freud's favorite sister, as neurotic as he, married a lawyer, Heinrich Graf, who died not long afterward. Her son Hermann lost his life during the First World War, and her daughter Cäcilie (Mausi) committed suicide in 1922 after having been abandoned by her lover during pregnancy.[39] Maria married a distant cousin from Bucharest, Moritz Freud, with whom she had five children:[40] among them one was stillborn and two others met with violent deaths (a suicide and an accident). Married to Valentin Winternitz, Paula had a daughter, her only child, and remained

a widow after that union.[41] As for Adolfine, the youngest, she remained single and served as governess for her mother, who humiliated her in numerous ways.

At the heart of this kinship organization in which women were still deprived of all access to trades, in which cousins and close relatives married among themselves, sometimes with age differences that quickly turned wives into widows, Freud very early became an astute observer of the evolution of the bourgeois family and of the passage from an ancient model—the one embodied by his father and grandfather—to a new model: love matches based on the free choice of one's spouse.

As he observed several families close to his own, he amused himself by inventing relations between mothers, fathers, and children that were actually only transformations of the family order he himself was facing. And this is why he was so sensitive to the idea that the father was in the process of losing his original omnipotence and had to share his power henceforth with the mother.

The family order in which Freud had been immersed in his childhood and adolescence rested on three foundations: the authority of the husband, the subordination of women, and the dependency of children. By granting the mother a central place, at the price of encroaching on paternal authority, the new order also sought the means to place under control something that, in the imaginary of late nineteenth-century society, threatened to give free rein to a dangerous irruption of the feminine, that is, to the sexuality known as "hysterical" or "nervous," deemed all the more devastating in that it would no longer be subordinated to the maternal function.

To avoid this highly dreaded "anthropological disaster," which moreover had as its background an actual decline in the birth rate and fertility in the West,[42] doctors and demographers asserted that women must above all be mothers so that the social body would be capable of resisting the presumed tyranny of feminine sexual pleasure; as they saw it, liberated from its constraints, that pleasure was apt to destroy society.

If the young Freud, in the grip of carnal desire, preferred to see in each girl the shadow of her mother, to the point of falling in love with the mother, it is surely because he was fascinated by the irruption of feminine desire. Far from rejecting it or deeming it threatening to society, he

wanted to grasp its significance, explore it, describe it in words. And in the same context he adopted two apparently contradictory attitudes: one aimed at eroticizing all intrafamilial relations, even imagining transgressions and depravity that existed only in his fantasies, while the other tended, on the contrary, to rationalize the supposedly dangerous character of the sex drive and to repress it. This repression would be the condition for a true emancipation of human sexuality. This regularly recurring dialectic between an affirmation of the creative value of eroticization and the necessity of keeping it under control was to be a constant in Freud's life and in his work.

At a very young age he was attracted by the myths of ancient Greece, which allowed him later on to transpose into the clinical setting, where late nineteenth-century neuroses and neurasthenias were treated, a great origins narrative based on various forms of duality: between the Titans, primordial divinities, and the gods of Olympus, conquerors of the ancient telluric forces; between a pleasure principle and a reality principle; between the irrational and the rational, or between a destructive drive (Thanatos) and a drive toward life (Eros); and so on.

Adherence to such a dialectic already attested to the politics of friendship that characterized the Freudian psychic universe: the indispensable friend is destined to be the indispensable enemy. Always inclined toward decisive and exclusionary formulations, Freud defined himself endlessly, in relation to those around him, as a bold contradictor, always prepared to defend an extreme position and pay the price. And he attributed that ardor not only to a construction that grew out of his childhood relations with his nephew John but also to an ancestral legacy: he felt capable, he said, of sacrificing his life with the same enthusiasm that the Hebrews had demonstrated in defending their temple.

During his secondary school years, Freud had good professors and was an excellent student, at the head of his class. Nevertheless, he did not hesitate to serve as spokesperson for his classmates to protest against an unpopular teacher, or one they considered ignorant. In June 1869, several students were penalized for having gone to places "of ill repute." Freud was not among them; he seemed to be interested only in knowledge and culture. He is not known to have had any significant liaisons before his marriage, and when Marie Bonaparte, always curious about sexual

matters, asked him whether he had had sexual relations in his youth and whether, like the other young people of his generation, he had frequented brothels in Vienna, he responded by rejecting the question.[43] Freud never spoke of his sexual life before marriage, and this gave rise to a host of rumors and sweeping judgments.

At the point when Freud was preparing to enter the university, free-market liberalism seemed to be spreading rapidly in the Austro-Hungarian Empire. And yet, for several months, an extremely serious financial crisis had been in the offing. It broke out in May 1873, at the same time as a cholera epidemic, provoking a series of bankruptcies and failures that spread throughout Europe. Ruined by an economic system to which they had enthusiastically subscribed, the liberals gradually lost their illusions, while national minorities made demands that challenged the relative stability of the two-headed monarchy. The urbanized Viennese Jews were then accused of destabilizing the markets. Journalists stigmatized the Jews' alleged "machinations," and caricaturists delighted in spreading their venom in the press. Here and there drawings cropped up representing stockbrokers with hooked noses and frizzy hair.

Once again, in this context, Jews were held responsible for setting in motion a process of social transformation that was going to lead to an evolution of moral standards based on a new organization of the family. Hadn't the Jewish people, they asked, always been a wandering people without a fatherland or frontiers, an accursed people driven by an appetite for profit and always inclined to favor perverse forms of sexual commerce? Weren't they an incestuous and sodomite people by nature? Wasn't a Jew as dangerous as a homosexual, a transvestite, or a hysterical woman? Wasn't he guilty, by virtue of his supposed "femininity," of the destruction of the patriarchal family?

During that same period, Vienna had become the refuge for Jews from all over eastern Europe: Galicia, Hungary, Russia, Moldavia. Unlike Jacob Freud, they had succeeded, for the most part, in becoming integrated into the new liberal society, initially (for the first generation) as traders or bankers, then as editors, journalists, patrons, lawyers, writers, poets, scholars, philosophers, or historians. But as the crisis grew, this successful integration of the communitarian type became suspect in the eyes of the public, and aroused hatred and discrimination.[44]

The adjective "anti-Semitic" had appeared for the first time in Germany in 1860, used by an eminent Orientalist Jew from Bohemia to characterize a prejudice against those who were referred to at the time no longer as Jews but by the learned word "Semites."[45] In the face of this new form of hatred, the great emancipation movement of Haskalah, born of the Enlightenment, risked appearing henceforth as a sort of interlude. Denounced up to that point for belonging to a religion, the Jews were now stigmatized as belonging to a "race": that of the Semites. In 1879, the word left the sphere of scholarly debates among philologists to constitute, in the vocabulary of the undistinguished publicist Wilhelm Marr, the kernel of a new worldview, that of anti-Semitism.

Advocated by recently formed leagues, this vision ended up embodied in a movement that aimed to expel German Jews and send them to Palestine, and to stigmatize them as a class that was "dangerous" for the purity of the Germanic, or "Aryan," race. In a few short years, during the period leading up to the First World War, anti-Semitism spread throughout Europe in many different variants: biological, hygienist, racialist, and nationalist.

Confronted during his university years with this mutation of anti-Judaism into anti-Semitism, Freud identified increasingly with the hero of his youth: the Semitic general Hannibal. During the entire period of his studies, Freud scorned those who labeled him a "dirty Jew" or who expected him to recognize his "racial inferiority." On several occasions he did not hesitate to raise his walking stick to drive off the rabble that had peppered him with insults. In counterpoint, he cultivated the idea that by being excluded, as a Jew, from the "compact majority," he would be capable of preserving an independence of judgment that would enable him to defend himself more effectively against prejudices. Freud had very little taste for the "liturgies of the social body, the protesting choirs, the anonymous slogans chanted blindly."[46]

Thirsty for knowledge, dreaming of glory and conquest, he first imagined setting out on a political career, before deciding that he would be a philosopher, then a jurist, and finally a naturalist. He thought many times about embarking on an ocean voyage like Charles Darwin, the hero of modern science whom he admired the most because "his theories . . . held out hopes of an extraordinary advance in our understanding of the

world."[47] But he also compared himself to Christopher Columbus, the seafaring adventurer who discovered the New World. Dreaming of another identity, and always preoccupied with surpassing his father by gaining access, thanks to exceptional teachers, to a scientific culture, he began to become familiar with the philosophical debates of his time through contact with Franz Brentano, whose courses he attended.

A nephew of Clemens Brentano marked by the German Romantic school, Franz Brentano was a philosopher who would later be Edmund Husserl's teacher. In his courses in Vienna between 1874 and 1894, he set forth the principles of an empirical psychology centered on an analysis of the modalities of consciousness that would exclude all forms of subjectivity. In so doing Brentano professed to be renewing the theses of the German philosopher Johann Friedrich Herbart, who had been one of the founders of modern psychological science, in the lineage of Immanuel Kant and Johann Gottlieb Fichte. As such, Herbart had had numerous disciples in the German-speaking academic world, especially in Austria, where doctors and lay professors claimed to be perpetuating his teaching.

Anchoring his approach in a conception of the self that presupposed a relation to an alterity, a "non-self," Herbart had helped explode the classical notion of subjective identity. He advanced the idea that the human subject is divided into a series of atoms repressed at the threshold of consciousness, struggling with one another to invade consciousness. In other words, he had posited, during the first half of the nineteenth century, the principles of a so-called dynamic theory of the unconscious, where three poles entered into play: representation, drive, and repression.[48] A partisan of order and political conservatism, Herbart had been the initiator, in Germany, of a pedagogy that valued the knowledge of "experts" to the detriment of the inventive mind. Highly appreciated within the Viennese academic milieu, his work had made followers who then tried to reform the teaching of natural sciences and medicine. Even while remaining a theist and advocating the values of a reformed Catholicism, Brentano identified with Herbart's doctrine, and he took recourse to the notion of intentionality, connecting it with that of representation to designate the act through which consciousness was oriented toward an object. He also distinguished between two categories of mental acts: judgments of

affirmation and negation on the one hand, and the conjoined attitudes of hatred and love on the other.

Freud was to remember that lesson when he began to elaborate his own doctrine. But in the period we are considering, he still thought he was heading for a doctorate in philosophy. Helped by his friend and fellow student Josef Paneth,[49] he thus undertook to challenge Brentano's theism by invoking the materialism of Ludwig Feuerbach, a German philosopher who had just died and whose teaching was quite prominent in the Viennese culture of the 1870s. A critic of Hegelian thought, Feuerbach had maintained that the affirmation of transcendence led to alienation, and that, to escape from this one had to return to concrete humanity. Sensualism and a critique of religion: such were the theses that inspired the early Freud and that in fact helped, during this period, to detach him from philosophical speculation, which he deemed too abstract and above all too theological. Through Feuerbach's sensualism, Freud managed to take into account the difference between the sexes and the recognition of an alterity—an I and a thou; through the critique of alienation, he espoused the idea that religion was always an obstacle to the progress of human knowledge. The young Freud thus came to admire unreservedly this materialist philosopher whose life and thought he had discovered by reading Karl Grün's biography.

After battling Brentano—a professor he respected, who agreed to direct his thesis despite their differences—Freud gave up the idea of pursuing philosophy as a career, without betraying in the least his adherence to Feuerbach's materialism. In 1873, at age seventeen, he enrolled in the University of Vienna to begin scientific studies: anatomy, biology, zoology, physiology, and medicine. But since his fondness for denying himself pleasures freed him to gain access to what he considered essential on his own terms, he continued to let himself be seduced by speculative thought. This thought was moreover never absent from his undertakings, and after 1923 it ended up permeating all his work: "As a young man," he later said to Ernest Jones, "I felt a strong attraction to [philosophical] speculation and ruthlessly checked it."[50]

Endowed with an exceptional organization, the huge University of Vienna was growing rapidly at that point, despite serious financial difficulties. In the area of natural sciences, it stood out as one of the best in

Europe for its capacity to bring together brilliant scholars from throughout the German-speaking world who were often liberal in political terms, and in any case experienced in oratorical jousting and engaged in the most prominent controversies. They included Carl Claus, a professor of comparative anatomy and zoology who had introduced Darwinian thinking into Austria, and Ernst Wilhelm von Brücke, a physician and physiologist born in Berlin who had been formed in the great positivist and antivitalist current represented by Hermann von Helmholtz and Emil Du Bois-Reymond.

To understand the role played by the instruction Freud received in his later trajectory, especially in his development of a new materialist dynamics of the psyche, we must recall that physiology dominated the medical sciences at the end of the nineteenth century. Starting from the anatomo-clinical method according to which illness is the expression of an organic injury, the physiological approach conceived of such an injury as resulting from a functional modification of an organ.[51] But it also relied on Darwinian doctrine, from which it drew the means for speculating on the origin and evolution of living organisms as well as on the instinctive forces that subtend human activity. Thus the representatives of this doctrine were moved by a veritable crusading spirit, whose goal was to bring to the forefront, against the old Romantic medicine, the idea that the human organism was exclusively made up of physical and chemical forces.

In thirty years, and without constituting a school, the physiologists ended up being recognized as the representatives of a sort of avant-garde of medicine in the German-speaking context. They applied their model to neurology and psychology so as to unite them and detach them from speculative psychology. By the same token, they completely stopped taking subjectivity—in the philosophical sense—into account, while focusing their work on the primacy of observation. From this perspective, the problems of the soul and the psyche could only be resolved by a monist approach capable of bringing the phenomenon of consciousness into the field of physiology and thus into that of experimental science. For the young Freud, this involvement in physiology and evolutionism perpetuated an already long-standing commitment to materialist philosophy.

During the summer of 1875, he finally achieved his dream of going to Manchester to stay with his half brother. He prepared meticulously for

his trip, recited verses, wrote letters, plunged into English history and de-
clared himself to be a fanatic lover of all things English. He already aspired
"to become an Englishman." Despite the "fog, the rain, the conservatism,
and the drunkenness," he felt profoundly attracted by England, by its eco-
nomic and political system, by its literature, and by its cult of an experi-
mental science that seemed to him very far removed from the German
metaphysical tradition: "If I wished to influence a large number of people,"
he wrote to his friend Eduard, "instead of a small number of readers or
fellow scientists, England would be just the place for that purpose. A re-
spected man, supported by the press and the rich, could do wonders in
alleviating physical ills, if only he were enough of an explorer to strike
out on new therapeutic paths."[52]

Meanwhile, it was in Trieste, where Claus had founded an institute for
research on marine animals, that Freud undertook his first work in zo-
ology while discovering the Mediterranean world at the same time. Fas-
cinated by hermaphroditism, Claus had charged Freud with testing the
recent assertion of the Polish researcher Szymon Syrski, who claimed to
have discovered testicles in eels. After two stints on site and after exam-
ining four hundred specimens, Freud tried hard to confirm the hypothet-
ical "Syrski's organ," but more than anything he learned, because he
couldn't do otherwise, to comply with the requirements of experimental
science. He profited from his stay by taking an interest in the sensuality
of Italian women, whom he compared to goddesses.

Brücke, the leading figure in the Austrian school of physiology, had
succeeded in bringing together in a single program of instruction the
German tradition of laboratory research and the clinical outlook that had
emerged from Viennese hospital practices. A highly colorful character en-
dowed with a mane of red hair and a diabolical smile, this Berliner who
specialized in the physiology of the eye, digestion, and the voice was also
a lover of poetry and painting who did not hesitate to invent a "universal
script"—a pasigraphy—that he thought would eventually make it possible
to transcribe all the languages of the planet. He had a real power of seduc-
tion over his students, as much through his capacity to transmit the princi-
ples of the science of organisms as through his elitist, even tyrannical con-
ception of the university hierarchy. He appreciated talent, and promoted
the flourishing of intelligence in his disciples while helping them to

progress and to steer clear of opportunism. None of them was to be unfaithful to him. Quickly conquered, Freud viewed him as a master, admiring the penetrating gaze of his blue eyes, and especially the patriarchal authority that seemed to him immune to failure: the complete opposite of Jacob Freud.

It was in Brücke's laboratory that he met three brilliant physiologists: Sigmund Exner, Ernst von Fleischl-Marxow, and Josef Breuer. The last was already interested in "medicines of the soul," and thus on the one hand he studied mental illnesses, which were treated by psychiatry, and on the other he studied nervous illnesses, which fell under neurology.

All three men belonged to a scholarly community that had an air of nobility, in which interfamily relations, clinical exchanges, friendships, love interests, social ambitions, aesthetic tastes, and a desire to change life were all intermingled, supported by the most sophisticated anatomo-clinical science in the European world. Most of the members of this circle, whether they were rich or poor, came from the progressive liberal bourgeoisie. Accustomed to literary salons and cafés, they maintained ties with artists, writers, philologists, academics, and journalists. Some were Jews, the others weren't; some were free thinkers or Protestants or Catholics, but all were detached from the grip of a religious ideal that they judged antiscientific and obscurantist.[53]

After studying the sexuality of eels, Freud planned to go to Berlin, a city he admired, in order to enroll in the courses of Helmholtz and Du Bois-Reymond. He finally gave up that idea and pursued his work in zoology. A fervid evolutionist, through the magic of the microscope he devoted himself to the study of crayfish neurons under Brücke's direction, then to the spinal cord of one of the most primitive fish species (*Amocoetes Petromyzon*); this allowed him to move up to the central nervous system of humans. He next worked on developing a theory of the functioning of nerve cells and fibers, while continuing to follow a classical medical curriculum; he completed it with two semesters of training in Professor Carl Ludwig's chemistry lab. In short, at this time, Freud was on the verge of becoming one of the best researchers of his generation in anatomy, biology, and physiology.[54]

In March 1881, Freud completed his studies, defended his doctoral thesis, and was named to a position as assistant in his revered teacher's

Institute of Physiology. Meanwhile, he had fulfilled his year of obligatory military service, during which, to fend off boredom, he had translated the twelfth volume of the complete works of John Stuart Mill, devoted to the emancipation of women, Plato, the question of the working class, and socialism. The invitation to take on the task had come from Theodor Gomperz, who had approached Brentano; the latter had extolled the exceptional qualities of his former student. The product of a family of Jewish bankers and industrialists originally from Moravia, a polyglot, and a distinguished Hellenist, Gomperz suffered from crises of melancholia and exaltation. He conceived of culture *(Bildung)* and progress only in the form of a growing refinement in the use of languages.[55] Subsequently, Freud maintained excellent relations with the Viennese intellectual who had introduced him to the philological method, and he even served as Gomperz's wife's doctor.[56]

His qualities as a researcher notwithstanding, in the summer of 1882 Freud took Brücke's advice and decided to turn toward a career in medicine and thus to pursue his training in Vienna's General Hospital. Given his youth, he had no hope of succeeding his master as the head of the institute, since Brücke's two assistants, Exner and Fleischl-Marxow, were ahead of him.[57] In addition, lacking a personal fortune, he was already thinking about a very different future.

Thus after having manifested insatiable curiosity about the most highly developed natural sciences of his day, he learned to recognize the truth of Mephisto's admonition in Goethe's *Faust:* "No use your roaming scientifically, / Each learns what he can and only that."[58]

Loves, Tempests, Ambitions

As we have seen, Freud often asserted that his entire existence had been marked by the need to find an indispensable friend who was also an indispensable enemy. In 1899, referring to *Faust* in this regard, he pointed out that all his male friends had been incarnations of a figure from his childhood, his nephew John, "who had 'long since appeared before my troubled gaze'; they have been *revenants*."[1]

By calling on texts by Goethe on numerous occasions, Freud very early on laid claim to a status analogous to that of the prince of German letters, his favorite writer. Like Goethe, Freud admired *Weltliteratur,* universal literature, Greco-Roman civilization, the Orient, and the sensuality of primitive peoples. He liked to tell the story of the goldsmith Demetrios, who had opposed the Jews, the Christians, and the apostle Paul in 54 CE at Ephesus because the new monotheistic religion was hostile to the ancient divinities and to the trade in statuettes of the goddess Artemis: "Great is Diana of the Ephesians," the rabble-rousers would shout. And Freud, like Goethe, made the goldsmith the symbol of the artist's resistance to religious militancy, while reminding his readers that figures of the mother-goddess *(Ur Mutter)* had existed in all cults, from the primitive Oupis to the Virgin Mary.[2]

Freud saw himself as Goethe's heir. Like Goethe, he had been his mother's favorite, born "dark"[3] and promised a heroic destiny. Identifying as much with Mephisto as with Faust, very early in life he took on the mission of bringing into existence what the discourse of reason sought to mask: the dark aspect of humanity, its diabolical elements—in short, what was repressed, unknown, forbidden (sex), uncanny, irrational, the

pharmakon.[4] In addition, Freud shared with Goethe the cult of nature, an aversion to dogmatism, a passion for archaeology and for Italy, a rejection of metaphysics, and a prodigious capacity for maintaining lasting friendships and then dismantling them.

And it was in the purest tradition of *Sturm und Drang* (storm and passion)—embodied by Goethe and by his *Sorrows of Young Werther*[5]—that Freud, a twenty-six-year-old positivist, rationalist, Darwinian scholar seeking fame and adversity, specializing in the observation of marine animals, fell in love with Martha Bernays. Since the time ten years earlier when he had had strong feelings for Gisela Fluss, he had taken very little interest in young women. Suffering from inhibitions, anxiety, and neurasthenia, he periodically succumbed to somatic ailments: dizziness, fainting spells, cardiac and digestive disorders, migraines, inflammatory neuralgias, colitis. His body, which he called "our poor *Konrad*," never left him at peace. One day, he even came down with a light case of typhoid, and later had a mild form of smallpox. Under the onslaught of physical pain, this tireless worker quickly became a regular user of nicotine, first smoking cigarettes and then cigars, some twenty a day.[6] Only a man who suffered could accomplish anything, he thought, and when he was overtaken by well-being he could neither create nor think. In 1897, he declared that addictions were nothing but substitutes for masturbation: a primitive need proper to the human species that had emerged from the animal world.[7] How can we avoid recalling Darwin's famous declaration, which applies so aptly to the genesis and destiny of Freud's work: "The devil under form of Baboon is our grandfather"?[8]

Once again, we have a story of intersecting families and encounters. Born in Hamburg on July 26, 1861, Martha was the daughter of Berman Bernays, a merchant who dealt in linen and embroideries; Bernays had undergone bankruptcy and imprisonment in the wake of some bad business deals before settling in Vienna in 1869. Although they lacked wealth, the Bernays were of a higher social and intellectual rank than the Freuds. Berman's brother Jacob, Martha's uncle, was a celebrated German philologist attached to Orthodox Judaism; he had refused to convert, preferring to give up a professorial post in a Prussian university rather than betray his faith. A commentator on Aristotle's work, he had gone against the classical interpretation and brought to light the medical character of *ca-*

tharsis, which he viewed less as a purgation of the soul than as an ancestral therapy that had originated in the Hippocratic corpus and that enabled societies to reduce collective violence. The Greek tragic writers had then inherited this view. Although he never met Jacob Bernays, Freud admired this rigorous, ascetic scholar, a lover of men who had been the lover of the poet Paul Heyse, his former student.[9]

Martha was the fifth of six children, two of whom died in early childhood and a third as an adolescent. She was very attached to her brother Eli, who became the head of the family after Berman's death, and to her younger sister Minna, who did not resemble her in any respect. The three siblings lived with their mother, Emmeline, the daughter of shopkeepers and a practicing Jew; arrogant, selfish, and imbued with religious prejudices, she followed the Orthodox rite and, once married, sacrificed her hair in favor of a wig.

Engaged to Sigmund's sister Anna, Eli often visited the Freud family in the company of his mother and his sisters. One evening in April 1882, Martha made the acquaintance of the young man who was to become her husband. At the sight of this elegant young woman with delicate features and dark hair, wearing a dress with a close-fitting collar and dainty laced-up boots, Freud experienced an unfamiliar feeling; he was convinced all at once that this person, who was the complete opposite of his mother, would be the woman of his life. And so he let himself be overcome by this amorous state whose devastating effects he had always dreaded. During his long years of study, he had dreamed of nothing but science and fame, at the price of repressing his feelings.

Despite his unhealthy timidity, he worked quickly to conquer the young woman, who was being courted by others. In his desire to become the master of her affection, every day he sent her a rose accompanied by a line of Latin verse. On June 2, 1882, they became secretly engaged, and by mutual agreement decided to respect the Victorian conventions of their time, which forced them to endure a long period of prenuptial chastity. Freud had not completed his medical training and thus could not contemplate starting a family right away.[10]

In the late nineteenth century, young women from good society, subjected to an interminable period of engagement and gnawed by frustration, often fell into a hysterical neurosis that led them to specialists in

nervous illnesses. As for the young men, they frequented brothels or maintained liaisons with married women who were tired of an often monotonous conjugal existence. Freud chose abstinence, drugs, Romantic exaltation, and sublimation; all this combined to turn him into an excellent letter writer.

For years he and Martha, who lived in Wandsbek, near Hamburg, exchanged voluminous correspondence in which Freud showed himself to be by turns tyrannical, impetuous, jealous, melancholic, prolific, and capable of working out projects for daily life in minute detail, to the point of describing in advance how he saw the organization of his future household. Martha was to be his sweet princess, he declared, the one to whom countless gifts and elegant clothes would be offered. But she would also be obliged to restrict her activities to household management and the education of the children, and to turn her back on any project of emancipation. On every page Freud contradicted the theses of John Stuart Mill, despite the fact that he himself had translated a work by Mill devoted to the freedom of women.

Similarly, he contradicted himself by adopting prejudices and controlling behaviors in his private life that he had criticized in public contexts. Martha always replied rather firmly that she would not agree to be thus tyrannized, although she never managed to prevent her fiancé from manifesting his jealousy and rivalry toward the men with whom she was in regular contact—Fritz Wahle, in particular, a seductive artist who had dared to give her a kiss. Freud also forbade his dear, tender princess to manifest any familiarity with her admirers, or even to take the arm of a man when she had the pleasure of going to the skating rink. One day, he took umbrage at the fact that she had visited a childhood friend who had had intimate relations with her fiancé before their marriage. He wanted Martha to be in good health, worried about her weight and the paleness of her complexion. In a word, being in love and remaining abstinent made him unbearable, despotic, and irrational.

Convinced that he was more in love with Martha than she with him, he went so far as to reproach her for agreeing to marry him without true feelings for him. And he complained of the suffering he endured when he thought he saw evidence that she was struggling in vain to love him. In June 1884, he drew up the balance sheet of their relationship: "I forced myself upon you and you accepted me without any great affection. I know

that it has finally changed and this success which I wanted more than any-thing else, and the prolonged absence of which has been my greatest misery, gives me hope for the other successes which I still need. . . . Do you remember how . . . we were always fighting, and you would never give in to me? We were two people who diverged in every detail of life and who were yet determined to love each other, and did love each other. And then after no hard words had been exchanged between us for a long time, I had to admit to myself that you were indeed my beloved, but so seldom took my side that no one would have realized from your behavior that you were really preparing to share my life."[11]

Seeking the indispensable enemy once again, he began to detest Em-meline, Martha's mother, who felt the same way about him and who, un-like her daughter, did not view her future son-in-law as an exceptional being. She did acknowledge that he had some positive qualities: constancy, stubbornness, boldness. If Freud had once fallen in love with a girl because he admired in her the shadow of her mother, this time he set out to sepa-rate the mother from the daughter. He reproached the former for resem-bling a man and for having deprived him of the latter by leaving Vienna to live in Wandbek. Moreover, he openly made fun of the Bernays family's religious practices. He characterized the alimentary rituals and the obser-vance of *Shabbat* as obscurantist foolishness, and he instructed Martha to distance herself from them, or scoldings would ensue. Women's destiny, he said, was to leave father and mother behind in order to submit to the authority of the husband.

As Martha had charged her brother Eli with managing part of the dowry she had inherited from her uncle Jacob, Freud found a way to com-pete with his future brother-in-law; he went so far as to accuse him of dubious transactions while demanding that his fiancée break completely with her brother. In reality, Eli was the victim of blackmail on the part of a woman, doubtless a former mistress, who demanded money to bring up the child she claimed he had fathered. And he did spend the dowry intended for his sister. Indignant, Martha sided with Eli, whom Freud saw as a scoundrel. The hostilities ceased only with Eli's marriage to Anna in 1893.[12]

Just as Freud had needed an enemy in order to drag the woman he de-sired away from her surroundings, in the battle to win her love he turned to an indispensable friend: Martha's younger sister Minna. Throughout

the interminable engagement period, Minna was an accomplice and an intellectual ally capable of opposing Emmeline, especially in the arena of religion: "You don't love [your mother] very much," he wrote one day to Martha, "and are as considerate as possible to her; Minna loves her, but doesn't spare her."[13] This situation suited Freud's conception of an extended familial order, moreover. Starting in 1882, he claimed to be all the more attracted by Minna inasmuch as she was engaged to his Viennese friend Ignaz Schönberg. He found his future sister-in-law's intelligence and caustic wit charming to the highest degree. Thus he wrote her immensely tender letters in which he mentioned many confidential matters while calling her "my dear, my sister."[14] As Emmeline had not authorized Minna to become engaged to Schönberg, Freud sent Schönberg's letters to Minna by clandestine means. It was in part because of this subtle interplay between Martha, Minna, and the two friends that commentators have supposed that there was a liaison, undiscoverable in the archives, between Sigmund and his sister-in-law.[15]

Freud had become convinced that Minna resembled him and that she was as wildly passionate as he, even if, physically, she looked like her sister's twin. Consequently, he saw Schönberg—a wise and thoughtful man—as Martha's double, someone who preferred a strong, authoritarian woman to a sweet, delicate princess. And he deduced from this that the two couples would come to form a worthy quartet in which opposing temperaments would be blended harmoniously. Thus he thought he could reconstitute in his future life the ideal of conflictual fraternity to which he had been so attached from childhood on. But Schönberg, already suffering from tuberculosis, saw Minna for the last time in 1885 before meeting Freud in Baden; Freud deemed his condition hopeless. When Schönberg died, his friend was all the more stricken because, shortly before, his comrade Nathan Weiss, destined for a brilliant career as a neurologist, had hung himself in a bathhouse while returning from his honeymoon.

Composed in an often chaotic style, Freud's letters from this period attest to a real literary talent. His writerly verve enabled him to express his feelings in just a few lines; interrogating his unconscious and his drives, he used simple but well-chosen words to manifest his moods, his worries, his hesitations, and his ambivalence. Always ready to question himself and to introduce humor, in the middle of a furious torrent he could paint

a lucid and picaresque picture of himself and others, occasionally drawing portraits of immense subtlety. He sketched situations, reported anecdotes, or recounted his dreams, without ever falling either into scientistic jargon—despite the use of Latin terms—or into rose-tinted narratives. These letters offer a veritable lesson in novelistic anatomy.

But the amorous exaltation Freud manifested on numerous occasions had as one of its sources an excessive consumption of drugs. Between 1884 and 1887, while he was an assistant at the General Hospital, he showed considerable enthusiasm for the multiple properties of the plant known as coca (*Erythroxulum coca*) and the alkaloid extracted from its leaves, cocaine.[16] Known since the mid-nineteenth century for its tonic and euphoric effects, this substance had been discussed in numerous publications. Unhappy that he had been compelled to give up scientific research in favor of practicing medicine, Freud hoped to work toward a major discovery that would make him famous. Thus he threw himself into a historico-clinical study of the virtues of cocaine in the treatment of heart problems, depression, and conditions that resulted from morphine withdrawal.

From the outset, he tried cocaine experimentally on himself as a miracle cure that was supposed to allow him to combat his neurasthenia and the devastating effects of his sexual abstinence: "Woe to you, my Princess, when I come," he wrote to Martha in June 1884. "I will kiss you quite red and feed you till you are plump. And if you are froward, you shall see who is the stronger, a gentle little girl who doesn't eat enough or a big wild man *who has cocaine in his body.*"[17]

In his enthusiasm, moreover, he suggested to two of his colleagues, the ophthalmologists Carl Koller and Leopold Königstein, that they should use the analgesic properties of coca for eye surgery. And this is how Koller became the inventor of the first local anesthesia.

The cocaine episode, which led to delirious interpretations among many commentators,[18] has to be understood as an important stage in the young Freud's journey. He said one day that the study of coca had been an *allotrion*[19] for him, one that he had sought in vain to keep at a distance: a marginal but profound and essential moment. In other words, one has to acknowledge that through the use of this drug Freud confronted his "demon," his *hubris*, his excesses, the irrational part of himself that would always lead him to defy the order of reason, whether through his interest

in occult phenomena and telepathy or through his attraction to the most extravagant speculations. During this episode, he experienced the extent to which the drug can be both an evil and a remedy for evil, a diabolical tool capable of creating pathological mental states and then attempting to eradicate them. This passage by way of a drug, which lasted several years, was thus a way for him to lay the physiological approach to rest in favor of the study of psychic phenomena.

Practicing in a hospital allowed Freud to meet several prominent men of medical science and to be initiated in all the specialized fields: surgery with Theodor Billroth, dermatology with Hermann von Zeissl, ophthalmology and nervous illnesses in the clinic, psychiatry under Theodor Meynert, and finally internal medicine under Hermann Nothnagel, whom he compared to a giant Teuton out of the Germanic forests: "That man is not of our race. Blond hair and a face covered with fur, with two huge warts on his cheek and at the base of his nose."[20]

At the time, the growing influence of Viennese hospital-based medicine, linked to the profusion of patients from all over the German-speaking world, went hand in hand with an attitude particular to certain members of the medical establishment who were more interested in research, autopsies, and anatomo-pathology than in the therapeutic relationship. For them, the fascination with death took precedence over the desire to cure or to care for suffering bodies. At the time, the most advanced clinical art consisted in examining the body of a dying patient to identify the signs of an illness that only an autopsy would reveal. The young Freud faced this test when he spent all night at the bedside of a patient suffering from scurvy whom he suspected of undergoing a cerebral hemorrhage. Hour by hour he noted the progression of the symptoms and observed how a human being accomplished the passage from life to death.

Within the hospital, the mandarins showed indifference, even arrogance, toward their patients. The "therapeutic nihilism" so characteristic of the Viennese mind during the second half of the nineteenth century was flourishing. Convinced—rightly, moreover—that illnesses were part of life, these experts sought to understand and describe them rather than to cure them.[21]

Meynert, the leading practitioner of Viennese psychiatry, came directly from the tradition of anatomo-pathology that was most notably

represented by Carl von Rokitansky. Meynert was quite a colorful character, choleric and ambivalent, " 'striking enough in appearance—a huge head poised on a short body—disheveled locks that had an annoying habit of falling down over the forehead and had to be pushed back every so often.' "[22] Perhaps this way of being was not unrelated to the doctor's interest in mental confusion *(amentia)*? Taking his inspiration from the Herbartian model, he distinguished between the higher cortex, which he took to be an agency of socialization, and the lower cortex, the privileged area of the archaic. From this perspective, he assimilated the primary ego to the part of the unconscious that had genetic precedence, and the secondary ego to the instrument that controlled perception. Freud appropriated Meynert's theses in part in his *Project for a Scientific Psychology.*[23]

Meynert made his mark on the Vienna school of psychiatry with his emphatic insistence that all psychological phenomena could be traced back to an organic substratum. He developed a veritable "cerebral mythology" while maintaining a stance of therapeutic nihilism. He paid little attention to the psychiatric patients in his care, preferring to devote his time to studying the anatomy of the brain in order to come up with a "natural" classification of mental disorders.

In 1883, Freud spent five months studying under this scientist, who made a powerful impression on him. And it was while he was in Meynert's unit that he had the opportunity, for the only time in his life, to observe several dozen mentally ill individuals on whom doctors were inflicting various bodily treatments with no concern for what the patients might be saying. Freud clearly was not drawn to this form of madness (psychosis), and he shared neither Meynert's cerebral mythology nor his nihilism. Since he had abandoned research in physiology in favor of the practice of medicine, he found it necessary to take the therapeutic relationship into account. This led him to turn first toward neurology, and then toward the study of "nervous illnesses," the famous neuroses that were frequently observed in Western society and that led to personality disorders:[24] anxiety, hysteria, obsession, neurasthenia. He himself was a pure product of this cluster. In 1885, thanks to Meynert, Nothnagel, and Ernst Wilhelm von Brücke, he received the title of *privat-docent,* which allowed him to teach at the University of Vienna.

Josef Breuer, born in 1842, was the son of a rabbi, but he belonged to a generation of Viennese Jews eager to assimilate; like Freud, he too saw himself as destined for physiology.[25] Working in the laboratory of Ewald Hering, one of Brücke's rivals, Breuer began to study the problem of respiration; later, he became an assistant to the remarkable internist Johann von Oppolzer and opted for a career in medicine, focusing first on neurology and then on psychology, thus on nervous disorders. A humanistic practitioner, far removed from the therapeutic nihilism of the mandarins of the faculty of medicine, he had managed to weave a network of personal relations within the well-to-do bourgeoisie; he became the personal physician of his colleagues and numerous Viennese intellectuals, including Franz Brentano; Billroth; Rudolf Chrobak, a famous obstetrician; and Marie von Ebner-Eschenbach, with whom he carried on extensive correspondence. As Albrecht Hirschmüller writes, "Breuer's patients were not interested only in his medical skills: they found in him a personal friend, also a stimulating conversationalist and a doctor, all in one person. Breuer represented a kind of family doctor which had been prevalent in the early 19th century but which had become rare in the wake of increasing specialization towards the end of the century."[26]

Freud had met him around 1877, if not earlier, and he had taken his courses on kidney diseases while also establishing connections, as Breuer had, with Ernst von Fleischl-Marxow and Sigmund Exner. He gradually came to find steady support in this equable clinician. Once again, then, he fell under the charm of an indispensable friend, someone who could occupy the place of the older brother in his familial imaginary.

Breuer manifested great generosity toward his friends. He helped Freud financially and offered abundant enlightened advice, encouraging him, for example, to choose neurology rather than psychiatry, and to maintain the best possible relations with the Viennese bourgeoisie. Finally, having perceived Freud's immense curiosity for innovative or transgressive experiments, he pressed his younger colleague to take an interest in hypnosis, which was roundly detested by the subscribers to nihilism: they judged this technique of putting patients to sleep for therapeutic purposes unworthy of their scientific ideal. But Breuer persisted in remaining open to exploring this practice, which had developed out of the old magnetism. Brentano himself had spoken to Breuer about it very fa-

vorably after a visit with the physiologist Rudolf Heidenhain in Breslau; the latter was interested in altered states of consciousness,[27] which were thought to enable the unveiling of pathogenic secrets buried in the subconscious.

In 1880, Breuer took on the treatment of Bertha Pappenheim, a twenty-one-year-old Viennese woman from an Orthodox Jewish family who presented serious symptoms of hysteria. Freud, acquainted with Pappenheim's history, received his first patient afflicted with identical disorders four years later.

For everyone seeking to treat nervous illnesses during those years, the French school seemed to have advanced much further than the Austrian school. In the eyes of young researchers, Paris was the capital of the most highly developed knowledge in this area. Thus Freud applied for a scholarship to study under the man who was viewed throughout the Western world as the greatest specialist in hysteria: Jean-Martin Charcot, nicknamed the "Caesar" of the Salpêtrière Hospital.

Authoritarian, surprisingly handsome, occasionally slipping a hand into his black jacket so as to strike an imperial pose, often wearing a top hat, this doctor of modest origins was at the pinnacle of his career. Somber and taciturn, afflicted with a slight strabismus that contrasted with the regularity of his clean-shaven face, this character out of Hugo dreaded contact with human beings even though he appreciated society gossip. He adored animals and lived in the company of dogs and a little female monkey that attested to his interest in the circus and in unusual beings who were afflicted with neurological disorders. Known for his defense of Louis Pasteur's theses and for his fight against hunting and vivisection, this clinician of the gaze, an erudite aesthete, seemed to stand completely apart from the political battles that were tearing France apart in the second half of the nineteenth century.

Heir to Claude Bernard's experimental medicine, a symbol of the republican success of hospital-based medicine, Charcot had turned toward neurology and had described the terrible disease that bears his name in French: amyotrophic lateral sclerosis.[28] In 1870, while Prussian troops were laying siege to Paris, Charcot had decided to reform the organization of the asylum in his charge by separating the mental patients from the epileptics (those who were not mentally ill) and the hysterics. And this is

how he came to grips with the question of hysteria, which haunted the medical discourse of the day.

Familiar from time immemorial, this strange malady, which was henceforth known as neurosis,[29] had been viewed for centuries as the expression of a strictly female sexual madness of uterine origin. The convulsions and suffocations that traversed women's souls and bodies were attributed to demonic possession. The deceptive devil, it was said, entered into women's uteruses to turn them away from their anatomical destiny and prevent women from putting these organs at the service of the perpetuation of the human species.

In reality, a shift from a demonic conception of hysteria to a scientific approach had come about on the eve of the French Revolution, with Franz Anton Mesmer. Through the false theory of animal magnetism, Mesmer maintained that the nervous illnesses originated in an imbalance in the diffusion of a "universal fluid." This notion gave rise to an early form of "dynamic psychiatry,"[30] which prioritized "magnetic cures." A doctor merely had to induce a convulsive crisis in a patient—and the patients were most often women—in order to reestablish the lost fluidic equilibrium. Hysteria thus escaped religion and was regarded as an illness of the nerves that affected women deemed "simulators," that is, possessed by the demon of their sex. These were sorceresses without god or devil, viewed as all the more harmful to society in that they were suspected of transmitting a dreadful evil: syphilis. By exhibiting their sexualized bodies, it was said, they transgressed the procreative order and refused to be spouses and mothers.

Charcot criticized these theses and, during his celebrated Tuesday and Friday lessons, which were attended by doctors and intellectuals from across the political spectrum, he imparted his theory of the various aspects of the hypnotic trance: lethargy, catalepsy, clownism, somnambulism. Above all, by putting the madwomen of Salpêtrière—lower-class women in states of ecstasy and convulsion—on display, he demonstrated that their paralyses or their obscene gesticulations did not result either from demonic stimulation or from localized lesions, but rather that they originated in trauma. And he offered proof of this by causing the symptoms of the illness to disappear and then reappear. Blanche Wittmann, Augustine Gleizes, Rosalie Dubois, Justine Etchevery, and many

others who had been mistreated during their lives, raped or abused in childhood, were the heroines of these experiments conducted by a master whose somber clinical gaze approached genius. Their destiny was immortalized as much by painter André Brouillet's *Clinical Lesson at the Salpêtrière* as by the *Iconographie photographique de la Salpêtrière* produced by Désiré-Magloire Bourneville and Paul Regnard, a veritable monument honoring the visual representations of late nineteenth-century hysteria.

To prove that it was not a *mal du siècle,* a pervasive Romantic melancholy, Charcot characterized it as a functional illness of hereditary origin, and he asserted that its stigmata could be found in works of art from the past. He pointed out that the inquisitors, in their day, had condemned hysterical women for witchcraft. And, to rid hysteria of any uterine presumptions, he showed that it could also affect men, notably after trauma subsequent to railway accidents. He thus likened functional disorders (classical hysteria) to posttraumatic disorders (accidents).[31]

Charcot shared the doctrine of localization[32] with the German school, and he thought that the construction of modern medicine went hand in hand with the development of a rigorous system of classification. Without adopting nihilism as a principle, he spent very little time on curing or treating neuroses. He used hypnosis not for therapeutic purposes but to demonstrate the accuracy of his conception of hysteria. He was reproached for this by Hippolyte Bernheim, his rival from the Nancy school.

Charcot unquestionably introduced a new conception of hysteria. However, he was able to bring this about only because hysteria had become, throughout Europe, the expression of an impotent revolt on the part of women against a patriarchal power haunted by the specter of a possible feminization of the social body. In Vienna, this revolt remained confined within the circle of bourgeois families. But in Paris, the city of revolutionary uprisings, it took a turn that was all the more political in that state medicine saw itself as popular and republican.

Thus the women exhibited at Salpêtrière were unwitting successors to the sorceress figure who had been rehabilitated by Jules Michelet and of whom Arthur Rimbaud had become the bard when he celebrated, in 1872, "the hands of Jeanne-Marie," a heroine of the Commune who had been labeled a "hysterical crone" and tortured by troops from Versailles.

Brücke intervened in Freud's favor. In June 1885, Freud was given six months' leave from his functions at the hospital.[33] On October 13, still a regular user of cocaine, he moved into the Hôtel de la Paix on the Impasse rue Royer-Collard, a dead-end street in the heart of the Latin Quarter, in close proximity to the Sorbonne and the Pantheon.

He had been extremely happy at the idea of strolling through the streets of the City of Light, where the Jews had been emancipated for the first time in Europe. He went to the Père-Lachaise Cemetery to visit Heinrich Heine's tomb, and Ludwig Börne's. However, attached as he was to the ideals of the royal dynasties, he did not particularly like the revolutionary spirit. He regarded the French revolutionary epic as the expression of a sort of mental pathology after the manner of Hippolyte Taine and the late-century reactionaries obsessed by the memory of the Commune, which they designated as the equivalent of a crisis of hysteria.[34]

In adopting the discourse of the counter-Revolution and the anti-Enlightenment, which was one of the sources of modern anti-Semitism, soon to be embodied by Édouard Drumont,[35] Freud would have almost forgotten his love for Napoleon Bonaparte, the heir to Jacobinism. Always excessive, he soon passed harsh judgment on the people of Paris, found the women ugly and had very little appreciation for French gastronomy: "I have a bird's-eye view of Paris," he wrote Martha, "and I could become very poetic, I could compare it to a gigantic, dashing Sphinx that devours all the foreigners who can't solve its riddles and who knows what else? . . . Let it suffice for me to tell you that this city and its inhabitants really have nothing I find reassuring, the people seem to me to belong to another species altogether, I believe they are all possessed by a thousand demons and I hear them shout: 'To the lamp-post!' and 'Down with so-and-so!' instead of 'Sir' and 'Here is L'Écho de Paris.' I think they know neither modesty or fear; the women, like the men, rush to see nudity as they rush to see the cadavers in the Morgue or the horrible posters in the streets announcing a new novel in such-and-such a newspaper and giving a sample of its content at the same time. This is the people of psychic epidemics, historical convulsions of the masses, and it hasn't changed since Victor Hugo's *Notre-Dame de Paris*." And: "Place de la République, I saw a gigantic statue of the

Republic bearing the dates 1789, 1792, 1830, 1848, 1870. This gives an idea of the discontinuous existence of this poor Republic."[36]

If he found republican culture disagreeable, and if his puritanism sometimes made him forget his own spirit of rebellion, Freud nevertheless remained appreciative of quite diverse artistic manifestations. In Vienna, he had always enjoyed the theater and the opera, even though he stubbornly avoided cafés and other places he deemed too noisy. He went to the theater district in Paris as soon as he could to admire his favorite actress, Sarah Bernhardt, whose voice and gaze hypnotized the crowds he hated so much. Like Charcot, she transported onto the stage her era's questionings about the ambivalence of human sexuality, sometimes playing the roles of men confronting their femininity, sometimes embodying female characters inhabited by a masculine libido. In a melodrama by Victorien Sardou, which Freud described enthusiastically to Martha, Bernhardt was cast as Theodora, an accursed Roman empress dressed in sumptuous Byzantine costumes, in love with a patrician suitor who was unaware of her true identity.

Freud frequented the major cultural sites of the capital, and it was in Notre-Dame de Paris that he felt for the first time that he was in a church totally unreminiscent of those he had visited in his childhood with his Nannie. He promised himself that he would reread Hugo's novel, and he never tired of climbing onto the towers to stroll among the grimacing monsters and devils of the cathedral, even as he daydreamed of enveloping his fiancée in a fierce embrace.

He admired his master so much that, one evening at Charcot's home on the boulevard Saint-Germain when he found himself highly attracted by his host's daughter, he made a point of keeping his distance from her and remaining with "the old gentlemen." Remarking that she was ugly but made interesting by a "comic resemblance" to her father, he began once again to imagine what his life would have been like if, instead of falling in love with Martha, he had succumbed to the charms of Jeanne Charcot: "Nothing is more dangerous than a girl who has the features of a man one admires. People would make fun of me, then, I'd be chased away, and all I'd have left would be the memory of a lovely adventure. It's really better the way it is!"[37] That evening, he had absorbed a small

dose of cocaine, had had his beard trimmed and his hair cut, and he was proudly wearing his new clothes: a black suit, an impeccable shirt, a tie bought in Hamburg, and white gloves. He found himself handsome and overall was quite favorably impressed with himself.

On February 28, 1886, he left Paris for Wandsbek and from there he went to Berlin in order to follow the teachings of Adolf Aron Baginsky, a professor of pediatrics very involved with the city's Jewish community who had initiated a policy for the prevention of mental and physical ill-nesses in children. Freud presumably had opportunities in Berlin to discover what tortures and mutilations were being inflicted on children at the time in order to keep them from masturbating.[38]

Although he had little sympathy for the Hohenzollern Empire, Freud liked Berlin, a city that embodied in his eyes the quintessence of culture and science in the German-speaking world. The encounter with Berlin helped prepare him to exercise important functions in the department of neurology of the Steindlgasse, the leading public institution in Vienna for the treatment of children's diseases, headed by Max Kassowitz. In April, Freud set himself up provisionally as a doctor in private practice in Rathausstrasse and began to see patients sent by his friends. At the same time that he was finishing his translation of Charcot's work, he was dreaming of Martha, whom he was finally going to be able to marry despite his financial difficulties and the warnings of his future mother-in-law.

By virtue of cultivating abstinence and *Sturm und Drang,* sometimes in order to wallow in Romantic suffering and sometimes the better to project himself into the future, Freud never ceased to desire everything and its opposite. On the one hand, he saw himself as a patriarch living alongside a wonderful spouse devoted to household tasks and to their numerous progeny; on the other hand, he feared that once the period of engagement was over he would face the dreadful obstacle of "dangerous rivals," the household and the nursery, the husband who meets his friends in a café, the abandoned spouse, and so on.

Sigmund Freud and Martha Bernays were married in a civil ceremony at Wandsbek on September 13, 1886. Freud cherished the hope that this would suffice, and that he would not be forced to yield to the religious rituals that horrified him. But to his great disappointment he had to face reality: in Austria, their marriage would never be validated in the absence

of religious rites. He was thus compelled, the next day, to go through a ceremony at the Wandsbek synagogue conducted by Rabbi David Hanover. So he asked Elias Philipp, Martha's maternal uncle, to coach him in the Hebrew prayers and teach him how to maneuver when he passed under the canopy symbolizing the Temple. On the wedding day, very elegant and already sporting the beard of a distinguished gentleman, Freud was content to wear a frock coat and a top hat, thereby avoiding the need to wear the traditional garments.

As soon as he was settled in his new Viennese apartment on Theresienstasse, he forbade Martha to celebrate *Shabbat* or follow the rules of kosher cooking. None of his sons would be circumcised.[39] Rejecting rituals was the only way Freud could conceive of himself as a Jew in the sense of Judeity without having to deny his identity by some sort of conversion. Aware, as Spinoza had been, of his status as heir to a people that had soldered its historical unity not so much by the sacred doctrine of election as by the hatred it aroused on the part of other nations, he thus made his pride in being Jewish an intensely powerful ferment for resistance to all conformism.[40]

Martha passed from the status of feverishly desired fiancée to that of satisfied, respected, and de-eroticized spouse and mother. Between January 1887 and December 1895, she gave birth to six children: Mathilde, Martin, Oliver, Ernst, Sophie, and Anna. Freud had given the boys the first names of his favorite "heroes"—Charcot, Cromwell, Brücke—and the girls' first names were chosen from within a tightly circumscribed family circle: Mathilde, the wife of Josef Breuer; Sophie, the wife of Josef Paneth; Anna, the daughter of Samuel Hammerschlag. While Freud's daughters were thus "related" to Jewish families of the Viennese bourgeoisie that counted among their father's friends, his sons had a different, more symbolic type of designation; their names signified endogamy and the perpetuation of the home on the one hand, science, politics, and an exit from the ghetto on the other.[41]

In 1891, the family moved into quite a large apartment at 19 Berggasse. However, the following year Freud rented a second one on the ground floor where he could set up his office. Five years later, Minna came to live with them, to help her sister bring up the children and manage the household. This was a perfectly ordinary destiny in the extended families

of those days, where the place of the single woman—unmarried or widowed, daughter, aunt, cousin, sister—was defined according to strict criteria: second mother, household manager, indispensable companion.

As early as 1893, seeing that Martha was exhausted by her successive pregnancies, Freud decided to resort to abstinence once again. After a first failure that led to the birth of Anna, his last child, he refused to practice coitus interruptus or any of the various contraceptive methods used in the 1880s: condom, diaphragm, sponge. Scarcely forty years old, and suffering on occasion from impotence, he freed Martha from the perpetual fear of pregnancy by renouncing all carnal relations. She felt less anxious and he more curious to thrust himself into such an experiment, which aroused his imagination: he believed, in fact, that sublimation of sexual impulses was an art of living reserved for an elite, the only group capable of attaining a high degree of civilization.

The sex life of the greatest modern theoretician of sexuality thus presumably lasted nine years. However, up to age sixty, and even though he did not take advantage of the sexual freedom that he advocated in his doctrine, Freud had many erotic dreams, which he took particular pleasure in analyzing; moreover, he never stopped seeking "sexual" causes for all human behavior. Thus he was accused on a number of occasions of being a libidinous bourgeois, of practicing clandestine abortions, frequenting whorehouses, masturbating, and unhesitatingly concealing his sexual relations with his sister-in-law. Dozens of books, novels, and essays were published to "demonstrate" that throughout his whole life Freud had never ceased to dissimulate his sexuality, which was necessarily wild and transgressive. In reality, on several occasions Freud attempted to renew his carnal relations with Martha. But he felt old and awkward, and he finally gave up: "When I have totally overcome my libido (in the common sense), I shall undertake to write a 'Love-life of Mankind.'" And again: "My Indian summer of eroticism that we spoke of on our trip has withered lamentably under the pressure of work. I am resigned to being old and no longer even think continually of growing old."[42]

All the rumors about Freud's sex life were based on a reality reinterpreted again and again: endogamy on the one hand, the theory of substitutes on the other. Freud had been fascinated since childhood by the desire for incest, consanguineous marriages, transgressive interfamilial rela-

tions, awkward genealogies; in each girl he saw the negative or positive image of her mother or the inverted reflection of a sister, and in every governess he saw the substitute for a mother, an aunt, or a grandmother. Similarly, he viewed every son or son-in-law as the heir to a father or grandfather, or else as the accomplice of a brother.[43] And this is why he made Minna his "second spouse," his sister, his confidant at every turn—on the condition, however, that she never occupy Martha's place.

In September 1897, four months after Emperor Francis Joseph had resigned himself to validating the election of Karl Luger—an admirer of Drumont and the head of the anti-Semitic wing of the Christlichsoziale Partei (Christian Social Party)—as mayor of Vienna, Freud joined the B'nai B'rith lodge, a humanitarian Jewish association with charitable and cultural aims, before which he gave some twenty talks over time. Alongside his "brothers" by alliance, he claimed bonds with Judaism of an ethical nature, bonds that had nothing to do with any sort of "belief." Freud remained a nonbeliever, and he voted for the Liberal Party even though he associated with Social Democrats.

His encounter with Charcot had been decisive. Not only because the latter's conception of hysteria had opened up new perspectives on psychic life and the reality of human sexuality, but because that master belonged, much more than Brücke, to a line of scientists whose influence extended well beyond the confines of the academy. Known throughout the world, Charcot was first and above all a "seer" endowed with an imaginative power in perfect harmony with Freud's most extravagant dreams. Had he not gone so far, even as he was severing hysteria from any reference to an anatomical substratum, as to whisper in the ear of the young Freud, in love and convinced of his own talent, that even the most pertinent theory remained powerless in the face of a reality that contradicted it? "Theory is good; but it doesn't prevent things from existing": Freud would always remember this categorical imperative.[44]

For all the scientists of the period, in Europe and North America, the study of sexuality was the great question of the century to come, and hysteria seemed to be its key element, a focus of interest far beyond the debates among specialists. And it is undeniable that Charcot was not only a master for Freud: he was the master through whom an entire continent had been conquered, the continent of sexuality.

To be sure, the honest Breuer had led Freud along the path toward elucidation of neurotic phenomena by showing him the importance of psychic determinism in the etiology of hysteria. But as a rigorous practitioner, concerned with experimental verification, he doubted everything, constantly expressed reservations about his own hypotheses, and advised Freud to be extremely prudent. Breuer loved Freud and Freud loved Breuer. But Freud, under the influence of the love he felt for Charcot, did not know how to be prudent.

This is why, on October 15, 1886, invited to give a lecture before the prestigious Imperial Society of Doctors in Vienna, he committed the error of not producing original work, as tradition demanded; instead he served as spokesman for Charcot's theses on male hysteria and hypnosis. Convinced that the leading lights present in the room were unaware of the French master, Freud delivered a talk in proper form. He thus credited Charcot with being the first to discover that hysteria was neither a simulation nor a disorder of the uterus, forgetting that these facts were already well known in Vienna.[45] In addition, he failed to note that the quarrel between Vienna and Paris had to do with the distinction between functional and traumatic hysteria, which Charcot refused to recognize.[46]

As a result, Freud was harshly criticized by Heinrich von Bamberger, Emil Rosenthal, and especially Meynert, who was very hostile to hypnosis. Freud reacted with great bitterness and became firmly convinced, as were his hagiographers later on, that he was detested owing to his brilliant innovations as a solitary scientist. However, this was not the case.[47]

Breuer and Freud often discussed their patients and traded notes on their experiences. Both practiced the treatments that predominated at the time: electrotherapy, balneotherapy, hydrotherapy. Breuer was fond of the cathartic method, brought back into use by Jacob Bernays. It allowed patients to eliminate pathogenic affects and then to "abreact" them by reliving the traumatic elements to which they were linked. Freud eventually turned to this approach as well. In the fall of 1887, though, he turned rather to hypnotic suggestion, which was a real bone of contention not only among Viennese doctors but between the Paris and Nancy schools. By seeing himself as a "hypnotizer," Freud was seeking a way out of therapeutic nihilism through a dynamic doctor-patient relationship. Standing up to the medical experts who had criticized him for his use of cocaine

and for his praise of Charcot, he meant to play to the hilt the role of transgressive rebel that suited him so well. And, by the same token, he was distancing himself from the teachings of Salpêtrière.

A professor of internal medicine at Nancy, Bernheim had adopted the hypnotic method used by Auguste Liébault, and he treated only patients capable of entering into a hypnotic state. If, on the eve of the 1789 Revolution, the marquis Armand de Puységur had opened the way to the idea that a master—a member of the nobility, a doctor, a scientist—could be limited in the exercise of his power by a subject capable of putting up resistance, at the end of the nineteenth century Bernheim showed that hypnosis was no longer anything other than a matter of verbal suggestion. During this period, clinics focused on speech were being substituted for clinics devoted to observation, and Bernheim contributed to the dissolution of the last vestiges of magnetism by inverting the relation described by Puységur, at the price of reducing hypnosis to suggestion.

At bottom, then, Bernheim accused Charcot of artificially creating hysterical symptoms and manipulating patients—whereas the logic of the fusion between hypnosis and suggestion led Bernheim to maintain that the effects achieved by hypnosis could result from a suggestion made in the waking state, a process that would soon be designated as psychotherapy.

In the summer of 1889, accompanied by Anna von Lieben, a patient from the Jewish aristocracy of Vienna whom Charcot had already treated, Freud paid a visit to Bernheim before going back to Paris to attend two international congresses. He observed Bernheim's experiments with suggestion, had stimulating discussions with him, and undertook to translate his book.[48] Without turning his back on what he had learned from Charcot, he borrowed from Bernheim the principle of a therapy that opened the way to a talking cure. While he did not enter into the quarrel between the two schools, he very quickly noticed that suggestion worked only in certain circumstances, most particularly in a hospital setting. He preferred to use the cathartic method, although without banishing hypnosis, and this led him, moreover, to take into account the erotic element present in treatment, that is, transference.[49] In his autobiographical account, Freud recalls an illuminating experience: "It related to one of my most acquiescent patients, with whom hypnotism had enabled me to bring about the most marvellous results, and whom I was engaged in relieving

of her suffering by tracing back her attacks of pain to their origin. As she woke up on one occasion, she threw her arms round my neck. . . . I was modest enough not to attribute the event to my own irresistible personal attraction, and I felt that I had now grasped the nature of the mysterious element that was at work behind hypnotisms. In order to exclude it, or at all events to isolate it, it was necessary to abandon hypnotism."[50] After that Freud retained from hypnosis only the position of the patient lying on the sofa; he took a seat behind the patient in order to see him or her without being seen. As for Anna von Lieben, a fine chess player afflicted with madness and obesity, given to unrestrained consumption of caviar, champagne, and drugs, never sleeping at night, she was Freud's principal patient during that period, his prima donna.[51] And in her family, Freud was called *Der Zauberer* (the magician). But Freud was subsequently rejected, as he failed to cure Anna of her addiction to morphine either through hypnosis or through the cathartic method.[52]

After his marriage and his establishment as a specialist in nervous illnesses, Freud lacked an interlocutor who was far enough away to allow him to use his incomparable epistolary talents once again. The waiting period lasted a year, until the day in the fall of 1887 when, on Breuer's advice, a certain Wilhelm Fliess, a doctor from Berlin who specialized in pathologies of the nose and throat,[53] came to study with Freud while finishing his training at the General Hospital in Vienna. Of the same generation as Freud, Fliess identified as strongly as Freud did with Darwinism and with Hermann von Helmholtz's positivist school. Fliess was the son of a not very successful grain trader who tended toward depression; his Sephardic Jewish family had settled in the Margraviate of Brandenburg in the seventeenth century.

It is hard to know what Fliess really felt in this volcanic friendship that seized Freud once again. Unlike his correspondence with Martha, the correspondence between the two men could never be completely reconstituted; only Freud's letters have survived.[54] A new *Sturm und Drang!* Freud wrote very fast, multiplying abbreviations and Latin words, mixing in everything he was learning about the sexual life of his patients and that of Viennese families: fathers, mothers, sisters, daughters, servants. He classified and organized, offered numerous clinical portraits, and manifested frenetic enthusiasm over each letter received or sent.

In short, from their very first meeting, Freud fell under the charm of this doctor who did not resemble any of his Viennese friends and contemporaries, not even Breuer, who, despite his legendary prudence, admired Freud just as much as Fliess did.

Endowed with solid medical and scientific training, Fliess nevertheless belonged to the long lineage of Promethean scientists featured in Romantic literature and of whom one finds traces in the work of Thomas Mann. A subscriber to a mystical and organicist theory of sexuality, he was Freud's double, in a way, his "demon," his "other," arousing in Freud the highest intellectual excitement. By virtue of loving each other, opposing each other, taking each other as witness to the most intimate aspects of everyday life or relating case histories to each other while building up the boldest hypotheses, but also by virtue of meeting each other in various European cities during "congresses" at which they were the only listeners and the only speakers, they came to see each other as twin brothers and had their picture taken with the same beards, the same clothes, and the same look; they distributed this portrait to their friends.

In 1892, Wilhelm Fliess married Ida Bondy, one of Breuer's patients; five years later, Ida's sister Melanie married Oskar Rie, the Freud family's doctor and Sigmund's partner in tarot games. Wilhelm and his wife had a son, Robert, who became a psychoanalyst, while Oscar and Melanie had two daughters, Margarethe and Marianne. The first married Hermann Nunberg and the second Ernst Kris, both disciples of Freud. A family story, unquestionably!

Heir to a scientific approach in full mutation, where the most rational, the most innovative, and the most extravagant explanations concerning the relations between soul and body were intermingled, Fliess, who suffered from unexplained migraines, never doubted his own hypotheses, which he took for established certainties as soon as they came to mind. Passionate about art, mathematics, biology, history, literature, and archaeology, he had fallen into the habit of establishing relationships between all sorts of pathological manifestations of human life that actually had nothing to do with one another. His approach was thus all the more fascinating, in that it relied on a conception of science in which there was no room for doubt, and which was based on sometimes delirious speculations.

When he met Freud, Fliess was in the process of developing a doctrine articulated around three axes: a clinical approach to neuroses, a physiological theory of periodicity, and a biomedical and cosmological representation of human bisexuality.

Having described a clinical entity labeled "nasal reflex neurosis,"[55] Fliess found its causes sometimes in organic disturbances connected with various illnesses—including migraines—and sometimes in disorders originating in the genital organs. Thus he established a relationship between nasal mucous membranes and genital activities, and he concluded that a link existed between the nasal passages, female menstruation, pregnancy, and childbirth. Whence the idea that the symptoms of this "neurosis," just like migraines and other aftereffects of menstruation, obeyed a regular rhythm of twenty-eight days. To which Fliess added another cycle of twenty-three days, which he saw as the male equivalent of the female menstrual cycle. And as both cycles were manifested in both sexes, he deduced the existence of a fundamental bisexuality of the human being, which was translated, as he saw it, by a physiological bilaterality, each human being at once man (on the right) and woman (on the left). On the strength of this knowledge of periodicity and human bisexuality, he thought he could determine with certainty the critical dates of the cycles that predetermined birth, illness, and death.[56]

Convinced that the various troubles of his "poor *Konrad*" could thus be relieved or cured by treating the nasal cavities, Freud had Fliess—whom he compared to a "Kepler of biology"—operate on him twice. For a time, he suffered from abscesses. Fliess tried in vain to wean him from his addiction to nicotine, which increased when he stopped taking cocaine. As they were reaching the age of maturity, the two men undertook scientific calculations to determine birth and death dates using Fliess's theory.

During this period, Freud feared that he would die before he had seen Rome, his promised land, or before he had achieved his master goal: the passage from neurology to psychology. However, he continually put off traveling, invoking his famous calculations. When Ida was pregnant at almost the same time as Martha, Fliess predicted the birth of a daughter and Freud that of a boy, whom he would name Wilhelm. But fate decided differently: Fliess had a son (Robert) and Freud a daughter (Anna).

While Fliess was advancing in an increasingly irrational exploration of human bisexuality and at the same time advocating dangerous operations on the nasal cavities, Freud was constructing all sorts of hypotheses about the human psyche. In 1895, in a manuscript of roughly a hundred pages, *Project for a Scientific Psychology,* conceived as a treatise on psychology for the use of neurologists, he offered his friend a general outline of his neuropsychological approach to memory, perception, and consciousness. In it he described the characteristics of the so-called normal psychological phenomena. Unlike Fliess, Freud was constantly subject to self-doubt as he sought to make psychology a natural science far removed from the project of reducing psychic phenomena to organic disorders.

He posited a certain number of correlations between the structures of the brain and the psychic apparatus, trying to represent psychic processes as so many states quantitatively determined by material particles, or neurons. He distributed the latter among three distinct systems: perception (w neurons), memory (c neurons), and consciousness (v neurons). As for the energy transmitted (quantity), it was governed, in his view, by two principles, inertia and constancy, and its source was sometimes the external world, conveyed in that case by the sensory organs, and sometimes the internal world, that is, the body. Freud's ambition was to relate all the workings of the psyche, pathological and normal alike—desire, hallucinatory states, functions of the ego, dream mechanisms, and so on—to this neurophysiological model.

The need to "neurologize" the psychic apparatus amounted to creating a "cerebral mythology" once again. Freud quickly became aware of this, and he gave up the project in favor of constructing a purely psychic theory of the unconscious.[57] From then on, he characterized his earlier writing on the topic as delirium, babbling, or gibberish.

By virtue of his new perspective, which led him to explore unconscious phenomena, he considered that the origin of neurotic symptoms—and in particular those that characterized hysteria—lay in sexual traumas experienced in childhood. This coincided with what he had retained from Charcot's teaching. And he used the terms "seduction" and "attack" for the childhood sexual abuse experienced by his patients, who often recounted these episodes during treatment with an abundance of details, accusing a father, an uncle, or a family friend.

However this may be, between 1892 and 1895, the beautiful young Emma Eckstein was the principal victim of the clinical exchanges and the theoretical divagations in which Fliess and Freud were engaged.[58]

Born into the progressive Jewish bourgeoisie and highly involved in the Austrian feminist movement, Eckstein seems to have been a victim, as a child, of an excision deemed "therapeutic" that was intended to keep her from masturbating. For a long time she suffered from gastric problems and painful menstrual periods. Freud, who was close to her family, took her as his patient for a cathartic treatment at no charge, and went to see her in her home. He convinced himself that her pains could be associated with the nasal mucous membranes; thus he asked Fliess to make the trip to Berlin to operate on her nose. Fliess removed the anterior third of Eckstein's left middle nasal passage.

Two weeks after the operation, the young woman experienced terrible pain caused by infectious secretions of pus, which gave off a fetid odor. A piece of bone had been broken, provoking hemorrhages. Worried, Freud called on his friend Ignaz Rosanes, who, while cleaning the wound, noticed that Fliess had left a piece of iodine-soaked gauze in the nasal cavity. A heavy flow of blood ensued. Freud almost fainted, and took refuge in the room next door. After drinking a glass of cognac, he returned to the patient, who greeted him with these words: "So this is the strong sex."[59] Eckstein lived with aftereffects of this surgical intervention for the rest of her life; the necrosis of the bone in her nose was irreversible.

Seriously affected by this episode, Freud felt that he and Fliess had behaved irresponsibly toward Eckstein, although she never reproached them for their errors. But to exonerate his friend, Freud noted that Eckstein had already suffered from violent nosebleeds starting in childhood. Eckstein resumed treatment with Freud. Listening to her talk about her fear of going into shops, he deduced that this phobia stemmed from a seduction scene that had occurred when she was about eight years old: a shopkeeper had tried to fondle her. In Freud's view, the scene had been repressed, but it was the source of the symptom of which Eckstein complained.[60]

Subsequently, having put forward the hypothesis that confessions by hysterics of seductions experienced in childhood resembled confessions of sexual relations obtained in earlier times under torture by inquisitors,

Freud was astonished to see Eckstein confirming his thesis by relating a scene in which "the diabolus" had planted needles in her fingers and then put a piece of candy over each drop of blood. And once again he exonerated Fliess, who moreover still refused to recognize his error.[61]

Emma Eckstein became the first woman psychoanalyst in what became known as the Freudian school. Between 1905 and 1910, she wrote several articles and exchanged letters with Freud, who continued to be unaware of the multiple causes from which her psychic and somatic disorders stemmed. After an unhappy love affair, she attempted suicide. But neither her nephew Albert Hirst,[62] who gave Kurt Robert Eissler a poignant account, nor any doctor succeeded in curing or even understanding her.[63]

Aware of the enduring mystery, but refusing to acknowledge that he could have been mistaken so many times, Freud predicted that Eckstein would never recover. An incredible prophecy! Paralyzed by an inexplicable ailment, she spent the last years of her life lying in bed among her books.

In light of this episode, one may well wonder who invented the alleged abuses and other perverse lapses that were said to be concealed at the heart of honorable families: Freud himself, or the female patients who led him to believe in the existence of a systematic enterprise of seduction of children on the part of adults? On this topic, Breuer, who was preparing a study of hysteria with his protégé at the time, always maintained serious reservations as to the traumatic etiology.

For years, then, Freud let himself be captivated by Fliess, and the latter locked him into a conception of science in which neither error nor experience nor the search for truth had a place, given the degree to which certainty governed speculative work. One can see from his correspondence, however, that over time Freud evolved in the opposite direction from Fliess. Even as he consciously refused to cast doubt on his friend's hypotheses, he gradually moved away from them, by way of denials, ambivalence, and contortions, as if the inner work that was going on without his knowledge were leading him to doubt what he was affirming as a true scientific undertaking.

In fact, during the time of his contact with Fliess, he gave up neurology, broke finally with Breuer, invented psychoanalytic treatment, renounced

his theory of seduction, called on Greek tragedy to shore up his theory of the unconscious, and prepared the major work that was to make him one of the most important thinkers of the twentieth century, *The Interpretation of Dreams*. Like Emma Eckstein, Fliess was a primary victim of the combat Freud was waging against himself. Whereas Fliess was celebrated in his lifetime for his contributions to medical biology, he was judged harshly by posterity as a fiend for numbers, a delirious thaumaturge, the last witness to the dying medicine of the Romantic era. His work was so thoroughly forgotten that it persisted only in elucidations of the history of psychoanalysis.[64] And Freud himself always refused to be linked to the Romantic tradition.

At the dawn of the twentieth century, after so many years of shared follies, after having been united through marriages among close friends within an extended intellectual family, and against the background of the double flowering of modernity in Vienna and Berlin, the two friends separated and never saw each other again. Freud was the splendid beneficiary of their fifteen years of friendship, which culminated in a disaster for Fliess and a triumph for psychoanalysis.[65]

The break was extremely violent. In July 1900, the two men met at Lake Achen. Fliess accused Freud of showing animosity toward him, and Freud reproached Fliess for not recognizing the value of his discoveries.

Not long afterward, Freud laid out his theory of bisexuality to Hermann Swoboda, an Austrian jurist who was undergoing analysis with him. That same evening Swoboda talked about Freud's theory with his friend Otto Weininger, a well-known Viennese Jewish writer who published his only book a year later: *Sex and Character*, a veritable manifesto of bisexuality and hatred toward women and Jews.

Some time later, Weininger committed suicide. He rented a room in Beethoven's former home and shot himself in the heart.[66]

Fliess came across Weininger's book in 1904, and like Swoboda and Paul Julius Moebius,[67] he felt that he was a victim of plagiarism; he accused Freud of having stolen his ideas throughout the entire period of their friendship. The "idea theft" affair was the talk of the town, and Freud acknowledged his debt to Fliess.[68] But he also knew that, unlike plagiarism, there was no such thing as idea theft, and that the theory of bisexuality permeated all contemporary scientific work. Originating in

Darwinism and embryology, this theory reactivated in part the foundational myths of ancient Greece. To be sure, Freud felt guilty for having talked to Swoboda, but he never subscribed to the fantasy of idea theft.[69] As for bisexuality, he later made it a central concept of psychoanalytic doctrine that no longer had much in common with Fliess's representation of bilaterality.

Freud nevertheless remained haunted by the episode of a friendship that, through lengthy meanderings, had made him a different man. Without daring to admit it openly, he destroyed Fliess's letters and, when Marie Bonaparte bought his own letters from a merchant in 1936, he strenuously opposed their publication.[70]

Relying then on his own conception of paranoia, Freud explained to Sándor Ferenczi in 1910 that the idea of linking paranoid knowledge to a homosexual investment and theoretical knowledge to a rejection of that investment had come to him from a painful reactivation of the break with Fliess: "Since Fliess's case, . . . [a] piece of homosexual investment has been withdrawn and utilized for the enlargement of my own ego. I have succeeded where the paranoiac fails."[71] This theory was debatable, at the very least.

Freud had nevertheless thought he could separate himself from this swatch of his history. In August 1897, he claimed that he was undertaking a "self-analysis"—a way of calling into question, without saying so, the entire system of thought he had developed up to that point. But this episode too ended in a fiasco. Freud had first explained to Fliess that his principal patient was himself. Then he had analyzed his own dreams, following up with a declaration that he understood nothing about what was happening within himself. Believing for a time that "self-analysis" had really gotten under way, he ended up admitting that it was impossible: "My self-analysis is still interrupted. I have now seen why. I can only analyse myself with objectively acquired knowledge (as if I were a stranger); self-analysis is really impossible, otherwise there would be no illness. As I have come across some puzzles in my own case, it is bound to hold up the self-analysis."[72]

Invented in an attempt to get out of an impasse, the elusive concept of self-analysis met with success in the Freudian community, which received the idea that only Freud, as the "founding father" of the discipline, had

really practiced an investigation of the self that could serve as an initiatory model for the entire genealogy of filiations to come. He was said to be "self-engendered," and, as a result, any contextual history of the origins of psychoanalysis would have to be disqualified to the benefit of a mythology of the "great man."

Such was the position of Ernest Jones in 1953. From this perspective, he presented Fliess as a fanatic false scholar and Freud as a hero of science capable, from the height of his "splendid isolation," of inventing everything without owing anything to his epoch. And on this basis he plunged into a psychoanalytic interpretation of history that was to be taken up for decades by the Freudian community, to its own great detriment: a veritable legend in place of history, according to which Fliess occupied with respect to Freud the position of paranoid seducer and father substitute whom Freud eventually managed to shed by dint of his own genius.

We know very well that such legends do not stand up to historical studies. Even if every new discipline owes its pronouncements to a "founding father," this father instituted a discursivity that cannot belong to him alone, since, if it is rational, it engenders an infinite possibility of discourses capable of being reinterpreted in their turn.[73]

Another much more interesting interpretation of this episode was provided by Freud at the beginning of his break with Fliess. In a letter dated May 7, 1900, right after his forty-fourth birthday, he reaffirmed that, in order to think, he needed contact with a friend who could reveal to him his "feminine" aspects. And, after emphasizing that no scholar could know in advance what the judgment of posterity would be, he added, "No critic . . . can see more clearly than I the disproportion there is between the problems and my answers to them, and it will be a fitting punishment for me that none of the unexplored regions of the mind in which I have been the first mortal to set foot will ever bear my name or submit to my laws. When breath threatened to fail me in the struggle I prayed the angel to desist, and that is what he has done since then. But I did not turn out to be the stronger, though since then I have been noticeably limping. Well, I really am forty-four now, a rather shabby old Jew."[74]

Freud is alluding here to the famous passage in Genesis that recounts Jacob's nocturnal combat with the angel. Alone in the night, Isaac's son,

Abraham's grandson, struggles until dawn with a mysterious adversary; Jacob does not know his sex and does not know that he is at once God and God's emissary (Elohim and the angel). Understanding that he will not conquer the man, the angel wounds him in the hollow of his thigh so that Jacob becomes lame. And when the angel seeks to flee, Jacob demands a blessing. Triumphant over his adversary but wounded for life, the third patriarch embodies the idea that the greatest victory of man is the one he wins over himself and his arrogance.[75]

And it is indeed through this thematics, inherited from the sacred text, that Freud carried out his break with Fliess while inventing a destiny for himself: that of a wounded man who was preparing himself for perpetual combat against men and against himself. Such was his state of mind in 1900 at the moment when, like the third patriarch, he thought he had made a discovery whose future he would never master, considering himself too old and too "lame" to put it to work.[76]

This adventure confirms, if confirmation is needed, that every scientific undertaking is punctuated by the passage from error to truth. No theory, however rational or logical, is ever exempt from the irrationalism that it claims to want to avoid. In other words, in his later works Freud never fully sheds the vestiges of his deviations from the path of rationality—or of his lifelong struggle with the angel; traces of these deviations and this struggle can be glimpsed in his correspondence with Fliess.

The Invention of Psychoanalysis

In 1895, the hysteria of all the women observed by a large number of scientists remained a mystery. It was left to novelists and their heroines—from Flaubert to Tolstoy, from Emma Bovary to Anna Karenina—to give these women a human face: that of individuals waging an impotent revolt that led to suicide or madness. No matter that the existence of masculine hysteria was asserted in Paris and Vienna alike; the "illness" seemed to strike women above all.

The paradigm of "THE hysterical woman," gradually abandoned during the twentieth century,[1] remained linked to a state of society in which women had no means other than the display of a suffering body to express their aspirations to freedom. If, in the late nineteenth century, mad or half-mad women from the outskirts of Paris had served as the objects of study in the development of a clinical practice based on observation (that of Jean-Martin Charcot), Viennese women, welcomed in the secrecy of a private office, were the major players in the construction of an approach based on listening: a practice focused on internal rather than external states. Unlike the Parisian working-class women, the bourgeois women of Vienna had the right to a private life, to a sense of intimacy. Their existential distress allowed male scientists to develop a new theory of subjectivity. Through their mute presence and through clinical narratives that disguised their real lives, these women were at the origin of the invention of psychoanalysis: an unspeakable origin that historians have a duty to retrace.

It is no surprise, then, that *Studies on Hysteria,* published in 1895 by Freud and Josef Breuer, had such an impact on writers, owing to the fact

that patients as well as doctors had the floor, even if only the doctors were authorized to retrace the histories of their patients.[2] In the course of these case studies, readers of the time watched the clinic of the gaze being abandoned in favor of a clinic of transferential relations: a renewal of the dynamic treatment inherited from the old magnetizers.

But the real novelty lay in the fact that the two authors took the opposite course from the cold descriptions larded with technical terms of which their contemporaries, doctors of the soul, were so fond. Eager to strike the imagination, Freud and Breuer skillfully privileged novelistic narratives over clinical case studies, and they took care to penetrate in a literary fashion into the intimate geography of the familial turpitudes of their day, in order to give unusual, lively accounts of the everyday dramas of the private insanity dissimulated under the appearances of complete normality: "She told me," Freud writes, "that her mother had herself been in an asylum for some time. They had once had a maid-servant one of whose previous mistresses had spent a long time in an asylum and who used to tell her horrifying stories." And again: "She began talking about her family, and in a very roundabout way got on to the subject of a cousin. He was rather queer in the head and his parents had all his teeth pulled out at one sitting. . . . [She later related] how she had nursed her sick brother and he had had such fearful attacks as a result of the morphine and had terrified her and seized hold of her. . . . She had had some fearful dreams. The legs and arms of the chairs were all turned into snakes; a monster with a vulture's beak was tearing and eating at her all over her body."[3]

The women whose anguish Freud and Breuer unfolded would doubtless never have imagined that their stories—real or invented—could be thus exposed to the public, given that their "illness" was still so suspect in the eyes of the representatives of medical science: paralysis, cramps, tics, hallucinations, grimaces, terrors written on their faces, anxieties, fears, and especially sexual obsessions accompanied by narratives of childhood trauma and abuse.

Always concerned with fleshing out what he was discovering, Freud had pushed a very hesitant Breuer to go ahead with publication, in particular regarding the astonishing history of Bertha Pappenheim, a young Viennese woman from the upper Jewish bourgeoisie whose treatment

took place between 1880 and 1882. But Breuer resisted, as he was very un-
satisfied with the results achieved with this patient: after a therapeutic
marathon during which she had developed an impressive series of symp-
toms (hallucinations, paralyses, coughing fits, and so on),[4] Pappenheim
had been sent to the Bellevue sanatorium in Kreuzlingen, a magnificent
clinic on the shore of Lake Constance directed by Robert Binswanger. In
this idyllic spot, she had joined the elite among the wealthy mentally ill
patients from all over old Europe. A morphine addict who had not over-
come any of her anxieties, she had subsequently been admitted to a
number of other clinics before returning to her family.[5]

In 1895, Breuer was no longer using the cathartic method, and he did
not want to interpret the fact that patients might want to seduce their
therapists as a transferential phenomenon. Freud, on the contrary, thought
that Pappenheim's treatment brought not only proof of a sexual etiology
but also that, as it considerably preceded Pierre Janet's experiments with
patients presenting the same symptoms,[6] it allowed him to demonstrate
that his French rival was not, as Janet himself believed, the inventor of
this type of treatment. Freud had the last word and his enthusiasm car-
ried the day. Although he was fully acquainted with Pappenheim's story
(she had been a friend of Martha Bernays, moreover), he could not do
without Breuer's collaboration, since the latter was better known and had
introduced the method.

In their presentation of the work, the two authors emphasized that
their choice had not been dictated by scientific considerations: "Our ex-
perience is derived from private practice in an educated and literate so-
cial class, and the subject matter with which we deal often touches upon
our patients' most intimate lives and histories. It would be a grave breach
of confidence to publish material of this kind, with the risk of patients
being recognized and their acquaintances becoming informed of facts
which were confided only to the physician. It has therefore been impos-
sible for us to make use of some of the most instructive and convincing
of our observations."[7]

Thus the authors had to focus on slices of life without exposing truths
apt to disturb the social order that the physicians and patients shared. The
women treated by Breuer and Freud belonged to an extended family: they
were often friends, sisters, or cousins of the doctors' wives, in whose eyes

they might become rivals. And then, if these women presented such symptoms, it meant that those same spouses might be unwitting bearers of the great scourge of hysteria. So all the treatments had to be presented as therapeutic successes rather than as "experiments" whose validity could have been immediately challenged. Otherwise, what was the point of publishing such studies?

This, then, was the state of mind in which Freud and Breuer found themselves on the eve of their book's appearance. Breuer had doubts about everything; he stressed physiological causality and refused to fall back on sexual etiology alone; moreover, he feared virulent attacks on the part of his colleague Adolf Strümpell, who asserted, as did Richard von Krafft-Ebing and many others, that the patients, through their symptoms, were leading the doctors astray. For his part, Freud maintained that the mental dissociation encountered in hysterical symptoms was triggered by a psychic defense mechanism and by reminiscences tied to a childhood sexual trauma. Confident in his own destiny and convinced of the accuracy of his theory of seduction, he was quite determined to challenge nihilism by proving the curative value of psychotherapy: "When I have promised my patients help or improvement by means of a cathartic treatment I have often been faced by this objection: 'Why, you tell me yourself that my illness is probably connected with my circumstances and the events of my life. You cannot alter these in any way. How do you propose to help me, then?' And I have been able to make this reply: 'No doubt fate would find it easier than I do to relieve you of your illness. But you will be able to convince yourself that much will be gained if we succeed in transforming your hysterical misery into common unhappiness. With a mental life that has been restored to health you will be better armed against that unhappiness.' "[8]

The two authors did not agree. But they found common ground on the question of reminiscences and on the necessity for affirming that the eight patients whose cases they presented had been cured, if not of their illnesses, at least of their symptoms. "Fraülein Anna O.," "Frau Emmy von N.," "Miss Lucy," "Katharina," "Fraülein Elisabeth von R.," "Fraülein Mathilde H.," "Fraülein Rosalie H.," and "Frau Cäcile": the real identity of five of these women was revealed by historians beginning in the 1960s.[9] Their names were Bertha Pappenheim, Fanny Moser, Aurelia Öhm, Anna

von Lieben, and Ilona Weiss.[10] None of them was "cured," but nothing justifies a claim that their existence was not transformed by the experience of treatment.

In this respect, these *Studies,* viewed as the birth record of psychoanalytic practice, related only hypnotic and cathartic treatments. To this was added a method of concentration through pressure on the skull or on a thigh, a method Freud used (in the case of Ilona Weiss, "Miss Lucy") in order to persuade his patients to tell him whatever came to mind.

As for the "founding case," that of "Anna O.," it was nothing other than an experiment in treatment that fascinated Freud but that had been carried out by Breuer. Pappenheim herself never admitted to being Anna O. And the patients whose cases were reported in the *Studies on Hysteria* never recognized themselves in the portraits Freud had produced on the basis of his notes. Thus Ilona, questioned one day by her daughter, responded that she remembered that the famous "bearded doctor from Vienna" to whom she had been sent had tried, against her will, to convince her that she was in love with her brother-in-law. In this story, however, neither of the protagonists can be suspected of lies or distortion. As presented by the two scientists, the case studies do not bear much relation, in general, to the lived reality of their patients.

Let us simply say that this gap is a measure of the dialectical opposition between two regimes of subjectivity—that of the doctor on the one side, that of the patient on the other—and that these regimes express a division inherent in the relations between insanity as it is voiced and the discourse of psychopathology, a division between self-awareness and critical awareness: on one side, the anonymous existence of a patient immersed in distress; on the other the rationality of a clinical gaze that remains at a distance from the distress the better to grasp it.

In this respect, we may note that case studies are always constructed as fictions, short stories or literary vignettes designed to validate scientists' hypotheses. Hence the necessary revisions that generally bring to light the extent to which the patient rejects the validity of a reconstructed discourse of which he feels he is the victim.

This was Pappenheim's attitude. After her sessions with Breuer and the rest of her therapeutic journey, she rejected everything that had to do with her treatment and she demanded that her family never supply any infor-

mation about this episode of her life.[11] On several occasions she manifested strong hostility toward psychoanalysis, refusing to offer any comments whatsoever about the legendary fate of Anna O., especially after the publication of *Studies on Hysteria*. Was she cured of something? Yes, without question. Would her life have been the same if she had never met Breuer? No one knows.

By a sort of sublimation, Pappenheim managed to convert her pathological symptoms into humanitarian activity, to such an extent that in just a few years she became a major figure in German Jewish feminism. After serving as director of an orphanage in Frankfurt, she traveled to the Balkans, the Near East, and Russia to conduct investigations into white slavery. In 1904, she founded the Jüdischer Frauenbund, a league of Jewish women intended to promote women's emancipation through work. She wrote countless articles, tales, and plays for children before crossing paths with Martin Buber and Gershom Scholem. Hostile to Zionism, and as pious and authoritarian as her mother had been, she spoke out against the emigration of Jews from Germany. She died in 1936, three years before Freud, after having barely escaped persecution by the Nazis.

While Pappenheim pursued a public existence, Anna O., her hated double, met a quite different fate. Convinced that Breuer had been frightened by the sexual character of the amorous transference onto him from his patient, between 1915 and 1932 Freud gave—most notably to Arnold Zweig[12]—several versions of the end of that treatment, reconstructing after his own fashion the story of his break with his old friend. Seeking to demonstrate that what was at stake in this rupture was a difference of opinion regarding the sexual etiology of hysterical neurosis, he asserted that Anna had once manifested all the symptoms of a phantom pregnancy. Fearing for his reputation, Breuer fled, according to this account, while Mathilda, his wife, attempted suicide out of jealousy.

Taken up again by Ernest Jones, the fable of this nervous pregnancy was transformed, in 1953, into a veritable novel of the origins of psychoanalysis, pitting the "fearful" Breuer against the "stout-hearted" Freud. According to this version, Breuer literally "fled" to Vienna with his wife for a new honeymoon during which his daughter Dora was conceived. And Jones goes further, indicating that Breuer called Freud in as a consultant on an identical case ten years later. When Freud declared that the

symptoms of this new patient revealed a phantom pregnancy, Jones says, Breuer could not bear this repetition of a past event: "Without saying a word he took up his hat and stick and hurriedly left the house."[13]

At all events, the break between Freud and Breuer was inevitable. Not only because they did not share the same view of how to approach neuroses, but because Freud could not bear being contradicted by a man who had been his benefactor. Eager to assert himself at a point when his passion for Wilhelm Fliess was growing, and unable to master his pride, once again he transformed the intimate friend into an enemy.

In 1925, when Breuer died, Freud came to regret his attitude upon learning that his former protector, many years after their break, had continued to take an interest in his work. Now seventy years old and famous, Freud confessed to Breuer's son how mistaken he himself had been for decades: "What you have to say regarding your father's attitude towards my later works was new to me, and its effect was like a balm on a painful wound which had never healed."[14]

It was thus in this conflictual climate that Freud attributed to Breuer, in March 1896, the invention of a new method for exploring the unconscious: *psychoanalysis*.[15] But in fact he himself had already been practicing psychoanalysis for six years, placing the patient on a short bed decorated with Oriental rugs and cushions, gifts of a certain Mme Benvenisti. Over time, he had gotten into the habit of sitting behind this couch, the better to hear the flow of the patient's words.[16] A veritable manifesto against Charcot's French heirs, the text in which the word "psychoanalysis" appeared for the first time contained the first major Freudian classification of the neuroses.

In this text, the author also asserted that the sacrosanct heredity so prized by psychiatrists, psychologists, and advocates of therapeutic nihilism could in no case explain the origin of a neurosis. The true cause lay, as he saw it, in an actual trauma experienced in childhood. With such a conception of psychic disorders, Freud was carrying out a sort of therapeutic revolution. He maintained in effect that, thanks to the new talking cure invented by Breuer and taken up by Freud himself, psychic disorders could be heard, treated, and sometimes cured. For this it sufficed that the origin of the problem be brought to light by the patient himself with the help of the therapist and according to the earlier technique of avowal.

Thus he was reconnecting, unwittingly, not only with Franz Anton Mesmer's legacy but also, in a much more distant way, with the great principle of confession inherited from the Counter-Reformation and especially from the Council of Trent, which had made avowal a sacrament, an intimate exercise without visual or physical contact between the confessor and the penitent.[17] Willingly or not, Freud was also the heir, more or less, of certain Catholic traditions; his cherished governess had initiated him to this religion while serving also as his "teacher in sexual matters."[18]

And to respond to the accusations of those who maintained that the confessions of hysterics were not trustworthy, or that they were induced by the doctors themselves, Freud became the vigorous defender of suffering patients, even as he embarked on a ferocious attack on late nineteenth-century family life. He was thus justifying, after the fact, the validity of the cases exposed in the *Studies on Hysteria*.

Most often, he said, girls were victims of abuses committed by their older brothers, who had been initiated into sexuality by a governess or a servant. But, worse still, Freud asserted that in the bosom of every family there was an "early attempt," always committed by an adult on a child generally between two and five years old.

Hence his classification of the neuroses based on the difference between the sexes: obsessional neurosis on one side, hysterical neurosis on the other. According to Freud, the first resulted, for boys, in active participation in the aggression to which they were subjected; the second led, in girls, to passive acceptance of abuse: "The importance of the active element in sexual life as a cause of obsessions, and of sexual passivity for the pathogenesis of hysteria, even seems to unveil the reason for the more intimate connection of hysteria with the female sex and the preference of men for obsessional neurosis. One sometimes comes across a pair of neurotic patients who were a pair of little lovers in their earliest childhood—the man suffering from obsessions and the woman from hysteria. If they are a brother and sister, one might mistake for a result of nervous heredity what is in fact the consequence of precocious sexual experiences."[19]

On May 2, 1896, Freud, as bold as ever, again presented his theory of seduction before the Association of Psychiatry and Neurology of Vienna. He received an icy reception, especially on the part of Krafft-Ebing, a

specialist in sexology and perversions, who characterized his communication as a "scientific fairy tale,"[20] emphasizing once again that hysterics' "confessions" might very well have been obtained through the effect of a suggestion induced by the doctor. Freud felt persecuted once again by the mandarins of the faculty. And yet, fifteen months later, he would have to admit that his theory did not hold up.

In the meantime, he continued to wander. When Jacob died, on October 23, 1896, Freud felt real pain at the recollection of his weak father, who had played such an important role in his life, with Jacob's way of associating the most profound wisdom with a manner of being full of fantasy: "By the time he died, his life had long been over, but at a death the whole past stirs within one."[21]

Three months later, Freud persuaded himself that the unfortunate Jacob had behaved like every other adult, child abusers all: "[He] was one of those perverts and is responsible for the hysteria of my brother (all of whose symptoms are identifications) and those of several younger sisters. The frequency of this circumstance often makes me wonder."[22] However, as he was hardly inclined to think of himself as a father who felt guilty desires for his progeny, he began to doubt his own theory.

A subscriber to abstinence, Freud gave himself over, as we know, to all sorts of substitute passions, including lust for travel. Beginning in 1895, in the grip of a strong desire to explore the high points of Greco-Roman culture and Renaissance art, he had decided to defy his fear of railway accidents and his obsessive concern with border crossings and go to Italy every year.[23] In September 1895 he had discovered the marvels of Venice. A year later, accompanied by his brother Alexander and Felix Gattel, he embarked on a long journey in Tuscany, and the following year he visited Venice again before heading down toward Siena, Orvieto, Perugia, Arezzo, and Florence. After that, accompanied by Minna, then Alexander, then Sándor Ferenczi or his daughter Anna, he kept on being drawn toward the south: first Rome, then Pompeii, Naples, Ravello, Sorrento, Capri, Palermo, Syracuse, and Athens.[24] Fascinated by Egyptology, an admirer of Jean-François Champollion, he often dreamed of visiting the banks of the Nile to see the former land of the pharaohs, though he never managed to do so.

The fact remains that in September 1897, intoxicated by his search for a subterranean world similar to the one described in a poem by Heinrich Heine, he sent Fliess a letter in which he declared that he was seeking in Italy a "punch made of Lethe," an intoxication of forgetting, a new drug, a source of creativity: "Here and there I get a draft. One savors the strange kind of beauty and the enormous creative urge; at the same time my inclination toward the grotesque, perverse-psychological gets its due."[25]

This first plunge into the intoxication of travel in Italy was the last act of a long reflection that led Freud to renounce his theory of seduction when he returned to Vienna: "I no longer believe in my *neurotica*. . . . I would have grounds for feeling very happy. The hope of eternal fame was so beautiful, and so was that of certain wealth, complete independence, travel, and removing the children from the sphere of the worries which spoiled my own youth."[26] Too late, nevertheless, to do justice to the unjustly suspected Jacob!

Since he had never subscribed to the critiques of those contemporaries who viewed his theory of seduction as the validation of a falsification induced by suggestion, Freud ran up against a complex reality. It was certainly unthinkable that all fathers were rapists. But neither could all hysterics be considered fakers or compulsive liars when they asserted that they had been victims of abuse. So it was necessary to put forward a hypothesis that could account for two contradictory truths: sometimes hysterics invented scenes that had not taken place, and sometimes, when the scenes had actually occurred, they did not suffice to account for the formation of a neurosis.

By abandoning his *neurotica,* Freud was distancing himself not only from neurology and physiology but also from sexology, a discipline linked to psychiatry and biology whose object was to study human sexual behavior in order to set forth norms and describe pathologies.

Concerned with hygienics, nosography, and the description of "aberrations," the major sexologists of the late nineteenth century—Krafft-Ebing, Albert Moll, and Havelock Ellis—were less preoccupied with therapeutics than with erudite research into the various forms of sexual practices and identities: homosexuality, bisexuality, transvestism, pedophilia, zoophilia, and so on. In short, they were interested first and foremost in the

question of sexual perversions and their origins in childhood. If the paradigm of the hysteric woman had invaded the entire field of the study of neuroses, the two major figures of "non-procreative sex"—the homosexual and the masturbating child—were the preserve of sexologists, hygienists, and pediatricians, who left to psychiatrists, heirs of the alienists, the task of dealing with insanity, that is, with psychoses.

By giving up the idea that the bourgeois family order could be based on the alliance between a perverse parent and an abused child, Freud shifted the question of the sexual causation of neuroses onto a terrain that no longer belonged to sexology, nor did it belong moreover to psychiatry or psychology. He was leaving the realm of describing behaviors for that of interpreting discourse, considering that the famous sexual scenes described by patients could stem from fantasies, that is, from subjective or imaginary representations. And he added that even when an instance of seduction had actually occurred, it was not necessarily the source of a neurosis. Thus he accepted simultaneously the existence of fantasy and that of trauma. And he emphasized that, thanks to the psychoanalytic method (exploration of the unconscious and treatment by way of talking), the therapist should henceforth be able to discern several orders of reality that are often confused: real sexual abuse, psychic seduction, fantasy, and transference.

But one still had to ask what the place of the real child was in these stories of avowed or fantasized seductions.

For some time the child's body had already been an object of predilection for hygienists and physicians. And hundreds of books recounted the harmful effects of childhood masturbation in the genesis of neuroses and perversions. Freud had taken an interest in that question in 1886 during his sojourn in Berlin, in the unit of the pediatrician Adolf Aron Baginsky.[27] And as someone who had himself been a child in a large family before becoming a father himself, attentive to his numerous offspring, he had never ceased to see himself as an informed observer of real or fantasized carnal relations that spread trouble at the heart of family relations.

The whole debate during the second half of the nineteenth century bore on the question whether a child could be born, if not insane, at least perverse, and whether this particular "insanity" was manifested by a specific sexual practice—masturbation—whose harmful effects had not been

previously recognized. Since it was now acknowledged that children were sexual beings—and not merely inert objects disguised as adults—a legal, social, and psychic framework had to be defined for them. Having acquired the right to exist, children had to be protected against themselves and against attempts at seduction that endangered their integrity.

Consequently, and still from the perspective of the child who had to become a "normal" adult well integrated into the family order, it was also necessary to convince children, in their innermost being, that learning how to live required going through formidable physical and psychic training intended to make them better. Such were the principles of a perverse education, practiced in particular in Germany, that consisted in making children acknowledge that the corporal punishments inflicted by adults made them better people and allowed them to combat their own vices in order to reach a "sovereign good" and, better still, to want to achieve that goal.

Among the theoreticians of this "dark pedagogy,"[28] Gottlieb Moritz Schreber made his reputation by writing manuals through which he claimed to be providing a remedy for the decline of society by creating a new man: a pure mind in a healthy body. Supported initially by the Social Democrats, Schreber's theses were later adopted by the Nazis. Daniel Paul Schreber, a mentally ill jurist, was subjected to this insane education, which left traces in his *Memoirs* that were later discussed by Freud.[29]

If pediatrics was rooted in the philosophy of the Enlightenment, the annexation of the domain of childhood by psychiatric discourse took place at the end of the nineteenth century with the beginning of the great wave of medicalization of all human behaviors through sexology, criminology, and psychology. Thus was the notion of childhood innocence demolished by psychiatric science, to the benefit of several contradictory theses. From the perspective of Darwinism, it was believed that children, born without humanity, bore in themselves, in their bodies and thus in their genital organs, the vestiges of a not-yet-surpassed animality. But it was also believed that, if children exhibited perversions, this way of acting emanated from their souls and thus from a vice proper to humanity itself.

It was at this time that masturbation began to be viewed as the chief cause of certain forms of delirium that were manifested not only in children but also, later, in all so-called hysteric subjects. Both groups were

categorized as suffering from "sexual disorders": the former because they engaged without limits in the practice of solitary sex, the latter because they had experienced as children—or asserted that they had experienced—traumas of a sexual nature identical to those induced by masturbation (abuse, seduction, rape, and so on).

The idea of the dangerous nature of masturbation had been masterfully articulated by Jean-Jacques Rousseau, not only in 1762 in a famous passage from *Émile*—"Once he knows this dangerous supplement . . ."[30]—but also in the *Confessions,* published posthumously in 1780: "I had felt the progress of the years; my restless temperament had finally declared itself, and its first, very involuntary, eruption, had given me alarms about my health that depict the innocence in which I had lived until then better than anything else. Soon reassured, I learned that dangerous supplement that fools nature and saves young people of my disposition from many disorders at the expense of their health, their vigor, and sometimes their life."[31]

A century later, far from being seen as a "dangerous supplement," masturbation was viewed, along with homosexuality, as the greatest of the perversions, as perilous exposure to madness and death—in short, as a loss of substance that aimed to "stand in for" nature, to act in its place,[32] to impose a culture of sex that broke with the natural order of the living world. As a result, only human beings were deemed responsible for the seduction they carried out on themselves by their mania for autoeroticism. Confident in the progress of the rapidly expanding surgical art, children's doctors recommended a preventive remedy for this pathology: excision or cauterization of the clitoris for girls, circumcision for boys. In addition, all sorts of "therapies" were invented to come to grips with the onanist plague: antimasturbation corsets, erection sheaths, devices to spread girls' legs apart, injunctions and threats of castration, handcuffing, and finally legal charges brought against wet nurses accused of "abuses."

But in order to apply such "treatments" and to proffer such threats, it remained necessary to prove the existence of sexual excitement. Within families, then, systematic efforts were made to uncover traces of the infamous practice. Every inflammation of the genitals, every swelling or bruise, every appearance of herpes or rash was examined under a magnifying glass. But masturbation was conceptualized not only as the fruit

of a solitary practice but also as an "anonymous" pleasure that sometimes presupposed the presence of something other: rubbing, an unknown hand, clothing, a tactile or olfactory sensation. Long after the victory of Louis Pasteur's theses, there still lingered a belief in the fable according to which all sorts of infectious or viral diseases originated in the practice of masturbation.

But what was the origin of the masturbatory impulse?

On this level, there were two opposing hypotheses, each establishing a link between autoeroticism and seduction. If masturbation was a "dangerous supplement," that meant that it was induced by the culture and the environment. And if this was the case, it was then important to know whether the child himself was his own seducer as soon as he became a social being, by passing from nature to culture, or whether the seduction was the work of a corrupting adult abusing the child. The whole debate over the question of trauma on the one hand, and theories of infantile sexuality on the other, stemmed from these two hypotheses, both of which Freud ended up abandoning at the same time that he gave up any conception of masturbation as a "dangerous supplement."

Such was the impulse behind the great surgical *furia* that washed over Europe from 1850 to 1890, striking masturbating children as well as hysterical women. Were they not both, like the "invert" (homosexual), moreover, the most flamboyant actors of this "dangerous supplement"? At all events, they had in common, in the eyes of the medical profession, a preference for autoerotic sexuality as opposed to procreative sexuality.

In abandoning his *neurotica,* and in defining the original conditions of a therapy of avowal, Freud was exploring an unprecedented way of conceptualizing human sexuality. Far from insisting on describing rapes, sexual pathologies, erotic practices, or instinctual behaviors ad nauseam, and rather than drawing anatomical charts awash with measurements and assorted calculations or evaluations, or decreeing norms, or cataloging all the sexual aberrations, he extended the notion of sexuality, making it a universal psychic disposition and the very essence of human activity. It is thus less sexuality in itself that became primordial in his doctrine than a conceptual cluster that made it possible to represent sexuality: the drive, the source of unconscious psychic functioning; the libido, a generic term designating sexual energy; anaclisis, or relational process; bisexuality,

a disposition proper to any form of human sexuality; and finally desire, a tendency, an accomplishment, an infinite quest, an ambivalent relation to others.

As the positivist scientist that he was, nourished by physiology and experimentation in the animal realm, Freud thus turned in 1897 toward the construction of a theory of love—or Eros—as the masters of Western philosophy had done before him. But as a good Darwinian, fully permeated by the legend of Faust and his pact with the devil, he asserted not only that the Christian principle of loving one's neighbor as oneself went against the aggressive nature of the human being, but that the acquisition of subjective freedom was achieved via the acceptance of an unconscious determinism: "I is an other."

No longer wishing to be a philosopher, Freud was convinced that his doctrine had to be above all a science of the psyche, capable of subverting the field of psychology; its foundations would come from biology, from the natural sciences. In reality, he was launching something quite different: a revolution of the intimate that grew out of the shadows of the Enlightenment and the dark side of Romanticism, a revolution that was at once rational and haunted by the conquest of subterranean rivers. Ulysses searching for a promised land populated by specters, mirages, temptations: such was the promise of the Freudian voyage to the heart of the unconscious, which was defined as an "other stage," and which presupposed an organization of kinship structures that could account for the modalities of a new familial order of which Freud sought to be the clinician but in which he was also the actor.

Marked, as was his entire generation, by the famous "dramas of fatality" that put on stage terrible histories of kings, princes, and princesses against a background of incest and parricide, Freud had wanted to be the privileged witness to the sickness of families that was ravaging Vienna within the very heart of the Habsburg imperial dynasty. In these spectacles, which horrified him, "fate" intervened in the form of a deus ex machina that allowed a young couple crushed by paternal power to free themselves from the weight of a deceptive genealogy.

And it was in thinking about one of these, and after having yet again evoked his childhood and his amorous feeling toward his Jewish mother and his Christian governess, that, in a letter to Fliess dated October 15,

1897, he had the brilliant idea of comparing the fate of the turn-of-the-century neuroses to that of a hero of Greek tragedy: "Every member of the audience was once a budding Oedipus in phantasy, and this dream-fulfilment played out in reality causes everyone to recoil in horror, with the full measure of repression which separates his infantile from his present state."[33]

But to his theatrical construction Freud immediately added the character of Hamlet, the melancholic prince who hesitated to avenge his father and kill his uncle, who had become his mother's husband. And he made this prince of Denmark a feminized hysteric haunted by the memory of having desired his mother: "How can one explain . . . his hesitation to avenge his father by killing his uncle . . . ? How better than by the torment roused in him by the obscure memory that he himself had meditated the same deed against his father because of passion for his mother?"[34]

Oedipus, the most distressing figure conceived by Sophocles in the trilogy he devoted to the Labdacid family, thus became the archetype of the modern neurotic in Freud's writings, Freud having deliberately distorted the history of this noble and generous tyrant given to excess and condemned by the oracle to learn that he was not who he thought he was. Sophocles's Oedipus was indeed the murderer of his father (Laius) and the husband of his mother (Jocasta), but he did not know his father's identity any more than he desired that mother who had been attributed to him by the city of Thebes after he had solved the riddle of the Sphinx, a riddle having to do with the three stages in human development (childhood, maturity, old age). Oedipus, father and brother of the children he was to have with his mother, would end his days in exile, accompanied by Antigone, his accursed daughter, who was condemned never to procreate. This Oedipus has nothing in common with the one reinvented by Freud, guilty of a double desire: the desire to kill his father and the desire for sexual possession of his mother's body.

In the late nineteenth century, following the excavations that had led to the discovery of the sites of Troy and Mycenae, a return to the Greek tragedians, to the mythologies of antiquity and the thematics of excess (hubris) was the order of the day. In the unfolding of these ancient sagas that pitted men against gods, in which the men, subjected to fate, were never viewed as guilty of their actions, the thinkers of modernity thought

they were seeing, as in a collective catharsis, the unfolding of the contemporary story of the death throes of a patriarchal system that they rejected but to which they were attached: that of the imperial European presence.

The structures of kinship proper to the Labdacid family, the one singled out by Sophocles, fascinated historians because they seemed to confirm, quite as much as they blocked, the arrival of the dreaded apocalypse: the potential erasure of the difference between the sexes. In the long history of the Labdacids, the women, the men, and their descendants are in fact condemned never to find their places except under the sign of madness, murder, and defilement until the final extinction of their *genos*.

In counterpoint, in the story of the Atrides, every crime has to be punished by another crime, and each generation, guided by the Erinyes (the Furies), has to avenge and expiate the crimes of the preceding one. Thus Agamemnon, king of Mycenae, who has sacrificed his daughter Iphigenia, has his throat cut by Clytemnestra, his wife, with the complicity of her lover Aegisthus, who is the son—conceived in incest—of Thyestes. The mother avenges her daughter, and thus Orestes is compelled to avenge his father by killing his mother and Aegisthus with the help of his sister Electra. At the end of the cycle,[35] Apollo and Athena put an end to the rule of crime and establish law and justice in the polity. Orestes, who has gone mad, is purified; the Erinyes, divinities of vengeance, become the Eumenides (Benevolents), and the order of civilization wins out over the wild, incestuous, destructive order of nature.

Just as the story of the Labdacids displays an implacable, ahistorical self-destruction of the subjectivity of each of the actors, generation after generation, so the story of the Atrides indicates that civilization can bring an end to the hubris of men and of gods. On one side, we have the tragedy of the unconscious, of self-destruction and monstrosity; on the other, we have history, politics, and the advent of democracy. Given this difference, we can understand why, in 1897, Freud chose the Labdacid family as his genealogical model, a family guilty of destroying itself in the environment of Thebes, an almost "Viennese" polity, endogamous, closed off and turned inward on itself: a madness internal to the psyche.

If, for Freud, Sophocles's Oedipus embodied the unconscious as conceptualized by psychoanalysis, Shakespeare's Hamlet, an early seventeenth-

century Christian prince, made it possible to theorize a "guilty conscience." A Copernican subject, Hamlet does not yet achieve Cartesian doubt about the foundations of rational thought. Anxious and weak, he can neither remain a prince nor become a king, since he does not even have the assurance of "being or not being." In the Freudian system, Hamlet is a sort of Christianized Orestes, guilty and neurotic.

By inventing a modern subject divided between Oedipus and Hamlet, between an unconscious that determines him without his knowledge and a guilty conscious that shackles him in his freedom, Freud conceived of his doctrine as an anthropology of tragic modernity, a "family romance":[36] the unconscious tragedy of incest and crime, he said, is repeated in the drama of a guilty conscience. This conception of the subject no longer had anything to do with any sort of medical psychology. As for psychoanalysis, it was an act of transgression, a way of surreptitiously listening to words, taking them in without seeming to hear them or define them. A bizarre discipline, a fragile combination uniting soul and body, affect and reason, politics and animality: I am a *zoon politikon*, a political animal, said Freud, citing Aristotle.

Thus, at a time when vast research programs based on the study of facts and behaviors were being developed throughout Europe, Freud was turning to literature and origin myths to give his theory of the psyche a consistency that, in the eyes of his contemporaries, could in no way claim to stem from science: not from psychology, which enumerated behaviors and sought to be objective; not from anthropology, which sought to describe human societies; not from sociology, which studied social realities; and not from medicine, which had defined norms and pathologies based on organic and physiological variations in the wake of M. F. X. Bichat, Claude Bernard, and Pasteur. And yet Freud declared that he was the inventor of an authentic science of the psyche.

It is easy to understand, then, why this strange revolution in the sense of one's most intimate self, contemporaneous with the invention of the art of cinematography, another great factory for manufacturing dreams, myths, and heroes, managed to interest writers, poets, and historians while it was rejected by supporters of the positive sciences, the very ones Freud wanted to convince. Unwittingly faithful to the darker strains of Romanticism, he espoused the idea of the Greek tragedians according to

which man is an unconscious actor in his own destruction, owing to the very fact that he is anchored in a genealogy that he does not control. A twisting of reason into its opposite, a quest for the obscure part of the self, a search for death at work in life: such was the nature of the excavations undertaken by the inventor of psychoanalysis at the dawn of the twentieth century. About this movement, countering Freud's own view, Thomas Mann would later say quite rightly that, in psychoanalysis, one was dealing with "Romanticism turned scientific."

From his childhood on, Freud had always admired rebellious heroes: conquerors, founders of dynasties, adventurers capable of simultaneously abolishing the law of the father and symbolically reinstituting the sovereignty of a vanquished or humiliated paternity. By linking Hamlet's fate to that of Oedipus, he was assigning psychoanalysis an imperial position, to be sure, at the heart of what would later be called the human sciences, but a position impossible to define: it lay between rational knowledge and the savage mind, between medicine for the soul and the technique of confession, between mythology and therapeutic practice.

Freud was in fact carrying out a symbolic revolution: he was changing the way an entire era looked at itself and its ways of thinking. He was inventing a new origin narrative in which the modern subject was the hero not of a simple pathology but of a tragedy. This Freudian invention was to mark minds for a century. But even as he updated the Oedipal tragedy, Freud also took the risk of enclosing his narrative within a "complex," thus creating the conditions for a reduction of his doctrine to a family-oriented psychology. He would need thirteen years to give body to this Oedipus complex, without devoting the slightest publication to the notion. It was present everywhere in his work, but it was subject to very little elucidation in the end. Not until 1910, shortly after he wrote his essay on Leonardo da Vinci, did Freud use the term *Ödipuskomplex* for the first time.[37]

Freud viewed the "Dora case" as the first psychoanalytic treatment he had undertaken. And yet, if we look closely, we note that the patient to whom he had assigned this pseudonym, Ida Bauer, resembled the other young Viennese women of the affluent Jewish bourgeoisie whose fates he had evoked in *Studies on Hysteria*. Once again, he was confronting a familial pathology, as a doctor and also as a specialist in nervous disorders. And once again, with immense narrative talent, he wrote an account

that could be read as a novel by Stefan Zweig or Arthur Schnitzler. The victim of a quartet of cynical adults, one of whom had tried to abuse her sexually when she was thirteen years old, Ida was forced by her father to enter treatment with Freud.

A leading industrialist, Philipp Bauer, blind in one eye and syphilitic, had come down with tuberculosis in 1888, which had led him to live in Merano, in the Tyrol region, with his wife, Katharina, and his entire family. There he had become acquainted with Hans Zellenka, a less successful businessman than he, married to a beautiful Italian woman, Giuseppina or Peppina, who suffered from hysteric disorders and regularly frequented sanatoriums. She had become Bauer's mistress and she stayed with him in 1892 when he had a detached retina.

At the time, Bauer had returned to Vienna and was living on the same street as Freud, whom he consulted about an attack of paralysis and mental confusion of syphilitic origin. Satisfied with the treatment, he then sent Freud his sister, Malvine Friedmann, who was seriously neurotic and embroiled in a disastrously tormented married life. She soon died of emaciation, which had developed very quickly.

Like her husband, Ida's mother, Katharina, had been born into a Jewish family that had originated in Bohemia. With little education or intelligence, she suffered from constant abdominal pains, which were passed down to her daughter. She had never taken an interest in her children, and since her husband's illness and the resulting disunity, she presented all the signs of "housewife psychosis": without understanding anything about her children's aspirations, she devoted all her days, if we take Freud at his word, to cleaning and maintaining the family apartment and all its furnishings, to such an extent that it had become almost impossible to use and enjoy the home. The daughter paid almost no attention to her mother, criticized her harshly, and had completely exempted herself from her mother's influence. For there was a governess who supported Ida: a modern, "liberated" woman, she read books on sexual life and informed her pupil about this in secret. In particular, she opened the girl's eyes to the relation between her father and Peppina. Still, after having loved her and listened to her, Ida turned against her governess.

As for Ida's brother Otto, he dreamed above all of escaping the family quarrels. Whenever he had to choose a side, he aligned himself with his

mother. At age nine he was deemed a child prodigy; he had even written a play about the end of Napoleon's reign. Later, he rebelled against his father's political opinions, though he approved of the latter's adultery. Like his father, Otto Bauer was to lead a double life, marked by secrecy and ambivalence. Secretary of the Social Democratic Party from 1907 to 1914, then assistant to Victor Adler at the Ministry of Foreign Affairs in 1918, he was to become one of the major figures of the Austrian intelligentsia during the period between the wars.

In October 1900, when she was eighteen, at her father's insistence Ida went to see Freud and embarked on a treatment that lasted exactly eleven weeks. Afflicted with various nervous disorders (migraines, coughing fits, aphonia, depression, suicidal tendencies), she had been subjected to a second offense. Long since aware of her father's "fault" and of the lie that undergirded their family life, she had refused once again the amorous propositions made to her by Hans Zellenka on the banks of Lake Garda, and then she had slapped him. The drama had broken out when she had been accused by Hans and by her father of making up the seduction scene out of whole cloth. Worse still, she had been disavowed by Peppina Zellenka, who suspected her of reading pornographic books, in particular Paolo Mantegazza's *Physiology of Love,* published in 1872 and translated into German five years later. The author was a Darwinian sexologist abundantly cited by Krafft-Ebing, and a specialist in anthropological descriptions of the major human sexual practices: lesbianism, onanism, masturbation, homosexuality, fellatio, and so on.

By sending his daughter to Freud, Philipp Bauer hoped that the doctor would agree with him and would work on putting an end to the girl's alleged sexual fantasies. Far from subscribing to the father's expectations, Freud set off in a completely different direction. In eleven weeks, and through the analysis of two dreams, one about a fire in the family home and the other about the father's death, he reconstituted the unconscious truth of the drama. The first dream revealed that Ida frequently practiced masturbation and that in reality she was in love with Hans. But Freud's evocation also revealed a repressed incestuous desire involving her father. As for the second dream, it allowed Freud to go even further in the investigation of Ida's "sexual geography," and in particular to bring to light her thoroughgoing knowledge about adult sexual life.[38]

Freud realized that the patient could not bear the "revelation" of her desire for the man she had slapped. He thus launched into risky and erroneous interpretations of the fact that an attack of appendicitis had been the result of a fantasy of childbirth. Ida refused to let herself be pinned down by this discourse. So he let her leave when she decided to discontinue her treatment.

At first favorable to Freud's approach, the girl's father quickly noticed that Freud had not accepted the hypothesis that Ida had made up the whole story. As a result, he lost interest in the matter. For her part, Ida did not find in Freud the consolation she expected from him. At that time, in fact, he did not yet know how to handle transference in treatment. Similarly, as he emphasized in a note in 1923, he was incapable of understanding the nature of the homosexual bond that united Ida to Peppina: "If Freud used dry language with his patient," Patrick J. Mahony writes, "he did not use calm language; he was stirred up and showed it in tones of irony, frustration, irritation, bitterness, vengeance, and self-indulgent triumph."[39]

In short, Freud had doubts, and he resisted the temptation to apply his brand-new theory to the story of that unhappy hysteric girl so as to make her a "case." Ida escaped him. But whatever she may have said about it later, he had nevertheless freed her in part from the straitjacket of a pathogenic family.

Ida never got over her rejection of men. But her symptoms decreased. After her short analysis, she got her revenge for the humiliation she had suffered by making Peppina admit her liaison and Hans his attempt at seduction. She then reported the truth to her father, and broke off all relations with the couple. In 1903, she married Ernst Adler, a composer employed in her father's factory. Two years later she gave birth to a son who eventually had a career as a musician in the United States.

In 1923, subject to new disorders (vertigo, tinnitus, insomnia, migraines[40]), she called Felix Deutsch, one of Freud's disciples, to her bedside. She told him her whole story, spoke of men's selfishness, her frustrations, and her frigidity. As he listened to her complaints, Deutsch recognized the famous "Dora" case. He affirmed that she had forgotten her past illness and that she showed immense pride at having been the object of a famous text in psychiatric literature. She then discussed Freud's

interpretations of her two dreams with Deutsch. When he saw her again, the attacks had ceased.[41]

The Dora case was to become one of the most discussed cases in the entire history of psychoanalysis, even more than that of Bertha Pappenheim; it has given rise to dozens of articles and essays, a play, and several novels. It brought together all the ingredients of late nineteenth-century sexuality that were the delight of writers and doctors of the soul: hysterical irritation, homosexuality, the obsession with venereal disease, the exploitation of women's and children's bodies, the pleasures of adultery.

Even before abandoning his *neurotica,* Freud devoted a good part of his time to the study of what had attracted him most for years: the analysis of dreams. A habitual drug user, he readily gave himself over to an intense dream life, and he kept a journal of his dreams. He dreamed often, and in a disordered way: he dreamed about forthcoming trips, about his colleagues, about daily life in Vienna, about anodyne facts or, on the contrary, about important events having to do with life, food, love, death, or kinship.

Throughout his nocturnal wanderings he assailed his rivals, put himself in risky situations, relived scenes from his childhood, dreamed that he was dreaming, then dreamed another dream in the midst of the first, before finding himself at the heart of a city in ruins, populated with statues, columns, or buried houses, where he roamed the streets while losing himself in the archaeological labyrinth of his guilty desires. He dreamed in several languages, in several strata; he dreamed about sex, contemporary politics, anarchists' attacks, the imperial family, Hannibal, Rome, anti-Semitism, atheism, mothers, fathers, uncles, wet nurses.

He dreamed: he invented hieroglyphs and projected himself into literary characters, traversed rivers or wandered at great length through European museums to contemplate paintings by his favorite artists. In his dreaming, he reviewed all the works of Western culture, cited names of cities, places, or famous or unknown scholars. And this is how he began to write the book in which he claimed to be founding his new theory of the psyche. Initially it took the form of a sort of encyclopedia, revised over and over, before it settled down into an initiatory journey punctuated with great moments of exaltation, doubt, anguish, and melancholy.

In the course of this new *Sturm und Drang*, between 1895 and 1900, during which he was in conversation with himself without ever ceasing to address Fliess as if he were addressing Mephisto's double, Freud fell into the habit of referring to *The Divine Comedy*, sending enemies and adversaries to hell. He collected 160 dreams, including 50 of his own and 70 reported by friends and family members, and composed a vast poem in free verse populated with dreams in every genre: about Bismarck, a gray horse, Casimir Bonjour, a monograph on botany, Fidelio, a dead child on fire, a lynx on the roof, his own myopic son, Julius Caesar, Napoleon, Oedipus in disguise, a dead father, Giuseppe Tartini's sonata. This book, as he stated in the 1908 preface, had "a further subjective significance for me personally—a significance which I only grasped after I had completed it. It was, I found, a portion of my own self-analysis, my reaction to my father's death, the most poignant loss, of a man's life."[42] A strange remark, which confirms in any case that in his eyes the father was mortal and the mother immortal.

In turning to this exploration of the psyche, paralleling Dante's voyage and Ulysses's wanderings, Freud was aware that he was in the process of creating, almost unwittingly, a magisterial work that was leading him into the dark forests of his own unconscious in full turmoil. This "science of dreams," coming out of the Romantic tradition, mobilized interrogations on infantile sexuality and on the origin of neuroses even as it found support in a return to the gods and heroes of ancient Greece. Through this voyage into the depths of the soul, Freud saw himself as the messenger of a rejected, denied, repressed reality: "It seems to be my fate," he said one day to Jones, "to discover only the obvious: that children have sexual feelings, which every nursemaid knows; and that night dreams are just as much a wish fulfillment as day dreams."[43]

Aware of approaching the banks of a continent that had been known since the dawn of time and invaded in particular during the second half of the nineteenth century, Freud decided to read the most pertinent books on the question; thus he devoted the first eighty pages of the first chapter of his great book to a critical analysis of what his predecessors had written, from Aristotle and Artemidorus of Daldis to his closest contemporaries, the very ones who, shedding the idea that a dream was a premonition, a "key to daydreams," or the expression of a physiological activity induced

by sensory or somatic stimuli, had made dreams an object of knowledge and self-knowledge: Gotthilf Heinrich von Schubert, Eduard von Harmann, Johannes Volkelt, Adolf Strümpell, Havelock Ellis, Albert Moll, Joseph Delboeuf, Yves Delage, Wilhelm Griesinger, and many others, especially Alfred Maury, Karl Albert Scherner, and Hervey de Saint-Denys.[44]

All these authors, and especially the last three, had come up with techniques for investigating the part of human life protected by sleep. They had noticed that dreams were distorted expressions of inadmissible thoughts, repressed desires, childhood memories, or sexual fantasies touching on fundamental taboos: incest, masturbation, perversion, madness, transgression. Several of them had already formulated the hypothesis that rational deciphering of the rhetorical figures associated with the structure of dreams would allow specialists in nervous illnesses to care better for their patients. And while certain authors asserted that dreams were similar in nature to psychotic syndromes, others emphasized that oneiric activity served as a spontaneous remedy for the disorders of subjects suffering from perversions. The subjects, in fact, were said to be able to stage their sexual aberrations during sleep, the better to dismiss them when they were in a waking state. In short, when Freud set out on the path of dream analysis, he had simultaneously to receive an inheritance and to set himself apart from it.

Thus, far from referring, as his predecessors had done, to "dream life," or to a way to direct one's dreams, he decided to produce a synthesis of all possible modes of approach to the question of dreaming in general and dreams in particular, and to present his *Traumbuch* as the manifesto of a new understanding of human subjectivity. Hence the choice of a noteworthy date—1900 and not 1899—and an astonishing title: *Die Traumdeutung.* Through this generic term ("the interpretation of dreams"), Freud reestablished a connection, above and beyond scientific experimentation, with the tradition of soothsayers.[45] Not dreams but "THE dream," not two words, *Deutung des Traums,* but a single label that connoted the idea of offering the public a definitive, universal summing-up, similar to a bible that would be at the same time a treatise on oracles and the expression of a science of the psyche.

For the epigraph, Freud chose a line from book VII of the *Aeneid* ("*Flectere si nequeo Superos, Acheronta movebo*" [If heaven resists me, I'll

rouse Acheron][46]), in which Juno defends Dido, queen of Carthage, against Aeneas, a fallen Trojan and the future founder of Rome. Unable to convince Jupiter (the god from on high) to allow Aeneas to marry Dido, Juno appeals to Alecto, one of the Erinyes from the Acheron, a sort of bisexual Gorgon capable of unleashing the instinctual passions and the armed forces in the camp of Aeneas's allies. Abandoned by her lover, Dido commits suicide, and, when Aeneas rejoins her in Hell, she refuses to forgive him; he will speak to her ghost.

With this epigraph, Freud mobilized in a single sentence not only the essence of his doctrine on sexuality—the drives reactivated by the subterranean powers of Hell—but also some of the major signifiers of his own history. First of all, we encounter the expression of his revolt against the longed-for and unattainable imperial city, the city that Hannibal, a Freudian hero par excellence, had not managed to conquer, thus failing to avenge his father, Hamilcar. Identifying with Hannibal, Freud always felt guilty, as we know, that he had not given up his theory of seduction before the death of his father, whom he had unjustly suspected of abusing his daughters.

But Juno's curse, in Virgil's work, could also be related to Freud's ambivalent political attitude toward the Austrian monarchy and especially toward its most formidable representative, Count von Thun,[47] with whom he reported having a confrontation. The scene took place on a train platform in Vienna on August 11, 1898, when Freud was leaving on vacation. That day, he encountered von Thun, who was on his way to the emperor's summer residence, where economic agreements with Hungary were to be concluded. Even though von Thun did not have a ticket, he shoved the conductor aside and settled into a luxurious car. Freud then began to whistle the valet's tune from Mozart's *Marriage of Figaro:* "If the Count wants to dance, I'll play the guitar." Figaro was of course making fun of Count Almaviva, who was courting Figaro's fiancée.

The next day, Freud had a "revolutionary dream" in which he identified with a student who had contributed to the outbreak of the revolution of 1848. And he saw another Jewish doctor appear: Victor Adler, a former fellow student whom he had once challenged to a duel. In another scene, after fleeing the political stage, he found himself on a station platform. But instead of confronting von Thun, he was accompanying a blind

man to whom he was holding out a urinal. In interpreting this dream, Freud determined that the old man was a stand-in for his own dying father, whom he had challenged as a child by urinating in his bedroom. He had thus substituted for the hated image of von Thun that of his father in his death throes.

How could one not see in this dream the illustration of Freud's destiny and of his conception of power, according to which every society can trace its origin back to a conflict between a tyrannical father and a rebellious son who is compelled to put his father to death? Freud later made this the theory behind *Totem and Taboo,* and he came back to it again in "Moses and Monotheism."

But in 1900 Freud also announced, via the epigraph borrowed from Virgil, his firm intention to celebrate the primacy of psychoanalysis over politics and to make his newly developed doctrine the instrument of a revolution: to change human beings by exploring the hidden face of their desires.[48]

In a letter written to Werner Achelis in 1927, Freud said that he had come across that quote while reading a pamphlet published by Ferdinand Lassalle in 1859 against the Habsburg monarchy, deemed obscurantist: "You translate *'acheronta movebo'* as 'moving the citadels of the earth,'" he said to his interlocutor. "But it means 'to stir up the underworld.' I had borrowed the quotation from Lassalle, in whose case it was probably meant personally and relating to social—not psychological—classifications. In my case it was meant merely to emphasize the most important part in the dynamics of the dream. The wish rejected by the higher psychic structures (the repressed dream wish) stirs up the mental underworld (the unconscious) in order to get a hearing. What can you find 'Promethean' about this?"[49]

As Carl Schorske points out, there was great similarity between the young Freud's political choices and Lassalle's.[50] Both men rejected Roman Catholicism and the Habsburg dynasty. But above all, Freud posited a parallelism between the social revolution sought by Lassalle and the one to which he aspired.

Celebrating drives, legends, myths, and popular traditions was a way for Freud to attack the mandarins and the representatives of official science. And the recourse to dreams and their interpretation amounted to a

proclamation that the power of the imaginary, decoded by an ambitious expert, could just as well be embodied in a vast movement capable of challenging political power. Under the mask of a Hannibal endowed with the wit of a Figaro, Freud created a myth, that of the solitary hero immersed in "splendid isolation"[51] and confronting a world hostile to his genius.

By virtue of this emblematic construction, he began to see himself as the master of a revolution in sexuality placed under the sign of a new science, psychoanalysis. And yet Freud had so much self-doubt that he saw himself as the object of all sorts of persecutions: "I pictured the future as follows:—I should probably succeed in maintaining myself by means of the therapeutic success of the new procedure, but science would ignore me entirely during my lifetime; some decades later, someone else would infallibly come upon the same things—for which the time was not now ripe—would achieve recognition for them and bring me honour as a forerunner whose failure had been inevitable. Meanwhile, like Robinson Crusoe, I settled down as comfortably as possible on my desert island."[52]

During this period, Freud was neither isolated nor rejected, however; he was actually perceived as a brilliant doctor with a promising future. And while he saw himself as a rebel, the sexologists considered him a conservative, and the mandarins of medical science as a "literary type."

Had it been drafted as a sumptuous poem, *The Interpretation of Dreams* would not have enabled the imposition of a new approach to the human psyche. And this is why, even as Freud adopted a style for the book that could render an account of the novelistic aspects of dream life, he was determined to make the work a theoretical and clinical manifesto of unequalled force and modernity.

In two fundamental sections of the book, he sets out his interpretive method: it is based on free association, that is, on listening to what the dreamer expresses as his or her thoughts are given free rein without any discrimination among them. From this perspective, the dream ceases to be a fixed utterance and instead becomes narration, a work in movement, a veritable deformed or censored expression of a repressed desire whose signification is to be deciphered. And to explain the modalities of dreaming, Freud distinguishes a manifest content—the account of a dream by an awakened dreamer—and a latent content that is gradually brought to light thanks to the associative process.

According to Freud, two major operations structure the rhetoric of dreams: displacement, which transforms the primordial elements of the latent content by means of a shift, and condensation, which brings about a fusion among several ideas from the latent content so as to end up with the creation of a single image in the manifest content.

Throughout the famous seventh chapter of his book, which has elicited a great deal of commentary and which constitutes a book in itself, immersed, as it were, in the vast whole of the *Traumdeutung,* Freud sets up his conception of the psychic apparatus—or its first topography—on the basis of the "manuscripts" he had sent to Fliess, which had been inspired by all the theories of the psyche put forth by nineteenth-century thinkers. Thus he distinguishes between the conscious, the equivalent of consciousness; the preconscious, an agency accessible to the conscious; and, finally, the unconscious, an "other stage," a place unknown to consciousness. But while this last term had been in use for centuries and had been theorized for the first time in 1751, Freud made it the major concept of a doctrine that broke radically with the old definitions: the term no longer referred to a superconscious, a subconscious, or a reservoir of derangement, but to a place instituted by repression, that is, by a process aiming to maintain apart from any form of consciousness, like a "defect in translation," all the drive-related representations capable of becoming sources of displeasure, and thus capable of troubling the equilibrium of subjective consciousness. In the Freudian system of the first topography, repression is for the Acheron what the unconscious was for Oedipus and the preconscious for Hamlet.

What is most astonishing about this undertaking, through which Freud explained that dream analysis is "the royal road to the unconscious," is that his *Traumbuch* aspired to universality; he constructed it on the model of what Vienna had become for the intellectuals of his generation: a city divided between hate and love whose repressed grandeur inspired a real attraction for those thinkers. They were drawn not only to the atemporality and the deconstruction of the self that were experienced in Vienna, but also to the invention of a very strange modernity centered on the return to an ancestral past. In the words of Hugo von Hofmannsthal, Vienna was then, in the imaginary of Freud's generation, the "monstrous residence of a dead king or an unborn god."[53]

How could one fail to see in the famous dream of "Irma's injection," interpreted countless times,[54] the illustration of the "family romance" that united Freud with Vienna?

In the summer of 1895, a patient given the pseudonym Irma had been in treatment with Freud. Observing that she was not getting better, he suggested interrupting the treatment, but she refused. He then spent a few days with his family at the Bellevue residence, in the hilly section of Vienna, where Oskar Rie joined him after spending some time with Irma's family. Rie had several criticisms of Freud's treatment, and Freud wrote up his observation to present it to Breuer. During these few days, Martha was to celebrate her birthday and receive her friend Irma.

During the night of July 24, Freud dreamed that he met Irma at an evening gathering and told her that it was his fault that she was still suffering. Nevertheless, when he examined her he discovered grayish spots in her mouth that looked like small nasal conchae or symptoms of diphtheria. He summoned Dr. M., who limped and offered words of consolation. Freud then brought in two other friends, Leopold and Otto; the latter administered an injection of trimethylamine to cure the infection, which he himself had caused by using a dirty syringe.

Freud thought that this dream was of capital importance, noting that it was the first one he had submitted to detailed analysis (some fifteen pages). In his eyes, the dream was about the satisfaction of a desire that exonerated him from all responsibility for Irma's illness.

There is a link between the major importance that Freud attributed to this dream and the operation of autofiction in which he was engaging under the cover of impeccable rationality. Just as much as the realization of a desire or the affirmation of a completed interpretation, this dream in fact contained a sort of family romance concerning the Viennese origins of psychoanalysis. In it we find Oskar Rie (Otto), who was Fliess's son-in-law, Ernst von Fleischl-Marxow (Leopold), Josef Breuer (Dr. M.), and finally a condensation of Emma Eckstein and Anna Lichtheim, the daughter of Samuel Hammerschlag (Irma): the quintessence of the Viennese Jewish woman at the turn of the century.[55]

At the very moment he was presenting himself as the inventor of a doctrine that was to revolutionize the world, then, Freud was dreaming about the failure of his treatment of Emma. He attributed the responsibility

to Fliess—through the intermediary of Rie, embodied by Otto—and to Emma herself. Then he took his revenge on his critics by transforming his friends into adversaries. At the same time, he justified his choices vis-à-vis Breuer, and he remembered that his own daughter Mathilde had nearly died from diphtheria. He freed himself next from his guilt toward Fleischl-Marxow; and, finally, countering the mandarins of medical science, he asserted that dreaming could absolutely not be reduced to an expression of brain activity.

On June 12, 1900, he wrote to Fliess, "Do you suppose that some day a marble tablet will be placed on the house, inscribed with these words: 'In this house on July 24th, 1895, the Secret of Dreams was revealed to Dr. Sigmund Freud'?"[56] And on July 10, feeling exhausted and not prepared to take on other major problems, he had the impression of entering an intellectual hell and making out, in the darkest heart of its various strata, "the outline of Lucifer-Amor."[57]

Until 1929, Freud continued to revise this inaugural book, deepening his analysis and adding lists of reference works along with two contributions from his friend and disciple Otto Rank.

For a long time, the idea that the *Traumbuch* had been badly received prevailed. Accredited by Freud, on the same basis as the myths of "self-analysis" and "splendid isolation," this exaggerated presentation of one of the major works by the founder of psychoanalysis was repeated by Jones and by generations of practitioners. In his preface to the second edition, in 1908, Freud himself referred to the "deathly silence" that had greeted the book; a year later, he was still complaining that his work was not being taken seriously. Thus the reality invites more nuances, especially when we know what the intellectual and scientific life of the day was like.

For Freud had expected this work to be a best seller. Above all, he had expected to be hailed by psychologists and doctors as a true genius of science. The reality was very different. To be sure, the work was listed by virtually all the major journals in European medicine and psychiatry. On average, only seventy-five copies a year were sold over a period of eight years, enough, however, to ensure Freud an international reputation.[58] Moreover, even the attacks and insults he had to bear, along with the polemics that the book provoked, may well attest to an advance of the Freudian doctrine in the fields of psychiatry and psychopathology.

At the same time, the reception of the *Traumdeutung* in literary, philosophical, and artistic milieus (and in particular by the avant-gardes and the surrealist movement[59]) gradually helped guarantee for Freud the eminent place that was to become his in the history of Western thought.

As early as 1897, Hermann Nothnagel and Krafft-Ebing had proposed Freud as a candidate for a professorship at the University of Vienna. After numerous administrative hassles, and even though he had never taught, since he had opted for a career as a city doctor, in 1902 Freud finally obtained the highly desired nomination as an extraordinary professor,[60] which meant that his work was beginning to be recognized. From this point on, he would be Herr Professor, "the Professor."

At this point, there was already a before Freud and an after Freud. But he himself focused on his own destiny; he was simultaneously lucid, triumphant, and bitter, doubting and not doubting his own genius; he seemed not yet to want to become aware of the event of which he was the demiurge.

PART TWO

The Conquest

The Belle Époque

ON JANUARY 4, 1926, Freud confided to Marie Bonaparte that he had been quite disappointed by *Du côté de chez Swann:* "I don't think Proust's work can last. And that style! He always wants to go deeper, and he never ends his sentences!"[1]

If Freud so decisively failed to appreciate Marcel Proust's work, the author of *À la recherche du temps perdu* returned the favor: he never made the slightest allusion to Freud's work, although it had been enthusiastically received between 1910 and 1925 by the Parisian literary milieu, from André Gide to André Breton. In 1924, struck by this mutual ignorance, the editor of *La nouvelle revue française,* Jacques Rivière, sought to explain in a series of well-attended lectures he was giving at the Théâtre du Vieux-Colombier how thoroughly both Freud and Proust had explored dreams, the unconscious, memory, and sexuality, in parallel but dissimilar approaches.[2]

While Freud and Proust, each in his own way, were modern narrators of the exploration of the self, they also both viewed the mother, or her substitute, as the first object of attachment to which human beings turn. And this idea led the writer and the scientist alike to a conception of love according to which each human being desires to be loved by another just as he or she had been loved by a mother—or, in the absence of a mother figure, just as he or she would have wanted to be loved. As for homosexuality, which they called "inversion," Freud and Proust both defined it as the consequence of a bisexuality that was necessary to civilization and to the perpetuation of the human race. Without bisexuality, as they

saw it, men would be subjected to an excess of virility; little inclined to sublimation, they would be condemned to perpetual extermination.

Beyond these analogies, which introduced new perspectives at the dawn of the twentieth century, Freud and Proust were both quite attracted by the seductions of an aristocracy in decline that had merged with the bourgeoisie; giving up on the exercise of political power, this class was focused on the quest for the self, seeking in this way to regain access to lost time: the illusion of an existence devoted to its own end. Jewish but de-Judaized, Freud and Proust saw themselves as outsiders in the society in which they were immersed while remaining attached to that society's way of life and family traditions. They both offered lucid descriptions of the various spheres of this world, which was very much their own: the great bourgeois families, the social climbers, the domestic servants, the fringe elements. And since À la recherche du temps perdu ended in the aftermath of the First World War, it is hard to avoid observing that Proust's work featured the history of a social class whose European ideal had been traversed, since the rise in nationalism and anti-Semitism, by the conviction that it could only outlive itself by transforming each individual destiny into a work of art.

Freud's earliest patients and disciples thus resembled Proustian characters, cultivating the anguish of being themselves alongside the happiness of a personal freedom finally conquered in the bosom of a profoundly inegalitarian society, in which living conditions remained wretched for workers, peasants, and the poor.

Devoted to self-seeking, the cult of art, and the values of free-market liberalism, members of the well-educated class of the Belle Époque put all their hopes in science. From another perspective, at the heart of the rapidly changing continent, the Jews of Vienna were also actors in a significant period of ferment that seemed likely to go on forever. Having realized the ideal of moving beyond the ghetto, they displayed in dazzling ways the many facets of their multiple identity. They were engaged in an ongoing quest for a future whose reality would be projected into the past: scientific rationality and the resurrection of myths for Freud; the dream of a return to the promised land for Nathan Birnbaum and Theodor Herzl; the fantasy of a "red Vienna" for Viktor Adler and Otto Bauer; an ideal of destruction and satirical reconstruction of the German language for Karl

Kraus; nostalgia for a fusion between the French and German Enlightenments for Stefan Zweig; the affirmation of a Jewish and Austrian novelistic aesthetic for Arthur Schnitzler; the development of a new musical formalism for Gustav Mahler and Arnold Schönberg. All these Jews who were no longer Jewish sought to express the hidden face of a utopia that could supplant the dying world in which they knew themselves to be the principal actors.[3]

Even as he adopted the attitude of a Spinozan Jew, Freud always manifested the signs of the ambivalence associated with the late nineteenth-century Jewish identity crisis. He spoke unhesitatingly of "the Jewish race," of "racial belonging," and of "differences" between Jews and "Aryans," using the latter term to designate non-Jews. When he was exasperated by his early disciples, he was quick to call them "Jews" unfit to recruit allies for the new doctrine. However, the use of such expressions never led him to promote a psychology of racial difference, as he explained one day in a letter to Sándor Ferenczi: "On the matter of Semitism there are certainly great differences from the Aryan spirit. We can become convinced of that every day. Hence, there will surely be different world views and art here and there. But there should not be a particular Aryan or Jewish science. The results must be identical, and only their presentation may vary. . . . If these differences occur in conceptualizing objective relations in science, then something is wrong."[4]

Distressed that he was not more widely recognized, Freud seemed to be unaware that his "splendid isolation" was only a fantasy and that his work on dreams was actually receiving as much praise as criticism. He was scarcely conscious that he was living at a moment in which states of mind and soul had become an object of passion for a generation of obsessive introverts. Overcome by doubt, he perceived in the surrounding culture only what allowed him to nourish his own neurasthenia and his status as a solitary genius. Thus he was unaware that in reinventing Hamlet and Oedipus he was producing, in the subject lying on a couch, a faithful reflection of a character drawn by Alfred Kubin in 1902: a headless naked man, contemplating an immense melancholic head set on the ground, its mouth half-open, staring at him with its blind eyes.[5]

During this period, Freud wore a beard trimmed carefully by his barber every day. Somewhat stooped as he walked briskly, dressed in clothing

that was slightly too large but sober and elegant, he always looked visitors straight in the eye, as if seeking to show that he never missed a thing. He spoke German with a Viennese accent, in a clear, low voice, and he had a tendency to recount the facts of everyday life with the help of fiction. When he remarked on an act of forgetting or a misfire, if his interlocutor tried to explain it away in rational terms, Freud was intransigent, and his condemnation came down like a cleaver.[6] He worked sixteen to eighteen hours a day; he used a horse-drawn carriage when he had to make house calls, and he insisted that his household adhere to strict mealtimes. As for Martha, she had become a rigid housewife, attached to the immutable rituals involved in the proper management of her home.

Highly erudite and exceptionally intelligent, Freud read and spoke English, French, Italian, and Spanish perfectly. He wrote German in Gothic script, and he understood Greek, Latin, Hebrew, and Yiddish. *"Mare nostrum,"* he would say, characterizing himself as a Mediterranean, as distinct from the Celts, the Germans, the Prussians, the Scandinavians, the Americans, or the Swiss. He was a pure product of Viennese culture, a veritable Babel of sumptuous European sonorities. Neither a gourmand nor a gourmet, he nevertheless did not refuse certain pleasures of the table. He hated fowl and cauliflower; he did not appreciate the refinements of French gastronomy, but he had a pronounced taste for little Italian artichokes, boiled beef, and roasts with onions. He had no patience for any form of negligence. While he was endowed with a ferocious sense of humor, he was essentially lacking in charm. He tolerated neither lapses in language nor sloppy dressing, and he showed a certain disdain for people who were overweight. He did not like to go to the theater or dine in town; he did not dance the waltz, and he was not at ease when he had to mix with aristocratic high society.

Nevertheless, he bestirred himself willingly to attend an opera by Mozart, his favorite composer. Gallant and polite, he was happy to offer women flowers; he had a predilection for orchids and even more for gardenias. He enjoyed chess well enough, but he preferred tarot, devoting his Saturday evenings to it in the company of brilliant doctor friends Oskar Rie, Leopold Königstein, and Ludwig Rosenberg. He had a telephone installed in 1895, finding the instrument detestable but necessary; never-

theless, the telephone did not deter him from maintaining his celebrated correspondence on a daily basis.

Like all Viennese doctors at the beginning of the twentieth century, he employed four domestic servants: a cook, a maid, a governess, and finally a servant who opened the door to his patients. He generally took at least two months' vacation each year, between mid-July and late September. It was during these periods, and especially in August, that he spent time with his children, reserving the following month for his travels. He liked to bathe and swim on the beaches of the Adriatic. "Uncle Alexander," Martin Freud wrote, "was with us, and he and father were seldom out of the water, becoming completely sunburnt so far as the decorous bathing-costumes of the last century would permit. These costumes covered men's shoulders and even parts of their arms. Ladies of that era were even worse off: they had to cover their legs with long black stockings. I cannot recall ever having seen my mother or her sister in bathing-costumes, either on the Adriatic coast or at holiday places where there were lakes. It is probable that both were much too modest, or vain, to show themselves even in nineteenth-century bathing costumes; possibly they could not swim."[7]

This Belle Époque was the happiest of Freud's life. In a few short years he conquered the Western world, traveled frenetically in pursuit of a map of the unconscious of which he had been dreaming since his childhood, founded an international movement, and surrounded himself with a group of disciples who, after reading *The Interpretation of Dreams* with enthusiasm, helped to spread and shape his doctrine as no scholar among his contemporaries had been able or willing to do: not Pierre Janet, not Theodore Flournoy. Like socialism, feminism, and the ideas of the literary and philosophical avant-garde during this period, psychoanalysis became a symbol of an astonishing revolution of the mind.

Traces of this joy in existence are found in *The Psychopathology of Everyday Life,* which was written serially and published in two parts in a journal in 1901 before it appeared in book form;[8] Freud went on to revise and augment it endlessly over the years. Just as the analysis of dreams brought to light the nocturnal continent of thought, this new work, more modern in some respects, showed that the unconscious manifested itself continuously through the normal phenomena of psychic life in all waking

individuals in good health. This text was received with delight by writers, poets, linguists, structuralists, authors of detective stories, and Jacques Lacan.[9] With infinite pleasure Freud took hold of words, syntax, discourses, and narratives, finding omissions, slips of the tongue, mistakes, lapses, untimely gestures, and screen memories. All this linguistic material, he said, simply betrayed truths that escaped a human subject and that constituted themselves as organized knowledge, in a formation of the unconscious of which the subject remained unaware.

Before Freud began to focus on the matter, a number of authors had already reflected on the status of "free association," emphasizing that it allowed analysts to decipher, in a subject, a component unknown to him or her. Hans Gross, a German magistrate and the founding father of criminology, had become interested, for example, in slips of the tongue and in their value as clues to false witness in certain cases. His students had perfected a method of analysis—an "associative test"—that could be used during inquiries and investigations.[10]

But Freud went much further: he declared that these forms of *lapsus*— mistakes and other failures—were manifestations of repressed desires, often sexual in nature, that radically contradicted the subject's conscious intention. As always, he drew on numerous anecdotes from private life, his own or that of someone close to him. He drew on the German prefix *ver-* as the basis for a logical table of all the failures of discourse: *versprechen* (to commit a *lapsus* in speaking, or a slip of the tongue), *verhören* (a *lapsus* in hearing), *verlesen* (a *lapsus* in reading), *verschreiben* (a *lapsus* in writing), *vergriffen* (a *lapsus* in gesturing or acting), and *vergessen* (to forget words or names). This analysis was supplemented by a study of beliefs, instances of "luck," and superstitions.

Should we be surprised to find that this book, devoted to betrayal and how to detect it, set the stage for the break between Freud and Fliess, against a background of Freudian slips and reciprocal accusations? Be that as it may, while Freud was completing the first part of the text, adding an epigraph from *Faust* that had been identified by Fliess himself,[11] he still sought to convince himself that his work would be ill received: "I have taken a tremendous dislike for [this work], and I hope that others will take an even bigger dislike to it. It is entirely formless and contains all sorts of forbidden things."[12] And alongside these words—or "forbidden things"—

he affixed the three Christian crosses of conjuration to which the power of healing an illness or lifting a spell was traditionally attributed.

Once again, he was mistaken: this luminous book was greeted enthusiastically by a broad public; it not only contributed to his renown, it also helped to popularize the concept of the unconscious.

And while Freud was still engaging in self-doubt and feeling more persecuted than ever, he dreamed of leaving Vienna behind once again as he contemplated an object in his collection: "[A] fragment of a Pompeiian wall with a centaur and faun transports me to my longed-for Italy." And he added, thinking about his sojourn in Paris, *"Fluctuat nec mergitur."*[13]

In September 1900, in a letter to Martha written in Lavarone, a small city in southern Tyrol, Freud had written a sentence that sums up both his love of travel and his desire to reach Rome and then flee farther south: "So why are we leaving this ideally calm, lovely place with its wealth of mushrooms? Simply because there is only a week left, if that, and our heart, as we have observed, tends toward the south, toward the figs, the chestnuts, the laurels, the cypresses, the homes adorned with balconies, the sellers of antiquities, and all the rest."[14]

A year later, on September 2, 1901, accompanied by Alexander, he finally took possession of Rome, the city so often desired, bypassed, rejected: "Arrived in Rome after 2:00, changed my clothes at 3:00 after a bath and became a Roman. It's unbelievable that we didn't come here years ago. . . . Noon, facing the Pantheon, this is what I've been dreading for years! It is almost deliciously hot, and this means that a marvelous light is spreading everywhere, even in the Sistine Chapel. For the rest, one gets on divinely if one isn't forced to scrimp. The water, the coffee, the food, the bread: excellent. . . . Today I put my hand in the Bocca della verità and swore that I would come back."[15]

The trip to Rome was not only the accomplishment of an imagined revenge. The city was also the site of great archaeological promises, of reconnections with the timeless nature of femininity. Rome, for Freud, was an antidote to Vienna, a remedy, a drug. The promised land, the shining city, the kingdom of popes and Catholicism, Rome sent Freud back to his search for an elsewhere. A bisexuated city, a city idolized as much for its feminine charms as for its masculine power: "Unlike his approach to either England or Paris," Carl Schorske emphasizes, "his

perspective on Rome is Jewish, that of the outsider, but it is a double one. On the one hand, Rome is masculine, the citadel of Catholic power, and his dream-wish, as a liberal and a Jew, is to conquer it. On the other hand, other of his wishes show Rome as feminine: Holy Mother Church, promising gratification, is to be entered in love."[16]

In the depths and ruins of Rome, Freud became acquainted with the delights and violence of forbidden knowledge. In Rome's topography he discovered the secret of infinite pleasures: of taste, of vision, of hearing, of the soul. Like Goethe before him, he felt transformed by the Italy he found in Rome.

Three years later, when he spent five days in Athens, after a long sea crossing that had brought him from Trieste to Corfu, he finally visited the Acropolis: "I put on my finest shirt for the visit to the Acropolis. . . . It surpasses everything we have seen up to now and everything we have been able to imagine."[17]

Arriving at the foot of the Parthenon, he thought once again of his father. But in the land of the Olympians, it was less a matter of avenging him, as in Rome, than of expressing once again the degree to which access to Greek culture had allowed him to surpass Jacob. In the rain, Freud whispered into Alexander's ear the words that Napoleon Bonaparte had addressed, on the day of his consecration, to his brother Joseph: "What would our father have said?"[18] And at the very moment when he was identifying with Bonaparte, Freud felt himself traversed, as in a Proustian narrative, by a powerful sense of guilt. By adhering fervently to this classical culture, had he not renounced part of his Jewish identity? He also had the feeling that everything he was seeing truly existed, and not simply in books. "I am not worthy of such happiness," he thought, even as he was experiencing a sense of déjà vu, or déjà vécu: a double consciousness, a cleavage. He became aware of something strange, like a life already lived, as if what he was seeing then and there were not real.

He returned to this thematics in a book that he himself viewed as a diversion, and yet it marked the final stage in the trilogy of his maturity devoted to dreams and slips of the tongue and other unintended blunders: *Jokes and their Relation to the Unconscious.*[19]

Once again, Freud presented himself as an authority on family affairs, and especially as a "Jewish matchmaker" *(Schaden)* telling stories about

beggars *(Schnorrer)* that served as vehicles for expressing, through laughter, the large and small problems of the central European Jewish community confronted by anti-Semitism. Endowed with a corrosive humor, Freud loved to collect anecdotes that allowed him to make fun of himself and those around him by laughing at the darkest realities. This was a way of paying his respects to Yiddishland, the territory of his ancestors, dealers in oil and cloth—a land to which he would never return.

It was a celebrated book by Theodor Lipps,[20] a philosopher of empathy, that led Freud to look into the relation between jokes and the unconscious. This did not keep him from drawing on Henri Bergson or on Georg Christoph Lichtenberg's aphorisms, as well as on the comic tales told by Heinrich Heine or Cervantes.

In the new book, Freud began by studying the technique of jokes inasmuch as they make it possible to dramatize, socially and psychologically, the mechanism of pleasure in the presence of at least three protagonists: the author of the joke, the addressee, and the onlooker. But, as he showed, this did not suffice to reach the joke's ultimate objective, which was skepticism. A joke, as a formation of the unconscious, has to attack a fourth partner, a much more abstract player: the supposed reliability of judgment. Thus a joke is always, according to Freud, a sort of nonsense. It lies when it tells the truth, and it speaks the truth from the angle of lies, as attested by a famous Jewish story: "'Two Jews met in a railway carriage at a station in Galicia. 'Where are you going?' asked one. 'To Cracow,' was the answer. 'What a liar you are!' broke out the other. 'If you say you're going to Cracow, you want me to believe you're going to Lemberg. But I know that in fact you're going to Cracow. So why are you lying to me?'"[21]

If Freud saw dreams as expressions of the accomplishment of a desire leading to a regression toward thinking in images, he saw jokes as producers of pleasure authorizing the exercise of a ludic function of language. Its first stage, he emphasized, is child's play, and the second is joking. "For the euphoria which we endeavour to reach by these means is nothing other than . . . the mood of our childhood, when we were ignorant of the comic, when we were incapable of jokes and when we had no need of humour to make us feel happy in our life."[22]

Children and childhood occupied a central place in Freud's life. And since, in his view, all the emotional problems of adults originated in

childhood, he undertook to write a short work in which he spelled out his theories on infantile sexuality and on human sexuality more generally: *Three Essays on the Theory of Sexuality.*[23]

After the sumptuous trilogy from the turn of the century, which was an autobiographical narrative as much as an exploration of the various formations of the unconscious, Freud was now taking on a field that had been studied for years by educators, doctors, legal scholars, and sexologists. Nevertheless, contrary to a persistent legend, he was not the hero of a great dismantling of the "green paradise of youthful loves."[24] In 1905, when he undertook his new project, the field had already been explored extensively by contemporary scholars, who were convinced, as I have suggested, that children were perverse polymorphous beings. However, Freud helped deconstruct the child's universe still further by describing infantile sexuality as a "perverse polymorphous disposition." His choice of the term "theory of sexuality" *(Sexualtheorie)* deliberately marked a break with earlier approaches, since Freud used the term to designate both the hypotheses posited by scholars and the "theories" or phantasmic representations invented by children—and sometimes by adults—to resolve the mysteries of copulation, procreation, giving birth, and the difference between the sexes.

Playing on that ambiguity, Freud set forth with humor, and without resorting to psychiatric jargon, all the knowledge he had accumulated on the subject, whether from his own childhood or from contact with his children. He spoke without embarrassment or obscenity about suckling, defecation, playing with excrement, the various ways of urinating, and the uses of "dirty words." In short, he presented children under the age of four as beings who experienced sexual pleasure, cruel and barbaric creatures capable of indulging in all sorts of experiments that they would have to give up in adulthood. Hence the idea of the series of phases—anal, oral, genital, and, later, phallic—borrowed from the theory of evolution and charged with defining the stages of subjective life according to the objects chosen: feces, breasts, genitalia.

Freud added that infantile sexuality recognized no laws and no taboos, and that it was directed toward all possible goals and objects. And that is why the "theories" made up by children constitute a form of magical

thinking: babies come into the world via the rectum; human beings—men and women alike—give birth through the navel; and so on.

In a limpid, direct style, Freud tore away the old *libido sexualis* from medical discourse and made it a major determinant of the psyche: the goal of human sexuality, he said, is not procreation but the exercise of a pleasure that suffices in and of itself, and escapes from the order of nature. Sexuality is based on a drive (an impulse) that is manifested through a desire that seeks satisfaction by fixing on an object. To be sure, sexuality has to be controlled, but it must by no means be eradicated by corporal punishment.

By building his sexual doctrine around the terms "drive" *(Trieb)*,[25] "libido," "stage," and "desire" or "quest" for the object, Freud freed children—and thus adults as well—from all the accusations that late nineteenth-century medical practices had fostered, in an effort to repress the manifestations of childhood sexuality, and especially the charges emanating from "dark pedagogy." So a masturbating child was envisaged, from this new perspective, not as a savage creature whose evil instincts had to be tamed, but as a prototypical human being in progress. Freud normalized "sexual aberrations" by freeing them from all approaches couched in terms of pathology or in terms of innate dispositions comparable to "defects" or signs of "degeneracy."

In a perfectly natural way, he proceeded to analyze sexual perversions in adults, all the practices that were treated so flamboyantly by the sexologists of his day (pedophilia, fetishism, zoophilia, sadomasochism, inversion, and so on). But instead of drawing up a catalog of such practices, Freud sought to relate them to structures linked to specific stages of a subject's evolution. In this context in particular, he represented homosexuality not only as the consequence of a bisexuality present in all human beings, but as an acquired component of human sexuality: an unconscious universal tendency. Hence the famous formula he had already come up with in 1896 according to which neurosis is, in a way, the negative of perversion.

With this book, which he revised repeatedly, Freud opened the way to the development of child psychoanalysis and to a vast reflection on human sexuality. He pleaded for social tolerance toward the various forms

of sexuality—homosexuality in particular—and he insisted that adults not lie to children about where they come from.

Freud's work thus inaugurated an original way of thinking about the universal aspects of sexuality. Over the years, the new approach contributed both to the extinction of sexology—even though that field had been its primary matrix—and, in the second half of the twentieth century, to the surge in works by historians and philosophers on the history of Western sexuality, from Michel Foucault through John Boswell to Thomas Laqueur.

Once again, Freud had convinced himself that his new book was destined to stir up a scandal when it was published, and that it would make its author "universally unpopular." With every new printing, he complained of the bad reception that awaited it. In reality, in 1905, the work was greeted by mostly favorable articles, although it was not distributed widely. However, a few years later, as the psychoanalytic doctrine was spreading throughout Western societies through an organized movement and new publications, Freud's work on childhood sexuality was viewed in retrospect as pernicious, obscene, pornographic, scandalous, and so on.

Just as Freudianism was beginning to achieve international recognition, then, the accusations of pansexualism arose. At this point, resistance to the new theory of sexuality expressed in *Three Essays* became an obvious symptom that the doctrine was making progress.[26]

In 1909, in a fierce attack on psychoanalysis, the German psychiatrist Adolf Albrecht Friedländer asserted that psychoanalysis owed its success to a supposed "Viennese mentality" that attributed major importance to sexuality.[27] In so doing he was returning to the nationalist thesis of the *genius loci,* a notion that had come into fashion with the rise of anti-Semitism and the psychology of national or ethnic groups; it claimed that any given nation could be not only different from but also superior to another. On this basis, the accusation of pansexualism could serve as a warhorse for a fast-growing, primal anti-Freudianism. The term made it possible in effect to assert that Freud's doctrine was merely the expression of one culture seeking to dominate another.

In France, where Germanophobia was especially pronounced, Freud's sexual theory was conflated with a barbaric vision of sexuality, said to be Germanic, "Teutonic," or "Boche." The French contrasted the sup-

posed Cartesian luminosity of their own "civilization"[28] with what they took to be German *Kultur,* while in the Scandinavian countries and in northern Germany, on the contrary, Freudianism was accused of privileging a "Latin" conception of sexuality unacceptable to the Nordic "mentality."

During this period, Freud accepted requests for brief consultations from a number of figures in the art world who were curious to meet him; some left original accounts of their meetings, portraits that revealed the enthusiasm of a man who believed in his own power to decipher enigmas.

In 1905, the young Swiss poet Bruno Goetz, who was taking courses on Hinduism in Vienna, was afflicted with acute facial neuralgia. Freud had read some of his poems. For an hour, Goetz talked to him about his father, a ship's captain on long-distance voyages, and spoke of his own unfortunate love affairs with certain girls and a certain sailor whom he smothered with kisses. After obliging the poet to recall a childhood memory connected with the god Poseidon, Freud told him that his case was not suitable for analysis. Finally, in a paternal tone, he recommended that he eat well, including meat, and gave him a prescription and an envelope containing two hundred crowns, representing them as "a small payment for the pleasure which your poems and the story of your childhood have given me."[29]

Some time later, when he saw the poet again, he warned him against reading the Bhagavad Gita, which might plunge him into a state of annihilation. The neuralgia disappeared. "I am a doctor," Freud said, "and want to help, to the best of my ability, the many whose present lives are an inner hell. It is not in any afterlife but here on earth that most people go through hell, as Schopenhauer has quite rightly seen. My knowledge, my theories and methods have this as their object: to make men conscious of this hell so that they may escape from it. Only when they have learned to breathe freely will men perhaps rediscover what art can be. For the moment, they are misusing it, treating it as a narcotic in order to escape from their worries at least for a couple of hours. For them it is a kind of schnaps."[30]

A year later, Bruno Walter, conductor of the Imperial Court Opera, consulted Freud for pain in his arm that kept him from playing the piano and conducting. Instead of beginning treatment with him, Freud advised

him to travel to Sicily. The trip allowed the musician to discover the Greek temples there, to his amazement, but it did not cure his neuralgia. When Walter returned, Freud advised him to resume conducting, and used suggestion by offering to "take responsibility" himself for the risk of failure; he persuaded his patient to stop thinking about the pain. Later, Walter tried autotherapy, inspired by a book by the Romantic author Ernst von Feuchtersleben on the diatetics of the soul. He eventually overcame his handicap, retained his admiration for Freud, and advised his friend Gustav Mahler, who was suffering from melancholia, to see the psychoanalyst.[31]

After several cancelations, the two men finally met in Leyden on August 26, 1910, for four hours, during which they took a long walk through the city streets. "I take it," Freud remarked to Mahler, "that your mother's name was Maria. I should surmise it from various hints in your conversation. How comes it that you married someone with another name, Alma, since your mother evidently played a dominating part in your life?" With astonishment, "Mahler then told him that his wife's full name was 'Alma Marie' but that he called her 'Marie'!"[32] During the conversation, Mahler succeeded in understanding why his music was "spoiled" by the repetitive intrusion of a banal melody. In his childhood, following a particularly violent domestic row between his father and his mother, he had fled into the street and had heard a street organ playing a popular Viennese song; that tune had stuck in his memory and came back in the form of a bothersome melody.[33]

Freud did not yet see that at the heart of this Belle Époque, which had so often dreamed of a great blossoming of post-Enlightenment Europe in the wake of advances in industrialization and democracy, a mutual hatred among nations was taking shape, a dark foreshadowing that would lead that Europe, through the First World War, to its own annihilation.

By dint of contemplating itself in the mirror of its own boredom, the most cultivated bourgeoisie in the Western world had neglected to take the great poverty of the masses into account. And psychoanalysis, invented by a Jew of the Haskalah, the Jewish Enlightenment, a Teutonic science for some and a Latin science for others, was already experiencing the consequences: "We failed to see the writing on the wall in letters of fire," Stefan Zweig wrote later about that "world of yesterday." "Like King

Belshazzar before us, we dined on the delicious dishes of the arts and never looked apprehensively ahead. Only decades later, when the roof and walls of the building fell in on us, did we realize that the foundations had been undermined long before, and the downfall of individual freedom in Europe had begun with the new century."[34]

Disciples and Dissidents

PSYCHOANALYSIS, A STRANGE DISCIPLINE at the intersection of archae-
ology, medicine, literary analysis, anthropology, and psychology that
plumbs beneath the depths of intimacy, was never reduced by its inventor
to a clinical approach to the psyche. From the outset, Freud sought to
make it a full-fledged system of thought, one that could be conveyed by
a movement of which he would be not the leader but the master. Thus
he inscribed his teaching within the legacy of the great philosophical
schools of ancient Greece, adding a certain secularized tradition from
Judeo-Christian messianism. At a time when feminism, socialism, and
Zionism were all developing, Freud too dreamed of conquering a new
promised land and becoming a modern-day Socrates. And to carry out
his project, he could not limit his horizons to university teaching. He had
to found a political movement.

At age forty-four, he had acquired real notoriety within a vast move-
ment of renewal both in psychology and in the dynamic psychiatry that
had been spreading throughout Europe since the late nineteenth century,
against a background of challenges to the illusions of religion and in-
creasing unbelief. Freud began to gather around himself, informally at
first, a group of disciples who for the most part were not fully integrated
into the Viennese academic world. Rudolf Reitler, a physician from a bour-
geois Catholic family who specialized in thermal treatments, was the
first practitioner in this inner circle. Max Kahane, a melancholic French-
speaking doctor of Romanian origin and one of Freud's childhood friends,
was passionately interested in hypnosis and multiple therapies; he accom-

panied the movement in the beginning, although he did not subscribe to Freud's theory of sexuality.[1]

In the fall of 1902 Reitler and Kahane participated, along with Alfred Adler and Wilhelm Stekel, in the creation of the Wednesday Psychological Society (Psychologische Mittwochs-Gesellschaft, or PMG), the first such circle in the history of the psychoanalytic movement.[2] They were soon joined by Paul Federn, who liked to compare himself to the apostle Paul or to a subaltern officer of the psychoanalytic army; Hugo Heller, an editor and bookseller, came next, then Max Graf, a musicologist, Eduard Hirschmann, a tenacious psychobiographer, and finally Isodor Sadger and his nephew Fritz Wittels, both fanatic Freudians and misogynists.[3]

Immersed in the Viennese spirit, almost all Jews in their thirties (born between 1865 and 1880), these men adopted the custom of meeting after dinner on Wednesday evenings in Freud's home. At each session, seated around an oval table, they followed the same ritual: they placed the name of the prospective speakers in an urn, then listened in silence to a talk by the one whose name had been drawn at random. During a short pause, they drank black coffee and ate delicious cakes. They then plunged into interminable discussions, smoking cigars and cigarettes all the while. It was forbidden to read a paper written in advance, and no woman came in to disturb the banquet at which Freud was, in spite of himself, the secular prophet. During that period, and for a limited time, he always had the last word, and everyone seemed to venerate him. Without the dialogue he maintained in those days with this first generation of disciples, he would never have been able to nourish his own work as he did, continually revising it in the light of what each member of the group brought him.

These men, who did not yet practice psychoanalytic treatments, often compared themselves to paladins. Intellectuals and militants, they were quite representative of the culture of *Mitteleuropa*. In creating this inner circle, they were seeking to calm their anxieties and give substance to their dreams of a better world. When they spoke about their clinical cases, they were most often referring to themselves: to their often tumultuous private lives, their complicated family genealogies, their neuroses, their Jewish identity, their psychic and sexual troubles, their rebellion against their fathers, and often their deep melancholia.

In a word, they formed a sort of extended family, and they resembled their patients, who were from the same social class. A number of them were in treatment with Freud for their pathologies, and several began to treat their own family members, or else sent them to see Freud or one of their colleagues. Spouses, lovers, and sisters thus became patients and, later, therapists. As for the children of the members of this first circle, they were the first to experience the Freudian treatment, which some of the disciples began to practice in 1904.

Thus the Viennese musicologist Max Graf was introduced to Freud by Olga Hönig, who had been Freud's patient in 1897, just as he was abandoning the seduction theory.[4] Two of Hönig's brothers had committed suicide, and she herself had suffered from a serious neurosis. When Graf visited Freud, he asked him whether the young woman's mental state would allow her to marry him; Freud gave his blessing. In 1902, Graf joined the Wednesday group. Six years later, under Freud's direction, he treated his own son Herbert. He had begun to take notes on the way the child talked about sexuality by asking direct questions and by handling his "pee-maker." Under the name "little Hans," Herbert Graf was to become a famous case, one that allowed Freud to illustrate his theories on infantile sexuality and to give decisive momentum to the psychoanalysis of children. Freud had thus treated the boy's mother, and after the father had become his disciple, he allowed the latter to serve, under his direction, as the analyst of his own son. In these early days, the history of psychoanalysis was essentially that of a reconstituted family.[5]

Wilhelm Stekel, a doctor and a prolific writer, regarded Freud as a Christ figure and himself as an apostle. He adopted the master's sexual theories with a sectarianism that had to do with his own neurotic problems. Suffering from a pathological compulsion to masturbate, he was treated by the Professor during eight sessions without being freed of his symptoms. Freud admired his talent and his inventiveness, and borrowed certain themes from Stekel that he later put to good use in his own work, most notably on dreams and on repression. Very quickly, however, he became quite exasperated with his disciple, to the point of viewing him as an "absolute pig" and wanting to break with him.[6]

If Alfred Adler was the first major dissident in the history of the psychoanalytic movement, which he left in 1911, it was because, unlike Stekel,

he never adhered to the Freudian theses. Within the Wednesday community, he was already developing an original system of thought centered on the priority of the self: his individual psychology owed nothing to the colleague whose companion and rival he was for nine years. Born to a family of Jewish shopkeepers from the German-speaking community in Burgenland, a much more prosperous group than the one in Galicia, Adler attached much more importance to communal and fraternal bonds than to intrapsychic and genealogical relations. Whereas Freud made the family the keystone of his theory, to such an extent that he sought to apply his Oedipus complex to all societies, Adler saw the family as a changing community whose status needed to be studied by sociology, history, and anthropology. In his eyes, neurosis was the consequence of a struggle between the feminine and the masculine, and it derived from a feeling of inferiority that was repressed at the time a child first came into contact with sexuality. Adler was interested in Marxism, and after he married Raïssa Epstein, who had ties to the Russian intelligentsia, he spent time with Leon Trotsky. On top of everything else, Adler was never able to regard Freud, his elder by fourteen years, as a father figure to whom he would have to submit unconditionally.

Not only was Adler never a Freudian, not only was he completely unable to accept the mythology of the Labdacids, but he never had the kind of relation Freud had with his own Jewish identity. Although Adler was not imbued, as Karl Kraus and Otto Weininger were, with a sense of "Jewish self-hatred," in 1904 he sought to escape his condition by converting to Protestantism—which did not keep him from leading the life of a free thinker and a subscriber to reformist socialism.[7] He was already aware at that point that he could not be a disciple like the other members of the inner circle, and he began to challenge the idea that sexual causality could be the central pivot of a virtually ontological conception of the family and of a child's incestuous fixation on the parent of the opposite sex. The battle and then the break between the two men were inevitable. The one, an elegant and cultivated member of the bourgeoisie, endowed with university titles and sure of his genius, wanted to build an army of missionaries; the other, less brilliant and suffering from a lack of academic recognition, was seeking a forum for discussion and exchange: "Adler's theories were departing too far from the right path, and it was time to

make a stand against them. He forgets the saying of the apostle Paul the exact words of which you know better than I: 'And I know that ye have not love in you.' He has created for himself a world system without love, and I am in the process of carrying out on him the revenge of the offended goddess Libido."[8]

In May 1906, for his fiftieth birthday, a group of disciples offered Freud a bronze medal engraved by Karl Maria Schwerdtner and based on a superb art nouveau design by Bertol Löffler that the Professor used as his ex libris.[9] The front side showed Freud's bust in profile, while the back featured a stylized representation of Oedipus facing the Sphinx. Naked and leaning on a walking stick, this Viennese Oedipus, pensive and muscular, did not resemble any known portrait of Sophocles's character. Nor indeed did the Sphinx, represented as a somewhat witchlike modern woman whose animal aspect was clearly less important than the human aspect. The engraved Greek inscription had been chosen by Paul Federn, and it made no reference to the "Oedipus complex" but rather to the real meaning of Sophoclean hubris: "Who divined the famed riddle and was a man most mighty."

Reading these words, Freud seemed momentarily to forget his own redirected interpretation of Sophocles's tragedy and to remember with emotion that, during his university studies, he used to look at the busts of famous professors and tell himself that one day, perhaps, his own would be installed, accompanied by the famous citation.[10]

That year, the editor Hugo Heller sent a questionnaire to Freud and several other intellectuals asking them to name ten good books that they would always like to have at hand. Freud replied on All Saints' Day, emphasizing to the editor that for him it had not been a matter of selecting masterworks of world literature, but rather companions, "good friends" to whom "one owes a part of one's knowledge of life and view of the world."[11] And he gave ten names and ten titles in no particular order: Multatuli (the pseudonym of Eduard Douwes Dekker), *Letters and Works*; Rudyard Kipling, *The Jungle Book*; Anatole France, *Sur la pierre blanche* (On the white stone); Émile Zola, *Fécondité* (Fruitfulness); Dmitry Merezhkovsky, *The Romance of Leonardo da Vinci*; Gottfried Keller, *Die Leute von Seldwyla* (The people of Seldwyla); Conrad Ferdinand Meyer, *Huttens letzte Tage* (The last days of Hutten); Thomas Babington Macaulay, *Critical and*

Historical Essays; Theodor Gomperz, *Griechische Denker* (Greek thinkers); Mark Twain, *Sketches.*[12] Thus two French writers, one Dutch, two Swiss, two English, one Russian, one Austrian, and one American, all attached to the Enlightenment tradition. A work on the beauty of the jungle opposed to the artifices of modern life, another against colonialism, another on the abolition of slavery, a fourth on archaeology, another on the love of Greece, one on motherhood (its author was an important Dreyfusard), one on the apologia of a Prussian reformer, another on Dionysiac pleasures, another on the life of the greatest Renaissance painter, and a final work devoted to stories of the macabre treated humorously by a writer who defended the Jews. Freud had agreed to comply with a sort of associative test that authorized his readers and future exegetes to come up with a multitude of interpretations of his life and his work. Like Oedipus, the solvers of riddles indulged to their hearts' content.

During that period, Freud brought into his inner circle a young autodidact, a twenty-six-year-old apprentice lathe operator, Otto Rank.[13] The son of an alcoholic jewelry maker who came, like Adler, from Burgenland, Rank suffered from rheumatoid arthritis and was as preoccupied with that malady as with his own physical unattractiveness. In addition, he had been a victim of childhood sexual abuse and he suffered from a phobia that kept him from touching anything at all without wearing gloves.

Freud was extremely fond of him and quickly came to see him as an adoptive son. He encouraged him to enroll in the university and get a doctorate in philosophy. Above all, he named him secretary of the Wednesday society and made him responsible for transcribing the meeting notes. The inner circle thus became an important site of memory, and Rank was its first archivist. In the minutes, carefully preserved and eventually transmitted to posterity, Rank related the birth of a movement, making himself the messenger of the dialectic thinking developed in the group.

In 1907, the society still had twenty-one active members when Freud decreed its dissolution. Concerned at that point with respectability, and seeking to marginalize certain Viennese members who were overly enthusiastic, fanatical, or dissident in his eyes, he created a formal body, the Vienna Psychoanalytic Association (Wiener Psychoanalytische

Vereinigung, or WPV), the first psychoanalytic association in the history of Freudianism. He abolished the rule that required each member to take the floor under certain conditions, and in its place he instituted a set of procedures based on the de facto existence of a hierarchy between the master and his students, or even several masters and their students. Above all, Freud supported the entry of "foreign" disciples into this new institution, in particular Max Eitingon, Sándor Ferenczi, Karl Abraham, Carl Gustav Jung, and Ernest Jones.[14]

Thus the first core group of Freud's principal disciples took shape between 1907 and 1910; these men—they were all men—gradually helped internationalize the movement. They practiced psychoanalysis in most cases after pursuing treatment with another member of the group, with Freud himself, or with Federn or Ferenczi. The Socratic banquet was followed by a sort of Academy, riddled with quarrels but having as its main function the launching of a politics of psychoanalysis no longer centered in Vienna: it turned first toward Europe and later toward North America. To ensure the transmission of psychoanalytic knowledge, Freud and his disciples, with the help of Heller, founded three journals: the *Jahrbuch für Psychoanalytische und Psychopathologische Forschungen* in 1909, the *Zentralblatt für Psychanalyse, Medizinische Monatsschrift für Seelenkunde* in 1910, and finally *Imago*, two years later. The first was addressed to the general public, while the second was the organ of the international movement and the third was more aesthetic in inspiration.[15]

In contact with the members of this new circle, Freud resumed the intense letter-writing activity that he had been missing since his break with Wilhelm Fliess. On a daily basis, he wrote some ten letters in Gothic script in which he dealt with theoretical, clinical, or political questions as well as with everyday matters. In Freud's correspondence, the use of the familiar *Du* was reserved for family members and childhood friends; it was never used with disciples, male or female, who were addressed for example as *Lieber Herr Kollege, Herr Doktor, Lieber Freund,* dear Jones, *Liebe Marie, chère Princesse, Liebe Lou, Verehrter Freund und liebster alle Männer.*[16]

Freud asked all his correspondents for news of their spouses and their children; he took an interest in their health and never forgot their birthdays. Each disciple had a singular place in these exchanges, and he spoke to each about the others in a way that established a link among them,

passing through him. He sometimes produced contradictory statements on the same day, and he often committed real indiscretions on the pretext of sharing confidences with one of them about another, and vice versa. These men, whose mission was henceforth to found schools and groups in their own milieus and to spread the new doctrine, were all militants devoted to the cause of what they viewed as the greatest revolution of the twentieth century. None of them was servile, and none doubted the genius of the one they had chosen as master. Freud was part of their families, their private lives, their personal histories.[17]

This progress toward internationalizing the psychoanalytic movement was at the origin not only of the various doctrinal or transferential conflicts that arose but also of the construction of an official history based on the "hero legend." Over the years, Freud was regarded by those around him as a solitary thinker unfairly attacked but gloriously triumphant over his enemies, whether these were outside the inner circle or within it. In 1914, he added to that legend himself by publishing a contribution to the history of the psychoanalytic movement in which he asserted that psychoanalysis was his "thing" *(die Sache):* "For psycho-analysis is my creation; for ten years I was the only person who concerned himself with it, and all the dissatisfaction which the new phenomenon aroused in my contemporaries has been poured out in the form of criticisms on my head."[18] Eleven years later, at the request of an editor, he wrote a self-presentation *(Selbstdarstellung)* in the same vein, in which he exposed his "ego-history" and the subjective genesis of his discoveries.[19]

Magnificently written, these two works brought together the chaotic history of the origins of psychoanalysis in a mythical but plausible narrative, structured by the Freudian duality of a humiliated father and a rebellious son elevated to a heroic destiny. In the meantime, Freud added to this construction the idea that psychoanalysis as a discipline presupposed a decentering of the subject as it passed through three narcissistic humiliations: no longer being the center of the universe, no longer being outside the animal world, no longer being master of one's own house.[20] Not content to assign an Oedipal origin to his doctrine, Freud—who had earlier identified himself with Hannibal and with Napoleon Bonaparte— henceforth saw himself as the heir to Copernicus. A new confirmation of an enduring concern: how to proceed in such a way that his movement

could be referred to an epic of origins: a *chanson de geste,* with its fables, myths, pious tales, and images.

In 1908, the first major reunion of the new "Freudian psychologists" took place in Salzburg. Forty-two people from six countries participated, and they agreed to meet in Nuremberg two years later. In 1910, determined to bring psychoanalysis out of the "Viennese Jewish ghetto," with Ferenczi's collaboration Freud founded the Internationale Psychoanalytische Vereinigung (IPV), nicknamed the Verein (Association).[21] And he entrusted the leadership to Jung. In his address to the group, Ferenczi engaged in a brilliant exercise in insiders' history by distinguishing three major stages in the psychoanalytic movement: the "heroic" period (1896–1907), during which Freud had built his little circle; "Jung's" period (1907–1909), which had allowed Freud to implant psychoanalysis on the terrain of psychiatry; and finally the "American" period (1909–1910), which followed Freud's transatlantic trip.

After this sweeping introduction, Ferenczi asserted the need for the movement to yield to rational discipline, even as he gave evidence of great lucidity as to the fate of organizations: "I know the excrescences that grow from organized groups, and I am aware that in most political, social, and scientific organizations childish megalomania, vanity, admiration of empty formalities, blind obedience, or personal egoism prevail instead of quiet, honest work in the general interest."[22] Until 1918, after Salzburg and Nuremberg, the Verein held its congresses every two years in the German-speaking world of the old empires: Weimar (1911), Munich (1913), Budapest (1918). After the war, the choice was broadened between 1920 and 1936 to include the Netherlands, Switzerland, and Great Britain: The Hague, Berlin, Salzburg, Bad Homburg, Innsbruck, Oxford, Wiesbaden, Lucerne, and Marienbad.

A typical representative of the Budapest intelligentsia, Ferenczi was the son of a Jewish bookseller of Polish origin who had supported the people's springtime by espousing the cause of liberalism. Brought up in the spirit of the Enlightenment by a father he adored, Ferenczi had plunged enthusiastically into medical studies while maintaining the conviction, shared with the other intellectuals of his generation, that it was going to be necessary to rid Hungary of its past-oriented dreams in order to transform it into a modern country resembling the Western democracies.

Thus, from the outset, and unlike Freud, he was open to the debates led by avant-garde journals about art nouveau (*Jugendstil*), the emancipation of women, sexual freedom, and the expansion of the new sciences of man. In 1905, at age thirty-two, and after having worked at the Saint-Roch hospital, he had set up a private office where he practiced general medicine, neurology, and psychiatry while also serving as a medical expert in tribunals. Immersed in Darwinism, passionate about hypnosis, spiritism, telepathy, occultism, and mythologies, he was fascinated by the study of drugs and psychosomatic phenomena; as cultivated in literature as in philosophy, he had taken up the defense of homosexuals—the "Uranians"—in a courageous text presented to the Budapest Medical Association.

Leaning on the work of Magnus Hirschfeld,[23] Ferenczi refuted all stigmatizations and opposed the theory of degenerescence, upholding the idea of a bisexuality proper to the human species. And he cited Plato, Leonardo da Vinci, Michelangelo, Oscar Wilde, pell-mell: "No one punishes humans who love each other in a heterosexual way. Similarly, homosexuality, to the extent that it causes no damage to society, should not be sanctioned. Jurists are sometimes right to protect the interests of our society, but not to punish someone for a benign act. In doing that, they are inevitably rejecting beings of great value but with unfortunate instincts who become the prey of wretched, unsavory individuals. This is not in society's interest."[24]

Sensual, feminine, and sensitive to the suffering of his patients, Ferenczi met Freud in 1908 and became his closest disciple, not a crown prince or an heir but an adoptive son beloved by the master, so much so that Freud dreamed of giving him his daughter Mathilde in marriage. Ferenczi called himself a "paladin," a "great secret vizier," or an "astrologer of the heart"; he loved to visit clairvoyants in Budapest. He did not hesitate to plunge into controversies; he rejected Freud's authoritarian tendencies without ever dreaming of breaking with him. Over a quarter century the two men exchanged 1,200 letters: a treasure trove of clinical and theoretical invention punctuated with confidences and invaluable testimony about the customs and daily lives of the Freudians of the Belle Époque. Much more of a therapist than Freud, Ferenczi invented the notion of countertransference, and throughout his life he never stopped

modifying the principles of treatment and introducing special empathy into his relations with his patients and his students.

Like most of the disciples in the first circle, he intermingled his treatments with his private life and family affairs. In 1908, he accepted his mistress, Gizella Palos, as a patient in analysis; her divorce from her first husband had not yet been finalized, and her oldest daughter, Magda, was married to Ferenczi's brother Lajos. Three years later, he decided to analyze Elma, Magda's younger sister, who suffered from depression and with whom he quickly fell in love. In a succession of letters he confided his difficulties to Freud, who delighted once again in his activities as a "Jewish matchmaker" and a great connoisseur of intrafamilial affairs. He had lived through identical situations himself, whether by falling in love with a girl whose mother attracted him or by seeking to drag a fiancée away from the influence of a mother even as he established complicity with the other daughter. Moreover, he never stopped wondering about the desire for incest characteristic of the human species,[25] and about the question of the relations between love and transference.

In a blend of desire, love, and transference, Ferenczi decided to marry Elma even as he pressed Freud to take her as a patient in analysis. Some time later, he backed off and renounced the marriage after having analyzed his countertransference on the master's couch. Believing that he loved the daughter, he actually loved the mother, whom he ended up marrying when he saw that she cared for him. In 1919, rereading their exchange of letters in which the whole "recent history of the developments of psychoanalysis" was recorded, Ferenczi sent Freud his wholehearted thanks for his solicitude: "On this occasion, there arose in me like a gleam the insight that, since the moment in which you advised me against [marrying] Elma, I have had a resistance against your own person which could not even be overcome by the attempt at a [psychoanalytic] cure, and which was responsible for all my sensitivities. With the ucs. [unconscious] resentment in my heart, I, as a loyal 'son,' nevertheless followed all your suggestions, left Elma, again turned to my present wife [Gizella], with whom I have stayed, despite countless temptations from other quarters."[26]

While Freud showed considerable affection for Ferenczi, he maintained a certain distance from Abraham. Affable, attentive, eloquent, cultivated,

until his early death in 1925 Abraham remained an intelligent orthodox adherent to the psychoanalytic doctrine, a "rock of bronze," as Freud put it. Abraham devoted all his energy to implanting shared ideas in the Berlin psychiatric milieu, and to organizing a solid association of clinicians. He was the only disciple who did not turn to Freud for advice on affairs of the heart or on potential sexual relations with his patients; nevertheless, he analyzed his own daughter Hilda Abraham when she was six years old (she later became a psychoanalyst), and he published her "case" in an article in 1913.[27] In December 1907 he went to Vienna to meet Freud, who had received a visit some months earlier from Eitingon, from Zurich, whom he analyzed during "evening strolls."

The second son of a family of Orthodox Jews from Belarus, Eitingon was a fervent Zionist, accustomed to an itinerant life since childhood. He was twelve when his father, a wealthy fur trader, had settled in Leipzig; Max went to school there before beginning his university studies as an auditor, first in Marburg, then in Heidelberg. In 1902, after choosing to become a psychiatrist, he had had an assistantship in the Burghölzli clinic in Zurich with Eugen Bleuler, and there he met Jung and Abraham; he rejoined them in Berlin, where he remained until his definitive departure for Palestine in 1934.[28] In February 1920, after the collapse of the Central powers, Eitingon created his life's great work, out of his love for psychoanalysis: the Berliner Psychoanalytisches Institut (BPI), the first training institute, which would serve as a model for all the others later established throughout the world.[29] Throughout his tumultuous existence, he put his fortune at the service of his institute; in the context of a "policlinic,"[30] he also offered free treatments to the poor, while other patients had to pay. In 1930, he had singlehandedly become "the heart of the entire international psychoanalytic movement," according to Jones.

Located on the wooded hill in the Reisbach sector, the huge Burghölzli hospital, founded in 1870, took in patients afflicted with mental disorders. The architects had been at pains to build the edifice with its back turned toward the lake, so as to keep the sight of the water from inmates tempted by suicide. Under the leadership of August Forel and then Bleuler, a new approach to mental illness had been imposed, at the dawn of the twentieth century, in the heart of the prestigious fortress that was to become, over the years, an obligatory stop for all specialists. In this context, the

Freudian opening to the world of dreams and the unconscious aroused enthusiasm: the young therapists of madness looked at the work being done in Vienna as an innovation apt to bring psychiatric knowledge out of its therapeutic nihilism.

In 1898, when Bleuler took over as head of the hospital, psychiatry practiced in the German language—which had spread throughout Europe and into the rest of the world—was still dominated by Emil Kraepelin's nosography. A contemporary of Freud, Kraepelin had developed a rigorous classification of mental illnesses while remaining attached to a repressive view of madness that included very little effort to improve the patients' lots. Despite its power, Kraepelin's system was already splintering in reaction to the advances being made by an approach based on listening to subjects. To hear the patients' suffering, decipher their language, understand the meaning of their delirium, and establish a transferential relationship with them: such was the therapeutic program advocated by the Burghölzli hospital team.[31]

In 1911, drawing on his long-term project on early-onset dementia (dementia praecox), Bleuler synthesized his approach by assigning the label "schizophrenia" to a form of mental illness characterized by incoherent thought and delirious behavior. Without giving up on the idea of an organic etiology, he situated the illness within the field of psychological disorders, and he characterized it by dissociation of the personality (*Spaltung*) and a turning inward on the part of the subject (autism).[32]

Although he did not share the Freudian conception of sexuality, Bleuler proposed to integrate the psychoanalytic approach into the treatment of psychoses. Hence the analogy: just as Freud had transformed hysteria into a modern paradigm of neurosis, Bleuler invented schizophrenia and made it the structural model for mental illness in the twentieth century.

When Jung, who was Bleuler's assistant at the time, got in touch with Freud in October 1905, the latter already knew that the encounter would be decisive for the history of his movement. Up to that point, psychoanalytic treatment had seemed to be reserved for neuroses; now, outside of Vienna and far from Berlin, the continent of psychoses seemed to be opening up for it: a new "promised land." Psychoanalysis was an urban phenomenon that went hand in hand with the transformation of the traditional family, and it presupposed the confrontation of subjects with

themselves, whereas psychiatry, a medical discipline, remained dependent on a collective conception of care for the psyche. Moreover, since the mid-nineteenth century, the organization of asylums had been taking place outside cities, in natural settings. The trend presupposed the creation of temporary or permanent living spaces capable of filling in for inadequate families that could not take care of their afflicted relatives. Thus large public or private hospital spaces had been developed, modeled on boarding schools and sanatoriums, where doctors, nurses, and caretakers lived together with patients. Thanks to its federal organization and its privileged geographic situation, along with an intense pedagogical tradition rooted in Calvinism, Switzerland, with its numerous lakes and mountain regions, had become in just a few decades one of the European countries with the most prosperous clinics. Like Bleuler and the entire team at Burghölzli, Jung never touched a drop of alcohol. With his intimate knowledge of mental illness, he was strongly drawn to psychotic patients. He never feared their threats, because he knew he was strong enough to fight back; he worked with them to organize dances and costume balls.

For the first time, Freud was about to have a young disciple of exceptional intelligence. One of Bleuler's most brilliant students, Jung owed Freud nothing, and he was already known for his own work on free association and the psychogenesis of mental illnesses.[33] From the start, Freud wanted to turn this talented—and sometimes mythomaniacal—pastor's son into a crown prince who would be all the more useful, Freud believed, in that he was neither Jewish nor Viennese. By granting such a place to this thirty-year-old man who dreamed, as Freud did, of a glorious destiny, he thought he could protect psychoanalysis from the dreaded characterization as a "Jewish science," which went hand in hand with the accusation of "pansexualism."[34] As a result, during that period, he refused to recognize that his cherished heir designate, whom he frequently compared to Joshua,[35] maintained an ambiguous relation, to say the least, with the "Jewish question."[36] "Be tolerant," Freud wrote to Abraham in 1908, "and do not forget that really it is easier for you to follow my thoughts than it is for Jung, since . . . you are closer to my intellectual constitution through racial kinship, while he as a Christian and a pastor's son finds his way to me only against great inner resistances. His association with us is therefore all the more valuable. I was almost going to say that it was only

by his emergence on the scene that psychoanalysis was removed from the danger of becoming a Jewish national affair."[37]

Just as Freud was the heir of a rationalist conception of science and of a universalism that did not tolerate any form of relativism, so Jung had come out of an entirely different tradition in which were mingled esoterism, antimaterialism, spiritism, occultism, enthusiasm for the spiritual, an attraction to the subliminal unconscious and the phenomena of multiple personalities,[38] and finally the psychology of peoples. As a neurologist and a physiologist, Freud cultivated abstinence even as he based his doctrine on the primacy of the sex drive. Jung, as a psychiatrist and a reader of philosophical texts (Kant, Nietzsche, and Hegel), saw himself rather as adhering to a broadened conception of the libido, understood as "vital energy." At once a polygamist and a Calvinist, Jung did not hesitate to multiply amorous adventures with his patients, whom he was to turn into disciples.

The relationship between the two men was passionate at first, before it became conflictual and then hostile. After the break in 1913, Freud accused Jung of giving in to the "black mud of occultism," while Jung experienced his rupture with Freud as a liberation, although he was soon overcome by a crisis of melancholia.[39] Throughout his life, he remained aware of the supremacy of Freud's doctrine over his own,[40] even though he felt that he was socially superior to Freud; in his eyes, the latter was only the son of a lower-class Jewish tradesman married to a poor woman.[41] As for Freud, convinced of the value of his own system of thought, once again he turned out to have loved a man whom he first regarded as a son and a disciple, before transforming him into an enemy.

Jung had had a disturbed childhood, so much so that he was haunted, once he reached adulthood, by terrifying memories that made him hate Jesuits and the Catholic Church, and which reminded him of the extent to which a phantasmic sense of unworthiness had been present all through his school years. No doubt he had been reminded that he was the grandson of another Carl Gustav (called "the Eldest"), a doctor and the head of the university in Basel; a tenacious legend made this Carl Gustav out to be an illegitimate son of Goethe's.

Short tempered, resistant to the patriarchal order and subject to frequent fainting spells, the young Jung took refuge very early in the con-

templation and study of the major texts of Western civilization, before he turned toward medicine. He had acquired an intuitive knowledge of mental illness within his own family, especially in the case of his mother, Emilie Preiswerk, whom he observed as she gave herself over to spiritism, in the company of her own father, an "illuminated" pastor, along with her brother and her nieces. When Jung began to exchange what was to become a very rich correspondence with Freud, he had the feeling that he had crossed paths with a messiah capable of saving him from his own "unworthiness" in relation to a sexual advance: "Actually—and I confess this to you with a struggle—I have a boundless admiration for you both as a man and a researcher, and I bear you no conscious grudge. So the self-preservation complex does not come from there; it is rather that my veneration for you has something of the character of a 'religious' crush. Though it does not really bother me, I still feel it is disgusting and ridiculous because of its undeniable erotic undertone. This abominable feeling comes from the fact that as a boy I was the victim of a sexual assault by a man I once worshipped."[42]

Jung became Bleuler's assistant in 1895; he defended his thesis on the case of a young female medium afflicted with somnambulism, who was later discovered to be his cousin, Hélène Preiswerk. In Jung's study, actually a disguised autobiography, he painted a terrifying picture of the familial universe of his patient while treating her in a scornful fashion, reducing her to a subject of observation and emphasizing that her parents were mentally ill. The text, well received by Theodore Flournoy, nevertheless stirred up a storm of indignation.[43]

Jung then had the opportunity to escape his family by marrying a beautiful, intelligent, wealthy, and distinguished woman, Emma Rauschenbach. His wife's fortune allowed him to write without needing to worry about his income, but also to live in privileged conditions while frequenting the best circles of the upper bourgeoisie in the financial world of German-speaking Switzerland. Despite the servitude of her position as mother and wife, worn out by her numerous pregnancies and wounded by her husband's many infidelities, Rauschenbach became Jung's disciple after undergoing analysis with him.

On March 3, 1907, a very elegant presence as usual, Rauschenbach accompanied her husband to Vienna for his first meeting with Freud. The

latter greeted him at his hotel holding a bouquet of flowers. Intimidated, Jung had asked Ludwig Binswanger to go with him to this so eagerly anticipated encounter. A nephew of Otto Binswanger, the head of the famous Kreuzlingen clinic where Bertha Pappenheim had spent some time, the young Ludwig ardently desired to make the acquaintance of this master whom he so admired.[44]

Impressed by Rauschenbach, who was so different from the women around him and who most notably was from a different social class, Freud was at his most amiable. The guests were invited to share a meal with the entire family, but it quickly became obvious to the others how impatient the two men were to find themselves alone, to begin a dialogue that went on long into the night.[45] Jung spoke without stopping for three hours, and Freud finally interrupted him, suggesting that they converse in an orderly fashion. The exchange went on for ten hours, and each man had the feeling that he was sharing convergent opinions with the other. Jung was struck, however, by the "complete" absence of "philosophical awareness" on the part of his interlocutor, by his "positivism," and by the extravagant importance he accorded to sexual theory.

While the men were conversing, a loud noise coming from the library made them jump. Convinced that the source was a phenomenon of "cataleptic externalization,"[46] Jung, always on the alert for voices from the beyond, announced that a second noise would soon be heard. Freud judged his guest's superstitions "pure hogwash," while Jung thought he detected a mark of terror on his host's face when a second cracking noise occurred.

Convinced of the depth of Freud's genius, Jung was nevertheless certain at the outset that his own neurosis would be an insuperable obstacle in their relations. On his side, in spite of his fear that Jung would not live up to his hopes, Freud invited him to join his circle without suspecting that his new colleague, imbued with a sense of his own superiority, would quickly come to look at the other members as "a medley of artists, decadents and mediocrities."[47] In reality, from this first meeting on, Freud and Jung both found themselves in an intolerable situation vis-à-vis the other. Freud believed he had found an heir apt to adhere to his doctrine, and Jung thought he had met a father capable of loving him. But at the very moment when each was trying to convince himself of the power of

their union, the son was already rebelling against the father, while Freud was worrying that this imaginary Joshua would become his chief rival.

In addition, neither of the two protagonists was willing to see, at that point, that the Freudian invention was hardly suited, strictly speaking, to the psychiatric clinic. Yet the majority of the Professor's students—Jung first and foremost—were psychiatrists who thought, quite rightly moreover, that the psychoanalytic method, inherited from the dynamic approach, was going to transform the way Western society looked at mental illness from top to bottom. And if Freud viewed this discipline as a promised land to be conquered, the psychiatrists looked at psychoanalysis as the weapon that would allow them to achieve that conquest.

At all events, the psychoanalytic way of thinking in fact proceeded from a genuine rejection of the prevailing notions in psychiatry and medical psychology. Although Freud admired Philippe Pinel, he never used the alienist vocabulary: mental state, personality, character, doubling, clinical psychology, alienation, behavior, and so on. He did not prescribe remedies, did not think about the way asylums were set up, and did not concern himself with the way the collective life of mentally ill patients was managed. He took into account only speech, language, sexuality, neurosis, life, death. In his eyes, human destiny was organized around intimate forces, dynamic principles, psychic topographies. In short, Freud defined psychosis as the unconscious reconstruction of a delirious reality, and he inscribed it in a tripartite structure by virtue of which it was differentiated from neurosis and perversion.

Neither a psychiatrist nor a sexologist, Freud rejected all forms of nomenclature. And by the same token he never seriously thought that mentally ill patients could be psychoanalyzed, because in their case the unconscious was already laid bare. Thus, when he had to deal with an individual case of mental illness, he always tried to "neuroticize" it. Freud was first and foremost a doctor of the psyche, a humanist who worked with words, dreams, and mythologies, a physician of solitary suffering, a man of science trained in neurology and physiology. The world of psychiatry, with its normative classifications, its asylum universe, its observations of bodies and behaviors—this world organized politically as a state within the State, the closed world of Bleuler, Jung, Binswanger, and many others—was not his.

The morning after their memorable first meeting at 19 Berggasse, Freud engaged in his favorite exercise by asking Jung and Binswanger to tell him their dreams: "I no longer remember Jung's dream," Binswanger said later, "but I remember how Freud interpreted it. The interpretation tended to show that Jung wanted to dethrone [Freud] so as to take his place. As for me, I dreamed of the entrance to the house at 19 Berggasse, which was being remodeled just then, and I dreamed of the old light fixture hastily covered over because of the construction. Freud's interpretation, which did not strike me as particularly convincing . . . was that the dream contained the desire to marry his (eldest) daughter, along with the denial of this wish, since he declared . . . 'I am not marrying someone who is from a house where there is such a dilapidated light fixture.'"[48]

Freud and Jung went on pursuing their passion for interpreting dreams for a long time. Both of them, like all the disciples in the first circle, were certain that henceforth, thanks to their shared doctrine, the unconscious had made a spectacular entry into the everyday life of European societies. It was as though it would soon no longer be possible to immerse dreams in sleep, to conceal them in the depths of nocturnal life, since, through the miracle of Freudian interpretation, man himself had become the embodiment of dreams. This was the maxim of the new day, which the poet Joë Bousquet later summed up in a striking formulation: "There were signs that a time was coming when people would no longer dream, man having become the dream."[49]

The Freudians of this generation were convinced that the symbolic revolution they represented had to be extended to all realms of thought. Psychoanalysis had to be "applied" to literature, to the study of myths and religions, to the science of history, to anthropology, to art, and to the entire set of human productions. Intense discussions were pursued within the Wednesday society, later in the WPV, in an effort to distinguish applied psychoanalysis from the "pathography" that had been developed while medical discourse was pressing its own authority over the lives of the mentally ill.

It was in this context that Jung received, with great pleasure, the essay Freud devoted to a novel by Wilhelm Jensen, *Gradiva, ein pompejanisces Phantasiestück* (Gradiva, a Pompeian fantasy).[50] The young man from Zurich, too, loved to recount dreams and compare literary texts to clinical

narratives. And he was already interested in the great cosmic mythologies and in Orientalism. He knew, in this connection, that Freud had been seduced by a famous bas-relief representing a Greek girl walking, her garment slightly raised to reveal her sandal-clad feet, one solidly on the ground and the other lifted so that only the tips of her toes seemed to graze the earth. Such was Gradiva, a mysterious woman, molded in stone, draped in a tunic with disorderly folds, and advancing with warlike footsteps toward an unknown destination: Was she going into battle, or did she want to give life?

Published in 1903, Jensen's story brought together all the themes of turn-of-the-century love stories: confusion between delirium and desire, omnipresence of ancient ruins, dead women, mourning, and evanescent passions. Freud was so drawn to Gradiva that he acquired a cast of the bas-relief and hung it on his office wall.

In Jensen's short story, Norbert Hanold, a young archaeologist, falls in love with the woman in the bas-relief, who captivates his gaze. In a nightmare he sees her as a victim of the eruption that had engulfed Pompeii in the first century CE. Convinced upon awakening that his dream revealed a truth, he leaves for Pompeii after noticing a silhouette in the street that resembled Gradiva's. On his visit to the ruins, he believes he is meeting Gradiva when he spots a very real young woman, Zoé Bertgang, whose name means "the woman who shines by her way of walking." Understanding the mental state in which Hanold finds himself, she tries to cure him and succeeds, by managing to bring repressed recollections up from his memory. In fact, she lives in the same city as he, and as children they had been good playmates.

One can understand how Freud could have been seduced by this text, to which Jung himself had drawn his attention. The story seemed to stage the mechanisms of the unconscious and of dreams, while at the same time attributing to the fictional characters the respective roles of patient and therapist. Thus Freud could find support for the thesis according to which the dreams invented by writers could be interpreted in the same way as those of patients. Better still, such narratives offered perfect illustrations of something he had asserted to Arthur Schnitzler: "I have often asked myself in astonishment how you came by this or that piece of secret knowledge which I had acquired by a painstaking investigation of the

subject, and I finally came to the point of envying the author whom hitherto I had admired."[51]

Freud wanted to go further, but he ran up against serious difficulties. In fact, after sending Jensen a copy of his book, he received in response a friendly letter acknowledging his understanding of the story. But, acting on the advice of Jung, who had pointed out to him two other texts by the same writer, he imagined that Jensen had experienced an acute incestuous desire for his younger sister, who was handicapped by a club foot. Once again he was mistaken, and was rejected. Annoyed by Freud's questions, Jensen explained in the end that he did not have a sister but that in childhood he had indeed experienced amorous feelings toward a friend, a girl who had died young. Thus *Gradiva* came to acquire an incredible posterity, especially among the surrealists. According to the Freudian concept of neurosis, Hanold had all the traits of a hysteric. But, for Jung, Jensen's novel was the expression of true delirium, in the psychiatric sense of the term.

Madness was something Freud constantly encountered among his patients and his disciples, who found in the Oedipean tragedy of sons rebelling against their fathers the echo of their own rebellions.

It was in this context that Otto Gross came into contact with the Freudian adventure. An only child, Gross had been reared as a prince by his parents, who saw him as a prodigy of intelligence.[52] His father, Hans Gross, a friend of Richard von Krafft-Ebing and an admirer of Freud's early writings, dreamed of associating his gifted offspring with his own work. Thus he gave Otto a privileged education, without reproaches or constraints, which contrasted markedly with the theses that he was defending and that he was putting at the service of forensic science. An enthusiast in the struggle against the so-called degeneration of societies, this well-known penologist sought in fact to combat prostitution, homosexuality, perversions, and pornography not only by police repression but also by the interdiction of novels deemed "immoral." He lashed out against "masculinized" women, anarchists, vagabonds, and gypsies, whom he saw as "dishonest and thieving."

Subjected for years to the love of this father whose delirious theories seemed to be absolutely rigorous and above all in keeping with late nineteenth-century racialist ideology,[53] Otto Gross became a brilliant psy-

chiatrist. However, shortly after earning his doctorate, he signed on as a shipboard doctor on the Hamburg–South America line and indulged in various drugs: cocaine, opium, morphine, and so on.

When he returned, after several placements in neurological clinics in Munich and Graz, he underwent an initial detoxification treatment in the Burghölzli clinic. In 1903, he married Frieda Schloffer, and through her made the acquaintance of Marianne Weber (the wife of the sociologist Max Weber) and also the von Richthofen sisters, with whom he had relationships.[54] Appointed as a university lecturer with a degree in psychopathology, Gross served as Kraepelin's assistant in Munich and became enthusiastic about Freud's work even as he demanded that he himself be viewed as a prophet. After meeting Freud, who was not unhappy to have the son of such a celebrity as a disciple, Gross turned toward the practice of psychoanalysis while frequenting the intellectual milieu of the Schwabing district in Munich, where the disciples of Stefan George and Ludwig Klages mingled early in the new century. As Jacques Le Rider emphasizes, Nietzscheanism in that context took the form of a metaphysics of the "cosmogonic eros," in which nostalgia for an archaic Dionysism inspired by Johann Jakob Bachofen's mythological research on "matriarchy" was manifested.[55]

It was via this cult, and by advocating sexual immoralism and ecstatic practices, that Gross militated in favor of psychoanalysis, seeking to counter his father's theses and highlight everything the latter condemned: the fragility of beings, hedonism, pleasure, matriarchy, abnormality, feminism, women's rebellion: "Degenerates are the salt of the earth" and "The healthiest state for a neurotic must be sexual immorality," he would say. In short, he combined Freudianism and Marxism to spell out a "program" of sexual liberation that would later be taken up, but differently, by Wilhelm Reich and the Freudo-Marxists.

In May 1908, coerced by his father, he was admitted to the Burghölzli clinic for a second detoxification treatment, accompanied by his wife, Frieda, whom he subjected to his whims. Freud, who had drafted a certificate in his favor, asked Jung to supervise Gross's withdrawal, hoping that he himself could then take him as a patient in analysis, though this did not happen. Even as he vaunted his own worth as a theoretician, Jung issued two successive diagnoses: obsessional neurosis, then dementia

praecox. Thus Gross became a disciple-patient caught between a master and another disciple, himself a future dissident. Thanks to Gross, in a way, Jung could maintain, in relation to Freud, the validity of the notion of dementia praecox that Freud was resisting. Jung first undertook to see Gross as an absolute madman, then became attached to him without managing to help him; he even reached the point of viewing him as a twin brother.

Gross ate nothing but vegetables cooked according to his specifications; he was unkempt, he never washed or shaved, and he used opium alongside the medications prescribed for withdrawal. He put on several layers of clothing when it was hot, required that all lamps be lighted, wandered the corridors of the asylum and scribbled drawings on the walls and floors; he slept with a pillow pressed over his head.

The treatment ended disastrously. After a manic phase, Gross fled the clinic and sought treatment next from Stekel, with no greater success. In the Burghölzli clinic, Jung also took care of Frieda, who made clear to him the benefits of their common erotic emancipation, while she told Jones how much she suffered from her situation and from her husband's escapades.[56]

Most of Freud's disciples soon came to look at Gross as a dangerous extremist apt to harm the movement. Depraved, immoral, an anarchist, fiercely attached to the thematics of revolution by way of sex, Gross was dismissed without ceremony by Freud, who suddenly decided that he was distorting the psychoanalytic cause. This did not prevent Gross from continuing to practice and identify with Freudianism. After creating a scandal by treating a young woman who was rebelling against parental authority, he lived with an anarchist woman painter who killed herself in 1911. Accused of incitement to suicide, then institutionalized several times, finally pursued by the police, who continually hassled him for "subversive activities," he brought his wandering life to an end in 1920, after his father's death and the fall of the powers, on a sidewalk in Berlin, carried off by hunger and cold.

Clearly, Freud did not know what to do with the disciples who were mentally ill, transgressive, inventive, and talented;[57] in some ways they took his doctrine literally, while reading into his texts things that were not there, in an effort to launch a much more extreme revolution of self

and society than Freud had in mind. A mediocre clinician of mental illness, but concerned first and foremost with building a movement that could serve as a support for his theses, the Professor felt obliged to satisfy public opinion with proof that his acolytes were honorable therapists. Thus he was always quite unjust toward those who, through their excesses, gave his doctrine a very different face, one that recalled to him Fliess's delirium and his own early divagations.

In this respect, Freud did not have as much room to maneuver as writers and poets did: he had undertaken to build a movement that would be accepted by science. An impossible mission, of course. Still, under these conditions, how could he have seen that the cult of orthodoxy always ends up feeding sterility of thought along with its deviances and its transgressions?

Franz Kafka would thus be more perceptive than he, giving a strikingly convincing portrait of Gross: "He made me think of the consternation of Christ's disciples at the foot of the cross."[58] In contrast, Max Weber, who had become acquainted with psychoanalysis by way of Gross's extravagances, proved to be quite severe toward Freud and his disciples, judging that psychoanalysis brought no new ethical demands to humanity and that it threatened to lead to the replacement of scientists by "directors of souls."[59]

In 1908, Jones was the man of the hour, the one who could bring Freud what Jung did not offer him: the political means necessary for the transmission of his work, for the normalization of psychoanalytic practice and the worldwide extension of the Verein.

Born in Wales to a lower-middle-class provincial family, Jones had a difficult childhood under the authority of a father who believed that children should not commit any acts of insubordination; he turned toward psychiatry after studying with the great neurologist John Hughlings Jackson. When he became acquainted with Freud's early writing, Jones was convinced that psychoanalysis was bringing a new rationality to the world, and he learned German so he could read *The Interpretation of Dreams* in the original.

The education he had received led him, like many others, to rebel against the established order and the prevailing moral standards in an England that was still very Victorian. Very early on he had developed an

acute awareness of sexual practices, and he spoke of them with a frankness that did not sit well with his entourage—a way of challenging the law of the father. And as he was also seducer of women, accustomed to maintaining multiple liaisons, he could not be indifferent to the new Freudian theory of sexuality. Thus he began, in 1906, to practice psychoanalysis spontaneously. A year later, in Amsterdam, he met Jung at a neurology conference, and was invited to work with him at the Burghölzli clinic, where he was introduced to the new psychiatry even as he witnessed the downward spiral of Gross and Frieda.[60]

On April 30, 1908, after the Salzburg conference, Jones paid a visit to Freud in the company of Abraham Arden Brill, a psychiatrist who was born in Galicia but emigrated to the United States around 1890 after violent conflicts with his father, an officer in the imperial army. Jones wanted to meet Freud, while Brill wanted to become Freud's analysand and his American propagandist.

The result of this visit was disastrous for Jones but beneficial to Brill, to whom Freud entrusted the translation of his works without noticing that this capricious disciple did not know English well or that, most importantly, he dreamed of adapting the Viennese doctrine to a so-called American mind.

In the early phase, Jones displeased Freud. Hence the following exchange with Jung: "Jones is undoubtedly a very interesting and worthy man, but he gives me a feeling of, I was almost going to say racial strangeness. He is a fanatic and doesn't eat enough. . . . He almost reminds me of the lean and hungry Cassius. He denies all heredity; to his mind even I am a reactionary." And later: "I find the racial mixture in our group most interesting; [Jones] is a Celt and consequently not quite accessible to us, the Teuton and the Mediterranean man."[61]

In a first phase, then, Freud felt no sympathy toward this "Celt" who came from a different world from his own. Jones expressed no interest in *Mitteleuropa,* understood neither the baroque follies of imperial Vienna nor the dreams of melancholic atemporality that haunted the first circle of disciples. Jones was neither Jewish, as they were, nor fascinated by spiritism and Ouija boards, as Jung was, and while he respected Ferenczi's clinical genius, he had no inclination for telepathy or the seers of Budapest. A conservative, a pragmatist, more a neurologist than a psychiatrist,

and very favorably disposed toward the emancipation of women in a country in which feminism was at the forefront of every conflict, he rejected the idea that psychoanalysis was the bearer of a possible social or philosophical revolution. Thus he sought to connect it with medicine while inciting it to launch debates with other disciplines, especially anthropology, which was rapidly expanding in the English-speaking world at the time. In short, having come from the extreme edge of Europe and as a pure representative of the liberal values of one of the most powerful Western democracies, Jones was historically, politically, and geographically the man of the future of psychoanalysis.

Never seeking to seduce a master in whose company he could have found some paternal support, Jones aspired solely to serve a "cause" and to defend it, if necessary, at the price of turning against its founder and being unfaithful to him. From the outset, he positioned himself with respect to Freud as an heir whose fidelity went well beyond attachment to the person. And Freud had to admit that this tireless worker, who had no desire to "surpass the father," brought him not only the effectiveness he needed in the organization of his movement and the much-touted exit from the "Viennese ghetto," but also the opening to the new world of which Freud dreamed: the kingdom of Shakespeare and Cromwell and, beyond the oceans, that of New England. And since Jones did not succeed in deciphering his Gothic script, Freud agreed to write his letters from that point on either in Latin characters or in his "poor English."

In London, the situation of this new disciple was hardly enviable. After being publicly denounced by the brother of one of his patients who was seeking a divorce, Jones was accused of having spoken crudely about sexuality to two children to whom he had been administering a test. To be sure, he had just been exonerated after a night in prison, but he decided to leave Great Britain and settle with his companion Loe Kann[62] in Canada, where he lived for four years. He began to write to Freud while he was living in Toronto. As opposed to Brill, he was recognized very quickly as the best organizer for implanting Freudianism in the New World, most notably with the creation, in 1911, of the American Psychoanalytic Association (APsaA).[63]

Freud understood how right he had been, despite his original reticence, to bind the fate of his movement to this Welshman whom he did not like

but who was to play a considerable role, for better and for worse, in the history of Freudianism. Whatever he may have thought of Jones, the Professor had found in him the indispensable friend who would never be his enemy.

As soon as he arrived in Toronto, Jones faced a difficult situation. On the one hand, he came up against religious movements that rejected any rational approach to the psyche and sang the praises of miraculous cures, and on the other he had to deal with partisans of a whole trend in dynamic psychiatry marked by the work of Pierre Janet and Morton Prince. Prince was a leading specialist in multiple personalities and a pioneer within the Boston school of psychotherapy, which was engaged in an all-out war against Freudian theory. In the name of a clinical approach deemed more "scientific," these specialists looked at Freudians as proponents of a new religion. As for the Toronto bourgeoisie, Jones found it detestable, narrow minded and obscurantist.

He soon fell victim to a campaign orchestrated by one of the Puritan leagues of the New World, which equated Freudianism with a sexual demon and psychoanalysis with a practice of debauchery and libertinage. He became a veritable scapegoat, accused of all sorts of imaginary crimes: inciting young people to masturbate, distributing obscene postcards, or sending adolescents from good families to prostitutes. One of his special enemies was Sir Robert Alexander Falconer, a Presbyterian minister and university president; Jones was also taken to court by the famous Emma Leila Gordon, Canada's first woman doctor and a member of the very puritanical Women's Christian Temperance Union. Gordon accused him of sexually abusing a hysterical, delirious woman, a morphine addict whom Jones had had in treatment and to whom, moreover, he had foolishly given money to get her to stop blackmailing him. The affair turned into a tragedy when the patient sought to kill him before trying to commit suicide. After having served the purposes of a "league of virtue," the woman was banished from Ontario.

Prevented from pursuing his work in this witch-hunting environment, Jones considered moving to Boston. In 1910, in fact, the sympathetic James Jackson Putnam, who had converted to the Viennese doctrine despite his own puritanism, contemplated getting Jones a position at Harvard, even though he hesitated to support him because of the latter's proclivity for

speaking about sexuality before a reticent public.[64] Finally, the attempt failed, and Jones left Canada during the summer of 1912 to settle in London.[65]

A year later, acting on Freud's advice, he spent two months in Budapest to undergo analysis with Ferenczi; at the same time, Jones asked Freud to take over the treatment of Loe, who had been terrified by her stay in Toronto and was taking morphine to relieve her pain from pyelonephritis. The daughter of a wealthy family from the Dutch Jewish bourgeoisie, Loe was attractive, witty, and generous, and she did not appreciate hearing others interpret her situation in ways that she felt were inaccurate. Nevertheless, she agreed to see Freud. He found her delectable, and tried to cure her frigidity and her abdominal pains, which he took to be hysterical symptoms. At this point there arose a transferential entanglement of the type that was very characteristic of the earliest psychoanalytic treatments.

If Jones was not yet aware that Loe was in the process of leaving him, he rightly suspected indiscretions on the part of Freud and Ferenczi in her regard. And in fact Freud kept his favorite disciple informed of the course of the young woman's treatment, while the Hungarian shared Jones's confidences with the master. In September 1912, Loe settled in Vienna with Lina, her maid, and Jones was urged by Freud—according to the famous rule of abstinence of which he was so fond—to remove himself "sexually" from his patient. Four months later, Jones became Lina's lover, while Loe fell in love with Herbert "Davy" Jones (nicknamed Jones II), an American millionaire whose family owned zinc mines in Wisconsin. Out of loyalty to the first Jones, Loe accompanied him to London to help him financially in his effort to reestablish a clientele.

On the eve of the war, in Budapest, she married Herbert Davy, with Rank and Ferenczi as witnesses. Skeptical toward psychoanalysis, she nevertheless became friends with Anna Freud, and maintained good relations with the Professor. She was never cured of her addiction to morphine or her frigidity. But the treatment did allow her to separate from Jones.[66]

Always inclined to intervene in the amorous adventures of his disciples, Freud used psychoanalysis to interpret the meanings of the conflicts that arose, not only in their lives, but at every stage in the constitution of his

movement. Thus he looked at his closest supporters as so many patients, and they themselves responded to his demands. They all shared the same interest in exploring their own unconscious, their dreams, their private lives. They analyzed one another endlessly, while also exposing their clinical cases at their meetings or in their correspondence. In short, during this period the master's disciples developed a veritable mania for interpretation,[67] forgetting that interpretation must never cross the line into delirium, or serve as a drug, or nourish sexual pleasure; otherwise it risked harming the cause of psychoanalysis.

In addition, Freud engaged in systematic interpretations with regard to political or doctrinal conflicts, tossing about willy-nilly the sacrosanct Oedipus complex, which his imitators were gradually transforming into a familialist psychology. Thus he applied his concepts not only to literary texts but also to the most banal conflictual situations. And he refused to see that this evolution threatened to make psychoanalysis a new theology that would make it possible to neutralize all forms of contradiction or engagement.

Clearly, this slippage offered partial support to the anti-Freudians, who viewed psychology as a "dangerous method" and rejoiced in the spectacle of dissent. How could one not see that the great pioneers of this magnificent doctrine passed their time in behaving, in their daily lives, like beings incapable of controlling their passions? They were playing with fire.

In 1906, Freud was called on by Jung to consult on the case of a Russian girl, Sabina Spielrein, who came from the Jewish merchant milieu in Rostov.[68] She had been hospitalized in the Burghölzli clinic on August 17, 1904, following a psychotic episode and after having passed from a clinic to an asylum without ever seeing any improvement in her condition. Her destiny was to become emblematic of the saga of the earliest female psychoanalysts.

According to the report Jung wrote in September 1905, Spielrein had been brought up by neurotic parents whose marriage had been arranged by their own parents. Terrified by "sexual things," Spielrein's mother spent her time traveling, staying in the finest European hotels and buying jewels and luxurious clothes. As for the father, mentally ill and suicidal, he beat his children, his son in particular, and insulted his daughter. At age seven, Spielrein already spoke several languages; as an adolescent, she ended up

experiencing sexual excitement at the sight of her father's hands, which had struck her brother's nude buttocks before her eyes. Afflicted with a compulsion to masturbate accompanied by rituals linked to anal eroticism, she had developed the habit of folding back her foot so as to press it against her anus in order to hold in her stool, while feeling a voluptuous sensation at every attempt to free her intestines. When she arrived in the Burghölzli clinic, at age nineteen, she seemed to take orgasmic pleasure in her rituals and her onanism even as she yelled out convulsively against all and sundry.

Jung presented her case to Freud in 1906, stressing that he had treated the young woman as a "psychotic hysteric." But Freud put forth an interpretation of his own devising: according to him, Spielrein suffered from anal autoeroticism with a libidinal fixation on her father and a repressed perversion.[69]

Somewhere between 1906 and 1909, Jung told Freud that Spielrein had fallen in love with him, to the point that it had become an unpleasant scandal. The reality was quite different. During the treatment, Jung had in fact become his patient's lover, and their liaison lasted several years, during which she pursued medical studies. Jealous and desperate, Rauschenbach spread the word about the affair and informed the young woman's parents. Panicked, Jung finally admitted the truth to Freud, who sided with his cherished crown prince.

Cured of her symptoms, Spielrein became a different woman, as much through her love for her therapist as through the treatment: a classic trajectory, specific to transferential and countertransferential relations. Thus she dreamed of getting involved in supporting the great cause of psychoanalysis. However, she was still in love with Jung—who, for his part, continued to feel a guilty attachment toward her—and she wanted to have his child; she wrote to Freud, who advised her to let go of a relationship without a future in order to invest in another object.

In 1911, she defended her thesis on the case of a psychotic woman treated at the Burghölzli clinic.[70] Then she gave a lecture at the WPV in which she presented her theses on the drive to destroy, stressing that this drive ran through the sex drive.[71] Freud later drew inspiration from this hypothesis, modifying it in his development of a new conception of the duality of drives.

The same year, Spielrein married a young Russian Jewish doctor, Pavel Naoumovitch Scheftel, to Freud's great delight; at this point, Freud wanted to hear nothing more about Jung, or about his own critique of Theodore Herzl and Zionism, or of the danger to psychoanalysis of being written off as a "Jewish science": "I am, as you know," he wrote to Spielrein, "cured of the last shred of my predilection for the Aryan cause, and would like to take it that if the child turns out to be a boy he will develop into a stalwart Zionist. He or it must be dark in any case, no more towheads. . . . We are and we remain Jews."[72]

In the course of the entanglement between Freud and Jung, Spielrein thus played an essential role in the evolution of the relations between the one who was her lover and the one whose cause she espoused. Seeking to avoid a break between the two men, she was, for each, and by virtue of a terrible "ruse of history," the one who revealed the degradation of a situation that marked the end of a certain era of psychoanalysis, a moment of fervor during which only men—disciples or dissidents—were authorized not only to engage in intellectual jousting matches but also to believe themselves to be the only possessors of knowledge of the psyche, based on the decline of patriarchal authority and the revolt of the sons. Henceforth, there would be a different configuration, in which the place of women and the analysis of female sexuality—and not only the hysteria clinic focused on young Viennese women suffering from their memories—served as the stakes in an essential combat in the history of psychoanalysis.

Starting in 1919, then, women made their entrance into the history of the psychoanalytic movement: among the very first, we can identify Hermine von Hug-Hellmuth, Tatiana Rosenthal, Eugénie Sokolnicka, Margarethe Hilferding, and the famous Lou Andreas-Salomé.[73]

In September 1911, at the congress of the Verein in Weimar, Goethe's city, Freud was surrounded by some fifty disciples from a number of different countries. In a photo taken before the entrance to a major hotel, he can be seen perched on a stepladder. In an understanding with the photographer, he had chosen to conceal his small stature in order to look like the master of the spot, alongside Jung, on his left, and Ferenczi, on his right. Farther away, one sees Abraham, Jones, Brill, Eitingon, and Hanns Sachs, in some disarray. All the Viennese were present, along with

Bleuler and many others: Oskar Pfister, the Swiss Alfons Maeder, Karl Landauer, the Swede Poul Bjerre, Ludwig Jekels. In the first row, eight women had taken their places in elegantly arranged chairs, one wearing a hat and the others bareheaded, all shod in little boots and laced up in corsets. Frau Emma Jung, straight backed and proud; Fräulein Toni Wolff, disturbing in her uncanny strangeness; *Liebe* Lou, glowing with beauty. Spielrein was not among them.

During this moment of great happiness, Jung was still the preferred crown prince, and Ferenczi the beloved son. Facing this gathering of men and women who had agreed to pose before the camera obscura, Freud launched into a sparkling commentary on *Memoirs of My Nervous Illness* by Daniel Paul Schreber, a mentally ill jurist and former president of the court of appeals in Saxony. The author of this strange autobiography was the son of a doctor, Daniel Gottlieb Schreber, an enthusiast for "dark pedagogy" who had become famous in Germany because he wanted to provide a remedy for society's downfall by creating a new man, shaped by exercises in orthopedic gymnastics: a pure mind in a sound body.[74]

When Daniel Paul Schreber, the son, wrote the story of his life, after initial treatment at the mental health clinic in Leipzig, he had succeeded in getting out of the asylum by demonstrating that his mental illness could no longer be used as a justification for confinement. He asserted that God, his persecutor, had entrusted him with the salvational mission of turning into a woman in order to give rise to a new race of humans. Freud represented him as a paranoid who was rebelling against paternal authority, and he analyzed Schreber's delirium as stemming from repressed homosexuality and from an effort to reconcile himself with the image of a dead father transformed into a divine presence.

Freud concluded his study by evoking the myth of the eagle and the sun, which he had gotten from Jung. Relying on what Schreber had said about his relation with the rays of the sun and his inability to procreate and to take his place in a genealogical order, Freud emphasized that in the ancient myths eagles, who flew in the highest reaches of the atmosphere, were regarded as the only animals who conversed with the sun, a symbol of paternal power, an intimate relation. Thus they imposed on their offspring the test of looking straight at the sun without blinking; to fail meant being thrown out of the nest. Freud gave the myth new life in

the present by affirming that modern neurotics contained, hidden away inside, the relics of primitive humanity:[75] every son has to confront his father, at the risk of death, to prove his own legitimacy. Once again, Freud laid out the story of a son's rebellion against a father: a mad son whose madness had been engendered by that of a father devoted to delirious educational theories that appeared perfectly normal at the time: a case of "soul murder." Schreber's story had many features in common with that of Gross, but Freud said nothing about this, and was presumably unaware of it. However, Gross had already commented on the work, in 1904.[76]

The Schreber case became a classic, discussed and revisited by dozens of psychoanalysts who, unlike Freud, took into account the "educational theories" of Schreber's father in the genesis of his madness.[77] From an entirely different perspective, Elias Canetti considered the case in 1960 in *Masse und Macht*,[78] making Schreber's system of thought one of the paradigms for the conspiracy theory of power characteristic of the twentieth century. And he proposed to bring back to light the subterranean delirium of this famous paranoiac, the better to compare him to the surge of obscure forces that would end up triumphing over democracy by reversing the order of legal sovereignty, turning it into its opposite: the hideous figure of a unique ego, abolishing alterity, reason, and thought.

In 1909, Freud had agreed, at the request of the patient's parents, to begin psychoanalysis with a twenty-five-year-old Viennese writer, the baron Viktor von Dirsztay, known for his extravagances and periods of delirium. The baron's father, a Hungarian Jew who belonged to the nobility, had made his fortune in banking and business. A friend of Kraus and Oskar Kokoschka, von Dirsztay suffered from a serious psychosis and a skin disease that he attributed to the scorn he felt for his family and the shame he felt about his origins. Over more than ten years, in three series of sessions, he came to 19 Berggasse to recount his suffering.

Like Schreber, he felt that he was a victim of "soul murder." Caught in an entanglement that found him opposed sometimes to Kraus and sometimes to Freud, he ended up feeling persecuted by psychoanalysis and was admitted to several sanatoriums for the mentally ill, including the one run by Rudolf von Urbantschitsch, one of the founders of the Wednesday society.[79] After these experiences, von Dirsztay wrote a novel about his "case" in which he featured a diabolical double that was leading

him to his death. The mad baron, who believed himself bewitched, eventually ended up accusing Freud and Theodor Reik of destroying him. In 1935, he committed suicide along with his wife, who had also been treated at the Steinhof psychiatric hospital for a serious psychosis.[80] Such was the fate of this Viennese Schreber, an aesthete and a bohemian, said to be one of Freud's disciples; his case was never published, but simply mentioned in certain exchanges of letters and in the press.

In 1912, while Freud was grappling with this new "soul murder," after commenting on Schreber's *Memoirs*, Jung too took an interest in the thematics of the sun, but in a very different way. He had treated a psychotic patient, Emil Schwyzer, who had been admitted to the Burghölzli in 1901; when Schwyzer looked at the sun, he saw a *membrum erectum* (an erect phallus). He was convinced that he could "influence the climate" by making the erect member move in keeping with movements of his head. Far from likening the phallic appendix to a substitute for paternal power, Jung related this delirium to the liturgy of Mithra, an Indo-European divinity.[81] Whereas Freud reinterpreted myths in the light of psychoanalysis, Jung saw mythologies as the expression of an archaic unconscious that characterized each people and gave rise to psychological types. The two theses were incompatible. Jung returned to the ancient subconscious of spiritualists and sorcerers, believing that modern man was the direct heir of his ancestors, whereas Freud drew from origin myths instruments capable of finding metaphors, in language, for the condition of modern man.

After 1913, the year of the break between the crown prince and the master, and on the eve of a murderous war that was to change the destiny of psychoanalysis as much as that of Europe and of women, Freud never again felt the same enthusiasm for a disciple, and Jung was never again attracted by a father whose love he so longed for.

As for Sabina Spielrein, whose status changed from patient to clinician, she was the first woman in the psychoanalytic movement to have a real career, and thus to enter into a history from which women had been excluded except insofar as they settled for the roles of patients or wives. She met a tragic end. After participating in the rise of the psychoanalytic movement in Russia, she was exterminated with her two daughters by the Nazis in Rostov-on-Don in July 1942.

The Discovery of America

As was the case throughout Europe, scientists on the East Coast of the United States, under the rising impetus of dynamic psychiatry, were seeking to solve the problem of nervous illnesses. In a country founded by the descendants of the Puritans whom Freud so admired, the American democracy took its inspiration from the Declaration of Independence of 1776; it was based as much on an individualist conception of human freedom, including religious freedom, as on the creation of a federation of states. Through its founding fathers, the American citizenry saw itself as the new interpreter of the Bible, and as the heir to the old alliance between God and Israel. During the entire first half of the nineteenth century, the spread of psychiatry had coincided with the development of state mental hospitals and a system of insurance that took in indigent mental patients, while numerous foundations and private establishments were devoted to the treatment of madness.[1]

At the time Freud was invited to discover the New World, two major trends were competing in the treatment of "soul sickness": on one side, somaticians attributed the origin of psychic disorders to a neurological substratum while advocating "educational treatment"; on the other, psychotherapists criticized the excesses of somaticism and sought legitimacy while refusing to be classified as "healers." All the great American specialists in mental disorders—Morton Prince, Adolf Meyer, William James, James Jackson Putnam, G. Stanley Hall—were very well acquainted with the European theses. They spoke several languages, had traveled, and kept up with the publications of specialists such as Pierre Janet, Theodore Flournoy, Eugen Bleuler, Jung, and Freud.

If neurology, psychiatry, and psychology played a capital role in the rise of psychic treatments, "civilized morality" remained an essential component in the development of the various therapeutic approaches. In this profoundly religious country, the ideologues of the new industrial society were in fact convinced that the progress of civilization depended on the stability of the monogamous family and on the exercise of control over sexuality.[2] In this context, the construction of a civilized morality entailed placing absolute value on love-based marriage, as opposed to arranged marriage, and thus entailed a radical condemnation not only of all forms of "fornication"—masturbation, sodomy, fellatio, and so on—but of all forms of sexual relations outside marriage, for men and women alike. Terrified by the power of sexual energy (or the libido), whose harmful effects were discovered in the convulsed bodies of hysterical women, defenders of the Protestant ethic had set out around the turn of the century on a crusade against its potential decay. To be useful to an industrious family, the libido had to be channeled, desexualized, measured, or else oriented toward activities deemed profitable, such as pedagogical or economic pursuits, and it had to be controlled even within bourgeois marriages. Thus, countering the interdiction on pleasure outside marriage— tantamount to a requirement of abstinence—proffered by the leagues of decency, there was a symmetrical desire to struggle, within marriage, against female frigidity and male impotence. A good "civilized union" thus presupposed the constraint of "normalized" sexuality, based as much on intercourse itself as on orgasms and procreation. But in exchange, outside the bonds of marriage no "normal" sexuality was allowed.

This position was very different from that of Freud, who argued on the contrary that the repression of sexuality was the cause of neurosis but that lack of control over the sex drive was nevertheless not a solution to the problem. In other words, in his eyes, the ideal of a "civilized morality" rested not on the preservation of the monogamous family or conjugal fidelity, but on the necessary sublimation of the drives in favor of creative activities. To be sure, Freud thought that the mind ought to win out over the senses, but he also knew, because he had chosen to practice sexual abstinence himself, that such abstinence could not be imposed on subjects in the name of a hygienicist morality based on religious principles.[3]

It was in this context that the psychologist Hall, sympathetic to Freud's views, invited the Professor to give several lectures at Clark University in Worcester, Massachusetts, on the occasion of the twentieth anniversary of the university's founding. Known for his "manias"—he went about barefoot—and convinced of the validity of the Freudian theories on sexuality, this leading specialist in childhood and adolescence, a supporter of hygienics, did not realize the extent to which Freud, despite his misgivings, dreamed of America, all the more so because he felt that he was held in contempt in Europe. Besides, Freud loved to travel; he admired Abraham Lincoln, wanted to see porcupines, and dreamed of conquering a new promised land.

When he learned that Jung had been invited to the same celebration, after Ernst Meumann, a specialist in childhood, had withdrawn, Freud asked Sándor Ferenczi to accompany him, at his own expense. For several weeks, Ferenczi focused primarily on the clothing he would have to wear during the Atlantic crossing, in first class, aboard the magnificent *George-Washington*, the jewel in the Norddeutscher Lloyd-Dampfer line; it was equipped with elegant cabins, smoking rooms, ornate private rooms, Marconi antennae, chaise longues with wraps and shawls, and several levels of interconnected decks. Would there be balls requiring formal evening dress? What food would be served? What digestive disorders would he have to worry about? What would the barber be like? And the bathroom? Armed with his Baedeker and books and clothes piled up in a trunk, Ferenczi prepared for his trip in minute detail, while suggesting that Freud read scholarly books on America.[4] Freud did nothing of the sort.

The three men met on August 20, 1909, in Bremen, the day before they were to embark, and they had a joyful lunch in an excellent restaurant. Pressed by Freud and Ferenczi, Jung decided to break his oath of abstinence, and he drank some wine for the first time in nine years. Freud interpreted this act as an oath of allegiance in his favor, and the interpretive manias of the two companions were off and running, with Ferenczi, who had no desire to enter into the great game of "wild" analysis, as their audience.

That evening, Jung invited his two friends to dinner at his hotel, and he began at once to tell them the legend of the mummified bodies of prehistoric men, the *Moorleichen*, which had been found in German peat

bogs; no one knew how they had died. Seized by anxiety, Freud fainted. When he came to, he explained that this story translated a vow by the son to put the father to death. Furious, Jung rejected Freud's interpretation, enumerated everything that the "Cause" owed to him, and reproached Freud for giving in to a projective delirium.[5]

During the crossing, while observing the movements of the ocean, Freud and Jung continued to play at analyzing one another. Thinking of the glass coffins located in the lead cellar of the Bremen Cathedral, Jung recounted a dream during which he had seen two human skulls lying on the floor of a grotto. Freud hastened to reassert that his friend unconsciously desired his (Freud's) death.

While the master was accusing his heir apparent of wanting to "kill the father," Jung was surreptitiously becoming aware of his own inner evolution. In reality, his fascination with grottos and mummies, vestiges of the past, corresponded to his conception of the unconscious. Jung had never espoused the Freudian theory of an unconscious conceived in terms of agency, woven of repressed content and manifesting itself in the words of ordinary language. He had never accepted the idea of that "other stage," the structural stage dear to Freud, internal to subjectivity and lacking any connection with any sort of anteriority. He had never been inspired by the model of the Greek tragedians.

Jung was already imagining the possible existence of something beyond the unconscious, a form of primal representation that each individual would bear as a patrimony belonging to all humanity. Grottos, caves, the archaic, ancestral genealogies, phantoms, crypts, and unavowed secrets were among the themes that led him to this conviction, that is, to all that Freud judged irrational and highly unscientific. What divided the two men was not Jung's desire to "kill the father," but rather the impossibility on both sides of sharing a common conception of clinical practice, the psyche, and sexuality: "It was my first inkling," Jung wrote later, "of a collective a priori beneath the personal psyche. This I first took to be the traces of earlier modes of functioning. . . . I would not have been able to present to Freud my own ideas on an interpretation of the dream without encountering incomprehension and vehement resistance. I did not feel up to quarreling with him, and I also feared that I might lose his friendship if I insisted on my own point of view."[6]

Jung promptly explained that the skulls were those of Freud's wife and his sister-in-law. Freud didn't believe it, and, later, he lashed out angrily when he discovered that Jung sympathized with William Stern, a Berlin psychologist who opposed psychoanalysis and was a proponent of "intelligence quotient" measurements. Freud called Stern a "pitiful Jew."[7] Nevertheless, enchanted by the transatlantic voyage and by the strong friendship that always bound him to his disciple, he showed good humor in noting that he appeared on the passenger list under the name *Freund* (friend). And he was truly delighted to meet a steward who was reading *The Psychopathology of Everyday Life* and enjoying it.

As the ship approached the shores of the New World, and after attending a farewell dance the evening before, Freud reacted with intense emotion. He had dreamed of America, and now America lay before him, having promised him, by way of a prestigious invitation, that psychoanalysis would soon leave the confines of the "Viennese environment" for good. As the liner glided silently through the mouth of the Hudson and dropped anchor on the evening of August 29 in the port of Hoboken, New Jersey, Freud saw the immense Statue of Liberty holding up its flame. He turned to Jung at that point and uttered these words: "Won't they get a surprise when they hear what we have to say to them!"[8] In January, he had written to Ferenczi, "By the way, we could soon be 'up shit creek' the minute they come upon the sexual underpinnings of our psychology."[9]

To deal with what awaited him, Freud had made the right decisions: he had not drafted any lectures in advance, and he had chosen, against Jung's advice, to speak in German to his fully German-speaking audience; most importantly, he had decided to address the sexual question head on.

Abraham Arden Brill was waiting for the three men on the dock, accompanied by Bronislaw Onuf, the chief physician on Ellis Island. Once the formalities had been completed, Brill took them to the Manhattan Hotel, at the corner of Madison Avenue and Forty-Second Street. For five days, ignoring their digestive problems and their fatigue, he showed them around New York: the Metropolitan Museum and its Greek and Egyptian antiquities, the Museum of Natural History, the psychiatry department at Columbia University, and various neighborhoods, including Chinatown, Harlem, and the amusement park at Coney Island. Freud saw a movie for the first time. He got around by taxi; he wanted to visit a former

school friend, Sigmund Lustgarten, and also Eli Bernays and his wife, but they were all away on vacation. He observed posters written in German, Italian, and Yiddish; the last sometimes included Hebrew characters, to his great surprise. He wrote to Martha about several restaurant meals, evoking for her benefit the taste of the coffee, fruits, bread, mushrooms, and meat. He was becoming accustomed to the company of a new urban population, that of the American melting pot. At times, he had the feeling that the mix was simply the reverse image of the populations found in *Mitteleuropa*.

Spending hours in Central Park, he talked with Jung about the difference between peoples and "races," and especially between Jews and "Aryans." The conversation touched once again on dreams. Freud had a urinary weakness that Jung interpreted in Freudian fashion as an infantile desire to attract attention to himself. Then he took Freud back to his hotel to subject him to a more "in-depth," "Jungian" analysis.

Where Freud saw stories of murdering the father in Jung's dream, in his colleague's dreams Jung sought unconscious feminine mysteries buried in an archaic grotto. And since Jung was interested only in representations evocative of his own polygamy, he was convinced that, under the cover of abstinence, Freud was dissimulating blameworthy activities, inflammatory material: that is, sexual relations with his sister-in-law Minna. So he decided to relieve his friend by making him confess his pathogenic secrets.[10] Arguing that his own authority was at stake, Freud refused to participate in the exercise, and Jung deduced from this that Freud was demeaning him, even as he convinced himself that he had cured Freud provisionally of his symptoms.[11]

Such were the senseless jousts, then, in which these two great representatives of the new approach to the psyche engaged, having been invited to present their clinical and scientific work to the highest academic authorities in New England. Each had his own way of wielding the instruments for exploring the psyche so as to make the other suffer.

Ernest Jones joined Jung, Freud, and Ferenczi on the eve of their departure for Worcester. During a dinner at Hammerstein's Roof Garden, he advised Freud once again not to go too far onto the terrain of sexuality—to no avail. On September 5, they moved into the Standish Hotel. The next day, Jung and Freud had the privilege of staying in Hall's

home at the same time as James, a celebrated psychologist who found Freudian theory dangerous—"a dangerous method"—and Freud's interpretation of dreams incomprehensible. He felt closer to Jung, owing to the latter's interest in parapsychology, spiritualism, and faith healing. Freud longed to convince him of the solidity of his doctrine, and James wanted more than anything to meet the extravagant Viennese doctor who had shaken up the world of psychology. They walked to Worcester together and Freud remembered James with feeling as an already very sick man who was facing death with serenity.

On September 9, for the first time in his life, at dinner in his hosts' home Freud was served by uniformed black domestics wearing white gloves. Hall might well align himself with his guest's sexual theories, but the fact remained that he was heir to an old family of Puritan farmers. Jung seemed flattered by the welcome but he nevertheless wrote to Emma that he had little appreciation for the "solemnity of great virtue" of this "stiff" family. To distance himself from it, he indulged in all sorts of pleasantries intended to make the servants laugh. A subscriber to the hierarchy of the "races," he felt closer to his "African brothers"—whom he saw as anchored in a primitive genealogy—than to the civilized white men of the East Coast. Freud, who saw each human being, beyond all differences, as a universal subject, a singularity, made no remarks, for his part, on his host's domestic servants.[12]

On September 7, after a long discussion with Ferenczi about what he was going to say, Freud launched his series of five lectures before an audience of illustrious scholars, among them the anthropologist Franz Boas; the physicists Albert Michelson and Ernest Rutherford, both Nobel Prize winners; William James; and many others.[13] Adapting perfectly well to the pragmatism demanded by his American listeners, he embarked on a stunning presentation of his clinical work and his theories, without consulting any notes. And in order not to take a proprietary approach to his doctrine, he spoke very highly of Josef Breuer, the inventor of the word "psycho-analysis," and he presented the case of "Anna O." with enthusiasm as the story of a fantastic cure, unaware that Bertha Pappenheim had come to America to speak about prostitution, in a visit coinciding with his. He went on to set forth his method for interpreting dreams, his concept of repression, his treatment technique, and his vision of hysteria.

Finally, he approached the question of infantile sexuality directly, evoking the case of "little Hans" and establishing a parallel with Jung's presentation of the "Ana case."[14]

At every step in these exposés, Freud gave concrete examples. So, to explain the "instinctual impulse of desire," he evoked the possible presence of a "heckler" coming in and disturbing the unfolding of his lectures. If such an event were to occur, he said, persons present in the room (the "resistances") would quickly make themselves known and drive the heckler from the amphitheater: it would be a matter of a repression that would allow the course to continue in peace. But once outside, the heckler could very well make still more noise and disturb the speaker and the audience in a different but no less intolerable way. This was what Freud called the symptom: a displaced manifestation of a repressed unconscious movement.

He then compared the psychoanalyst to a "mediator" who would be capable of entering into negotiations with the heckler so that he could return to the amphitheater after promising to stop disturbing the audience. The task of psychoanalysis was thus to lead the symptom back toward its place of origin, that is, toward the repressed idea.

These lectures offered a kind of synthesis of the early Freud, the optimistic Freud of the Belle Époque, convinced that he had brought to the world the impetus for a revolution in the way the intimate workings of the human psyche were construed. At this time, it was not yet a question of narcissism, metapsychology, complex topographies, or the death drive. Freud talked about the libido, healing, and manifestations of the unconscious in daily life. Beyond that, with regard to sexuality, he was adroit enough to quote the positivist works of Sanford Bell, a researcher at Clark who had compiled a sample of 2,500 cases of children: "[Bell] carried out his work in what we in Europe would call 'the American manner'. . . . It would not astonish me if you were to attach more credence to these observations made by one of your closest neighbours than to mine."[15]

Unanimously appreciated, these five lectures in Worcester were triumphantly received in the local and national press. In a fine article, Hall characterized the Freudian concepts as new and revolutionary, although this did not prevent him from taking an interest later on in Alfred Adler's theories, to Freud's intense ire. On September 10, during a formal meeting,

Freud and Jung both received the title of doctor of laws *honoris causa* from Clark University. This would be Freud's only university distinction. For Jung, on the contrary, it was the first in a long list: he was so proud of it that upon his return to Zurich he ordered new stationery with the heading "Med. CG JUNG, LL.D."

Freud had the feeling that his American moment marked the end of his isolation: "At the time I was only fifty-three," he wrote in 1925. "I felt young and healthy, and my short visit to the new world encouraged my self-respect in every way. In Europe I felt as though I were despised; but over there I found myself received by the foremost men as an equal. As I stepped on to the platform at Worcester to deliver my *Five Lectures on Psycho-Analysis,* it seemed like the realization of some incredible day-dream: psycho-analysis was no longer a product of delusion, it had become a valuable part of reality."[16]

In the group photo taken the day of the ceremony, we see Freud and Jung, dressed in frock coats, standing in the first row alongside Hall, Meyer, Boas, and James; behind them stand Jones, Brill, Ferenczi, Michelson, and Rutherford. Among these men wearing beards or mustaches, some holding canes or hats in their hands, in the last row on the right, we find Solomon Carter Fuller, born in Liberia, the grandson of American slaves who had gone back to Africa. The first black psychiatrist of the professorate at the medical school of Boston University, he was well acquainted with Europe, and with Germany in particular, because he had been the student of Alois Alzheimer in Munich before he became one of the American pioneers studying Alzheimer's disease. He also practiced psychotherapy, and he had attended Freud's lectures with interest.

No woman appears in the photograph, yet it was a woman, the feisty Emma Goldman, a famous anarchist, who offered the liveliest commentary on the visit. While she was studying to be a midwife in Vienna in 1896 she had had the opportunity to attend Freud's courses. In Worcester, she would have very much liked to intervene from the floor, but the "authorities" refused: too explosive, too dangerous, too hysterical, they said. "The most important event of our Worcester visit," she wrote in her autobiography, "was an address given by Sigmund Freud. . . . I was deeply impressed by the lucidity of his mind and the simplicity of his delivery. Among the array of professors, looking stiff and important in

their university caps and gowns, Sigmund Freud, in ordinary attire, un-assuming, almost shrinking, stood out like a giant among pygmies."[17]

"In a little over a year," Linda Donn writes, "Freud had moved from a small gathering in Salzburg to a position of one among equals within the broad discipline of psychology."[18] Jones returned to Chicago, but Jung, Freud, and Ferenczi went on with their trip. They visited Niagara Falls, then crossed Lake Placid on their way to Keene Valley in the Adirondacks.

Like many members of the East Coast aristocracy, Putnam had pur-chased a piece of land surrounded by maple, spruce, and pine trees. Freud, who loved forests and wilderness, was stunned by the sumptuous land-scapes and by his hosts' lifestyle in their old farmhouse, which had been transformed into a country home complete with reception rooms, a library, bathtubs, fireplaces, and cigars everywhere. To welcome the visi-tors, the Putnam family had decorated the guests' quarters in black, red, and gold, the colors of imperial Germany, forgetting that none of them was German. But it hardly mattered. Jung sang old German songs, and Ferenczi helped Freud get over a "nervous appendicitis" that was simply a manifestation of his usual digestive difficulties *(Magenkatarrh)*. Freud found American food completely dreadful, and he refused to drink the ice water he was served; he asked for Rhine wine wherever he went.[19]

After much effort and many long walks, he finally came across some-thing he'd dreamed of seeing, a porcupine—a dead one, unfortunately. To console him, the Putnams gave him a statue of the animal, which he kept on his desk. He had long been fascinated by the parable on socia-bility related by Schopenhauer, his favorite philosopher: "A company of porcupines crowded themselves very close together one cold winter's day so as to profit by one another's warmth and so save themselves from being frozen to death. But soon they felt one another's quills, which induce them to separate again. And now, when the need for warmth brought them nearer together again, the second evil arose once more. So that they were driven backwards and forwards from one trouble to the other, until they had discovered a mean distance at which they could most tolerably exist." Schopenhauer concluded that sociability was inversely proportional to a person's intellectual value and that human wisdom consisted in remaining apart from society and cultivating inner warmth.[20]

He may have conquered the New World, but Freud nevertheless continued to see America as a "mad machine": "My success will be brief," he soon confided to Barbara Low. "The Americans treat me the way a child treats a new doll: fun to play with, but soon to be replaced by another new toy."[21]

A few years later, psychoanalysis became the most popular "mental treatment" on the North American continent. It swept away the old somatic doctrines, took psychiatry's place, mocked the leading principles of civilized morality, and aroused the enthusiasm of the middle classes. One can thus understand the furor that was unleashed in its wake against this pessimistic European who was disinclined to adhere to the axis of good and evil where sexuality was concerned. Had he not stirred up trouble in 1909 in the persecuted conscience of the Puritans? In fact, the Americans received psychoanalysis with acclaim for what it was not—a therapy for happiness—and they rejected it sixty years later because it had not kept that unfulfillable promise.

Jung and Freud were dangerous for each other like two porcupines, as psychoanalysis was for America and America for psychoanalysis. Freud knew this, but he did not yet know that his doctrine was destined to become more and more "American" just as, after a devastating first war and the exile of Freud's principal disciples, Europe was destined to fall prey to Nazism.

After a period of fainting spells, disagreements and disputes, "wild" interpretations and somatic ailments, the break between Freud and Jung took concrete form in the summer of 1912, when Freud rushed to Kreuzlingen to see Ludwig Binswanger, who was suffering from a malignant tumor.[22] Freud had let Jung know he planned to visit and expected to see his colleague at the bedside of their mutual friend. Thus he neglected to make the detour by way of Küsnacht, the home that Jung had just set up on the shores of Lake Zurich: yet another misunderstanding. Then there was the fourth congress of the Verein in Munich, followed by somber discussions about an article Karl Abraham had devoted to Amenhotep IV, the son of the pharaoh, and finally Jung's 1912 publication of *Psychology of the Unconscious (Wandlungen und Symbole der Libido)*, a work that proposed a complete desexualization of the notion of libido.

During all this time, Freud continued to extend his doctrine to the elucidation of artistic and literary enigmas. Like a Sherlock Holmes, he enjoying decoding the unconscious life of "great men." Leonardo da Vinci had always belonged to the pantheon of the elect to whom Freud devoted his unrestrained admiration.

In October 1909, just after his return from the trip to America, he decided to write about this universal genius of the cinquecento. Left-handed, homosexual, vegetarian, attracted by "bizarre and grotesque heads," known for leaving his works unfinished, an engineer, a sculptor, an anatomist, a caricaturist, an architect, admired in his own lifetime by all his contemporaries, the illegitimate child of the wealthy notable Piero da Vinci and a humble peasant woman, Leonardo was celebrated and protected by princes and kings, from Ludovico Sforza and Lorenzo de Medici to Francis I.

Freud announced his project to Jung as if he were undertaking to conquer a new continent: "We must . . . take hold of biography. I have had an inspiration since my return. The riddle of Leonardo da Vinci's character has suddenly become clear to me. That would be a first step in the realm of biography. But the material concerning L. is so sparse that I despair of demonstrating my conviction intelligibly to others."[23]

Freud was convinced, in particular, that the great Leonardo's erotic life was a perfect illustration of one of his own hypotheses about the theories of infantile sexuality; he deduced that Leonardo had been sexually inactive or homosexual and that he had "sublimated the better part of his sexuality into an urge for research" while remaining caught up in a "notorious inability to finish his works."[24] And he added that he had recently come across an identical set of symptoms in a neurotic patient who was not a genius. Once again, then, he was formulating a hypothesis that he hoped could be verified in light of the facts.

To produce his essay, he relied on unchallengeable sources, almost all translated into German: Edmondo Solmi's biography, Smiraglia Scognamiglio's study of da Vinci's childhood and adolescence, Giorgio Vasari's classic study, that of the French art historian Eugène Müntz, da Vinci's own *Treatise on Painting* and his *Notebooks*.[25] But Dmitry S. Merezhkovsky's fictionalized biography was the one on his nightstand, and the

source of a good portion of his hypotheses. In this well-documented historical novel, the Russian writer drew a portrait of Leonardo by imagining that Giovanni Boltraffio, one of the artist's students, kept a secret diary about his master. This allowed Merezhkovsky to make the painter a character in conformity with his own dualist concepts of paganism and Christianity: two irreconcilable universal trends, as he saw it, one turned toward God and the other turned away. The novelist thus painted Leonardo as a sort of heretical, irreverent, feminine Antichrist who never approached women because he was horrified by physical possession. This interpretation of a riven, unbelieving Leonardo, attracted as much by the smiles of androgynous angels as by monstrous faces, who had undertaken to destroy the Holy Scriptures through his art, appealed to Freud, who was well acquainted with the other works of the Russian writer.

Like virtually all of Leonardo's biographers, Merezhkovsky did not mention the painter's active homosexuality; he settled for alluding to his ambiguous relations with his master, Andrea del Verrocchio, and with two of his students, Boltraffio and Francesco Melzi. At the beginning of the twentieth century, to dare to speak bluntly of da Vinci's sex life was still an act of subversion that risked provoking a major scandal.[26] However, the fact of the artist's homosexuality was known, even if it was not named. It sufficed to consult the archives to learn that the painter had come close to being burned at the stake after being denounced, on April 9, 1476, by "officers of the night" working for the city of Florence for "active sodomy" on the person of Jacopo Saltarelli, an apprentice silversmith and notorious prostitute. Leonardo spent two months in prison before being released for want of proof; the experience did not keep him from continuing to have young lovers. Later, moreover (in 1505), he said that he had been condemned in his youth for acts that he still practiced in his adult life and that were probably even more condemned at that point.

He had taken into his home one Gian Giocomo Caproti, nicknamed Salai (the devil), a graceful young thief with curly hair and an enigmatic smile who became the artist's pupil and later painted a portrait depicting a nude Mona Lisa. Leonardo did not have "ambiguous relations" with men, then; he had hidden affairs throughout his life, at the risk of death. It is highly unlikely that he was, as Freud thought, a "sexually inactive"

man who converted his sexuality into an "urge for research" through sublimation. Until his death he lived with Melzi, whom he made his heir.

Freud was clearly projecting his own cult of abstinence onto this greatly admired genius. In fact it was Freud himself, not Leonardo, who had converted his sex drive into a creative drive. At all events, the genesis of this homosexuality still had to be explained. And Freud knew that many mysteries remained to be cleared up in the great man's life, in particular a childhood memory carefully recorded in the *Notebooks*. There, Leonardo explained why he so loved birds, to the point of imagining machines capable of transforming men into flying angels: "It seems that I was always destined to be so deeply concerned with vultures; for I recall as one of my very earliest memories that while I was in my cradle a vulture came down to me, and opened my mouth with its tail, and struck me many times with its tail against my lips."[27] Freud cited the German version of this text, in which the word "vulture" *(Geier)* appeared, but in a note he added the original version in Italian, where Leonardo referred to a different bird of prey called a *nibbio* (kite), which should have been translated into German as the word *Hühnergeier* or *Gabelweihe*. In this version, cited by Scognamiglio and drawn from the *Codex Atlanticus,* da Vinci said that the bird's tail had come in "between my lips" and not that it had "struck" him on his lips.[28]

Understandably fascinated by this astonishing childhood memory, which seemed to come straight out of *The Interpretation of Dreams,* Freud did not notice the error in translation. But was he not forgetting that a word is not a myth? Trying to solve the puzzle of the link between Leonardo's homosexuality and his childhood memory, he thus hypothesized that the painter had been inspired by the myths of Egyptian civilization in which the word "mother" was written by means of a pictogram referring to the image of a vulture, an animal whose head represented a maternal divinity and whose name was pronounced *Mout.* And he associated this representation with the Christian legend in which a female vulture opened its vagina to be fertilized by the wind, thus embodying the immaculate virgin.

By relating these two myths to Leonardo's childhood memory, Freud deduced that fellatio via the tail was only the repetition of a more ancient situation, that of the infant taking the mother's breast into its mouth. The

memory of the vulture and the passive connotation associated with it thus had to be understood in relation to the painter's childhood: he had been reared by his mother, Catarina, as the exclusive object of her love, without a father with whom to identify when his sexuality began to emerge. This is the way, Freud explained, that a male homosexual represses love for his mother after having been fixated on her, and then "finds the objects of his love along the path of *narcissism*."[29]

Up to this point Freud had been content with contradictory declarations on the subject of masculine "inversion." Male homosexuality derived, as he saw it, not from heredity but from bisexuality, from a predisposition or from autoeroticism. But with regard to da Vinci, he spoke for the first time of a fixation on the mother and of a narcissistic choice that excluded identification with the father. And he was obviously trying to solve the mystery of the *Mona Lisa*'s famous smile, which had been defying viewers of the painting for four centuries, to the point of making all the specialists who looked at it go off the deep end. Goethe saw it as the purest incarnation of the eternal feminine, the equivalent of what the Greek ideal had brought to classical statuary. For Freud, Leonardo had simply painted his mother's smile, a mother transfigured by her child's gaze. Thus the lovely heads of angels and adolescents admired by the painter were all simply reproductions of his own person as a child, and the smiling women were replicas of Catarina, who had once manifested this smile, while he himself had lost it.

Audacious as ever, Freud proceeded to another juxtaposition, between *La Gioconda* and *Sant'Anna, la Vergine e il Bambino con l'agnellino* (*Sant'Anna Metterza*, in English *The Virgin and Child with Saint Anne*), asserting that this second painting was a sequel to the first.[30] Leonardo had painted Saint Anne holding back her daughter, Mary, who was gesturing in an attempt to keep Jesus from trying to play with the sacrificial lamb. Anne embodied the church, while Mary knew that her son was to die. The first figure held back the second, who held back the third, and each actor in the trio was presumed to know that Jesus's passion and redemption were inevitable.

Forgetting that the theme of *Sant'Anna Metterza* was common in the painting of the quattrocento, and that Leonardo had drawn sketches for this canvas before his encounter with Mona Lisa,[31] Freud claimed to make out the presence of two mothers here: Catarina on the one hand, and the

legitimate wife of Leonardo's father, Donna Albiera, on the other. The two women were the same age and had the same smile, according to Freud: "When Leonardo was received into his grandfather's house before he had reached the age of five, his young step-mother Albiera must certainly have taken his mother's place where his feelings were concerned, and he must have found himself in what may be called the normal relationship of rivalry with his father. As we know, a decision in favour of homosexuality only takes place round about the years of puberty. When this decision had been arrived at in Leonardo's case, his identification with his father lost all significance for his sexual life, but it nevertheless continued in other spheres of non-erotic activity."[32]

Not only did Freud attribute two mothers to Leonardo, but he explained that the identification with the father proved damaging for the painter, since, feeling that he was the father of his own works, he was no more concerned with them than his father had been with him. Hence the permanent incompleteness. Finally, the love of birds and the dream of flying referred, in Freud's reading, to an infantile desire to engage in an intense sexual activity that was then converted into an unprecedented ability to create unusual objects that resembled children's toys. Vasari reported, moreover, that Leonardo made hollow, lightweight animals into which he blew to make them fly, and that he attached wings to the back of a big lizard, adding eyes, horns, and a beard to scare his friends.

Freud's invention of a Leonardo for the new century was rightly greeted as a tour de force. In its style, it resembled a coming-of-age novel—somewhere between Balzac and Conan Doyle—that drew the reader into an occult world where the strange androgynous figure of la Gioconda reigned like an enigmatic goddess: "the only truly beautiful thing I have ever written," he said of it in 1919.[33] Countering the psychologists of his day, Freud had attached the story of modern neurotics to the paired names of Hamlet and Oedipus, and now, confronting the sexologists, he gave the name Leonardo to every representative of the ancient "cursed race." In the aftermath, he changed his mind repeatedly as to the best clinical approach to male homosexuality.[34]

In notes added in 1919, he commented on the drawings, showing that in one of them da Vinci had merged the bodies of Mary and Anne, as in a process of condensation, so that they could not be distinguished from

one another except by their faces. Freud also analyzed one of the painter's famous drawings of an act of sexual intercourse, and he deduced from this picture that da Vinci had treated the female genital apparatus with a certain negligence.

For years, his disciples and friends made a game of finding unconscious riddles in paintings. In 1923, Oskar Pfister thought he saw the outline of a vulture in the drapery surrounding the two women in *Sant'Anna Metterza*. In fact, by playing with interpretations that were nevertheless perfectly rational, Freud inscribed himself unwittingly in the straight line of descent of a symbologist and hierogamic literature that took the mysteries of da Vinci's life and work as its theme, making this universal painter the emblem of a sexualized vision of the Holy Scriptures.[35]

In the Leonardo essay Freud also responded to Jung, who was fond of this type of literature. He no longer spoke of the murder of the father, but of the early link to the mother, as if to show that the latter occupied a place just as determining, symbolically, as that of the father in a child's evolution. In this text, the mother is situated not in terms of natural self-evidence but in terms of a structural position. Through this study, then, Freud refined his conception of the Western family, although this meant taking the risk of transforming a great origins narrative—the very one he had invented—into a commonplace psychology.

It was in fact right after he finished his brilliant essay on Leonardo that he used the term *Ödipuskomplex* (Oedipus complex) for the first time.[36] He claimed to be translating clinically, against the background of the primal scene of fantasized coitus, the history of the boy's desire for his mother and his rivalry with his father. After explaining all the scorn that a little boy feels for prostitutes when he discovers that his mother resembles them in that she sleeps with his father, Freud underscored the point: "He begins to desire his mother herself in the sense with which he has recently become acquainted, and to hate his father anew as a rival who stands in the way of this wish; he comes, as we say, under the dominance of the Oedipus complex. He does not forgive his mother for having granted the favour of sexual intercourse not to himself but to his father."[37]

It was on the occasion of a new incursion into a continent that he proposed to explore—anthropology—that Freud went back to his thematics of the murder of the father; between 1911 and 1913, he published four brief

essays that were later combined under the title *Totem and Taboo,* one of his finest works.[38] Like hysteria, totemism attracted the attention of scholars in the late nineteenth century. It consisted in establishing a connection between a natural species (an animal) and an exogamous clan in order to account for a hypothetical original unity of various ethnographic phenomena.[39]

The book took the form of a Darwinian fable about the origin of humanity, the omnipotence of thought, and the relation of human beings with the gods. Thus it went counter to the evolution of modern anthropology, which at the time had given up the search for origin myths in favor of travel and expeditions to study the customs, languages, and histories of primitive peoples. And here was a Viennese scholar who had never traveled outside the Western world, purporting to explore a terrain that he knew only from books. In short, Freud proposed to mobilize myths and royal dynasties once again just when modern scientific knowledge—from Boas to Bronislaw Malinowski—was making a radical break with all the old theses about the opposition between the primitive and the civilized, the animal and the human, and especially with the colonial thematics of the hierarchy of the races.

But Freud did not want to abandon the Oedipus complex that he had just theorized; against any and all opposition, he meant to make it a universal complex proper to all human societies and at the origin of all religions. Here is the basic structure of his narrative, as it was presented with feverish excitement to all his disciples in the WPV. In a primeval period, men lived in small groups or hordes, each of which was subject to the despotic power of a male who appropriated the females for himself. One day, the sons of the tribe, rebelling against the father, put an end to the reign of the savage horde. In an act of collective violence, they killed the father and ate his corpse. However, after the murder, they repented, disavowed their crime, and invented a new social order by simultaneously instituting exogamy—giving up possession of the women of the clan represented by a totem—and totemism, based on a taboo against murdering the substitute for the father (the totem).

Totemism, exogamy, prohibition of incest: these constituted the model common to all religions, monotheism in particular. From this perspective, the Oedipus complex was, according to Freud, nothing other than

the expression of two repressed desires (the desire for incest and the desire to kill the father) contained in the two taboos characteristic of totemism: the taboo on committing incest and the taboo on killing the totem-father. The Oedipus complex thus had to be seen as a universal paradigm, since it translated the two fundamental interdictions of all human societies.

To construct this fable, Freud relied on evolutionist literature. First, he borrowed Darwin's famous account of the primal horde, recorded in *The Descent of Man;* then he added the theory of recapitulation, according to which the individual repeats the principal stages of the evolution of species (ontogenesis repeats phylogenesis); finally, he incorporated the idea of the heredity of acquired characteristics, a thesis popularized by Jean-Baptiste Lamarck and taken up again by Darwin and Ernst Haeckel. From James George Frazer—the author of the famous epic *The Golden Bough,* the story of the murderer-king of Latin antiquity who was killed by his successor, whereas he himself had acquired his power from the murder of his predecessor—Freud borrowed a view of totemism as an archaic mode of thought characteristic of so-called primitive societies. From William Robertson Smith, he took up the theses of the totemic meal and the substitution of the clan for the horde. From James Jasper Atkinson, he drew the idea that the patriarchal system came to an end with the rebellion of the sons and the devouring of the father. Finally, from the work of Edward Westermarck, he adopted perspectives on the horror of incest and the harmfulness of consanguineous marriages.[40]

While Freud saw savages as the equivalent of children, and while he retained the stages of evolution, in contrast he denied all theories predicated on the "inferiority" of the primitive state. As a result, he did not represent totemism as a less elaborate mode of magical thinking than spiritualism or monotheism: he saw it rather as a relic found in all religions. For the same reason, he compared savages to children only in order to prove the correspondence between infantile neurosis and the human condition in general, and thus to set up the Oedipus complex as a universal model. Finally, he shed new light on the prohibition of incest and the origin of societies. On the one hand, he rejected the very idea of origin, asserting that the famous horde existed nowhere: the original state was in fact the form internalized by every subject (ontogenesis) of a collective

history (phylogenesis) that was repeated from generation to generation; on the other hand, he emphasized that the prohibition of incest was not derived, as Westermarck believed, from a natural feeling of repulsion toward this practice on the part of human beings, but that there was on the contrary a desire for incest and that this desire had as a corollary the prohibition instituted in the form of a law and of a categorical imperative. Why, indeed, would an act that so horrified the collectivity have been prohibited? In other words, Freud offered anthropology two themes that came out of his doctrine: moral law and guilt. In place of the origin there was a real act: the necessary murder; in place of the horror of incest, there was a symbolic act: the internalization of the taboo. From this perspective, every society was founded on regicide, but humanity exited from murderous anarchy only to the extent that the regicide was followed by a sanction and by reconciliation with the father's image, for this image alone authorized conscience.

Totem and Taboo was thus in the first place a political book, Kantian in inspiration, as much as it was a manifesto against the psychology of peoples that Jung held dear. I shall also offer the hypothesis that it was, in addition, the fruit of the trip to America, during which Freud and Jung had so often addressed the question of the mixing of "races" and "ethnic groups," especially in New York. The two men held completely divergent opinions on the subject, and *Totem and Taboo* was proof of this. With his study on da Vinci, Freud had privileged the relation to the mother in response to Jung; with this new study, he returned to the rebellion against the father in order to mark a radical break both with Jungian relativism and with all forms of colonialism.

His book proposed, finally, a theory of democratic power centered on three requirements: a founding act, law, and renunciation of despotism. Nevertheless, *Totem and Taboo* was not received as a political text but as a serious contribution on the part of psychoanalysis to anthropology. It did not arouse the indignation that might have been expected, but it did receive severe critiques—often justified, moreover. In fact, not only did Freud remain attached to the frameworks of the evolutionism from which early twentieth-century ethnology was freeing itself, but he also claimed jurisdiction over a domain about which he knew nothing, without taking contemporary work into account. The critique formulated in 1920 by the

American anthropologist Alfred Kroeber, a specialist in North American Indians, proceeded along these lines; it was taken up again by numerous representatives of the discipline.

It was basically through the resistance it aroused that for more than sixty years *Totem and Taboo* nourished debates that are still going on today. Jones was an active participant in the arguments, especially with Malinowski; subsequently, new quarrels and questions came up with Géza Róheim and Georges Devereux.[41]

Totem and Taboo was Freud's last major work in the Belle Époque: a Rousseau-like reverie on the passage from nature to culture that evoked the Daniel Paul Schreber case to some degree, on the clinical level. The text had all the freshness of the messianic ideals with which the early Freudians were imbued. Reading this book leaves one with the impression of seeing Freud strolling about in the heart of a wilderness populated by the adventure stories he had so loved in his childhood. He traversed the geography of myths and beliefs by way of books from a bygone era with the same vivacity as when he was on vacation in Italy, dazzled by Leonardo, or heading south in search of an undiscoverable Gradiva.

Years after the American trek, once the break had become definitive, Jung was assailed by hallucinations and was afraid he was losing himself in an abyss of ignorance to the point of forgetting that he lived in Küsnacht and that he had a wife and children. He had lost a master, a friend, an accomplice. On both sides, the break had been extremely violent, despite the efforts of Jung's wife: like Sabina Spielrein, Emma tried to prevent the two men from burning their bridges. Even as he continued to practice psychiatry, Jung experienced states with which he was very familiar because he had diagnosed them in his patients. When he emerged, he surrounded himself with lovers and disciples. With Emma, who had come close to divorcing him, he set up a school of psychotherapy—analytic psychology—and plunged into the exploration of imagoes, then archetypes. He never saw Freud again. Still, like Freud, for the rest of his life he continued to think back on what had united and then separated them.

In September 1913, steeped in sadness, Freud went to Rome once again, convinced that the city's incomparable beauty was more and more indispensable to him. He detoured by way of Bologna to rejoin Minna, who accompanied him in his travels. To his daughter and son-in-law, Sophie

and Max Halberstadt, he wrote, "Of course, you must come here one day. But there is no real urgency; as the years pass, the visit becomes more and more substantial, and perhaps you are still too young. For now, you should be excited about your own home and find it much more interesting than the most beautiful and most eternal of cities."[42] He also wrote to Anna, "Papa to his future traveling companion." Minna was exhausted by the rushed visits her brother-in-law imposed. As for Freud, he was already imagining his youngest daughter in Minna's place. In the meantime, seated in a café, he distributed chocolates to the children of a traveler, who was not really surprised to note how much this brother and sister—Minna and Sigmund—resembled each other.[43]

Every day, as he had done the year before, he visited San Pietro in Vincoli to contemplate the imposing statue of Moses sculpted by Michelangelo for the tomb of Pope Julius II. This is where he noticed that the prophet held the Tables of the Law upside down and that, in his rage against his people, Moses was about to let them fall when he regained control of himself: calm followed the storm. As Freud maintained, with this work that had taken years to complete, "the relation that one has with a love child," he identified with Michelangelo, who had made Moses the quintessential example of the human capacity for self-mastery.[44] After the Greek tragedies, America, and the torments of the break with Jung, the time had come for Freud, through the prism of his attachment to the Italian Renaissance, to take an interest in a new story of the murder of the father, which led him to a reflection on his own Jewishness. He had taken a first step in this direction, moreover, in his superb Darwinian reverie on the origin of societies. In March 1914, in *Imago,* he published his essay on Michelangelo's Moses anonymously. He had doubts about his own hypotheses.[45]

In the meantime, Jones had taken Jung's place and had created the Ring (or Secret Committee) in order to bring the most faithful disciples back together: Abraham, Hanns Sachs, Otto Rank, and Ferenczi. Anton von Freund, a Hungarian industrialist, was part of the group until his death in 1920, and Max Eitingon rejoined in 1919. For Freud, thus surrounded by his six favorites, including the one who would end up financing the movement's publishing house, it was a matter of constructing a rational project that could preserve the doctrine from all forms of deviance: it had to reject

obscurantist mythologies, spiritism, and magical thinking; hold firm on the question of sex; train clinicians who would no longer be afflicted with pathological disorders; struggle against charlatans; and so on. Jones sought to bring together fighters who would be capable of responding to external enemies so that Freud himself could concentrate exclusively on developing his work and thus be relieved of the leadership role.

Inspired by the model of nineteenth-century secret societies, the Ring was thus conceived as a gathering of Knights of the Round Table: the members enjoyed equality and shared sovereignty with the master, who could decide nothing without them. But the initiative was also a way of reconnecting with the principles of Hippocratic medicine: developing schools based on the relation between a master and a disciple. The horizontal axis on one side, the vertical on the other: Freud would return to this theorization of power in 1921 in "Group Psychology and the Analysis of the Ego."[46] To seal the alliance with his new paladins, he shared with them an intaglio from his collection, which they had engraved on a ring of gold. Still invested with the Olympian ideal, he himself wore one that represented Zeus.[47]

Once the war was over, and once the sacred union against Jung was a thing of the past, new conflicts broke out among the paladins themselves, and ultimately put an end to the great adventure, after the circulation within the group of an impressive number of letters: the *Rundbriefe*.[48]

In July 1914, summering in Karlsbad, Freud did not imagine for a moment that the war would go on and on, nor that it would entail millions of deaths, nor that the Europe he knew, the cradle of psychoanalysis, would disappear forever. To his sister Maria (Mitzi), he confided how old and tired he felt: "Martha and I have heart problems. . . . We have become the old generation."[49] And in a letter to Ferenczi, he referred to the surprising "Sarajevo assassination," without imagining the consequences that that event could have on his own rapidly expanding movement.

In Berlin, Abraham for his part was thinking solely about getting rid of Jung's partisans, while he concentrated on organizing the fifth congress of the Verein, to be held in Dresden. In London, Jones, much more lucid, anticipated that Germany and Austria would be the losers in this war of a new type. Anna Freud was staying with him, and he felt that she would be safer in England than in Vienna. Still, he arranged for her return. None

of the committee members dreamed of looking at him as an enemy, and Freud himself wrote to him in English, knowing that the mail would be opened.

On November 9, 1914, Freud announced to Ferenczi that the voice of psychoanalysis could no longer be heard in the world, now that the cannons had begun to fire. As in Tolstoy's novel, peace was followed by war, speech by wounded bodies, dialogue by hatred. Everywhere, university professors sent their diplomas *honoris causa* back to the friends who had become enemies.[50]

With the publication of an article on narcissism in 1914,[51] Freud was in the process of revising his doctrine and producing an alternative to Jung's "desexualized libido," relying in part on the work of Abraham, a clinician specializing in psychoses. He was no longer content to speak of the libido as a manifestation of the sex drive; he sought to show that it could be transferred to the ego. And from this he deduced the simultaneous existence, in the psyche, of an opposition between the libido of the ego and the libido of the object, between primary narcissism, a primal state of life, and secondary narcissism, which evolves toward a withdrawal of investments in objects. Thus he opened the way to a reflection on disorders of subjectivity that went well beyond his previous views regarding the genesis of the neurotic conflict. From then on, the subject was no longer simply Oedipus transformed into Hamlet, but Narcissus guilty of contemplating his own image to the point of dying from it: this was a way of emphasizing the extent to which the human beings of the new century were inhabited by the deep and permanent desire to destroy themselves while destroying the other.

The war seemed to prove Freud right.

The War of Nations

WHILE HE CLAIMED to hate Vienna and the dual monarchy as much as he hated the Prussian spirit, Freud was so surprised by the war that he began to support the Triple Alliance strongly; he hoped for an Austrian victory, and he fulminated against France, the Serbs, and Russia. He didn't believe for a moment that France and England would win, or that the Americans would offer support, or that the empires of Central Europe would disappear.

He had not noticed the rise of popular nationalist fervor against the last imperial dynasties, nor the growth in hatred that over some six decades had gradually supplanted the optimism of the "springtime of the peoples." He had not yet realized that the bourgeois "nobility" of the Belle Époque—a class so self-involved that it had remained unaware of the wretchedness of the disinherited—was in its death throes. Before the outbreak of hostilities, Freud had been acquainted with war only from his reading—Alexander, Caesar, Napoleon, Homer—and from memories of his military service, during which he had played at being an army doctor, with his nurses at hand to fight off his neurasthenia. In the short run, facing the real deployment of arms, he was not at all inclined to condemn England, in any case, even though he regretted that it was not on the side of the three empires—Prussian, Austro-Hungarian, and Ottoman.

Thus he found himself in contradiction with the evolution of the Verein, which encompassed doctors from virtually all the European countries and the United States: a new generation aspired to a psychoanalysis that was no longer centered in Vienna and thus no longer tied to the Freudian ideal of paladins united in the Ring. More than anything

else, the war shattered the progress of the movement and erected artificial frontiers between intellectuals, researchers, doctors, writers, and psychologists.

This first twentieth-century war was unfolding in the skies and at the bottom of the oceans, at sea and on land, in muddy trenches ravaged by toxic gasses and strewn with mutilated corpses. It had nothing in common with the wars of earlier centuries, when great armies faced each other in broad daylight, with their gaudy colors and their trumpets, their bloody knife fights and songs of victory and death.

All at once this war shifted the conflicts internal to psychoanalysis onto another stage, and from the outset it forced the Freudians to give up their congresses and their activities, to suspend their exchanges of letters and their editorial output. In short, it obliged them to take an interest in something other than their scientific work and their ludicrous war against "the brutal sanctimonious Jung,"[1] or against the "Zurichois," who moreover never shared in the furor of the other nations. Switzerland, Spain, the Netherlands, and the Scandinavian countries did not enter into any of the coalitions.

With the exception of Hanns Sachs, who was exempted owing to his myopia, all the members of the committee were called up, one by one. Max Eitingon left first, in 1915, as a surgeon in the Austrian armed forces; he was sent to Prague and then to northern Hungary. Karl Abraham was also called up as a surgeon in a large hospital in East Prussia. Otto Rank was sent to Kraków in a heavy artillery unit. Sándor Ferenczi was assigned as a medical officer with the Hungarian hussars; he later went to Budapest as a psychiatrist in a military hospital, which allowed him to resume his activities. He never gave up his faith in psychoanalysis, and he conducted a treatment on horseback with an officer of his regiment who was suffering from trauma after being struck by a shell. Ferenczi was also trying to solve his problems with his wife, Gizella, during this period.

Remaining alone in Vienna with Sachs, Martha, Anna, and Minna, Freud entered into wartime fearing every day that his three sons and his son-in-law (Martin, Oliver, Ernst, and Max Halberstadt), who had enlisted or been called up in the artillery, the corps of engineers, or other branches of the military, would be victims of the butchery.[2] His nephew Hermann Graf, Rosa's only son, was the only one who never came back; he was

killed on the Italian front in July 1917. Rudolf Halberstadt, Max's brother, met the same fate.

In reality, from the very start of the conflict, and despite his bellicose mood and his certainty that Germany would win, Freud understood that the war would be long and deadly, and that it would change the world in which he lived from top to bottom: "I do not doubt that mankind will survive even this war," he wrote to Lou Andreas-Salomé in November 1914, "but I know for certain that for me and my contemporaries the world will never again be a happy place. It is too hideous. And the saddest thing about it is that it is exactly the way we should have expected people to behave from our knowledge of psycho-analysis. Because of this attitude toward mankind I have never been able to agree with your blithe optimism. My secret conclusion has always been: since we can only regard the highest present civilization as burdened with an enormous hypocrisy, it follows that we are organically unfitted for it."[3]

Once again, Freud was asserting that his doctrine revealed the darkest aspects of humanity, and he sought confirmation of the accuracy of his hypotheses in the events, just as he did, moreover, in literary texts, myths, and legends. By the same token, he failed to see that his reflections, and in particular his recent study on narcissism, were not exempt from the lethal evolution of the world he had known and was already starting to miss. Freud thought of himself as the creator of a doctrine, without imagining that that doctrine could also be the product of a history that he did not control. Psychoanalysis was his "thing" *(die Sache),* and he saw it at work everywhere.

The happy period that included his trip to America, his passion for Jung, and his firm belief in the benefits of psychoanalytic treatment was over. And it was in fact during this time of war that he began to refashion his system of thought. Whether he liked it or not, the war was getting to him from all directions. He was irritable; he committed one solecism after another; he told Jewish jokes to stave off anguish. His libido, he said without really believing it, was solidly mobilized in favor of Austro-Hungary.[4] As for his theory, it is not at all clear that he could have summarized it at that point.

Freud's dream life and fantasies soon took a new turn. He dreamed that his son and his disciples had died; he dreamed about the dispersal of

his movement, about dreadful injuries, about battlefields covered with anonymous corpses. In a word, he was invaded night and day by the idea that the deadly force of unconscious drives threatened the highest forms of human civilization.[5]

And it was while thinking about this question, in April 1915, that he wrote an essay about war and death in which he radically contradicted his initial bellicose enthusiasm. In this despairing text, which announced all the hypotheses to come, he began with vibrant praise for the European society that grew out of Greco-Latin culture and was imbued with the scientific Enlightenment, in order to show to what extent this new war was leading the most enlightened humanity not only to a lowering of all moral feeling and to a dangerous disillusionment, but also to a re-awakening of all possible forms of cruelty, perfidy, and betrayal, the very forms that were thought to have been abolished by the exercise of democracy and the reign of civilization. And it is for this reason, he said, that the "citizen of humanity finds himself completely at a loss before the world that has become foreign to him: his great country ruined, common goods devastated, his fellow citizens divided and humiliated."[6]

In other words, Freud took note of the fact that this war, engendered by nationalism and the mutual hatred between peoples, translated the quintessence of a desire for death proper to the human species. It came to remind modern subjects of their position as heirs in a genealogy of murderers and to reconnect them with a base of archaic drives whose contours Freud himself had described in *Totem and Taboo*. War thus authorized them to transgress the prohibition on putting others to death. Worse still, in this conflict, the Professor observed that no one was capable any longer of recognizing the prerogatives of the wounded and of doctors owing to the abolition of the distinction between combatants and civilian populations.

In a dramatic tone, he stressed the fact that this war disturbed man's relation to death in an unprecedented way. A "natural" phenomenon, he said, death is the necessary outcome of every life and everyone has the duty of preparing for it. But, since our unconscious is inaccessible to its representation, in order to accept it we still have to deny its existence, put it out of play, or even dramatize it in an identification with an idealized hero. Yet modern warfare, with its power of massive destruction, abolished

in human beings the recourse to such imaginary constructions capable of preserving them from the reality of death.

Evoking Achilles's response to Odysseus,[7] Freud took up the classical idea of an opposition between a glorious death, the heroic death of warriors who chose a short life, and a natural death following a long and peaceful life. And he implied that contemporary warfare erased the boundary between the two deaths, since it hurled soldiers—anonymous individuals—into the daily reality of their immediate finitude even before they had had the time to identify with anything at all. Thus this war laid bare, he said, the most ancestral feature of mankind: the pleasure of generalized murder beyond heroic death and natural death. If cruelty was making a comeback during this troubled period, then it was because civilization had never managed to eradicate it. Despite their humanization and access to culture, human beings would thus always be other than what they believed themselves to be. In the deepest layers of their psychic life, a barbarian was always ready to stir.

And Freud concluded his essay with a definitive profession of faith: "We recall the old saying: *Si vis pacem, para bellum.* If you want to preserve peace, arm for war. It would be in keeping with the times to alter it: *Si vis vitam, para mortem.* If you want to endure life, prepare yourself for death."[8]

At age fifty-nine, Freud was thus encountering the kingdom of the dead. He was thinking as much about his own death and that of those closest to him as about the death of combatants lost in the "polar night" of a war from which he saw no way out and which he compared to "repugnant craftsmanship." Minna and Martha already called him the "dear old man." Four months before the hostilities began, during the night of March 10–11, 1914, he had become a grandfather for the first time, with the birth of little Ernst (nicknamed "Ernstl") Halberstadt, Sophie's son, who would be the "child with the spool" whose play Freud would describe several years later: "Very strange! An oldish feeling, respect for the wonders of sexuality!"[9]

In the fall of 1914, he learned that his cherished half brother Emanuel had died, at age eighty-one; according to Freud, Emanuel had not been able to tolerate the war. On his own sixtieth birthday, in May 1916, he wrote that he too had crossed the threshold of old age, that nothing should

be postponed any longer, that his heart and his arteries had grown old, and that physically he was not the man his father had been at the same age.[10]

He left Vienna on several occasions, to visit first his daughter, then Abraham's wife, and finally his beloved friend Ferenczi. Freud's patients were fewer, his savings were melting away, his family members were suffering from poverty; there wasn't enough food, the living areas weren't heated, and tuberculosis threatened the most impoverished or the most fragile individuals. The bitter *Konrad* was faltering; Freud had sore throats, a swollen prostate, and other bodily disorders. In 1917, when he was sixty-one, he tried once again to stop smoking. But against all rational logic he succeeded in convincing himself that the painful swelling he felt in his mouth was a consequence of his abstinence, and he began to light cigars with a vengeance to sharpen his intellectual faculties.[11]

His awareness of the atrocities of the war and the physical presence of death in his life and in his body led Freud to give himself over to the creative solitude that he liked so much and that was associated with his smoking, with a certain masochism as well, along with his cult of sexual abstinence. Only a man who suffers can accomplish anything, he thought, even as he constantly asserted that the passion for cigars did not belong in the realm of psychoanalysis. Despite years of work on himself, Freud was as neurotic as ever.

In 1896, in a letter to Wilhelm Fliess, he had already used the term "metapsychology" to characterize his overall conception of the psyche in order to distinguish this conception from classic psychology. Armed with this term, he sought to realize his old dream of devoting himself to philosophy, or rather of defying philosophy. Later on, in *The Psychopathology of Everyday Life*, he had asserted even more clearly that knowledge of the psychical factors of the unconscious was reflected in the construction of a supraperceptible reality, which science was transforming into a psychology of the unconscious. And he had thus taken on the task of decomposing the myths relating to good and evil, immortality, and the origins of humanity, by translating metaphysics into a metapsychology.

In other words, if metaphysics was the study, in philosophy, of the first causes of being and existence—and thus of realities separate from

matter and lived experience—then metapsychology ought to be the parallel study of psychic reality, that is, of everything that escapes consciousness and material reality. By this speculative undertaking Freud meant to found psychoanalysis as a new discipline detached from psychology. Up to that point, he had always anchored his doctrine in psychology without ever theorizing the idea that his doctrine might subvert psychology.

Competing in this way with philosophical knowledge, which he viewed as a paranoid system, Freud was challenging psychology, the discipline that had once allowed him to leave neurology behind. An excessively ambitious undertaking—for he claimed to be making psychoanalysis a full-fledged "science" situated somewhere between psychology, philosophy, and biology; he refused to view it as a "human" or social science on the same footing as anthropology or sociology.

Starting in 1915, then, under the rubric of "metapsychology," he developed a set of models defined by the fact that they took into account dynamic, topographical, and economic viewpoints at one and the same time. Through the dynamic approach, he related psychic processes to their unconscious origins, and thus to the drives. Along the topographical axis, he defined places: the conscious, the preconscious, and the unconscious.[12] Finally, via the economic perspective, he distinguished among the various domains of psychic energy.

And it was in this perspective that, between 1915 and 1917, under the name *Metapsychology,* he brought together five austere, complex essays that broke with his earlier writings: "Instincts and Their Vicissitudes," "Repression," "The Unconscious," "A Metapsychological Supplement to the Theory of Dreams," and "Mourning and Melancholia."[13] He proposed to distinguish between two groups of instincts, or drives: the drives aiming at self-preservation, and the sex drives. He brought to light various reversals of drives with opposing objects, goals, persons, or pairings: sadism and masochism, voyeurism and exhibitionism, passivity and activity. And he drew a dark picture of the multiple facets through which human beings take pleasure in seducing, showing off, tormenting themselves by tormenting others, hating even while pretending to love.

Regarding repression, a major concept, Freud invented a sort of cartography of its ruses, its shapes, its twists and turns, its withdrawals, its

persecutions directed at the subject, even as he distinguished between primal repression, fixation, repression properly so-called, and finally the return of the repressed, with its representatives, its represented, its "quota of affects," its mechanisms of substitution at work in the principal neuroses: phobia, anxiety, hysteria, obsessional neurosis.

In this new light, the unconscious no longer had much to do with *The Interpretation of Dreams,* according to Freud. To be sure, it was still accessible only transposed or translated into a dream, a *lapsus,* a misfire, or a somatic conversion. But it was also something else: a hypothesis, a process "in itself," a form derived from humanity's ancient animal nature revisited and corrected according to a principle borrowed from Kantian philosophy. And Freud indicated that the unconscious psyche must never be substituted for the perception of consciousness, even if the former remains less unknowable than the external world. In this respect, he recast psychoanalysis as a psychology of the depths, articulated around the primacy of the unconscious—with the repressed contents taken into account—over the conscious and the preconscious, which were always in the process of formation.

As he approached the vast continent of melancholia, so magnificently described in every historical period by poets, philosophers, and, in recent times, "alienists," Freud did not try to compete with such texts, all the less in that he himself had already depicted Hamlet, the early seventeenth-century prototype of the melancholic prince, as a hysteric. It sufficed to try to integrate melancholia into his metapsychology, and thus to pull it away both from psychiatric nosography and from the philosophical tradition so as to redefine it as a sort of narcissistic delirium.[14] The times were propitious for such a reflection. Women, dressed in black, replaced the men fallen in combat by taking over economic activities in their respective countries. Far from looking at melancholia as one of the major components of the human condition, Freud defined it as the pathological form of mourning: a disorder entailing self-punishment. Before publishing his manuscript he sent it to Abraham, who had already compared mourning and melancholia and who offered a number of remarks in response. Freud thanked Abraham and quoted him. Thus he brought the torments of melancholia into a process of libidinal regression and abandonment of unconscious investment.[15]

Freud emphasized that, in the work of mourning, the subject gradually manages to detach himself from the lost object, whereas in melancholia he thinks he is responsible for the death that has occurred; he either denies the death or believes he is possessed by the deceased or suffering from the same illness that brought about the death. Confronted with this irremediable loss, he feels unworthy and believes that his moral conscience is judging and persecuting him. Freud will later call this form of consciousness, or conscience, the "superego."

Freud planned to write twelve essays and bring them together in a set to be called *Elements for a Metapsychology*. But he had misgivings, and he finally abandoned seven texts, of which only one has been rediscovered: *Overview of the Transference Neuroses*.[16] Constructed as an exchange with Ferenczi,[17] but as a "phylogenetic fantasy," this set of texts had been conceived as a sequel to *Totem and Taboo*. It grew out of a "bioanalytical" speculation that had led Freud to extend the theory of neuroses and the theory of the murder of the father at the origin of mankind. In other terms, he claimed to be proceeding to a recapitulation of phylogenesis by ontogenesis.[18] Thus he asserted that there is an analogy between the evolutionary stages of the human species and those of the neuroses. If the chronological order of the neuroses shows that, in individual development, anxiety hysteria comes first, followed by conversion hysteria and later by obsessional neurosis, this indicates that these three types of neurosis have their equivalent in a phylogenetic history of humanity, situated between the beginning and the end of the Ice Age.[19] One would thus find the trace, in every human being, of a neurotic regression corresponding to a stage already present in phylogenesis. At the dawn of the Ice Age, in this view, humanity became anxious, and then entered into a conflict between self-preservation and the desire to reproduce: hence the appearance of an anxiety hysteria. The following phase saw an overevaluation of thought and language, corresponding to an obsessional neurosis, that is, to a religious conception of the world. There followed, in Freud's text, a new version of the story of the "struggle for existence," converted into a psycho-phylogenetic fable: the primitive horde; the murder of the father; sons united by their homosexuality; women immersed in an unknown, "dark" continent; the return of the father figure in paranoia;

identification with the dead father, situated between mourning and melancholia.

Once again Freud reinvented the components of his kinship system to make it a model for understanding the psyche. One can see why he hesitated to make his speculations public and actually destroyed several manuscripts. His ambitious metapsychology was, to say the least, obscure and faltering. As for the idea of giving psychoanalysis a foundation in perfect symmetry with that of biology, it amounted to making psychoanalysis a "metabiology," as Ferenczi had hoped. Freud indeed acknowledged at this point that he wanted to present the "calling card" of psychoanalysis to the biologists.[20]

Aware of the fragility of his hypothesis, Freud abandoned it, although he did not give up the idea of transposing the mechanisms of evolution into the field of psychoanalysis. To that end, he began to read Jean-Baptiste Lamarck's *Zoological Philosophy*,[21] not so as to oppose Lamarckism to Darwinism[22] but rather to show that the Lamarckian idea that "need . . . creates organs" was nothing other than a way of taking into account the "power of [unconscious] ideas over one's own body," vestiges of which he saw in hysteria: in brief, as he put it, "the omnipotence of thoughts." "This would actually supply a [psychoanalytical] explanation of expediency," he added; "it would put the coping stone on [psychoanalysis]. Two big principles of change (of progress) would emerge; the change through adaptation of one's own body, and the subsequent change through transformation of the external world (autoplastic and heteroplastic), etc."[23]

Freud took up this thesis again in 1920, in increasingly speculative texts, without ever providing a more robust content for his metapsychology—which would never prove useful, moreover, except as a support structure for a few attempts to psychologize psychoanalysis. A meager consolation.

While this change of perspective was being shaped, Freud continued teaching at the General Hospital in Vienna, drawing audiences of a hundred or so: students, doctors, parents, friends, and future disciples, including Max Schur, Edoardo Weiss, and Anna Freud. A new generation was emerging. As was his custom, Freud spoke without notes, and for his final academic year he decided to present, in twenty-eight lessons, the principal findings from what he still called "a young science": a synthesis

of *The Interpretation of Dreams, The Psychopathology of Everyday Life,* and *Three Essays.*

In addition, he included a series of presentations on psychoanalytic technique, transference, and the definition of neuroses. In this new effort to introduce psychoanalysis, Freud reaffirmed forcefully that the first object choice of a human being is always incestuous, that in a man it is directed toward the mother and sister and in a woman toward the mother and then toward the father and brother, and that only a severe prohibition makes it possible to hold this instinctual tendency in abeyance; it remains present forever in adult sexuality.

As soon as these lectures were published, they met with overwhelming, worldwide success.[24] The work nevertheless continued to feed rumors about the alleged "incestuous" organization of family life at 19 Berggasse. More than ever, psychoanalysis was received by its enthusiastic defenders—writers, philosophers, and poets—as a liberating revolution apt to change human destiny, and by its adversaries as a false science that threatened the order of the family, the benefits of religion, and the patriotic sentiments of populations: a lubricious way of thinking produced by a degenerate brain and a dying empire.[25]

During this period, Freud was dreaming of a Nobel Prize. His young friend and former student Robert Bárány, a Hungarian doctor, had been named a laureate in 1914 for his work in physiology on the vestibular apparatus of the ear; Bárány had designated Freud as his candidate. But on what grounds, and in what discipline? Despite his worldwide reputation, the Professor had not been recognized either as a scientist or as a writer. As for psychoanalysis, it was not part of any field of academic knowledge. Freud would never win the prize he had so desired.

Although he was not a proponent of Marxism, Freud welcomed the October Revolution that ended Russian participation in the war; similarly, whereas he was in no way an advocate of Zionism, he approved the Balfour Declaration, which opened the way for the creation of a Jewish national homeland in Palestine.[26] In November 1917, he was so pessimistic that he wanted to dream of better days.

As the end of the hostilities approached, the members of the committee went on the warpath against one another. Determined to take the fate of the movement in hand and make sure it landed on the side of the victors,

Ernest Jones attacked Abraham while supporting Ferenczi. Against Abraham, who wanted to organize the fifth congress of the Verein in Berlin, he stressed that such a move risked getting psychoanalysis dismissed as a "Boche science"; with Ferenczi's agreement, he chose Budapest as the meeting site. Freud approved this option. Each of the "paladins" knew that Hungary would soon be separated from Austria: Budapest, the cradle of a certain Ferenczian ideal of psychoanalysis proper to *Mitteleuropa*, was at the height of its glory.

The congress took place on September 28 and 29, 1918, at the Hungarian Academy of Sciences; it was attended by representatives of the Hungarian, German, and Austrian governments and by forty-two psychoanalysts, among them Géza Róheim, who was to become an American anthropologist, and a significant number of women, wearing discreet hats and flowing dresses. With the exception of Freud, all the men were in uniform. Melanie Klein, a brilliant student of Ferenczi's, met the master for the first time and attended his lecture on "Lines of Advance in Psychoanalytic Therapy."[27]

Instead of improvising as usual, Freud read his paper, which was stupefying to say the least. Arguing against his earlier views and against his own practice, but also against Ferenczi, he announced that psychoanalytical treatment should take place *"as far as is possible, under privation— in a state of abstinence."*[28] He did not go so far as to say that the patient should be deprived of all sexual activity, but he put forward the idea that the patient should be forbidden to profit from the initial results of the treatment. Without this rigor, he said, the patient risked falling back into irremediable failure.

Not content to oppose therapeutic empathy, and even though he disapproved of the puritanical approach adopted by his friend James Jackson Putnam, Freud announced that psychoanalysis was going to become a therapy for the masses—as it was in the United States—and that institutions that could offer successful treatment for free had to be created everywhere. In this way, the most impoverished populations could be helped to escape their condition. By advocating such a program of social hygiene, and by calling on the modern democratic nations to recognize the prophylactic value of psychoanalysis, Freud was in fact breaking with the old world. After his wanderings in the metapsychological labyrinth, he wanted

to believe that the treatment was no longer reserved for the Proustian figures of the upper bourgeoisie who were attached to a certain self-image—a class that had already faded away with the war.

And he called on the new generations to project themselves into the future:

> We shall probably discover that the poor are even less ready to part with their neuroses than the rich, because the hard life that awaits them if they recover offers them no attraction, and illness gives them one more claim to social help. Often, perhaps, we may only be able to achieve anything by combining mental assistance with some material support, in the manner of the Emperor Joseph. It is very probable, too, that the large-scale application of our therapy will compel us to alloy the pure gold of analysis freely with the copper of direct suggestion; and hypnotic influence, too, might find a place in it again, as it has in the treatment of war neuroses. But, whatever form this psychotherapy for the people may take, whatever the elements out of which it is compounded, its most effective and most important ingredients will assuredly remain those borrowed from strict and untendentious psycho-analysis.[29]

The question of war neuroses was discussed throughout the meeting in Budapest, with presentations by Abraham, Freud, Ferenczi, Ernst Simmel, and Viktor Tausk.[30] And the problem was fundamental: How could psychoanalysis be incorporated into the heart of society, in times of war and peace alike? Freud and his disciples were particularly interested in showing the difference between traumatic neuroses and ordinary neuroses, on the one hand, and between neurotic subjects and "healthy" subjects, both groups caught up in the turmoil of war, on the other.

The Freudians, who had long since abandoned trauma as a causal explanation of neuroses, now found themselves facing trauma again on a wholly different scale. Under these circumstances, it was impossible to deny that the horrors of war could have something to do with the appearance of disorders such as amnesia, terrors, nightmares, insomnia, and the like. Confronting the authorities of their respective countries, the psy-

choanalysts, who had been drafted for military service themselves, tried to explain that soldiers reacted differently to combat depending on whether they had been neurotic in civil life. Thus one soldier might present serious signs of shock without being depressed or anxious, whereas another soldier, who had not been under fire, could perfectly well fall into a state of shock at the very idea of finding himself face to face with the enemy. How should the soldiers afflicted by these neuroses be treated? Was the talking cure superior in all circumstances to electrotherapy, a real torture imposed on patients, or to hypnosis, which was deemed very effective?

These lectures were published in the context of the Internationaler Psychoanalytischer Verlag, a publishing house founded in January 1919 and financed by Anton von Freund, the jewel of the movement. Freud published his subsequent books there.

During the meetings, Hermann Nunberg proposed for the first time that one of the conditions required for becoming a psychoanalyst was to have undergone analysis oneself. Rank and Ferenczi opposed bringing a motion on the matter to a vote, but it was all for naught. The idea of analyzing the analysts—a didactic treatment and an analysis undertaken under supervision—gradually imposed itself over the years, starting with major experiments in Berlin. Freud saw fit to declare that the nerve center of psychoanalysis was in Hungary; he was wrong.

Two months later, the representatives of the Austro-Hungarian Empire signed the Armistice of Villa Giusti, the German plenipotentiaries met the Allies in the Rethondes clearing in northern France, William II abdicated, and Hungary became a republic. In the name of peoples' right to self-determination, and by virtue of the fourteen points drafted by U.S. president Woodrow Wilson, the various populations of the old Central and Balkanic Europe were redistributed within new borders defined a few months later by the Treaties of Versailles, Saint-Germain, and Trianon. Austria was now only an uncertain outline, "a grey, lifeless shadow of the old Austro-Hungarian monarchy."[31]

When the First Hungarian Republic was founded, Ferenczi, who was involved with progressive groups and the literary journal *Nyugat,* was recommended for a university teaching chair in psychoanalysis. Despite an initial negative report, the decree was signed by György Lukács, the

people's commissar for education and culture with the new government of Béla Kun; on March 20, 1919, Kun had instituted a Republic of Councils modeled on the Bolshevik revolution. On June 10, Ferenczi gave his first class in an amphitheater full of enthusiastic students.

On this occasion, Freud wrote an article that was published directly in Hungarian: "On the Teaching of Psycho-analysis in Universities."[32] Listing all the areas of study required for a student of psychoanalysis, he not only stressed the need for a good understanding of the history of psychotherapies, in order to grasp the objective reasons for the superiority of the psychoanalytic method, he also proposed a program that included literature, philosophy, art, mythology, and the history of religions and civilizations. He emphasized strongly that psychoanalysis must by no means limit its field of application to pathological disorders. The program Freud outlined was never established: not in Budapest, not in Vienna, not anywhere else in the world. Freud had taken the wrong path in seeking to impose psychoanalysis as a discipline in its own right. In reality, it owed its existence only to its own private institutions. In the upper reaches of university teaching, it could only find a foothold via other disciplines: psychiatry and psychology on the one hand, the humanities on the other. Thus it was split into two branches: a clinical branch, linked to the medical ideal of treatment, and a cultural branch, linked to philosophy, history, literature, and anthropology.

The fall of the Budapest Commune and the bloody repression organized by the troops of Admiral Miklos Horthy, who proclaimed himself the "Regent," put an end to the experiment. Ferenczi lost his position: "The most repugnant feature of Horthy's first decade," William Johnston writes, "was the White Terror of 1920. With a vengeance reminiscent of General Haynau's bloody assizes of 1849, torture was used indiscriminately, public whipping was reinstated, political murders were concealed, and Jews who had arrived as refugees since 1914 were expelled."[33]

Freud condemned the commune as much as he condemned Horthy's reign of terror: another misjudgment on his part. As for Jones, he profited from the situation, which allowed him to take over the Verein (IPV) and shift the nerve center of the movement toward the West, that is, toward the Anglophone world.

In 1919, the only patients Freud had left were a few Austrians and Hungarians. In Germany, his children had been ruined financially by the war, and he had to support them temporarily, while at the same time helping out some friends, in particular Andreas-Salomé, whom he supported on a regular basis until her death. While waiting for new disciples eager to train with him, he worked on perfecting his spoken English. Once again, he thought about settling someplace other than Vienna, Berlin, or London: "We have grown hungry beggars all of us here. But you shall hear no complaints. I am still upright and I hold myself not responsible for any part of the worlds [*sic*] nonsense." And he added, "Psychoanalysis is flourishing I am glad to learn from everywhere, I trust science will prove a consolation for you too."[34] Welcomed warmly in Vienna in September, Jones invited Freud and Ferenczi to lunch; they were starving.

Depressed after the fall of the commune, Ferenczi took steps toward emigrating to the United States. Freud stubbornly refused to let him go, even as he was neglecting his Hungarian disciple and turning more and more toward Jones for the organization of the international movement. Aware of belonging to the victors' camp and eager to pull the management of the Verein's affairs way from devastated Continental Europe, Jones began to deploy his pragmatic policies for normalizing the profession. He even defended the idea—which Freud opposed—that psychoanalysis should be exclusively practiced by doctors, as was the case in the United States.

With the same perspective, Jones imposed on the committee a decision that proved catastrophic for the future: he secured passage of a rule that excluded homosexuals from membership in any professional psychoanalytical association and kept them from becoming analysts, for "in most cases, they are abnormal." This astounding ruling was completely opposed to Freudian doctrine. It subjected the name of da Vinci to ridicule. The Berliners opposed it; warning his friends, Rank accused Jones of failing to take into account the different types of homosexuality.[35]

Thus homosexuals were once again treated as perverts by the very people who had distanced themselves from the racialist theses of the late nineteenth century. Of course this ruling did not prevent homosexuals

from becoming psychoanalysts, but they had to conceal their sexual orientation. The ruling encouraged the spread of a frightening homophobia among the worldwide psychoanalytic community, all the way to the end of the twentieth century.[36] This position on the part of the committee was all the more absurd in that Freud had supported an initiative by Magnus Hirschfeld in Germany that was aimed at abolishing paragraph 175 of the penal code punishing homosexual activity, especially on the part of men, by prison sentences and the loss of civil rights.[37]

Psychiatrists in the countries involved in the war had been called on by the military hierarchies to help ferret out "pretenders," who were viewed as deserters, unpatriotic or cowardly.[38] At the heart of the debate, the old question of the status of hysteria came back at full strength: Was it a true psychic illness, or dissimulation?

This was the context in which Julius Wagner-Jauregg, a famous organicist Viennese psychiatrist and asylum reformer,[39] was accused of abuse of authority for having classified as pretenders soldiers afflicted with traumatic neuroses, whom he had subjected to electroshock treatments.[40] The scandal arose in 1920 when Lieutenant Walter Kauders, a brilliant Jewish patriot in the Austrian army, brought a complaint against Wagner-Jauregg and his assistants, Michael Kozlowski in particular.[41] At that point, Freud was summoned as an expert witness before an investigatory commission led by Alexander Löffler; Julius Tandler was one of its members. Freud wrote a report and participated in the exchanges between the members of the jury, the accused, and the plaintiff.

In 1915, Kauders's skull was fractured by an exploded shell. After several stints in military hospitals, he remained half-dazed, walked with a cane, and suffered from migraines. Between November 1917 and March 1918, treated as a mental patient, he had been placed in isolation in the Wagner-Jauregg clinic before undergoing two "faradizations" administered with metal clips by Kozlowski, and he was classified as a malingerer:[42] "These unmistakable tortures were specially prepared psychologically. The patient is usually given to understand that he is about to experience a procedure which is known to be horrible. . . . The pains caused by brush faradization are indescribable. It feels as though innumerable drills are being driven right into the bones at a furious speed."[43]

Focused above all on using this platform to defend his doctrine, which was being attacked from all sides, Freud sidestepped the question of Wagner-Jauregg's responsibility and went on to produce an apologia of the psychoanalytic method. He emphasized first of all that doctors should be at the service of patients, not subject to the orders of a military hierarchy, and he challenged the usefulness of electrotherapy. In so doing, he exonerated Wagner-Jauregg of all responsibility in the matter, but regretted that the psychiatrist was not an ardent supporter of psychoanalysis. He affirmed nevertheless that Wagner-Jauregg was not a torturer, and that he had not committed any abuse of authority in his belief that such a treatment could be a remedy for malingering. In Freud's eyes, malingering was not at issue in this instance, for the good reason that "all neurotics are malingerers" and vice versa, to the extent that they "simulate without knowing it, and this is their sickness."[44] In other words, once again, Freud nullified the notion of simulation: one simulates only what one is.

Wagner-Jauregg, for his part, could not accept being defended in this way by a man he admired but whose reasoning he rejected. He did not accept either the idea that simulation was a neurosis or the principle according to which a psychiatrist, in wartime, ought to put himself at the exclusive service of the patient. He was acquitted nevertheless.

Freud had made the error of positing a diagnosis of neurosis without taking an interest in Kauders. And yet the lieutenant had much in common with a good number of his peers. He had had an authoritarian father, an older brother who committed suicide, a mentally ill half sister, and a childhood marked by the humiliation of being Jewish. He was undoubtedly neurotic, but above all he had undergone a serious trauma in the war, as Kurt Robert Eissler emphasized in 1979: "I would say that the Kauders case, despite its tragic aspects, contains at its core a truly Austrian comedy. A young man goes enthusiastically to war, becomes an officer, is wounded, and cannot go on, for whatever reason. . . . It is not known whether anyone in the courtroom saw clearly that Wagner-Jauregg and Freud were facing each other as representatives of two different worlds, one representing the point of view of expediency and the other that of humanity, which sees in man the sufferer caught in the toils of fate."[45]

The number of human victims of this First World War totaled some forty million people: military and civilian deaths accounted for slightly more than half this number, the rest being those who suffered from injuries of all sorts. The Allies lost five million soldiers, and the Central powers four million. Ernst Lanzer was among them.

Lanzer had met Freud in October 1907 when he was twenty-nine years old. He had had a childhood similar to that of many sons of the Viennese Jewish bourgeoisie; he could have come straight out of a novel by Arthur Schnitzler or Stefan Zweig. His father, Heinrich Lanzer, had married his wealthier cousin Rosa Herlinger, and this had allowed him to join the Saborsky company as an employee.[46] The fourth child of seven, Ernst had watched his mother wear herself out in successive pregnancies, and he judged that his father had become violent following financial setbacks. Ernst had been beaten as a child and treated as a "future criminal" by his father, because he had dared answer his father's insults in kind.[47]

At age five, he had taken refuge under his governess's skirt to fondle her genital organs. The result was a precocious sexuality and solid erections, often encouraged by the remarks of the servants. Like his brother, he had adopted "sexual habits" and a coarse way of speaking; he did not hesitate to ask his mother to "scrub his ass." In 1897, a young seamstress in his parents' employ made sexual overtures; he felt guilty when she committed suicide after he rejected her advances. Subsequently, he fell in love with Gisela Adler, a poor cousin, sterile and sickly, who displeased his father. Thus he felt that only Heinrich's death could remove the obstacle to the marriage he desired.

When his father did die, Lanzer was still prey to sexual rituals, even though he was a member of the Austrian army with the rank of private first class. Haunted by the phantom of his father, which disturbed his sleep, he fell into the habit of contemplating his own erect penis, using a mirror placed between his legs. Assailed without respite by suicidal thoughts and a desire to cut his own throat, when he first had sexual intercourse (at the age of twenty-six) he became aware that he was suffering from a psychic illness. He then went to Munich for a course of hydrotherapy, and he embarked on a sexual relationship with a servant girl, thinking all the while that achieving such satisfaction would make him capable of killing his father. He masturbated regularly, and engaged in

religious rituals. He saw several doctors, including Wagner-Jauregg, who brought him no relief.

In 1907, now a reserve officer, he went to Galicia to carry out military exercises, and there he became acquainted with a certain Nemeczek, a particularly cruel captain with a fondness for corporal punishment. Nemeczek told Lanzer the story of an Oriental torture in which a prisoner was forced to undress and kneel on the ground, bent over. A large pot with a hole in it was then attached to the man's buttocks with a leather strap; inside the pot a rat, deprived of food and agitated by a red-hot twig inserted through the hole, sought to escape the burning brand and penetrated the victim's rectum, inflicting bloody wounds; within half an hour, the rat died of suffocation, and the man was dead as well.[48] That day, during an exercise, Lanzer lost his pince-nez, and sent a telegram to his optician in Vienna asking for an immediate replacement. Two days later, the object was delivered to him through the intermediary of the same captain, who informed him that the mailing charges were to be reimbursed to Lieutenant David, the base supervisor.

Facing this constraint, Lanzer reacted deliriously; the story of the torture became entangled with that of the debt, and brought to the surface a memory of another episode involving money: his father had once contracted a gambling debt and was saved from dishonor by a friend who lent him the money he needed to pay it off. After completing his military service, Heinrich had tried to find the man again, but he had never succeeded and thus had never been able to honor his debt.

Such was the man who presented himself at 19 Berggasse on October 1, 1907. He began by evoking his childhood memories, and Freud kept a journal of the treatment, writing down the dialogue every evening. For once he had an ideal patient, truly afflicted with an obsessional neurosis just as Freud had described the disorder: a neurosis originating in a psychic conflict characterized by fixation of the libido in an anal stage. Hatred of the father, conjuring rituals, ruminations, doubts, scruples, inhibitions, consanguinary marriages, familial turpitudes, and the presence of brothers, sisters, uncles, aunts: in the face of such a "Freudian" story, the Professor would not need to construct a fiction in which the patient would not recognize himself. And since Lanzer was in search of a paternal authority that would allow him to understand the meaning of his neurosis,

a positive transference was formed between the two men, so much so that Freud could compel Lanzer to recount the terrible torture scene, while imagining that his patient felt, as he spoke, *"horror at pleasure of his own of which he himself was unaware."*[49]

Freud allowed himself to be insulted so that, through the painful path of transference, Lanzer could recognize the unconscious hatred that he felt for his father. And Freud solved the puzzle: it was the story of the punishment by rats, he said, that awakened Lanzer's anal eroticism. By making himself the advocate of physical punishment through rats, the captain had taken the father's place, in the patient's eyes, and attracted to himself an animosity comparable to the hatred that had once responded to Heinrich's cruelty. According to Freud, the rat took on here the signification of money, and thus of the debt, which was manifested during the treatment by a verbal association: "florin/rat" or "rate/rats [*Ratte*]." Indeed, from the beginning of the treatment, the patient had gotten in the habit of counting the sum of his payments with the refrain "So many florins, so many rats."[50]

In 1908, at the first congress of the Verein in Salzburg, Freud spent five hours presenting the *Rattenmann* case before an audience surprised by the logical construction of the narrative. For publication, he transformed the patient's statements by attributing interpretations to the patient that were in fact his own, and he left out several incidents. Moreover, he presented the father as an exemplary man and said almost nothing about the mother. For all this, it was not "a purely speculative construction," as some have claimed.[51] In any case, Lanzer felt that his four months of treatment had been beneficial, and that Freud's interpretation had freed him from his suffering and especially from his obsessions. He agreed, moreover, to allow his "case" to be made public.[52] Freud, for his part, asserted that the treatment had been completely successful.

In 1910, Lanzer married his dear Gisela, and in 1913 he became a lawyer. Enlisted in the imperial army in August 1914, he became a prisoner of the Russians in November and was executed. His mother died two months later. What would have become of him, had he lived?

With Lanzer, Freud had been confronted once again with a family tragedy and familial intermarriage, but certainly not with an Oedipus complex. The officer of the imperial army had read some of Freud's books,

and he had sought out the psychoanalyst as someone who solved riddles, an Oedipus occupying the place of the Sphinx, although there was never any question, during his treatment, of an unconscious desire for the mother.[53] Lanzer had indeed had the culpable wish to kill a deficient and brutal father,[54] but not to possess his mother, even when he remembered that he had gone to her for protection against the father he feared. His mother had remained an object of disgust for him; he was horrified by her nauseating odors, a result of intestinal problems. And he saw her only as a rigid, frustrated woman who had tried to keep him from marrying the love of his life and to marry him off to a Saborsky.

Rather than adding an interpretation that would refute or complete all those that have been put forward by psychoanalysts since the publication of this case, it is probably more useful to emphasize the extent to which Lanzer's story is representative of the earliest Freudian treatments, characterized as they were by the mutual entanglements of a certain state of the Western family—marked by the dismantling of patriarchal authority—and the primacy given to the capacity of an individual's speech to reveal the existence of these entanglements. Freud himself was the actor in this story, and he drew on it to refine his doctrine, confronted with the enduring risk of wandering in the labyrinth of the most extravagant interpretations or trying to pin down in detail the signification of an individual destiny.

To the injunction of an arranged marriage that would have been a repetition of his parents' union, Lanzer had opposed the virtues of a love marriage, without calling into question the consanguinity of cousins. Unlike other Viennese Jews, he had never sought to surpass his father, and his entry into military life did not allow him to resolve the conflict that opposed him to his family. His encounter with Freud made him the agent in his own existence, while the other, physical treatments that had been inflicted on him stemmed from therapeutic nihilism. Like many young men of his day, he did not have time to learn what would come next in his story, since death in combat was his fate: "The patient's mental health was restored to him by the analysis . . . ," Freud wrote in 1923. "Like so many other young men of value and promise, he perished in the Great War."[55]

On June 28, 1914, Sergius (or Sergei) Konstantinovitch Pankejeff was strolling in the Prater, thinking about his analysis with Freud, when he

heard the stunning news that Archduke Franz Ferdinand had been as-
sassinated by a Bosnian nationalist. His treatment had begun in January
1910, two years after Lanzer's ended, and from that point on, without any
awareness of the fact on his part, he was in a camp opposed to that of the
Austrian army officer who had also spent time at 19 Berggasse. From a
wealthy Russian aristocratic family, Pankejeff and his sister Anna had
been brought up in Odessa by three servants (Grusha, Nanya, and Miss
Owen) and several tutors. In their palatial residence, his alcoholic and de-
pressive father, Konstantin, led the active life of a liberal, cultivated man
while also organizing wolf hunts which Pankejeff very much enjoyed. In
the evening, after the outings, his mother, continually afflicted by phys-
ical ailments, often danced with her two children before a heap of trophy
animal skins.[56]

On both sides of the genealogy, the members of this pathological family
recall the characters in *The Brothers Karamazov*. Sergei's paternal grand-
father died an alcoholic, and his wife had sunk into depression. Uncle
Peter, his father's oldest brother, suffered from paranoia and had been
treated by the psychiatrist Sergei Korsakov. Fleeing human contact, he
lived like a savage among animals and ended his life in an asylum. Uncle
Nicholas, Sergei's father's second brother, had sought to kidnap the fiancée
of one of his sons and marry her by force. A cousin, the son of Sergei's
mother's sister, had been committed to an asylum in Prague, he, too, af-
flicted with a form of persecution delirium. As for Konstantin, he had
been treated by Moshe Wulff, one of Freud's first Russian disciples, who
also treated two schizophrenic cousins on the maternal side. When Kon-
stantin went to Munich to consult Emil Kraepelin, he received a diag-
nosis of manic-depressive psychosis, but the doctor was of no help at all.

Very early, Pankejeff was confronted with wolves and quite peculiar
tails. One day, Miss Owen, whom he detested, brandished long caramels
in front of him and compared them to pieces of snakes. On another occa-
sion, she untied her dress in back, and, shaking her body all over, cried
out, "Look at my little tail!" As for Anna, Pankejeff's cherished sister, a
bold, masculine girl, she teased him by imitating Miss Owen. Trying to
arouse his curiosity one day, she thrust an attractive picture of a girl under
his nose. But behind that sheet of paper she had hidden the portrait of a
horrible wolf standing on its hind legs and on the verge of devouring Little

Red Riding Hood. In love with this sister who was Konstantin's favorite child, Pankejeff spent time with her drawing trees, horses, wolves, drunkards, and greedy characters. When he was frightened, he took refuge in the arms of his Nanya, his adored nurse, a very pious woman who told him stories of saints, martyrs, and persecutions.

In 1896, when he was ten years old, Pankejeff showed signs of animal phobia. In 1905, his sister Anna committed suicide, and his father killed himself in turn two years later. During this period Pankejeff was in secondary school. He met a peasant woman, Matrona, from whom he contracted a venereal disease. He then sank into frequent depressions, which soon led him—through sanatoriums and asylums, rest homes and thermal baths—to become, like the rest of the family, an ideal patient in terms of late nineteenth-century psychiatric knowledge: a chronic melancholic subject to fits of exaltation and depression and always in search of an elusive identity. As much to win affection as to give himself some consistency, he offered each doctor a different version of his "case."

Initially treated by Vladimir Bekhterev, who used hypnosis, he next saw Theodor Ziehen in Berlin, and finally Adolf Albrecht Friedländer, after which he went to see Kraepelin in Munich; the last, recalling Pankejeff's paternal heredity, diagnosed manic-depressive psychosis once again. At the sanatorium in Neuwittelsbach, where he underwent a variety of treatments, all useless (massages, baths, and so on), Pankejeff, still very attracted by wet nurses and peasant women, fell in love with Teresa Keller, a nurse who was a little older than he and had a daughter (Else). This was the start of a love affair that was opposed not only by his family but also by his psychiatrist, who was convinced that this sort of relationship with an "inferior" woman would result in aggravating his madness.

Once back in Odessa, Pankejeff was treated by a young doctor, Leonid Drosnes, who decided to take him to Vienna for a consultation at 19 Berggasse. In a trenchant phrase, Freud stigmatized the therapeutic nihilism of his psychiatrist colleagues: "Up to now," he said to Pankejeff, "you have been looking for the causes of your illness in the chamber pot."[57]

The interpretation had a double meaning. Freud was targeting both the uselessness of the earlier treatments and the fact that Pankejeff's pathology involved continuing intestinal disorders, in particular chronic constipation. Wrongly, the master was convinced that this disorder had a psychic

origin. Thus he ordered the patient to stop taking the enemas that a student had been administering, because they promoted "subconscious homosexuality."[58]

On Freud's advice, Pankejeff moved to Vienna. While Drosnes followed the WPV seminars and was initiated into psychoanalysis, Pankejeff took fencing lessons and worked on his study of law. In the evenings, he went to the theater or played cards. He liked Vienna, the Prater, the cafés, the urban life that made him forget his childhood in a countryside populated by wolves and terrifying forebears.

Instead of forbidding him to see Teresa again, Freud asked him simply to wait until his treatment was over before seeing her. He did not oppose marriage: Teresa, he said, "is the breakthrough to the woman."[59] In a February 1910 letter to Ferenczi, he noted the violence of his patient's transferential manifestations: "A rich young Russian, whom I took on because of compulsive tendencies, admitted the following transferences to me after the first session: Jewish swindler, he would like to use me from behind and shit on my head. At the age of six years he experienced as his first symptom cursing against God: pig, dog, etc. When he saw three piles of feces on the street he became uncomfortable because of the Holy Trinity and anxiously sought a fourth in order to destroy the association."[60]

For the first time, Pankejeff had the impression that he was being heard, rather than simply being viewed as a sick person. The treatment helped give him an identity and helped bring him out of the existential void in which he had been maintained by the various doctors he had seen as he went from hospital to hospital. Above all, he had friendly relations with Freud, and ended up venerating him. Freud finally met Teresa and approved the marriage, which was celebrated in Odessa in 1914. Pankejeff felt that he was cured by then, and he asserted that the analysis had allowed him to marry the woman he loved.

With this patient, Freud had been confronted once again with a history that perfectly illustrated his conception of family neuroses: precocious sexuality; ambiguous sibling relationships; the role of governesses and corrupt nurses; seduction scenes; pathologies on the part of fathers, uncles, and cousins; the subjection of women; and so on. Thus he forgot that his patient suffered from incurable chronic melancholia; he saw him as a case of anxiety hysteria with an animal phobia that

was later transformed into an obsessional neurosis or an infantile neurosis.

In October and November 1914, it was in this state of mind and in the turmoil of the war that Freud set down the story of this depressive, ambivalent Russian, without using the "wolf man" label. At Pankejeff's request, the narrative was published in 1918 under the title "From the History of an Infantile Neurosis."[61] In it, Freud made no reference to what he had just written about melancholia. On several occasions, however, he later added notes to the original text.

Unlike the Rat Man case, in which the logic of the treatment was presented implacably, Freud allowed himself to tell Pankejeff's story through a painstaking biographical reconstruction; as the interpretation proceeded, he even "invented" events that probably never took place.[62] The entire narrative was centered on the patient's childhood and his sexuality.

The Freudian family portrait included the mother, the father, the sister, and three employees: the children's nursemaid (Nanya), the English governess (Miss Owen), and the servant (Grusha). According to Freud, who relied on the memories evoked by his patient during treatment, Pankejeff was the object of a seduction attempt by his sister Anna when he was three and a half; Anna reportedly showed him her own "bottom," and he then showed his to Nanya, who scolded him. As Freud told the story, when the boy was about ten, he tried to seduce his sister in turn, but she rebuffed him. As a result, he later preferred women of a lower social status than his own. It was while interpreting a dream Pankejeff had when he was four, and which he related and sketched during his treatment, that Freud reconstructed the origin of the infantile neurosis: "I dreamt that it was night and that I was lying in my bed. . . . I know it was winter. . . . Suddenly the window opened of its own accord, and I was terrified to see that some white wolves were sitting on the big walnut tree in front of the window. There were six or seven of them. The wolves were quite white, and looked more like foxes or sheep-dogs, for they had big tails like foxes and they had their ears pricked like dogs when they pay attention to something. In great terror, evidently of being eaten up by the wolves, I screamed and woke up."[63]

Relating this dream of white wolves to several of the patient's memories about his childhood sexuality, Freud invented, providing details of

unprecedented precision, an extraordinary "primal scene" *(Urszene)*[64] that would become famous in the annals of psychoanalysis and spark numerous commentaries. Pankejeff, about eighteen months old, had had malaria. "Probably for the very reason of this illness, he was in his parents' bedroom. . . . He had been sleeping in his cot, then, in his parents' bedroom, and woke up, perhaps because of his rising fever, in the afternoon, possibly at five o'clock, the hour which was later marked out by depression. It harmonizes with our assumption that it was a hot summer's day, if we suppose that his parents had retired, half undressed, for an afternoon siesta. When he woke up, he witnessed a coitus *a tergo* [from behind], three times repeated; he was able to see his mother's genitals as well as his father's organ; and he understood the process as well as its significance. Lastly, he interrupted his parents' intercourse" by crying out.[65] According to Freud, the dream about wolves was thus an inverted representation of an old scene of lovemaking. Pankejeff himself never acknowledged the existence of such a scene, but he always found it fascinating, emphasizing that it had given meaning to his existence. Sometimes he asserted that Freud had been right to reconstitute his unconscious psychic life in this way, and sometimes he doubted that the interpretation was well founded.

Two other episodes of Pankejeff's life were the objects of a series of interpretations. One concerned Grusha, whose buttocks, compared to butterfly wings, then to the roman numeral V, referred to the five wolves of the dream and to the hour at which the famous intercourse scene was thought to have taken place; the other had to do with a visual hallucination. In his childhood, Pankejeff had seen his little finger cut by a pocketknife, and had later noticed the nonexistence of the wound. Freud deduced that his patient had manifested, in this instance, an attitude of rejection *(Verwerfung)* that consisted in seeing sexuality only from the perspective of an infantile theory: intercourse via the anus.

After this great plunge into Pankejeff's childhood, Freud was certain that he had cured his patient. Until the spring of 1918, the latter lived in Odessa between his mother and Teresa, who did not get along well. He then resumed his studies and soon earned his diploma as a lawyer. As for Teresa, she had to leave Russia to be with her daughter, who died in Vienna. Pankejeff rejoined her there. The October Revolution had ruined

him, and the former wealthy aristocrat became a different man, a poor émigré without resources, obliged to take a job in an insurance company, where he worked until he retired.

The changes that had taken place in his life sank him into another depression, which led him to return to Freud. The latter welcomed him gladly, and at once made him a gift of the story of his case, which had just been published; he then began a new analysis, lasting from November 1919 to February 1920. If Freud is to be believed, this "post-treatment" made it possible to liquidate the last vestiges of an unanalyzed transference and cure the patient at last.

In reality, Pankejeff continued to present the same symptoms, which were aggravated by his mediocre financial situation. Freud helped him by taking up a collection within the circle of his Viennese disciples. This was the moment when the patient began to identify with the story of his case and actually see himself as the Wolf Man, calling himself *Wolfsmann*.

In 1926, still afflicted with the same symptoms, he consulted Freud once again, but the latter refused to treat him a third time and sent him instead to Ruth Mack Brunswick, a morphine addict who was almost as ill as Pankejeff. Freud was not only analyzing Ruth, her husband, and her husband's brother at the same time, but he also sent Muriel Gardiner to Ruth's couch the same year; as their respective analyses unfolded, Muriel became a friend and confidant to Pankejeff.

A follower of Klein's theories, after six months of treatment Ruth identified in her patient not neurosis but paranoia. In 1928, she published a second version of the case.[66] For the first time, she attributed to the patient the name he wanted to have and which would be his from then on: "the Wolf Man." She described him as a persecuted man, antipathetic, greedy, sordid, hypochondriac, obsessed with his appearance and especially with a pustule that was eating away at his nose. With respect to this new diagnosis, the psychoanalytic movement split into two camps, with the partisans of psychosis on one side, and the partisans of neurosis on the other. Pankejeff concluded that his second therapist was insane, that she had been incredibly hard on Teresa, but that she had helped him.

Still in 1926, at a moment when the terrible quarrel between Freud and Rank was becoming explicit, Rank criticized the Freudian interpretation of the wolf dream. From his perspective, it was impossible that a

four-year-old child could have had such a dream, and he asserted that what was really involved was a transferential wish on the patient's part. The child's bed, he said in sum, represented the couch, the trees were those that could be seen from Freud's office, and the wolves were simply stand-ins for the members of the committee whose photograph was on Freud's desk, or perhaps they stood for Freud's children. And Rank added that the dream confirmed his own theories on maternal transference and the birth trauma. In his eyes, the patient had dreamed of a "family tree," and this had awakened his infantile jealousy, in which Freud occupied, for him, the place of a mother equipped with a penis.[67]

Furious, Freud annihilated the theses of his cherished disciple by demonstrating, with supporting evidence, that at the time the patient recounted his dream he could not have seen the portraits of the committee members because, on the wall above the painting *A Clinical Lesson at the Salpêtrière*, there were only two or three portraits. And, to confirm this assertion, he asked Pankejeff to send him a written attestation: "There is no occasion for me to doubt the correctness of this recollection. . . . Also, as far as I know, the memory of this childhood dream never underwent a change. . . . The wolf-dream always seemed to me to stand in the middle of my childhood dreams. . . . I related the wolf-dream to you at the beginning of the treatment."[68] Following this episode, Freud charged Ferenczi with the task of attacking Rank's theses. A sad struggle, which ended, for Freud, with the loss of two of his best disciples.[69]

For generations of psychoanalysts, historians, and philosophers, the name Sergei Pankejeff remained unknown in the annals of psychoanalysis. All that remained, for several decades, was the story of the Wolf Man as it had been told by Freud and endlessly reinterpreted, in one outlandish theory after another, by prestigious commentators.[70]

Until the real life of Sergei Pankejeff was finally revealed, in two contradictory works,[71] his story had been impossible to piece together with clarity, since Pankejeff always went by the name of "the Wolf Man." Over the years, the former patient had turned into a sort of archive, a novelistic character from another century, ruined by two wars, a refugee in Vienna drawing his wolf tree ad infinitum, multiplying his dedications to psychoanalysts from around the world who wanted to hang the memory of a lost era on their office walls. Taken under the wing of the

Viennese psychoanalytical community, until his death in 1979 Pankejeff never stopped telling each of his interlocutors several different versions of his story.

Having become an expert on the reality of his own melancholia, he had learned to rival all those who commented on his "case." Had he not had the privilege, he used to ask, of being an unalterable part of Freud's work and the "friend" of a "brilliant thinker"? The anti-Freudians would assert in response that the unfortunate Russian was the victim of a criminal enterprise, and that Freud was a crook who manipulated his patients to make people believe that psychoanalysis was curing them.[72]

Two years after the Great War, during which Lanzer had died, but which Pankejeff had survived, Freud advanced the idea that a crime, in the form of the murder of the father, was at the origin of every society. But the only type of crime that really interested him was the crime connected with incest, and he made this the paradigm for all murderous acts. Armed with this hypothesis, Freud suggested that every society repeated this act in the course of its development. The act remained present as a "remainder" or a "relic" both in human communities and in individual lives, he noted, and this remainder must not be denied but rather reinterpreted as stemming from a prohibition. For this reason, Freud opposed the death penalty, not in his capacity as an ordinary citizen but because it was incompatible with the teaching of psychoanalysis: "Only the fact that mankind shrinks from facing facts, from acknowledging the facts of unconscious emotional life, delays the victory of the concept of capital punishment as murder sanctioned by law. My attitude concerning the problem of capital punishment originates, therefore, not in humanitarian reasons, but in the appreciation of the psychological necessity of the general human prohibition: 'thou shalt not kill.' . . . I profess to be an opponent of murder, whether committed by the individual as a crime or by the state in its retaliation."[73]

Freud envisaged his theory as a science that was designed to translate the psychic epic of the human species and its origin into the language of myths. Thus he was convinced that, in the world that was his, everything took place according to the myths he had constructed. In his clinical practice, in his daily life—with Lanzer, Pankejeff, and many others—he attempted to find his own scientific constructions. To be sure, the war

had brought his old bursts of optimism to an end and, in 1920, he saw death at work around him. But at the same time, his doctrine was being received triumphantly everywhere as a hygiene for life, as a new civilized morality, not only by the proponents of a new dynamic psychiatry but also and especially by writers who saw in it a sumptuous way of exploring the depths of the unconscious.

The Belle Époque and the murderous years were followed by a decade—at least for society's dominant classes—known as the Années folles, the Crazy Years, marked by an economic recovery and aspirations to all forms of revolution: literary, artistic, political, sexual, musical . . . The art of cinema, arriving from Hollywood, sought to bring an unprecedented representation of reality to the masses. Through the impetus of socialism, feminism, and psychoanalysis, everyone wanted to believe that the hierarchy between the classes and the sexes was about to disappear. The family was being transformed, divorce was more frequent, and the birth rate was dropping. In urban settings, the cult of bisexuality and of transgressive experimentation was flourishing: in Paris, in Berlin, in London, in New York. As for women, they were freeing themselves from their familial straitjackets and demanding the right to participate in political life. In a word, they were refusing to be reduced, as they had been formerly, to the status of stupid fiancées, mothers exhausted by a series of unwanted pregnancies, wives condemned to household chores.

In France, a country full of contrasts, psychoanalysis aroused all the more enthusiasm among writers in that it had been rejected, as a "Boche science" or as a "scientific obscenity," by a large part of the medical establishment. And when the surrealists highlighted the "Freudian revolution," Freud refused to hear their voices and did not really comprehend the admiration afforded him by André Breton and his friends. He continued to admire Anatole France and persisted in ignoring the importance of the literary avant-gardes even as he maintained a correspondence with Romain Rolland, a prolific writer and a close friend of Zweig; hostile to all nationalisms, Rolland had received the Nobel Prize for literature in 1915.[74] In short, Freud remained attached to "the world of yesteryear," and even more to the way he had envisaged this world by bringing it a revolution whose impact he probably did not appreciate. A strange, superbly Freudian contradiction.

Even as the war was winding down and new modes of life were emerging, a deadly flu struck and started a worldwide pandemic. It originated in China, hit the United States, passed through Spain in a mutated form, and spread throughout Europe. In just a few months, it killed more people than had been lost in the war.

In January 1920, Freud showed little sympathy for the aspirations of the young generations. Not very sensitive to the enthusiasms of modernity, he was preoccupied with thoughts of his own death and that of those closest to him, concerned with the aging of bodies and faces and with his old maladies: bladder and intestinal disorders, nasal suppuration. He feared that he would die before his mother, and he worried even more that, if it happened, she would have to be kept from learning the truth. When Jones told him about his own father's death, Freud consoled him, considering it a stroke of luck that the old man had not had to go on suffering too long from a cancer that would have eaten away at him little by little.

This was not the case for Freund, his friend and benefactor. Freud wrongly believed he had preserved Freund from a relapse by treating his neurosis, and he had to acknowledge this. His friend died on January 20 at age forty: "T. F. died yesterday, peacefully delivered from his incurable illness. For our cause a great loss, for me a keenly [felt] pain, but one which I have been able to assimilate during the past months. He bore his hopelessness with heroic and clear awareness and was no disgrace for psychoanalysis."[75]

Five days later, Sophie Halberstadt, weakened from the effects of an unwanted pregnancy, succumbed to flu-related pneumonia. Because the rail lines had been shut down, no one from Vienna could go to Hamburg for the burial. "The undisguised brutality of our time weighs heavily on us. Our poor Sunday child is to be cremated to-morrow. . . . Sophie leaves behind two boys, one aged six and the other thirteen months, and an inconsolable husband who will have to pay dearly for the happiness of these seven years. The happiness was only between them, not in external circumstances, which were war and war service, being wounded and losing their money, but they remained brave and cheerful."[76] And again: "So why am I writing? I think only that we are not together and that in this wretched period of imprisonment, we cannot go see one another. . . .

It is a brutal, absurd act of fate that has taken our Sophie from us, something in the face of which we can neither accuse nor ruminate, but only bow our heads under the blow, we poor humans without recourse, playthings of the higher powers."[77]

As much as Freud was touched by death, suicide, which was very frequent among Vienna intellectuals and psychoanalysts, left him cold. Attached to a heroic conception of death, deeply marked by Greco-Latin culture and dark Romanticism, he refused to view the act of suicide in psychiatric terms, seeing it, for good reason, as a right. But he was interested in it only to relate it to his conception of the difference between the sexes, or else to show that the desire to kill oneself stemmed from a reversal of the desire to kill. He thought that women did not kill themselves in the same way men did: men, he said, preferred to use weapons, that is, substitutes for the penis, whereas women tended to choose death by drowning, jumping out of windows, or taking poison—three ways, according to Freud, of giving birth or desiring a pregnancy.[78]

In other words, Freud, obsessed by primal murder, war, heroic death, and the idea of the biological finality of life, understood very little about voluntary death: a multifaceted crime against the self, present at the heart of all human societies, an unvarying challenge to all forms of authority. He found it amusing when someone announced his or her own suicide, and was fond of citing Mark Twain's telegram.[79] To be sure, Freud saw clearly that suicide was not an insane act, and he established a link between suicide and melancholia, even sometimes speaking of "deliverance" following an excess of psychic suffering, but he did not grasp the extent to which voluntary death could also be the expression of the highest freedom. In a word, he had a tendency to "psychologize" suicide.

And that accounts for his ferocity toward Tausk, one of his most brilliant first-generation disciples. Tausk had been brought up in Croatia by a tyrannical father and a persecuted mother. Like his lover Andreas-Salomé, who called him "Brother-animal,"[80] he had felt in himself the presence of a primitive force. Haunted by hatred of his father, Tausk had adopted an ambivalent attitude toward Freud, a mix of rebellion, adoration, and submission. During the war, he had spent time on the Serbian front before he returned to Vienna, devastated by the fall of the empire, and Freud had found nothing better than to plunge him into one of the

transferential triangulations he was prone to arrange. He had sent him to Helene Deutsch for analysis, Deutsch being one of his own patients at the time, imagining that he could control the progress of Tausk's treatment through her. However, in July 1919 Tausk took his own life by strangling himself with a drapery cord and shooting himself in the temple.

Freud wrote an effusive obituary in praise of Tausk. But in a personal letter addressed to Andreas-Salomé, he wrote: "Poor Tausk, whom you for some time favoured with your friendship, committed suicide on 3.7. He returned worn out from the horrors of war, was faced with the necessity of building up under the most unfavourable circumstances the practice in Vienna which he had lost by being called up for military service, had intended to remarry only a week later—but he decided otherwise. His farewell letters to his fiancée, his first wife, and to me were all equally affectionate, insisted on his clarity of mind, blamed only his own inadequacy and his failure in life; they gave therefore no clue to his last act." And Freud added, "I confess that I do not really miss him; I had long realized that he could be of no further service, indeed that he constituted a threat to the future."[81]

Once peace was restored, the members of the committee plunged into fierce internal battles. The psychoanalytic societies of London and Berlin had grown larger than the WPV, and the New York Psychoanalytic Society (NYPS) was also increasing considerably in membership. Ferenczi and Rank were more and more interested, as Jung had been earlier, in the "feminine" and "maternal" origin of neuroses and psychoses, rather than remaining focused on the murder of the father. Freud had always affirmed that the mother was the first love object of human beings, but by psychologizing the Oedipean tragedy he had transformed it into a "complex" that could not account for all aspects of the psyche. And the psychoanalysts of the new generation were seeking to detach themselves from the tutelary figure of the father set up as a totem. So they turned away from the originary crime to investigate the early attachment to the mother. In this context, with his application of the "active technique" Ferenczi was advocating a radical transformation of psychoanalytic treatment. At the Budapest congress he had already opposed Freud on the question of the "new paths." Now he was going still further.[82]

Instead of limiting themselves to producing interpretations aimed at extracting narratives of primal scenes from the unconscious, modern analysts should intervene during treatment with injunctions and prohibitions, according to Ferenczi. To the figure of the Sphinx, possessor of secrets and riddles, he contrasted the image of the benevolent, empathetic, feminine, sensual, maternal therapist concerned with alleviating the patient's suffering. In the light of such a revolution, Freud looked like an honored monarch reigning over an archaic kingdom.

Supporting Abraham, Jones sought for his part to professionalize the trade while fighting against Rank and Ferenczi in an effort to tilt the movement toward the Anglophone world. And the Allied victory seemed to confirm his judgment. Against Abraham, and despite the financial difficulties on the losing side, Jones imposed the choice of The Hague for the sixth IPV congress. He remained president until 1925, with Freud's support.[83]

In September 1920, before sixty-two participants, including a number of women, Abraham gave the opening address in Latin to avoid shocking the sensibilities of those on the winning side of the war. Nevertheless, the discussions took place primarily in German. And for another ten years or so, thanks to the creation of the prestigious institute, Berlin was to remain the nerve center of psychoanalysis as it expanded both eastward and westward. Freud delivered another of his lectures on dreams, using the occasion to revise his treasured *Traumbuch* once more, while Ferenczi described the active technique, Ludwig Binswanger dealt with psychiatric clinics, and Róheim spoke in English about totemism in Australia. The Dutch participants tended to mix with the English, while the Poles tended to exchange travel stories and ideas during long rides in automobiles, on boats, or on horseback. To conclude these joyous days of renewed acquaintances, a convivial banquet, organized by the victors, allowed the vanquished subjects of the old Central powers to stop seeing themselves as the pariahs of the new Europe.

Henceforth famous throughout the world, Freud was thus present at the worldwide triumph of his movement. But he was irritated, for the most part, and he missed the era when he had seen himself as a solitary discoverer. For in reality he did not accept the way his numerous disciples and admirers interpreted his doctrine and imbued it with the vibrant

rhythm of the Roaring Twenties, and he felt that an irreparable breach had been opened up between himself and the others: "I find the passage in your last Rundbrief [letter to the group] excellent," he wrote to Ferenczi, "where you say that we are all doing badly, but our cause is doing well. It really is such that the cause is consuming us and that we are being dissolved in it, as it were. And it is probably right that it is, only I would have wished for the younger, second analytic generation to be able to resist the solution for a while longer."[84]

In The Hague, Freud nevertheless experienced real happiness at the arrival, from the east bank of the Rhine, a quite extraordinary doctor, Georg Groddeck, accompanied by his mistress. In the midst of this learned assembly that was attempting to put the war years to rest and to normalize the training of practitioners, Groddeck declared, in effect, in a booming voice and a rather exalted tone, that he was "a wild analyst" and that he meant to cure organic illnesses with a psychic treatment adapted to that end. In 1900 he had founded a sanatorium in Baden-Baden, moreover, where he could apply his theories: a medicine of the "subject" with hydrotherapy, massages, a dietary regimen, and conversations between patients and caregivers. Ferenczi adored him and Freud had already expressed his enthusiasm: "I have to assert that you are a splendid analyst who had understood for ever the essential aspects of the matter. The discovery that transference and resistance are the most important aspects of treatment turns a person irretrievably into a member of the wild army." But he added, "Why do you jump from your beautiful basis into mysticism, cancel the distinction between mental and somatic, commit yourself to philosophical theories which are not called for? Your experience does not take you any further than the realization that the psychological factor is of an unimaginably great importance also in the origin of organic diseases?"[85]

Unlike a good number of Freud's disciples and patients, Groddeck had not suffered from paternal tyranny but rather from his mother's coldness; in his own eyes, his mother had eclipsed the figure of his father, whom he adored. Having been reared herself in the cult of an authoritarian father, Groddeck's mother had not been capable of transmitting to her children the affection required for their development. Afflicted with various organic ailments, four of the children had died young, and Georg

was the only survivor. His father, Carl Theodor, a noted doctor, headed a bathing establishment and was known for his ultraconservative positions. After the springtime of the peoples, he had published a book in which he likened democracy to a scourge, an epidemic apt to "contaminate" Europe and do away with all forms of self-awareness in individuals. This thesis, which came up again among sociologists who studied crowds, especially Gustave Le Bon, made Carl Theodor Groddeck a partisan of the chancellor Otto von Bismarck.[86]

Under pressure from his father, Georg embarked on a medical career by becoming the assistant to Ernest Scheninger, a marginal doctor who had become famous when he succeeded in treating Bismarck's various "ailments"—addiction to tobacco and drugs, obesity—by imposing a draconian regimen. An ultraconservative in his own right, Scheninger had transposed the principles of Prussian authoritarianism into medicine by instituting with his patients a relation of suggestion and absolute submission on which he made the treatment and the very nature of the cure depend. His motto—*Natura sanat, medicus curat*[87]—was taken up again by Groddeck in 1913 when his first book was published.[88]

Like his master and his father, Groddeck advocated the idea of "racial purity" and proposed that every German citizen married to a foreigner be deprived of his civil rights. In 1929, in his *Lebenserinnerunger* (Memoir),[89] he expressed regret for his earlier attitude and corrected it without ever renouncing the eugenicist utopia that underlay it, a perspective that was shared moreover by many German doctors and sexologists attached to the idea of "the improvement of the human species."[90] In the same book, he attacked psychoanalysis energetically, warning the reader against the dangers of a technique often poorly mastered by incompetent practitioners.

Groddeck had made an about-face very quickly. And Freud was fascinated by this doctor who reminded him of Fliess and the splendid delirium of an earlier era. In association with Groddeck, he could once again defy the medicine of his day, dream of conquering the territory of the body, imagine a friendship with a feminine double of Jung, defy Jones's tedious pragmatism, and indulge in speculation on the bisexual nature of humanity. In a word, in Groddeck Freud rediscovered his own youthful enthusiasm; it hardly mattered if some of his theses went against med-

ical science, since they took into account subjective suffering, which science had left aside.

At the Baden-Baden sanatorium, Groddeck received patients afflicted with all sorts of organic maladies against which the medicine of the day had proved powerless. In order to get the patients to participate in their treatment, he had the idea, starting in 1916, of giving talks addressed to them; he also created a journal, the *Satanarium,* in which he could express himself on the same basis as a therapist. Groddeck treated cancers, ulcers, rheumatisms, diabetes, claiming to find the expression of an organic desire in the traces of the illness. Thus in a goiter he found a desire for a child, and in diabetes a desire on the part of the organism to be sweetened. From the same perspective, he sexualized the organs of the body, assigning the optic nerve to the side of masculinity and the cardiac cavities to the side of femininity.[91]

This organic desire derived from what he called the id *(Es)*. With this neuter pronoun borrowed from Nietzsche, Groddeck designated an archaic substance anterior to language, a sort of wild irredentist nature submerging the subject's psychic structures, rather like Jung's "grottoes." The cure consisted in allowing the id, a source of truth, to surge forth in the subject.

A year after his encounter with Freud, he published a "psychoanalytic novel," *Der Seelensucher* (The soul-seeker),[92] in which he told the epic story of a man transfigured by the revelation of his unconscious who went around the world chasing after bugs and "soul pictures." Freud admired the author's picaresque style, which reminded him of Rabelais and Cervantes's *Don Quixote.* In 1923, Groddeck published the famous *Book of the It (Das Buch vom Es),*[93] in which he featured his epistolary relation with Freud through a set of fictitious letters addressed by narrator Patrick Troll to a friend. In this way he sought to popularize the concepts of psychoanalysis and his own doctrine. Freud appropriated the id while radically changing its definition. This was the point at which he began to change his tune and become irritated at this fanciful doctor whom he had liked so much and whom he now accused of sowing discord among his pack of disciples: "I am sorry that you want to erect a wall between yourself and the other lions in the congress menagerie. It is difficult to practice analysis in isolation. It is an exquisitely sociable undertaking. It

would be much better if we roared and cried together in unison and in the same boat, instead of grumbling in our different corners."[94] Freud refused to go to Baden-Baden, whereas Ferenczi went there to be treated and Jones and Abraham denounced a scandal. Finally, Freud declared that Groddeck had good ideas but that they could not be used for scientific research.

Thomas Mann can be credited with producing the finest available portrait of Groddeck. In *The Magic Mountain,* under the name Dr. Edhin Krokowski, the head doctor of the Berghof, he is presented as an old-style hypnotist, obsessed with sexuality, but not yet in possession of enlightened reason: "'Ah, Krokowski,' Settembrini exclaimed. 'There he goes, filled with all the secrets of our ladies. I beg you, please regard the delicate symbolism of his garb. He wears black to indicate that his particular specialty is the night. The man has but one thought in his head, and it is a filthy one.'"[95] Krokowski manifests a radical pessimism with respect to human health: he sees human beings only as subjects inhabited by illness. Shifting between materialism and occultism, he devotes himself to experiments in telepathy that plunge him into the Faustian universe of a disordered subconscious.[96] Such was the magnificent healer of whom Freud was enamored without ever really embracing his extravagances.

Whereas Karl Kraus and Otto Weininger associated Jewishness with a feminine essence responsible for the decadence of patriarchal civilization, Groddeck, on the contrary, proclaimed the necessity of rediscovering in each human being a primal bisexuality that had been repressed in the Jewish religion by the practice of circumcision. In his view, that practice favored the affirmation of man's unisexuality and the rejection of his feminine essence in the face of a bisexual and omnipotent God. By his hostility to the religion of the father, and in the name of a messianic quest for a femininity that he saw as the only thing capable of saving humanity, Groddeck thus rejected Judaism for reasons opposed to Weininger's.[97] And yet they shared the same problematics: on the one hand, Jews were likened to women when all the evils of civilization arose from femininity; on the other, they embodied evil by repressing the benefits of the feminine.[98]

In 1920, Freud was thinking much more about the worth of his discoveries than about his friendships. Although he was determined to devote

the time he had left to his work, he accepted the displacement of the activities of the psychoanalytic movement toward the Anglophone world. This is why he relied more and more on Jones for the management of the movement's affairs. As for him, he would henceforth be oriented toward three types of research: a speculative study on life and death, which went hand in hand with a reworking of his first topography of the psyche; an analysis of the collective mechanisms of social power; and an interpretation of the phenomenon of telepathy, which allowed him to plunge once again into the world of the irrational that never ceased to haunt him even as he defined himself as a rational thinker in the Enlightenment tradition.

PART THREE

At Home

Dark Enlightenment

AN ENLIGHTENMENT THINKER, Freud was heir to Kant and the idea that man had to escape all alienation in order to enter the world of reason and understanding. He welcomed the famous maxim about courage and the necessity of knowledge—"Dare to think for yourself"—and he believed it was possible to subject instincts to self-control. He was also convinced that the elite should guide the masses and not settle for serving as representatives of the people. In this, he remained attached to the figure of patriarchal authority, even though that authority had been somewhat eroded. But at the same time he saw himself as exploding the ideals of progress, since he regularly associated himself with Goethe's *Sturm und Drang,* with Faust and the "pact" with Mephisto, as well as with the dangerous supremacy of passion over reason. In this respect he belonged to the tradition of "dark Enlightenment"[1] through his ability to let himself be haunted by the demoniacal, the occult, the *pharmakon,* or the "uncanny" *(Unheimliche)*[2] and then immediately distance himself from it by invoking the ideal of science. And it is within this dialectic play between darkness and light that we can situate Freud as Nietzsche's heir, inasmuch as his project presupposes a will to transform Romanticism into science.

Even while claiming to be in Diderot's lineage, Freud had established himself as the inventor of a view of sexuality that, although intended to be rational, was nevertheless imbued with the memory of the great Sadean follies. As he said himself, he sought to be "an *advocatus diaboli,* who is not on that account himself sold to the devil."[3] And yet he rejected any legacy from philosophy. He even wanted to spare himself any debt in that quarter to the extent of considering philosophy an "unworthy ancestor."[4]

"I read Schopenhauer very late in my life," he said in 1925. "Nietzsche, another philosopher whose guesses and intuitions often agree in the most astonishing way with the laborious findings of psycho-analysis, was for a long time avoided by me on that very account: I was less concerned with the question of priority than with keeping my mind unembarrassed."[5]

Fascinated by death and love, by sex and desire, but concerned with offering intelligible explanations of the cruelest and most ambivalent aspects of the human mind, Freud confronted human subjects with their destiny: an unconscious that, without depriving them of their freedom, determined their fate without their knowledge. And Freud had a powerful urge to see psychoanalysis as a symbolic revolution whose primary vocation was to change human beings by showing that "the ego is not master in its own house." By this gesture, as we have seen, he had set himself apart from the psychologists and the sexologists of his day by using myths and dreams to make humanity's nocturnal life visible, quite apart from all the so-called sciences of behavior. Thus he gave an existential content to this domain rather than claiming to describe it with scientific instruments. What he borrowed from Darwin, moreover, was nothing other than what he was also taking from Sophocles: the tragic story of a man who, after seeing himself as a god, realizes that he is something other than what he had believed himself to be—he is a murderer, or the descendant of animals.

In addition, while he rejected the notion that psychoanalysis was Jewish by nature, Freud acknowledged the idea that the Jews, after following Moses to the desert, never renounced anything, and that they constantly invented substitutes in order to deal with what had been lost:[6] substitutes for a territory, a mother, a father, an ancestor, a god, an object. In other words, Freud drew on that tradition to conceptualize the universal questions of inheritance, genealogy, transmission, fidelity, and exile. He maintained that each loss allowed people to surpass themselves, and thus to accede to a kind of immortality—that of life's drives—even if, in their heart of hearts, there remained an attraction to the void, to death and self-destruction. As he saw it, human destiny was inseparable from the quest for something "beyond the self," beyond death and love. Hence the strictly sexual causality that he had invoked up to that point against Jung and all the dissidents no longer sufficed to explain pathologies and other neuroses, whether traumatic or not.

From this perspective, one could attribute to Freud the definition of man offered by Jean de La Fontaine: "As to mankind, I would have their lot infinitely better. We men should possess a double treasure; firstly, the soul common to us all, just as we happen to be, sages or fools, children, idiots, or our dumb companions the animals; secondly, another soul in common, in a certain degree, with the angels."[7]

Freud had thus invented a "discipline," one impossible to integrate not only into the field of physical or natural science but into that of the human sciences, an area that had been steadily expanding since the late nineteenth century. For scientists, psychoanalysis belonged to literature; for anthropologists and sociologists, it attested to a resurgence of the ancient mythologies; in philosophers' eyes it resembled a strange psychology that had sprung up both from Romanticism and from Darwinism, while psychologists saw it as putting the very principle of psychology in danger. Thus psychoanalysis was rejected by all academic disciplines, so decisively that it appeared to be the property of a master whose goal was to restore the Socratic banquet rather than to foster the growth of modern knowledge. And indeed the committee, with its sacred rings, its protocols *(Rundbriefe)*, and its oaths, seemed to legitimize such a view. As for the therapeutic aim of psychoanalysis, it fell neither into the field of medicine nor into that of psychology, even if some believed that psychoanalysis, as medicine for the mind, might "influence" psychiatry even though it had grown out of magnetism. In reality, the Freudian clinic consisted in an art of interpretation apt to obtain from the patient the confirmation of a construction that emerged through transference and the work of treatment. In this sense, it nullified therapeutic nihilism, which consisted in categorizing psychic illnesses without ever listening to the patient.

As someone who offered a renewed critique of familial genealogies, Freud was as much a theoretician of an elitist democracy as a thinker of the irrational. Thus he asserted that civilization alone—that is, the constraint of a law imposed on the omnipotence of murderous drives—allowed society to escape the barbarity that humanity itself so desired. And while Freud had never been a great reader of the Marquis de Sade,[8] he nevertheless shared with Sade the idea that human existence is characterized less by an aspiration to the good and to virtue than by the quest for ongoing pleasure in evil: the death drive, the desire for cruelty, the

love of hatred, the aspiration to unhappiness and suffering. For this reason, he rehabilitated the splendid idea according to which perversion is necessary to civilization, as *la part maudite,* the accursed share in societies.[9] But instead of anchoring evil in the natural order of the world, and rather than making man's animality a sign of racial inferiority, he preferred to maintain that only the arts and culture were capable of pulling humanity out of its own desire for self-annihilation.

In a fascinating book, Gilles-Gaston Grangier brings to light three major modalities of the irrational that come up in the history of science.[10] The first appears when a scientist has to confront the obstacle constituted by a set of doctrines governing the thinking of an era, doctrines that have become dogmatic, constraining, or sterile. The scientist then has to innovate; he has to challenge a dominant model by focusing on unexpected objects or bringing familiar objects viewed in a new light into the purview of science—for example, the unconscious, insanity, folly, the feminine, the sacred: in short, everything that Georges Bataille calls the heterogeneous. Recourse to this irrational component then makes it possible to resuscitate a figure of reason and to make a new start toward conquering a *different* rationality.

The second modality of the irrational appears when a mode of thought is in the process of becoming fixated in a dogma or in an overly constraining rationalism. To obtain reliable results and infuse this thinking with new vigor, the scientist must then set it into contradiction with itself in order to prolong the creative act that had presided over its birth.

The third modality concerns the adoption, by scientists or creators, of an entirely irrational mode of thought based on the abandonment of reason and the adherence to false sciences or to attitudes that entail systematic rejection of the dominant body of knowledge. This results in a validation of magic and the religious impulse, associated with a belief in the beyond or in the power of an uncontrolled ego. This third modality is generally accompanied by a vehement denial of the system previously adopted. It is easy to assign extreme revisionist deviations to this category, when they manifest hatred for what was previously an object of adulation.

These three modalities of the irrational can all be identified, as I have said on many occasions, in the history of psychoanalysis. However, Freud

always remained within the bounds of the first two, which are inherent to the very process of theoretical innovation. In a first phase, through his relation with Wilhelm Fliess, he found himself confronting irrationality in a biological context, and through a dialectical reversal this allowed him, up to 1915, to develop the principles of a new rationality. Then came the war years, a period of gestation of a new symbolic revolution.

In a second phase, from 1920 to 1935, once he had constructed his doctrine, Freud introduced doubt at the heart of the rationality of psychoanalysis. He meant in this way to combat the positivism that threatened psychoanalysis from within, by turning toward a speculative irrational. He then set forth the hypothesis of a death drive, which he applied to the analyses of "crowds"; next, he inaugurated a lengthy debate on the question of telepathy, even as he embarked on a fight against religion and in favor of lay psychoanalysis.

"Death is the mate of love. Together they rule the world. This is the message of my book, *Beyond the Pleasure Principle*."[11] Freud himself pronounced this judgment, in 1926, on the unprecedented work that he had sketched out between March and May 1919, influenced by the experience of the uncanny *(Unheimliche)*; the work seemed to renounce the very principles of pre-1915 psychoanalytic doctrine. In reality, Freud was increasingly coming to grips with the prospect of his own death.[12] But he was also trying to flesh out his metapsychology by inventing a new instinctual dualism. In the process, he invoked several great names in science, literature, and philosophy—Gustav Fechner, August Weismann, Torquato Tasso, Schopenhauer, Goethe, Theodor Gomperz, Plato—and also people in his own entourage: Sabina Spielrein, Sándor Ferenczi, and his own grandson Ernstl Wolfgang Halberstadt. In addition, he included references to the Upanishads and to nirvana.

Starting in 1911, he had maintained that two principles governed psychic life. One was aimed at procuring pleasure, and the other modified the first by imposing on it the restrictions required for adapting to the constraints of reality. And now, in 1919, as if to follow up on his conception of narcissism, he was prepared to replace these two principles by a new dualism: life and death. Beyond the speculative side of his reflection, Freud drew on a reality encountered in clinical settings. After so many years of therapeutic practice and cures that had not achieved the expected

results, he had observed that his theory of neurosis did not allow him to account for a phenomenon known to all specialists in psychic ailments: certain patients remained inaccessible to treatment of any sort at all. Worse still, when these patients were treated, they regressed; their condition worsened. It was as though, unconsciously and no matter how gifted the therapist may have been, the patients managed to obey a repetition compulsion that was apt to lead them toward self-destruction.

> The impression [some normal people] give is of being pursued by a malignant fate or possessed by some "daemonic" power. . . . The compulsion which is here in evidence differs in no way from the compulsion to repeat which we have found in neurotics. . . . Thus we have come across people all of whose human relationships have the same outcome: such as the benefactor who is abandoned in anger after a time by each of his protégés, however much they may otherwise differ from one another, and who thus seems doomed to taste all the bitterness of ingratitude; or the man whose friendships all end in betrayal by his friend; or the man who time after time in the course of his life raises someone else into a position of great private or public authority and then, after a certain interval, himself upsets that authority and replaces him by a new one.[13]

In these few sentences, Freud drew an uncompromising picture of all the unconscious attitudes through which subjects seek to destroy themselves, masochism being much more powerful in these instances than sadism.[14] He called this deadly pattern the "perpetual recurrence of the same thing."[15]

Not content to stop here, Freud deduced from this observation that the goal of all life is death, and that, in this struggle, the instincts of life only prolong the journey that ends up in death. Consequently, there were psychic forces, he believed, that acted "beyond the pleasure principle." And he took as an example of the significance of that "beyond" a game—the *Fort-Da*—that he had observed as it developed in his grandson Ernstl when the child was about eighteen months old.

When his mother was absent, Ernstl played at tossing small objects out of his bed while uttering the sound "o-o-o-o," in which a listener could recognize the German word *fort,* meaning "gone." One day he played the same game with a wooden spool attached to a string: he threw the spool while saying "o-o-o-o," then pulled the string and brought the spool back, greeting it joyfully with the word *da,* "there."

In this way Ernstl transformed a state of passivity or displeasure at his mother's departure into a situation under his control. Through this game, according to Freud, the child found a way of expressing hostile feelings that he couldn't acknowledge in his mother's presence, and a way of getting revenge for her disappearance. In other words, he was able to bear a disagreeable situation by the repetition of a separation that brought him an increase in pleasure. Such was the "repetition compulsion" that could also be observed in psychoanalytic treatment; it had very little to do with the reality of a genuine loss.[16]

Without purporting to generalize on the basis of this case, Freud nevertheless clung to an additional example. Eager to relate the condition of modern man to ancestral myths or to literary epics, he compared the destiny of compulsive neurotics to that of Tasso's hero in *Jerusalem Delivered*.[17] In the illustrious tradition of Homer and Virgil, this epic poem in twenty cantos tells the story of the First Crusade and the conquest of Jerusalem. A prototype of the victorious knight, Tancred, as melancholic a figure as Tasso himself, confronts the infidels, among them a blond Saracen warrior named Clorinda for whom he experiences a tormented, unrequited passion. Clorinda learns along the way that she was born to a Christian mother,[18] but Tancred challenges her to fight, believing he is combating an enemy knight. It is to be "war or death," he says, and she replies, "War and death you shall have . . . if you are seeking them." They fight through the night on foot, in close combat; at dawn, at the end of the long death struggle, Clorinda falls, fatally wounded. She refuses to tell Tancred her name, but she asks him to baptize her, and she lifts her hand to him in a gesture of pardon. Afterward, he declares, "I shall live amid my torments and my sorrows—my justice-dealing furies—a wanderer, driven mad; I shall tremble at the dark and solitary shades . . . and I shall bear the countenance of one ashamed and in horror of the sun that

discovered my misfortunes: I shall fear my own self and (always fleeing myself) I shall have myself always at hand."[19]

After Clorinda's burial, Tancred goes deep into the "strange magic forest" *(in den unheimlichen Zauberwald)*[20] that terrifies the crusaders, a dark forest populated by spirits and ghosts. There, he slices a cypress with his sword and hears his beloved's voice, lamenting that he has hurt her; her soul had taken refuge in the tree. After he has been saved by Hermine, another Saracen who has fallen in love with him, Tancred is taken to Jerusalem, which has been liberated by the Christians.

Freud borrowed from this poem the thematics of the hero condemned by destiny to produce his own unhappiness, endlessly.[21] Thus he accepted the idea that the death drive was so firmly anchored in the unconscious that it condemned the subject to remain forever under its sway. Curiously, though, he did not take the nocturnal combat between Tancred and Clorinda into account, even though it ought to have reminded him of the struggle between Jacob and the angel. And he said nothing at all about the hero's obvious melancholia. In reality, in this essay, Freud was struggling against himself. He made two opposing claims at once: the death drive dominates human life, on the one hand; on the other, it is unthinkable that life should be nothing but preparation for death. And he concluded that the death drives, however powerful they may be, are limited by the very fact that life reproduces itself, beyond death. The psyche is thus a battlefield, a nocturnal stage on which two warring elementary forces, Eros and Thanatos, are condemned to love and to hate one another for all eternity.[22]

It is thus understandable that Freud could have found his speculations confirmed in the most recent works of the German biologist Weismann,[23] even though Weismann contested the neo-Lamarckian theses on the inheritance of acquired characteristics while proposing a genetic model. Weismann established a distinction in living substances between a mortal part ("soma") and an immortal part ("germ plasma"), the latter serving to preserve and propagate the species. This unexpected analogy between Weismann's theories and his own allowed Freud to anchor his speculations in science, and no longer solely in mythology or literature.

But, in a new reversal, Freud began to rely on this analogy to translate the genetic model into a metapsychological mode of sorts. Thus he as-

serted that germ cells were proof of an "absolute narcissism": they too were carriers of a death drive. And he went so far as to say that the cells of malignant tumors, so destructive for the organism, could be "narcissistic in this same sense."[24] Thus he transformed the instincts into mythological entities, even into goddesses or demigoddesses.

Clearly, Freud used the genetic model borrowed from Weismann to reformulate his overall conception of the psyche. For the former instinctual dualism, he substituted a new one, and in place of the former levels of the initial topography—the conscious, the preconscious, and the unconscious—he introduced a second set: the ego, the superego, and the id.[25] Freud had certainly not discovered the working mechanisms of the psyche, but with this reformulation he made it possible to think about the question in a different way. Conceived as a chaotic reservoir, the id became the site par excellence of the death drives, an "amoral" entity, a god of the dark underworld, while the ego, more "moral," was in part, but only in part, incorporated into the id, like a melancholic hero, a sort of Tancred, heir to Oedipus. As for the concept of the superego, Freud made it the cruel, merciless censor of the excesses of the soul, and thus of the id and the ego. As he put it later, "Where id was, there ego shall be" (Wo Es war, soll Ich werden),[26] and he was to make this injunction a new task for culture, as important as the draining of the Zuider Zee.

After disowning all philosophical legacies, Freud now managed to introduce into his reformulation of the psyche two of the greatest names in German philosophy: Kant and Nietzsche. From the first, he borrowed the categorical imperative, transformed into the superego, and from the second, the "impersonal subjected to the necessities of being," taken up again by Georg Groddeck in the form of the id.[27]

Rather than letting the biologico-genetic model have the last word, Freud concluded "Beyond the Pleasure Principle" by evoking an episode from Plato's *Symposium* during which Aristophanes recounts the myth of doubled or whole humans. In the beginning, Aristophanes says in essence, humanity consisted of three species: man, woman, and the androgyne. Each being resembled a sphere composed of four hands, four legs, and two faces on a single head with four ears and two sexes. These original humans moved forward or backward. The male was born of the sun, the female of the earth, the androgyne of the moon. One day, they rose to

the heavens to take the place of the gods. At that point Zeus, seeking to punish them without exterminating them, decided to split them in two. However, each half, regretting its other half, tried to unite with the missing part, even if it meant dying of hunger or inaction. To bring that self-destruction to an end, Zeus moved the sex organs to the front of the bodies, allowing men and women to copulate and perpetuate the human race. Men who loved men, rather than giving birth to life, gave birth to the mind. The most accomplished beings would then, according to Aristophanes, be purely masculine. By virtue of this myth, love (Eros) would have originated from a tearing. Thus it is at once evil and the remedy for evil for humans, who never stop dreaming of an original state of fusion even as they never stop pulling away from it.

Freud relied only on a tiny part of Aristophanes's discourse,[28] and he declared that he was seeking to retranslate the history of the relations between Eros and Thanatos in physiological and chemical terms. Thus he once again did an about-face in shifting back from mythology to biology. Still, in the final chapter, he gave the last word to poetry, against the arrogance of a science that saw itself as a "catechism." Against scientism, but also against himself, against his own hubris as a scholar, he claimed the right to doubt, to speculation and uncertainty, citing Friedrich Rückert, a German Orientalist and translator of a *maqâmât* by Al-Harîrî, a eleventh-century Arab grammarian: "What we cannot reach flying we must reach limping. . . . The Book tells us it is no sin to limp."[29]

In writing the last line of this baroque essay, constructed after the fashion of a work in progress, Freud found himself, like Oedipus, a prince with a limp, interrogated by an androgynous Sphinx, who embodied absolute knowledge and the questioning of all knowledge at one and the same time. No doubt this text can be interpreted as the prophecy of a man who felt a real nostalgia for the world of yesteryear—that of the myths and dreams of his Viennese youth—and who nevertheless refused to deplore the lost greatness of former times or to adopt a discourse of decline invoking supposed catastrophes to come. Escaping into speculation allowed him to doubt everything, and to open a new path toward knowledge of the human psyche that was as much oriented toward life as toward its own destruction. In other words, even if this work bears obvious traces of the wartime context in which it had been conceived, it was at the same

time just as much the consequence of an evolution engendered by the work of thought.

Since Freud characterized the death drive as a mute force that gripped the psyche as much as the soma did, he could only detect its existence by falling back on interpretations drawn from literature, social reality, or individual behavior. The death drive, thus defined, was an entity that could not be found from the vantage point of biology: a chimera. The critics asserted in vain, then, that the causes of the Freudian speculation could not be traced to an intellectual undertaking but solely to external determinism.

For several years, in the Anglophone world, "Beyond the Pleasure Principle" was not well received. William McDougall, in 1936, called it "the most bizarre monster of all [Freud's] gallery of monsters."[30] But the most vigorous opposition of all came up at the heart of the committee, and among the other disciples. Max Eitingon and Ferenczi accepted the hypothesis, but Ernest Jones distanced himself, emphasizing that Freud had always suffered anguish about death, his own as well as that of those close to him, that he undertook constant calculations on this subject, that he dreaded growing old and trembled at the idea of bodily deterioration.[31] As for Fritz Wittels, he did not hesitate to psychologize Freud's invention further by purporting to demonstrate that the theorization of the death instinct was a reaction to the grief Freud experienced upon Sophie's death.[32]

Even before confronting such critiques, Freud had taken care to write to Eitingon, "The *Beyond* is finally finished. You will be able to confirm that it was half finished when Sophie was alive and full of health."[33]

"Half finished"! Such a phrase authorized all sorts of interpretations, including one that charged Freud with giving in to pure denegation. In 1980, Jacques Derrida showed that Freud had wished for the death of his little brother Julius, and that, when the boy died, he experienced a feeling of guilt that had never left him. And Derrida deduced from this that Freud treated his essay as a *Fort-Da* game in order to "send [himself] the message of [his] own death."[34]

Discussions about "Beyond the Pleasure Principle" were endless. The members of the American school could not accept its speculative side, which made Freud a "psychologist of the id" rather than a therapist of

the ego, in their eyes. Melanie Klein and her partisans took up the second instinctual dualism on their own account, in a strictly clinical fashion, suggesting that the death instinct contributed to the subject's installation in a depressive position consisting in anguish and destruction. The text, a pure product of the dark Enlightenment,[35] elicited the most comments in France, both on the clinical side and as a decisive moment in the history of philosophic thought.[36]

On May 6, 1921, for his sixty-fifth birthday, Freud received the original of the bust made by David Paul Königsberger: "A ghostly threatening bronze doppelgänger. . . . I very suddenly took a step toward really getting old. Since then, the thought of death never leaves me at all, and sometimes I have the feeling that seven organs are vying with one another for the honor of being allowed to make an end to my life. . . . But I haven't succumbed to this hypochondria, but rather observe it in a coolly superior way, somewhat as I do the speculations in the 'Beyond.'"[37] Divided between what he was and what he was doing, through "Beyond the Pleasure Principle" Freud had thus really sent himself a message whose ultimate destiny he did not claim to control. Once again, he elicited all sorts of vocal reactions.

For a long time he had wanted to extend his analysis of human societies, not in the direction he had taken in *Totem and Taboo,* but rather with the more political project of describing the path that led from the collectivity to the individual. Facing the challenge of social psychology, whose advocates were gaining momentum at the time, he wanted to construct a metapsychology that would account for the relations between the ego and the masses. Once again, he meant to respond to Jung—or rather to the specter of Jung—while adopting the same perspective as Hugo von Hofmannsthal and Arthur Schnitzler, who had both had the same project. In this effort, he did not hesitate to refer to the Aristotelian conception of man as a political animal. But it was from Gustave Le Bon, a multidisciplinary physician, that, in 1921, he borrowed the essential elements of his new research, which was much less speculative than his previous venture.[38]

An ideologue of the counter-Revolution, haunted by the memory of the Paris Commune and rejected in the university context, Le Bon saw himself as the founder of a people's sociology for the use of tyrants who

sought to get rid of the fear aroused by the very existence of "the people." In Le Bon's eyes, a crowd was a barbaric and hysteric assemblage, a sort of organic feminine substratum in which the individual was abolished, melting into the mass of a threatening body. A crowd moves like a Medusa, Le Bon said; it is traversed by irrational instincts and subject to all sorts of "contagions."[39] Thus is it capable of obeying bloodthirsty tyrants, insofar as it embodies the darkest forces of the human spirit: mental illness, irrationality, death, decadence. After describing the soul of a crowd, Le Bon called for the formation of a science that would help politicians become psychologists capable of controlling a crowd through the power of suggestion.[40]

Here, then, was a work Freud admired, one that in certain respects supported his aversion to the ideals of the French Revolution: "the people" is a dangerous entity as soon as it is granted too much power and transforms itself into a "crowd." And when Freud drew on the writings of William McDougall, the very McDougall who was to characterize "Beyond the Pleasure Principle" as a "monster," he was saying essentially the same thing: Freud indeed had a tendency to confuse "the people" with a crowd.

A psychologist of Scottish origin who had emigrated to the United States, McDougall supported eugenics and neo-Lamarckian theories about the heredity of acquired characteristics; contesting behaviorism, McDougall maintained the principle according to which man was inhabited by a dangerous gregarious "instinct" that pushed him to "glue himself" to his fellows. In 1920, analyzed by Jung, passionately interested in telepathy and parapsychology, McDougall had just published *The Group Mind*,[41] in which he set forth propositions—classic views at the time—about the inequality of the "races": "The few distinguished negroes, so called, of America such as Douglass, Booker Washington, Du Bois—have been, I believe, in all cases mulattoes or had some proportion of white blood. We may fairly ascribe the incapacity of the negro race to form a nation to the lack of men endowed with the qualities of great leaders, even more than to the lower level of average capacity."[42]

Freud shared with the ideologues of the fear of crowds the idea that the advent of mass society tied to the rise in industrialization endangered the relation of the elites to the people, at the risk of favoring tyranny. But, unlike the ideologues, he maintained that this dangerous collective

attitude on the part of crowds constituted the archaic part of individual subjectivity, and that in passing from one to the other—from the archaic level to a higher level of subjectivity—the human psyche advanced toward progress. He thus relied on Le Bon and on McDougall without calling into question their conceptions of crowds or of the inferiority of blacks in relation to whites. In so doing, he evaded the question that was being raised at the time by the founders of the social sciences, some of whom were modernists oriented toward a coherent explanation of crowd phenomena, while others advocated an instinctual or racialist conception of the soul of populations.

Freud distinguished between crowds with a leader and those without. He took as models two organized and temporally stable crowds—the church and the army—which were organized, according to him, around two axes: a vertical axis structuring the relation between the crowd and the leader, and a horizontal axis involving the individuals of a given crowd. In the first case, the subjects identify with an object set up in the place of their ego ideal (the leader); in the second, they identify with one another. Of course, Freud had imagined the possibility that the leader's place might be occupied not by a real person but by an idea or an abstraction: God, for example. And he referred to the Communist experience to show that the "socialist bond," substituting for the religious bond, risked liberating the same intolerance toward "outsiders" that had been unleashed during the Wars of Religion.

Drawing on his theory of identification, Freud attributed the primordial function to the vertical axis, on which the horizontal axis depended. Thus identification with the father, the leader, or an idea took priority, as he saw it, over relations among members of the same group. And it was from this angle that he took his distance from the theses of mass psychology, which continued to be based on the idea that suggestion or hypnosis—and not identification—accounted for the fascination that bound the masses to their leaders.

For years, this new Freudian thesis was used to interpret the way Fascism operated politically.[43] In reality, when he published this essay, Freud was thinking about the Communist experiment, to which he was deeply hostile from 1917 on, even though he had initially greeted it favorably as a sign that the war was coming to an end. As Michel Plon points out,

"Freud proposed a conceptual framework that made it possible to begin thinking through questions that twentieth-century sociology, history, and political philosophy—neglecting Machiavelli as well as La Boétie—were still quite unable to formulate."[44]

Freud thus clearly distanced himself from any thinking based on the hatred of specific peoples, on the rejection of democracy, or on a revitalized ideology of chiefdom. However, his lack of familiarity with twentieth-century revolutionary experience led to numerous errors, in particular with regard to the Russian psychoanalytic movement and its Freudo-Marxist disciples Wilhelm Reich and Otto Fenichel. In this area, part of Freud's approach—the most unconscious and the most repressed—can be said to have remained anchored in what he claimed to be denouncing. Taking Le Bon and McDougall as his models had not been a completely innocent move. Through them he called up, the better to exorcise it, the whole Jungian story of grottoes, caves, and crypts, the subterranean world of chaos and Titans.

Freud certainly did not expect the unprecedented use that his American nephew, Edward Bernays, would make not only of "Group Psychology" but also of his uncle's tobacco addiction. The inventor of a new art in the management of mass opinion in the 1920s, Bernays relied on Freudian concepts to develop a powerful publicity campaign in favor of the tobacco industry, Lucky Strike in particular, in a campaign aimed at women. Staying strictly within the lines of the feminist movement's politics of emancipation, he produced advertising films designed to prove that women should have the right to smoke on the same basis as men, and that for women a cigarette consumed in public was like a "liberty torch," the equivalent of an exuberant penis that they could display without the slightest restraint and so free themselves from male domination.[45]

While he was attempting to provide rational explanations for irrational phenomena, Freud began to plunge enthusiastically into the depths of fables from the Danube region. In 1921, in a letter to Hereward Carrington, an American specialist in spiritism[46] who had asked him what he thought about occult phenomena, Freud replied as follows: "If I were at the beginning rather than at the end of a scientific career, as I am today, I might possibly choose just this field of research." Then he asked Carrington not to mention his name, because he did not believe in the "survival of the

personality" after death, and because he was "interested in sharply demarcating psychoanalysis" as a science from "this as yet unexplored sphere of knowledge" so as not to create "any occasion for misunderstanding in this respect."[47]

As we have seen, this topic of "occult things" had arisen in Vienna during Jung's first visit to 19 Berggasse. It had resurfaced in 1910, when Ferenczi had claimed to be looking for seers and prophetesses in the Budapest region to prove to his adored master that there was such a thing as thought transmission. Freud had then ended the debate by mercilessly condemning, in the name of science, the telepathic experiences of a certain Professor Roth whom Ferenczi had brought to the WPV.

Nevertheless, starting in 1920 and continuing until 1933, the question of the occult returned to the forefront with the standardization, between London, Berlin, and New York, of the principal rules of didactic analysis, a process meant to make the Verein a movement organized according to the principles of positivist rationalism. In this context, in which the ideal of a scientific basis for psychoanalysis went hand in hand with the gradual institutionalization of principles for treatment, Freud once again came to the defense of telepathy. In the company of his daughter Anna and Ferenczi, he "made tables turn" and engaged in experiments in thought transmission during which he played the role of a medium while analyzing his own verbal associations.

Jones and Eitingon tried to curb his fervor at the time by arguing that the conversion of psychoanalysis into telepathy would increase the resistance of the Anglo-Saxon world to Freudian doctrine and would make that doctrine look like the work of a charlatan. In order to bring psychoanalysis into the scientific era and mark the definitive end of its moorings in the old Austro-Hungarian world populated by gypsies and magicians, Jones proposed to banish research into occultism from the international congresses. Freud agreed.

In 1921, however, he wrote an article (untitled) on these questions, intending to present it at the Berlin congress in 1922. Eitingon and Jones talked him out of it. He withdrew his text, which would ultimately be published posthumously in 1941. After this rejection, he returned to the fray, the same year, with another article, "Dreams and Telepathy," which

he published in *Imago*. Ten years later, he gave a lecture on the theme "Dreams and Occultism" in which he reintegrated the material from 1921 and in particular the case of David Forsyth,[48] who was to figure in "Psychoanalysis and Telepathy."[49]

According to Freud, occultism and psychoanalysis had both been treated with disdain by "official" science. And yet the progress of the sciences could have the additional effect of making thinkable what was once rejected in occultism. To be sure, he added, when one undertook to revive this type of questioning there was the risk of giving rise to new obscurantist forces. Hence the danger that the Professor had just pointed out in connection with his group psychology: irresponsible parties could decide to manipulate certain occultist techniques in order to lull a credulous public for their own purposes.

Freud went into this investigation wholeheartedly, falling back on his old passion for numbers, puzzles, and calculations. He thus reported with delight the story of a young man who had consulted a prophetess, giving her the birthdate of his brother-in-law. The prophetess had immediately declared that the brother-in-law in question would die of poisoning by oysters and crayfish. Stunned, the young man had observed that what had been predicted had already occurred: a great lover of fish, the brother-in-law had in fact nearly died of poisoning from eating oysters the year before. Freud concluded from this that a phenomenon of telepathy accounted for the prediction: the client's knowledge had been transferred to the seer by unknown pathways, excluding all known modes of communication. Positing the existence of "thought transference," Freud thus left the terrain of the occult and telepathy for that of psychoanalytic interpretation. Once again, he was playing with the devil even as he was playing the devil's advocate.

For Jones, all these stories of clairvoyance were pure rantings that endangered the politics of the Verein: "You might be a Bolshevist," he told Freud in 1926, "but you would not help the spread of psychoanalysis by announcing it." To which Freud replied, "It is really hard not to offend English susceptibilities. . . . I have no prospect of pacifying public opinion in England, but I should like at least to explain to you my apparent inconsistency in the matter of telepathy. . . . When anyone adduces my fall

into sin, just answer him calmly that conversion to telepathy is my private affair like my Jewishness, my passion for smoking and many other things, and that the theme of telepathy is in essence alien to psychoanalysis."[50]

The game Freud indulged in during all those years confirms well enough that for him it was a matter of proclaiming, against the overly rational primacy of science, a magical knowledge that escaped the constraints of the established order.[51] The fact that Freud insisted on assuming the role of a prophetess from the old Austro-Hungarian Empire, having fun pretending to believe in telepathy even as he was classifying it as a manifestation of the unconscious and of transference, is a good indication of what the specific status of psychoanalysis might be in its ambiguous relation with science as well as the recurrence of its interrogations into its origins. As Derrida was to emphasize in 1981, "So psychoanalysis . . . resembles an adventure of modern rationality set on swallowing *and* simultaneously rejecting the foreign body named Telepathy, to assimilate it and vomit it up without being able to make up its mind to do one or the other. . . . The 'conversion' is not a resolution or a solution, it is still the speaking scar of the foreign body."[52]

Families, Dogs, Objects

FREUD WAS WONT to describe the family as a source of great happiness, but also of endless cares. His doctrine was rooted in the idea that the family crucible served as ontological support for the concepts of psychoanalysis. His social world and his psychic universe were populated with fathers, mothers, sisters, brothers, nephews, and cousins suffering from pathologies and substituting for one another. All of them might have taken recourse to psychoanalytic treatment, so compelling was the question of sex and intimacy in the Western world of the late nineteenth and early twentieth centuries. In Freud's eyes, the familial community was the model par excellence for all forms of social organization. In it lay the power of life and its transmission.

At once liberal and conservative, Freud had built his thought and his movement on the basis of a communitarian model that owed nothing to the nation-state or its institutions. Whence a major contradiction: the more the Freudian movement became an international one, without fatherland or frontiers, the more the communitarian model on which it relied became obsolete. Ernest Jones was aware of this, and Freud suffered from it. He resorted, sorrowfully, to the values of "family solidarity" that he had drawn on in his doctrine, preserving them in private even though he did not hesitate to subvert them in theory. He thus surrounded himself with everything that allowed him maximal protection from the various forms of violence of his day: his household, his pets, the objects in his collections, and his archaeological explorations of the human psyche via the experience of the couch.

Freud's parents had been brought together in an arranged marriage, and Amalia had given birth to eight children in ten years; Sigmund on the contrary had married the woman of his choice, for love. And Martha had given him six children in eight years, after which the spouses had voluntarily stopped procreating. Of Freud's five sisters, only four had children: five for Anna Bernays—Judith, Lucia, Edward, Hella, and Martha—of whom three were born in Vienna and two in New York; two for Rosa Graf, Hermann and Cäcilie, both born in Vienna; five for Maria Freud—Margarethe, Lilly, Martha (Tom), Theodor, and Georg—of whom one was born in Roznau, two in Vienna, and two in Berlin; one for Paula Winternitz, Rose Béatrice, who was born in New York and who married the poet Ernst Waldinger.[1] As for Alexander, who married Sophie Schreiber late, he had just one child, Harry, born in Vienna.[2]

There were thus few manifest differences between the situation of Freud's parents—Amalia and Jacob—and that of their children. At one generation's remove, there were just as many women who were unmarried or widowed, and none had recourse to contraception or abortion. None of Freud's sisters had been able to pursue advanced studies and only one, Anna Bernays, had succeeded in settling abroad, by marrying Eli Bernays, Martha's brother. Among Freud's nephews and nieces, only one, Hermann Graf, lost his life during the Great War;[3] two others, Cäcilie Graf and Martha Seidman-Freud, committed suicide, and another, Theodor Freud, died in a drowning accident. All the members of this vast Viennese community married Jews; while they were not attached to an Orthodox form of Judaism, at least some of them took care to respect the rites.

Unlike Martha, Sigmund looked favorably on mixed marriages. But the society in which he lived was not very open to them. And, noting that his own children had all spontaneously chosen Jewish spouses, he concluded that family life among Jews was warmer and more intimate, and that solidarities were stronger.[4] He himself had been brought up in the heart of a community that banished mixed marriages.

Among Freud's six children, who lived through two deadly wars, only four had children of their own; one daughter (Anna) remained unmarried and another (Sophie) died of an illness. Like their parents but unlike their grandparents, Freud's offspring chose their spouses freely—all chose

Jews. But they had decidedly fewer children, thanks to contraception, and most became English citizens after fleeing the Nazi regime. Martin had two children (Anton Walter and Sophie), Oliver just one (Eva), Ernst had three (Stefan, Lucian, and Clemens), and Sophie Halberstadt two (Ernstl and Heinz).[5] Unlike their mother and their aunts, Freud's three daughters had some schooling, even though public instruction for girls was not obligatory in Vienna, and there were no real professional outlets.[6] Freud was concerned with marrying them well and inculcating the idea that they were born to be mothers and housekeepers. Nevertheless, he did not adhere to the Jewish precept regarding arranged marriages according to which a father is responsible for his daughter only to pass her along to another man. Very close to his daughters, Freud understood that they would never be like their mother and their grandmother, but—except for Anna—he did not want them to be emancipated following the model of his female disciples. Moreover, they themselves sought no destiny other than the one prescribed.

Freud loved deeply not only his wife, his brother, and his sister-in-law, but also his children and his grandchildren. With his children, he always manifested great generosity; he did the same with his nieces and nephews insofar as was possible. All the members of his family admired him unconditionally and all were aware of his genius.

His children lived through two world wars and remained united in adversity despite the ceaseless conflicts. They were all well versed in their father's doctrine, as was Freud's brother Alexander. Moreover, Freud's three sons all played a role in the psychoanalytic movement, and his youngest daughter became one of his disciples.

In the two-story rented apartment on the Berggasse, Freud lived like a patriarch in the old style. He had wanted to "shape" Martha so that she would conform perfectly to his image of the ideal wife. In vain: she resisted him, without ever deviating from a pacifist attitude. When he sought to quarrel with her, she turned inward. Thus he reproached her for repressing her aggressiveness, even as he regarded her with a sort of adoration.

Martha reared the children and reigned over the household, which included two and sometimes three domestic servants, but she did not meddle in her husband's intellectual affairs, even though he met with his

disciples at home. When a family member sought to change sleeping quarters or modify anything at all in the way the household space was organized, he or she had to turn to Martha.

Freud looked after his children's education, and he suffered when he was separated from them, especially after they married and left home. Very early on he had required them to learn through reading, rather than from him directly, about the realities of sexual life.

Minna, whom people called his "second wife" even before Jung spread the rumor that they were having a "liaison,"[7] occupied a bedroom contiguous to that of her sister and brother-in-law. She was always prepared to accompany her dear "Sigi" on his September travels. In August 1898, for example, she stayed with him in Maloja, in the Engadine valley, and on several occasions Freud experienced some embarrassment at being seeing alongside a woman who was not his wife. In 1900, on another trip, he had sold a number of old books from his collection so that Minna could go to Merano to treat a bronchial infection.[8] This was all it took for certain commentators to imagine a dark story about a clandestine abortion. And because Minna suffered later on from abdominal pain, it was easy to suppose that her pulmonary problems were just a pretext. Thus the rumor grew, especially after the publication of *Three Essays*. Forty years after Freud's death, this widespread rumor became the object of research by historians and commentators.[9]

Like Martha, her accomplice in everything, Minna put on weight, and as the years passed she had less and less concern for her femininity. When she answered the telephone, she was in the habit of saying "Frau Professor Freud," totally unconcerned about the gossip. Far from being a true "second wife," she behaved more like a playmate for her sister and brother-in-law's children; her attitude was all the more understandable in that she had no taste for the role of mother or wife in relation to anyone at all.

In the aftermath of the First World War, Freud was already famous, and by the same token he was detested throughout the world for what was taken to be his notion of "pansexualism" in its various declensions. In Vienna, he was accused of all sorts of depravity: immorality, incest, destruction of family values.[10] In France, Freud was called a *savant boche*, that is, a lubricious character consumed by a so-called Teutonic instinct.[11]

Charles Blondel even called his doctrine an "obscenity promoted to the rank of a science."[12]

The image of Freud presented through these attacks was in radical contradiction with his morals and his opinions. His critics forget that the master was himself a practitioner of sexual abstinence, a sublimating neurotic. And as he was not known to have any extramarital relations, a "real" sexual life had to be invented for him, preferably transgressive, so as to account for the repugnant character of his conception of sexuality.

In this regard, the endogamous mode of life he had adopted and the abusive use he made of his famous Oedipus complex, which had been popularized through all sorts of publications, authorized no end of caricatures. Karl Kraus went at it with gusto by affirming energetically that psychoanalysis, which purported to cure disorders of the mind, was itself such a disorder. To be sure, the flamboyant polemicist had been the victim of the fanaticism of the earliest Freudian circle, when Fritz Wittels had pronounced him afflicted with a case of Oedipal frustration.[13]

In his splendid autobiography, Elias Canetti tells how, during the 1920s in Vienna, the cult of the "Oedipus complex" had become so noxious that it tended to discredit the most innovative aspects of the Freudian doctrine. As much as Canetti supported the idea of interpreting wordplays and misfires, he nevertheless rejected the reduction of Sophocles's tragedy to what he saw as a psychology of "universal banter": "In some way or other," he wrote in 1980, "everybody (even posthumous sons) got his Oedipus; and eventually the whole company sat there in guilt, everyone a potential mother-lover and father-killer, hazily wreathed with mythical names—all of us secret kings of Thebes. . . . I knew who Oedipus was, I had read Sophocles, I refused to be deprived of the enormity of this fate. By the time I arrived in Vienna, the Oedipus complex had turned into a hackneyed prattle that no one failed to drone out; even the haughtiest scorner of mobs wasn't too good for an 'Oedipus.' "[14]

During this period, Freud was supporting an extended family: Amalia; Anna; Minna; his children and their spouses, often penniless; four sisters, intermittently; a domestic staff; and some of his disciples who had hardly any patients. On several occasions, he imagined marrying one or another of his daughters to one of his disciples. In reality, he wanted to keep them

all within his close family circle. Thus he regarded his sons- and daughters-in-law as his own children.

Mathilde, his eldest child, was in fragile health and had had several close brushes with death; an operation for appendicitis carried out by the surgeon who had operated on Emma Eckstein had left her unable to bear children. Freud had imagined marrying her to Sándor Ferenczi, but in 1909, in the synagogue, she married Robert Hollitscher, a textile tradesman who was not very good at business and who was always pessimistic; Freud characterized him as "tender and stout-hearted." The couple lived in an apartment near 19 Berggasse, which allowed Mathilde to visit her parents daily. Always very elegant, she affected a certain coolness, but she was devoted to her family; she shared a love of knitting with her mother and her aunt. She was able to earn a little money through her talents as a stylist, which allowed her to avoid depending entirely on her family.

Sophie, the prettiest of the daughters (to the point of arousing jealousy in Anna), was much less interested in intellectual pursuits than her two sisters. She loved dancing, evenings at the opera, social life, and youthful company; she did not feel at ease in this overly rigid family. In love with—and loved in return by—Hans Lampl, a school friend of her brothers and a future disciple of her father, she nevertheless had to give him up: her parents found him too young and deplored the fact that he did not have a job. In Hamburg, far from home, she met Max Halberstadt, a photographer distantly related to the Bernays family; she married him in the synagogue in Berlin. He was a believer. Freud adopted him as a son, eventually even granting him the commercial monopoly on his official portraits. Unlike his brother Rudolf, Max survived the First World War, although he was handicapped by a traumatic neurosis with headaches and depression. Long after his demobilization, he was a victim of the financial crisis and compelled, despite his real talent, to depend on his father-in-law, who pampered him and begged him to have confidence in the future.

Sophie rejected the destiny of her mother and grandmother. After the birth of two sons, dreading the prospect of another pregnancy, she sought her father's advice; Freud recommended that she resort to contraception by using a "pessary."[15] As much as he had been reluctant to use condoms himself, he was nevertheless now in favor, if not of abortion, at least of

birth control, which was being demanded at the time by feminist movements, even as the nations of Europe were adopting repressive laws against abortion.[16] When Sophie became pregnant again, accidentally, Freud encouraged her to accept the birth. He thought, wrongly, that her rejection of maternity had to do with Max's financial difficulties.

In 1920, weakened by her condition, Sophie fell ill with the flu and died in just a few days, despite the efforts of Dr. Arthur Lippman, an internist at Hamburg's general hospital. In a letter, devastated by grief and guilt, Freud confessed to Lippman that he had not appreciated the extent to which the unwanted pregnancy had modified his daughter's physical and mental state: "My daughter's unfortunate fate seems to me to entail a warning that is not often taken seriously enough by our corporation. In the face of an inhuman law devoid of empathy, which imposes the pursuit of a pregnancy even on a mother who does not want it, the doctor clearly ought to consider it his duty to teach appropriate and inoffensive means for preventing unwanted pregnancies—in the context of marriage."[17]

To relieve Max, Mathilde took charge of Heinz (Heinerle), and Anna took care of Ernstl, who became her first "adopted" child and, later, her analysand. The two were thus second mothers to their sister's children. When Heinz died, on June 19, 1923, as a result of miliary tuberculosis, Mathilde was once again deprived of what she most desired. From then on she continued to busy herself with her nieces and nephews. As for Freud, in despair at this loss, which occurred three months after the discovery of his own cancer,[18] he continued to love Max and to help him financially, even after the latter's remarriage: "Whoever was happy once in marriage is easily happy again."[19]

Freud had always been convinced that family happiness was modeled on the great cycle of life and death and the substitution of one desired object for another, provided however that the repetition compulsion was not morbid in nature. Thus he thought that, if a lost being were replaced by another, that other would be loved only because he was taking the place of the one who had been loved before him. Such was the Freudian philosophy of happiness.

None of Freud's three sons resembled him and they did not resemble one another. But all of them participated in the advances of the

psychoanalytic movement, and in the lives of their father's disciples. Martin thought highly of himself. He practiced fencing, fought in duels, wrote poems, was a poor student, and had multiple relations with women. After studying law for a time, he volunteered for military service in 1914, and he experienced the war as the happiest period of his life. In combat he had shown insolence and humor and had faced up to danger; within the family, he was said to have neither a superego nor an unconscious. When he married the beautiful, elegant Ernestine (Esti) Drucker, from a wealthy family, Freud found her "much too pretty" to be part of the household. In reality, he judged her "unreasonable, abnormal," and not well suited to put up with his son's escapades.[20] According to the rule that he himself had instituted, he obliged her to give her firstborn the name Anton, in memory of von Freund, and to call her daughter Sophie.[21] Esti worked, refused to continue getting pregnant, and suffered from her condition as a dependent and betrayed woman. Despite the support of his father and his father-in-law, Martin underwent numerous financial reversals. In addition, he quarreled with his wife, and they ended up separating. For several years, until the period of exile beginning in 1938, he was in charge of managing the publishing house.

Oliver, his mother's favorite child, was never able to practice a real trade, in times when an economic crisis had followed on the heels of war. When he moved to Berlin, after a breakup and a divorce, he asked Max Eitingon to take him as a patient for analysis. Feeling that he was too close to the family, Eitingon refused, and it was Franz Alexander, a Hungarian by birth and a future American citizen, who accepted this demanding task. Freud insisted on paying for the treatment. Oliver married Henny Fuchs, a painter, with whom he had a daughter, Eva. Freud loved this neurotic, fragile, and odd son who suffered from fierce rivalry with his more brilliant younger brother, Ernst.

After earning a diploma in architecture in Munich, Ernst fell in love with Lucie Brasch, a dazzling and melancholic woman with blue eyes and blond hair from a wealthy banking family. They were married in Berlin on May 18, 1920, in the presence of Karl Abraham and Eitingon, who, like Ernst, made known their sympathy for the Zionist movement. Lucie was able to charm Freud, and between them they obliged Ernst to spend three

months in the Arosa sanatorium to treat the tuberculosis that he had contracted during the war.

Ernst adored his wife to such an extent that he began to call himself Ernst L. Freud, adding the initial "L" (for Lucie) to his name in order to underline the "symbiotic" existence he was enjoying with her. "It is very hard to live with my heart always aflame, never at rest," Lucie wrote.[22] Between 1921 and 1924 she gave birth to three sons: Stefan Gabriel, Lucian Michael, and Clemens Raphaël, nicknamed the "archangels." Lucie devoted herself to the family cause, while Ernst had an exceptional career thanks to the psychoanalytic movement. He worked as an architect for Eitingon, Abraham, Karen Horney, René Spitz, Sandor Rado, Hans Lampl, and, later, Melanie Klein. In addition, he took charge of setting up the famous "policlinic" and then the sanatorium at Tegel that Ernst Simmel had established. By his modernist choices, he broke with the stifling aesthetic of the Viennese interiors so appreciated by his father: carpets on carpets, heavy draperies, overloaded windows, walls covered with paintings, furniture invaded by objects. Freud had little interest in this aspect of his son's talent. Indeed, when Freud resettled as an exile in London, Ernst arranged what was to be his father's final residence in the purest Viennese style of the previous era, for which he himself had no nostalgia whatsoever. More German than Austrian and more English than German, Ernst came close to emigrating to Palestine, at the request of Chaim Weizmann, who wanted Ernst to direct the construction of his home.[23]

Freud always said that his last daughter's birth coincided with that of psychoanalysis. And since he had associated his invention with a family romance populated by melancholic princes and idle princesses, it is hardly astonishing that this daughter reported a dream to him in 1915 that referred to their common history: "Recently I dreamed," she wrote, "that you were a king and I was a princess, and that someone wanted to separate us through political intrigues."[24]

It was for love of Anna that Freud incorporated a new circle into the family, consisting of dogs: "Our two dogs," he would say one day, "the faithful Wolf and the gentle Pekinese Lun Yug, are the latest additions to the family."[25] In 1914, he sent his daughter a postcard from Brion showing a chimpanzee wearing clothes and combing its hair in front of a mirror:

"Miss a very intelligent female ape doing her toilet."[26] Whereas Anna liked males, Freud particularly appreciated the company of female chow chows, long-haired creatures resembling miniature lions. He began to show a particular attachment to them starting in 1920, as is attested by his exchanges with two women who adored them as much as he did: Hilda Doolittle and, even more, Marie Bonaparte.[27] He preferred red-coated dogs to black ones, and he saw dogs as exceptional beings on which civilization (*Kultur*) had no hold. Consequently, he said, one could love them entirely, since they embodied "an existence perfect in itself," devoid of ambivalence—a nonhuman life, then, but one that reminded man of something of a state anterior to himself. Were not dogs ready, at every moment, to hail their masters and bite their enemies? Freud did not hesitate to associate the affection he felt for the canine race with an aria from Mozart's *Don Giovanni*.[28]

At no time, however, did he question the attribution of the symbolic function to humanity alone. On the contrary, because he was a Darwinian and because he had defined his discovery as the third narcissistic wound inflicted on man, Freud knew that there was a clear break between humanity and animality: that of language and culture. This is why he emphasized that civilization had no hold on animality, on that delicious "non-human life," devoid of hatred. One could add that, for the same reason, perversion and sexual pleasure in evil do not exist in the animal kingdom.[29]

In point of fact, when he described his household, Freud placed the "human occupants" and the "State of dogs" on the same level, where the females, whom he nicknamed *les dames,* were in the majority: "Yofi sits as usual on the floor, emblematic, heraldic," Doolittle would report. "[Freud] told me that Yofi's first husband was a black chow and Yofi had one black baby, 'as black as the devil.' It died when it was three-quarters of a year old. Now . . . [Freud] said, if there are two puppies, the father's people have one, but if only one, 'it stays a Freud.'"[30]

When Yofi (Jofi) died, Arnold Zweig, who knew Freud's passion for dogs, wrote to him as follows: "Jofi was a foster-child, as devoted to you as any real child and with a wiser heart than most of our children."[31]

Freud, who had adored Cervantes's "Colloquy of the Dogs," loved nature and animals, especially those he encountered on the grounds of the

Villa Borghese among the ancient statues and columns: peacocks, ga-
zelles, pheasants. Animality was a constant, appearing in his reports on
clinical cases, in his own dreams and in those of his patients, in his evo-
cation of the earliest societies, in his essay on Leonardo da Vinci, and in
Totem and Taboo: rats, wolves, birds, horses, vultures, chimeras, demons,
or Egyptian gods. His attraction to dogs—and especially to females of the
species—made him reject cats as overly feminine, overly narcissistic,
overly foreign to alterity. And it was with considerable malice that he
lashed out one day, unjustly, against Mirra Eitingon, the wife of his de-
voted disciple: "I don't appreciate her. She has a catlike nature, and I don't
appreciate cats either. She certainly has her share of the charm and grace
of a cat, but it's no longer an adorable young kitten."[32]

Nevertheless, in 1913, Freud had been seduced by a "narcissistic cat"
that had come into his office through a partly open window. Without
showing any concern for his presence, she had settled on his couch and
complacently inserted herself among the objects in his collection. Freud
was compelled to recognize that this cat did no harm to the things
piled on his desk, and he began to observe her, to like her, and to feed her.
He enjoyed looking at her oblique, glazed green eyes, and he viewed
her purring as the expression of true narcissism. He had to make a spe-
cial effort to get her to pay attention to him. Their relations lasted for a
while, until the day he found the cat burning up with fever on his couch.
She succumbed to pneumonia, leaving behind the memory of the
"playful charm of true egoism" characteristic of felines, which Freud
later described so well in his article on narcissism.[33]

Anna had not been wanted by either her mother or her father, and she
spent her youth struggling to exist, then competing with her aunt Minna
for access to knowledge of her father's work. In January 1913, she allowed
her jealousy toward her sister to burst forth: "I am no longer embroidering
Sophie's cover and I always feel a little bad when I think that I would like
to have finished it. Naturally I think very often about Sophie's wedding
but I am actually indifferent about Max."[34]

It was during this time that Freud's lack of understanding of his
daughter's true sexual inclinations became clear. Anna had alluded, in a
letter, to her "bad habits" (masturbation): "I don't want to go through
this again," she wrote in the same letter. Convinced that Anna, whom he

nicknamed "my only daughter," had converted her old rivalry with So-
phie into jealousy of her sister's husband, he exhorted her not to be afraid
of being desired by men. He did not yet suspect that she was actually
jealous of her sister and not of Max: she was attracted by women.

In July 1914, when she had called on Jones, Freud had gotten the idea
that she was running a risk: "I know from the most reliable sources that
Dr Jones has serious intentions of wooing you. . . . I know . . . that he is
not the right man for a more refined feminine person."[35] And to Jones, he
had explained that Anna was not yet asking to be treated as a woman,
"being still far away from sexual longings and rather refusing man."[36]

At the time when he was forbidding his daughter to let herself be
courted by his disciple, Freud did not perceive that Anna was much more
attracted by Lou Andreas-Salomé, of whom she was actually dreaming,
than by Jones. But Jones was aware of this: "She has a beautiful character,"
he wrote to Freud later, "and will surely be a remarkable woman later
on, provided that her sexual repression does not injure her. She is of course
tremendously bound to you, and it is one of those rare cases where the
actual father corresponds to the father-imago."[37]

The attachment was reciprocal, and Freud never hesitated to send away
the Viennese disciples who were charmed by Anna: August Aichhorn,
Siegfried Bernfeld, Lampl. For her part, she continually sought to be close
to her father, especially during the war period when she pursued a course
of study to become an elementary school teacher.

Worried that Anna would remain an old maid, Freud observed that on
the strength of taboos and repression his daughter drove men away even
though she wanted to be a mother. And it was to "awaken her libido" that
he suggested to her, in October 1918, that she should go into analysis with
him.

The treatment took place in two phases: between 1918 and 1920, then
between 1922 and 1924. As their mutual attachment strengthened, rein-
forced by the analysis, and to which, through a crisscrossed correspon-
dence, Andreas-Salomé was the principal witness, Freud was obliged to
acknowledge that, if Anna's libido were "awakened," her "object choice"
by no means led her toward men.

At that time, Freud was treating a young woman, Margarethe Csonka,
whose parents belonged to the great Austrian bourgeoisie of Jewish or-

igin that had converted to Catholicism. Carefree and worldly, loving the luxury and freedom that her fortune and her elegance afforded her, she had always been attracted by women, though without desiring sexual relations with them. Thus she had rejected the advances of her friend Cristl Kmunke, whose lesbianism was completely overt. In 1917, Margarethe experienced a delirious passion for the flamboyant baroness Leonie von Puttkamer, a demimondaine from the Prussian nobility, supported by men and going out openly with women. Sumptuously dressed and wearing fabulous hats, Leonie liked to walk along the finest avenues accompanied by an immense wolfhound on a leash. She enjoyed strolling around cafés and through markets to find fruits in which she delighted, without the slightest concern for the penury from which the Viennese were suffering just as the empire, already in full decline, was experiencing its last glittering moments.

Leonie found it amusing to see Margarethe following her everywhere, idolizing her, serving her, and indulging in the pose of a troubadour straight out of chivalric literature. One day, surprised by her father on the arm of the baroness, Margarethe fled to escape his gaze. Leonie dismissed her. Margarethe then attempted suicide, and her father, Arpad Csonka, obliged her to consult Freud to bring an end to the scandal of this homosexuality deemed intolerable. He wanted to see her married at once.[38]

Lacking any desire to go into analysis, Margarethe nonetheless decided to obey the paternal injunction. Freud accepted her, even though he knew perfectly well that he would never manage to change the sexual orientation of this patient. In any case, he never regarded her as "ill." Still, he asked her to respect the principle of abstinence and to stop seeing the baroness during treatment.

Margarethe then began to lead a double life. At every session, she invented dreams and family stories in keeping with the Freudian doctrine, while she complained to the baroness about her therapist's interpretations: "You know that he has been questioning me for some time about my parents and my brothers, and that he wants to know everything about them. Last time he was particularly insistent about the youngest one. Imagine what he told me today: that I would have liked to have a child by my father, and obviously since it is my mother who had one, that is why

I hate her and my father too, that is why I turn completely away from men. It's revolting."[39]

Freud discovered the double game Margarethe was playing and stopped treating her. Her father was satisfied to know that his daughter had followed a treatment, and Margarethe was delighted to be able to continue living as she liked. By way of farewell, Freud told her, "You have such crafty eyes that I would not like to meet you in the street if I were your enemy."[40]

In reality, he profited from this experience, using it to modify further his definition of homosexuality. While he confirmed that homosexuality was indeed the consequence of bisexuality, he claimed to be convinced that, in the case of an exclusive choice, it stemmed from an infantile fixation on the mother. Among boys this choice excluded women, he said, while among girls it provoked disappointment with regard to the father. In Margarethe's case, this radical rejection of the father had been translated by the choice of a substitute for the mother, and, in treatment, by a negative transference onto the analyst. And Freud added, "It is not for psycho-analysis to solve the problem of homosexuality. It must rest content with disclosing the psychical mechanisms that resulted in determining the object-choice, and with tracing back the paths from them to the instinctual dispositions. There its work ends, and it leaves the rest to biological research, which has recently brought to light, through Steinach's experiments, such very important results concerning the influence exerted by the first set of characteristics mentioned above upon the second and third.[41] Psycho-analysis has a common basis with biology, in that it presupposes an original bisexuality in human beings (as in animals)."[42]

Freud thus attributed the ultimate explanation of homosexuality to biological causality, even after asserting its psychological origin: this audacious new interpretation seemed to contradict his previous positions. In addition, from then on he distinguished innate homosexuality from acquired homosexuality.

It seems clear that Margarethe suffered from something other than her homosexuality. Still, she resumed her life as a lesbian, falling repeatedly in love with women with whom she failed to find sexual satisfaction. She attempted suicide several more times before she entered into a loveless marriage with Baron Eduard von Trautenegg, who was more interested

in the Csonka family fortune than in his wife. Both had to convert to Protestantism to marry, because Eduard had divorced his first wife and could not take a second while remaining a Catholic.

When Eduard aligned himself with the National Socialist Party after the Anschluss,[43] he benefited from the situation and had his marriage with a Jewish woman annulled while taking control of her fortune. Margarethe was left destitute in every sense, being no longer either Catholic or Protestant. She became Jewish again, even though she had never really been Jewish in the first place and had little love for Jews. With no husband, moreover, she risked being regarded as a notorious homosexual. She thus left Austria. After an immense trek that kept her traveling endlessly around the world in search of herself, decidedly drawn to women and faithful to her dog, always compelled to avoid settling down, she returned to Vienna and died a centenarian, after having offered differing versions of her treatment to psychoanalysts and researchers dazzled by her adventure dating back to a bygone era.

The way Freud conceived of feminine homosexuality, on the basis of that encounter with Margarethe, could not help him grasp what was happening in Anna's analysis. How could he imagine, in this case, an unconscious infantile fixation on the mother and the rejection of a father who disappointed her? Freud himself had forbidden his daughter to let herself be seduced by men, and especially by his disciples. For her part, she dreamed of being the disciple of her adored father, and she rejected her mother's fate. In other words, Freud found himself confronted with a reality that contradicted his theory.

If Margarethe's treatment, devoid of therapeutic value, turned into a fiasco, that of Anna Guggenbühl, a young Swiss psychiatrist trained in the Burghölzli clinic, was successful, according to the patient's testimony. Anna G. began seeing Freud at age twenty-seven, of her own free will and with a positive transference.[44] Having been engaged for years to a school friend, and having had many amorous adventures, she doubted that she really wanted to marry her fiancé. Her desire was waning, even though her family had already planned the wedding. Determined to understand the unconscious reasons for her hesitation, she left her parents and her job all the more willingly in that she was eager to meet the person whom she viewed as the greatest listener of her time. As a virtuoso of

lightning-fast interpretation, Freud listened to her and then explained that her conflict with her fiancé was taking place at the "higher stage" of her life. To understand its significance, he added, she would have to explore the "intermediary stage," which had to do with her neurotic relation with a brother, and then the "lower stage," totally unconscious, which was that of her relation with her parents.

In other words, he declared that Anna G. was in love with her father, that she wished for her mother's death, and that it was her attachment to her brother, a substitute for her father, that explained her ongoing hesitation waltz. He told her that her lovers were substitutes for her brothers, and that was why they were the same age, although they were less mature than her brothers. The treatment ended when Freud told Anna that she was under the influence of a desire to defy her parents. And one may suppose that the lifting of the repressed desire to be caught up in her own defiance led her to break off her engagement, to disobey her father, and to choose her own destiny.[45]

. . .

In 1922, while she was preparing her first presentation for the WPV, Anna Freud, once again in analysis with her father, was aware of how attracted she was to women, and confided her uneasiness to Andreas-Salomé: "For the first time, I have had a daydream with a feminine protagonist. It was even a love story, and I haven't stopped thinking about it. I wanted to exploit it and write it down, but Papa found that it would be better for me to let it go and to think about my presentation. So it has left me, but if I still remember it in July, I'll write it down anyway. Unfortunately, only known people appear in it."[46]

Anna's talk was not unrelated to this matter. Indeed, its theme was young children's punishment fantasies, following upon her father's famous article "A Child Is Being Beaten," in which Freud described the case of a little girl whose childhood fantasies closely resembled those his own daughter had described to him. And Anna in turn analyzed them as someone else's, explaining that the dreamer had succeeded in substituting "lovely stories" for the memory of those scenes.[47]

In 1923, Anna explicitly decided to renounce marriage. Her father soon nicknamed her "Antigone," then offered her a German shepherd, Wolf

(or Wolfi), who became part of the household at once. To Andreas-Salomé, he confided his distress. He feared that Anna's "genitality" was doing her a disservice and he admitted that he was not managing either to free her from him or to separate himself from her.[48]

If Anna's treatment by her father allowed her to assert herself as the head of a school, surrounded by Freud's best disciples at the heart of the *Kinder-seminar,*[49] it was to have the damaging consequence of making her hate her own homosexuality. Throughout her life, Anna manifested hostility toward the idea that homosexuals could practice psychoanalysis. Against her father's opinion, she was convinced, as was Jones, moreover, that homosexuality was an illness.

Sometime after the end of her second series of sessions on her father's couch, Anna met the woman who was to be her lifetime companion: Dorothy Tiffany Burlingham. Born in New York, the granddaughter of the founder of Tiffany and Co., Dorothy had married a surgeon, Robert Burlingham, who was afflicted with manic-depressive psychosis. To escape his bouts of madness, she had gone to Vienna, determined to treat her own phobia and to entrust to the Freud family the fate of her four children: Bob, Mary ("Mabbie"), Katrina ("Tinky"), and Michael ("Mikey"). After a preliminary interview Anna accepted the first two for treatment, and suggested to Dorothy that she go into analysis with Theodor Reik.

Very quickly, the two women saw themselves as twins, and spent their free time driving around the outskirts of Vienna in Dorothy's Model T Ford. Freud loved to accompany them. They got in the habit of wearing identical clothing, as they developed intimate relations that closely resembled those of lesbians. But Anna categorically denied the existence of a sexual relationship with her new friend—a way of remaining faithful to the only man she ever loved, her father.

Once the treatment with her father had ended, Anna chose Max Eitingon as a confidant, and then adopted a new friend, Eva Rosenfeld, a Jewish Berliner from a well-to-do family and the niece of Yvette Guilbert, a French singer Freud admired. She helped Eva overcome the death of two of her children from dysentery. In 1927, with Eva and Dorothy, Anna founded a private school intended to take in children who were in treatment with her or with other disciples from the family circle, children whose parents were also undergoing analysis in Vienna. Among these was

Peter Heller, who later married Dorothy's daughter Tinky: "The Burlingham-Rosenfeld school," he wrote later, "was a marvellously promising, privileged experiment, animated and inspired by a purer, more humane, and more sincere ideal of humanity than any school I ever went to. It was suffused with a genuine sense of community and housed in a light, sunny, warm place."[50]

Still in 1927, Anna pressed Dorothy to go into analysis with Freud, which allowed the latter to have a better grasp of the nature of their relationship. He welcomed a new visitor at the same time: a female chow chow named Lün-Yu, who got along extremely well with Wolf.

Happy and free, Anna and Dorothy soon acquired a small farm with a vegetable garden and some animals; the two families spent their vacations there. In the fall of 1929, while the world was under the threat of the American stock market crisis, Dorothy and her four children moved into an apartment at 19 Berggasse. She was thus just one floor away from Freud—whom she viewed as God the Father—and his couch. Thanks to the installation of a direct telephone line, she could talk to Anna at night without disturbing the household: an astonishing enactment of the telepathic utopia that haunted Freud's imaginary and Ferenczi's during this troubled time.

Thus Anna realized her desire for motherhood by becoming, via psychoanalysis, the "coparent" and therapist of Dorothy's children, in addition to her role as the adoptive mother and analyst of her nephew Ernstl. As for Freud, he saw himself more than ever as the happy patriarch of a reconstituted family subjected to the erosion of the old patriarchal authority, the very process that had given rise to psychoanalysis: "Our symbiosis with an American family (without husband)," he wrote in 1929, "whose children my daughter is bringing up with a firm hand analytically, is getting more and more established, so our needs for the summer are shared. Our two dogs, the faithful Wolf and the gentle Pekinese Lun Yug, are the latest additions to the family."[51]

From the beginning of the century, Freud had had a passion for antiquities;[52] these were as indispensable to his daily life as his cigars or the characters in the Greek tragedies, as necessary to his horizon as Rome, Athens, or Egypt. Having read many more works on archaeology than on psychology, he had transformed his house at 19 Berggasse into a veri-

table museum: "It is only after one has reconstructed the mental atmosphere and scientific pieties of the late nineteenth century," Peter Gay wrote, "that the full measure of Freud's revolution emerges. Yet he made his revolution in the most unrevolutionary of surroundings. Its banners and slogans are all invisible."[53]

A whole set of inanimate figures—Greek, Chinese, Egyptian, preColumbian—inhabited the various rooms of Freud's residence. As in a silent film, objects from ancient civilizations let their shadows and their light glide over the lives of dogs and human. More numerous every year, they proliferated within an abundant décor, amid an accumulation of rugs covering floors, armchairs, and sofas, along with colored fabrics covering the walls. Some twenty figurines, among the most moving and most disparate, presided upright on Freud's desk, across from his manuscripts. Each was credited with its own personality, and each helped maintain the creative spirit of the master of the premises. As soon as Freud came into the room where he received his patients, in the presence of his chow chow, he greeted his Chinese sage, situated at the edge of his desk, surrounded by a statuette of Imhotep on the left—the god of knowledge and medicine—and a minor Egyptian divinity on the right. Thus the guardians of body and soul kept watch over the doctor's sessions with patients and his writing exercises.

Everywhere, showcases, pieces of furniture, bookshelves, and Oriental porcelains filled the space of the labyrinthine house, where no empty place was tolerated, as if each item—a pastel of the Abu Simbel temple; a stone Janus, Horus, Anubis, Nephtys, Isis, and Osiris; a cast of the Gradiva; a bas-relief of the death of Patroclus; a camel from the Tang dynasty; assorted Buddhas—embodied at one and the same time the three provinces of psychic life and the upsurging of an ancestral drive that was immediately repressed. Amid this profusion of images, hieroglyphics, funerary signs, and sacred statuettes, men and animals mingled, the traces of a Jewish memory emerged in the half-light: Rembrandt's etching of Jews in the synagogue, an engraving by Theodor Kruger representing Moses holding up the tablets of the law, a Hanukkah menorah, and finally two Kiddush goblets arrayed in front of Egyptian statuettes.[54]

Freud also collected paintings: a reproduction of André Brouillet's famous *Clinical Lesson at the Salpêtrière*, Jean-Auguste-Dominique Ingres's

Oedipus and the Sphinx, Henry Fuseli's *Nightmare,* Albrecht Dürer's *Kiss of Judas,* and so on. Then there were dozens of photographs: medallions featuring mothers, sisters, and children, portraits of disciples or of women Freud admired, for example Andreas-Salomé, Bonaparte, and Guilbert.[55]

In August 1922, Rosa Graf's daughter Cäcilie Freud committed suicide by swallowing an overdose of barbital. Unmarried and pregnant, she exonerated her lover. Whatever her motives, in a letter to her mother, who was thus left without descendants, she explained that it was very simple to die, that it even brought a certain joy. Profoundly shaken by that act, Freud did not hesitate to evoke the troubled future of Austria. He was well aware of the political conflicts that were agitating the new republic, whose capital, which had been nicknamed "Red Vienna," was governed by a coalition of Social Democrats and Christian Democrats influenced by the principles of Austrian Marxism. He observed the rise in power of the anti-Semitic and pan-Germanist populists, who were denouncing the ambitious social programs of the Left. He was also aware that the latter were looking for new scapegoats in denouncing foreigners, and more particularly the Jews who had come from Poland, Romania, and Ukraine.

For the time being, though, Freud continued to rail against American president Woodrow Wilson, whose "fourteen points" he could not forgive. He did not believe for a moment in the Wilsonian conception of the right of the peoples of the former empires to govern themselves, and he saw Wilson's project only as an attempt to Balkanize central Europe. In short, he held this enlightened president responsible for the misfortunes of those whom he claimed to be liberating from the yoke of their masters. Far from respecting the vanquished peoples, he had treated them with contempt, as Freud saw it. Freud's views had just been reinforced, moreover, by a book by the American journalist William Bayard Hale, who denounced Wilson's overblown style while referring to the psychoanalytic method.[56] Freud had had some correspondence with Hale, which helped maintain a certain anti-Americanism on his part, Jones's recommendations notwithstanding. Neither Freud nor anyone in his entourage had any idea, at the time, of the role Adolf Hitler would play in the history of psychoanalysis.

Freud was always preoccupied with his health. On several occasions, he had noticed a suspicious lesion in his mouth on the right side of the

palate, and he had chosen not to worry too much about it. Rather than give up tobacco, he preferred to think that he was suffering from a simple leukoplakia.[57] However, on April 20, 1923, he had a tumor removed that was said to be "benign," which he called an epithelioma. At that point he decided to consult his old friend Max Steiner, the cofounder of the Wednesday society. Steiner advised him once again to stop smoking, but he did not reveal the cancerous nature of the tumor.

Felix Deutsch, his disciple and personal physician, who had noted the presence of this lesion on April 7, also refused to tell his revered master the truth for fear of frightening him, but he recommended a new operation. Freud was known to the greatest professors of medicine in Vienna, and he could have chosen one of the best at the outset. Instead, he turned to Marcus Hajek, an otorhinolaryngologist, certain that Hajek would reassure him completely. He was not mistaken. This doctor, who could have been Wilhelm Fliess's double, proceeded to a new excision of the tumor, which ended in disaster, with terrible bleeding.[58] Subsequently, Freud had to go through a useless round of radiation therapy, which resulted only in aggravating his pain. He still did not seek to know the truth, wholly absorbed as he was at the time by the death of little Heinz (Heinerle), his "dear child." At the end of June he left for Gastein with Minna, then went to Tyrol and finally to Lavarone, where his family joined him.

At the end of August 1923, the members of the committee found themselves in San Cristoforo at the foot of the mountain where Freud was staying. During this period, they were engaged in fierce disputes over the "active technique." In addition, Otto Rank and Ferenczi were feeling marginalized by the Berliners, Abraham and Eitingon, while Jones was still trying to develop psychoanalysis outside the German-speaking world. Refusing to take part in the argument, Freud stayed in his hotel, and only Deutsch and Anna joined the group to share a dinner in San Cristoforo. This was the moment when Freud's chief disciples became aware of the seriousness of his cancer.[59] And since a new operation was necessary, they plunged into a tumultuous discussion without deciding for all that to tell Freud the truth.[60] They let him leave for a last trip to the south. In 1913, Freud had promised to initiate Anna into his love of Rome; nothing and no one would be able to keep him from carrying out this project. Together, father and daughter walked through the city for hours on end.

According to an itinerary established with rigor, they visited Capitoline Hill, the Pantheon, Tivoli, and the Sistine Chapel: "These are our last days," Freud wrote to his other children. "To make our departure easier, the sirocco has started to blow again and the reactions of my jaw make me suffer more than ever. Anna is gay as a lark. She even tried an operetta today."[61]

Freud subsequently broke with Deutsch, whom he called a "wretched coward." Then he reconciled with him. But in 1927 he chose a new physician, Max Schur, who had attended his lectures in 1916 and who ended up taking care of Freud until he died. Born to a family of Jewish émigrés from Poland, Schur took charge of his prestigious patient after having undergone a full-fledged analysis with Ruth Mack Brunswick. Younger than the disciples of the first circle, Schur admired Freud but without venerating him to the point of lying to him.

Well before this encounter, when he returned from his most recent trip to Rome, Freud had already decided to seek out Hans Pichler, an Austrian stomatologist considered to be one of the greatest European specialists in maxillofacial surgery. Trained at Northwestern University in Illinois, during the war Pichler had acquired exceptional dexterity in repairing the faces of gravely wounded patients.

Pichler saw Freud on September 26, 1923, and on October 4 he subjected him to a serious ordeal by removing a considerable portion of his upper jaw and the right side of his palate. On November 13, he operated again, and continued for a total of twenty-five additional operations. In 1931, he sought the help of his American colleague Varaztad Kazanjian, a former honorary major in the British Army famous for his innovations in perfecting the best dental prostheses designed for patients with seriously damaged faces. Thus Freud was able to benefit from the progress of facial surgery following the First World War.[62] Nevertheless, he endured torments during the remaining sixteen years of his life.

The "prosthesis" made its appearance among the objects in Freud's collection, amid the books, cigars, dogs, and patients, in the everyday universe of the Professor and his entourage. Damned prosthesis, horrible monster, instrument of torture, ill-fitting object: these were some of his terms for the nameless thing that disturbed his ailing body. To each of his correspondents, Freud described the intruder, without ever giving up

smoking: *"Lieber* Max, I have been taken over by the state of tension pro-
voked by the prosthesis. Eating, drinking, and speaking are moments that
I dread." *"Lieber* Lou, nothing more irritating than a bodily substitute that
has begun to rebel, a thing that is only an artifice, like a pair of glasses,
false teeth, or a wig. . . . Little arrangements with this intrusive and life-
saving object, that is, the hope of managing to converse without thinking
about my mouth. . . . All the recent interventions presented as inevitable
have nevertheless been useless." And in 1931, speaking of Kazanjian: "He
has Charlie Chaplin's smile. . . . This magician has given instructions for
making a temporary prosthesis half as big and half as heavy as the current
one. It allows me to chew, talk, and smoke at least as well as before."[63]

Freud had to undergo several types of operations: some under local an-
esthetics and sedation, others under general anesthesia. After each one,
he had difficulty speaking, and over the years it became harder and harder
for him to eat; he also suffered from deafness in his right ear, so he was
obliged to adjust the placement of his couch in order to hear his patients
correctly. The prosthesis constantly had to be cleaned, readjusted, and re-
positioned, at the price of endless pain. When Freud was unable to put it
back in place, he called for Anna's help; she sometimes struggled with the
"monster" for an hour: "Far from inspiring resentment or disgust," Gay
wrote, "this physical closeness only tightened the bonds between father
and daughter to the utmost. He became as irreplaceable for her as she had
become indispensable to him."[64]

The Art of the Couch

SEVERAL DOZEN ARTICLES OR BOOKS have been devoted to Freud's patients and to his fortunes after he established his practice first as a nerve specialist, then as a psychoanalyst, and finally as a trainer of analysts. By consulting the archives in the Library of Congress along with various testimonies or narratives about reconstituted or published cases, it has been possible to establish that during his professional life Freud treated a little more than 170 patients. While no two were alike, most of them came from the wealthy or well-to-do bourgeoisie. Other treatment stories may well emerge in the future, although such finds are unlikely to change much in the way historians look at Freud's complex clinical practice.[1]

Between 1895 and 1914, patients came from the Central European empires and from western, northern, and southern Europe, whereas after 1920 they came from the North American continent or the United Kingdom, that is, from the "victors." At this stage in his life, Freud essentially became the analysts' analyst, even while continuing to consider psychoanalytic treatment as a family affair. He analyzed not only his daughter but also friends of his other patients, as well as several of his disciples, their spouses, or others in their intimate circle. We know that he respected none of the technical rules established by the psychoanalytic societies. It is important to note that these "rules" were instituted over time starting in 1918, and it was out of the question for the psychoanalytic movement to oblige Freud to adhere to them. How could Freud be compelled to subject himself to analytic treatment and then to supervision in order to become an analyst? How could he be prohibited from analyzing his family members or close friends and their spouses when, up to

1920, the members of his first circle had not yet formulated these rules, and in fact the rules were only applied in the IPV (the Verein) as the psychoanalyst's trade became professionalized?[2] In reality, the rules were developed by the first circle for the generations to come.

Starting in 1920, an essential change came about in the history of information about the "cases." Instead of being reconstructed by Freud as clinical narratives, the treatments conducted during the period between the two wars were related by the analysands themselves in the form of testimonies, autofictions, or notes transmitted to posterity, and published by historians or other interested parties. In other words, where this period is concerned, it is through the gaze of an analysand relating his or her treatment that one can evaluate and retrospectively understand Freud's clinical work, rather than through accounts published by Freud himself. The difference is considerable.

We know, furthermore, that the patients whom Freud took on as suffering from an "illness," both before and after 1914, were more or less obliged by their entourage to seek treatment: this was the case for all the women in the *Studies on Hysteria,* as well as for Ida Bauer, Margarethe Csonka, and many others. Under these conditions, the treatments were not very likely to be experienced as "successes," especially when the patients were young women rebelling against their families; in the eyes of these young women, Dr. Freud appeared as a lubricious figure or as in league with their parents. In contrast, the patients who came to 19 Berggasse of their own accord for analysis generally felt satisfied. Whence a paradox: the treatments were all the more "successful" insofar as they resulted from free choice on the part of the subject. Later, Freud theorized in fact that no psychoanalytic experience was possible without the patient's full adherence. It is also noteworthy that, during this period, the more an analysand aspired to become an analyst, the more chance the treatment had of being therapeutic before it became didactic, because the patient was committing himself or herself to a cause. As a result, generally speaking, the most successful cures—that is, the most satisfying from the viewpoint of the subjects themselves—were those that resulted on the one hand from a conscious will and on the other hand from a militant engagement.[3]

The great majority of Freud's patients were Jews suffering from neuroses, in the very broad sense in which this term was used during the first

half of the twentieth century. The neuroses were often mild, but sometimes quite severe; the latter would later be characterized as "borderline," or even as psychoses. A number of these patients were intellectuals, often famous musicians, writers, creators, doctors, and so on,[4] who wanted not only to be treated but also to experience the "talking cure" with the founding father. Generally speaking, they made their way to 19 Berggasse after a trek during which they had been examined by the leading figures in the European medical world: psychiatrists or specialists in all types of nervous ailments. And whatever may be said to the contrary, especially after 1914 they had been confronted with the famous "therapeutic nihilism" that so well characterized the state of mental medicine at the time.

In this respect, the immense success of psychoanalysis was the consequence of Freud's invention of a system for interpreting psychic disorders, a system based on great narrative epics that had more to do with solving riddles than with psychiatric nosography. On the couch of this highly original scientist, who was experiencing physical suffering himself, surrounded by his sumptuous collections of objects and by his surprisingly beautiful dogs, patients could see themselves as the hero of an adroitly composed theatrical scene containing princes and princesses, prophets, fallen kings, and queens in distress. Freud told stories, summarized novels, read poems, and evoked myths, Jewish tales, jokes, and narratives of sexual desire buried in the depths of the soul: as he saw it, any such material could serve to endow modern subjects with a mythology that brought them back to the splendor of humanity's origins. On the technical level, Freud justified this position by asserting that the goal of a correctly conducted analysis—that is, a successful one—was to convince the patient to accept the truth of a skillful construction quite simply because such a construction produced a benefit above and beyond the mere recovery of a lost memory. In other words, a successful treatment was one that allowed subjects to understand the underlying cause of their torments and their failures, and to move beyond these obstacles the better to satisfy their desires.

Every day, Freud saw eight patients for fifty-minute sessions that were repeated six days a week, for several weeks and sometimes several months. Some treatments turned out to be interminable, punctuated by reversals

and returns. Freud also welcomed other patients for simple consultations, medical treatment, or a few sessions of psychotherapy. He generally took no notes during the sessions, and his entire art of the couch consisted in an initiation to travel: Virgil guided by Dante in the *Divine Comedy*. While he recommended abstinence, he never obeyed a rigid principle of "neutrality," preferring a "floating attention" that allowed unconscious activity to occur. He talked, intervened, explained, interpreted, made mistakes; he smoked cigars without offering any to his patients, which provoked varying reactions. He occasionally evoked certain details of his own life and mentioned his own tastes, political choices, and convictions. In a word, he involved himself in the treatment, convinced that he would overcome the most tenacious resistances. And when he did not succeed, he tried to understand why, at the very moment when he abandoned all hope of success. Moreover, he sometimes committed indiscretions, informing his correspondents about the content of his sessions with patients, or reading to certain patients letters that he had received about them, letters that should have remained confidential.

Freud kept his accounts from day to day in a special datebook *(Kassa-Protokoll)*[5] and talked endlessly about money in his letters. Between 1900 and 1914, he had acquired a social status equivalent to that of the top professors of medicine, who also received private patients, moreover.[6] He was thus as wealthy as the most prominent practitioners of his generation, and his life style was similar to theirs.

During the war, his revenues collapsed along with the Austrian economy. But starting in 1920, he began to reconstitute his fortune by receiving not only patients from the former empires who had been ruined by the financial crisis and the currency devaluations, but also wealthy foreign psychiatrists and intellectuals, often American, often seeking to be trained in psychoanalysis. Freud thus gradually became the analysts' analyst.

Whenever he could, he had his patients pay cash. Over the years, he managed to place assets abroad; their returns were added to his quite considerable royalties. And while he earned less than a psychiatrist practicing in New York or London, he was decidedly better off than his German, Hungarian, and Austrian disciples, who had had to struggle to survive in a disastrous economic context. In October 1921, wanting Lou

Andreas-Salomé to come to Vienna, as she had expressed a desire to do, he wrote this: "If your freedom of movement has been impaired by the rupture of all communication with your homeland, I hope you will allow me to send you from Hamburg the money for your journey. My son-in-law looks after my credit in marks there, and through my earnings in sound foreign currency (American, English, Swiss), I have grown relatively *wealthy*. But I want to have *some* pleasure out of this new wealth myself."[7]

For the purpose of comparison, we can observe that Freud asked 10 florins per hour in 1896; in 1910, between 10 and 20 crowns per session; in 1919, 200 crowns, or 5 dollars for an American patient (the equivalent of 750 crowns), or a guinea—worth a little more than a crown sterling (600 crowns)—for an English patient who was not particularly well off. In 1921, he considered asking 500 or 1,000 crowns, then set the hourly price at 25 dollars, which did not prevent him from charging certain patients lesser amounts.[8]

At times, Freud was unable to repress an unjustified but ferocious anti-Americanism, so that he would declare, for example, that his disciples from across the Atlantic were good for nothing but bringing him dollars. Once he declared before a stunned interlocutor that the Statue of Liberty could be replaced "by a monkey holding up a Bible."[9] On another occasion he asserted before one of his students who was in analysis with him that the Americans were so stupid that their mode of thinking could be reduced to a ridiculous syllogism: "You Americans are like this: garlic's good; chocolate's good—let's put a little garlic on chocolate and eat it!"[10]

The defeat of the Central European empires and the growing preponderance of American psychoanalysts in the international movement were profoundly humiliating to Freud. He suffered at having to charge all his patients, and he was in favor of the idea that institutions should eventually be able to offer free treatment to the most impoverished patients. Generally speaking, he was horrified by the American way of conceiving of democracy, individual liberties, and the right of people to govern themselves: "The Americans," he said one day to Sandor Rado, "transpose the democratic principle from the political realm to that of science. Everybody must be president, by turns. So they are incapable of accomplishing anything at all."[11]

Freud had always thought that psychoanalytic treatment was unsuit-
able for people who were unintelligent, unsophisticated, too old, or suf-
fering from melancholia, mania, anorexia, or episodic states of hysterical
confusion. He also excluded psychotics and people suffering from perver-
sions "who did not wish to be reconciled with themselves." Starting in
1915, he added to the category of nonanalyzable persons those suffering
from serious narcissistic neuroses, and those overwhelmed by the death
drive or by destructive impulses that were chronic and impossible to sub-
limate. And later on, when Sándor Ferenczi proposed to take him as an
analysand, he responded humorously that, for a man in his seventies
suffering from tobacco addiction and a cancerous lesion, there was no
possibility of successful treatment. In contrast, Freud declared that the
psychoanalytic approach was indicated to treat hysteria, obsessional
neuroses, phobias, anxieties, inhibitions, and sexual disorders. But he
added that treatment could succeed only with intelligent individuals en-
dowed with a moral sense and apt to want to commit to it.

In 1928, he acknowledged very clearly to his Hungarian disciple Istvan
Hollos, an artisan of asylum reform, that he did not like psychotics: "I have
finally admitted to myself that I didn't like those patients and that I resented
them for being so different from me and from everything human. It is
a curious sort of intolerance that makes me ill suited, of course, for
psychiatry. . . . If I were to behave in this case the way the doctors who
preceded us behaved toward hysterics, is this a result of a bias of the intel-
lect ever more clearly affirmed, the expression of hostility toward the id?"[12]

If we were to take these declarations literally, we might think that,
according to its founder, psychoanalysis is only appropriate to sophisti-
cated subjects capable of dreaming or fantasizing, aware of their condi-
tion, concerned with improving their well-being, manifesting a morality
above all suspicion, and apt to be cured within a few weeks or months,
by virtue of a positive transference and countertransference. Yet we know
perfectly well that most of the patients who came to 19 Berggasse did not
correspond very closely to this profile.

In other words, from the beginning of the twentieth century on, there
was a major contradiction between the conditions of treatment advocated
by Freud in his writing and the reality of his practice with his patients.

And Freud was all the more conscious of this in that he had revised his doctrine: in "On Narcissism: An Introduction" and in "Beyond the Plea-sure Principle" he had described cases about which he doubted that any form of therapeutic treatment could succeed. And yet, through opposi-tion to nihilism (but under the pressure of financial necessity, and always eager to take up a challenge), he accepted for analysis persons said to be "unanalyzable" in the hope that he would manage, if not to cure them, at least to attenuate their suffering or modify their existential condition.

As we have already seen, these patients—afflicted with mania, psychoses, melancholia, suicidal or self-destructive impulses, perver-sions, masochism, sadism, or narcissism—consulted other specialists, who achieved no more success than Freud.[13] But only Freud was accused of all sorts of turpitude, during his lifetime and even more so after his death: accused of being a charlatan, a swindler, rapacious, and so on.

This is why it is so important to study certain treatments in detail, both some of the most disastrous and some of the most successful. Let me stress first of all that of the 170 patients accepted by Freud—all categories combined—some 20 or more drew no benefit at all from the treatment, and about 10 rejected it and ended up hating the therapist. Most of them took recourse to other therapies, under identical financial conditions and without obtaining any better results. No researcher to date has been able to say what would have become of these patients had they never done any-thing at all to treat their suffering.

At the beginning of the twentieth century it was in Trieste, a baroque port village then under Austrian domination and a passageway between *Mitteleuropa* and the Italian peninsula, that one of the most unusual clin-ical adventures in which Freud ever engaged took root. In October 1908 a young medical student named Edoardo Weiss turned up at 19 Berggasse; Weiss had strongly admired Freud ever since he had read *The Interpreta-tion of Dreams.* He was the son of a Jewish industrialist from Bohemia who had made his fortune in the cooking oil business: "When I was get-ting ready to leave," he said to Kurt Eissler, "Freud asked me why I was in such a hurry. I told myself then that he was happy to meet someone coming from Trieste. In the past, he himself, as we know, vacationed in that Julian city. He loved Italy and was delighted at the idea that someone from Trieste was interested in his work. I was nineteen years old at the

time. When the visit was over, I asked him how much I owed him for the consultation, and he replied in a charming way that he accepted nothing from a colleague."[14]

Freud did not want to carry out the analysis of someone who was to introduce his doctrine to Italy and who was one of his best disciples. So he sent Weiss to be trained on the couch of Paul Federn, who became Weiss's teacher and friend even in exile in America.

Very similar to the Viennese of the Belle Époque, the Triestine intellectuals saw themselves as "irredentists." In a complex way they claimed not only their Italian identity but also a profound attachment to European culture, which made them sensitive to all the major movements of the literary and artistic avant-garde. As for the de-Judaized Jewish intellectuals from the commercial bourgeoisie, whether wealthy or penniless they aspired to the same emancipation as the Viennese, even as they unleashed a ferocious and melancholy critique of the Habsburg monarchy. In short, they felt more Italian than Austrian, more Jewish than Italian, and sufficiently tormented by familial neuroses to be attracted by the idea of exploring their subjectivity.

At the time when Weiss was committing himself to the cause of psychoanalysis, Italo Svevo—a pseudonym for Ettore Schmitz—was also interested in Freud's work, which was being discussed with passion by the Triestine intelligentsia: a veritable "cyclone," according to Giorgio Voghera.[15] Svevo, too, came from a family of Jewish businessmen; he had married his cousin Livia Veneziani, whose wealthy parents had converted to Catholicism; her brother Bruno, a homosexual, smoker, and drug addict, was one of Weiss's childhood friends. While developing friendships with Umberto Saba, a Triestine poet soon to be analyzed by Weiss, and with James Joyce, who taught English at the Berlitz School in Trieste, Svevo, who smoked as much as Freud, published two unsuccessful novels. And when he met Isidor Sadger in 1911, while summering in Bad Ischl, he told him about his dependence on tobacco.[16]

In his professional life as a businessman running his in-laws' company,[17] Svevo appeared perfectly normal; in private, however, he was assailed by sexual and homicidal fantasies. He dreamed of devouring his wife bit by bit, starting with her boots. He was visibly jealous and eccentric, and constantly imagined biting his wife's face. In this way he so closely resembled

a character in a novel that Joyce took inspiration from him in sketching the portrait of Leopold Bloom in *Ulysses*. Joyce would also remember Livia and her "long blond tresses" when he was beginning *Finnegan's Wake*.

As for Olga Veneziani, Livia and Bruno's mother, she seemed to have come straight out of one of Freud's major case narratives. A frenetic woman, she detested her son-in-law, while suffering the escapades of a husband who deceived her. Always at the boiling point,[18] she was so smitten with her only son that she saw him as a genius, a glorious musician, and a great businessman. From childhood on, Bruno Veneziani was subject to severe convulsions; he was treated with no results whatsoever by Augusto Murri, one of the leading lights in positivist medicine at the time.[19] Under the grip of this extremely wealthy mother given to excesses, he experienced a feeling of horror and led a rowdy, openly homosexual life.

On the advice of Weiss and his mother, Veneziani consulted several psychoanalysts: Wilhelm Stekel, Sadger, Rudolf Reitler, Karl Abraham. Then, between 1912 and 1914, he visited Freud's couch intermittently; it took Freud a long time to recognize that no treatment would overcome the pathologies he was seeing, given the patient's strong desire to maintain them. On October 31, 1914, exasperated, Freud asserted that there was nothing to be done with this "bad case," and Abraham stressed, in a communication with Freud, that the narcissism of this terrible patient was eluding all forms of interpretation.[20] Struck by the radical failure of his brother-in-law's treatment, and by the sums invested in it, Svevo became deeply embittered, convinced that psychoanalytic treatment was dangerous: it was useless, he would say, to try to explain what a man is. Only a novel experienced as self-analysis would make it possible, according to him, to refrain from "treating life," given the knowledge that life itself is a mortal malady.

Veneziani returned to Trieste. During the war, Svevo undertook to translate some of Freud's texts; at the same time, he was thinking about writing a new novel that would deal with a false psychoanalytical cure and the tobacco addiction of a man afflicted with the syndrome of "the last cigarette." How could one put a stop to such an addiction, except by never making the slightest decision to give it up? A Freudian question par excellence.

In 1919, Veneziani, still addicted to morphine, resumed his endless trek in search of a cure at his mother's insistence, just when Svevo was beginning to write the story of his double, Zeno Cosini—which was also the story of Schmitz and Weiss. And it was at this point that Weiss encouraged Veneziani to head back to Freud's couch and to participate in the meetings of the WPV. But Freud reacted negatively to this suggestion: "I think he does not represent a favorable case. He lacks two things: first, a conflict between his ego and the requirements of his drives, which leaves him satisfied with himself and suffering from the antagonism of external circumstances; second, he lacks a semi-normal ego that would be capable of cooperating with the analyst. Without these, he always tries to dupe the analyst and to get rid of him by pretense. Whence the existence in him of an extremely narcissistic ego, resistant to all influence, and served, unfortunately, by personal talent and gifts."[21]

Freud pointed out that Olga did not want to let go of her son, and he recommended that the patient be sent to the Baden-Baden sanatorium. Veneziani went directly there for three successive periods of treatment by Georg Groddeck, during which he met a new lover but did not give up his addiction. He then migrated to the Bellevue clinic in Kreuzlingen for treatment by Ludwig Binswanger; there he was at leisure to confront the melancholic suffering of a good part of the elite among the European intelligentsia. Finally, unhappier than ever, he returned to Trieste. Periodically committed to the psychiatric hospital there, he took on the role of a character in a novel, incompetent and decadent, similar to the hero depicted in 1923 by his brother-in-law in *Zeno's Conscience*. From the depths of his unhappiness, he became a spectator of the great catastrophes of Europe, always in search of an impossible alterity.

After Olga's death in 1936, having inherited the largest share of the family fortune, Freud's former patient settled in Rome and embarked on an illusory career as a baroque concert artist. Two years later, right before he emigrated, Weiss sent him to a Jungian colleague, who took him in hand and proposed that he translate some of Jung's works. Finally, Veneziano found peace with a lover who helped him escape persecution by the Fascists. He died in 1952, "his liver riddled with pains and poisons," after having sold half of the shares in the family factory to buy himself a harpsichord.[22]

Drawing on the story of these wanderings, which allowed him to avoid the experience of the couch even though he had dreamed of being analyzed by Freud, Svevo invented one of the most fascinating characters in twentieth-century literature: Zeno, a modern antihero tormented by his own lack of consistency, his melancholia, his addiction to tobacco, and the absurdities of a life doomed to failure. In short, Svevo was the first writer of his generation to create from whole cloth a Freudian patient in the first quarter of the twentieth century, a chronically ill individual confronted with an impotent and vengeful psychoanalyst (Dr. S.), haunted by the death of his father and the power of women, competing with a suicidal alter ego and ultimately dreaming of a grandiose catastrophe that would blow up the planet: "An ordinary man . . . will invent an incomparable explosive. . . . And another man, also ordinary, but a bit sicker than others, will steal this explosive and will climb up at the center of the earth, to set it on the spot where it can have the maximum effect. There will be an enormous explosion that no one will hear, and the earth, once again a nebula, will wander through the heavens, freed of parasites and sickness."[23]

Keeping himself deliberately at a distance from literary modernity, especially when it was inspired by his work, Freud never took an interest in *Zeno's Conscience*. As for Weiss, he refused to write a review of the book, despite a request from the author. Worse still, thirty years after the author's death, Weiss continued to assert that the novel in no way reflected the psychoanalytic method and that he himself bore no resemblance to Dr. S.[24] Once again, like most psychoanalysts, he sought a reflection of the Freudian doctrine in literary works, without conceding the slightest importance to the way in which that doctrine had contributed to a renewal of literature.

Years after his own death, Weiss was in turn the expiatory victim of his own method when certain commentators, armed with the Freudian doctrine, explained that his rejection of the novel lay in a negative countertransference toward Svevo, who allegedly committed the sacrilege of not respecting Weiss's "paternal authority."[25]

Veneziani's fate finally resembles those of Otto Gross, Baron Viktor von Dirsztay, Viktor Tausk, Horace Westlake, Frink, Carl Liebman, and many others.[26] These men were in some sense the antiheroes in the his-

tory of the Freudian saga. Forgotten, rejected, or mistreated by the official historiography, then revalorized by the anti-Freudians, they formed a sort of accursed community that no historian could ignore any longer without completely failing to understand the complexity of the Freudian adventure.

After 1920, Freud ought to have been able to experience great happiness in contemplating the immense success that psychoanalysis was reaping from one end of the planet to the other. During this period, it was perfectly clear that his cause was progressing, yet he drew very little satisfaction from it. It was as though he feared that, after his ideas had been rejected, they would eventually be accepted only to be distorted. Concerned about all the "deviations" that his contemporaries were imposing on his doctrine, he wondered what "the rabble" would do when he was no longer alive. Like many founders, Freud chose to be a ferocious guardian of his own concepts and inventions, at the risk of legitimizing the idolaters or the simpletons.

And it was in this state of mind that he welcomed to 19 Berggasse so many patients from the conquering countries, especially America; they brought him currency as they came to be trained as psychoanalysts while also seeking to understand themselves better. Freud might well grumble, but he was obliged to admit that these treatments, briskly carried out in English with cooperative disciples, brought him a possible future for psychoanalysis of which he had not even dreamed. Thus he had to temper his anti-Americanism and acknowledge that other promised lands were opening up to his doctrine: France, the United Kingdom, the United States, Latin America, Japan, and so on.

Born in New York to a family of Jewish tailors from Ukraine, Abram Kardiner, a thirty-year-old doctor, came to Vienna in October 1921 to embark on treatment with Freud, as did several of his compatriots during the same period: Adolph Stern, Monroe Meyer, Clarence Oberndorf, Albert Polon, and Leonard Blumgart.[27] Passionate about anthropology, rejecting dogmas, Kardiner was already a practicing analyst, having undergone a first treatment, which he deemed insufficient, on Frink's couch.

Over a six-month period Kardiner told Freud the stories of his parents, impoverished migrants fleeing anti-Semitic persecution: their arrival on Ellis Island, their search for work, his mother's death from tuberculosis

when he was three years old, the prayers uttered in a language he did not understand, the fear of unemployment, hunger, then the appearance of a new mother, a Romanian, for whom he felt a strong sexual desire. Kardiner talked about his taste for music, about discovering his Jewishness and the Yiddish language, then anti-Semitism; he spoke of his desire to become a great doctor, and of his interest in minority communities—the Indians, the Irish, the Italians: the famous "melting pot," which was not unlike the one in *Mitteleuropa*.

Kardiner also evoked memories of his adolescence. His stepmother suffered from a malformation of the uterus that prevented her from having more children, a fact in which he rejoiced. As for his father, Kardiner recalled that he had insulted and beaten his mother, whom he had married without love. It was under the influence of Kardiner's adored second mother that his father had been able to become a true husband devoted to his family. After a difficult love affair with a girl, followed by a period of depression, Kardiner had embarked on medical studies, thus moving from the status of a naturalized American Jewish tailor's son to that of a brilliant intellectual seduced by psychoanalysis and culturalism. He nevertheless suffered from intense anxiety, which made him fragile in everything he did in life.

He recounted two dreams to Freud. In the first, he saw three Italians urinating on him with raised penises; in the second, he was sleeping with his stepmother. Kardiner was clearly an ideal "Freudian patient," intelligent, capable of dreaming, suffering from a phobic neurosis, with an amorous fixation on a stepmother who was a substitute for a mother victimized by a persecuting father, who had entered an arranged marriage before emigrating. But Kardiner himself simply sought this experience with the Viennese master, without manifesting the slightest idolatry. Although he admired Freud, he was quite prepared to challenge the master's interpretations.

This wasn't the case for Oberndorf—the founder, along with Abraham Arden Brill, of the New York Psychoanalytic Society—who was in treatment with Freud at the same time as Kardiner.[28] Freud held him in contempt, judging him stupid and arrogant.[29] Oberndorf was much more faithful to him than Kardiner was, however, even though he was very reserved—and rightly so—about the maniacal determination of psycho-

analysts to look for "primal scenes" everywhere. He was already convinced that the old-style treatments were no longer suitable for modern times.[30]

On the very first day of his analysis, he recounted a dream in which he was taken toward an unknown destination inside a carriage drawn by two horses, one white and one black. Freud knew that his patient, born in Atlanta to a sadistic family, had had a black nursemaid in his childhood to whom he was very attached. Thus, right at the start he gave this dream a devastating interpretation by declaring to Oberndorf that he would never succeed in marrying because he was unable to decide between a white woman and a black one. Beside himself, Oberndorf discussed this dream with Freud and with Kardiner for months on end. He felt all the more humiliated in that he was already a seasoned analyst, trained on Federn's couch and himself adept at interpreting dreams. According to Kardiner, he remained a bachelor and Freud continued to hold him in contempt.

With Kardiner, Freud had reasons to be much happier than with Oberndorf. Like a seer from the Danube, he explained to his patient that the latter had identified with his mother's unhappiness (thus attesting to an "unconscious homosexuality"), that the three Italians in his dream represented his father, by whom he had felt humiliated, and that the break with his fiancée repeated a primal abandonment that would never be produced again because he had gotten over it on his own. Regarding another dream, Freud explained to Kardiner that the latter wanted to remain submissive to his father so as not to "wake up the sleeping dragon." On two points—the unconscious homosexuality and the submission to the father—Freud was mistaken, and his patient became aware of this.

At the end of six months, Freud found that Kardiner was quite well analyzed and predicted a magnificent career for him, with exceptional financial success and good fortune in his love life. His forecast was right on target. In 1976, after Kardiner had left psychoanalytic dogmatism behind and challenged both the generalized Oedipeanism and the canonical interpretations of repressed homosexuality or the law of the father, he recalled his months at 19 Berggasse with delight: "From my present vantage point, Freud's analysis was a brilliant performance, done with speed and accuracy. What made Freud such a great analyst was that, at

least at that time, he never used theoretical formulations, but made his interpretations in simple language. Except for the use of the concept of the Oedipus complex and unconscious homosexuality, he dealt with the material as it had occurred in life. As an interpreter of dreams, he was brilliantly insightful and intuitive." As for Freud's error concerning "the sleeping dragon," Kardiner observed, "The man who had invented the concept of transference did not recognize it when it occurred here. He overlooked one thing. Yes, I was afraid of my father in childhood, but the one whom I feared now [in 1921] was Freud himself. . . . He could make me or break me, which my father no longer could."[31]

This testimony is all the more interesting in that Kardiner had come to Vienna because he thought that his analysis with Frink had been in-sufficient. He did not know at the time that the latter's treatment with Freud had been very difficult. To be sure, Kardiner had perceived Frink's aggressiveness, but he had not uncovered any signs of psychosis in the analyst. More dogmatically Freudian than Freud himself, Frink had in-terpreted Kardiner's relation with his father as an Oedipal death wish: "You envied him the possession of your stepmother," he had said.[32] And this erroneous interpretation had induced in Kardiner renewed anxiety and a legitimate desire to end treatment. Without seeking to harm Frink, Freud disqualified him. But at the end of the analysis, he confided his fears to Kardiner. Therapeutic problems no longer interested him, he said: "I am much too impatient now. I have several handicaps that disqualify me as a great analyst. One of them is that I am too much the father. Second, I am much too occupied with theoretical problems all the time."[33]

In April 1922, after Kardiner had declared to Freud that psychoanal-ysis could not harm anyone, Freud showed him two photographs of Frink, one taken before his analysis (October 1920) and the other a year later.[34] In the first, Frink looked like the man Kardiner had known, but in the other he looked haggard and gaunt. Was it really the experience of the couch that had produced the metamorphosis? Kardiner had many more doubts about this than Freud,[35] who never succeeded in getting out of the nightmare of that tragic treatment, which intermingled conjugal relations, adultery, psychoanalytical endogamy, and diagnostic error.

Born in 1883, Frink was neither a Jew nor a son of European emigrants, neither wealthy nor neurotic. Endowed with exceptional intelligence, he

had plunged into studies in psychiatry quite early and had become a psychoanalyst. Suffering from manic-depressive illness since his youth, he had been analyzed by Brill and then welcomed into the heart of the NYPS before he published, a few years later, a veritable best seller that helped spread the popularity of Freudianism in the Western Hemisphere.[36] In 1918, he had become one of the most highly respected psychoanalysts of the East Coast; however, he still suffered from manic and depressive crises with delirium and suicidal tendencies. He divided his life between his legitimate spouse, Doris Best, with whom he had had two children, and his mistress Angelika (Angie) Bijur, a former patient and a wealthy heiress married to Abraham Bijur, a prominent American industrialist who had been analyzed by Frink and then by Thaddeus Ames.[37]

Pressured by his mistress to divorce his wife, Frink went to Vienna to undertake treatment with Freud, in order to decide which one was to be the woman of his life. Angie consulted Freud in turn; he advised her to divorce her husband and marry her lover. Otherwise, he indicated, Frink risked becoming homosexual, in a more or less disguised fashion; at the same time, in his treatment of Frink, he diagnosed repressed homosexuality. In reality, Freud was quite seduced by this brilliant man whom he called a "very nice boy"; whether he would "prove steady depends on a complete change in his private affairs."[38] He encouraged Frink to take Brill's place.

It was impossible for Frink to accept such a diagnosis. And yet, blinded by Freud's hold over him, he made the decision to leave Doris and marry Angie. Scandalized by this behavior, which he deemed contrary to all ethics, Abraham Bijur drafted an open letter for publication in the *New York Times,* in which he treated Freud as a "great charlatan doctor." He entrusted a copy to Ames, who sent it to Freud, emphasizing the danger that this affair would pose to the NYPS if it were revealed by the press. To Ernest Jones, who was trying to put out the fire, Freud declared that Angie had misunderstood his remarks. He stressed nonetheless—and he believed this firmly—that society tolerates adultery better than divorce between two unhappy persons living together but seeking to remarry.[39] This amounted to acknowledging that he had indeed pushed Frink and Angie to divorce their respective spouses, in keeping with his belief that they no longer got along with them.

In other circumstances, Freud made different decisions, especially when he was convinced that adultery was just a symptom of an unresolved problem with a spouse who was still loved. In short, as much as he condemned adultery, he also favored a "good separation," provided that it ended up with a new marriage. In the affair in question, Freud was seriously mistaken about Frink. And he persevered by sending him a foolish letter: "I have required of Angie that she not tell outsiders that I have advised her to marry you, because you risked a nervous decompensation. . . . May I suggest to you that your idea that she has lost part of her beauty could be transformed by the idea of acquiring part of her fortune? You complain of not understanding your homosexuality, which implies that you are not conscious of your fantasy of wanting to make me a rich man. If everything goes for the best, let us change this imaginary gift into a real contribution to the psychoanalytic fund."[40]

Like all his disciples, Freud contributed to the financing of the psychoanalytic movement. In this connection, it is not astonishing that he could have expressed the idea that Frink too could participate in the financing by a gift in order to cure his fantasies. As for the interpretation according to which a woman who has lost her beauty in her lover's eyes could be desired for her fortune, this stemmed from a traditional conception of the bourgeois family. Thus Freud behaved with his patient as a sort of old-style paternal marriage arranger, blending the couch and conjugal counseling. This was evidence that he had understood nothing of Frink's condition; he took his patient to be an intelligent neurotic who was repressing his homosexual impulse toward his father. Once he was free to marry his former mistress, Frink experienced overwhelming guilt, and he went back to Vienna in November 1922. During an episode of delirium, he imagined that he had fallen into a tomb and, during the treatment sessions, he paced back and forth so frenetically that Freud engaged a doctor, Joe Asch, to watch over the patient and monitor him at his hotel. The situation worsened when Doris died of pneumonia after her former husband's marriage to Angie. Frink then asserted that he had loved his first wife and began to assault the second.

In May 1924, Freud was compelled to disavow his patient, declaring him mentally ill and unfit to direct the NYPS: "I settled all my hope upon his person, yet his reactions during psychoanalysis were of a psychotic

nature. . . . When he saw he was not permitted to have free satisfaction to his infantile desires he broke down. It was the same in his relation to his new wife, on account of her hardness in money matters he did not get all the tokens of her affection, he had pressed her for."[41] Admitted at his own request to the psychiatric clinic of Johns Hopkins Hospital in Baltimore, and treated by Adolf Meyer, Frink learned that Angie was seeking legal separation. After a life spent alternating between exaltation and melancholia, he died forgotten in 1936.

Forty years later, his daughter, Helen Kraft, found his correspondence with Freud in Adolf Meyer's papers, along with several documents whose content she made public, accusing the master from Vienna of having been a charlatan.[42] Taking advantage of the situation, subscribers to anti-Freudianism accused Freud of having manipulated all his patients; under their pens, the latter became victims of the perfidies of his doctrine. The psychoanalysts, for their part, remained calmly oblivious to the clinical errors of their idolized master.

After this episode, Freud's hatred of America and the Americans became even more pronounced, triggering a stinging, lucid response from Jones: "I remember Pitt's saying: 'One cannot indict a whole nation'. They are human beings with the same potentiality as others. . . . In fifty years they will be the arbiters of the world, so that it is impossible to ignore them. At all events, I shall persevere in my endeavours to strengthen the slight foothold [psychoanalysis] has there."[43]

During these years, in the Bloomsbury district of London, the nonconformist elite in literature, the sciences, economics, and the arts was gathering around Virginia and Leonard Woolf, Lytton and James Strachey, Dora Carrington, John Maynard Keynes, and Roger Fry. Motivated by a fierce will to demolish the Victorian spirit and put an end to imperial wars, they had been conscientious objectors and had refused any involvement in the massive butchery of the trenches; they made known their desire to transform the customs of British society, institute equality between men and women, combat imperialism, and temper the mercantile ardor of capitalism.

Thus they defended, as much by their sexual practices as in their writings, a new conception of love that would allow all the so-called natural tendencies of beings to flourish without being repressed, in particular

homosexuality and bisexuality. Originating in the English intellectual bourgeoisie and trained in some of the best universities of the realm (for example, Trinity College in Cambridge), the "Bloomsburies" admired Freud's work, viewing puritanism as a threat to civilization and claiming to oppose it through an ethical and aesthetic ideal based as much on liberalism as on Socialism. With support from Jones, the English school of psychoanalysis emerged at the heart of this splendid critical modernity, at the same time as postimpressionism.

In 1917, Leonard and Virginia Woolf founded a prestigious publishing house, Hogarth Press, intended as an outlet for writers they admired. A year later, Hogarth published Lytton Strachey's biography of four eminent Victorians: Florence Nightingale, Thomas Arnold, Charles Gordon, and Edward Manning. But he described them from a somber perspective, the better to criticize, through their actions, the negative aspects of Victorian politics: narrow-minded evangelism, colonialism, a repressive educational system, a selfish humanitarianism. Moreover, he spoke out in favor of the writer's right to interpret facts freely and to introduce himself or herself into the narrative. In this sense, he renewed the art of biography, offering an intimist perspective that was not far removed from that of psychoanalysis.

Furthermore, Strachey was as interested as Freud in the tormented lives of the heroes of the British monarchy. And that is why, after writing a satire of the eminent Victorians, he devoted two books to the love lives of two great queens: Elizabeth and Victoria. They had in common the fact that, toward the end of their lives, they allowed themselves to be dominated by lovers whose very existence countered the ideal that their reign had exemplified.

As we know, for more than a decade, from 1587 to 1601, Elizabeth nurtured an intense passion for her very young cousin, Robert Devereux, Count of Essex, who beleaguered her with the idea that the highest functions of the state ought to be awarded to him. To shore up his influence over the aging queen, who was prey to dark sexual torments, he provoked and threatened her, withdrew abruptly into his own castle and expressed rancor and bitterness in order to obtain her forgiveness; he would then come back and resume his exhortations. To put an end to all the madness,

which threatened to plunge the realm into anarchy, Elizabeth, although consumed with grief and suffering, had him put to death. She had never consented to sexual relations with him. In his book, Strachey drew a picture of the mysteries of the baroque age and Elizabeth's implacable determination to embody an image of perfection in keeping with her legend, rather than lowering herself to the status of an ordinary woman.

Similarly, he focused on describing the passion Victoria felt, after the death of Prince Albert, for the latter's former squire, James Brown. Transgressing her own codes, the queen made this brutal and vulgar protégé the instrument of her revenge against a reign during which she had sought to conserve the appearance of the greatest perfection.[44]

As for Keynes, who was to become one of the greatest economists of the twentieth century, he shared with Freud not the inverted memory of the heroic dynasties, but a frank hatred for the Treaty of Versailles. Having been part of the English delegation during the Paris negotiations, he had spoken out against the French policy that consisted in humiliating Germany. In 1919, he had written a pamphlet denouncing that "Carthaginian peace," prophesying that its consequences would be disastrous for Europe and that it would arouse unmanageable popular resentment in the German-speaking world and at the heart of the old dismantled empires.[45] He was not mistaken.

For a long time, James Strachey, Lytton's brother, had wanted to go to Vienna to be trained on Freud's couch in order to become a psychoanalyst. He could not afford to pay for treatment at the same rate as the American psychiatrists, however. Thus he asked Jones to intercede on his behalf, and Jones complied at once. Eager to develop a winning politics in America, Jones was aware, on the one hand, that Freud would never get on well with his American disciples and, on the other hand, that the English movement was apt to constitute a useful counterweight to the future American power.

James was thus, for Jones, just the right man. Intelligent, cultivated, refined, elegant, caustic, tolerant, lacking any merchandizing tendency, and devoid of pragmatism, he was already engaged in an intellectual cause of which psychoanalysis was a part. At age thirty, he was not seeking a substitute father with whom he could compete, nor a brother who would

dominate him, nor a mother who would resemble his sister, nor a re-placement for an abusive nursemaid. Nor was he prey to repressed homosexuality. He was neither a Jew nor a migrant, nor was he moti-vated by any desire except to put his writing talents at the service of an adventure of the mind that he saw as extraordinary. A self-declared bi-sexual, falling in love with young men who resembled women and with women who resembled young men, he suffered from no particular pa-thology and had received a remarkable education in an astonishing, aty-pical family that cultivated the love of books and liberties. At the very most, he suffered from a permanent symptom of indecision, and from a difficulty in speaking associated with a sort of world-weariness.

In 1920, he married Alix Sargant-Florence, who became his lifelong companion. She too came from a nonconformist family. Her mother, a committed feminist who was already a widow when her daughter was born, had pushed her to pursue advanced studies, and it was at Newnham College, Cambridge, that she discovered Freud's work. From childhood on she refused to wear women's clothing, and at age twenty, after a bout of anorexia, she experienced her first severe depression.

When she met James, she fell madly in love, and he found her very ap-pealing: "a real boy," he wrote. Gifted with a lively intelligence, she al-ways tried to dissimulate her condition behind a veil of laughter, though this did not deceive Virginia Woolf, who characterized her in terms of a "sepulchral despair." Like James, Alix suffered from a certain inability to choose an activity that she would enjoy, while also suffering from depres-sive states and bouts of heart palpitations.[46] She wanted to become in-volved in the psychoanalytic movement.

In August 1920, James and Alix moved to Vienna, and in October James began his analysis with Freud.

> Each day except Sunday I spend an hour on the Prof.'s sofa. . . .
> The Prof himself is most affable and as an artistic performer
> dazzling. . . . Almost every hour is made into an organic aesthetic
> whole. Sometimes the dramatic effect is absolutely shattering . . .
> you feel dreadful things happening inside you, and can't make
> out what they could possibly be; then he begins to give you a
> slight lead; you suddenly get a clear glimpse of one thing; then

you see another; at last a whole series of lights break in on you; he asks you one more question; you give a last reply—and as the whole truth dawns upon you the Professor rises, crosses the room to the electric bell, and shows you out at the door. That's on favorable occasions. But there are others when you lie for the whole hour with a ton weight on your stomach simply unable to get out a single word.[47]

Clearly, Freud did not behave the same way with James as with his American patients. Kardiner realized this when he spoke of his treatment with James and with John Rickman, who was also in analysis with Freud. The master spoke a great deal with the Americans and very little with the English. Kardiner humorously deduced from this that Freud's attitude had given rise "to the 'English' school of psychoanalysis, in which the analyst says nothing at any time other than 'Good morning' and 'Goodbye.' And this can go on as long as four, five, or six years."[48] Rickman, for his part, had the impression that Freud's silence and his "absences" were caused by his illness. Well versed in archaeology, he also noted that Freud had purchased some fake statuettes and that he did not distinguish very well between Greek and Egyptian objects.[49]

Kardiner's testimony on the silent treatments that went on and on—as was standard practice in the 1950s—does not correspond to the Viennese experience of the 1920s. We have to suppose, rather, that Freud had no need to impose a given interpretation on James, and that he simply felt antipathy toward Rickman.

The Professor lacked the curiosity to take an interest in Virginia Woolf's work, but he admired Lytton Strachey's and he was impressed by James. As for Alix, while she had not intended to submit to analysis, on the occasion of one of her "crises" she asked James to organize a course of joint treatment for the two of them, which was contrary to the very ethic of psychoanalysis. Interested by the reactions and counterreactions provoked by this experiment, Freud decided nonetheless to analyze Alix and James together. In the winter of 1922, he declared them fit to practice analysis, but he strongly advised Alix to consult Abraham. A wise decision: Abraham was at the time one of the best clinicians for treating melancholia.

A few weeks after the dual analysis—which had continued, with interruptions, until the winter of 1922—Freud proposed to James that he translate several of his works. "In the Stracheys," Perry Meisel and Walter Kendrick wrote, "Freud found the precise embodiment of what England, his favorite country, meant to him. He saw in them the appropriate sensibility for rendering his work into the only tongue besides German to which he deeply responded—the language of his favorite poet, Milton, a language embellished with the wry urbanity of contemporary aestheticism."[50]

With Alix's help, James finally found his path: he achieved the great work of his life in the complete translation of Freud's work into English, the future *Standard Edition*—such was the success of this analysis founded on a transference onto Freud's language more than onto his person. James's goal, his culture, his training, his adherence to the Bloomsbury spirit fit very well with Freud's ideal, given that the master had seen himself as a writer and a man of science simultaneously.

The earliest translations, produced by Brill, were mediocre. Before he met James, Freud had been concerned only with spreading his ideas abroad, without worrying too much about the manner in which a translator could capture his style, transpose his concepts, or establish a veritable critical apparatus with notes and a scholarly bibliography listing sources and references. James began by publishing three volumes of *Collected Papers* with Hogarth Press; it was Jones who had the idea of producing a complete edition and having the American psychoanalytic societies finance the work, even though the enterprise was to be placed under the aegis of Great Britain.

Aware of the fact that the American psychoanalytic movement was likely to grow, Jones, as we have seen, was concerned with reinforcing English power. In 1919, he had founded the British Psychoanalytical Society (BPS) to replace the former London Psychoanalytical Society (LPS) that had been created in 1913; he subsequently gathered a large number of members, including Barbara Low, Rickman, Sylvia Payne, Joan Riviere, Ella Sharpe, and Susan Isaacs. In 1920, he brought out the first issue of the *International Journal of Psychoanalysis (IJP)*, the first psychoanalytic review in English; it became the official organ of the Verein, then of the International Psychoanalytical Association.

James sought to honor Freud's work, but he was never servile. His work reflected his own orientations. Thus he had a tendency to neglect everything that connected Freud's texts with German Romanticism and *Naturphilosophie;* he gave priority instead to its medical, scientific, and technical aspects. This bias was expressed in the choice of certain Latin and Greek words on the one hand, and by a certain "anglicizing" on the other. Thus, to translate the *Es* (French *ça*), the *Ich (moi)*, and the *Überich (surmoi)*, he used the Latin pronouns *id, ego,* and *superego;* for *Besetzung* (French *investissement*) and *Fehlleistung (acte manqué)*, he used Greek terms: *cathexis* and *parapraxis*. Finally, he made the mistake of translating *Trieb* (French *pulsion*) as "instinct," on the pretext that the term "drive" *(trajet, conduite)*—which was adopted later—was unsuitable.

James thus helped accentuate the irreversible process of anglicizing Freud's doctrine. His translation has been subject to constant criticism, unjustly, moreover; it was Bruno Bettelheim—having become Anglophone himself after his emigration to the United States—who proved to be the most virulent critic. In 1982, in a work that received a great deal of attention, *Freud and Man's Soul,* he reproached James for having deprived the Freudian text of its "German soul" and its "Viennese Spirit."[51]

When James returned to London to embark on another treatment with James Glover and establish himself as a psychoanalyst, Alix, who had just recovered from pneumonia contracted in Vienna, stayed in Berlin. For a year, she had time to discover a different way of practicing psychoanalysis, which she found dazzling. The society established by Abraham was "at the height of its splendid decadence,"[52] and the imperial city shone with its brightest lights before the catastrophe of 1933. There Alix met the elite among the German-speaking psychoanalytic movement, whose members would soon emigrate to the United States or elsewhere: Hanns Sachs, Rado, Franz Alexander, Otto Fenichel, Felix and Helene Deutsch, Hans Lampl, Karen Horney, and Ernst Freud. She became familiar with the ambivalences of the city, in which the newest ideas and the most barbaric intolerance could be found side by side, amid frivolity, fratricidal eruptions, and glittering quagmires. In the cafés and cabarets, one could encounter Bertolt Brecht, George Grosz, and all sorts of audacious artists seeking new ways to live and think.

Alix learned to speak perfect German, discovered how numerous Jews were in the psychoanalytic milieu, and tasted the pleasures of parties and the theater. One day, she met the famous, charming, and dowdy Dr. Wilhelm Fliess, with his dwarflike appearance and his big stomach. He had changed very little, and he asked her if a member of her family might have died since the beginning of the year; this was the only way to explain, according to him, why she was suffering from a fever with swollen tonsils.

But it was with Melanie Klein, established in Berlin since 1921 and in analysis with Abraham after a stint on Ferenczi's couch, that Alix had a revelation about what clinical depths psychoanalysis could reach. She did not want children herself, but she understood very quickly that Klein's lectures and presentations on the analysis of young children, the archaic relation to the mother or the precocity of the Oedipus complex, upset the classic Freudian perspective by allowing an earlier understanding of the genesis of neuroses and psychoses. Whereas Freud claimed that a three-year-old boy was completely unaware of the existence of the vagina, Klein maintained a contrary position, on the basis of her own observations; she claimed that every male child wanted to insert his penis in his mother's vagina. In other words, if, for Freud, a male child was a wild narcissistic being who went through "stages" and had to be trained, for Klein he was closer to a sadistic cannibal seeking to copulate with his mother, and haunted by an inner world woven of fantasies, hatred, madness, and anxiety.

In Salzburg in April 1924, at the eighth congress of the IPV, Klein gave a talk on the analysis of young children in which she asserted that the pronounced preference for the parent of the opposite sex appeared as early as the second year, and that the mother was perceived by her son from then on as terrifying and castrating. She had made these "discoveries" in analyzing her own children.[53] Separated from her husband, Klein had associated her daughter Melitta early on with her own passion for the psychoanalytic cause. The latter pursued medical studies in order to become a psychoanalyst. In Berlin, Melitta frequented the couches of the leading lights of the movement—Sachs, Max Eitingon, Horney—while feeling hated by her mother, who already saw her as a rival. This is where she met and then married Walter Schmideberg, a cultivated Viennese psycho-

analyst, an alcoholic, and a homosexual, trained within the ranks of the WPV. The subsequent relations between Klein and her daughter are among the most painful in the history of psychoanalysis.

For the time being, Alix admired Klein's charm, her eroticism, her verbal powers, and her determination, which hid, in fact, a good deal of suffering from depression. As Alix spent time with Klein, without knowing much about her history, she discovered that a woman could hold a place equal to that of a man in the development of psychoanalytic theories. From the vantage point of Berlin, then, she took her distance from Vienna, and she dreamed of helping Klein become English, just as James, during the same period, persisted in trying to make Freud a British scholar. Alix later became Klein's translator, after having introduced her into the BPS.[54]

In the meantime, in Berlin, Alix gave English classes. On January 31, 1925, disguised as Cleopatra, Klein took Alix to a masked ball organized by Socialists. The two women danced all night. Two weeks later, the policlinic celebrated its fifth anniversary under the leadership of Eitingon, and everyone had the impression that the psychoanalytic movement was firmly anchored, and for years to come, in the heart of Berlin. However, on December 25, Abraham died at age forty-four from an infection resulting from an abscess probably caused by cancer. Klein had already left for England with Alix. Devastated, Freud was losing one of his most fervent disciples.[55] At the time, Rickman had already set up a psychoanalytic institute in London modeled on the one in Berlin. Thus the English psychoanalytic movement was beginning to take on considerable proportions, while the Berliners continued to see themselves—as opposed to the Viennese—as the avant-garde of European Freudianism.

Just as Freud understood nothing about the literary modernity that was taking inspiration from his work, he was similarly unaware of the new art of the century, cinematography, which came into being at the same time as psychoanalysis. And yet there was great proximity between the modes of approaching the unconscious that these two art forms deployed. Convinced that his doctrine must in no case be popularized by means of moving pictures, Freud believed that only speech could give access to the unconscious. A new contradiction: Had he himself not asserted that dreams were a way to travel into a space beyond reason, to make a

visual voyage woven of words and speech? In reality, he failed to understand the cinematographic art just as he failed to understand the broader expressionist movement, which asserted its will to express, by harsh colors or lines of fracture, a vision of tormented, driven, violent, chaotic subjectivity, traversed by a fantastic imaginary.

To be sure, one can understand that Freud refused to lend his support, at the price of $100,000, to Samuel Goldwyn's project of producing a film about famous love affairs. But when Sachs was invited by Hans Neumann, toward the end of the 1920s, to participate in drafting a scenario for *Secrets of a Soul,* which was to be directed by Wilhelm Pabst, a filmmaker of Austrian origin, Freud adopted the same negative attitude, though the project was a completely different one. Freud declared that the abstractions of his thought could not be represented in a plastic form. He did not see to what extent silent black-and-white film had already invaded the realm of dreams, with its superimpositions, its fade-out techniques, its subtitles, its camera movements capable of abolishing past and present, of gliding from one decor to another, from one face to another, or of representing primal scenes, memories, bizarre objects while simultaneously linking hallucinations to a skillfully reconstituted reality.

A masterpiece of expressionist cinema, *Secrets of a Soul* was thus produced without Freud's approval, and without even arousing any interest on his part. Werner Krauss, already a well-known actor, interpreted the role of Professor Matthias, a man haunted by murderous desires involving sabers and knives, who was cured by psychoanalysis. This was the first film inspired by Freud's theses.[56] Sachs had written a short work, "The Mystery of the Unconscious," which served as an instruction manual for the film, and his name figured among the credits along with that of Abraham. Both had gotten beyond Freud's disapproval; Freud was left with little recourse but to confide his hostility toward the modern world to Ferenczi: he liked neither movies nor women with boyish haircuts.

On March 25, 1925, during the first projection in Berlin, in the large screening room in the Gloria Palast, the press greeted the film enthusiastically: "From one image to the next, we discover Freud's thought. Every shift in the action could be one of the propositions of the henceforth so celebrated analyst of dreams. . . . Freud's students can rejoice. Nothing in

the world could have brought them publicity with so much tact. But the people of German cinema can also be proud."[57]

When Jones attended a screening of the film in Berlin, he had nothing to say about its aesthetic quality, but he found it damaging for psychoanalysis. He deplored the fact that in New York it could be supposed that Freud had given his consent to the undertaking, which was at the origin of a new controversy between Viennese and Berliners.[58] Jones did not even mention Pabst's name in his biography of Freud. In the aftermath, the relations between Freud's heirs and filmmakers remained hostile.[59]

While Freud never took an interest in modern art, he never lost his preoccupation with certain mysteries that surrounded his favorite artists. Thus, for several years, defying his disciples from the 1920s, he adhered to a conspiracy theory concerning Shakespeare's identity. All the Freudians of the first circle shared his idolatry for the great English dramatist, and all allowed themselves, as they did with Leonardo da Vinci, to engage in endless speculation about each of the characters in his theater and especially Hamlet, the first prototype of the modern neurotic.

In the mid-nineteenth century, with the rise of the science of history and of the Romanesque art that was linked to it, the idea had surfaced that Shakespeare's works had to have been produced by someone other than Shakespeare. Those who endorsed this thesis claimed to be opposing the "official" history by declaring that Shakespeare had not been born in Stratford and that he was only a figurehead whose name the empiricist philosopher Sir Francis Bacon had borrowed.[60] The "anti-Stratfordians" thus imagined the existence, in the late sixteenth century, of a conspiracy intended to protect the real author of the work, who, in their eyes, could in no case be the son of a glove maker, a tradesman in skins and wool who came from the peasantry. But why Bacon? Because Delia Salter Bacon, a maniacal American playwright, the author of a best seller on the question published in 1857 and a subscriber to this thesis, had gone to Shakespeare's tomb and claimed to have wrested all his secrets from him. In her wake, a slew of puzzle solvers had imagined that Bacon, a former friend of the Count of Essex, could not take the risk of being perceived as an entertainer. The anti-Stratfordians manifested "absolute fanaticism and

subscribed to conspiracy theories that bordered on paranoia," Peter Gay wrote. "In the late 1880s, the prominent American politician Ignatius Donnelly, a populist with a weakness for outlandish causes, launched— or rather popularized—the fashion of reading the works of Shakespeare as a gigantic cryptogram."[61]

The polemic was started up again in 1920 by Thomas Looney, a school-master who adhered to Auguste Comte's positivism; Looney took up the same arguments in attributing the paternity of Shakespeare's works not to Bacon, this time, but to Edward de Vere, the Count of Oxford.[62] Un-like the other anti-Stratfordians, Looney claimed to be relying on scien-tific theses, and he demonstrated such erudition that his arguments looked like the antithesis to a monomaniacal delirium. Everything pointed to a great solitary scholar bringing his brilliant discovery to the world. Thus he managed to convince several authors and critics of the validity of his great revision of the official truths, Mark Twain among them.[63]

Nothing could have better seduced Freud, who, during this period, manifested great interest in occult phenomena, detective stories, and fantastic tales. He too saw himself as a solitary and grandiose solver of riddles, the inventor of a doctrine that had been rejected by official science. Had he not been an admirer of Fliess's theses? Had he not deciphered the enigmatic life of da Vinci by accepting the idea that a vulture was present in one of the painter's best-known works? Despite warnings by James Strachey and Jones, who tried in vain to talk him out of taking the new "Oxfordian" thesis seriously, he began to believe in Looney's extrapolations.

Convinced, after a detailed "examination" of the facts, that the author of Shakespeare's works could only be a man of letters with a passion for theater, a world traveler of high social rank, Looney had sought for years to find someone who might correspond to this social and psychological profile. He finally detected in de Vere all the indications he needed to shore up his thesis. The fate of the Count of Oxford dovetailed with his hypothesis, and Looney added to this certainty the idea that Hamlet was the author's "double," someone who devoted a cult to his father and hated his mother. In other words, he unwittingly made Hamlet a substitute for de Vere, a Freudian character haunted by his Oedipus complex.

Freud never renounced this revisionism, of which he himself would soon be a victim, for he adored rumors. In December 1928, in a long letter to Lytton Strachey, responding to the receipt of the biography of Elizabeth and Essex, he asked Lytton's opinion about one of his hypotheses: Freud thought that in the character of Lady Macbeth there was a hidden portrait of Queen Elizabeth, the two women being similarly tortured by a murder. And he added that Macbeth and his wife in fact formed a single divided character, both embodying the fate of the virginal, murderous, depressive, hysterical queen. Above all, he reasserted his belief in Looney's thesis, even as he took the precaution of saying that he "felt ignorant" and that he was not fully convinced of the Oxfordian hypothesis. He added, however, that de Vere resembled Essex in the extreme, before plunging into an implausible interpretive spiral: "Of an equally high heritage to Essex's, and equally proud of it, he also embodied, like Essex, the type of the tyrannical nobleman. Besides, he certainly emerges in Hamlet as the first modern neurotic. Also, in his youth, the queen had flirted with him; perhaps if his mother-in-law[64] had not campaigned so energetically for her daughter, he would have come still closer to Essex's fate. He was surely an intimate friend of Southampton. Essex's fate cannot have been indifferent to him. But enough. In any case, I have the feeling that I ought to beg your especial pardon for this second writing style of mine."[65]

Lytton never answered Freud. At the time, he could have usefully advised Freud to be skeptical of the Oxfordian hypothesis. A year later, Freud no longer had any doubts. Thus he recommended Looney's book to Smiley Blanton, a great specialist in the Shakespearean question. Bewildered, Blanton came close to interrupting his treatment, imagining that the Professor, a man of science and reason, had gotten lost in foolish nonsense.

To explain these divagations, Jones imagined that Freud had identified with Looney's thesis because he had unconsciously projected himself into a family romance in which he could have been the son of his half brother Emanuel, a more prosperous businessman than Jacob, and that his Oxfordian fantasy would thus be merely the translation of a desire to change part of his own family reality.

Rather than adding an Oedipal interpretation to a Freudian digression on Shakespeare's multiple identities, we may hypothesize that Freud always

remained in part the heir to a certain late nineteenth-century mode of thought that represented human society as divided between rational questing and attraction to the occult, between logical minds and paranoid delirium. From this standpoint, Freud resembles both Giovanni Morelli, the inventor of a method for distinguishing authentic works of art from imitations, and Sherlock Holmes,[66] the famous fictional detective, a past master in the art of solving an enigma by the simple observation of a few traces: ashes, hairs, threads, bits of skin. Of course, all these methods for deciphering could, like psychoanalysis, be turned in the opposite direction and used to fabricate false enigmas, whose presumed existence was supposed to bring proof of the validity of the approach used to interpret them. Thus questioning the historicity of an event or a person led to the substitution of fables for facts, then to the presentation of these "facts" with impeccable rigor as so many riddles to be deciphered, in order to demonstrate that they concealed conspiracies: Napoleon did not die at Saint-Helena; Jesus was married and had children; a certain king is actually his own twin brother . . .

And if Freud, despite the enduring nature of his doubts, got so carried away when it was a matter of bringing false enigmas to light, it was also because he had been obsessed since childhood by the idea that the people he observed around him—father, mother, aunts, sisters, brothers, multiple sibling groups—were never what they seemed, but rather substitutes for a permanent alterity: a father generated by an ancestor, a mother in place of a nurse and vice versa, a brother who could be the father, Saint Anne confused with Mary, and so on. And behind the alleged or denied father, and beyond the substitute mother, there was the outline of a "family romance" through which the subject was always other than what he thought he was: son of a king or of a hero, murderer of a father, tyrant, commoner, abandoned child sleeping with his mother, impostor, and so on. From this thesis arose the necessity of deciphering insignificant elements in the unconscious that could be referred back in turn to mythic traces.[67]

One can never insist enough on the extent to which Freud, a man of the Enlightenment and a decipherer of the real mysteries of the human psyche, strove continually and simultaneously, as a counterpoint to his attachment to science, to confront the obscure forces characteristic of

human beings in order to bring their subterranean power to light—at the risk of getting lost in them himself.

Such, for him, were the stakes of the passion he brought to deciphering a rumor that was in fact a pure invention, as if he were dealing with an authentic enigma. This rumor seemed to conform to his theory of infinite substitutions, and thus he was obsessed until the very end of his life by one question: So who is it that is always concealed beneath the name of a "great man"?

Among Women

FROM THE 1920s ON, women were increasingly present in the psycho-
analytic movement, within which, moreover, there were several ongoing
debates about women's lives and practices, on such topics as motherhood,
child psychoanalysis, and feminine sexuality. Just as women were de-
manding the right to exist as full-fledged citizens, they were also starting
to take their places among the ranks of psychoanalysts, and not only as
spouses. In this process, they brought a new perspective on how to think
about treatment. In addition, the responsibility for analyzing children ini-
tially fell to them. This function, designated "educational," did not
oblige them to undertake medical studies, which were still reserved for
men. From this standpoint, we can say that child analysis favored women's
emancipation. If female psychoanalysts were often analyzed by their
spouses or colleagues of their spouses, they in turn analyzed their children
or entrusted that task to others.

In 1924, Otto Rank and Sándor Ferenczi, who had already proposed
technical innovations in the way treatments were carried out, sought to
transform the Freudian vision of the family to make it better adapted to
postwar modernity. Early in the year, Rank started the battle by pub-
lishing an iconoclastic book, *The Trauma of Birth,* triggering a defensive
reaction on the part of Ernest Jones and Karl Abraham.[1] Criticizing the
conception of the Oedipal organization of the psyche, which he found too
rigid, based as it was on the preponderant place attributed to paternal au-
thority, Rank supported the idea that at birth every human being experi-
enced actual trauma. According to him, this first separation from the
mother became the prototype of an anguish that was more determining

for human subjectivity than the Oedipal triangulation. In this way Rank relaunched the old debate on the traumatic origin of neuroses.

Rather than refuting this thesis, of which he disapproved, Freud demanded "proofs." He seemed to forget that he himself had condemned, among his own adversaries, the abusive recourse to the famous experimental model: "One would have to require," he wrote to Ferenczi, "that, first, and before any extensive applications, it be demonstrated statistically that firstborn, difficultly and asphyxically born children, on average, reveal a greater disposition to neurosis, or at least to the production of anxiety in childhood."[2] And he added that it was also necessary to study children born by caesarian section. Unable to supply such "proofs," Rank was then accused by Jones and Abraham of being neither a doctor nor an analyst, just as new rules making training analysis obligatory were about to go into effect at the IPV congress in Bad-Homburg.[3] The mania for interpretation regained the upper hand at once: Rank, they said, had not resolved his conflict with the father figure. Thus he was obliged to enter into analysis, for a few sessions, with the revered master. A wasted effort!

In reality, Rank did not want to continue to depend on Freud. Tempted by new technical advances, and eager to leave Vienna, with his wife,[4] he went to the United States, which for Freud amounted to a real betrayal. Rank gave lectures and seminars, was very well received, and asserted that, without betraying the master's doctrine, it was necessary to take mothers into account from now on, and to develop the principle of brief therapies. When he returned to Vienna, Freud adopted a conciliatory approach, not wanting at any price to break with this disciple of whom he was so fond. But Rank, energized by his American triumph, thought only about leaving again. In December 1925 he left Vienna once more, and then returned. In a great fit of masochism, he engaged in self-criticism, humiliated himself, and recognized that he was afflicted with a complex of rebellion against the father.

For his part, Ferenczi proceeded to maintain, in *Thalassa,* that every human being was nostalgic for the maternal breast and that, to avoid being detached from it, everyone sought to regress to the watery depths of a fetal state.[5] This approach to psychoanalysis via the metaphor of the crypt was accompanied by technical innovations. According to Ferenczi,

if the analytic session repeats a sequence of the history of the individual, and if, in addition, ontogenesis recapitulates phylogenesis, one has to wonder what traumatic state is repeated symbolically by ontogenesis during the session itself.

In a first phase, and despite his disagreement with the birth trauma theory, Ferenczi supported Rank's position, for he shared the latter's idea that the bond with the mother should be explored well beyond the Freudian conception of the Oedipus complex. This was no help. In April 1926, Rank definitively pulled away from Freud to pursue his own destiny. As a gift marking the separation, he offered Freud the complete works of Nietzsche: twenty-three volumes bound in white leather. Freud had never wanted to read the work of this philosopher to whom he owed so much, as his cherished disciple had told him many times. Grief stricken but as ferocious as ever in his way of rejecting his best friends, he wrote the following to Ferenczi about Rank: "He received much as a gift and accomplished much in return, so we're even! But on his farewell visit I didn't see any occasion for the expression of extreme tenderness; I was honest and hard. But we can make the sign of the cross over him. Abraham was right."[6] Freud continued to reproach Rank for his interpretation of Sergei Pankejeff's wolf dream.

He nevertheless took the trouble to respond, in a hastily written text: "Inhibitions, Symptoms and Anxiety."[7] While he took Rank's position into account, Freud avoided the pitfall of attributing a traumatic reality to the process of birth itself. He thus acknowledged the idea that a paradigmatic, even phantasmic, value could be attached to the separation from the mother, but he sidestepped the question of the unpleasantness that could be caused, especially in the United States, by the idea that any birth—normal or with forceps—could be the cause of existential anguish or neurosis.

Without breaking with Freud, Ferenczi nevertheless took his distance through his technical innovations, but also by relaunching the question of repressed trauma and sexual abuse that act like psychic "imprints," like wounds that cannot heal and are capable of damaging the ego.[8] Jones seized the opportunity to combat Ferenczi relentlessly, all the more so in that he could tolerate neither his penchant for telepathy nor Freud's unwavering friendship with him. In this quarrel between the Ancients and the

Moderns, Freud was no more correct than Rank. For if the thesis of birth trauma was erroneous from the experimental standpoint, it opened the way to a new conception of separation anxiety. Freud acknowledged this. And he was honest enough, subsequently, to revise his position and to recognize the merits of his dear Rank. Too late.[9]

In the meantime, Jones was in the process of winning his battle to ensure the supremacy of the Anglophone world over continental Europe: this was a way for him to be unfaithful to Freud even while remaining faithful to what he believed was the future of psychoanalysis. He had understood right away, as Alix Strachey had, that the only serious way of challenging the original Viennese doctrine—centered on the primacy of the law of the father—was through a new approach to the twinned questions of child analysis and feminine sexuality.

Up to this point, while Freud had conceived his Oedipus complex according to the model of the nuclear family (father, mother, child), he had also assigned to each family member a place that made it possible to clear up only the genesis of the neuroses and conflicts that were formed in childhood. He developed a critical view of the bourgeois family, which he explored from the starting point of his famous Oedipal structure without noticing the dangers of this psychologizing of psychic life, a process that initially represented an authentic innovation but would end up subject to ridicule.

He thought that a child was always and necessarily the child of a man, or of his substitute, who embodied paternal authority, and of a woman, or her substitute, who had displaced her libidinal investment toward maternity. Consequently, the child, in the Freudian sense, was viewed, to be sure, as a full-fledged subject, but if he or she had to be treated for pathological conditions it was necessary to proceed "within the family," and never before the age of four or five. Indeed, Freud had undertaken to analyze Herbert Graf through the discourse of the boy's father, and by accepting his mother on the couch. And when he understood that his own daughter wanted to be a mother without necessarily giving birth, he accepted the idea that she could form a family with a woman who had left her husband, provided however that both women were, thanks to the benefits of psychoanalysis, just as much educators as parents. For Freud, the happiness of existence rested on a triptych: educational ideal, happy

motherhood, accomplished fatherhood. Imbued with this model, the Viennese school had at first been favored by Ferenczi. In 1913, he had thus described the case of a five-year-old child, Arpad, obsessed by fowl and given to crowing like a rooster.[10]

On her side, in the company of August Aichhorn and Siegfried Bernfeld, who cared for delinquent, handicapped, traumatized, or poor children, Anna Freud pursued her career by devoting herself to the education of children through psychoanalysis.[11] And Freud supported her only to the extent that he was convinced, as were his earliest Viennese disciples, that the psychic treatment of children had to be carried out through the mediation of parental authority. "We assume," he wrote to Joan Riviere in October 1927, "that the child is a creature of its drives, with a weak ego and a superego that is only in the process of formation. In adults we work with the help of the strengthened ego, so it is not a betrayal of analysis, if our technique takes into consideration the different conditions in children and supports the ego during analysis against the overpowerful drive-id [*Trieb-Es*]. Ferenczi wittily remarked that, if Mrs. Klein is right, then children really no longer exist. Of course, experience must have the last word. Hitherto I have only seen that, in children, analysis without education worsens the condition and has an especially bad effect on neglected asocial ones."[12]

Freud's arguments were perfectly acceptable. It was still necessary for parents to agree to entrust their offspring to psychoanalysts at a time when childhood pathologies were treated by psychiatrists or pediatricians. In the absence of patients outside the psychoanalytic circle, experimental treatments were carried out on children of analysts or of people close to them. This was not a self-evident solution and could even be a source of fraud.

In 1919, Hermine von Hug-Hellmuth, a member of the WPV in analysis with Isidor Sadger, the most misogynist of all Freud's disciples, drew on her own childhood memories to create a work presented as the authentic journal of an adolescent girl named Grete Lainer. In his preface, Freud affirmed that the diary was "a gem. Never before, I believe, has anything been written enabling us to see so clearly into the soul of a young girl, belonging to our social and cultural stratum."[13] Everyone admired this pioneer in child psychoanalysis, endowed with real literary talent, but no

one noticed that she was not only a forger but also a devotee of "wild" analysis. For several years, her young nephew Rolf Hug had lived in her home and had been submitted to her Oedipal religion. No aspect of this poor boy's behavior escaped the interpretive vigilance of his aunt: his infantile sadism, his repressed desire for his mother, his instinctual sexuality, his fixation on objects or on parental substitutes. In September 1924, in a fit of rage, he strangled her.

The Viennese psychoanalytical community was all the more tarnished by this scandal in that Hug, sentenced to twelve years in prison, claimed that he had been a victim of psychoanalysis. In 1930, he demanded reparations from Paul Federn, president of the WPV at the time. Meanwhile, of course, the *Diary,* which had been quite successful, had been withdrawn from circulation. Freud had allowed himself to be hoodwinked by a fraud that sprang directly from his doctrine.

Melanie Klein did not share Freud's conceptions of the family. And what she had learned from her own family kept her from any temptation to blend pedagogy and psychoanalysis. Born to a Galician father and a Slovakian mother (both attached to Orthodox Judaism), she had had an unhappy childhood.[14] Her mother, a beautiful and cultivated woman, held her husband in contempt; for his part, he favored his oldest daughter, who was unattractive and not very intelligent. Thus Melanie turned to her brother for refuge. Reared without principles or ethics, a witness to her parents' incessant disputes, she married a man she did not love— Arthur Klein, a cousin on her mother's side—and had three unwanted children.[15] She embarked on the psychoanalytic adventure with a fervor that resembled a mystic conversion: she sought revenge against unhappiness and wanted to conjure away her melancholic existence.

Despite her brilliance, Klein attached no importance to the real lives of children or to their upbringing. Nothing interested her but the unconscious processes that she could uncover in small children. The privileged seat of all forms of hatred and immorality, the family in the Kleinian sense was to Freud what Picasso's canvases were to classical painting. The noses, the mouths, the faces were the same, but disturbed, displaced, dislocated. As for Klein's visions of childhood, they could evoke a painting by Max Ernst: nightmares, mineralized nature, a nocturnal reconstruction in which animality, humanity, and liquid elements were mingled.

Klein staked a claim to Oedipal psychology, but she accentuated its features dangerously, the better to immerse herself in the child's so-called pre-Oedipal universe: a maternal crypt, the child's appropriation of the interior of the mother's body, voracious greed, tumult, intense fear of punishment, anxiety, psychosis. In this respect, she was more "modern" than the classic Freudians, closer to a nineteenth-century literary model than to one from the twentieth century. And this is what fascinated Alix Strachey. In very little time, Klein conquered most of the British psychoanalysts, Jones in particular: he had her analyze his own children.

In her eyes, it was necessary to abolish all the barriers that prevented the therapist from gaining access to the child's unconscious. Thus she countered Freud's notion of "protection" with a doctrine focused on the *infans*—a child from two to three years old, that is, a toddler, a child who does not yet speak but who is already no longer a nursling because he has repressed the inner nursling.

Freud may have been the first to discover the repressed child in the adult, but Klein was the first to identify in the child what is already repressed, that is, the nursling. As a result, she proposed not only a doctrine but also a framework necessary to the exercise of specifically infantile treatments: an appropriate decor, a specially adapted room with simple, sturdy furnishings, including a small table and chair and a small couch. Each child was to have his own toy box reserved for treatment, with small houses; figures of humans, farm animals, and wild animals; and blocks, balls, marbles, and art materials: scissors, string, pencils, paper, and modeling clay.

This conception of the clinical approach to children went hand in hand, for Klein and her partisans, with a recasting of the doctrine of female sexuality. Borrowing his models from Darwinian biology, Freud supported the thesis of sexual monism and of a "male" essence of the human libido. The latter derived from his own clinical observations of children's sexual theories; it was aimed neither at describing the difference between the sexes on the basis of anatomy nor at settling the question of the female condition in modern society.

Remaining within the perspective of a single libido, he claimed that, in early childhood, girls were unaware of the existence of the vagina and made the clitoris play the role of a penis equivalent. Thus, as he saw it,

girls had the impression that they were equipped with a castrated organ. As a function of this dissymmetry, evolving around a single pole of representations, the castration complex, he said, is not organized in the same way for the two sexes. Each has a different destiny, not only in anatomical terms, but also under the effect of the different representations attached to the anatomical features. At puberty, the vagina belongs to both sexes: boys see penetration as a goal for their sexuality, while girls repress their clitoral sexuality. But earlier, when boys see that girls do not resemble them, they interpret the absence of a penis in girls as a threat of castration for themselves. At the moment of the Oedipus complex, a boy detaches himself from his mother and chooses an object of the same sex.

Girls' sexuality, according to Freud, is organized around phallicism: they want to be boys. At the Oedipal moment, a girl desires to have her father's child, and this new object is invested with a phallic value. Unlike the boy, the girl has to detach herself from an object of the same sex, the mother, in favor of an object of the opposite sex. For both sexes, attachment to the mother is the primary element.

This analysis of "penis envy" was based on an empirical observation, made by Freud during a specific period of time, on which he relied to build his theory of infantile sexuality. From this perspective, which was in keeping with what children themselves said, Freud noted that girls identified with boys. Hence the psychoanalytic dogma that we find again in Abraham, for example: women unconsciously desire to be men because, in their childhood, they have experienced penis envy and have wanted to have a child with their father. The fact that this thesis is empirically correct does not mean that it is universally applicable, for, insofar as it is in phase with infantile subjectivity, it can change in response to transformations imposed by society.

Even though he was a partisan of sexual monism, Freud deemed erroneous any line of argument that affirmed the instinctual nature of sexuality. In his eyes, there was no such thing as a "maternal instinct" or a female "race," except in fantasies and myths constructed by men and women. As for the difference between the sexes, Freud took his inspiration from Greek myths and reduced it to an opposition between a separating *logos*—the male principle symbolized—and a profuse archaism, a state of maternal disorder anterior to reason. Hence his famous formula,

"Anatomy is destiny."[16] Contrary to what has been said, Freud never maintained that anatomy was the only possible destiny for the human condition. And he borrowed that formula from Napoleon, who had sought to inscribe the history of peoples to come in politics rather than in references to ancient myths.[17]

In other words, with this formula Freud, even though he had a very high regard for the ancient tragedies, nevertheless conceived of the great issue of the difference between the sexes in terms of a modern and more or less political dramaturgy. The stage described by Freud was thus inspired by the stage of the world and war as conceived by Napoleon.

In sum, we can say that if, for Freud, anatomy was part of human destiny, in no case did it represent, for every human being, an uncrossable horizon. Such is indeed the theory of freedom that stems from and is inherent in psychoanalysis: one must recognize the existence of destiny the better to free oneself from it. Moreover, Freud said, in the end, that anatomy never suffices to determine what is feminine or masculine.[18]

On the clinical level, the existence of a single libido did not mean that a libido could not be bisexual. On the contrary, it accounted for that possibility: in the Freudian perspective, no subject could possess a pure male or female specificity. In other words, if sexual monism is a solid hypothesis, this means that, in a subject's unconscious representations—whether that subject is male or female—the difference between the sexes, in the biological sense, does not exist. Bisexuality, which is the corollary of that monist organization, thus affects both sexes. Not only does the attraction of one sex for the other not stem from complementarity, but bisexuality undermines the very idea of such an organization. Whence the two distinct modes of homosexuality: feminine, when a girl remains "soldered" to her mother to the point of choosing a partner of the same sex, and masculine, when a boy makes a similar choice to the point of denying his mother's castration.

The Freudian thesis of the so-called Viennese school was supported by certain women, in particular Marie Bonaparte, Helene Deutsch, and Jeanne Lampl-De Groot. But it was contested, as early as 1920, by other women of the so-called English school: Klein, Josine Müller, and many others. Just as they challenged the primacy granted to the law of the father, to Freudian "phallocentrism," and to the educational ideal in the psycho-

analytic approach to children, these women criticized, and quite rightly, the extravagant Freudian hypothesis according to which girls had no sense of a vagina, and they opposed a dualism to the idea of a "female nature." Moreover, in treating children, they did not perceive this supposed absence of a sense of the vagina, nor the role attributed to the clitoris as a penis substitute. Under these conditions, the English school renewed the idea of a "female nature," that is, of a difference based on anatomy, where Freud had relativized it by placing the nonconscious differentiation between the two sexes in the category of a single male principle and an Oedipal organization in terms of dissymmetry.[19] In other words, the partisans of the English school were more "naturalist" than Freud: they believed that one is born a woman once and for all, whereas Freud said, rather, that womanliness is constructed with the help of representations. Whence the idea that women see themselves as failed or deficient men *(hommes manqués)*.

It was at the Innsbruck congress, in September 1927, under Max Eitingon's presidency, that a no-holds-barred war broke out between Anna Freud and Klein. The latter arrived, luminous and masterful, surrounded for the first time by her supporters, who were astounded by her statements about the "precocious stages of the oedipal conflict," though these were no longer "stages" but rather "phases" or "intrapsychic positions." Suffering increasingly from his cancer, Freud had decided to withdraw from the movement. Jones, who supported the theses of the English school, both on the analysis of children and on the question of female sexuality, did not try to put out the fire. He had succeeded in isolating Ferenczi and in creating a growing tension between Freud and his Hungarian disciple, deemed "paranoid," whereas in fact Ferenczi had good reasons to feel persecuted. Jones wanted to dissolve the committee and was already dreaming of holding the Verein meeting in England. Once again, his policy was coherent.

The debate over women and children took on considerable historical scope. This new quarrel between Ancients and Moderns initiated a change of paradigms tied to the transformations of Western society. And from this standpoint, English society, based on liberalism, empiricism, and individualism but also on culturalism, was more apt than continental Europe to welcome the Kleinian theses, which were deemed more

"feminist," more democratic, and more egalitarian than Freud's, for the latter still expressed strong attachment to a patriarchal model. It should be noted that this debate took place at a moment when the feminist movement was expanding internationally, paving the way, via the suffragists' efforts, to the legal and political emancipation of women. Traces of this development can be found in Virginia Woolf's *Three Guineas,* published in 1938. The author encouraged women to recognize their difference. Convinced that the warrior instinct, in that era, was peculiar to men, she compared masculine sexism to the triumphant fascisms of Germany and Italy, although she did not rule out the possibility that the phenomenon might be cultural rather than sexual in nature.[20]

Freud complained to Jones about the campaign orchestrated by the Kleinians against Anna. He was particularly disturbed to see that the lovely Riviere, a product of the English aristocracy and connected to the Bloomsbury group, had let herself be seduced by the Kleinian theories. Melancholic and insomniac, she had been perfectly analyzed by Freud, and he had great respect and deep affection for her, whereas Anna detested her. Riviere knew how to keep her distance without ever giving in to any sort of Kleinian idolatry.

In September, Jones wrote to Freud to confirm his disagreement with Anna's positions, but he attributed her resistances to the inadequacy of her analysis with her father: another occasion to psychologize scientific conflicts, the stakes of which were nevertheless unmistakably historical and political. Freud had acted the same way against Jung, and then Jung against Freud, then Jones against Rank, and so on. Once again, a vigorous debate between two different approaches to a single reality was interpreted by the protagonists themselves not as a change of paradigm but as an Oedipal affair.

Jones nevertheless reaffirmed his unswerving fidelity toward the master and his daughter. Freud did not want to get involved in that struggle even though he continued to think that the Kleinian path was erroneous, even as he acknowledged that experience would be the ultimate arbiter. But he was offended by the fact that the positions of the English school were already fixed even before Anna entered the debate:

In the behavior of the English toward Anna, two points remain inexcusable: the reproach, which is not customary among us and offends

against all good practice, that she was not analyzed sufficiently—put forward by you publicly and in private—and Mrs. Klein's remark that she believed Anna is avoiding the Oedipus complex on principle. With more good will, this misunderstanding could easily have been avoided.

More disconcerting to me than these tempests in a teapot are the theoretical statements of Riviere, especially because I have always had such a high opinion of her understanding. Here I must reproach you with having carried tolerance too far. If a member of any of our groups expresses such mistaken and misleading basic views, that is good reason for the group's leader to give that person a private lecture, but not a case for which one seeks to ensure the widest publicity, without critical comment.[21]

Experience gave the upper hand, against Freud, to Klein's theories, which took root throughout the world, among psychoanalysts specializing in early childhood, as London gradually imposed its leadership in the organization of psychoanalysis worldwide. But they were corrected and modified everywhere in an "Anna-Freudian manner," that is, in the sense of the integration of a pedagogic model into the process of treating children.[22]

Armed with his Oedipal psychology, his belief in the clitoris as a penis substitute, and his conviction that girls were aware of the inferiority of their "little penis," Freud had remained trapped in a conception of women, femininity, and love life that had arisen out of German Romanticism and *Naturphilosophie*. While his doctrine of sexual monism pulled him away from naturalism, he continued to bring it to bear on the way he looked at women and the "nature" of femininity. Once again, his positions were extremely complex, and Freud spent a good deal of time contradicting and combating himself.

He thought women were more passive than men, more bisexual as well, and that as a result female homosexuality was different from male homosexuality, that women's need to be loved was greater than men's, and that on the pathological level, by the same token, women were more masochistic than men, since their need to be loved readily turned into sexual pleasure in mistreatment. At the same time, he asserted that women develop a taste for sexual perversions only under the influence of men. He insisted on the fact that, in childhood, girls saw themselves

as "foreshortened" and worthless, and that they resented their mothers for having given birth to them as women rather than as men: they had "penis envy." He saw relations between a man and a woman in terms of complementarity, a view that ran counter to his doctrine of sexual monism. A woman must be the sweet companion of a man, he said, and she gains nothing by practicing a professional activity or pursuing studies, since her natural condition is to maintain three "inevitable" relationships with men: as genitrix, companion, and destroyer, three forms through which the image of the mother passed during the course of a man's life—his mother herself, the lover he chose in his mother's image, and, ultimately, the earth mother who welcomed him once again to her breast.

As a good Darwinian, well versed in the theory of the "stages" of evolution, and a great decipherer, like Oedipus before the Sphinx, of the riddle of human destiny, that is, of the three ages of man, Freud always claimed that women embodied for men three forms of femininity: the desirable girl, the beloved spouse, and the mother who loved her newborn child more than her adolescent son. In other words, a woman as conceived by Freud encompassed within herself not only the three types of femininity referring to the nurturing earth, and thus to birth and death, but also, like the three Moirai of Greek mythology (the Roman Parcae), three modalities of fate. In each woman, he thought, man rediscovers three goddesses from Olympus: the "spinner" who manipulates the spool on which existence unfolds, the "fateful" one who holds the hourglass, and the "inflexible" one who cuts the thread of life. Whence the fact that, for him, women's greatest contribution to culture had been the invention of weaving.[23]

To flesh out the underlying hypothesis of this representation of women, Freud relied on one of his favorite characters: King Lear. In Shakespeare's play, the mad monarch is determined to find out which of his daughters loves him the most, and he sentences the best of them, Cordelia, to exile, an act that leads to the collapse of his kingdom and his family line. Thus, at the end of the tragedy, recognizing his mistake too late, he holds Cordelia's lifeless body in his arms: "But it is in vain that an old man yearns for the love of woman, as he had it first from his mother; the third of the Fates alone, the silent Goddess of Death, will take him into her arms."[24]

The father of three daughters, surrounded in his residence at 19 Berggasse by three women (Martha, Minna, and Anna), Freud found in Greek mythology and in Shakespeare's dramas the echo of his conception of the three functions of femininity—the woman-mother, the lover-spouse, the goddess Earth—that offer themselves to a man during his lifetime. He seized particularly upon the thematics he found in the judgment of Paris, in one of Charles Perrault's tales ("Cinderella"), in a tale by Apuleius ("Cupid and Psyche"), and also in a famous scene from Shakespeare's *Merchant of Venice*, a comic version of the tragedy of King Lear. In *The Merchant of Venice*, young Portia is forced by her father to take as her husband the suitor who, from among the three caskets presented to him, chooses the right one. The three caskets are made of gold, silver, and lead, respectively, and the "right" one is the one containing the girl's portrait. Two of the rivals have already withdrawn without success, having chosen the gold and the silver caskets. Bassanio, the third, decides on the lead one and wins the fiancée, who had inclinations in his favor even before the trial.

According to Freud, each casket represented a type of femininity, and Portia, represented by lead (a "mute" metal), is the simplest of the three women, the least troublesome: she loves and she remains silent. In this, she resembles the faithful Cordelia, "the dead one."

Freud liked women who were faithful and intelligent, not too beautiful but knowledgeable about life and devoted to their offspring, and he was in favor of their access to civil rights. He had a horror of adultery and a strong dislike for courtesans and brothels. He railed against the misogyny of certain of his Viennese disciples and certain doctors in his milieu who looked at women as beings physiologically inferior to men. This inequality, he said, did not exist in the unconscious: it is a phantasmic construction. Moreover, he saw hatred and denigration of women as one of the unconscious roots of anti-Semitism.

And just as he had described infantile sexuality on the basis of theories invented by children, as he built his doctrine of sexuality he took into account not only masculine representations of femininity but also feminine representations of masculinity. This is one of the reasons why he contradicted himself so constantly over the years.

If women, according to Freud, feel deprived of a penis, men, if they are to gain access to women other than their mothers, need to overcome

the respect that mothers impose on them. And, he added, they have to integrate the idea of incest with mothers or sisters. Freud explained that this passage from the mother to *the other woman* was expressed in the need felt by men to engage in sexual relations with women of lower social standing than their own, noting that one frequently sees a "tendency . . . in men of the highest classes of society to choose a woman of a lower class as a permanent mistress or even as a wife."[25]

Freud preferred a good divorce to a bad marriage, and he thought that the use of condoms frustrated women by depriving them of orgasms on the same basis as coitus interruptus. From the 1920s on, however, he thought that female contraception was far preferable to the other means available for controlling procreation. A charming puritan, he adored seducing women with words. His epistolary art, in which he was virtually a genius, was as rich as his carnal desires were limited, and his erotic imagination as luxuriant as his sexual practice was impoverished. In his heart of hearts, he wondered about one of the most obvious and best-known cleavages in amorous relationships: how to keep love and desire united in men. "Where they love they do not desire," he said, "and where they desire they cannot love."[26] Oddly, he did not want to see that women were as subject as men to this cleavage, and that they too could presumably choose a man of lower social standing as lover or husband.

These diverse representations of women had shocking aspects, not only for generations of feminists but also for the women present in the psychoanalytic movement at the time. Once again, moreover, these representations were in contradiction both with the Freudian doctrine of female sexuality and with Freud's attitudes toward women in general. For, rather than encouraging them to take up knitting or weaving, he pushed them to engage in a professional activity and to ensure their societal independence. He knew that the familial organization to which he adhered in his personal life would not last, and that the women and men of future generations would be very different from the ones he had known: he saw the traces of that evolution in the lifestyles of his own children, even if he denied this and wanted to see them in his own image. Convinced, rightly, that his doctrine, while it was quite remote from the feminists' struggles, played a major role in the emancipation of women, he saw himself as a man of the past who had not himself benefited from

the sexual revolution that he had brought to Western society. The twentieth century was in a sense more Freudian than Freud himself.

Without mentioning Amalia, Freud did not hesitate to assert that only the relation to the son brought a mother unlimited satisfaction. And he added, "A mother can transfer to her son the ambition which she has been obliged to suppress in herself, and she can expect from him the satisfaction of all that has been left over in her of her masculinity complex. Even a marriage is not made secure until the wife has succeeded in making her husband her child as well and in acting as a mother to him."[27] In other words, for Freud, every woman is first of all a potential mother whom man needs to belittle in order to make her a sexual object. As a result, he said, the starting point for a sexual relationship lies in orality: sucking the breast or its substitute. Every man repeats this initial choice in his life: finding the mother in multiple forms, from passion to hatred, from happiness to despair.

Even as Freud was developing a rational theory of sexuality, by opposing the visions of ideologues haunted by terror of the feminine, he was taking up again on his own account the ancestral idea according to which women are for men the greatest mystery in the entire history of civilization. Men, he said, have always feared the secret, terrifying power held by women, and they are not about to free themselves from it. Let us recall Tiresias here. Man and woman at once, he knew the mystery about which gods and men wondered: Which one, man or woman, benefits most from sexual congress? Consulted by Zeus and Hera, he had dared to assert that women drew from coitus nine times more pleasure than men did. Having betrayed the so savagely protected secret of orgasmic pleasure, he was struck blind by Hera but rewarded by Zeus, who gave him the gift of prophecy and the power to live for seven generations.[28]

And it was in fact this mythology that Freud appropriated in terms that came both from dark Romanticism—"What does a woman want?"—and colonial literature: "After all, the sexual life of an adult woman," he said in 1926, "is a 'dark continent for psychology.' "[29] On that occasion, he was alluding to a best seller by the British journalist Henry Morton Stanley, who had explored the Congo in the late nineteenth century, bringing back from his expedition a naïve and paternocentric vision of Africa, a continent depicted as dark and bewitching, feminine and wild, not yet explored

by civilization.[30] And it was to that "dark continent," toward which the civilizing mission of the West was oriented, that Freud compared the sexual life of women. By way of that slogan, which met with lasting success, he expressed as much the fear of the white man in the face of a continent reinvented by colonial discourse as the anxiety experienced by Man (in the generic sense) before the excesses of female sexuality: untamed nature, an obscure zone, a mystery not yet cleared up by science, and so on. Is it not likely that Freud had experienced that same terror, very early in his life? Had he not expressed a certain fear in the presence of the black chow chows? He himself was born "dark."

However this may be, the Freudian doctrine in question was in large part a masculine representation of women and femininity inherited from the late nineteenth century.[31] Freud knew this, and he asserted that only more modern women, trained in psychoanalysis, would be capable in the future of understanding so-called pre-Oedipal female sexuality. Posterity proved both approaches—Freudian and Kleinian—right, along with many others that were more productive.[32]

From 1920 on, Freud's principal female disciples or patients were quite different from those in his family. Englishwomen, Americans, Germans, Austrians, almost all were from the upper social classes, and they all had acquired a degree of independence and a way of life that contrasted not only with those of the pioneers in the first generation of the WPV but also with the situation of the women of 19 Berggasse, as with those of Freud's mother, sisters, and daughters.

Until the 1920s—with just a few exceptions—the women psychoanalysts who were present in the movement had remained in the men's shadows. Henceforth more visible, having shed their corsets and their wide skirts, they made their second entrance into history writ large by becoming full-fledged actors in the psychoanalytic movement. If most of them suffered from melancholia, boredom, or various neuroses, often owing to a troubled familial or marital context, they found in psychoanalysis the means to gain access to a trade, to engage in a cause, to transform their existence, or more simply to participate in an intellectual adventure. This was true in particular of Deutsch, Hilda Doolittle, Edith Jacobson, Ruth Mack Brunswick, Dorothy Burlingham, Riviere, Marianne Kris, and Margaret Stonborough-Wittgenstein.[33]

Two very different women, Lou Andreas-Salomé and Bonaparte, one German and one French, neither a Jew, played major roles in the second part of Freud's life, becoming part of his circle of disciples and of his close family circle as well. Each received a ring symbolizing their initiation into the Ring.

Born in Saint Petersburg, five years younger than Freud, Andreas-Salomé belonged to the German aristocracy. Early on she chose to devote herself to intellectual life and to refuse to submit to the norms of bourgeois marriage. An emblematic figure of the narcissistic femininity that she brought to incandescence, she thought that women were freer than men. The latter, she said, were constrained by their culture to practice a domination that could only leave them feeling guilty. In contrast, women, who were capable of giving themselves fully in sexual intercourse, experienced neither shame nor embarrassment. This was the perspective from which she conceived of sexual intercourse as a physical passion that is exhausted once desire has been satisfied. Consequently, only intellectual love, based on absolute fidelity, is capable of being sustained over time. In a text on eroticism published in 1910, Andreas-Salomé commented on one of the great themes of literature, from Emma Bovary to Anna Karenina, according to which the separation between amorous folly and conjugal tranquility, usually impossible to overcome, had to be fully experienced. She knew that her arguments in favor of marriages in which each partner was authorized to practice regenerative sexual freedom were somewhat far fetched, not only because they went against the moral commandments of religion, but because they were incompatible with the powerful possessive instinct rooted in men.

Nevertheless, throughout her life she never stopped putting this separation into practice, shrugging off invective, rumors, and scandal. After Nietzsche, Freud was dazzled by this woman who shook up his existence: they shared the same pride, the same excesses, the same energy, the same courage, even the same way of loving and possessing the chosen love objects feverishly.[34] The one had chosen sexual abstinence with the same strength and the same will that drove the other to satisfy her desires. They had a common intransigence, and the certainty that friendship should never mask divergences or impinge on the freedom of either partner.

In June 1887, Lou had married the German Orientalist Friedrich-Carl Andreas, who taught at the University of Göttingen. The marriage was not consummated, and it was Georg Ledebourg, founder of the German Social Democratic Party, who became her first lover, some time before Friedrich Pineles, a Viennese doctor. This second liaison ended in an abortion and a tragic renunciation of maternity. Andreas-Salomé then moved to Munich, where she met the young poet Rainer Maria Rilke. "If I was your wife for years," she wrote in her memoirs, "it was because you were the first *truly real* person in my life, body and man indivisibly one, unquestionably a fact of life itself. . . . We were siblings—but from a time before incest had become sacrilege."[35]

Andreas-Salomé's espousal of the Nietzschean conception of narcissism, and more generally of the cult of the ego, characteristic of the turn-of-the-century *Lebensphilosophie,* paved the way for her encounter with psychoanalysis. In all her texts, as Jacques Le Rider points out, she sought in fact to rediscover a cosmogonic eros capable of compensating for the irreparable loss of the feeling that there was a God.[36] It was in 1911, in Weimar, that she met Freud for the first time. At that point she was the lover of Poul Bjerre, a young Swedish psychoanalyst fifteen years her junior: "Time had softened her features somewhat," her biographer Heinz Frederick Peters wrote, "and she added a touch of femininity by wearing soft fur pieces, boas and capes, over her shoulders. . . . Her physical beauty was matched, if not outshone, by the brightness of her spirit, her *joie de vivre,* her wit and her warm humanity."[37]

Freud fled from feminine beauty, and at first he mistrusted the attraction he felt for this exceptional woman. Very quickly, however, he came to love her for the intelligence of her soul, her passion for living, her unshakeable optimism. She embodied all the facets of the femininity that was so familiar and at the same time so foreign to him. In fact, she seemed to contradict his thesis about the three states of female life, because she had remained a desirable young girl without becoming a mother, and a mature woman who refused to take on the role of a spouse and homemaker but never gave up her sexual activity. Rather than seeing her as a mystery, Freud offered her the highest form of love of which he was capable: a friendship that entailed elegance, seduction, and courtesy, along with an intellectual exchange such as he had never had

with any of his disciples or other interlocutors. For the first time, he would not transform the indispensable friend into an indispensable enemy.

Freud was aware, from their very first meeting, that Andreas-Salomé hoped to be admired, even to be freed of her own overly strong personality, and that she had experienced tragedy in giving up motherhood. From then on he understood that she truly wanted to devote herself to psychoanalysis and that nothing would stop her. That is why he accepted her immediately among the members of the WPV. Her silent presence attested in everyone's eyes to a continuity between Nietzsche and Freud, between Vienna and German culture, between literature and psychoanalysis. It was evident that Freud was in love with her, and that is why he would insist forcefully, as if to defend himself against what he was experiencing, that that attachment had nothing to do with any physical attraction.

Having moved to Vienna in 1912, Andreas-Salomé attended as many of the meetings organized by Alfred Adler as she did those organized by Freud's circle. Jealous, Freud left her alone but did not hesitate to call his rival a "repugnant character." One evening, suffering from Andreas-Salomé's absence, he wrote, "I missed you in the lecture yesterday and I am glad to hear that your visit to the camp of masculine protest played no part in your absence. I have adopted the bad habit of always directing my lecture to a definite member of the audience, and yesterday I fixed my gaze as if spellbound at the place which had been kept for you."[38]

She soon espoused the Freudian cause exclusively, and it was then that she fell in love with Viktor Tausk, the most handsome and most melancholic man in Freud's circle. He was almost twenty years her junior. Alongside Tausk, Andreas-Salomé was initiated into analytic practice, visited hospitals, observed cases that interested her, and met Viennese intellectuals. After each Wednesday meeting, Freud took her back to her hotel, and after every dinner, he plied her with flowers. One day, a particularly fanatic disciple indulged, with her, in one of the group's favorite sports: the mania for interpretation. While she was knitting, as many women did at the time, he pointed to her and remarked that she seemed to experience pleasure in practicing continual intercourse, as symbolized by the movement of her needles. She did not respond.

Andreas-Salomé belonged to the same world as Freud, and she shared the same values and the same elitist representation of Belle Époque Europe; she was unaware of its dark side. Thus she was surprised by the outbreak of the First World War. While Freud emphasized that this conflict resembled an instinctual eruption buried in the popular unconscious, Andreas-Salomé saw war in general as a sort of vampire that sucks blood to appease man's need to destroy himself: "We are all and always murderers of our own selves and of each other. That is perhaps unavoidable but because of it our guilt is terribly universal and our only means of redemption is to accept it as such. . . . When I had understood that I realized with astonishment that for this reason I would have fought too, if I had been a man, and if I had borne sons I would have sent my sons to war."[39]

Freud was clearly on the side of the vanquished, but for Andreas-Salomé the war represented an even greater collapse. On which side would she have fought? With the Russians, or the Germans? She did not share the nationalist sentiments of her compatriots in the German-speaking world, but even so she could not support the anti-German combat of her Russian brothers. Thus she viewed the unleashing of hatred as a fratricidal struggle internal to her own subjectivity. And at the time of the October Revolution, she proved resolutely hostile to Bolshevism. Earlier, she had admired the Russian revolutionaries and their utopian ideal, but now, like Count Pierre Bezukhov[40] during the advance of Napoleon's troops on Moscow, she saw only the tragedy that was befalling her country. And Freud responded to her in the same tone: "Revolutions, I believe, are acceptable only when they are over; and therefore they ought to be over very quickly. What the human beast needs above all is restraint. In short, one grows reactionary, just as incidentally did the rebel Schiller in the face of the French Revolution."[41] Neither Freud nor Andreas-Salomé had understood the deep misery of the populations.

After the war, Andreas-Salomé spent six months looking after sufferers of traumatic neuroses in a work camp in Königsberg. While Freud manifested increasing pessimism about the deadly tendencies of humanity, Andreas-Salomé rediscovered her joie de vivre as she began to devote herself to the practice of psychoanalysis in Göttingen. For years she was thus present in the psychoanalytic movement on the same basis as Freud: always in the background and always close to the familial circle that had

welcomed her but that was already giving way to the new generation of young Anglophone practitioners, who were less fettered by the memory of yesteryear.

With Andreas-Salomé, Freud finally encountered an interlocutor whom he could treat as an equal, as a foreigner, and as a woman in his family. Thus he encouraged her to become the protector of his daughter, with whom he was having so much difficulty. And by receiving the secrets that Anna shared with her about her own analysis, her sexuality, her troubles, she became Anna's second therapist: she supervised the treatment carried out by Freud on "the girl Anna" even as she welcomed with tact and with gourmandise the savor of this relationship. With Anna, Andreas-Salomé talked about shawls, fur trimmings, fur coats, and the long garments that reminded her of her Russian youth impregnated with Tolstoy's novels. Between confidences, Anna talked to her about the smell of brioches and their shared love of dogs and of mushroom harvesting.

Over the years, Freud and Andreas-Salomé watched each other age while also witnessing the decomposition of the Germany of Goethe and Nietzsche of which they were heirs. In 1931, for the seventy-fifth birthday of her cherished professor, Andreas-Salomé devoted a book to him, in which she expressed her gratitude and her disagreements, especially regarding the mistakes made by the movement about artistic creation and about faith, which Freud reduced to a form of alienation: the book was a plea against the dogmatism that was already firmly rooted. Freud responded that she was bringing a feminine order to the ambivalent disorder of his own thought.[42] One could hardly put it better.

Andreas-Salomé had very little opportunity to encounter Marie Bonaparte, who was twenty years younger. Opposites as much by their culture, their lifestyles, and their relation to Freudianism as by their origins, the two women nevertheless had in common the vibrant love they felt for Freud. Andreas-Salomé had come from a world in its death throes; Bonaparte was a conqueror holding high the virile banner of her great-great-uncle; she identified with the name much more than with the imperial pomp: "If anyone ever writes my life story, it should be titled 'The Last Bonaparte,' for that's what I am. My cousins from the imperial branch are only Napoleons."[43] If, for Freud, Andreas-Salomé was the embodiment of intelligence, beauty, and freedom, something like *the* woman, Bonaparte

became rather the daughter, the student, the patient, the disciple, the exceptional translator, the devoted ambassador, the lover of chow chows, and the organizer of the French psychoanalytic movement, over which she was to reign in a sometimes disastrous manner for decades.

She reconciled Freud with the France he loved: that of Voltaire, Anatole France, Balzac, Sarah Bernhardt, Philippe Pinel, Jean-Martin Charcot, and Zola. But she had no more interest than he did in the real representatives of literary modernity, the surrealists in particular, despite the central role they played in the introduction of psychoanalysis in France. He called her *Prinzessin* (his princess), and when she purported to compete with the *other woman,* he exclaimed, "Lou Andreas-Salomé is a mirror; she has neither your virility nor your sincerity nor your style."[44]

The daughter of Roland Bonaparte, who was Lucien Bonaparte's grandson, Bonaparte had lost her mother at birth and had been brought up by a father who was solely preoccupied with his work in anthropology and by a paternal grandmother who was a veritable domestic tyrant, avid for success and notoriety. Thus Bonaparte bore in herself the suicidal anguish that was often found among the heirs to European dynasties in the early twentieth century, who were condemned to wander in a simulacrum of their lost grandeur. Having inherited, from her mother, an immense fortune that she didn't know how to handle, she resembled a character from the great Freudian theater of the early days: a true princess prey to an aristocratic neurosis and in search of a master who would be at once her father, her mother, her king, and her ancestor.

Still, never forgetting her Corsican origins and her position in the Bonaparte genealogy, which had made her a rational republican attached to the ideals of the most highly developed science of her day, she did not manifest the slightest nostalgia for the old world, even if her arranged marriage with Prince George of Greece, a homosexual and lover of her uncle Valdemar, a Danish prince, had raised her to the rank of royal grandeur, of highly honored monarchic nobility. In reality, even though she was attached to the codes and rituals of her caste, Bonaparte made fun of all conformist theories; she had multiple amorous affairs and suffered from an unconquerable frigidity, which led her to become smitten with all the sexological theories of her day. Haunted by her inadequate femininity, someone whose name and kinship ties were linked as much to the

kingdom of Hamlet as to the tragedy of Oedipus or to the bridge at Arcola (the site of a famous battle in which Napoleon led the successful charge against the Austrians), how could such a princess have avoided a Freudian destiny?

When she met Freud in Vienna on September 30, 1925, on the advice of René Laforgue,[45] she was on the verge of suicide. She moved, with her chambermaid, into a suite at the Bristol Hotel where she was received with all the honors due her title of Royal Highness, Princess of Greece and of Denmark. She found the place lugubrious.

Under the pseudonym A. E. Narjani, she had just published, in Belgium, an article in which she praised the merits of a surgical operation that was fashionable at the time: it consisted in shifting the clitoris closer to the vagina so as to transfer the clitoral orgasm toward the vagina.[46] She believed that this was a remedy for female frigidity and she tried the operation herself in Vienna, but she failed to achieve any results.[47]

Freud initially mistrusted this famous, worldly woman who spent fortunes buying clothes and maintaining her lifestyle. In response to Laforgue, who extolled the princess's intellectual merits, her desire to undertake training and therapeutic analysis, he required that she be able to speak German or English, forgetting that she was as European as he and as polyglot as most of his disciples. At bottom, he had little inclination to concern himself with a person he deemed frivolous. And yet with her, from 1925 to 1928, he carried out, in stages, one of the most successful treatments in the entire history of his practice: he kept her from suicide and from numerous destructive transgressions. Bonaparte recorded the unfolding of this analysis in her *Sommaire,* adding notes, reflections, and confidential remarks about Freud of considerable interest for all historians.

From the very beginning of her treatment, Bonaparte was the beneficiary of a strong interpretation. Following her account of a dream in which she saw herself in her cradle witnessing scenes of sexual intercourse, Freud asserted in a peremptory tone that she had not only heard these scenes, like most children who sleep in their parents' bedroom, but that she had seen them in broad daylight. Stunned, and always concerned with material evidence, she challenged this assertion and protested that she had not had a mother. Freud held his ground and objected that the wet nurse had been present. Finally, she decided to question her father's half brother,

who looked after the horses in her childhood home. By evoking before him the high scientific import of psychoanalysis, she made him confess his former affair with the nurse. Somewhat ashamed, the old man related how he had made love in broad daylight in the presence of Bonaparte's cradle. She thus had in fact witnessed scenes of sexual intercourse, fellatio, and cunnilingus.

This interpretation has to be compared to the one given to Pankejeff. In that first case, Freud had invented a primal scene that had never occurred but that had allowed the patient to give a meaning to his dream about wolves. In the second, the patient refused to believe in the existence of that scene, which, however, had been verified as having actually taken place. In each case, the notion of a "primal scene" took on the value of a myth, referring to an unconscious genealogy.

With this woman who showered him with gifts, Freud thus proved his clinical genius. During the analysis, he kept her from an incestuous relation with her son, and he explained why patients must not take their clothes off during treatment sessions. In addition, he refused to answer the questions she asked him about his sexual life, and he gave her to understand that she must not exhibit herself in front of him. As he himself was undergoing painful surgical procedures, he scarcely had the means, in such a transferential situation, to interpret the orgasmic pleasure Bonaparte experienced when she handled a scalpel.

By integrating herself into the psychoanalytic movement, Bonaparte took part in the debate over female sexuality in a very personal way. She in fact transformed the Freudian doctrine into a psychological topology of the biological instincts, a topology that differed from the approaches of both the Viennese and the English schools. She distinguished three categories of women: the demanders, who sought to appropriate the male penis; the accepters, who adapted to the reality of their biological functions or their social role; and the renouncers, who detached themselves from sexuality.[48]

Freud was clearly fascinated by these stories of cut-off clitorises and he found in Bonaparte's insistence on surgery a "biologized" echo of his own theses. And this is why he offered her *Neger-Eros*, the famous work by the Viennese anthropologist Felix Bryk devoted to the practice of excision among the Nandi. The author showed how the men of that tribe

sought, through excision, to feminize the bodies of their partners to an extreme extent by suppressing the last vestige of the penile organ. And he pointed out to her that that operation did not abolish the women's capacity to experience orgasm; otherwise the men of the tribe would not have allowed it.

Once again, Freud dealt in ambivalence. On the one hand, he told Bonaparte that no surgery would be able to solve the problem of female frigidity, and on the other he encouraged her to do research in that area. It was all she needed. She hastened to undertake investigations into her fetish subject; she was to repeat that gesture throughout her life.

Such was the interpretive limit encountered by Freud in Bonaparte's treatment: he never succeeded in keeping his dear princess from pursuing her muddled quest for an unfindable femininity. Must we not see in this failure the sign of the impossible situation in which Freud found himself, unable to escape the infernal spiral of the "cut-off clitoris," a veritable *dark continent* of his own thinking about the feminine?

PART FOUR

The Final Years

Between Fetish Medicine and Religion

As MEDICINE BECAME more and more scientific, national governments found it increasingly necessary to regulate therapeutic activities. Although it was fully integrated into the field of medicine, psychiatry saw itself as all the more rational in its classifications in that it did not rely on the same clinical criteria as those used by the rest of the medical field. Nevertheless, in transforming a "crazy" person into a "case," that is, into a "sick" person, it had come closer to traditional medicine in the sense that the subject was conceived simply as an object that could be entered into a nosographic framework. And it was on this terrain that Freud, coming out of neurology and psychology, had built his discipline as a branch of psychology, while also harking back to the dynamic tradition of Franz Anton Mesmer: magnetism, hypnotism, suggestion, catharsis, and finally transference.[1] Psychoanalysis restored speech to the subject and relaunched the old idea according to which the patient, rather than the doctor, possessed the power to come to terms with mental suffering.

However, by creating institutions for the purpose of training practitioners throughout Europe and in the Western Hemisphere, after the First World War Freud and his disciples could no longer escape the regulations that various countries were gradually adopting in order to protect patients from pretenders, impostors, drug peddlers, and other unauthorized therapists known at the time as "charlatans."

Every society, as we know, has a place for the figure of the charlatan, owing to the very fact that a society can only reproduce itself by clearly defining whom it includes and whom it excludes by virtue of the norms it has settled on. Thus a charlatan, whatever he or she is called, is always

a figure of heterogeneity. Defined as "the accursed share,"[2] charlatanism is what eludes reason or the *logos:* the devil, the excluded, the sacred, stains, instincts, the unmentionable. But by the same token it encompasses drugs (the *pharmakon*), the purveyor of drugs (the *pharmakos*), and the scapegoat or the martyr, who must be punished so that civil society can regenerate itself. A charlatan is thus a dual being, one who accepts a sanction and is at the same time the very condition of any sanction. Whether a poisoner or a healer, a tyrant or a miserable wretch, the charlatan is the *other* of science and reason, the *other* of ourselves.[3] On this theme, Freud, a man of the dark Enlightenment who had been a cocaine enthusiast, found himself on familiar ground, between nostalgia and the practice of a scathing humor. He suffered more every day from the two-headed intruder that impeded his speech: the prosthesis that he called his "muzzle" and the cancer that was spreading inexorably.

Psychoanalysis, then, had been regarded by the medical authorities as a strange entity, as a charlatanic intrusion. After all, Freudian doctrine invoked Oedipus, a sage among sages but also a monster and a stain, even though the new movement had been created by a bourgeois elite: doctors, men of letters, lawyers, all holding university degrees. The accusation of charlatanism can be explained in part by the fact that Freud viewed psychoanalysis as a separate, full-fledged discipline that only "initiates" were authorized to practice. Hence his hostility to the creation of university programs designed to teach psychoanalysis, even though he himself taught in a university framework. In other words, he himself labeled in advance as a "charlatan" any person who might teach the Freudian doctrine without having been analyzed.

Moreover, like Ernest Jones, was he not concerned with eliminating from his movement any practitioner deemed "dangerous," psychotic, deviant, suicidal, or transgressive, and also any "unauthorized" analyst? Otto Rank and Sándor Ferenczi ended up paying the price of this exclusion. And yet Freud himself had strayed from this path by supporting psychotics and pretenders—such as Horace Frink and Hermine von Hug-Hellmuth—and by taking a dangerous interest in all sorts of occult phenomena. And since the upholders of scientific medicine were hunting down charlatans at the time, the psychoanalysts were ideal prey.

The trouble began in Austria in 1924, when Freud sent Newton Murphy, an American doctor who wanted to pursue psychoanalytic treatment, for

analysis with Theodor Reik. Freud had not noticed that this patient, seemingly neurotic, presented signs of psychosis. Unhappy with the treatment, Murphy turned against his analyst and lodged a complaint against him for the illegal practice of medicine. Even before this incident occurred, the physiologist Arnold Durig, a member of the High Council on Health of the City of Vienna, had asked Freud for an expert opinion on the analysis practiced by nondoctors, called "lay analysis" *(Laienanalyse)*.[4] The opinion rendered had convinced the authorities, and the matter took on considerable proportions in February 1925 when Reik was forbidden to practice psychoanalysis; the situation was all the more dramatic for him because he had no other source of income. For more than a year, the question of the definition of charlatanism inflamed minds in the German-speaking world and in the North American press alike. Such an interdiction threatened to harm women psychoanalysts most of all, since far fewer of them had diplomas than their male counterparts, but it was also a threat to all those who with good reason claimed that the discipline Freud had invented went far beyond the framework of medicine for the mind. The richness of the psychoanalytic movement had to do with the diversity of those who had taken it up. Coming from all over Europe, almost all polyglot, the Freudians had acquired a vast culture in the areas of science, literature, sociology, philosophy, and anthropology. Few of them were self-taught. The determination to push them into a single mold contributed to a real lowering of their social and ideological power to intervene.

Always ready to fight the WPV, Wilhelm Stekel, president of the Association of Independent Medical Analysts, threw himself into the battle against lay analysis, forcefully denouncing the scandal related to the Hug-Hellmuth affair and the abuses committed by Freud's disciples. Forgetting that he himself was subject to dark pathological states, he reaffirmed his thesis according to which an overly prolonged analysis led necessarily to suicide.[5] But he did not spell out how medical doctors could be better clinicians of the mind than nondoctors. As for the terrible Karl Kraus, he let loose once again in *Die Fackel,* asserting that the popularity of Freudianism was disrupting tourism in Vienna: everybody in the world, he claimed, was squeezing into the palaces of the old Habsburg capital to have the honor of lying on the couch at 19 Berggasse. Julius Wagner-Jauregg, for his part, even though he himself had been the victim of an

accusation of poor treatment, did not hesitate to write a report stipulating that only doctors should have the privilege of practicing Freudian analysis.[6]

Accused of "sabotaging" treatments, the nonmedical psychoanalysts thus became scapegoats. Unquestionably, what was happening constituted a new attack on psychoanalysis itself. For the assailants knew perfectly well that, in the realm of psychic treatment, the status of medical doctor did not prevent diagnostic errors or the divagations of patients suffering from mental illness or melancholia, who were often doctors themselves. For a long time, psychiatrists, despite being doctors, had already been periodically labeled charlatans by their colleagues, or charged with being as mentally ill as their patients—and sometimes they actually were. In reality, as we have seen, in the early 1920s the preoccupation with safety took precedence over concern about the clinical qualities of doctors or nondoctors.

However, another question was being raised: How would a nonmedical analyst be able to tell the difference between a symptom of hysteria and an organic illness? It was all very well to say that an analyst who had had medical training could make mistakes even more frequently than a lay analyst who was concerned with proving himself as a diagnostician, but in the end the conclusion was that a practitioner had to have a degree in medicine rather than in philosophy or psychology. Only child psychoanalysis was excepted, as it was associated with a form of pedagogy.

Reik, who came from a midlevel bourgeois Jewish family, had met Freud in 1911. From the outset he viewed the Professor as a father. Freud was as fond of him as he was of Rank, and he advised Reik to give up the medical studies he was contemplating, the better to devote himself to historical and anthropological research. Jones and several other disciples were jealous of Reik, and they made fun of his arrogance, his way of submitting to the master, of always justifying the critiques that Freud addressed to him.[7]

In Vienna, Reik was known as the enfant terrible of psychoanalysis, the "king's fool," or "Simili Freud." He indulged in imitating the master with a sort of passion that only translated the enthusiasm of the transference and countertransference of which he himself was a brilliant theoretician. He looked like Freud, sported the same beard, smoked Freud's cigars, spoke like Freud, but he never dared call himself Freud's friend:

"No, I'm not his friend," he confided one day, "one can't be the friend of a genius."[8] This identification with the figure of the "great man" did not prevent him from being an original author, and that is why Freud maintained an exemplary fidelity toward him, as he was able to do when he recognized an authentic talent among those close to him. He helped Reik financially, sent him patients, and entrusted him with intellectual and political tasks, without ever hesitating to criticize his disciple when he deemed it necessary.

With Reik, the love of Goethe had preceded the love of Freud. But, having failed to become a great writer himself, he took on the task of reading the totality of the poet's work. Later, he discovered in Freud the sublimated image of a Goethe transfigured by psychoanalysis. In this context the poet's work became for him the inexhaustible source of all possible forms of autobiographical expression, a way of telling one's life story without appearing to yield to the ceremonial of the personal journal. Like Freud, he thought that writers and poets had deeper access to the unconscious—in particular to their own unconscious—than the specialists of the mind. Thus literary works ought to serve as models, not only for writing up clinical cases, but for the psychoanalytic method itself, as a scientific exploration of subjectivity.

Goethe's work thus occupied a privileged place at the heart of this apparatus. Disguised as a model of Freudian introspection, it allowed Reik to project his own history onto that of the narrator of *Poetry and Truth,* that is, onto an autobiography that was itself reinterpreted in the light of psychoanalysis and Freud's writings. Goethe, as we know, delighted in cultivating self-dissimulation, declaring readily that no man can ever know himself. That did not keep him from confessing and speaking abundantly about himself. For that reason, he was already one of the authors most studied by the German-speaking psychoanalytic community during this period.[9] His *Faust* was the object of numerous interpretations, as many as *Hamlet* or *Oedipus.*

When he was the victim of an accusation of charlatanism, despite having doctorates in psychology and philosophy, Reik was all the more destabilized in that his Viennese colleagues offered no support whatsoever. Unable to remain indifferent to his disciple's fate, Freud reacted on March 8, 1925, by writing a letter to Julius Tandler, whom he had gotten

to know well in the aftermath of an affair involving war neuroses. Tandler was a municipal councillor in charge of welfare and health; a year earlier, he had helped obtain the title of "honorary citizen of the city of Vienna" for Freud. Although he was a Social Democrat, a prominent personality in "Red Vienna," Tandler was known for his conservative positions. Hostile to the admission of women to universities and opposed to the liberalization of abortion, he nevertheless defended the interests of psychoanalysis in an alliance with Karl Friedjung, a Social Democrat as well, a Zionist pediatrician who belonged to the WPV, and a pure representative of the end-of-century Viennese culture for which he had remained nostalgic.[10]

In his letter, Freud stressed that psychoanalysis was neither a science nor a technique belonging to the medical profession, and that it was not taught as such in the Faculty of Medicine:

> I see in the decree of the municipality an unjustified impingement in favor of the interests of the medical corporation to the detriment both of patients and of scientific research. Therapeutic interests are protected when the doctor has the exclusive privilege of deciding whether a given patient can be submitted to an analytic treatment or not. These are decisions I have made myself in all the cases Dr. Reik has treated. I claim the right to send a patient who finds it tiring to walk and whose feet hurt to an orthopedist, when I can diagnose flat feet in this patient, instead of prescribing pain medication and electric shock treatment. If the official authorities, from which official psychoanalysis has had so little satisfaction, now want to consider it as an active medication, even dangerous in certain cases, they ought to require certain guarantees before allowing such treatment to be administered lightly by lay analyses, whether they are doctors or not.[11]

This intervention and Reik's visit to Tandler did not have the expected outcome, and that is why Freud went on the offensive again in September 1926 with an astonishingly amusing text, "The Question of Lay Analysis," subtitled "Conversations with an Impartial Person."[12] By "impartial," he meant someone who resembled Durig as much as Tandler. As for the prin-

cipal protagonist, who was supposed to respond, Freud attributed to him the role of lay analyst, who possessed the true interpretation and a highly subtle listening ability. In its form, this work was inspired by a literary picaresque tradition that Freud knew well—that of Cervantes. But it was rather from Plato that he borrowed the idea of creating a dialogue between two protagonists who were opposed to one another but respectful of the other's opinion. With these "Conversations," he was clearly putting on stage two aspects of himself, while recalling yet again how much he identified with the interminable one-on-one combat between the angel and Jacob, Faust and Mephistopheles, Hamlet and the ghost, Leonardo and his vulture, the one always being a substitute for the other.

Much more than the controversies over female sexuality and child psychoanalysis, the controversies over lay analysis provoked a lasting upheaval in the international psychoanalytic movement. The holders of three positions were involved: the opponents of any form of lay analysis; the supporters of lay analysis who were hostile to any form of restriction; and the partisans of a lay analysis practiced within the framework of very strict rules, with a preference for the acquisition of medical training, especially in psychiatry.

The first group was supported by virtually all North American psychoanalytic societies, whose members were concerned with fighting a no-holds-barred battle against healers, sects, shamans, and seers, all of which were numerous in the United States. The second group was aligned with Freud, Ferenczi, and German-speaking Europe; it included Rank, Ernst Kris, Anna Freud, Hanns Sachs, Siegfried Bernfeld, and others. Members of the third group, supported by Jones and the English school, saw themselves as liberal and pragmatic. They counted among their ranks numerous lay practitioners of the first order: Joan Riviere, Melanie Klein, and James and Alix Strachey.

As these controversies unfolded, all sorts of arguments were invoked, especially regarding the treatment of psychoses and the relation that psychoanalysis should maintain with future advances in chemistry and biology. But since the Americans, beginning with Abraham Arden Brill, made medical degrees obligatory in their institutes, they had to face Freud's fury: he was more and more convinced that psychoanalysis in the

United States had become the handmaiden of psychiatry. In reality, psychoanalysis had expanded to such an extent in that country that it occupied, on the medical side, the place held by the psychiatric tradition in Europe, even as it was assimilated, on the lay side, to an "autotherapy of happiness": "The word 'psychoanalysis' is as well-known here as it is in the Far East," Bernfeld wrote in 1937. "Freud's name is less well-known, and it is pronounced 'Frud'. . . . Even people with little education know that psychoanalysis cures worries, marital troubles, lack of success, and other disagreeable situations, even if they seek out a more certain therapy at the Liquor Bar."[13]

Forgetting that he had dreamed, with Jung, of invading the promised land of psychiatric knowledge, Freud had come to think that medical training could even be harmful to the practice of psychoanalysis by nondoctors.

Finally, in May 1927, Reik's case was dismissed; the plaintiff had been disqualified owing to the vagaries of his testimony. The American press announced that an American had lost his case "against Freud." For some time afterward, lay analysis in the strict sense seemed to have been saved, but for Reik the damage had been done. Persecuted by those close to him, ridiculed by Stekel and Kraus, he never managed to find peace again in Vienna. Thus he decided to move to Berlin. Integrated into the BPI, he trained students and participated for five years in the spectacular rise of psychoanalysis in Germany, which ended with the advent of Nazism.

So Freud lost the battle of lay analysis. What had been at stake, at bottom, was simply the claim that psychoanalysis could not be reduced to any constituted body of knowledge. The discipline would never succeed in imposing itself as such in the academic realm, and those who had fought for lay analysis were gradually compelled to earn university diplomas and, above all, to submit to regulations imposed by the state. During the second half of the twentieth century, most of them became psychologists.[14]

After fighting to defend lay psychoanalysis against the doctors, Freud set out to attack religion. He sought to protect analysis against the priests who saw themselves as confessors or pastors of souls, depending on whether they were Catholic or Protestant. And he feared that they too, like the doctors, wanted to annex his doctrine to their practice. Once

again, he imagined assigning a status to his doctrine that did not yet exist and that would in fact never exist. Seeing himself as an unbeliever, Freud had always represented himself as the worst enemy of religion, which he considered an illusion, though this did not keep him from taking an interest in it in various ways.[15]

Like Jean-Martin Charcot and so many other scholars of the period, specialists in sicknesses of the mind, Freud had looked into the phenomena of possession, seeking to wrest their signification from representatives of the church and from the exorcists. In 1897, he had enjoyed reading the *Malleus Maleficarum,* a terrible manual published in Latin in the late fifteenth century and used by the Inquisition to send alleged witches to be burned at the stake.[16] Ten years later, he gave a talk in which he compared obsessional neurosis to a "private religion."[17] Finally, in 1923, at the request of Privy Councillor Rudolf Payer-Thurn, he studied the case of Christoph Haitzmann, a Bavarian painter afflicted with convulsions in 1677—eight years after he had signed a pact with the devil—who was then cured by an exorcism. Freud undertook to make the devil a substitute for the father, and he showed that in reality the painter, who became Brother Chrysostome, was never cured. In a monastery in Mariazell, Haitzmann continued to be visited by the devil as soon as he drank a little more than was reasonable. Freud ultimately contrasted the benefits of psychoanalysis with the failures of exorcism and criticized the religious practices of ancient times as more or less incompatible with the Enlightenment.

The hysterical woman viewed as a sorcerer, the devil substituting for the lubricious father, religion as a translation of a constraining neurosis that originated in childhood or in primitive times: these were the themes through which Freud purported to approach the question. Once again, this reasoning was severely flawed, in that phenomena of possession were interpreted in retrospect as pathological cases that only psychoanalytic science could clear up. Acting in accordance with his mania for interpretation, Freud thus exposed himself, along with his disciples, to a critique that hardly served the interests of his doctrine. And yet, by making up such fictions, he also helped introduce into the historian's work a model of subjective intelligibility that positive science excluded: he gave meaning to the ancient delirium that seemed to be reincarnated in the modern subject.[18] Here as elsewhere, his fondness for the devil led him to observe

a narrative field from an unprecedented angle, even though he tried to appropriate it for himself in an erroneous way. As he told it, Haitzmann's drama resembled something like Nathaniel Hawthorne's *The Scarlet Letter,* especially when it involved the various apparitions of the devil equipped with an extended penis in the form of a snake and topped by large breasts, a veritable projection of a maternal sexual emblem onto the erectile organ that was substituting for the father. Or when Freud set out to describe the "later neurosis" of the unfortunate painter, who was terrified by feminine visions, confronted by the voice of Christ and then by the impossibility of distinguishing the divine powers of the Spirit from those of evil. In the last phase of his account, Freud came down in favor of the demon, who was still present despite all the avowals of cure. Mephisto, the permanent friend, the indispensable enemy, also came back in the text of an ambivalent narrator prey to his own torments. Freud or Haitzmann?

With *The Future of an Illusion,*[19] Freud went after the institution itself, confronting religion as a system of control. In so doing, he was responding to Romain Rolland, who had sent him a copy of his play *Liluli,* dedicated to "the destroyer of illusions." In this "Aristophanesque" farce, the writer created a satire out of the illusion personified by a naïve young woman who was sowing discord among her interlocutors. As for Freud, after stating yet again that the idea of civilization depended on the introduction of a rampart that compelled men and women to renounce their instinctual drives, he emphasized that the religious ideas that served this purpose, holding humanity under constraint, were crumbling as they were refuted by science and rationality. Nevertheless, as a necessary illusion, religion did not have to be subjected to a truth criterion; it did not have to confront a reality test. As an infantile neurosis in a Copernican and Darwinian world, Freud said, religion was destined to be overcome. From a man who visited Italian cities repeatedly and who was deeply imbued with the values of Western civilization, which was as much a legacy of the medieval period as of the Renaissance, the argument seemed rather weak—all the more so in that the psychoanalytic technique of avowal was obviously related to confession.

But at bottom, if the Professor reduced religion to an illusion, he anticipated that religion was in the process of imposing itself as a culture.

At the time, Catholicism was combating Freudianism as vigorously as Freud was attacking religion. But the church meant to do this in a rational manner, as attested in Italy by the work of Father Agostino Gemelli, a Franciscan monk, doctor, and former student of Emil Kraepelin. Gemelli sought to integrate work in experimental psychology with neoscholasticism. He had founded a School of Psychology in Milan within the Catholic University of the Sacred Heart; he drew on Pierre Janet's theories in responding to the overly "sexual" doctrine of the Freudians.

Unquestionably, Freud thought that psychoanalysis could cure modern subjects suffering from the loss of the religious illusion; the risk was that psychoanalysis would supplant it and fail, following the pattern of Socialism, which had not succeeded in wiping out religion.

In his hatred of revolutionary Socialism, which he saw as a substitute for a new religion, Freud targeted not only the 1917 October Revolution but also a lifelong enemy, Alfred Adler, whom he reproached—the height of irony!—for his mania for interpreting: "Before me," he wrote to Ferenczi, "is also an interview that [Adler] gave about Mussolini (The World, Dec. 26, '26). Perhaps you haven't read it and don't yet know how Fascism can be explained. I will tell you: from Mussolini's infantile inferiority and his striving to compensate for it. Now it is dead certain that Adler would have given the same explanation if Mussolini had introduced, e.g., a homosexual social order in Italy, according to which normal coitus is punished by imprisonment, or a Trappist regime, in which talking is forbidden as unpatriotic. The only phenomenon to which he hasn't yet applied his famous theory is Socialism, because he, himself, belongs to it."[20]

In the last part of *The Future of an Illusion*, Freud took his disciple and friend Oskar Pfister to task. Pfister, a pastor in Zurich, had come to see him in Vienna in 1909, and had taken his side during the major conflict with Jung. Freud appreciated his generosity and his optimism; he knew very well that this "dear man of God," as he called him, saw himself as the heir to treatments for the soul *(Seelsorge)* and that he would never renounce his faith. Pfister had committed to the Freudian cause because he had been disturbed from his early years on by the spectacle of moral degradation linked to industrialization, and by the inability of the old abstract theology to respond to the anxieties of modern men and women.[21] He saw himself as a pedagogue.[22] In 1919, he had founded the Swiss

Society of Psychoanalysis (SSP), and he had had to confront the opponents of lay analysis, in particular Raymond de Saussure,[23] who criticized him for the brevity of his treatments.

A nonconformist incapable of any sort of idolatry, Pfister did not hesitate to criticize Freud. And while he thought that psychoanalysis was heir to the tradition of the "testimonial pastorate of souls," much more than to the Catholic confessional tradition, he was convinced that these two forms of therapy aimed at freeing the subject through access to the truth of the soul and the restoration of love. Thus he responded to *The Future of an Illusion* with a brilliant essay published in 1923 in the journal *Imago:* "L'illusion d'un avenir."[24] Here he asserted, rightly, that true faith was protection against neurosis, and that Freud's position was itself an illusion. According to him, Freud misunderstood the significance of mystical experiences, which had nothing to do with religion. Freud was unaware, moreover, that this mode of knowledge of the mysteries of God and of faith, expressed in flamboyant literary narratives, had always been contested by the churches. "How remote from me," Freud would write to Rolland, "are the worlds in which you move! To me mysticism is just as closed a book as music."[25] But he also admitted, on the subject of death, that every intelligent individual knows "a limit beyond which he can become mystical and enter into his most intimate being."[26] Friend Pfister had put his finger on a "Freudian unthought," present between the lines in the master's work. *The Future of an Illusion* was a bad book and Freud knew it.

Beyond the lively exchange with Pfister, another dialogue was unfolding in the shadows between Freud and Carl Liebman, a young American suffering from fetishism, and whose profile, barely hinted at, can be sensed at several points in Freud's correspondence without ever coming clearly to the surface. Between a famous scholar whose existence was dazzling and an anonymous patient immersed in an obscure life of suffering, a relationship had developed, starting in 1925, that was to prove significant for the development of psychoanalytic concepts. Between the lines of a confrontation with Pfister, two orders of reality were opposed once again: the critical consciousness of a doctor on the one hand, and the tragic consciousness of a patient on the other—a divide between reason and unreason, between clinical thinking and madness.

The young Liebman, born in 1900, came from a family of German Jewish tradesmen who had become American in the mid-nineteenth century; his great-grandfather Samuel Liebman had founded the famous Rheingold Beer company. Named after his grandfather, Carl had spent his childhood in the splendid mansion that his father, Julius Liebman, had had built in Brooklyn. Like a fictional character from the early part of the century, he too resembled many other patients of Freud who were afflicted with multiple, virtually incurable pathologies. He had always felt different from other adolescents. When he was five years old, while his nurse was bathing him along with his sister, he had had a great fright. The nurse had threatened to "cut off his penis" as "she had done to his sister" if he continued to complain about being dried vigorously with a towel. Subsequently, he very often manifested extreme sexual excitement when he saw boys wearing athletic supporters,[27] all the more so in that he himself avoided participating in sports and refused to climb trees. The young Liebman, a tall, thin, studious boy who spoke several languages, avoided all contact with girls. He was obsessed with the survival of his sperm, which he called his "spermanimalcules," and when he ejaculated he saw himself as a mass murderer. Once he even thought he had killed a baby. At Yale, where he pursued studies intended to make him the brilliant heir to one of the wealthiest dynasties in the United States, he was mocked as a "fairy."[28] He soon got into the habit of masturbating compulsively and wearing a jockstrap under his clothes all the time: a fetish.

After completing his studies, the young man sought help from an American psychoanalyst. Dissatisfied, he went to Europe on his own in order to become an "artist." In Zurich, in 1924, he consulted Pfister, who recognized the extreme seriousness of his condition and sent him to Eugen Bleuler for a consultation. After a forty-five-minute interview, Bleuler offered a diagnosis oscillating between obsessional neurosis and schizophrenia. He finally opted for "mild schizophrenia," and added that Liebman had told him about his hand-washing compulsion and his conviction that he was constantly under observation by people in the street. During the conversation, Liebman had fiddled with all the objects in the office, including an ashtray, without concern for its dirtiness. Bleuler recommended an analytic treatment and the choice of a trade that could free him from his symptoms.

On December 21, 1924, Freud responded favorably to Pfister's request, and on February 22, 1925, he agreed to accept the young man for treatment, for a fee of twenty dollars. In May, before he had even seen Liebman, he met with the patient's parents, Julius and Marie, whom he found much too ready to make "sacrifices" for their son. After hesitating, and pointing out to Pfister that it was probably preferable to let Liebman "go to his ruin" as an effect of his lack of sociability, he finally welcomed the young man in September. But he quickly became aware of what bad shape Liebman was in, and he wrote to tell the parents that treatment might not ever lead to any improvement. Nevertheless, as time passed, he began to feel a real attachment to the young man, although he remained convinced that Liebman suffered from a psychosis (paranoid dementia), that he was not open to any change, and that he would not hesitate to commit suicide as soon as he had the opportunity. Thus, once again Freud accepted for analysis a patient for whom no treatment seemed possible. But if he, the great specialist of mental illness, refused to see this type of patient, who would do so in his place? He decided, then, to go to battle for him.[29]

At this point, swept up in the reworking of his theory and his clinical practices, and in the context of the great debates over female sexuality, Freud was reflecting on the best way to account, structurally, for the difference between neurosis, psychosis, and perversion. He distinguished the principal figures of negativity capable of denoting the difference and of serving as markers in a characterization of the defense mechanisms at work within that trilogy.

In 1923, Freud defined what he called a denial or a disclaimer (*Verleugnung*)[30] to characterize a defense mechanism through which a subject refuses to recognize the reality of a negative perception, and in particular the absence of a penis in women. The idea of a negative hallucination, invented by Hippolyte Bernheim, had long since been accepted in psychiatry and was common currency in the literature: recognizing the reality of something that does not exist, the better to deny it. Two years later, in an exchange of letters with René Laforgue on the question of scotomization, Freud forcefully reasserted his choice of the term "denial" to characterize this defense mechanism, and at the same time he put forward another term, denegation *(Verneinung),*[31] to characterize a

different defense mechanism through which the subject expresses in a negative way a desire or a thought whose existence he is repressing. For example, in a sentence such as "She's not my mother," uttered by a patient in talking about a dream, what is repressed is identified in a negative way without being accepted. Freud by then associated denial with the process of psychosis—negation of an external reality with the reconstruction of a hallucinated reality—and he associated denegation with a neurotic process. But how, in this framework, could one characterize the defense mechanism associated with perversion? To answer this question, Freud used the notion of splitting *(Spaltung)*, which was also present in psychiatric literature, and used in particular by Bleuler to designate phenomena of dissociation of consciousness or discord leading to mental alienation or a serious identity disorder: the schism, for example, presented in schizophrenia.

While in Freudian clinical practice denial, in the sense of rejection of reality, characterizes psychosis, and while denegation is specific to neurosis, the form of denial proper to perversion is found "between the two," to the extent that it is also the expression of a split that produces the coexistence, within the ego, of two contradictory attitudes, one that consists in denying reality and the other in accepting it. In this perspective, Freud brought the discord back to the core of the ego *(Ichspaltung)*, whereas dynamic psychiatry situated it between two psychic structures and characterized it as a state of incoherence rather than as a structural phenomenon. On that basis, Freud brought perversion into a continuum between neurosis and psychosis. In neurosis, there is a repression of the demands of the id; in psychosis, there is a rejection of reality; in perversion, there is a split between knowledge and belief: "I know that a given thing does not exist but I do not want to know anything about this nonexistence." For Freud, always quick to reduce any conflict to a sexual cause, this denial of nonexistence signifies that a subject does not want to know anything about the absence of the penis in women and thus substitutes something else for it, in conformity with his belief.

Without ever attempting to draw up a catalog of sexual perversions, as the sexologists had done, Freud could not avoid addressing the question, owing to the very fact that he accepted for analysis patients about whom it was difficult to say whether their condition entailed psychosis

or perversion. And this was especially true of fetishists, whose cases were particularly fascinating for all specialists in mental illness. According to the author of *Totem and Taboo,* who adored animals and divinities, and who regarded primitive peoples as children and childhood as a stage anterior to adulthood, fetishism was above all a form of religion.[32]

As a religion, fetishism is characterized by the transformation into divinities of animals and inanimate beings to which magical power is attributed. But as a sexual perversion, this individualized religion becomes pathological when the subject can form attachments only with inanimate objects that are always venerated as parts of female bodies. In this sense, Freud considered that fetishes—shoes, clothing, or specific body parts (feet or shiny noses, for example)—were substitutes for a penis. And he concluded that there were no such things as feminine fetishes, since, he said, for women, the entire body is fetishized and not a particular object or body part. As he saw it, so-called female fetishism was thus only a manifestation of the narcissization of the body. This is why Freud seemed not to recognize the existence—rare, to be sure—of authentically fetishist women.[33]

He had reached this point in his reflections when he received Liebman. Aware that he was dealing with a difficult case, and especially that this was an unhappy young man whose parents wanted at all costs to see him conform to the very high social aspirations they had for him, Freud tried with all the means at his disposal to give meaning to his anxieties, his delusions, his compulsive practice of masturbation, and his fetishism. During the sessions, rather than remaining behind the couch, he walked back and forth, stepping around his dog or gesturing with his cigar, anxious himself that he might not have any hold on the pathology of this patient, who became convinced that the Professor was refusing to regard him as a real, virile man, because Freud did not offer him a cigar.

At a certain point in the treatment, in conformity with his hypotheses about the perverse denial of the absence of a penis in women, Freud explained to his patient that his fetish was a substitute for his mother's penis (or phallus).[34] That was why he wore a jockstrap. And Freud added that that piece of clothing served to hide his own genital organs completely and thus to deny the difference between the sexes. Accordingly, the fetish expressed the idea that while sometimes the woman is castrated,

sometimes she is not and then the man is. In other words, if we follow Freud, Liebman's fetish served to dissimulate all possible forms of the absence of a penis, and thus to deny the existence of the difference between the sexes. Freud added that, in his childhood, Liebman must have experienced a shock in discovering that his mother did not have a penis. No doubt he also thought about the threat of having his penis cut off?

He also deduced from this whole story that Liebman must have seen, as a child, an ancient statue in which the sex organ was concealed behind a fig leaf, and that the scene had constituted for him the first moment of an outline of his current fetish. After delivering this interpretation of a hypothetical "primal scene," Freud instructed Liebman to stop masturbating, the only way, as he saw it, to come to an understanding of his symptoms: "I am trying hard," he wrote to Pfister, "to get him deliberately to resist his fetishist masturbation to enable him to corroborate for himself all that I have discerned about the nature of the fetish. But he will not believe that such abstinence will lead to this and it is essential for the progress of the treatment. On the other hand, I feel a great deal of sympathy for him, and cannot make up my mind to send him away and risk a disastrous outcome. So I am continuing with him, though perhaps if I give up work he will leave me in any case."[35]

Drawing support from Liebman's story, Freud hastened to write an article on fetishism in which he universalized the idea, already sketched out in his book on Leonardo da Vinci, that fetishes have the same goal and meaning in all cases: "The fetish is a substitute for the penis. . . . I hasten to add that it is not a substitute for any chance penis, but for a particular penis and quite special penis that had been extremely important in early childhood but had later been lost. . . . To put it more plainly: the fetish is a substitute for the woman's (the mother's) penis that the little boy once believed in and—for reasons familiar to us—does not want to give up."[36]

Freud had already advanced a similar hypothesis in a letter to Jung with regard to Oedipus's "swollen foot," stressing that this was most probably a reference to the mother's erect penis.[37] In his 1927 article, he designated Liebman's fetish as "an athletic support-belt [*Schamgürtel*] which could also be worn as bathing drawers."[38]

On the strength of this interpretation, Freud believed he could bring his patient relief. However, Liebman continued to masturbate compulsively.

For a time, he locked himself away in his hotel room, cut off from the world. Freud was clearly right in thinking that the jockstrap was actually a substitute for a genital organ, but he stubbornly continued to call it by the old German name *Schamgürtel,* literally "belt of shame." At the time, the word also referred to an article of clothing derived from the Latin *sublicaculum,* a folded or rolled strip of cloth used to cover a man's genitals and buttocks. Since we know that the analysis was conducted partly in English, we may wonder why Freud did not simply translate "athletic supporter" by *suspensorium.* For, far from wearing a belt of shame, concealing the difference between the sexes, Liebman exhibited, on the contrary, by means of his fetish, a symbol of the phallic pride that he so admired among the young male athletes of his university. Under his clothing, he was actually concealing what he lacked most of all: a member covered with a sheath and enhanced by a "shell."[39] Was this the equivalent of the mother's missing penis? Freud insisted on saying so, but there is no proof.

In any case, we can imagine the shock the young man must have felt when Freud told him that his fetish referred to a primal scene in which he presumably discovered that his mother lacked a penis. To be sure, this interpretation could account for his old terror of the cut-off penis. But it in no way echoed what the fetishized athletic supporter meant to him, as a familiar garment on university campuses. Liebman nevertheless took in Freud's assertion even while denying it. And Freud interpreted this rejection as a sign of resistance. Still, he noticed a slight improvement in his patient.

One can wonder how Liebman would have reacted if Freud's interpretation had been different, and if instead of calling the fetish a belt of shame, the analyst had represented it as the symbol of phallic pride, even if it meant seeing it as a substitute for the mother's missing penis. In that case, would the young man have rejected the interpretation so forcefully? No one can say. It does seem, in any case, that no advice, no help, no therapy, no interpretation, could affect the condition of this young man, who was so alienated from himself and so wrapped up in the mystical contemplation of his own destruction.

Careful not to be untruthful, Freud wrote to Marie Liebman. He let her know that her son was suffering from paranoid schizophrenia, but

that he was hopeful, as well as fearful, for the future. The analysis went on for three more years. Once again, despite his pessimism about the outcome, and despite the fear he felt at the idea of Liebman's possible suicide, Freud prolonged the treatment, although the psychosis was burgeoning despite the work accomplished. Liebman grew more and more attached to his illustrious analyst as he plunged deeper and deeper into obsession and madness. When Freud understood that, even with all the attention he was giving his patient, he would never manage to make him better, he sent him to Ruth Mack Brunswick, convinced that a woman would be better able to make herself understood. The results she obtained were no better.

One last time, in 1931, Liebman went to see Freud before returning to the United States. He stopped in Paris for several sessions of analysis with Rank, who diagnosed a birth trauma. His parents had him followed by a detective, and he soon became aware of this. After a period of wandering and succumbing to material and psychic misery, just as the economic crisis was reaching new heights, he returned to the family circle and was employed by his father as a chauffeur.

Some time later he attempted suicide, by stabbing himself in the chest with a hunting knife; Brill made the decision to have him committed as an inpatient to the sumptuous McLean Hospital at Harvard, where wealthy patients were admitted, as they were at Bellevue in New York. But Liebman wanted to pursue analysis with Freud's American disciples, as he continued to venerate the master. His mother was opposed. He then began to tell everyone who would listen that thanks to Freud he had discovered the origin of his illness: the sight of his mother's missing penis. He suffered greatly from the stupidity of his prisonlike existence, and complained often of its emptiness, punctuated by exercises with modeling clay and required participation in games of pool or pottery making. To this ordeal he preferred the turbulence of his Viennese years, during which he had heard all sorts of stories about missing penises, whether shameful or cut off.

Over the years, after trying to escape, he became a celebrated case, subjected to every possible treatment connected with "progress" in asylum psychiatry: electric shocks, convulsion therapy, topectomy. In the aftermath, he never forgot his adored fetish, and whenever visitors came to

hear the legendary story of his treatment with the Professor, surrounded by chow chows and cigars, he would repeat, as he did every day with his doctors and nurses, "I am my father's penis."

Such was the destiny of this unforgettable patient of Freud's, inhabited by madness, incurable; his treatment was never the subject of an authentic narrative by any of its protagonists. It remains forever present between the lines of a work, a correspondence, and an archive, like the archaeological trace of an advance toward death in two parallel existences, Freud's and Liebman's, the one glorious and the other obscure.

From 1929 on, Freud experienced a certain lassitude in the exercise of his profession. Suffering increasingly from his cancer and from the treatments inflicted on him, he lost weight and was less able to tolerate difficult cases, even when they brought him the material comfort he needed to support his family, his close associates, and the psychoanalytic movement. Seeking diversions, he patronized a bookstore run by Emy Moebius and her friend Gerty Kvergic, the Fremdsprachige Leihbibliothek, a store frequented by diplomats that specialized in lending foreign-language books. Minna, who went there on Freud's behalf, brought him back detective novels by Dorothy Sayers and Agatha Christie, which he adored. Moebius became and remained a family friend until she emigrated to the United States.[40]

The future was dark: an economic crisis in the United States, a newly installed Fascist regime in Italy, the rise of Nazis in the German-speaking world. Once again Europe seemed vulnerable to the destructive drive that Freud had described so well. He designated with scorn what he characterized as the "riffraff": the imbeciles, the raging masses, the stupidity of the times. In July 1930, he was still dreaming of the Nobel Prize when the city of Frankfurt awarded him the Goethe Prize, not only because "his psychology had enriched medical science," but because his work had contributed to literature and the arts. Very honored, he declared that Goethe would unquestionably have been passionate about the discoveries made by psychoanalysis.

Freud was more and more obsessed with death, and, when Amalia died at age eighty-five, following a terrible gangrene of the leg, he was relieved; he had dreaded that she would be told one day that her son had preceded her to the grave. Opposed to religious rites and exhausted by his own suf-

fering, he did not attend the funeral: no grieving, no pain. He was convinced, however, that, in the depths of his unconscious, this death was going to cause an upheaval in his life. This turned out not to be the case.

Freud had lost his father before he had produced his work, but his mother died only nine years before his own death: she had had the time to contemplate the glory of her adored "Sigi." She was buried next to Jacob according to the Jewish rites. A few days later, Adolfine took refuge at 19 Berggasse. She had been her mother's principal support, her scapegoat as well. Henceforth her family was reduced to her brother, her sisters, and her nieces and nephews. Freud welcomed her warmly even though, generally speaking, he paid little attention to his sisters when they came, every Sunday, to call on Martha and Minna.

At this time he had already begun writing his *Diary (Kürzeste Chronik)*, a sort of informal personal journal in which he jotted down laconic notes every day about the events that seemed important: what happened to his dogs, the objects in his collections, the weather, family affairs, deaths, visits, the little details of daily life, current politics. He thus inaugurated a new narrative style, somewhere between journalistic writing—short forms—and catalogs of names, things, and lists. A minimalist literature, a bare-bones description of reality that aspired to no interpretation.

Despite his illness, Freud had retained all his intellectual faculties. He grew increasingly fond of his children, his grandchildren, and his women: Lou, Anna, Minna, Martha, Dorothy, Marie. To the two women in his service, Anna and Maria, he added a third, Paula Fichtl, age thirty-seven; she was the former governess of Dorothy's children. Martha liked her. The daughter of an alcoholic miller from Salzburg, she had been placed in domestic service as a child, without ever wanting to start her own family. She fled men like the plague after each new adventure. With the aging Freuds, she found a true substitute family.[41] The Professor thus lived at 19 Berggasse surrounded by six women, each with a well-defined task.

Moreover, he followed attentively the love affairs and conjugal relations of the other members of his family, those of his nephews and nieces in particular. He handed out pocket money generously to his grandchildren. Two new interlocutors, both Jews, took on great importance in his correspondence: Stefan Zweig, a politically conservative, profoundly European and anti-nationalist Viennese writer, already famous throughout the

world;[42] and Arnold Zweig, a writer from Berlin, a Zionist, Socialist, and Communist, who lived in Palestine beginning in 1933. Neither one was a disciple, and neither moved from the status of friend to that of enemy.

Stefan Zweig addressed all his dedicated works to Freud, and he reminded him endlessly how much contemporary writers—Proust, Joyce, and others—were in his debt. But Freud never responded, and for good reason: he remained entirely ignorant of their work. This often led him to be quite hard on Zweig, in particular when the latter wrote an essay, *Mental Healers,* in which he compared three lives, those of Franz Anton Mesmer, Freud himself, and Mary Baker Eddy, the American founder of the sect known as Christian Science, which claimed to cure illness through ecstasy and faith.

If Freud could acknowledge that Mesmer had been the initiator, beyond magnetism, of the procedure of suggestion, he did not view himself as Mesmer's heir. He was too attached to a mythological and genealogical conception of the science of history; it was hard for him to accept the notion of long duration that was already dear to historians. Worst of all for him, just as the battle over lay analysis was raging, was to be lumped together with Eddy, who embodied everything that the psychoanalytic movement rightly wanted to stay away from, even if that sometimes meant rejecting the master himself. And Freud responded to Zweig by asserting that Eddy was mentally ill: "We know that in a fit of frenzy the raving lunatic releases energies which normally are not at his disposal. The mad and wicked side of the Mary Baker Eddy phenomenon is not sufficiently brought out [in Zweig's presentation], nor is the unspeakable grimness of the American background."[43]

As for the portrait Zweig had drawn of him, Freud did not recognize himself in it. He thought that the writer saw him as a petit bourgeois and reproached him for forgetting to say that he preferred archaeology to psychology. In reality, Zweig's "characterological" portrait was a sort of literary construction, midway between fiction and reality. Zweig transformed Freud into a luminous being, robust and healthy, a tireless, solitary worker, standing up to gods and men, imbued with impeccable courage. Still, he described the changes in his body and face in an oddly familiar way, opposing the younger years to those of old age as if he had projected onto Freud his own rejection of the future: "Now that the bony

structure of the visage has become more conspicuous, there has been revealed something harsh and unconditionally militant—the expression of an indomitable, almost mordant will. In the early portrait the glance was simply contemplative, but now it is piercing and gloomy; the brow is deeply furrowed, as if with bitterness and suspicion."[44]

Zweig often relied on the Freudian technique of dream analysis, in particular by using the narrative device of integrating the main story into another story. And after writing his famous novella *Twenty-Four Hours in the Life of a Woman (Vierundzwanzig Stunden aus dem Leben einer Frau),*[45] inspired by an epistolary novel by Constance de Salm, a princess in the nineteenth century who hosted a salon and had herself been inspired by *La princesse de Clèves,* Zweig sent it to Freud.

The motif of this story was the amorous passion of an old English lady (Mme C.), who confided to the narrator a memory from her youth while the narrator was trying to understand the flight of another woman staying in a hotel on the Riviera. Freud appreciated this story, which brought to mind a case study in which the narrator purportedly took the place of the therapist, liberating an anonymous female patient from the weight of her past. The English lady recounted her vain attempt, twenty-five years earlier, to save a young pianist from his passion for gambling. But he had rejected her love and fled; she had then suffered for years over the guilty relations she had had with him and that had transformed her existence. She had learned, ten years later, that he had killed himself.

According to Freud, the motif of the tale was that of a mother who initiates her son into sexual relations in order to save him from the dangers of onanism. But she is unaware that she herself suffers from a libidinal fixation on her son; thus her destiny has caught up with her. Freud added, "What I am saying is analytic and is in no way attempting to do justice to literary beauty."[46] When he was willing to refrain from imposing his doctrine on the texts he had before him, Freud was capable of excellent interpretations. But the signification of the story interested him much more than its form, even if the story had been inspired by his own writings.

Around the same time, Freud entered into a warm relationship with Thomas Mann, someone he respected deeply and viewed as a great novelist, even though he had no real familiarity with the author's work. In

1929, Mann produced one of the finest texts ever written on the work and the person of the Professor: *Freud's Position in the History of Modern Thought*.[47] Freud did not recognize himself in this dazzling portrait that depicted him as a destroyer of illusions, heir to Nietzsche and Schopenhauer, capable of exploring all the forms of the irrational and of transforming Romanticism into a science. Thus he preferred to think that Mann was speaking of himself rather than of psychoanalysis and its inventor. "Mann's essay is certainly an honour. It gives me the impression that he had an essay on Romanticism ready to hand, when he was requested to write something about me. . . . However, when Mann says something, it has real substance."[48]

Freud had never given up the idea of making psychoanalysis a "pure" science, comparable to "infinitesimal calculus." Thus he was seriously mistaken about German Romanticism, whose legacy he rejected. In March 1932, Mann paid a call on Freud at 19 Berggasse for the first time; he was warmly received by Martha and Minna, two of his ardent readers, who saw him as a compatriot, born as they had been in northern Germany.

During the same period, a new "enemy" made his appearance in Freud's Viennese circles: Wilhelm Reich, born to a Jewish family in Galicia, as Marxist as he was Freudian, and more a sexologist than a psychoanalyst. For ten years he occupied a place formerly held by a string of mad doctors—Wilhelm Fliess, Otto Gross—whose presence seemed to go hand in hand with the flowering of the psychoanalytic movement. Among them Reich was by far the most interesting, and the most fertile: "We have here a Dr. Reich," Freud wrote to Lou Andreas-Salomé in 1928, "a worthy but impetuous young man, passionately devoted to his hobby-horse who now salutes in the genital orgasm the antidote to every neurosis."[49]

It was to this Freud of the 1930s, his waning years, that the great anatomist Tandler, an enthusiast for medical eugenics, euthanasia, and the elimination of "lives unworthy of being lived," devoted a cruel portrait, little known but extraordinarily acute. A Moravian by birth, Tandler had participated, as we have seen, in the rise of psychoanalysis in Vienna, and he looked at his friend Freud as the dark part of himself, his enigmatic double in a way, as Viennese as he was himself. In a personal notebook,

which he kept secret, he described Freud as a wild old man capable of destroying all of humanity's illusions, someone who "massacred values," a virtuosic autocrat who had an unprecedented mastery of the German language. A leader, a truly hard man, who could have been Bismarck if he had not been Jewish. An exceptional man in any case, someone who took pleasure, like a detective, in trapping his interlocutors through brilliant arguments, a thinker endowed with an intense but constantly repressed instinctual life, someone who sought to form "sex hunters" *(sexus)*, stubborn, opinionated, a quibbler, cruelly dissecting human cruelty, observing in solitude, as if through a peephole, a detestable world.

The Freud described by Tandler seemed to come straight out of a novel by Mann or Tolstoy, a tormented soul, a lively, excessive nature, imbued with unlimited vitality and overflowing wit: "A powerful race, great inner tenacity, very strong vitality that gives this old man the penetration of youth. This aged man, truly aged, has always had passionate enthusiasms but he suffers from an inhibition of his will. . . . When he builds a system, it manifests a natural logic. And when this man builds something, one has the feeling that a vital riddle has been solved. And that construction always proceeds from an intellect of incomparable acuity."[50]

Freud never knew what his friend had written about him. But on November 7, 1929, he noted "anti-Semitic incidents" in his diary.[51] That morning, several Nazi students had taken Tandler to task, in front of the Institute of Anatomy, shouting, "Death to the Jews!" In October 1931, Freud made a financial contribution to Tandler when the latter was organizing "Winter Support" intended to help victims of the financial crisis.

Tandler died in Moscow in 1936, while he was carrying out a humanitarian mission there. Unlike Freud, he received recognition for his various beneficent activities. The Viennese authorities gave his name to one of the most famous squares in the old imperial capital: Julius Tandler Platz. What twenty-first-century traveler remembers the role this man, so typically Viennese, played in Freud's life?

Facing Hitler

IN 2007, in an outstanding book on Freud's last years, Mark Edmundson, an American academic, drew on an idea dear to historians—but also to Thomas Mann—by establishing a parallel between two Viennese lives during the Belle Époque: the infamous life of the young Adolf Hitler, twenty years old in 1909, and the dazzling life of the rising star Sigmund Freud. The former was to become the biggest assassin of all time, destroying Germany and committing genocide against the Jews and against humanity in its essence; the latter was to become the most famous and most controversial thinker of the twentieth century. "In almost every way," Edmundson remarks, these men "were what the poet William Blake would have called 'spiritual enemies.'"[1]

Born in a milieu of downgraded farmers, mistreated by a stupid and violent father who had married his unhappy young cousin, the young Hitler hated the whole world and Austria most of all; he dreamed that it was doomed to fall one day under the control of Wilhelmian Germany. In Linz, his schooling was marked by repeated failures. A young Jew who was to become a celebrated philosopher, Ludwig Wittgenstein, attended the same school; Hitler despised him already. Very early on, the future führer let himself fall under the sway of the symbols and incantations of pan-Germanic nationalism, which he would use later on as a spearhead in his fight against the Jews. He was opposed to his father's nationalism, as his father was very attached to the greatness of the Habsburg Empire.

After his parents died, Hitler went to Vienna in the hope of making his fortune as a painter and an architect, but he was twice denied admis-

sion by the Academy of Fine Arts. This rejection heightened his hatred for the world of culture, the arts, and the mind. Convinced of his own genius, he often went to the opera, disguised as a dandy, to listen fervently to Wagner's music. Nevertheless, he scorned Vienna as an "immobile" city, permeated by the feeling that it faced imminent death, and he kept his distance from its various "miasmas": prostitution, unbridled sexuality, hysteria, immoral literature, homosexuality, decadent painting and architecture.

In short, Hitler rejected the city's most telling innovations, from which he was excluded. Lazy, lacking talent, preferring to give in to affects rather than to thought, he asserted a fondness for animals that reinforced his hatred of humans. He never ate meat, he drank neither alcohol nor wine, and he was convinced that tobacco was the scourge most harmful to people's health. From the depths of his misery, he saw himself as a remarkable humanist and an excellent poet; he imagined redesigning Vienna, transforming it into a paradise worthy of a regenerated humanity. He too was drawn to the German eugenic medicine that would end up supporting racial segregation.

In short, Hitler accumulated all the pathologies that could have made him an ideal Viennese patient, a case right out of Richard von Krafft-Ebing's nomenclature, revised and corrected in the light of "Beyond the Pleasure Principle":

> If Hitler and Freud passed each other on the street on an afternoon in the cold late autumn of 1909, what would each of them have seen? In Hitler, Freud would have seen a rank denizen of the crowd, a street rat (Freud was no populist). But he probably would have felt sorry for the unfortunate man as well. For his part, Hitler would have seen a Viennese burgher (he despised the upper middle class), and probably would have recognized Freud as a Jew. Hitler would have drawn back in shame at his threadbare overcoat and his broken-down shoes. If things were bad enough, he might have extended a hand to beg. Whether Freud gave or not—he could well have; he was generally good-hearted—would have made little difference: the encounter would still have left the young Adolf Hitler seething.[2]

In 1925, with the publication of *Mein Kampf,* Hitler set his sights on the objects of his hatred: Jews, Marxists, the Treaty of Versailles, the so-called inferior races. And he asserted his aspirations: to become the leader of a new Reich, purified of all the quagmires of an alleged degeneration, a leader capable of taking revenge on the winners of the Great War, who had humiliated Germany. At this point in time he bore a very close resemblance to the figure of the leader as Freud had described him in "Group Psychology": the man who had no need to love anyone—the ultimate version of narcissistic madness, denial of alterity, and withdrawal into oneself. The deteriorating political, social, and economic situation of Europe—and especially of the German-speaking world—had reached a point at which the advent of such a personality was possible. Freud had conceived of this in the abstract, without imagining for a moment that it could exist in the form of a man who would seize power in Germany twelve years later.

In 1939, sixty years before Edmundson's brilliant commentary, Mann, in exile on the West Coast of the United States, had already thought about the question of parallel lives, the monster and the sage, when he published a strange, Freudian essay that gave rise to considerable controversy: *Bruder Hitler* (Brother Hitler).[3] He knew that Freud had moved to London, surrounded by his family, and that he had only a few months to live.

Unlike Bertolt Brecht and the other Germans in exile, Mann refused to make a black-and-white distinction between the Germany of the Enlightenment and the Germany of Hitler's barbarianism. To be sure, he knew perfectly well that Goethe's Germany was very different from that of the Nazis, but he felt genuine clinical curiosity about the "monster," and he wondered how such an overturning of values could have come about in one of the most civilized countries in Europe. How was it possible that the opposite of what traditional German culture, under the Weimar Republic and the old Bismarckian empire alike, had venerated most highly—knowledge, competence, science, philosophy, progress— could have come to power? Hitler was a failure, an "asylum bum," a "deviant" *(Verhunzung),* an "ugly little duckling" who thought he was a swan, a "charlatan," a "scullery Lohengrin," Mann wrote. In short, he was precisely the opposite of what the Protestant ethic had fashioned over decades, the opposite of the most civilized invention of the *Aufklärung.* And

suddenly he had succeeded in conquering a people where Social Democracy had failed: "Drive Hitler out," Mann had written in 1933, "that miserable wretch, that hysterical impostor, that low-born non-German, that knight of the power industry, whose entire art consists in using the repugnant talent of a medium to seek a sensitive chord in the populace and make it vibrate in the obscene trance in which an incredibly lowly oratorical gift has put it."⁴ And Mann refused, rightly, to indulge in any comparisons between Napoleon and Hitler: "It is really going too far to speak in one breath of the great soldier and the blackmailing pacifist, the fighter and the coward whose role would be played out on the first day of actual armed conflict. That earlier figure is stamped for ever on men's memories, a classic Mediterranean bronze. Hegel called him the 'world-spirit on horseback.' And shall we compare that all-embracing brain, that immense capacity for toil, that embodiment of the revolution and tyrant harbinger of liberty, with the pitiable idler and incapable, the fifth-rank visionary, the stupid foe of social revolution, the sly sadist and plotter of revenge, the representative of 'temperament'?"⁵

To explain the reversal that had transformed a monster from the void into a dictator of a new Germanic order, Mann emphasized that he had to be regarded as an inverted "brother," that is, as the unconscious part of German culture, its shadowy part, as irrational as what Freud described under the term "instinct" could be: an impressive projection of the unconscious into reality. And rather than closing one's eyes before that vile brother, Mann called on his contemporaries to look evil in the face, the better to counter it with illusion-free rationality.⁶ And he added, "A man like that must hate psychoanalysis! I secretly suspect that the rage with which he marched on a certain capital was ultimately aimed at the old analyst who lived there, his true and essential enemy, the philosopher who unmasked neurosis, the great destroyer of illusions, the one who knows what's what and knows a great deal about genius."⁷

Hitler: this was the man, so well described by Mann in Freudian terms, who was to become the worst enemy of the great destroyer of illusions and of the city of Vienna, the first cradle of psychoanalysis.

Unlike Mann, Freud once again needed time to understand that the world was facing war of a new type, not a war between nations but something like the very expression of a principle of destruction aiming, through

the extermination of a so-called race (the "Semites"), to wipe out the human species and replace it with another "race" (the "Aryans"), the only one authorized to exist on the planet. In 1915, had he not affirmed that the Great War, a product of nationalism and of advances in the techniques of massive destruction, translated the quintessence of a desire for death anchored in the human species? Now, confronting the rise of Nazism in Germany, he did not yet perceive the nature of the death machine launched by National Socialism. He was not the only one in this situation.

The fact remains that in July 1929, when he put the finishing touches on a new book that was a sequel to *The Future of an Illusion*, he did not suspect that he had just written the book that would be the most read, and the most translated, the darkest no doubt but also the most luminous, the most lyrical, the most poetic of all his books: *Civilization and Its Discontents*. He had devoted his time to that work while on holiday at Berchtesgaden, in the Bavarian Alps, the preferred residence of Princess Marie-Elizabeth de Saxe-Meiningen, who had not survived the fall of the German monarchies. Very close by, perched high up on the Obersalzberg, stood the house where Hitler received the leaders of the National Socialist Party (NSDAP), starting in 1927.[8]

Freud initially thought he would call this essay *Das Glück und die Kultur* (Happiness and culture), then he came up with *Das Unglück in der Kultur* (Unhappiness in culture), but he finally settled on *Unglück, Unbehagen* (Unhappiness, discontentment).[9] In any case, beyond the anxiety he felt with regard to modern times, he meant to put forth a manifesto in favor of human happiness: a hymn in praise of love, progress, science, and the Platonic republic.

After reminding his readers that religion no longer offered any remedy for frustration, Freud asserted that the main sources of the modern subject's unhappiness lay in the absence of ideals, which reduced the subject to three determining factors: the biological body, the external world, and relations with others. Confronted with this finitude, and having become a sort of "prosthetic god" *(Art Prothesenengott)*, a human being had no way to escape suffering except to invent new illusions, on the basis of three unconscious choices: neurosis (anxiety, conflict), intoxication (drugs, drink), or psychosis (insanity, narcissism, delusion).

But an entirely different path was possible, Freud explained: access to civilization (to culture), which was the only possible avenue that could allow, through sublimation,[10] domination of destructive drives, that is, control over the state of nature, that savage, barbarian state that has been a component of the human psyche from the time of the ancient "savage hordes." Freud emphasized that those human beings who had given up the religious illusion could expect nothing from any return to "nature." As he saw it, the only way to achieve wisdom, that is, the most exalted of freedoms, consisted in an investment of the libido in the highest forms of creativity: love (Eros), art, science, knowledge, and the ability to live in society and to commit oneself, in the name of a common ideal, to the well-being of all. Hence this apologia for happiness—or "the good life"— in progress, which Louis Antoine de Saint-Just would not have disavowed. And Freud launched into an unconditional defense of the technical and scientific achievements of the twentieth century: the telephone, ocean liners and airplanes, photography, phonographs, domestic hygiene, cleanliness, and so on.

He added that, since "man is a wolf to man," there is no way to break with his primal self-destructive drive, except to consent to live with his fellow man.[11] Thus Freud based all social relations on the existence of the family (the germinal cell of society) on the one hand, and language on the other: "The man who first flung a word of abuse at his enemy instead of a spear was the founder of civilization."[12] And he went on to declare that the first man who had given up the pleasure of urinating onto a flame was also the hero of a great conquest of civilization—control of fire—since in that way he was giving a woman (his indispensable alter ego) the means for maintaining a household.[13] Here Freud was tacitly—and justifiably— parodying Jean-Jacques Rousseau on the origins of inequality: "The first person who, having fenced off a plot of ground, took it into his head to say *this is mine* and found people simple enough to believe him, was the true founder of civil society. What crimes, wars, murders, what miseries and horrors would the human Race have been spared by someone who, uprooting the stakes or filling in the ditch, had shouted to his fellows: Beware of listening to this impostor.' "[14]

Unlike Rousseau and the heirs of the Enlightenment philosophers, Freud did not believe that it would be possible to abolish inequalities.

Convinced that the instinctual forces are always more powerful than rational interests, he maintained that no society could be built on the basis of renouncing aggression, conflict, and self-assertion. But he argued nevertheless that language and law provided the only means for moving from the state of nature to the state of culture. He had already defended this thesis in *Totem and Taboo*. But now he was transforming it into a genuine political program, articulated around a psychoanalytic philosophy, an ideology, a representation of the world (Weltanschauung).[15]

In short, Freud was affirming simultaneously that civilization was a source of disappointment for human beings, because it forced them to give up their impulses, and that it was also a rational necessity for them, as long as it did not lead to excessive repression of the sexuality and aggressiveness needed for every sort of existence. Hence the discontent. Civilization is a remedy for unhappiness, he explained, only to the extent that it also creates unhappiness, by imposing constraints and shattering illusions. The life drive (Eros) is conceivable only because it opposes the death drive, and because it is articulated with constraint, with destiny, with the need for humans to live together (Ananke).

Equipped with this manifesto, Freud thus issued three challenges at once: to "the American way of life," which favored excessive individualism and thus led to economic disasters; to Catholicism, which was based on love for one's neighbor and thus ignored the human fascination with self-destruction; and the Communist revolution, which maintained an unshakeable belief in the illusion of human equality and thus purported to abolish one of the major wellsprings of human drives: the desire for wealth. In other words, Freud was flatly rejecting all modern beliefs in the advent of a "new man" who would be wholly "liberated" from the grip of the past. In this way, he was criticizing the utopia of the "new Jew" as much as the American dream of escaping the past and the Communist project of abolishing social classes. Finally, it is clear that he was rejecting all forms of dictatorship. At the very end of his essay, referring again to the dialectic between Faust and Mephisto and to Jacob's struggle with the angel, he insisted that the advent of scientific progress could always turn in the opposite direction: "Men have gained control over the forces of nature to such an extent that with their help they would have no difficulty in exterminating one another to the last man.

They know this, and it accounts for a large part of their current unrest, their unhappiness and their mood of anxiety. And now it is to be expected that the other of the two 'Heavenly Powers,' eternal Eros, will make an effort to assert himself in the struggle with his equally immortal adversary."[16]

In reality, this manifesto countered these three conceptions of society—religious, individualist, and Communist—with a representation of humanity based on psychoanalysis. Freud was as skeptical of democracy, which threatened to give too much power to the uneducated masses, as of dictatorships, which simply parodied the noble figure of authority in dangerous ways. Over these forms of government, he preferred a republic of elites based on the Platonic tradition and that of constitutional monarchy: a people enlightened by a sovereign concerned with the common good. This was, moreover, the reason he supported—as did Mann, Albert Einstein, and José Ortega y Gasset—the project of his Austrian compatriot Richard Nikolaus von Coudenhove-Kalergi, whose goal was to restore European unity by founding it on a common reference to Greco-Latin culture and Christianity.[17]

Once again, Freud made the city of Rome the major signifier of his doctrine of civilization. He knew that he would never go back to Italy, that the imperial city, the site of all his desires, was henceforth forbidden territory.[18] He knew that the sound of boots echoed there and that between the Coliseum and the Pantheon one would find the sinister emblems of the Blackshirts. And rather than believing in the new man, whatever the projected form, he emphasized that civilization was nothing but the expression of a constant reconciliation between past and present, between archaeological time—that of the unconscious—and the time of consciousness projected into the future:

> Since we overcame the error of supposing that the forgetting we are familiar with signified a destruction of the memory-trace—that is, its annihilation—we have been inclined to take the opposite view, that in mental life nothing which has once been formed can perish—that everything is somehow preserved and that in suitable circumstances (when, for instance, regression goes back far enough) it can once more be brought to light. . . .

Now let us, by a flight of imagination, suppose that Rome is not a human habitation but a psychical entity with a similarly long and copious past—an entity, that is to say, in which nothing that has once come into existence will have passed away and all the earlier phases of development continue to exist alongside the latest one.[19]

In other words, *Kultur,* according to Freud, was the same construct he had been advancing since *The Interpretation of Dreams,* one that unified all the stages of human time and thus made "I is an other" the sole "promised land" reserved for the modern subject. An instinctual id, buried in the ruins of an ancestral genealogy; an interdictive superego, symbolizing an inaccessible happiness; and an ego divided between memory and history. Such was, then, in 1930, the basis for the hope for a better life that Freud promised his contemporaries. In this system, Rome was conflated with Vienna and Vienna with 19 Berggasse, a site populated with all the ornaments of the ancient civilizations, the last refuge of a *Mitteleuropa* in its death throes, where visitors flocked from all over the world. At this moment, the name of Hitler had not yet appeared anywhere in the master's writings.

Civilization and Its Discontents was a best seller. When it was reissued in 1931, Freud added some laconic words to the final sentence: "But who can foresee with what success and with what result?" At this point he was thinking about the electoral victory the Nazis had won on September 14, 1930. The NSDAP had become the second most important political party in Germany, behind the SPD (Social Democratic Party) and ahead of the KPD (Kommunistische Partei Deutschlands; the German Communist Party). Hermann Göring, Joseph Goebbels, and Heinrich Himmler entered the Reichstag. Wiped out by the economic crisis, the country had more than four million unemployed citizens.

In 1932, Einstein was asked by the standing committee on arts and letters of the League of Nations to collect testimony from intellectuals in favor of peace and disarmament. Einstein thus wrote to Freud, whom he had already met, "Man has within him a lust for hatred and destruction. In normal times, this predisposition exists in a latent state, it emerges only in unusual circumstances; but it is a comparatively easy task to call it into

play and raise it to the power of a collective." Einstein asked the great connoisseur "of man's instinctive life" to enlighten him.[20]

Freud hastened to reply by a political manifesto, an extension of *Civilization and Its Discontents:* "Why War?"[21] Against the masters who sought to become dictators, and against the oppressed who sought to overthrow those masters, Freud anticipated a great return to the Platonic symposium, proposing that the League of Nations create an international republic of sages, a community of elite individuals who had "subjected their instinctual lives to the dictatorship of reason" and were capable, through their own authority, of imposing on the masses a genuine state of law based on the renunciation of murder. Everything that promotes civilization, he said, contributes to the weakening of the impulse to make war. Once again, he was proposing to the great leaders of the world an art of national governance that was in keeping with the doctrine of psychoanalysis.

Even though his doctrine had always been the vector of a representation of the world, of an ideology, of a political project, and of an anthropological body of thought, all based on the renunciation of murder and the institution of a state of law, Freud had never stopped contradicting himself by affirming that psychoanalysis was not a Weltanschauung.[22] He used this term to designate what he called "a specifically German concept, the translation of which into foreign languages might well raise difficulties."[23] In philosophy, the term referred to the idea of a metaphysics of the world, an overall conception of the human condition in the world. But for Freud, bent on making psychoanalysis a science of nature (which it never was), the expression was unsuitable. In his eyes, it was in league with philosophical discourse, religion, and political commitment, that is, with all sorts of illusions and other mental constructs that scientific reason—and thus psychoanalysis—was duty-bound to deconstruct. Moreover, in 1932 he openly mocked philosophy once again, representing it as a sort of small, limited-use religion: "Philosophy is not opposed to science, it behaves like a science and works in part by the same methods; it departs from it, however, by clinging to the illusion of being able to present a picture of the universe which is without gaps and is coherent, though one which is bound to collapse with every fresh advance in our knowledge. . . . Philosophy has no direct influence on the great mass of mankind; it is of

interest to only a small number even of the top layer of intellectuals and is scarcely intelligible to anyone else. On the other hand, religion is an immense power which has the strongest emotions of human beings at its service." Freud went on to cite the famous "derisive comment" made by one of his favorite poets, Heinrich Heine: "With his nightcaps and the tatters of his dressing-gown he patches up the gaps in the structure of the universe."[24]

Similarly, as in *Civilization and Its Discontents,* he offered up vibrant praise of scientific progress, the better to lash out pell-mell at Bolshevism, Marxism, and the obscure Hegelian dialectic, even though he asserted that he did not understand that dialectic very well, since he attributed the formation of social classes to the ancestral struggles among human hordes—or "races"—that differed very little from one another.

Freud thus continued to interpret the struggle of peoples to emancipate themselves according to the model laid down in *Totem and Taboo.* By the same token, he acknowledged that "Russian despotism was already doomed before it lost the War, because no amount of inbreeding among the ruling families of Europe could have produced a race of Tsars capable of withstanding the explosive force of dynamite."[25] In other words, he attributed the defeat of the Russian Empire just as much to the progress of scientific technologies as to the inability of the royal dynasties, as a result of their inbreeding, to renew themselves. Like the Labdacids, they were doomed to self-destruction. Freud seemed to forget that his argument did not suffice to explain the collapse of the ancient empires.

By seeking in this way to separate himself from philosophy and from the theory of history in order to make psychoanalysis a science, even as he maintained his mythographic analysis of the imperial dynasties and his conception of a republic of the elect, Freud made a mistake. For it was in the name of this rejection of any Weltanschauung that the idea was developed—with his assent—that since psychoanalysis was a science, it had to remain "neutral" in the face of all social change, and thus "apolitical."[26] In other words, even though he had criticized scientism and positivism, even though he claimed to be challenging scientific rationalism through his interest in occultism, even though he had invented an original conception of the "archaic" history of humanity, he refused to see

that his doctrine carried with it a politics, a philosophy, an ideology, an anthropology, and a movement toward emancipation.

Nothing was more contrary to the spirit of psychoanalysis than to disguise it as a so-called positive science and to keep it apart from all political commitment. After having criticized religion so strongly, Freud thus took the risk, in the name of "neutrality," of seeing his doctrine transformed into a catechism. This attitude was devastating for the psychoanalytic movement during the period between the wars, when it was confronted by the worst barbarism Europe had ever known. Among the Freudians, Ernest Jones was most vigilant in applying this "neutralist" line to which the master had given his stamp of approval.

Outside continental Europe, Jones had become the chief organizer of the psychoanalytical movement. A good pragmatic disciple who militated for a medical conception of the practice of treatment, he was thus simultaneously the one who destroyed the original Freudianism—that of Romanticism and *Mitteleuropa*—and the one who saved a community that, faced with the rise of Nazism, had no choice but to seek exile in the Anglophone world.

In the name of that neutrality and that apoliticism, Jones offered no support to the Freudians on the left in Germany and in Russia—Freudo-Marxists in particular—who sought to connect the century's two revolutions: the first aiming to transform the subject by exploring the unconscious, the second seeking to transform society through collective struggle.

In 1921, with the help of the Russian psychoanalytic movement, Vera Schmidt had created a pedagogical house in Moscow: the experimental Children's Home. She had taken in some thirty children of leaders and officials in the Communist Party in order to bring them up according to methods combining the principles of Marxism and of psychoanalysis. Thus the traditional educational system based on bullying and corporal punishment had been left behind. But the enterprise was based on the utopia of a possible abolition of the patriarchal family in favor of educational methods that privileged collective and egalitarian exchanges. The program also dictated that teachers go into analysis and that they not repress the children's sex play. In other words, Schmidt's pedagogical ideal attested to the new spirit of the 1920s, through which the dream of

a possible fusion between individual freedom and social equality was expressed.

In this context, accompanied by her mathematician husband Otto Schmidt, Vera had gone to Berlin and Vienna to seek support for the home from Freud and Karl Abraham. Their discussion bore essentially on the way the Oedipus complex should be treated in the framework of collective education. Clearly, this experiment did not adhere to the principles of Oedipal psychology. For that very reason, it was severely criticized by the Soviet Ministry of Health.

Freud would have liked to help the Schmidts, but Jones preferred to support not the Moscow psychoanalytic group but rather that of Kazan, which advocated a policy favorable to doctors and much more neutral toward Marxism. At the end of lengthy proceedings, and despite the provisional support of Lenin's wife, Nadezhda Krupskaya, the experiment was terminated. Criticized as much by the Freudians as by the Soviet regime, which was increasingly imbued with the Stalinist mindset, Vera Schmidt was also criticized by her friend Wilhelm Reich, who visited her in 1929. Already famous in Germany, Reich deemed the experiment insufficiently revolutionary.[27]

If we look at the debate over sexuality as it had been developing since the late nineteenth century, Reich's position was in reality symmetrical to Jung's. If Jung was in effect desexualizing sex in favor of a sort of élan vital, a "vital force," Reich was proceeding to desexualize the libido in favor of a biological genitality based on the blossoming of an orgiastic happiness from which the death drive was excluded. After having belonged to the Austrian Social Democratic Party, he had joined the KPD, where he was a fervent militant, constructing a worker-oriented mythology according to which the genitality of the proletariat was exempt from the bourgeois pathogen. Thus he did not hesitate to assert that neuroses were rarer in the working class than in the higher levels of society. Here was a new argument against the notion of the death drive.

Reich soon created a Socialist Society for sexual information and research, as well as sexual hygiene clinics intended to provide information to salaried workers (Sexpol). His admiration for Freud was boundless, whereas Freud's attitude toward him was disproportionately ferocious. He dreaded Reich's madness, his fame, and his political commitment. As

for Freud's disciples, they did everything they could to get rid of a man who upset their conformity, disturbed their convictions, and reconnected with the Fliessian origins of Freud's doctrine, origins whose importance they sought to relativize. This attitude led them, in 1934, to make a number of political mistakes.

As I have made clear, Freud had never stopped claiming his Jewish identity even though he refused to submit to the rituals of Judaism. Similarly, he felt himself to be Jewish only because he opposed the Zionist project of reconquering the Promised Land. In a word, Freud was a diaspora Jew who did not believe that the answer to anti-Semitism could be translated, for Jews, as a return to some particular territory. Even though he quite often supported the implantation of Jewish colonies in Palestine, he showed great prudence regarding the project of founding a "State of Jews." This is attested by the way he answered Chaim Koffler, a Viennese member of Keren Hayesod,[28] when Koffler asked him, along with other intellectuals from the diaspora, to support the Zionist cause in Palestine and the principle of allowing Jews access to the Wailing Wall. Let us note that, from 1925 on, thanks to the intervention of Chaim Weizmann, who sought to create a structure for official instruction in psychoanalysis in Israel, Freud had become a member of the Board of Governors of the University of Jerusalem, along with his English disciple David Eder.[29]

This did not keep him from declining Koffler's proposal:

Dear Doctor,

I cannot do what you ask. My unwillingness to involve the public with my name is insurmountable and not even this present critical occasion seems to warrant it. Whoever wishes to influence the crowd must express something that resonates and creates enthusiasm but my sober estimation of Zionism does not allow me to do so.

I certainly have a great deal of sympathy for their endeavours; I am proud of our university in Jerusalem and am pleased that our settlements are flourishing.

But, on the other hand, I do not believe that Palestine can ever become a Jewish State or that both the Christian and Islamic world will ever be prepared to entrust their holy places to Jewish care. To me it would have seemed more sensible to establish a Jewish homeland on a

historically unencumbered soil; I do know that with such a rational plan one could never have won the enthusiasm of the masses or the financial backing of the rich. Also, I regretfully admit that the unworldly fanaticism of our fellow Jews must bear some responsibility for awakening the mistrust of the Arabs. Nor can I summon up any trace of sympathy for the misguided piety that has made a piece of Herod's wall into a national relic, thereby provoking the natives' feelings.

Now judge for yourself whether I, with such a critical attitude, am the right person to act as the comforter of a people whose unfounded hopes have been shattered.

Yours respectfully, Freud[30]

On the same day, February 26, 1930, Freud sent Einstein another letter, taking up the argument again point by point: abhorrence of religion, skepticism toward the creation of a Jewish state in Palestine, solidarity toward his "Zionist" brothers (whom he sometimes called his "brothers by race"), and empathy, finally, toward Zionism, even though he did not share its ideal with its "misguided piety." Once again, Freud expressed his pride in "our" university and "our" kibbutzim, but he reiterated that he did not believe in the creation of a Jewish state because, he said, the Muslims and the Christians would never agree to entrust their sanctuaries to Jews. Thus, as Peter Gay reports, "he regretted to see the 'unrealistic fanaticism' of his fellow Jews awakening the suspicion of the Arabs."[31]

Freud clearly had the intuition, then, that the question of sovereignty over sacred sites would one day be at the heart of an almost unresolvable quarrel not only among the three monotheisms, but among the two sibling peoples residing in Palestine.[32] He feared with good reason that an abusive colonization would end up pitting anti-Semitic Arabs against racist Jews around an idolized stretch of wall.

Whereas Freud demonstrated great lucidity on the question of his own Jewishness and on the future of the Jews in Palestine, he manifested real blindness with respect to the nature of Nazi anti-Semitism and the appropriate political response to the question of the survival of psychoanalysis in Germany, Austria, and Italy during the bleak years between the

wars. Once again, the reference to Weltanschauung served as the pretext for adopting a dangerous neutrality.

As soon as he was in power, Hitler implemented the National Socialist doctrine, whose central thesis aimed at the extermination of all the Jews in Europe inasmuch as they were characterized as an "inferior race." This plan was to apply to all persons considered "defective" or inconvenient for the social body. Thus homosexuality and mental illness were treated as equivalents of Jewishness. In this context, the craftsmen of the Reich's new medicine added to their agenda the destruction of psychoanalysis, along with its vocabulary, concepts, works, movements, institutions, and practitioners. Among all the schools of dynamic psychiatry and psychotherapy, psychoanalysis was the only one to receive the label Freud so dreaded: "Jewish science." As for the cleansing program, it was orchestrated by the sinister psychiatrist Matthias Heinrich Göring, a cousin of the marshal.

A Lutheran and a pietist, Heinrich had been Emil Kraepelin's assistant before he took an interest in hypnosis and then adopted the theses of Alfred Adler's individual psychology. He went on to take Jungian psychology as his model, imagining that he would make it the prototype of a new Hitlerian psychology centered on the superiority of the German soul. Pragmatic and dogmatic, conservative and narrow minded, a committed and fearsome Nazi with the appearance of a nice grandfather with a big beard, he vilified the power of Freudian theory, which he saw as the fruit of what he hated most in the world: "Jewish" universalism linked to the *Aufklärung*. He quickly became known as the führer of psychotherapy.[33]

In March 1933, like many other Austrians, Freud did not perceive the danger that Nazism posed for his country. He believed that he was protected by the laws of the republic, and, despite the advice of his foreign friends, he rejected the possibility of leaving Vienna: "It is not certain that the Hitler regime will also overpower Austria; it is, of course, possible, but everyone believes that it will not reach the height of brutality here that it has in Germany. There is certainly no personal danger for me, and if you assume life in oppression to be amply uncomfortable for us Jews, then don't forget how little contentment life promises refugees in a foreign country, be it Switzerland or England. Flight, I think, would be

justified only in the case of lethal danger, and incidentally, if they kill you, it's one kind of death like any other."[34]

Refusing to see that Nazism was going to spread throughout Europe, Freud thought that Chancellor Engelbert Dollfuss, a conservative and a nationalist, an ally of Mussolini, was the person best situated to resist the Austrian Nazi Party, which sought to promote the annexation of Austria (the Anschluss) by Germany as quickly as possible. To be sure, Freud had no sympathy for this Fascist dictator, a Catholic and a reactionary, but he thought that the establishment of an authoritarian regime would be the lesser of two evils for the Jews. Thus he accepted Dollfuss's dissolution of basic liberties:[35] the right to strike was abolished, the press was censored, Socialists and Marxists were persecuted. And when, on February 12, 1934, the chancellor crushed the general strike launched by Socialist militants in a bloodbath, Freud remained "neutral": "We passed through a week of civil war. . . . No doubt, the rebels belonged to the best portion of the population, but their success would have been very shortlived and brought about military invasion of the country. Besides they were Bolshevists and I expect no salvation from Communism. So we could not give our sympathy to either side of the combatants."[36]

Freud did not confuse Communism with Nazism. He recognized the revolutionary ideal behind the Bolshevik revolution, whereas he saw the Hitlerian barbarity as a major regression toward humanity's most murderous instincts. But, when he was confronted with the reality of Fascism and Nazism, it took him time to understand that no negotiation was possible. He did not look at Hitler head on, he avoided pronouncing his name, and he had not read *Mein Kampf*—just the opposite of Mann.[37]

This was the context in which Edoardo Weiss, who had been living in Rome for two years, paid a visit to Freud on April 25, 1933. Weiss had thought of fleeing Fascism on several occasions, but the master had strongly advised him to stay in his own country, convinced that no other prospect was open to him elsewhere, despite the incessant attacks by the Catholic Church, and in particular by Father Wilhelm Schmidt, head of the Pontifical Museum of Ethnology in the Lateran, who denounced Freudianism as a pernicious theory that was responsible, on the same basis as Marxism, for the destruction of the Christian family. Freud stubbornly refused to entertain the idea of emigrating to the North Amer-

ican continent. In his eyes, the fight to rescue and maintain psychoanalysis had to be carried out in Europe.

The fact remains that Weiss came to Vienna this time in the company of Giovacchino Forzano and the latter's daughter Concetta, whom he was treating for agoraphobia and a serious case of hysteria. As he had not succeeded in handling this difficult treatment properly, he asked Freud to intervene as supervisor in the girl's presence. The experiment was a success, and Weiss was able to continue Concetta's analysis, writing to Freud to ask for advice.[38]

A playwright marked by the work of Gabriele D'Annunzio, Forzano had become a close friend of Mussolini, with whom he had written a three-act play about Napoleon's "Hundred Days."[39] The authors appropriated the emperor's image in a grotesque way, making Napoleon prefigure *Il Duce*. To seduce Freud, to whom he was entrusting the future of his daughter, Forzano brought the German edition of the play with him to 19 Berggasse. On the frontispiece, he had written a dedication in the name of both authors: "To S. F. who will make the world better, with admiration and gratitude."[40] And that is why he asked the Professor to give him, in turn, a photograph and one of his books, signed and addressed to Mussolini. Eager to protect Weiss, who was organizing the psychoanalytic movement and who had just brought out the first printing of the *Rivista italiana di psicoanalisi*, Freud went to his library to find a copy of *Why War?* and wrote a dedication destined to give rise to violent polemics: "For Benito Mussolini with the humble greetings of an old man who recognizes in the man of power a champion of culture."[41]

While he admired conquerors, Freud abhorred dictators; this is clear from all his writings, and even more from the choice he made of a book for Mussolini. But there was no way he could get around Forzano's proposal. So he handled it with humor, paying homage to a "man of power" who took himself for Napoleon and Caesar combined but who had started archaeological digs that delighted the humble sage of Vienna.[42]

Freud was convinced, wrongly, that Weiss was on good terms with Mussolini, as he wrote later to Arnold Zweig. The reality turned out to be much more complex. A protector of psychoanalysis, connected to Weiss, Forzano in fact received no support whatsoever from Mussolini, who had no intention of opposing the Catholic Church. Moreover, on

June 20, 1933, the dictator denounced psychoanalysis as a "fraud" orches-
trated by a Pontifex Maximus."[43] Ultimately, despite an appeal to Galeano
Ciano, Weiss could not prevent the Propaganda Services from sus-
pending the publication of the *Rivista*.[44] Worse still, Fascist diplomats
ordered a ridiculous investigation into the activities of the WPV intended
to prove that Sigismond (*sic*) Freud maintained suspect relations with the
anarchist thinker Camillo Berneri,[45] and that his disciples were engaging
in mercenary operations supported by the Socialists and the Communists.
As a result, no Italian psychoanalyst could enroll in the WPV.[46]

Three months after Hitler took power, the Nazis ransacked the building
housing the Institute of Sexology, dispersing the archives, documents,
books, objects, and all the iconography collected by Magnus Hirschfeld
on the various minority forms of sexuality. They ruined decades of work
and research, even as Ernst Röhm, the head of the strong-arm forces and
a notorious homosexual, had just joined the government, a year before
being assassinated himself on Hitler's orders.

Hirschfeld was not in Berlin that day; he was in Switzerland for med-
ical treatment. He decided to go into exile in Paris and then in Nice, where
he died, desperate at having seen his life's work collapse. In a very short
time, the cafés, cabarets, meeting places, and other institutions that had
made Berlin the most flourishing city in Eastern Europe during the 1920s,
and the city most open to homosexuals, were reduced to nothing: occu-
pied, closed, looted, destroyed.[47]

On May 11, 1933, Goebbels ordered the burning of twenty thousand
"Jewish" books. The auto-da-fé continued all night in the Opernplatz; the
spectacle brought together professors, students, and SS and SA sections.[48]
They all paraded around gleefully, brandishing torches, singing patriotic
hymns, and reciting incantations: "Against the class struggle and materi-
alism, I consign to the flames the books of Marx and Kautsky, against the
exaltation of the instincts and for the ennobling of the human soul, I con-
sign to the flames the writings of Sigmund Freud."[49] From Vienna, Freud
retorted: "What progress we are making. In the Middle Ages they would
have burnt me; nowadays they are content with burning my books."[50]

What a statement! Freud would have done better to say that burning
"Jewish" books would lead to burning not only the authors of the books
but the Jews themselves, along with other representatives of "races"

deemed "inferior." He still thought that Nazism was only the expression of a recurring anti-Semitism. How could he imagine, at the time, that what he had written in 1930 about man's capacity to destroy himself could be realized so very rapidly? He had been thinking during that period about the "American way of life," never about Europe.

In an article published in September 1933, accompanied by vile caricatures, a Nazi journalist asserted that "the Jew Sigmund Freud" had invented an "Asiatic" method destined to destroy the German race by obliging human beings to obey their destructive drives and thus to "enjoy orgasmic pleasure for fear of dying." He accused the Viennese master of wanting to foster among the young all sorts of transgressive sexual practices: masturbation, perversion, adultery.[51] Thus it was necessary, in his eyes, to get rid of the scourge. Such was Goebbels's program for destroying that "Jewish doctrine."

After proclaiming that Mein Kampf would be his guide when it came time to implement his mental health program, Göring made a special effort to attract favorable attention from the Freudians who wanted to collaborate with the regime: Felix Boehm and Carl Müller-Braunschweig were the first to sign on; Harald Schultz-Hencke and Werner Kemper soon followed. Members of the Deutsche Psychoanalytische Gesellschaft (DPG), these four men were mediocre figures, jealous of their Jewish colleagues. The advent of National Socialism was a windfall for them in terms of career advancement. Feeling inferior to those whom they saw as overlords, they became valets to the executioners.

In 1930, the DPG had ninety members, most of them Jews. As early as 1933, they started heading for exile. During this period the letters exchanged between Max Eitingon and Freud became all the more tense: they used coded language, as their letters were subject to censorship. Isolated at the heart of the BPI, Eitingon was soon pressured into resigning, while Jones, hostile to the Freudian Left in Germany—Otto Fenichel and Ernst Simmel, among others—and eager to reinforce Anglo-American power, relied on Felix Boehm to support the policy of collaboration with the new regime. This policy now consisted, under the Nazis, in maintaining an allegedly "neutral" approach, in order to preserve psychoanalysis from any contamination by the other schools of psychotherapy that had been introduced into the heart of the new "Aryanized" BPI.

Hostile to that line, Eitingon insisted on waiting to make his decision until Freud had spelled out his own opinion in writing. In a letter dated March 21, 1933, the master did just this, stressing that his disciple had to choose from three solutions: (1) work toward ending the activities of the BPI; (2) collaborate in maintaining the BPI under Boehm's leadership "so as to survive in unfavorable times"; or (3) jump ship, at the risk of leaving the Jungians and the Adlerians to seize the jewel, which would oblige the IPV to disqualify the BPI.[52] At that point, Freud had opted for the second solution, the "neutralist" solution advocated by Jones, which was to lead, two years later, to the wholesale Nazification of the BPI under Göring's control. However, Freud did not want to impose it on Eitingon, convinced as he was—wrongly—that Austria was not threatened by Hitler. He believed the country was protected by Austrofacism.

On April 17, he congratulated himself that Boehm had gotten Reich, whom he hated, out of his way (Reich was excluded from the IPV before emigrating to Norway, then to the Americas), and also Schultz-Hencke, an Adlerian Nazi who rejoined the BPI very quickly. In the face of Freud's blind conviction that psychoanalysis could survive under Nazism, Eitingon nevertheless decided to stay faithful to Freudianism as well as to Zionism. In April 1934, without reproaching Freud in the slightest, he left Germany to settle in Jerusalem. There he reconnected with Zweig and founded both a psychoanalytic society and an institute modeled on the one in Berlin, thus creating the basis for a future Israeli psychoanalytic movement.

When Sándor Ferenczi died, on May 22, 1933, after a bout of pernicious anemia, and with the old kingdom of psychoanalysis reduced to ashes, Freud felt the need, as always in such circumstances, to react immediately. When he was dealing with "traitors" to the cause, with enemies or others who had become "useless" in his eyes, Freud knew how to grasp with a single stroke of the pen the essence of a moment in someone's life worth preserving in the annals of his movement. He had a sense of memory rather than of history. Regarding Ferenczi, his companion from the outset, with whom he had always refused to break, Freud sought to mask his sorrow behind the outline of a clinical appraisal. Thus he offered Jones a psychoanalytical interpretation of the conflicts that had accompanied Ferenczi as he faced death, a questionable interpretation to say the least:

A mental degeneration in the form of paranoia developed with uncanny logical consistency. Central to this was the conviction that I did not love him enough, did not want to acknowledge his work, and also that I had analyzed him badly. His technical innovations . . . were . . . regressions to his childhood complexes, the main grievance being that his mother had not loved him—a middle child among 11 or 13—passionately or exclusively enough. So he himself became a better mother, even found the children he needed, among them a suspect American woman to whom he often devoted 4–5 hours a day. . . . After she had left, he believed that she influenced him through vibrations across the ocean. . . . He credited her with the oddest childhood traumas, which he then defended against us. In this confusion his once so brilliant intelligence was extinguished. But let us keep his sad end a secret between us.[53]

There is no evidence that Ferenczi had become paranoid. Evidence to the contrary is found in his clinical diary,[54] in which he reproached Freud for his increasing lack of interest in the therapeutic aspect of psychoanalysis, his hostility toward psychotic patients, his lack of empathy in treatment, his anti-Americanism. It is quite clear that these reproaches were partially justified. But one has to conclude that Freud and Ferenczi were both right, the former in his critique of the return to an exclusively traumatic explanation of mental disorders, the latter in his observation of the divagations of a treatment technique much too focused on frustration and the search for a univocal explanation. The fact remains that Ferenczi really was persecuted by Jones and criticized unfairly by the orthodox Freudians. He had chosen to remain faithful to Freud, who had never disclosed to him what he secretly thought about his disciple's mental state. In his last letters, Ferenczi demonstrated great lucidity about himself and about the evolving European catastrophe. On April 9, 1933, he had sent Freud a letter including these words: "Everything is quiet here in Budapest; who would have thought, ten to fifteen years ago, that my fatherland would be a relatively calm place on the European continent."[55]

As he had done for Abraham, Freud wrote Ferenczi's obituary. He recalled the happy years of the trip to Worcester and the foundation of the

IPV, adding that one day, perhaps, the "bio-analysis" dreamed of by the marvelous clinician of Budapest would emerge. He also evoked the differences between Ferenczi and himself, even as he asserted that Ferenczi had played an exceptional role in the history of analytic science. After penning these final parting words to his lifelong friend, he felt drained and deeply uneasy.[56]

If Freud had lost his best disciple, Jones had lost his analyst and his adversary; from that point on, Jones had a major role to play in the master's inner circle. He soon became the central actor in the psychoanalytic movement, before making himself the first biographer of the one whose policies he was presumably carrying out. In this way, at the heart of the storm, he ended up taking charge, from London, of implementing the "rescue" of psychoanalysis.

At the thirteenth congress of the IPV, which took place in Lucerne in August 1934 at the very moment when Jewish psychoanalysts were exiting from Nazi Germany, Reich was banned from the Freudian community owing to his "Bolshevism," which was deemed dangerous for psychoanalysis. However, Reich was opposed—in contrast to Jones, and quite rightly—to any form of collaboration with Nazism; he called for the dissolution of the DPG. Excluded from the German Communist movement as a leftist, he had just published his major work, *The Mass Psychology of Fascism*,[57] which responded directly to Freud's work on group psychology. Far from seeing Fascism as solely the product of a politics or an economic situation, he saw it as the expression of an unconscious structure, and he extended that definition to the collectivity, emphasizing that it resulted from a lack of sexual satisfaction on the part of the masses.

Freud's mistaken judgment about Reich, with which Eitingon disagreed, is attested by a report Boehm wrote in August 1934 after a visit with Freud: "Before we left, Freud expressed two wishes: firstly, that Schultz-Hencke should never be elected to the Board of our Society. I gave my word that I would never sit on a Board together with Sch.-H. And secondly, he said: 'Free me of Reich.'"[58]

Compelled to go into exile in Norway, and treated as a psychotic by the Freudians, Reich began to feel still more persecuted, and his paranoia increased. As of 1936 he had turned his back definitively on psychoanalysis and created, in Oslo, an institute for biological research on sexual eco-

nomics, which brought together doctors, psychologists, educators, sociologists, and kindergarten teachers. At the same time, he invented a new method, vegetotherapy, which was to become orgonotherapy; it was a matter of associating talking therapy with interventions on the patient's body. In this perspective, Reich attributed neuroses to a rigidity or a shrinking of the organism; they had to be treated by muscle-relaxing exercises in order to liberate the "orgasm reflex." Subsequently, attracted by the theory of bions (particles of vital energy), he gave free rein to his fascination with physio-biological theories, attempting to reconcile the cosmogonic themes cherished by Romanticism with the quantitative technology proper to sexology.[59]

Jones had picked the wrong enemy in fighting the Freudo-Marxists, and now he agreed to collaborate with the Nazis, even as he was helping Jews leave Germany for the English-speaking world. In 1935, he presided officially over the session of the DPG during which the nine Jewish members were forced to resign. Only one non-Jew opposed that farce: his name was Bernhard Kamm. He left the DPG out of solidarity with those excluded. He too followed the path of exile: he settled in Topeka, Kansas, in Karl Menninger's famous clinic, a veritable nerve center for all the psychotherapists in exile from Europe. Freud characterized this whole affair as a "sad debate." From this point on, the Freudians who had gone over to Göring ended their letters with the phrase "Heil Hitler."

While the Nazis were destroying psychoanalysis in Berlin, Freud continued to receive his patients in Vienna: among them, the American poetess Hilda Doolittle (H. D.), lover of Ezra Pound and of Annie Winifred Ellerman (known as Bryher); Doolittle had already been analyzed in London by a Kleinian for chronic depression. She gave an account of her treatment with Freud in two stages, eleven years apart (1945 and 1956): first, a verbatim report, and then a reinterpretation in the form of a narrative. In these two texts, she provided luminous accounts of Freud's interventions, which focused on her dreams, but she also bore witness to daily life in the household, and to her encounters with Freud's other patients, psychoanalysts for the most part. After that experience, she went on doing analytic work with other therapists. In the English-speaking world, her work, her life, and her account of her analysis gave rise to a considerable number of works devoted to lesbianism and gender studies.[60]

Joseph Wortis, an American psychiatrist born into a milieu of Jewish and Socialist intellectuals, also went to Vienna in 1934 to meet Freud, encouraged by Adolf Meyer and provided with a letter of recommendation from Havelock Ellis. He was doing research on homosexuality. In rebellion against all forms of transferential submission, he refused to enter into treatment, but Freud obliged him to do so, at least for a four-month period, as Freud deemed that, in order to undertake such research, one had to have gone through the clinical experience of psychoanalysis. As a result, Wortis behaved like a veritable detective, to Ellis's great delight, for the two maintained an active correspondence.

In the end, the analysis did not take place, but the two men plunged into a violent, intimate intellectual struggle that turned Wortis into a radical anti-Freudian; he would be obsessed for the rest of his life with the specter of the Viennese master. However, he pulled off the coup of collecting Freud's confidential remarks on his own life, on his disciples, friends, and worldview; Wortis thus produced a document of great interest to historians. Despite his illness and his difficulty speaking, Freud could manifest intense ferocity toward his enemies during this period, as though, anticipating his own end, he did not hesitate, even before an adversary, to give free rein to judgments that in other periods he would have preferred to conceal.[61]

Like the Freudians, Jung collaborated with Göring, from Zurich. He had succeeded Ernst Kretschmer as director of the Algemeine Ärztliche Gesellschaft für Psychotherapie (AÄGP, General Medical Psychotherapy Society). Founded in 1926, this association sought to unify the various schools of European psychotherapy under the aegis of medical knowledge. A journal, the *Zentralblatt für Psychotherapie,* was created in 1930 to spread the work of the AÄGP.

Kretschmer was an internationally renowned psychiatrist and the head of neuropsychiatry in Marburg; he had always made it his mission to bring all the branches of psychiatry and psychotherapy—including psychoanalysis—together in the AÄGP, provided that all the practitioners involved were medical doctors. At the Dresden congress in 1932, he had paid homage to Freud's work.[62] However, once Hitler had gained power, Kretschmer could no longer aspire to reach his goal; thus he preferred to resign the presidency of the AÄGP. The German branch of the society

and the *Zentralblatt,* published in Leipzig, were Nazified by force during that same period. At this point, the German psychotherapists, eager both to satisfy the regime and to maintain their national and European activities, asked Jung, the AÄGP vice president, to take over the presidency. Kretschmer, who enjoyed great prestige in Germany, was left alone by the Nazis during the war.

Wanting to ensure the domination of analytic psychology over the entire range of schools of psychotherapy, Jung agreed to become president of the AÄGP and thus to collaborate with Göring. In so doing, he claimed to be protecting both therapists who were not medical doctors, who had formerly been marginalized by Kretschmer, and Jewish colleagues, who had lost the right to practice in Germany. In reality, he had been chosen by the German practitioners because the advocates for "Aryan" psychotherapy, who were fiercely opposed to Freudian thinking, had confidence in him.

Pressed by Walter Cimbal and Gustav Richard Heyer, Jung thus plunged into an adventure that he could easily have avoided. As evidenced in a letter addressed to his disciple Rudolf Allers, who was to emigrate to the United States, he accepted all the conditions regarding the *Zentralblatt* that Göring dictated: "It must unquestionably be a 'conformed' editor, as he would be in a far better position than I to have the right nose for what one can say and what not. In any event it will be an egg-balancing dance. . . . Psychotherapy must see to it that it maintains its position inside the German Reich and does not settle outside it, regardless of how difficult its living conditions there may be." And Jung added, "Göring is a very amiable and reasonable man, so I have the best hopes for our collaboration."[63]

Jung began right away to publish texts favorable to Nazi Germany. The first appeared in 1933. Under the title "Geleitwort" ("Editorial"), he set forth a classic understanding of the differences among races and mentalities, each one being endowed, according to him, with a specific "psychology":

> It will . . . be the primary task of the *Zentralblatt* to give impartial appreciation to all objective contributions, and to promote an over-all view which will do greater justice to the basic facts of

the human psyche than has been the case up to now. The differences which actually do exist between Germanic and Jewish psychology and which have long been known to every intelligent person are no longer to be glossed over, and this can only be beneficial to science. In psychology more than in any other science there is a "personal equation," disregard of which falsifies the practical and theoretical findings. At the same time I should like to state expressly that this implies no depreciation of Semitic psychology, any more than it is a depreciation of the Chinese to speak of the peculiar psychology of the Oriental.[64]

On June 26, 1933, while he was in Berlin for a seminar, Jung granted a radio interview to his disciple Adolf von Weizsäcker, a neurologist and a psychiatrist who had become a Nazi. On that occasion, von Weizsäcker presented the master from Zurich as an eminent Protestant from Basel and as "the greatest researcher in modern psychology." Cleverly, he declared that Jung's theory of the psyche was more creative and closer to the "German spirit" than that of Freud or Adler. Then he led Jung to draw a laudatory portrait of Hitler and of Germany's fine young people, and to condemn the European democracies as "mired in parliamentarianism." Jung ended the interview by proposing that nations "enrich themselves" by applying a program for renewing their souls based on the cult of the leader: "As Hitler said recently," Jung declared, "the leader must be able to be alone and must have the courage to go his own way. . . . [The leader] is the incarnation of the nation's psyche and its mouthpiece. He is the spearhead of the phalanx of the whole people in motion. The need of the whole always calls forth a leader, regardless of the form a state may take."[65]

Refusing to acknowledge that Nazification aimed to drive all Jews from the profession of psychotherapy, and then to exterminate them, Jung did not admit, either, that a good number of the German Jungians with whom he was collaborating on the *Zentralblatt* had adopted the theses of National Socialism.[66] In this respect, his conduct was no more honorable than that of the second-rate Freudians in Berlin. They too thought they were protecting the integrity of psychoanalysis in the face of deviations: they too considered the long-bearded "grandpa-führer" as a likable and reasonable man. However, if Jung could accept this collaboration without hesitation,

it was also because his conception of the unconscious was for the most part in harmony with the one advocated by the partisans of "Aryanized" psychotherapy. Taking up a theory of the difference between the races, Jung saw the individual psyche as the reflection of the collective soul of populations. In other words, far from being an ideologue of racial inequality, along the lines of Georges Vacher de Lapouge or Arthur de Gobineau, Jung saw himself as a theosophist in search of a differential ontology of the psyche. Thus he wanted to establish a "psychology of nations" capable of accounting both for the fate of the individual and for the collective soul. He divided the archetype into three structures: the *animus* (image of the masculine), the *anima* (image of the feminine), and the *Selbst* (the self), the true center of personality. In his eyes, the archetypes formed the basis for the psyche, a sort of mythical patrimony proper to a humanity organized around the paradigm of difference. Armed with his archetypal psychology, Jung put the Jews in the category of uprooted peoples, condemned to wander, and all the more dangerous in that, to escape their psychological denationalization, they did not hesitate to enter the mental, social, and cultural universe of non-Jews.

It was in this context that he evolved toward an inegalitarian concept of the archetypal psyche. Previously, he had adopted an approach couched in classically differentialist terms. But in April 1934 he published a long article in the *Zentralblatt* titled "Zur gegenwärtigen Lage der Psychotherapie" ("The State of Psychotherapy Today") in which he defended National Socialism while asserting the superiority of the Aryan unconscious over the Jewish unconscious. This text, sadly, became famous and was to have enormous influence over Jung's later destiny and that of his movement.

All the ingredients were in place for transforming Freud's theory into an obscene pansexualism tied to the Jewish "mentality." Jung seemed to forget that some twenty-five years earlier he had defended psychoanalysis against arguments of the same type, which compared it to an epidemic spawned by the decadence of imperial Vienna. Here are some excerpts:

> The Jews have this peculiarity in common with women; being physically weaker, they have to aim at the chinks in the armour of their adversary, and, thanks to this technique which has been forced on them

through the centuries, the Jews themselves are best protected where others are most vulnerable. . . . As a member of a race with a three-thousand-year-old civilization, the Jew, like the cultured Chinese, has a wider area of psychological consciousness than we. Consequently it is *in general* less dangerous for the Jew to put a negative value on his unconscious. The "Aryan" unconscious, on the other hand, contains explosive forces and seeds of a future yet to be born, and these may not be devalued as nursery romanticism without psychic danger.

The still youthful Germanic peoples are fully capable of creating new cultural forms that still lie dormant in the darkness of the unconscious of every individual—seeds bursting with energy and capable of mighty expansion. The Jew, who is something of a nomad, has never yet created a cultural form of his own and as far as we can see never will, since all his instincts and talents require a more or less civilized nation to act as host for their development. The Jewish race as a whole—at least this is my experience—possesses an unconscious which can be compared with the "Aryan" only with reserve. Creative individuals apart, the average Jew is far too conscious and differentiated to go about pregnant with the tensions of unborn futures. The "Aryan" unconscious has a higher potential than the Jewish; that is both the advantage and the disadvantage of a youthfulness not fully weaned from barbarianism. In my opinion it has been a grave error in medical psychology up till now to apply Jewish categories—which are not even binding on all Jews—indiscriminately to Germanic and Slavic Christendom. Because of this the most precious secret of the Germanic peoples—their creative and intuitive depth of soul—has been explained as a morass of banal infantilism, while my own warning voice has for decades been suspected of anti-Semitism. This suspicion emanated from Freud. He did not understand the Germanic psyche any more than did his Germanic followers. Has the formidable phenomenon of National Socialism, on which the whole world gazes with astonishment, taught them better?[67]

In letters he wrote in 1934, Jung complained several times that it had become impossible to speak about the Jews without being accused of anti-Semitism. When the attacks multiplied, he attributed them to an

anti-Christian polemic: "The mere fact that I speak of a difference between Jewish and Christian psychology," he wrote to James Kirsch, "suffices to allow anyone to voice the prejudice that I am an anti-Semite. . . . This hypersensitivity is simply pathological and makes every discussion practically impossible. As you know, Freud previously accused me of anti-Semitism because I could not abide his soulless materialism. The Jew directly solicits anti-Semitism with his readiness to scent out anti-Semitism everywhere."[68]

Even as he reproached the Jews for creating the conditions of their persecution, Jung claimed to be helping them become better Jews. In a letter to his student Gerhard Adler dated June 9, 1934, he approved of the idea Adler had advanced that Freud was in a way guilty of having detached himself from his Jewish archetype, from his Jewish "roots." In other words, in keeping with his own theory, Jung was challenging the Freudian model of the Jew without religion, the Enlightenment Jew. He condemned the modern figure of the de-Judaized Jew who was guilty, according to him, of denying his Jewish "nature": "So when I criticize Freud's Jewishness I am not criticizing the *Jews* but rather that damnable capacity of the Jew, as exemplified by Freud, to deny his own nature."[69] At pains to bring the Jews back onto the terrain of a psychology of difference, Jung paid close attention to the evolution of his own Jewish disciples in exile in Palestine. Finally anchored in the new Promised Land, they could become truly Jungian. To Erich Neumann, who had settled in Tel Aviv, he wrote a letter dated December 22, 1935, in which he scolded the "cultivated [European] Jew" who was "always on the way to becoming a 'non-Jew.'" In contrast, he praised the Palestinian Jews who had finally found their "archetypal soil": "I find your very positive conviction that the soil of Palestine is essential for Jewish individuation most valuable. How does this square with the fact that Jews in general have lived *much longer* in other countries than in Palestine? . . . Is it the case that the Jew is so accustomed to being a non-Jew that he needs the Palestinian soil *in concreto* to be reminded of his Jewishness?"[70]

In other words, Jung was a Zionist out of anti-Semitism, while Freud rejected Zionism because he did not believe for a moment that the Jews would find a solution to anti-Semitism by conquering the Promised Land. To the end, Freud remained a Jew of the diaspora, a universal Jew, while

his former disciple clung to the idea that the Jews could survive only by making sure that they were anchored in an actual territory: thus the promised land of the unconscious, internal to subjectivity, was opposed to the archetypal territory.

If one looks closely at Jung's texts, one notices that he sometimes used the famous language of the Third Reich, *Lingua Tertii Imperii* (LTI), which the philologist Victor Klemperer described so well, a sort of Hitlerian jargon attributing value to the most simplistic German terms in order to facilitate propaganda. An enterprise aimed at destroying the richness of the German language, the LTI ended up contaminating the discourse and writings of those who collaborated with the regime. Texts written in this "newspeak" often multiplied references to the alleged specific characteristics of Jews, always designated as inert or nomadic, contemptible, nihilistic "things" set apart from humanity, in contrast to "Aryans," who were represented as grand, sublime, the quintessence of all forms of "racial" superiority.[71]

In this respect, one can usefully compare the respective positions of Jung and Martin Heidegger, a fierce enemy of psychoanalysis. Considering that the Jews "had no world" and that psychoanalysis was kin to nihilism, the philosopher remarked in a notebook dated 1940–1941 that one must not "express too much outrage against the psychoanalysis" of the "Jew Freud," as the supporters of racial biologism were doing, but he added at once that this was a form of thought that did not tolerate being and that reduced everything to the instincts and to a withering of instinct. He too used the jargon of the Third Reich.[72]

Just as Jung excluded diaspora Jews from any access to "Jewish individuation," Heidegger excluded Jews from thinking humanity, reducing them to the morass of instincts. In both cases, the anti-Semitism that did not want to speak its name claimed to be eliminating the Jewish mind from the world scene, inasmuch as that mind was thought to have given rise to a specifically Jewish doctrine. For Jung, psychoanalysis lacked an "archetypical ground"; for Heidegger it was a nihilism bearing the name of the Jew Freud. Jung and Heidegger had in common their adherence to a sort of anti-Judeo-Christian and polytheistic theology.[73]

In 1936, Göring finally realized his dream. He created his Deutsches Institut für Psychologische Forschung und Psychotherapie (German In-

stitute for Research in Psychology and Psychotherapy), soon called simply the Göring Institute. To emphasize the triumph of Nazism over psychoanalysis, he established the institute in the home of the prestigious BPI, a symbol of the Freudian power that he had sought so eagerly to abolish. In this site he brought together Freudians, Jungians, independents, and Adlerians, each of whom detested the others.

Throughout the war, some twenty Freudians thus pursued their therapeutic activities and their provincial quarrels while defending a "good psychoanalysis" under the banner of the Göring Institute and under the heel of the Nazi regime. In the name of an alleged rescue operation, these men dishonored themselves by collaborating in the destruction that would have taken place in any case; it would have been preferable for it to have taken place without them. They adhered to the language of the Third Reich, accepted the systematic eradication of the entire Freudian vocabulary, and, whatever they may have asserted later in their own defense, they refused to treat Jewish patients, who were moreover excluded from all treatment and sent off to the camps.

In May 1936, the celebration of Freud's birthday took on considerable proportions. Covered with honors, the illustrious scholar, henceforth confined to Vienna, received gifts and letters, as if all those who paid him homage—H. G. Wells, Romain Rolland, Albert Schweitzer, among many others—were aware that his situation was desperate: "Until a short time ago," Einstein wrote, "I was only aware of the speculative force of your thought and of its powerful influence on our contemporary view of the world, and was unable to make up my mind about the intrinsic truth of your theories. However, I recently happened to hear about certain, as such insignificant, cases, which convinced me that any differing explanation (an explanation different from the doctrine of repression) was excluded."[74] That day, Freud's niece, Lilly Freud-Marlé, sent him three essays that she had written expressly for him and that touched his heart, so conscious was he of the inexorable dispersion of the members of his family who were already in exile.[75]

The next day, he was visited by Ludwig Binswanger and Mann, and the latter came back on May 14 to Freud's villa in Grinzing,[76] where he often stayed, to read him the speech on the "life already lived" that he had given in Freud's honor at the Akademische Verein für Medizinische

Psychologie. This time, Freud was so impressed that he did not object when the writer classified his work as part of the patrimony of philosophy and characterized Freud himself as a son of Nietzsche and of Schopenhauer, then as a "pioneer of a humanism of the future": "Science," Mann said, "has never made a discovery without being authorized and encouraged thereto by philosophy."[77] Mann concluded his eulogistic remarks with a vibrant appeal for human freedom, while stressing the resemblance between Freud and Faust. The two men then embarked on a long conversation about the name of Joseph, the biblical hero, son of Jacob, grandson of Isaac; but also a historical person, brother of Napoleon Bonaparte, always very present in Freud's writings. In January, Freud had written a text on the subject for a book in honor of Rolland.[78]

Mann and Freud were both passionate about Egyptology, and Mann had begun to write a vast biblical novel devoted to Joseph, the last of the patriarchs. In the last book in Genesis, Joseph, Jacob's favorite son, enjoyed inciting the envy of his eleven brothers, to whom he recounted two prophetic dreams: in the first, eleven sheaves of grain bowed down to his own, and in the second, eleven stars bowed down to him. For challenging his brothers, Joseph was first thrust into a cistern, then sold for twenty pieces of silver to the Ishmaelites, who took him to Egypt. There, he was purchased by Potiphar, the commander of the pharaoh's guard; he was put in charge of Potiphar's household, and he resisted the illicit passion Potiphar's wife felt for him. God watched over his destiny. Thanks to Joseph's talents as an interpreter of dreams, he became viceroy of Egypt. At the end of a life in exile, having reached a position of power, he pardoned his brothers and reconnected with his father, who blessed the children born to Joseph's wife, Asnah, daughter of Potiphar, and designated him the chief heir to the divine alliance with Abraham's lineage. As he lay dying, Joseph prophesied the Exodus. In his wake, Moses took care, as he led the Hebrews toward the Promised Land, to take the bones of Jacob's son with him.

In other words, at the very moment when Freud was taking an interest in Moses, after having been inhabited all his life by the struggle between Jacob and the angel, Mann was writing a four-part novel in which he made Joseph a modern hero, a sort of Narcissus overwhelmed with privileges by a father who was subject throughout his life to a perpetual struggle. Con-

vinced that his fine appearance and his intellectual superiority would bring him power and glory, Joseph wrapped himself in his mother Rachel's wedding cloak, arousing his brothers' jealousy. And suddenly his fate thrust him into servitude. After having been a slave, he devoted all his talents as an organizer to the Pharaoh Akhenaten (Amenhotep III). In the process, he supported the transformation of the ancient mythologies into a monotheistic religion and became the embodiment of a progressive humanist.

A Jew and an Egyptian, a pragmatist and a manager, Mann's Joseph was the hero of a spirituality that could only be realized in exile and in the affirmation of an unprecedented subjectivity in the face of a father still attached to an archaic universe. Through this saga the writer sought to bring back into the light, confronting Nazism, the thesis of the predestination of the patriarchs of Israel, revised and corrected by the humanism that inspired him.

Freud had read the first three volumes of the tetralogy, which were published between 1933 and 1936,[79] and he was inspired by them to send Mann an astonishing interpretation of the place occupied by Joseph's life in the destiny of Napoleon Bonaparte. According to Freud, Joseph served as a model for the emperor, alternately sublime and diabolical. Freud started from the idea that as a child Napoleon had experienced intense hostility toward his older brother Joseph and that, in order to take his place, he had converted his primal hatred into love, while maintaining some elements of the old aggressiveness that was later focused on other objects. Adored by his mother, Napoleon eventually became a father substitute for his brothers and developed an outsize passion for Josephine, the female incarnation of Joseph. As Freud saw it, the emperor's love for the young widow, even though she treated him badly and was unfaithful, was thus merely the product of his identification with Joseph. But to assume fully his role as substitute for his older brother, Napoleon set his sights on Egypt, making a further connection with the life of Jacob's son. In this way the Egyptian campaign marked a sublime moment in the Napoleonic epic, since it allowed Europe, and thus Freud himself, to discover the vestiges of a fabulous civilization and to open a field of new studies to archaeology. In Freud's narrative, by repudiating Josephine, Napoleon became unfaithful to his myth and orchestrated his own decline, turning

himself into a diabolical tyrant. An incorrigible dreamer, he played the same role Joseph had played in Egypt, only to contribute to his own destruction and Europe's.

Like most nineteenth-century novelists, from Balzac through Hugo to Tolstoy, Freud had always been interested in the heroic destiny of this modern conqueror who admired science, was hostile to religious obscurantism, and had transformed the European world while giving Jews civil rights and fostering their assimilation. Freud had paid homage to Napoleon, moreover, when he recalled that Isaac Bernays, Martha's grandfather, had benefited from the civil code introduced by the French occupier when he enrolled as a university student and later became the chief rabbi of Hamburg. Moreover, the duke of Reichstadt belonged to the Habsburg line on his mother's side.[80] Freud seemed at that point to have forgotten that in his youth he had admired André Masséna, a Freemason and an imperial marshal with whom he shared a birthday and whom he took to be a Jew.

As a good Anglophile, he considered the emperor a pure product of French Jacobinism, even as he proclaimed that Napoleon's family history was of the greatest interest for psychoanalytic doctrine and that the man showed signs of genius and "magnificent class." Moreover, the romantic destiny of this man who had met Goethe and who embodied the determination of an entire epoch to break with mythologies of origins in order to ensure the advance of a new historic consciousness had aroused enormous interest in the Freudian community. Jones had been the first to talk to Freud about the story of Joseph and Napoleon's Oriental complex; after him, Ludwig Jekels and Edmund Bergler had each devoted an essay to Napoleon's life and his fraternal or paternal complex.[81]

The fact remains that, in his exchange with Mann, Freud had recalled his own visit to the Acropolis and the disturbance he had felt in observing that his own destiny was so different from that of his father.

The interest of the exchange with Mann lay in the similarity between the two undertakings. Like the writer, Freud mobilized Egyptology to translate the biblical history of Judaism into a novel of modern Jewishness, a Jewishness through which a hero forced into exile was the product of two identities: one Jewish, the other Egyptian. Mann had chosen Joseph and Freud Moses, as if each writer were seeking in his own way to

illustrate the greatness of the diaspora Jewishness that was destined for genocide. Mann eventually finished his book on the West Coast of the United States, in company with Brecht, Theodor Adorno, and Fritz Lang; Freud completed his in his home in London, surrounded by his family. Thus each managed to preserve, from the depths of exile, the beauty of the German language, the only possession Hitler could never take away from them.

In August 1936, Jones presided over the fourteenth congress of the IPV, held in Marienbad. He proposed to abandon the German acronym in favor of that of the International Psychoanalytic Association (IPA). The choice was justified since, from that point on, English was the majority language in international exchanges, and the exiles from the old *Mitteleuropa* spoke it perfectly. While the partisans of Melanie Klein and those of Anna Freud were confronting one another once again, and Melitta Schmideberg, supported by Edward Glover, was battling her mother, Jacques Lacan, a French psychiatrist already known in his own country, made his entrance into the international psychoanalytic movement by giving a presentation on the "mirror stage." After ten minutes, Jones cut him off. Lacan then went off to the demonstrations of the infamous Eleventh Olympiad in Berlin. Confronted by this spectacle, which horrified him, and after the humiliation visited on him by Jones, he felt that the time had come to carry out a second "Freudian revolution." He produced a manifesto, "Beyond the 'Reality Principle,' "[82] intended as a corollary to "Beyond the Pleasure Principle." At the time, no one on the IPA scene yet suspected what impact the Lacanian reworking of Freud's work was to have.

In November, during a WPV meeting, Boehm noted, as did Anna Freud, that many students were taking courses in psychoanalysis at the Göring Institute. At this point, Freud was beginning to realize that the policy of "rescuing" psychoanalysis was probably not the best option. He asked Boehm to describe the situation for him, just before he resumed his attacks on Alfred Adler, recommending that no concessions be made to the partisans of the "psychology of masculine protest."[83]

Boehm had managed to pass for a defender of Freudianism while conceding that what was happening then in Germany would never have been tolerated by the movement a year earlier. The unacceptable was henceforth ordinary. He nevertheless proposed to invite a member of the WPV

to Berlin. "Who will you invite?" Freud asked. And Boehm put forward the name of Richard Sterba, the only non-Jew in the WPV, who was hostile, moreover, to any form of collaboration with the Nazis. "I will gladly accept an invitation," Sterba replied, "after one of my Jewish Viennese colleagues has been invited to speak at the Berlin Institute." Sterba wanted to believe that Freud completely disapproved of Jones's policy. This was not yet the case. An ominous meeting.[84]

At the Göring Institute, each member was concentrating on his or her own research and experiments. In the ranks of the defunct DPG, John Rittmeister, August Watermann, Karl Landauer, and Salomea Kempner were the main victims of this policy; they were exterminated or assassinated, as were several other Hungarian and Austrian therapists who did not succeed in reaching exile.

Some of Adler's German partisans also participated in this policy of collaboration. However, the Adlerian theses were never a focus for the Nazis, even though the founding father of individual psychology was just as Jewish as Freud. But unlike psychoanalysis, Adlerian psychology espoused a particularism that was foreign to Freud's universalism. In short, only psychoanalysis was considered a "Jewish science," owing to its claim to be applicable to human subjectivity as such. On this basis, it was subject to a much more radical condemnation. Not only its partisans but its very language and concepts had to be destroyed.

Doggedly engaged in combating one another, the Freudians, Adlerians, and Jungians who came together at the Göring Institute thus collaborated in their own eradication. To the end of his life Adler accused Freud of fraud and conspiracy,[85] while Freud continued to issue similar charges against his old rival: "paranoid, a little Fliess," and so on. When Adler died in Scotland in May 1937 during a lecture tour, Freud offered a vengeful statement: "For a Jew boy out of a Viennese suburb a death in Aberdeen is an unheard-of career in itself and a proof of how far he had got on. The world really rewarded him richly for his service in having contradicted psychoanalysis."[86]

Starting in the summer of 1934, Freud worked on his Moses essay, inspired by Mann's work and by their common reaction to the anti-Semitic persecutions. He had spoken of this project first to Zweig, then to Lou

Andreas-Salomé: "Moses was not a Jew," he said, "but a well-born Egyptian . . . a zealous supporter of the monotheistic faith, which the Pharaoh Amenhotep IV had made the dominant religion round about 1350 B.C."[87]

Andreas-Salomé had been delighted to learn of this new essay. But a year later, she mentioned her own physical decline, which coincided, in Göttingen, with the increasingly criminal advance of the Nazi furor. Pursued by the hatred of Elisabeth Förster, who had contributed, until her death in 1935, to the Nazification of Nietzsche's work, Andreas-Salomé had been forced to join the Association of Writers of the Reich, and then to fill out forms attesting that she belonged to the "Aryan race." Day after day she noted that her neighbors, galvanized by Hitlerism, decorated their shutters with flamboyant swastikas; they called her the "Witch." In a moment of distress, she drafted a text that she intended to entrust to an editor on her "Adherence to Today's Germany." But when she realized that it could be used as proof of her support for the regime, she tore it up. Her faithful friend Ernst Pfeiffer glued the pieces back together and kept it in his archives. Under the ambiguous title, Andreas-Salomé evoked the German soul rather than adherence to what Germany had become. And she used what had always been her own style: cult of nature, vitalism, aspiration to spirituality.[88]

When Freud learned of Andreas-Salomé's death, he immediately wrote her obituary, honoring the memory of the woman he had so loved: "Those who were closer to her had the strongest impression of the genuineness and harmony of her nature and could discover with astonishment that all feminine frailties, and perhaps most human frailties, were foreign to her or had been conquered by her in the course of her life."[89]

A few days later, an agent of the Gestapo broke into Andreas-Salomé's house and confiscated her library, dumping it into the basement of city hall. The justification for the requisition was that she had been a psychoanalyst, that she practiced a "Jewish science," that she had been Freud's friend, and that her bookshelves held works by Jewish authors.

More and more attached to the past and to his old friendships, in this very dark year Freud sought to return to the debate that had opposed him to his two favorite disciples, Ferenczi and Otto Rank. And that is

why he published two major articles in 1937 on psychoanalytical technique: "Analysis Terminable and Interminable" and "Constructions in Analysis."[90]

In the first, he emphasized that, through the hypothesis of a birth trauma, Rank was seeking to eliminate the psychic causality of neurosis. Similarly, he argued against the attempt to shorten the duration of treatment, stressing that the effort was tied to a historical conjuncture: "Rank's argument . . . was a child of its time, conceived under the stress of the contrast between the postwar misery of Europe and the 'prosperity' of America, and designed to adapt the tempo of analytic therapy to the haste of American life."[91]

As for Ferenczi, Freud criticized in this "master of analysis" the danger represented by the unending quest for a return to hypnosis as a substitute for analysis of the transference. And he added that the practice of psychoanalysis was the exercise of an "impossible task"[92] and that one could never be sure, in advance, of the result. The therapeutic effort, he said, oscillates between a bit of analysis of the id and a bit of analysis of the ego: in one case, one is trying to bring to consciousness something of the id, and in the other one is trying to correct the ego. Without this oscillation, according to him, there can be no therapeutic success. Consequently, the analyst is no more normal than his patient, and as an "active" partner he is subjected more than the patient is to the dangers of analysis. This is why, periodically, for example every five years, the practitioner "should . . . submit himself to analysis once more, without feeling ashamed of taking this step. This would mean, then, that not only the therapeutic analysis of patients but his own analysis would change from a terminable into an interminable task."[93]

This article showed that in 1937 Freud was still opposed to Ferenczi's method concerning control of the countertransference and the idea of active support for the patient. If the therapist's training is part of an endless task, this is because analysis of the analysts is never-ending, he said in effect, just as a cure is never ensured. The notion of infinite analysis thus conforms to the proverbial saying, "No sooner won than lost." Like Ferenczi, Freud thus asserted that treatment could not be reduced to institutionalization, and he put the future teacher in exactly the same position as the patient. Once again, he doubted the effectiveness of treatment but af-

firmed that the failures encountered in the process were also based on multiple factors: types of pathology, resistance on the part of patients, attitudes of the analysts. In short, beyond the criticism he addressed to Rank and Ferenczi, Freud took note of the difficulties that he himself had encountered in numerous treatments.

This text lent itself to many interpretations, and in particular to the idea that analysts, like patients, might one day have recourse throughout their lives to new "slices," in order to explore the causes of their pathologies indefinitely.

In the second, even more interesting article, Freud went back over the history of Sergei Pankejeff in order to distinguish between the notion of interpretation and that of construction. And he acknowledged that the constructions put to work in treatment could perfectly well be of the same nature as the patient's delirium.

Through these two interventions, Freud insisted on taking a stand, one last time, on a question that would turn out to be essential, long after his death, in the history of the psychoanalytic movement.

At this point, Rank was pursuing a dazzling career in the United States. Rejected by the IPA, he practiced short face-to-face treatments, and continually analyzed instances of *lapsus,* misfires, and dreams. One day, a patient asked to be accepted for treatment even though he had already been analyzed by four therapists: two Freudians, a Jungian, and an Adlerian. The man asserted that he had no sexual problems but that he needed help. Rank understood at once that the patient was looking for a way to defeat the treatment itself. Thus he agreed to help the man on one condition: that they would address the sexual issue. By this means, he indicated that no one could exercise control over the course of the analysis itself: neither the patient nor the therapist.

Rank quite often evoked the memory of Freud and his own Viennese youth with nostalgia. As for Freud, vexed, he believed that his former disciple had suffered for a long time from a manic-depressive psychosis that had worsened since his definitive departure for the North American continent.[94]

In Berlin, Hitler had consolidated his alliance with Mussolini. He gave support to the Spanish nationalists and seriously considered annexing Austria to the Great Reich. Under these conditions, Weiss had nothing

more to expect from Forzano, and Freud began to understand that Vienna was threatened along with psychoanalysis: "The invasion of the Nazis," he wrote to Jones in March 1937, "can probably not be checked; the consequences are disastrous for analysis as well. . . . If our city falls, then the Prussian barbarians will swamp Europe. Unfortunately, the power that has hitherto protected us—Mussolini—now seems to be giving Germany a free hand. I should like to live in England like Ernst, and travel to Rome, like you."[95]

Despite this observation, Freud still wanted to believe that Kurt von Schuschnigg, Dollfuss's successor in the chancellery, a man from the old imperial nobility, would manage to preserve the country's independence. He was mistaken. He refused to recognize the reality even as he perceived it—the exact same attitude he had experienced during his visit to the Acropolis. In November 1937, Stefan Zweig paid him a visit, emphasizing that there was a book to be written on the tragedy of the Jews: "When I think of Vienna and I become somber, I think of you. From year to year, your dark severity becomes more and more exemplary for me. And I feel bound to you with ever more gratitude."[96]

The policy of a supposed "rescue" of psychoanalysis, orchestrated by Jones and supported by Freud, was a complete failure that was to be translated, in Germany and throughout Europe, by a pure and simple collaboration with the Nazis, and even more so by the dissolution of all the Freudian institutions and by the immigration toward the Anglophone world of virtually all its representatives. If that policy had not been put in place, it would have changed nothing in the fate of Freudianism in Germany, but the honor of the IPA would have been preserved. And especially, the disastrous attitude of neutrality, nonengagement, and apoliticism would not have been reproduced later under other dictatorships, as it has been in Brazil, in Argentina, and elsewhere around the world.

Eaten away by his cancer, Freud was to witness, during the last two years of his life, the collapse and ruin of everything he had built: publishing houses destroyed; books burned; disciples persecuted, assassinated, or forced into exile; institutions dismantled; objects looted; human lives reduced to nothing.

Death at Work

DURING THE LAST YEARS of his life, Freud developed a close friendship with the diplomat and journalist William Bullitt, a dandy from a very wealthy family of Philadelphia lawyers and an adviser to President Woodrow Wilson. A great admirer of the October Revolution, he was sent on a mission to Russia and had met with Lenin for the purpose of restoring relations between the two countries. But the negotiations failed. Bullitt went on to participate in the Paris Peace Conference; he roundly criticized the Treaty of Versailles, which he deemed unacceptable for the vanquished. In the process he developed a strong hostility toward Wilson. In 1924, he married Louise Bryant, a beautiful anarchist militant, the former mistress of Eugene O'Neill and widow of the well-known journalist John Reed, author of *Ten Days That Shook the World;* Bullitt and Bryant had a daughter. In 1928, Bryant came down with Dercum's disease, a painful condition that caused her suffering and disfigurement.[1] She began to drink heavily and became subject to mental illness, which led her, on her husband's advice, to consult Freud. Bullitt was self-centered, choleric, emotional, and incapable of dealing with the situation; he assailed Bryant with constant criticism, and he separated from her when he became aware that she was having an affair with a woman sculptor, Gwen Le Gallienne. Worse still, he seized the opportunity to obtain custody of their daughter with the intention of removing the child from Bryant's life.

It was in May 1930, at the time of his divorce, that he met Freud in Berlin, at the Tegel sanatorium. Under treatment for pneumonia at the time, Freud was depressed and preoccupied with death; he listened to Bullitt with interest as the American described his plan to write a biography

of Wilson based on the numerous archives that were available to him. We may recall that Freud had become acquainted with the life story of the twenty-eighth American president from the book by William Bayard Hale, *The Story of a Style* (1920). So he offered Bullitt his services. He had always dreamed of writing a real psychobiography that would be very different, stylistically, from the literary essay he had devoted to Leonardo da Vinci. This time, thanks to the seductive diplomat, he would presumably be able to consult all the necessary documentation. But at this point the journalist Ray Stannard Baker was himself in the process of writing a monumental official biography of Wilson, and Bullitt knew that some ruse would be necessary to counter the shock in the face of such a rival. Hence his interest in drawing the Viennese master into the adventure; he also asked Freud to accept him for analysis. He simultaneously told his friend Edward Mandell House[2] about the project, urging him not to let the word get out.

In October, Freud was very happy to see Bullitt again for a few sessions of work and analysis, just after he himself had undergone a new operation. Together they examined more than a thousand typewritten pages and discussed, point by point, each important moment in Wilson's life and career. Freud then wrote a first draft of some sections of the future manuscript. Bullitt took responsibility for the others, and they decided to publish the work in the United States under Bullitt's direction. In January 1932, Bullitt transmitted to his coauthor the sum of $2,500 as an advance against the American edition; in the spring, a quarrel broke out about which no one has ever learned the details, but it did not seem to affect Freud very much. The following year, he declared that Bullitt was the only American who understood Europe and who wanted to do something for its future. Finally, after being named ambassador to Moscow by Franklin D. Roosevelt, Bullitt decided, in agreement with Freud, to let the work ripen; each man would sign the chapters he had written.

The work was published in English in 1967 after the death of Edith Bolling Galt, Wilson's second wife, and just before the death of Bullitt's wife.[3] Both authors' names were on the cover. When the book came out, it did not attract much attention from historians, politicians, or psychoanalysts.

Moreover, Freud's heirs believed they recognized the pen of the master only in the preface. To be sure, the style of the work was very different from that of Freud's other works. The book was a veritable psychobiog-

raphy, and the method adopted was in perfect conformity with Freud's theory of substitutions. In other words, Bullitt had succeeded in writing a book so faithful to Freudian doctrine that it seemed too slavishly Freudian to have been authored by Freud himself. It lacked the doubt, the ambivalence, the bold hypotheses that were so characteristic of Freud's customary approach.[4]

Virulently anti-American, the work offered an analysis of the madness of a statesman, seemingly normal in the exercise of his functions. Identifying from his earliest childhood with the figure of his father, a Presbyterian minister and a great preacher, Wilson had first seen himself, according to Bullitt, as the son of God, before converting to a religion of his own invention in which he attributed the place of God to himself; he had chosen to take up a political career in order to carry out his messianic dreams. When he became president, he had not yet traveled beyond the American borders; Wilson regarded the United States as the most beautiful country in the world, just as William Ewart Gladstone did England. He was utterly ignorant of European geography and did not know that several languages were spoken there. During the negotiations leading up to the Treaty of Versailles, it became clear that he had "forgotten" the existence of the Brenner Pass, and he delivered the Tyrolean Austrians to Italy without knowing that they spoke German. Similarly, when someone close to him told him that the Jewish community included a hundred million individuals spread over the four corners of the earth, he took it at face value. Hating Germany, he thought that its inhabitants lived like wild beasts.

Not content with this attack on Wilson, Bullitt asserted that, to carry out his foreign policy, Wilson had relied on some delirious syllogisms. Thus, since God is good and illness is bad, he deduced that if God exists, there is no such thing as illness. This type of reasoning allowed him to deny reality in favor of a belief in the omnipotence of his own discourse, which led him, according to the authors, to the diplomatic disaster. Thus he created the League of Nations before the discussion on the conditions of peace had begun; as a result, the victors, assured of American protection, could calmly slice up Europe and condemn Germany with impunity.

Wilson believed at the time, according to Bullitt, that in the "fourteen points" he had the key to universal brotherhood.[5] But instead of negotiating with his partners by discussing economic and financial issues, he

gave them a sermon on the mount. Then he left Europe, convinced that he had instituted everlasting peace on earth.

As for Wilson's "libido," Bullitt asserted that it was especially weak. Married first to Ellen Axson, a friend of a cousin, Wilson proceeded to marry Galt just a few months after Ellen's death. Both women were substitutes for his mother, Bullitt added, and they sufficed to satisfy his weak desires. Bullitt's conclusion: experience shows that men who have been happily married tend to remarry quickly. We can recognize here the Freudian thesis of substitutions: one woman substitutes for the mother, then a second substitutes for the first.

Whatever may have been at stake in the quarrel between Freud and Bullitt, this work was rejected by historians, suspected of being apocryphal by the Freudian community, and held in derision by the anti-Freudians; still, it was faithful in many respects to the Freudian conception of history. In effect, it described the encounter between an individual destiny, in which an unconscious determination intervenes, and a specific historical situation in which this determination plays a role. But it also calls to mind a reverie on a fallen hero. In any event, with his preface, which supported Bullitt's undertaking, Freud reinforced his own anti-Americanism, his hatred for egalitarian democracy, and his conviction that the old Europe had indeed been destroyed by an obscurantist Don Quixote.

Wilson's personality lent itself to such an analysis, and Freud had good reasons for detesting the fanatical idealist who claimed to be bringing to the peoples of Europe the right to govern themselves, as if these peoples had been completely ignorant of law and democracy. But this psychological portrait was defective in that it presented Wilson's neurosis and his posture as a visionary prophet who had repressed his hatred for the father as the only causes of what Freud and Bullitt viewed as the failures of his policy. They were forgetting the major role played by Georges Clemenceau. In addition, the hypothesis of the "weak libido" was far from confirmed; we know that, during his first marriage, Wilson had had a secret affair with another woman.[6] At bottom, it was the very principle according to which the interpretive method could be applied to historical work that was open to criticism. We know, moreover, how deleterious it can be, in this realm, to claim to illuminate an individual's destiny in the light of an alleged Oedipus complex.

The major affair of these last years, for Freud, was writing a "historical novel" devoted to the question of Jewish identity: *Moses and Monotheism*.[7] The genesis of this major work, unique in its genre and one of the most widely commented on works in the world, deserves to be spelled out, so closely is its history bound up with that of the advance of Nazism in Europe.

For a long time, and even before he discussed the figure of Moses with Lou Andreas-Salomé or Arnold Zweig or Thomas Mann, Freud had been obsessed with the first prophet of Judaism, who prefigured Christ for the Christians and preceded Mohammed for the Muslims. He especially admired the figure that Michelangelo had represented so magnificently, a Moses capable of governing his own drives, a Moses of the Italian Renaissance, a Moses of the Enlightenment, much more radiant than the Moses of the sacred text, a Moses who had brought his people out of lethargy by imposing laws, pointing to the Promised Land, and inventing a new life of the mind *(Geistigkeit)*.[8] Once again, confronting the resurgence of an anti-Semitism whose genocidal import he did not grasp, Freud asked himself why Jews had attracted so much hatred.[9] But in particular he raised the question of Jewish identity: How does one become Jewish?

As in *Totem and Taboo,* he intended to grapple head-on with the question of origins. The resemblance between the two works is striking: the same technique of juxtaposing diverse literary narratives, the same interrogation going against the grain of the contemporary social sciences, the same concern for privileging myths of origin so as to invent additional myths that facilitate the exploration of the unconscious psyche, the same fascination with exegesis and archaeology, the same determination to attach psychoanalysis as much to the sciences of nature as to the foundational power of myths.

In 1934, Freud began a first essay, titled "Moses, an Egyptian?" He found inspiration in Mann, Goethe, and Schiller, but also in a number of works by Egyptophile historians who were eager to offer "rational" interpretations of the biblical story. In drafting this text, Freud went back to a thesis, very much in vogue since the late eighteenth century, according to which Moses had been a high Egyptian dignitary, a partisan of monotheism who was put to death by his own people.[10] And he explained this

"Egyptianness" by drawing on the notion of "family romance" applicable, as Otto Rank said, to countless stories, legends, and myths, including that of Oedipus.[11] A child "exposed" by virtue of a destiny presumed to be tragic is taken in by a family that rears him. When he reaches adulthood, he discovers that he is not the person he thought he was, and he fulfills his destiny. In most instances the first family, the one into which the child is born, is of high rank, and the second family, the one in which the child grows up, is of modest standing. In the Oedipus story, both families are of high rank, and in the story of Moses, as it is presented in the Bible, the first family is modest (the Hebrews) and the second is of royal blood (the pharaoh).

Seeking to prove that Moses was an Egyptian, Freud proposed to invert the terms of the legend. The true family, of royal blood, he said, was the one that abandoned the child in a basket in the water, and the other, of modest status, was the invented family (the Hebrews). Thus the hero was presented as having descended from the heights to go toward the people of Israel in order to save them.[12]

In a second essay, "If Moses Were an Egyptian," Freud retraced the story of the birth of monotheism, starting with the reign of Amenhotep IV (Akhenaton) in the fourteenth century BCE. He took pleasure in this new plunge into an archaic history in which the most prestigious names of Egyptian antiquity appeared one after another, and he concluded that Moses, a highly colorful novelistic figure, had transmitted the religion of his fathers to the people of Israel.[13] He went on to impose the Egyptian rite of circumcision on the Israelites in order to prove that God had chosen them by this alliance.

To recount the rest of the story, Freud referred to the work of an exegete from Berlin, Ernst Sellin, who, in 1922, on the basis of a reading of the prophet Hosea, had put forward the idea that Moses had been the victim of a collective murder committed by his own people, who preferred to follow the cult of idols. According to Sellin, the Mosaic doctrine became an esoteric tradition that was transmitted by a circle of initiates. And it was on these grounds that faith in Jesus, another assassinated prophet and the founder of Christianity, was born. From Sellin's Christian interpretation of the biblical narrative,[14] Freud deduced that the Hebrews, once freed from their captivity, did not accept the new religion; instead, they

killed the man who saw himself as a prophet, then erased all traces of this murder from their memory.[15]

Following the hypothesis of Edward Meyer,[16] an Orientalist and an Egyptologist, Freud then associated that event with another, later biblical story, concerning the alliance forged by the Israelites with the Bedouin tribes settled in the Midian[17] region, whose god, Yahweh, was a brutal, impulsive deity. Within these tribes, another Moses, a Levite, had been welcomed by Jethro, whose daughter he married; he became a priest after fleeing the pharaoh's persecutions. These two stories had given rise to the biblical legend of a single Moses, founder of a religion that merged the ancient cult of Yahweh with the new monotheism imported from Egypt.[18] Freud adds that the archaic religion of Yahweh had squeezed out and then repressed Mosaic monotheism, which was much more intellectual. However, the latter tendency had resurfaced several centuries later, and Yahweh was endowed with the intellectual attributes of monotheism, while the split figure of Moses was reunified in the persona of a single prophet imposing the law of a single God: a God of the Word and of choice, bearer of a highly spiritual message.

Once again, Freud applied his doctrine of substitutions to this reinvented story, using his talent for solving enigmas: one Moses hides another, the other takes on the attributes of the first and vice versa, while the memory of the murder remains repressed. What is more, he found one of his cherished motifs in this story: the opposition between a primitive, obscurantist, destructive Moses and a law-giving, rational Moses.[19]

In 1937, between January and August, Freud published these two essays, while continuing to work on a third. Even before completing this last essay, he wrote two "preliminary notes," one in Vienna before March 1938, the other in London in June of that year. In the first, he summed up the political situation in Europe, taking into account the fact that Soviet Russia had not succeeded in wiping out "the opium of the people" (religion) of the new Communist society, even as it had granted individuals a certain measure of sexual freedom. Next, he noted that the Italian population was currently living under the yoke of an authoritarian regime, while Germany was regressing toward the darkest barbarianism. And he concluded that the conservative democracies had become, on the same basis as the Catholic Church, the guardians of cultural progress. He

declared that he did not want to shock his Austrian compatriots by pub-
lishing the last part of his study on Moses, which contributed once more
to the desacralization of monotheistic religion—and thus of the Judeo-
Christian tradition—by transforming it into a historical novel populated
by myths and neurotic heroes. And he claimed to be convinced that psy-
choanalysis had "no home that could be more valuable for it than the city
in which it was born and grew up."[20] At this point in time, Freud still
thought that his movement was protected by the Catholic Church and
by the Austrian government, which would be able, he believed, to resist
Nazism. And yet since March 1937 he had also been aware that nothing
could stop Hitler any longer. In short, on the eve of the Anschluss, he
knew without wanting to know, and kept hoping. In the second prelimi-
nary note, written in June 1938 after his exile in London had begun, Freud
did an about-face: "Then, suddenly, came the German invasion and Ca-
tholicism proved, to use the words of the Bible, 'a broken reed.' In the cer-
tainty that I should now be persecuted not only for my line of thought
but also for my 'race'—accompanied by many of my friends, I left the city
which, from my early childhood, had been my home for seventy-eight
years. I met with the friendliest reception in lovely, free, magnanimous
England. Here I now live, a welcome guest; I can breathe a sigh of relief
now that the weight has been taken off me and that I am once more able
to speak and write—I had almost said 'and think'—as I wish or as I must.
I venture to bring the last portion of my work before the public."[21]

It had taken five years, then, between the Nazis' seizure of power in
1933 and the Anschluss, for Freud to understand. But he was not the only
one who did not see Hitler for what he was. In any case, this misunder-
standing of the situation of Austria and of the nature of Nazism confirmed
the degree to which Freud, usually so lucid, was more attached to Vienna
and to his Viennese Judaism than he thought, and that his work was, much
more than he realized, the product of an immediate history that was out
of his control—which is what makes it so interesting, moreover. The more
he explored origin myths and interpreted sacred texts to bring them into
line with his own constructions, the more he was speaking of present
times, that is, of the mutations of anti-Semitism and their impact on the
redefinition of Jewish identity.

In the third essay, "Moses, His People and Monotheist Religion," Freud went back to the thesis of the two Moseses, the Midianite and the Egyptian, to link the destinies of Judaism and Christianity. The people chosen by the prophet, he said, killed the founding father but repressed the memory of the murder, a memory that would return with Christianity. Here Freud was inspired by the old Christian anti-Judaism to interpret it in a sense contrary to the classical approach, which represented Jews as the god-killing people. In so doing, he linked Judaism to Christianity, making the first the religion of the father and the second that of the son, and making Christians the heirs of a murder repressed by the Jews: "The old God the Father fell back behind Christ; Christ, the Son, took his place, just as every son had hoped to do in primaeval times."[22]

Still according to Freud, Paul of Tarsus both continued Judaism and destroyed it: by introducing the idea of redemption, he managed to ward off the specter of human guilt but at the price of contradicting the idea that the Jews were the chosen people. Consequently, by renouncing the visible sign of this choice, circumcision, he transformed Christianity into a universal doctrine capable of speaking to all human beings.

But Freud also asserted that hatred toward Jews was fed by their own belief in the superiority of the chosen people, and by the castration anxiety aroused by circumcision, the act that marked them as members of that group. According to him, the purpose of this rite was to ennoble the Jews and enable them to scorn everyone else, the uncircumcised. From the same perspective, he took literally—displacing its signification—the chief complaint of anti-Judaism, that is, the Jews' refusal to acknowledge the killing of God. The Jewish people, he said, stubbornly persist in denying the murder of the father, and the Christians keep on accusing the Jews of being god-killers because they have been freed from original sin ever since Christ, a substitute for Moses, sacrificed his life to redeem them. In other words, if Christianity is a religion of the son who acknowledges the murder and redeems it, Judaism remains a religion of the father who refuses to recognize the killing of God. And the Jews are no less persecuted for the murder of the son, of which they are innocent. Freud concluded that this refusal exposed the Jews to the resentment of other peoples.

After acknowledging that the history of the Jews cannot be separated from that of Christian anti-Judaism, Freud explained that modern anti-Semitism attested to a displacement onto the Jews of hatred of Christianity:

> All those peoples who excel to-day in their hatred of Jews became Christians only in late historic times, often driven to it by bloody coercion. It might be said that they are all "mis-baptized." They have been left, under a thin veneer of Christianity, what their ancestors were, who worshipped a barbarous polytheism. They have not got over a grudge against the new religion which was imposed on them; but they have displaced the grudge on to the source from which Christianity reached them. . . . Their hatred of Jews is at bottom a hatred of Christians, and we need not be surprised that in the German National-Socialist revolution this intimate relation between the two monotheist religions finds such a clear expression in the hostile treatment of both of them.[23]

In other words, if Judaism, a "fossil" religion, is superior to Christianity in its intellectual strength, but not suited for universality, the two must nevertheless be associated historically—in their very difference—in order to foster a Judeo-Christian culture capable of opposing modern anti-Semitism.

This approach consisted essentially in bringing to light the unconscious roots of anti-Semitism starting from Judaism itself, rather than continuing to regard it as a phenomenon external to Judaism. This was a way of returning to the problematics of *Totem and Taboo,* of which *Moses and Monotheism* was in fact a continuation. If society had indeed been engendered by a crime committed against the father, putting an end to the despotic reign of the savage horde, then by the institution of a rule of law in which the symbolic figure of the father was revalorized, this signified that Judaism necessarily obeyed the same scenario. And in fact the murder of Moses had engendered Christianity, based on the recognition of guilt: monotheism thus stemmed from the interminable story of the institution of that law of the father on which Freud had built his entire doctrine.

In so doing, Freud was obeying an injunction to return to the supreme authority of the Bible and to the religion of his father. But far from adopting the solution of conversion as a response to anti-Semitism, or the solution of Zionism, he redefined himself once again as a Jew without God[24]—a Jew of reflection and knowledge—even as he rejected Jewish self-hatred. I would venture to say that he was undertaking to detach Judaism from the feeling of Jewishness proper to nonbelieving Jews, getting around both the alliance with and the election by God, the latter being viewed as a sort of delirium. However, at the very moment when he was de-Judaizing Moses and making him an Egyptian, Freud was assigning to Jewishness, understood simultaneously as essence and as belonging, a position of eternity. This feeling, through which a Jew remains a Jew in his subjectivity even when he adopts a position of externality in relation to Judaism, was one Freud himself experienced, and he did not hesitate to assimilate it to a phylogenetic heritage. In certain respects, he remained faithful to the Judaism of Moses, from the standpoint of his ongoing claim of Jewish identity, and he assigned to psychoanalysis the mission of taking on the legacy of that particular Judaism, a Judaism converted into the Jewishness of the diaspora.[25]

With his *Moses,* Freud was fully aware that he was writing a kind of testament that bore witness as much to his refusal to leave Vienna—the city where an unprecedented fusion had been achieved between diaspora Jewishness and a new way of conceptualizing the universality of the unconscious—as to his desire to go into exile and to live at last in a place where the renaissance of his doctrine might come about. Hence his dream of living in England, the country par excellence of the alliance between a monarchic system and liberal democracy. This was doubtless for him a way of responding to the collapse of the old Enlightenment Europe, a response based on the alliance between the Spinozan spirit of dissidence and the three great mythical figures in Western culture that had always been present in the development of his doctrine: Oedipus, a tyrant in the Greek world; Hamlet, a Christian prince; and Moses, a Jewish prophet reinvented by the Italian Michelangelo and then Egyptianized by nineteenth-century German scholars. In 1938, that Moses, blazing with an overwhelming desire for England, was in Freud's eyes the complete opposite of the lamentable American Woodrow Wilson.

And in fact Freud feared the American democracy, which threw into discredit the very idea of a republic of the elect, favoring instead the domination of the masses. And he cursed Nazism, which gave free rein to the destruction of mankind by savage drives. Each side's modality of governance called into question the very notion of authority as Freud understood it. He was convinced, especially after the economic crisis of 1929 and the publication of *Civilization and Its Discontents,* that the unbridled quest for wealth was as dangerous as submission to tyranny. Thus he thought that America would eventually be devoured by its three demons: puritanical madness, the individual quest for sexual performance, and unlimited speculation. This is why only the old imperial Europe of the Habsburgs had continued to find favor in his eyes, for that Europe protected minorities and encouraged control of one's drives. But that Europe had been swallowed up by the First World War. The desire for England then came to the fore.

In 1938, only England could be a welcoming land for Freud. It ruled over an empire and had inherited a glorious past; it cultivated both individual freedom and respect for royal dynasties. Finally, it had always managed to resist dictatorial temptations, at the price of a regicide and the reestablishment of monarchic dignity. Freud liked Oliver Cromwell, the great protector of the Jews,[26] but he also admired the fact that the British royal families had not been removed from power—if only symbolic power—by some Jacobin republic. As Mark Edmundson writes, "Freud, one might say, was a patriarch who worked with incomparable skill to deconstruct patriarchy. He wrote and lived to put an end to the kind of authority that he himself quite often embodied and exploited."[27]

Moses and Monotheism, the testament of Freudian Jewishness in exile, gave rise to multiple contradictory interpretations. The first, by David Bakan, inscribed Freud's work in the tradition of Jewish mysticism.[28] The second—from Carl Schorske through Yirmiyahu Yovel to Peter Gay—brought into view, on the contrary, an atheist Freud, no longer centered on his Jewishness and prey to the double problematics of Spinozan dissidence and integration into German culture. The third, finally, that of Yosef Yerushalmi, tried to bring to light Freud's Judaic ambivalences in the face of his own Jewishness.[29] I share in the second and third approaches.

On the side of the Israeli scholars who specialize in Jewish history, Freud's work was little appreciated and unjustly criticized. Martin Buber reproached Freud for his lack of scientific rigor,[30] and Gershom Scholem, at least for a time, preferred Jung, who had become an increasingly fervent Zionist, even as his anti-Semitism and his support for Nazi Germany became increasingly apparent.

At the beginning of 1938, Freud's cancer spread to the base of one eye. Every week, the lesions in his mouth grew while the decaying tissues became more and more painful, requiring daily cleansing. Surgical operations and electrocoagulation slowed the progress of the disease. Eager to keep working and to keep his vigilance intact, Freud, who was growing visibly thinner by the day, refused to take painkillers. Despite the damage being done to his face and the increase in his deafness owing to postoperative infections, he insisted on maintaining a decent appearance. So he demanded that Hans Pichler remove an atheroma in his jaw that had grown so much that it kept him from trimming his beard: "Perhaps you will even notice that I've actually been beautified. Wasn't I disfigured by a sebaceous cyst, an atheroma, which you never mentioned, probably out of tact? I had that ornament removed."[31]

Unlike Freud, Hitler despised the Habsburg monarchy, and since the time when Austria had become a little republic and Vienna a city that was damaged but still proud of its imperial past, he dreamed of nothing but its utter destruction: "German-Austria must return to the great German mother-country," he had asserted in *Mein Kampf,* "and not because of any economic considerations. No, and again no: even if such a union were unimportant from an economic point of view; yes, even if it were harmful, it must nevertheless take place. One blood demands one Reich."[32]

In early 1938, then, Hitler was waiting impatiently for the right moment to intervene in Austria so as to carry out his project of fusion, the very project he had been dreaming of since his youth. He felt quite simply that he had been invested with the "grandiose" mission of conquering Vienna, appearing there in broad daylight like a ghost in the middle of a spring storm. So he summoned Kurt von Schuschnigg to the Berghof to force him to give over two ministries to Nazi sympathizers, most importantly the Ministry of the Interior to Arthur Seyss-Inquart, under threat of a military invasion. Schuschnigg accepted, then tried in

vain to organize a plebiscite to save Austria's independence; this set off a "hysterical" rage on the part of Hitler, who was convinced—rightly, moreover—that Italy, France, and England would not budge: "The die is cast," wrote Joseph Goebbels. "Push straight to Vienna. . . . The Führer is going himself to Austria."[33]

Desperate, Schuschnigg asked for British aid, which got him a cynical telegram from Lord Halifax: "His Majesty's government are unable to guarantee protection."[34] On March 11, Schuschnigg submitted his resignation, and, that evening, he gave a stirring speech on the radio, while in every Austrian city crowds were already on the loose attacking Jews, shouting "Death to Judas," glorifying Hitler's name, and occupying official buildings.

At 19 Berggasse, Freud listened to Schuschnigg's speech, which concluded with the words "God save Austria." On March 12, he noted on his calendar, *"Finis Austriae."* A second time, determined to fulfill to the end his role as patriarch of psychoanalysis, he witnessed the death throes of the world that had been his. And yet he knew he was at risk: he had received a visit from John Wiley, a friend of Bullitt and the consul general of the United States in Vienna, whose mission was henceforth to oversee his exile and that of his family. Wiley did not delay in alerting Cordell Hull, secretary of state under President Roosevelt, to the danger facing Freud, despite his age and his poor health.[35] In Paris, Bullitt went to the German embassy to warn Count Ferdinand Maria von Wilczek that the Professor must meet with no mistreatment. Finally, Dorothy Burlingham was charged with alerting the American embassy in Vienna by telephone in case there were any problems.

On March 13, at the moment when the Anschluss was officially announced, the board of directors of the WPV met at 19 Berggasse in Freud's presence, with Anna Freud presiding. Ernest Jones had let it be known that he wanted to utilize, in Vienna, the same policy of a so-called rescue that had been implemented in Berlin. The only non-Jew on the board, Richard Sterba refused to play the role of Felix Boehm and declared that he intended to leave Vienna with his family as quickly as possible in order to reach Switzerland and then the United States. Consequently, the group decided to disband the WPV and to install its headquarters wherever Freud chose to live. This was the first political act of a decentering

that was going to make psychoanalysis the equivalent of a diaspora Judaism. If Vienna ceased to occupy a central place in the movement—however contested this place was already—it meant that Freud could in turn leave Vienna in order to reinstitute, in exile and before he died, a foundation of a different order: this time, memorial in nature. Facing organized destruction, it was necessary at all costs to transmit to the generations to come what had been the story of his life, his doctrine, his teaching, and the first circle of his disciples: books, archives, manuscripts, letters, collections, working notes, verbatim records, collective memories, and so on. All that belonged henceforth to the future much more than to the past. It was imperative to save the traces, save the history, save the memory, save the recollections of Vienna. These tasks were as indispensable as saving lives, and as remote as possible from any spirit of collaboration with Nazism.

Freud clearly got the message the board members had addressed to him, and this time, renouncing any pretention of "rescue," he declared, "After the destruction of the temple in Jerusalem by Titus, Rabbi Johanan ben Sakkai asked for permission to open a school at Jabneh for the study of the Torah. We are going to do the same. We are, after all, used to persecution by our history, tradition, and some of us by personal experience, with one exception."[36]

More and more excited by the announcement of Hitler's arrival, crowds railed increasingly against the Jews, the Communists, and the Social Democrats. Freud had thought the Austrians less brutal than the Germans. He had been wrong: they surpassed their Nazi masters in ferocity to the point that even the Nazis were astonished. Forcibly dragged out of their offices, Jews were stripped on the spot of all their belongings, then transformed into "cleaning squadrons" under the supervision of bands of looters who beat them and insulted them with cries of "Heil Hitler!": "Hades had opened its gates and released its basest, most despicable, most impure spirits," the dramatist Carl Zuckmayer observed; Vienna had been turned "into a nightmare painting of Hieronymus Bosch."[37]

Hitler had prepared his entrance into Austria very well. He stopped first at Braunau am Inn, his birthplace, where a jubilant crowd awaited him. Next he went to Linz, where, deeply moved by the welcome proffered by the inhabitants, he wept as he gave a speech in which he assigned

himself the role of a hero designated by Providence to accomplish the holy mission of wiping out Austrian identity. Finally, on March 15, he spoke to a delirious crowd before his triumphal reception by the highest dignitaries of the Catholic Church, who did not hesitate to manifest their support for the Anschluss, for National Socialism, for anti-Semitic laws, and for all forms of crusade against Bolshevism.[38] Cardinal Theodor Innitzer, the primate of Austria, signed the declaration of fusion and in his own hand added, "Heil Hitler!"

In a very short time the plundering of Jewish businesses was complete; a *Nazi-Kommissar* was immediately invested with full powers of confiscation, liquidation, arrest, and encouragement of informers. Next, and very rapidly, came deportation toward concentration camps, which were not yet sites of extermination. Without fully believing the reports, Freud had learned of the existence of these camps from a newspaper, *Das neue Tagebuch,* published in France thanks to Leopold Schwarzchild, a German journalist in exile, the very one who later published Thomas Mann's "Bruder Hitler" in the United States.

Freud had thought that Austrian Catholicism would protect the Jews. Once again, he was seriously mistaken. As for Giovacchino Forzano, Edoardo Weiss's friend, he sent a useless missive to Mussolini: "I recommend to Your Excellency a glorious old man of eighty-two who greatly admires Your Excellency: Freud, a Jew."[39]

It was now becoming urgent to organize Freud's departure for England as quickly as possible. On March 16, 1938, Jones arrived in Vienna, followed the next day by Marie Bonaparte. Like the captain of the *Titanic,* who had refused to leave his ship, Freud asserted that he would never abandon his post. But Jones had the idea of countering him with another story, that of the officer on that same ocean liner who had been tossed to the surface of the water by the explosion of a boiler. During the investigation, he had been asked at what point he had left the ship, and he had replied, in effect, "I didn't abandon the ship, it was the ship that abandoned me." Freud recognized that this was exactly his case. And since Vienna had abandoned him to the Nazis, he agreed to emigrate to England.

But, in keeping with the decisions made by the board of directors of the WPV, he wanted to take his last Viennese disciples with him. Now, Jones knew that the Kleinians would never allow these disciples to enter

the BPI en masse. Besides, the British government was accepting Jewish refugees only within the limits of very tight quotas. Ultimately, the departure had to be negotiated by mobilizing all the forces present: Bonaparte, who was willing to commit her fortune and her relations; Bullitt, Wiley, and Hull, confident in their positions in the United States;[40] and Jones, who mobilized all his relations in London: his brother-in-law Wilfred Trotter, who sat on the Council of the Royal Society; Sir William Bragg, an eminent physicist and Nobel laureate; and Sir Samuel Hoare, minister of the interior and a member of the Conservative Party.

It was time. The day before, March 15, the headquarters of the publishing house, located at 7 Berggasse, had been requisitioned by members of the SA. Martin Freud, head of publications, was threatened by a hefty fellow who pressed the barrel of a pistol to his temple. He had not had time to destroy all the documents that proved that Freud held assets in foreign banks. The same day, another Nazi cohort organized a search of the family home. Martha remained cool and collected, treating the looters like ordinary visitors, inviting them to put down their weapons in the umbrella holder at the entrance. They confiscated several passports and took away six thousand shillings in exchange for an official receipt.

In the United States, a rumor spread that Freud had been executed by the Nazis. On assignment from a newspaper, a reporter went to Vienna and presented himself at 19 Berggasse accompanied by Emy Moebius. Martha received them and told them that Freud was resting at the moment.[41]

For her part, beginning on March 17, with help from Anna, Martha, and Paula Fichtl, Bonaparte tried to sort, organize, and pack the treasures Freud had accumulated over a lifetime. Always concerned with saving the traces, she gathered up important papers that the Professor himself would have thrown away or burned. Sharing the family's daily life, she was able to hide objects away and have them sent secretly from the Greek legation where she was lodging. She recuperated several gold pieces that Freud had set aside. One day, she hid under her skirts a bronze statuette representing the goddess Athena holding a libation goblet in her right hand and a lance in her left, with a Corinthian cap on her head and a breastplate on her chest decorated with a Medusa face. Knowing that Freud was attached to this warlike icon, which combined the virtues of combat with

those of intelligence, she had decided to save it and offer it to him when he came to stay with her in Paris. Freud had been granted the right to take his collections and some of his books with him. But, forced to leave behind in Vienna around eight hundred priceless volumes, he summoned the major bookseller Heinrich Hinterberger, who took away a considerable number of art books.[42]

On March 20, under the leadership of Jones, who was still attached to the idea of collaborating with the Nazis, the members of the WPV board of directors agreed to sign a protocol of agreement that put the WPV under the guardianship of the DPG. On instructions from Matthias Göring, Carl Müller-Braunschweig participated in that meeting, which instituted a sort of Anschluss of the Viennese by the "Aryanized" Berlin psychoanalysts, those same Viennese who had, however, refused any form of "rescue." The business manager of the publishing house, Martin Freud, signed the document, as did his sister Anna, Bonaparte, Eduard Hitschman, Heinz Hartmann, Ernst Kris, and Robert Walder.[43] By signing, the Jewish members of the committee were agreeing to their own marginalization, since this guardianship excluded them de facto from playing any role in the WPV. Furious at Sterba's absence, Jones noted that the *Shabbes Goy*[44] had shirked his duties.

A month later, comfortably settled in 7 Berggasse, now *judenfrei,* Müller-Braunschweig informed Sterba of his intention to transform the publishing house headquarters into an "Aryanized" institute, in order to ensure the so-called survival of psychoanalysis in Austria. And he asked Sterba, as the sole "Aryan" of the WPV, to go along with this sinister operation.[45] Sterba responded with an unqualified refusal. Before leaving to go into exile, he had time to note a large swastika hanging at the entrance to Freud's house. When he met Jones in London, he became aware that he had helped bring about the failure of the policy he did not support. But he was not granted a visa to settle in England, so he sought to join Wulf Sachs in South Africa, then went into exile in the United States. Freud and his daughter, for their part, had approved Jones's decision to put the WPV into custodianship, after having rejected Jones's "rescue" policy on March 13.

Anton Sauerwald, a former student of the eminent University of Vienna chemistry professor Josef Herzig, had also participated in the March 20 meeting. As a *Nazi-Kommissar,* he was in charge of dispossessing

the Jews of their fortunes in order to "de-Judaize the Austrian economy." Thus he was supposed to deal with the holdings of the Freud family, along with all the operations of the WPV and the publishing house. Violently anti-Semitic, he began by insulting all the non-Jews who had dared to get mixed up with "Jüdische Schweinereien" (Jewish pigs). But because he was dealing with an illustrious scholar whose dignity impressed him, he began to read several books on psychoanalysis and to set himself apart from the other Nazi functionaries. When he realized that Freud had made a fortune and had invested money abroad, he decided not to "denounce" him but, on the contrary, to help him obtain the authorizations necessary for his exile. He imagined recovering one day, to his own profit, the money thus saved from sequester, and to that end he collaborated with a lawyer, Alfred Indra, another dubious character who made his fortune in these troubled times by advising wealthy Viennese Jewish families who were subject to exorbitant ransoms. Close to the Wittgenstein family and connected with Marie Bonaparte, Dr. Indra, a former officer of the imperial army, a collector of art objects, an assiduous reader of Karl Kraus, and a lover of fox hunting and of witty remarks, passed as an admirable lawyer by implying to his clients that the Nazi authorities were stupid and easily deceived. He became Freud's lawyer and collaborated with all the members of his inner circle.[46]

On March 22, Anna Freud was taken to the Hotel Metropole,[47] the Gestapo headquarters, to be formally interrogated on her "subversive activities." Bonaparte demanded to be taken along, but the SS, impressed by her royal status, would have none of it. Anna skillfully succeeded in convincing her jailors that she was apolitical. Back at 19 Berggasse, she found Freud in a state of extreme agitation. He never found out that she had taken veronal with her in case she were tortured.

To avoid such intrusions in the future, the princess decided to stand guard on the steps: "A blue-back mink stole wound tightly over her shoulders, light-colored gloves on her hands and a huge seemingly fragile hat on her head. Beside her, a brown crocodile bag. Enveloped in a cloud of stephanotis, her favorite perfume, she squatted there."[48] Unknown to the Professor, Paula brought her tea or chocolate.

At that point, more than 7,500 people had already been arrested and tortured, and thousands of incarcerated Jews did not yet know where they were to be deported. In early April, a first train of prisoners deemed

"political" left for Dachau. Helped, or not, by Jones or by their foreign friends, the psychoanalysts fled, abandoning their assets, their homes, their furnishings, their clientele, their pasts, and sometimes various family members who could not follow them for want of visas or of "certificates of innocuousness" *(Unbedenklichkeitserklärung)* indicating that they had paid the famous exit tax *(Reichsfluchtsteuer)* that was required for every official exit.

Ernst Freud and Lucie, with her children Stefan, Lucian, and Clemens, had already left Germany and were living in London; Oliver, Henny, and their daughter, Eva, had settled in the south of France;[49] Max Halberstadt was living in South Africa with his second wife, Bertha, and their daughter, Eva. As for the young Ernstl Halberstadt, "the child with the spool," he planned to leave London and join his father in South Africa, after a trip through Palestine with Eitingon and then a return to Vienna: "I had had insolent good luck, I had not been forced out and nothing bad had happened to me. Furthermore, I was fortunate enough to be able to wait for my family in England."[50]

Albert Hirst, who had become a famous lawyer leading a courageous struggle against the death penalty, had just enough time to return to Vienna to help his family emigrate to the United States. After so many years during which he had borne a grudge against Freud, he finally realized that he had overcome his neurosis and his sexual problems. In 1972, he judged that he had had a "good life," thanks to God, to America, and to Freud.[51]

On April 19, Freud and his family celebrated the birthday of his brother Alexander, who was preparing to leave for Switzerland, and Freud gave him his collection of cigars. He had not given up smoking, but for the time being he had lost his taste for tobacco. Making an effort to overcome his Anglophobia, Alexander and his wife, Sophie Schreiber, planned to go to London and then emigrate to Canada. His son, Harry, was in Davos for medical treatment. After the war, Harry went back to Vienna as part of the American army.

While various negotiations were under way, Freud's family members wondered what to do about the four elderly aunts, women in their seventies who had long since given up all activities. Supported by their two brothers, Sigmund and Alexander, and by their sister, Anna Bernays-

Freud, they had had lives marked by tragedy. Adolfine Freud (Dolfi) had lived alone since Amalia's death, surrounded by Regine Debora (Rosa) Graf, Maria (Mitzi), and Pauline Regine (Paula) Winternitz, all three widowed, with three daughters among them, all living abroad. Margarethe Freud-Magnus, Maria's daughter, lived in Denmark, and her sister Lilly Freud-Marlé[52] was pursuing a career as an actress in London with her husband, Arnold Marlé; she occasionally benefited from her uncle's generous financial support. As for Paula's daughter, Rose Winternitz, who suffered from mental disorders, she had married the poet Ernst Waldinger and had just left Austria for the United States, where Paul Federn took responsibility for her.[53]

To be sure, Freud saw the danger that threatened his sisters, but he could not imagine that the Nazis would try to exterminate old people without activities or resources. He believed, as did everyone around him, that the anti-Semitic persecutions targeted first of all active Jews who had fortunes or exercised professions. In short, he was convinced that his sisters could emigrate a little later, after the disciples and the other members of the family. Besides, the taxes required to get them out were so exorbitant that he did not have the means to finance their departure, especially given that the British authorities required that exiles be able to meet their own needs once settled in Great Britain.

Freud had requested that he be accompanied by the fifteen persons who were under immediate threat: Martha; Minna; Anna; Paula; Martin; his wife, Esti; their children, Anton Walter and Sophie; Ernstl Halberstadt; Mathilde and Robert Hollitscher; Max Schur; his wife, Helen; and their children, Peter and Eva. Bullitt was convinced that Freud would not be able to pull together the sum necessary to organize this operation, even with Bonaparte's help; he offered to contribute $10,000 toward the departure of the "caravan."[54]

At this point, Freud and Alexander decided to give their four sisters the sum of 160,000 Austrian shillings, and they asked Indra and Sauerwald to manage this fortune while waiting for better times. When he left Vienna, after paying all the requisite taxes, Alexander was left with no money whatsoever, and in exile he had to fall back on friends and relatives for help. His fortune had been sequestered and his Nazi lawyer, Erich Führer, had taken advantage of the situation for his own personal enrichment.

After weeks of negotiations, Jones obtained entry visas for England and the work permits needed by Freud and those persons accompanying him. They still needed authorizations to leave Austria. Sent to evaluate Freud's collections, Hans von Demel, the conservator of the Kunsthistorisches Museum, advanced the sum of thirty thousand reichsmarks (RM), less than the amount required. On top of this there was the estimated taxable fortune—125,318 RM—on which Freud had to pay an additional tax of 31,329 RM. But since the assets of the publishing house and those in his own bank account had been seized, he was unable to pay this obligatory "debt." It was Bonaparte who paid the ransom.

Accompanied by Burlingham, Minna left on May 5, followed ten days later by Mathilde and Robert. Already separated from Martin, who had had numerous affairs, Esti took the train with Sophie and Anton Walter. She had always detested Freud, who did not like her and considered her clinically "mad," even as he sought to give her excellent advice, which she never followed. When she left for Paris, she left behind part of her family. Her mother, Ida Drucker, would be exterminated in Auschwitz.

Martin left Vienna on May 14 to rejoin Esti and their children in Paris, but he left there the next day without her, taking his son along to London. Sophie lived with her mother in Paris, and Anton Walter remained in London with his father. In June 1940 Esti and Sophie left for the south of France, then went to Casablanca and from there to the United States, where the Bernays family helped them out. A number of their Viennese friends died in the gas chambers.

Much later, when Sophie, who had become an American citizen, felt the need to criticize her grandfather's theories, she remembered that she owed him her life: "I thus owe it to my grandfather to be among the few lucky ones to have escaped Vienna before the murderous persecution of its Jews. When my brother, many years later, heard of my criticism of one of our grandfather's theories, he said to me: 'Without Grandfather the Nazis would have made lampshades with your skin.' "[55]

August Aichhorn,[56] also eager to preserve traces of the beginnings, asked Edmund Engelman, a Viennese photographer from a Jewish family in Galicia, to take a series of photos of the still-intact sites and to make portraits of Freud. To evade Nazi surveillance, Engelman had to do without flash and projectors. He brought along a Rolleiflex and a Leica,

two lenses, and as many rolls of film as he could fit into his briefcase. For several days he made black-and-white photos in minute detail of objects, furnishings, and rooms from different angles, showing in this way, between half-light and chiaroscuro, how much closer this dreamlike place was to an engraving by Max Ernst than to a Renaissance painting. Threatened by the Gestapo, Engelman had to leave Vienna in a hurry. Out of prudence, he left the photos with Aichhorn. But he came back just before Freud's departure: "Workers had already started to put the offices and apartment into shape. The floor had been scraped and polished. The ghost of the couch had disappeared."[57]

On June 4, Freud climbed onto the Orient-Express with Anna, Martha, Paula, and his dog Lün-Yu. Josephine Stross, a pediatrician, had taken the place of Schur, who had had to undergo emergency surgery for an acute infection from a ruptured appendix. On June 10, still in bandages and with a drain in his abdomen, Schur had to flee from the hospital in a wheelchair to escape from the Gestapo with his family. Thanks to the visa obtained by Freud and Jones, he made it to Paris and then to London.

The day of his departure, Freud signed an obligatory declaration drafted by Indra in which he acknowledged that he had been well treated: "[Declaration]. I Prof. Freud, hereby confirm that after the Anschluss of Austria to the German Reich I have been treated by the German authorities and particularly by the Gestapo with all the respect and consideration due to my scientific reputation, that I could live and work in full freedom, that I could continue to pursue my activities in every way I desired, that I found full support from all concerned in this respect, and that I have not the slightest reason for any complaint. [June 4, 1938. Pr Sigmund Freud.]"[58] For decades, historians, witnesses, and commentators were convinced that Freud had written in his own hand, at the end of this declaration, the following sentence: "I can most highly recommend the Gestapo to everyone." One more legend overreaching the reality, this was an absurd rumor. It was impossible, in fact, to make fun of an official document. Still, Martin asserted that his father had slipped in this statement at the end of the declaration.[59]

Freud and the four women traveling with him passed through several cities before reaching the French border. At several points Freud came close to succumbing to cardiac arrest, and Stross administered strychnine

and other stimulants. Finally, on June 5, at about 3:30 A.M., the convoy crossed the Rhine on the Kehl bridge. Freud exclaimed, "Now we are free."[60]

When the train arrived at the Gare de l'Est in Paris, Paula was very struck by the welcome extended to Freud, but she noted how lost he was amid the photographers and the journalists. He was accompanied by Bullitt, who was particularly elegant in his felt hat with a rolled brim and his lace pocket handkerchief, and Bonaparte, wearing a dress by a great couturier and a sable stole. Freud seemed to have come from another world. Martha followed him, enveloped in a wrinkled raincoat, holding her pocketbook in both hands, and Anna was smiling, her face half hidden by a pitiful wool toque that covered her forehead. Two luxurious automobiles with chauffeurs drove the exiles to the princess's property at Saint-Cloud. They spent the day there before heading for Calais to cross the Channel. In the photos, one sees Freud coiffed in a cap that has fallen onto his glasses, his body stretched out on a wicker sofa, his legs hidden under blankets, his face inert, his right cheek dark and hollow, his beard white. Lün is lying calmly at his left.

The next day, the travelers arrived at Victoria Station, greeted by Jones, his wife, and Ernst Freud. They turned Lün-Yu over to a veterinarian for the obligatory six-month quarantine, then settled into their temporary quarters on Elsworthy Road.

Upon his arrival, Freud reconnected with his nephew Sam, whom he had not seen since his sojourn in Manchester, and he acquainted himself with the many newspaper articles that announced his arrival; at the same time an avalanche of telegrams, letters, flowers, and gifts came pouring in. Anna gave him a Pekinese whom he named Jumbo, by antiphrasis. On July 17, writing to his brother Alexander, he told the story of his exile, emphasizing that Jones had run into many difficulties in dealing with the British authorities as he sought to bring in the émigrés, because of the risk that they would not find work; he remarked that Jones obtained many things, but only for analysts. He explained in his letter that he had helped Harry with a recommendation and he added that Martin did not yet know what he was going to do, that Robert had found a job, and that Minna was ill.[61] On September 27, he moved into a lovely house with his family, at 20 Maresfield Gardens, Hampstead; it had been fur-

nished by Ernst Freud following the Berggasse model. This was Freud's last home.

On October 11, he was visited by Sauerwald, who had probably come to ask him for money. When Alexander asked Sauerwald what he was doing in London, the latter said that the Viennese police had hired him as an explosives expert, but that in fact he was making explosives himself for secret Nazi organizations. A strange story! According to Schur, he explained that Hitler felt that he was in a "state of siege" because the Jews were too individualistic to be assimilated into the population. Thus they had to be eliminated, he said, but that did not prevent an individual acting on the personal level—even if he were a Nazi—from helping another, as he himself had done for the Freud family.[62]

During the eighteen months that remained to him, Freud had the great pleasure of being honored, visited, recognized, admired, and celebrated as never before. He felt free, too, and he was able to finish his book on Moses and write "A Short Account of Psycho-analysis," in which he synthesized his work and predicted the forthcoming discovery of powerful chemical substances that could act directly on the psyche. He reaffirmed that Shakespeare was named Edward de Vere, and he defended his *Ödipuskomplex*.[63]

While the cancerous tumors were multiplying in his jawbones, he witnessed the destruction of continental Europe. But he became aware at the same time of the power of his doctrine in the English-speaking world. On June 25, he received a delegation from the Royal Society, which invited him to sign its official book, the very one in which Charles Darwin's name appeared. He received many visits from writers and intellectuals. Brought by Stefan Zweig, Salvador Dali drew several sketches of his damaged face, according to the surrealist principle of "the spiral and the snail." Freud seemed indifferent, and he explained to the painter that day that he was interested only in classical painting, in which he sought to detect expressions of the unconscious, whereas, in surrealist art, he preferred to observe the expression of consciousness.

When Arthur Koestler came to see him, in the fall, he was stupefied to hear Freud murmur, about the Nazis: "Well, you know, they are *abreacting* the aggression pent up in our civilization. Something like this was inevitable, sooner or later. I am not sure that from my standpoint I can

blame them."[64] Once again, Freud asserted that the world in which he lived mirrored what he had described in his work. A Hungarian Jew born in Budapest, a right-wing Zionist, close to Vladimir Jabotinsky, and an astute connoisseur of psychoanalysis, Koestler was not unaware that his mother, Adele Jeiteles, had met Freud in 1890 for a consultation, and that she had condemned him in no uncertain terms.[65] Afflicted with chronic melancholia, she detested her own son equally (she called him a pervert), and he felt the same way about her, as his autobiography attests.[66] At their meeting, the two men did not discuss their Viennese youth.

When he was visited by his old Viennese friend Walter Schmideberg, Freud went further still and greeted him with a "Heil Hitler!"—as if he were finally consenting to pronounce, through this lugubrious joke, the reviled name of the destroyer of his work.[67]

The arrival of Freud's family was experienced as a veritable intrusion by the members of the British Psychoanalytical Society (BPS). The Kleinians had dominated the British association for years. They had developed their own theses, which no longer had much to do with Freud's original doctrines. In addition, they had marginalized the old Freudians, and they looked on Freud himself as a patriarch from another era, straight out of the nineteenth century. They found the standards of the women around him—Martha, Minna, Anna, Paula—rigid, their ways of speaking and dressing ridiculous. They did not understand the family rituals, the prim politeness, the glacial humor, the tastes in food. In short, they viewed these people as strange beings attached to old mythologies and largely closed to the new approach to the unconscious centered on positions, object relations, the psychotic core, and the destructive drives detected in very young children. The Kleinians and the Freudians did not speak the same language. In this context, Jones, who had always supported Melanie Klein, played an essential role in Anna Freud's integration into the heart of the BPS.

On July 29, 1938, in Paris, Anna Freud participated in the fifteenth congress of the IPA, under Jones's presidency. She read aloud the chapter of *Moses and Monotheism* devoted to the progress of the human spirit and the greatness of the British Empire. Freud had addressed to his partisans a violently anti-American message, in which he exhorted them to vigilance against any attempt to transform psychoanalysis into an all-purpose handmaiden to psychiatry. In his closing speech, Jones praised his policy

of "rescuing" psychoanalysis in Berlin without saying a word about the exile of the Jews or the exodus of the leading lights of the Freudian intelligentsia. And he took the liberty of congratulating himself on having the WPV put under guardianship.[68] After these sinister statements, the participants met for a reception in Saint-Cloud, in the gardens of the princess's sumptuous residence, where Freud had spent several hours.

Eitingon had come to Paris to participate in the congress. He then went to London for a final visit with Freud. At that point he had been accused of being an agent of the People's Commissariat for Internal Affairs (NKVD), and implicated in the kidnapping of General Yevgeni Miller, which had been organized by German Soviet double agent Nikola Sklobin, husband of the singer Nadezhda Plevitskaya, whom Eitingon knew well. Owing to his connections with Plevitskaya, it didn't take long for the rumor to grow. Was he not also the brother of Leonid Eitingon, a Soviet spy and an organizer of Trotsky's assassination by Ramon Mercader in 1940? Although there was no family relationship whatsoever between Leonid and Max, the legend of a Freudian and Stalinist Eitingon, a double and triple agent, a seller of furs, and an organizer of crimes, never stopped cropping up, and it persists even today in the writings of authors determined to demonstrate an alleged common destiny between the two *internationales,* Communist and psychoanalytic.[69]

En route for America, the Viennese exiles gathered in Paris mused one last time, before the apocalypse, about the Europe they had dreamed of, whose splendors they were never to see again. The great Yvette Guilbert, so admired by Freud, sang "Dites-moi que je suis belle" before a crowd subjugated by the power of her voice and her eighty years of age. In Italy, with the first anti-Semitic laws Mussolini handed the Jews over to be deported. In January 1939, Weiss, too, was forced to go into exile in the United States, leaving behind his sister, his brother-in-law, and his wife's family, all of whom were exterminated by the Nazis. Weiss never again wanted to recall the hopes he had placed in Mussolini through his friendship with Forzano.

The very day he moved into Maresfield Gardens, Freud, who had just undergone a dreadful new operation at the London Clinic, learned of the Munich Agreement, through which France and the United Kingdom turned Czechoslovakia over to Hitler. On that occasion, Neville Chamberlain, who had been greeted in London as the savior of peace, gave a speech

on the uselessness of fighting on behalf of a distant country unfamiliar to the English. Without too much conviction, Freud approved of this policy, which allowed the Nazis to annex the Sudetenland at once. "We too are grateful for this bit of peace without being able to rejoice in it."[70]

Three weeks later, for Koestler's newspaper, *Die Zukunft,* he wrote a short note in which, bringing together statements by Mark Twain and Richard Nikolaus von Coudenhove-Kalergi, he emphasized the extent to which the fight against anti-Semitism had to be led first of all by non-Jews.[71] During this time the Nazis continued their persecutions by exposing German and Austrian women whose heads had been shaved because they had been accused of having had sexual relations with Jews. During the endless Kristallnacht, the Nazis destroyed buildings, businesses, and synagogues, and deported thirty thousand people to the camps at Dachau and Buchenwald. In Vienna, a Nazi officer who had arrested Professor Arthur Freud, a militant Zionist born in Moravia, shouted victoriously: he was convinced that he had captured the famous psychoanalyst.[72]

The specter of Freud was to haunt the consciousness of Hitlerites for many years.[73] But Freud himself was worried about his sisters: "The latest frightful events in Germany aggravate the problem of knowing what to do for the four elderly ladies ranging from seventy-five to eighty years old. Maintaining them in England exceeds our possibilities. The money we left them on our departure, around sixty thousand Austrian shillings, may already have been confiscated. We are thinking about housing them on the Côte d'Azur, in Nice or nearby. But will that be possible?"[74]

To respond to these concerns, Bonaparte tried to get visas from the French authorities or, lacking these, from the Greek legation. In vain; it was too late. Completely lucid about the persecutions that were striking the Jews, the princess expended a great deal of energy in an effort to save lives. She even proposed to Roosevelt, in a letter dated December 12, that he create a Jewish state in Southern California to accept thousands of refugees as quickly as possible.[75] She herself would never accept the slightest suggestion of "rescue" in France, and she left for exile in February 1941.[76]

On December 7, Freud received BBC technicians at his home to record a speech he had written.[77] He spoke in English, his voice stifled by his prosthesis, and at the end of his message he added a sentence in German:

"At the age of eighty-two, I left my home in Vienna following the German invasion, and I came to England where I hope to end my life in freedom." This is the only recording we have in Freud's voice.

During the last year of his life, several silent films were made at Maresfield Gardens, some in color.[78] In each shot, we see Freud walking in his garden, increasingly hunched over, on Anna's arm, accompanied by Lün-Yu and Jumbo; his jaw is fettered by his "muzzle," and his lips move as though he were chewing some food. Immense suffering is stamped on his face.

Freud continued to receive many visits from his London friends and from all those who came to see him for a final good-bye before they left for other continents. He suffered increasingly, stretching out on the swing in the garden or on his couch, often covered with a mosquito net. He preferred to eat alone, sheltered from the gaze of others; he no longer had much appetite, moreover. A fetid odor began to emanate from his mouth, but in his eyes the flame of the god Eros still sparkled. Freud had always said that at the hour of his death he preferred to witness the shipwreck of his *Konrad* in full consciousness, rather than becoming senile or being felled by a stroke: he wanted to die in harness, like King Macbeth. He knew that Schur would look after him to the end, and would only then emigrate to the United States.

On the recommendation of Pichler, George Exner, a specialist in facial surgery, followed the terminal phase of the illness along with Trotter, Jones's brother-in-law, a member of the Royal Society, and a specialist in anticancer treatments. In February, Bonaparte arranged to have Professor Antoine Lassagne, the chief director of the Institut Curie in Paris, brought to London; he was forced to admit that no further surgery was possible. So as not to disappoint Anna and Minna, who still wanted to hope, he suggested an intensive treatment with X-rays rather than radium. And Freud commented, "There is now no further doubt that I have a new recurrence of my dear old cancer, with which I have been sharing my existence for sixteen years. At that time naturally no one could predict which of us would prove the stronger."[79] He then confided to his dear princess that he wanted it to be over.

At the beginning of March, a few days before the German edition of *Moses* appeared in Amsterdam, Jones organized a gala dinner at the Savoy

Hotel to celebrate the twenty-fifth anniversary of the foundation of the BPI, in the presence of Anna, Martin, Ernst, Virginia Woolf, H. G. Wells, and many others. Too weak to attend, Freud sent a message of support: "The events of recent years have so ordained that London has become chief venue and center of the psychoanalytic movement. May the society discharge the functions thus devolving upon it in the most brilliant manner."[80]

During the summer, Wells tried in vain to obtain British nationality for the dying man, in order to satisfy a youthful wish that had been dear to Freud since the departure of his brother to Manchester: "All that was necessary was a small private bill . . . I am extraordinarily sorry that it couldn't be done."[81] At the beginning of August, Freud stopped receiving his last four patients. Burlingham and Smiley Blanton continued with their training sessions until the end of the month.

On September 3, 1939, the day France and England entered the war against Germany, Jones said his good-byes to his old master. In this critical moment, he stressed that they were finally in the same camp, united against the same barbarism: "When England last fought Germany, twenty-five years ago, we were on opposite sides of the line, but even then we found a way to communicate our friendship to each other. Now we are near to each other and united in our military sympathies. No one can say if we shall see the end of this war, but in any case it has been a very interesting life and we have both made a contribution to human existence—even if in very different measure."[82]

Descended from an aristocratic family in Auvergne, Raphaël de Valentin, the invented hero of Balzac's *Peau de chagrin,* dreams of glory. Pushed by Rastignac, he abandons artistic creation to try his luck in the world until he loses everything and is contemplating suicide. It is at this point that he discovers a talisman, in an antique shop: a *peau de chagrin,* endowed with a magic power that allows him to realize all his desires. Like Faust, he does not want to give up anything, and he signs a pact with the devil, to his own misfortune. Every time he becomes intoxicated with his pleasures, the skin shrinks. To suppress one's feelings in order to live to an advanced age, or to die young while accepting the martyrdom of the passions: this is the pivotal choice of the novel, which stages the enigma of the human condition.

By choosing to read this book on the eve of his death, Freud confronted the image of his broken-down body and his slow death from lack of nutrition, to be sure, but above all he saw unfolding before his eyes the story of a bad life that might have been his, had he not survived his combat against himself. Freud was the man who had wanted to teach people to what extent they were inhabited by the desire for their own destruction, and he had told them that only access to civilization suffices to contain that drive. He thought that what happened to human beings was already inscribed in their unconscious minds even before they became aware of it, and he was convinced that the Oedipus complex was the name of that inscription. And yet it was not the complex that he was confronting at this moment, it was the *peau de chagrin,* Oedipus or Macbeth, that is, the limit of his freedom.[83] He was engaging in a final combat against the torture of death, at peace with himself at the moment when the world was going to war, the moment when the id was triumphing over the ego, the moment when disease was so ravaging the inside of his mouth that it surfaced on his cheek, the moment, finally, when the sirens blared above his home, announcing the first air raid alerts. He made the last diary entry of his life on August 25, with a brief notation: "War panic" *(Kriegspanik).*[84]

On September 21, Freud reminded Schur of the promise he had made to help him end things when the time came. He asked the doctor to speak to Anna, "and if she thinks it's right, then make an end of it." Living under such conditions no longer made sense to him.[85] Schur squeezed his hand and promised to give him an adequate dose of tranquilizer. He administered a first dose of three centigrams of morphine, then repeated the dose two more times, several hours apart. He knew that the so-called calming dose could not exceed two centigrams. He had thus chosen death through deep and continuous sedation.

Freud died on Saturday, September 23, 1939, at 3:00 a.m.[86] It was Yom Kippur, the holiest festival of the Jewish year, the Day of Atonement. During the day, practicing Londoners went to the synagogue to plead for forgiveness from the God whom Freud had treated so badly. Sandbags were piled up everywhere against enemy raids; certain statues had been moved and trenches dug.

That same day, at the other end of a Europe long deserted by the Freudians, Adam Czerniakow, a former chemical engineer, agreed to be named

by the mayor of Warsaw as president of the Judenrat (Jewish council), while in Sokolow Podlaski, a nearby district, the Nazis burned the synagogue. Czerniakow hid a flask containing twenty-four cyanide pills in a drawer.[87] He too would be able to die at a time of his choosing.

Freud's body was incinerated at the crematorium of Golders Green with no rites, and his ashes were placed in an ancient Greek vase decorated with scenes of offerings. Before a hundred people or so, Jones delivered his master's eulogy in English, recalling the names of all the members of the committee, dead or scattered: "If ever man can be said to have conquered death itself, to live on in spite of the king of Terrors, who held no terror for him, that man was Freud."[88]

After Jones spoke, Stefan Zweig delivered a splendid eulogy in German: "Thank you for the worlds that you have opened for us but which we must now travel alone without your guidance—forever faithful to you, in awe of you, our precious friend, Sigmund Freud."[89]

Zweig committed suicide in Brazil, at Petropolis, in February 1942.

Epilogue

FROM NEW YORK, where he had managed to emigrate, Harry Freud, Alexander's son, announced the death of their brother Sigmund to the four sisters who had remained in Vienna: "He has entered into the other world, which we hope will be a better one. . . . He spent his last days in his office, where his bed had been placed. From there he could see the garden, and in his best moments he could enjoy looking at nature. I hope you receive this news in peace. The other family news is good."[1]

In terms of peacefulness, the four old ladies were soon to be forced to live, like other persecuted women, in Alexander's old apartment. In the name of the punitive tax, the JUVA,[2] they were stripped of their assets, which were under the control of Erich Führer, the Nazi manager of Alexander's property. Harry alerted Alfred Indra, who tried to get in contact with Anton Sauerwald. But the latter had been called to the Russian front. On June 20, 1940, Indra made an urgent request to Harry for support. But all efforts were useless. On January 15, 1941, the four women sent a desperate letter to the lawyer: "We four sisters are limited to *one* room which has to serve as bed- and livingroom. As you know, we are somewhat sickly, often bedridden persons, and the proper ventilation and cleaning is thus impossible without danger to health."[3]

At this point, because they were more than sixty-five years old, they had been spared when the decision was made to send the first convoys to the work camps. But after the January 1942 Wannsee Conference, they were deported to the ghetto of Theresienstadt (Terezin), where Adolfine died of malnutrition on September 29, 1942.[4] As for the other three sisters, they were transported to extermination camps from which they never

returned: Maria and Paula to Maly Trostinec on September 23, 1942, Rosa Graf to Treblinka either on September 29, 1942, or on March 1, 1943.

On July 27, 1946, Samuel Rajzman, a native of Warsaw, gave the following testimony before the Nuremberg tribunal concerning Obersturmbannführer Kurt Franz, the commander in charge of the camp: "A train arrived from Vienna. I was standing on the platform when the people left the cars. An elderly woman came up to Kurt Franz, took out a document and said that she was the sister of Sigmund Freud. She begged him to give her light work in an office. Franz read this document through very seriously and said that there must be a mistake here, he led her up to the train schedule and said that in two hours a train would leave for Vienna. She should leave all her documents and valuables and then go to the bath-house; after the bath she would have her documents and ticket prepared to be sent to Vienna would be available to her. Of course, the woman went to the bath-house and never returned."[5]

After the death of their father and grandfather, Freud's children and grandchildren had to adapt, as did his disciples, to a world very different from the one they had known. They had to face wartime without having had the opportunity to enjoy a new peace. But this time, owing to their exile, they found themselves in the victors' camp, where they were regarded as intruders who had lost everything.[6] They never forgot that they were Jews, but as they gradually discovered the scope of the destruction that had fallen on their former world and on those who had not been able to escape, they sought to break with the horrors of the past. Like many victims who managed to survive, they then confronted the question of the extermination of the Jews. And several of them participated in the hunt for former Nazis.

A very gifted seamstress, Mathilde opened a dress shop in London, along with other exiled Austrians. Martin continued to live as before, solitary, seductive, and impecunious; he saw himself as "a sick old Jew." He ended up running a tobacco and newspaper stand near the British Museum. Oliver settled in the United States, in Philadelphia. He tried in vain to adopt a child who had escaped the genocide; later, he held a position as researcher in a transportation company, where he went by the title "Professor Freud." Ernst, a spoiled child thanks to the family fortune, the most elegant of the lot, pursued his career as an English architect. Two of

his sons had exceptional destinies: Lucian Freud was one of the most innovative painters of the second half of the twentieth century, and Clemens became Sir Clement, a politician, journalist, humorist, restaurateur, and nightclub owner; as an observer, he followed the Nuremberg trials as they unfolded, and he published his autobiography under the title *Freud Ego*.[7]

Lucian had fourteen children by several different women; Clement had five, including one adoptee; Stefan, the older, overlooked, marginal brother in the hardware business, spent his life quarreling with his brothers, who detested one another as well. Lucian's daughter Esther wrote several novels in which she recounted the various facets of her difficult existence between an absent father, whom she came to know only when she was an adolescent, and a tormented mother. She often evoked her father's silence about the events of the 1930s.[8] As for Lucian himself, icy, pernicious, magical, incredibly handsome, cultivating secrecy and provocation, identifying with his favorite painter, Velasquez, he adored his grandfather, whom he remembered very well, and he abhorred any form of anti-Semitic expression.

When he was about ten years old, already very original in his way of observing the world around him, he had insisted on "seeing Hitler," the absolute enemy. During a Nazi demonstration in Berlin, he had even photographed him,[9] so he would never forget his features and gestures. Stifled by a mother (Lucie) who maintained a fusional relationship with him, he got away from her control only through his creative genius. Unlike his grandfather, whom he resembled very closely, Lucian was interested not in speech but in the body in its very nudity, not in the repression of desire but in the libido in all its violence as a drive. To paint, he took off his clothes and required his models to do the same, even when he was doing portraits of family members, most notably his daughters. It was as though Lucian were actualizing the obscure component of Freud's work through his paintings; he saw himself as his grandfather's demonic heir. As much as he rejected the Oedipus complex, he regarded the Professor as a fabulous zoologist, fascinated by the animal world—the first scientist to determine the sex of eels. Lucian had an almost animal bond with the fantasized body of his grandfather.

He knew that he owed Freud his freedom, in part, and it was with intense emotion that he remembered the scene during which Marie

Bonaparte had intervened with the Duke of Kent to get English nationality for Ernst and his family. Because of this debt contracted toward the royal family, he offered Queen Elizabeth II, fifty-five years later, the portrait he had made of her. The work provoked as big a scandal as Freud's theories had: the press asserted that the painter had made a "travesty" of the sovereign's face by endowing her with a rugby player's collar and a blue chin that seemed to be covered with the beginnings of a beard. For committing such a sacrilege, one journalist suggested that he should be locked up in the Tower of London.[10]

Anton Walter, Martin's son, was much more political than his father; he joined the army and was charged with liberating the Zeltweg airport, in Styria, in 1945. Parachuting in under cover of night, he mentioned his name and to his great surprise was not too ill received by Austrian officers eager to see the war end. In the aftermath, promoted to the rank of captain, he specialized in the search for former Nazi criminals; through his investigations he helped bring to justice Bruno Tesch, whose company made Zyklon B for the camp at Auschwitz. Found guilty by the military in Hamburg, Tesch was condemned to death and hanged in March 1946. Through his tenacity Anton also contributed to the condemnation of Alfred Trzebinski, an SS doctor and torturer who specialized in experimental injections of bacteria in children. Later, having become a chemical engineer, Anton worked for various English companies until he retired.

As for his cousin Harry Freud, who enrolled in the American army, he too returned to Austria, in order to track down Sauerwald, whom he accused of having looted the family's property. Arrested and then tried by the American authorities, the former *Nazi-Kommissar* pled not guilty. His wife asked Anna Freud to present testimony, which she willingly provided in writing, affirming that Sauerwald had helped the family.[11] He was freed.

After her father's death, Anna decided to say in London and to live in the family home at 20 Maresfield Gardens, in Hampstead. After Martha and Minna died, she lived there with Dorothy Burlingham, who had come back from New York in 1940 and was convinced that she could no longer manage without her friend.[12] Together, they carried on with their activities in support of children by creating Hampstead Nurseries and the

Hampstead Child Therapy Clinic, a research center and a clinic where they applied their theories in close collaboration with the children they were caring for.

In 1946, from her close friend Kata Levy,[13] the sister of Anton von Freund, Anna learned what had happened to her four aunts, without yet knowing in what camps they had died. She immediately shared the information with her three cousins, Margarethe Freud-Magnus, Lilly Freud-Marlé, and Rose Waldinger. Anna felt guilty that she had not been more vigilant. For years, she condemned the Austrians and wanted to hear no more about the Berggasse. From London, nevertheless, she helped her old friend August Aichhorn reconstitute the WPV.

She confronted the question of extermination by taking responsibility, between 1945 and 1947, for six young German Jewish orphans, born between 1941 and 1942, whose parents had been sent to the gas chamber. Imprisoned in the Theresienstadt camp in the section for motherless children, they had survived by sticking together, deprived of toys and food. When they were housed at Bulldogs Bank, then entrusted to Anna (who reconnected with the German language on this occasion), they spoke a vulgar language among themselves; they rejected toys, destroyed the furniture, and were given to biting, hitting, screaming, masturbating, and insulting adults. In short, they had been able to survive only by forming a single entity that served them as a fortress. After a year of care, they returned to a normal life. Children of genocide and absolute abandonment, they were the first to experience a new psychoanalytic approach, which showed future generations that nothing is ever decided in advance and that, even in the most extreme situations, a new life is always thinkable.[14] In this area, Anna revealed her genuine gifts as a clinician.

She remained close to the Viennese friends who had settled in the United States. They loved her for her devotion, her integrity, and her sense of loyalty. With them, she could evoke nostalgically the past greatness of Freud's original movement. She remained the living memory of an era swallowed up by two world wars.

The legal heir, with her brother Ernst, of her father's work and archives, Anna chose Ernest Jones over her friend Siegfried Bernfeld to write the first authorized biography of Freud. Published in three volumes between

1953 and 1957, it was a magisterial work based on unchallengeable sources and archives. Through this biography, the Freudian diaspora could picture its own origins in the form of a history, an official history to be sure, but not a hagiography or a pious account. Jones privileged the idea that Freud, a solitary, universal scholar, had succeeded on the strength of his genius alone in pulling away from the "false sciences" of his day in order to reveal the existence of the unconscious to the world. The biographer made little effort to situate Freud's work or his person in the long sweep of history, and he said nothing at all about his own political endeavor to "rescue" psychoanalysis, about which he had no regrets. He hid the suicides, the wanderings, and the treatment narratives, and he dealt very harshly with Josef Breuer, Wilhelm Fliess, Jung, Wilhelm Reich, Otto Rank, and many others.

Above all, though, he transformed Freud into a scientist more English than Viennese, more positivist than Romantic, much less tormented in his choices than he had been in reality. In short, for the use of his contemporaries Jones built a memorial in honor of the prince and scholar he had served. This monumental biography gave rise to a huge historiographic debate that for forty years remained as lively as the quarrels among psychoanalysts.

No subsequent historian could avoid confronting this first biography written by a contemporary, someone who had been both his disciple and the organizer of his movement. To be sure, Jones had succumbed to the introspective illusion by painting a hero en route to his destiny; still, he was the first to have access to archives, the first to use a coherent methodology and adhere to it.

He incorporated Bernfeld's research into his work, while at the same time Anna was closely supervising the publication of Freud's correspondence, in particular the exchanges with Fliess.[15] She banished everything that, in her eyes, risked tarnishing the ideal image she had forged of her father, a hero without fear and without reproach, a "historically correct" Freud for a psychoanalysis that was pragmatic, rule governed, and soon fossilized.[16]

In 1972, Max Schur corrected Jones's version by giving Freud the more Viennese image of an ambivalent scholar, a user of cocaine, someone anxiety-ridden about death and hesitating between error and truth. He re-

vealed the existence of Emma Eckstein for the first time, opening the way for others to explore the stories of Freud's patients.

Anna and Burlingham led a happy but complicated life. They never agreed to be viewed as lesbians, even though they formed a real couple, and Anna never consented during her lifetime to acknowledge publicly that she had been analyzed by her father.

The children whom Anna and Burlingham had adopted and raised together, who had all been very troubled, came regularly to London. Bob remained on Anna's couch for forty-five years, and along with his sister Mabbie he was one of the ten cases related in the first part of *The Psychoanalytical Treatment of Children*.[17] He died, asthmatic and depressed, in 1969, at the age of fifty-four. Five years later, still in analysis in London and, episodically, in New York with Marianne Kris, Mabbie committed suicide at 20 Maresfield Gardens by taking barbiturates. Although she was Burlingham's favorite, she had never been able to endure the conflict between her psychotic father, who had been rejected by the Freud family, and her mother, who embodied in her eyes the world of health and soul healers.

Ernstl Halberstadt, a child of psychoanalysis like Anna and like Burlingham's children, was interested all his life in children, in the relations between infants and their mothers, in premature babies, in children all over the world: in Jerusalem, in Moscow, in Johannesburg. In search of an identity that could link him with his grandfather, he went by the name Ernst W. Freud so he would not be confused with his uncle. When Anna died, he went off to practice psychoanalysis in Germany, thus reconnecting in his practice with the language of his childhood. He was the only male descendant in the Freud family to become an analyst.

He often recalled his arrival in London and the bizarre—and very Freudian—behaviors of his cousin Lucian, estranged from his family, detesting his mother,[18] and dreaming of becoming a famous painter. One day, in a train, when he was sixteen years old, Lucian had suddenly stood up to grab a suitcase in which he was hiding a secret: "A horse's skull. He stared at it for a long time and then put it away: he had found the skull at Dartmoor and had become attached to it."[19]

The reconstruction of the life of the "great man" and the various publications being supervised did not suffice either to unify fully the psychoanalytic community that had scattered to the four corners of the

earth, or to give the Freudian movement the controlled and honorable countenance that it wanted to present to the public.

To complete the editorial and historiographic enterprise, it was still necessary to reconstruct an accurate recollection so that no one would forget the splendor of the *Mitteleuropa* that had been destroyed by Nazism. This would be the work of Kurt Eissler.

Born in Vienna in 1908, analyzed by Aichhorn, Eissler had emigrated to Chicago in 1938, leaving behind a brother who would be deported. Eissler had moved to New York after joining the medical service of the American army; as a captain, he was assigned to oversee consultations in a training camp. Entirely oriented toward the past, he manifested strong hostility toward the American school of analysis, which he reproached for abandoning Freud's original doctrines. Thus he decided to devote his life to constituting an archival corpus that would allow new generations to know Freud's life and work in the smallest details: a Viennese life, a European life. Bernfeld had been the first to think of doing this, but Eissler had shoved him aside, relying on Anna, as Jones had done for his biography. He got in touch with Luther Evans, the head librarian of the prestigious Library of Congress in Washington, DC, and Evans agreed to house the future Freud archives.

In February 1951, Eissler founded the Sigmund Freud Archives (SFA), with himself as curator, supported by an administrative board made up exclusively of psychoanalysts who were members of the IPA: Bertram Lewin, Jones, Willi Hoffer, Hermann Nunberg, and Bernfeld, along with some honorary members: Albert Einstein, Thomas Mann, and Anna.

During a thirty-year period, Eissler collected some fabulous treasure: letters, official documents, photographs, texts, and interviews with all those who had known Freud, including patients, neighbors, and the most anodyne visitors. All the psychoanalysts who had known Freud and most of his family members entrusted their documents and their testimonies to Eissler. With Anna's agreement, Eissler followed a policy that was as noteworthy on the archivistic level as it was disastrous for research. Anxious to classify, organize, master, and control the entire memory of a world of which he himself had known only the last moments, he refused to allow professional historians access to the archives, reserving the right of consultation exclusively to psychoanalysts duly trained in the seraglio

of the IPA. However, from the 1960s on, the latter were devoting themselves increasingly to clinical work, and were scarcely prepared in any case to undertake historiographical or even simply historical research.[20]

From 1970 on, the English language clearly dominated the historiographic work. Jones's massive tome was succeeded on the one hand by a dissident strain, and on the other by a scientific approach. Inaugurated by Ola Andersson in 1962, scientific historiography then blossomed with the innovative work of Henri F. Ellenberger. His *Discovery of the Unconscious,* which was my own starting point for research into the history of psychoanalysis in France,[21] was the first in fact to introduce *longue durée* into the Freudian adventure and to plunge psychoanalysis into the history of dynamic psychiatry. Freud emerged stripped down and looking like a scientist torn between doubt and certainty.

Ellenberger gave birth, unwittingly, to a revisionist historiography, critical in its first phase, especially with the publication by Frank J. Sulloway of a work devoted to the biological origins of Freud's thought, then radically anti-Freudian later on, via several essays—arising from "Freud bashers"—who made Freud out to be a swindler, a rapist, and incestuous; thus a dark legend grew in opposition to the golden one.

Similarly, works by American and English historians on fin-de-siècle Vienna (Carl Schorske, William Johnston), which were relayed in turn in France by those of Jacques Le Rider, transformed the way the social and political circumstances surrounding Freud's discovery were seen. Jones's Freud was succeeded by a man immersed in the movement of ideas that was shaking up the Austro-Hungarian Empire of the 1880s. That other Freud embodied, in a way, all the aspirations of a generation of Viennese intellectuals haunted by Jewishness, sexuality, the decline of patriarchy, the feminization of society, and finally a common will to explore the deep sources of the human psyche. As for dissident historiography, it took shape around 1975, with the publication of Paul Roazen's *Freud and His Followers.*

Starting in the second half of the 1970s, the conditions were thus ripe for the imposition of an authentic historical school of Freudianism. In this context, in the face of the emergence of scholarly works and critical approaches, the representatives of psychoanalytic legitimacy (IPA) lost ground and did not manage to prevent the historians from producing

works that departed from the official imagery. They retained only one monopoly: that of managing and controlling the famous archives residing in the Library of Congress.

Confronted with that reality, Eissler and Anna made a catastrophic decision by entrusting the establishment of Fliess's correspondence to Jeffrey Moussaieff Masson, a brilliant polyglot, a former professor of Sanskrit, and a disciple of Paul Brunton, a Jewish mystic who had himself been converted to Hindu spirituality by the guru Ramana Maharshi. Duly analyzed in the inner circle, Masson, seductive and intelligent, seemed to present all the qualities required to undertake the task. However, right in the middle of his research, the fortunate chosen one turned into a radical challenger. Imagining himself a prophet of a revised Freudianism, he began to believe that America had been perverted by an original Freudian lie. He thus asserted that Freud's letters enclosed a "secret." Freud, he said, had abandoned the theory of seduction out of cowardice, so as never to reveal to the world the atrocities inflicted by adults on innocent children. Freud, then, had invented the theory of the phantasm; he was a forger.[22]

The book Masson published on this theme in 1984 became one of the biggest best sellers in the history of American psychoanalytic literature.[23] He called the Freudian doctrine aggressively into question while reactivating the old debate between Freud and Sándor Ferenczi on trauma and sexual abuse. From then on, the author relied on the idea, very fashionable in the 1980s, that an immense Freudian lie had perverted America since Freud's triumph in 1909, a lie that went hand in hand with power based on oppression: the colonization of women by men, of children by adults, of affect and emotion by dogma and concepts.

Eissler never got over this disaster that he himself had instigated.[24] He was extremely fond of Masson, and he had imagined making him his successor at the head of the SFA; instead, he was forced to remove him from his position. A tireless worker, Eissler had never stopped responding with erudition to all the criticisms and attacks directed at Freud. And he would obviously have preferred to see the person he had trained continue along the same path.[25] What is more, he had imposed Masson on Anna, who did not trust him. Eissler had even thought of inviting Masson to oversee the transformation of 20 Maresfield Gardens into a museum.[26]

In the wake of this scandal, the revisionist American camp—especially Peter Swales, Adolf Grünbaum,[27] and many others—spent the next ten years tearing apart Freud's doctrine and Freud himself, the master having become once again a diabolical scientist guilty of engaging in sexual relations within his own family. As early as 1981, Swales, an iconoclastic author well versed in Freudianism and well acquainted with the archives, asserted, without offering the slightest proof, that Freud had had a sexual relationship with his sister-in-law, had gotten her pregnant, and then forced her to have an abortion. Eissler felt some sympathy for Swales, whereas Anna, overwhelmed by the events, no longer knew how to confront the revisionist madness.

In 1986, four years after Anna's death, the Freud Museum opened its doors. Over the years, it became an eminent center for research, exhibits, and conferences. One could see Freud's collections, his desk, and his library; twenty-five thousand documents were available for consultation.[28] In Vienna, after many twists and turns, a first Freud Museum had seen the light in 1971; it was a museum without objects, without furniture, without a library, a museum to the memory of what had disappeared in 1938—in short, a prelude to the second museum.

Following the Masson affair, the image of an abusive, rapist, lying, infamous Freud came to dominate the media with the publications of novels and essays about his undiscoverable sex life, while interest in psychoanalysis declined in Western societies—especially in France—and, among the more classical historians, a return to the biographical tradition began with the 1988 publication of the biography by Peter Gay, a historian who specialized in the Victorian era.

The crisis of the archives reached its culmination with the organization of a long-planned exhibit on Freud at the Library of Congress. Forty-two independent researchers, mostly American, signed a petition[29] addressed to James Billington, director of the Library of Congress; Michael Roth, commissioner of the exhibition; and James Hutson, head of the manuscript division. The signatories included excellent authors—Phyllis Grosskurth, Elke Mühlleitner, Nathan Hale, and Patrick Mahony—who rightly criticized the overly institutional character of the future catalog and asked that their own works be included. But to support this collective undertaking Swales and Grünbaum launched a virulent press campaign

against Freud, repeating the customary accusations. Alarmed by this witch hunt, the organizers preferred to defer the exhibit, even as numerous American journalists and intellectuals publicly manifested their hostility to these extremist positions.

It was in this context and at the initiative of French psychiatrist and psychoanalyst Philippe Garnier and myself that another petition was organized, in France, criticizing both the challengers and the organizers of the Library of Congress exhibit, the latter for being unable to impose their authority and remaining too attached to an old orthodoxy. Signed by 180 intellectuals and analysts from all over the world, representing many tendencies and many nationalities, this second petition met with considerable success.[30] The main effect of the anti-Freudian offensive by Grünbaum and Swales was to marginalize the other signatories and to privilege a stilted academic approach. Opened in October 1998, the exhibit at the Library of Congress in fact presented a Freud whose theories no longer mattered from the standpoint of science and truth: "It hardly matters whether Freud's ideas are true or false," Michael Roth insisted. "What matters is that they have impregnated our entire culture and the way in which we understand the world through films, art, comic books, and television."[31]

Notwithstanding the success in France of two best sellers, *Le livre noir de la psychanalyse* (The black book of psychoanalysis), a collective work bringing together the contributions of some forty writers, and *Le crépuscule d'une idole* (The twilight of an idol), a pamphlet by Michel Onfray, the theses of the "Freud bashers" did not take root in France in the university milieu, even with the rise of cognitive therapies. They were even rejected, after having been the delight of a certain written and audiovisual press avid for Freudian sensations.[32]

Nevertheless, they helped interject into public opinion a blurred image of Freud's life and work, an image sometimes based on the wildest rumors, which were presented in print as established truths. Hence my decision to undertake this biographical and historical work, at a time when the Sigmund Freud Archives were finally accessible to researchers, while a rich trove of publications and debates was proliferating on the Internet.

In April 2014, a few days before my departure for Washington, DC, accompanied by Anthony Ballenato, I went to the crematorium of Golders

Green in London, a site of secular burial across from the Jewish cemetery of the same name; it welcomes believers, nonbelievers, writers, Communists, actors, and free thinkers alike. I lingered before the mausoleums, the statues, and the Gothic-style crypts full of plaques, inscriptions, urns, and assorted objects. I knew that some time earlier, on New Year's Eve,[33] vandals had broken the window behind which the Greek vase containing the ashes of Sigmund Freud and Martha Bernays had been placed. Presumably seeking to steal objects of value, the thieves had knocked the urn off its large marble stand, leaving the visitor with the sad spectacle of a decapitated monument. They had then fled in a panic, without taking anything.

Looking at this damaged spot, covered with offerings and souvenirs where the ashes of other members of the Freud family and some close friends remain in small boxes, and listening to Eric Willis, head of the crematorium, tell me the long story of this scholar who had come to die in London, I could not help thinking that this profanation—or rather, this "beheading"—signified in fact that, seventy-five years after his death, Freud was still disturbing Western consciousness, with his myths, his princely dynasties, his traversal of dreams, his stories of savage hordes, of Gradiva on the march, of the vulture found in Leonardo, of the murder of the father, and of Moses losing the tablets of the law.

I imagined him brandishing his cane against the anti-Semites; putting on his finest shirt to visit the Acropolis; discovering Rome like a lover overcome with joy; lashing out at imbeciles; speaking without notes before Americans; reigning in his timeless dwelling amid his objects, his red chow chows, his disciples, his women, and his mad patients; waiting attentively for Hitler without managing to speak his name; and I tell myself that, for a long time yet, he will remain the great thinker of his time and ours.

Notes

Introduction

1. A specialist in the editions of Freud's work, Gerhard Fichtner (1932–2012) spent his life looking for Freud's unpublished writings and collecting his letters. See "Les lettres de Freud en tant que source historique" and "Bibliographie des lettres de Freud," *Revue internationale d'histoire de la psychanalyse* 2 (1989): 51–81. See also Ernst Falzeder, "Existe-t-il encore un Freud inconnu?," *Psychothérapies* 27, no. 3 (2007): 175–195.

2. The Conclusion, the Works Cited list, and the Bibliography provide all the indications needed for establishing the sources used in this book. The bibliography incorporates historiographic information that sheds light on the quarrels over the Freud archives; additional genealogical and chronological indications are found in the Family Tree. Most of the existing biographies are mentioned in one or more notes.

1. Beginnings

1. Louis Antoine de Saint-Just, *Rapport sur le mode d'exécution du décret contre les ennemis de la Révolution, fait au nom du Comité de salut public par St.-Just, le 13 ventôse, l'an 2 de la République* (Paris: Imprimerie nationale, 1794). [TN: Unless otherwise indicated, translations from the French are my own.]

2. Karl Marx and Friedrich Engels, *The Communist Manifesto,* trans. Samuel Moore with Friedrich Engels, introduction by David Harvey (London: Pluto, 2008), 31.

3. See Vincenzo Ferrone and Daniel Roche, eds., *Le monde des Lumières* (Paris: Fayard, 1999).

4. William Johnston, *The Austrian Mind: An Intellectual and Social History, 1848–1938* (Berkeley: University of California Press, 1972), 25–26. See also Jean Clair, ed., *Vienne: L'apocalypse joyeuse,* exhibition catalog (Paris: Centre Georges-Pompidou, 1986).

5. I addressed these problematics in Élisabeth Roudinesco, *Retour sur la question juive* (Paris: Albin Michel, 2009).

6. All the documents concerning the civil status of the Freud family have been published by Marianne Krüll in *Sigmund, fils de Jakob: Un lien non dénoué* (Paris: Gallimard, 1983 [1979]). See also Renée Gicklhorn, "La famille Freud à Freiberg" (1969) *Études freudiennes* 11–12 (January 1976): 231–238; Ernest Jones, *The Life and Work of Sigmund Freud,* 3 vols. (New York: Basic Books, 1953–1957), vol. 1, *The Formative Years and the Great Discoveries, 1856–1900;* Henri F. Ellenberger, *The Discovery of the Unconscious: The History and Evolution of Dynamic Psychiatry* (New York: Basic Books, 1970), 419–427; Peter Gay, *Freud: A Life for Our Time* (New York: W. W. Norton, 1988); Emmanuel Rice, *Freud and Moses: The Long Journey Home* (New York: State University of New York Press, 1990). Kallamon (Salomon) is sometimes spelled Kalman, Kallmann, or Kelemen. Tysmenitz may be transcribed as Tysmienica or Tismenitz. Freiberg is sometimes written Freyberg, or Příbor (Přbor) in the Czech language. For Jacob, one also finds Jakob; for Peppi, Pepi. See also Freud's letter to the burgomaster of the city of Příbor dated October 25, 1931, in *The Standard Edition of the Complete Psychological Works of Sigmund Freud,* ed. James Strachey (London: Hogarth Press and the Institute of Psychoanalysis, 1966–1974; hereafter *SE*), 21:259–260).

7. Sigmund Freud to Martha Bernays, February 10, 1886, in Sigmund Freud, *Letters of Sigmund Freud, 1873–1939,* ed. Ernst L. Freud, trans. Tania Stern and James Stern (London: Hogarth, 1970), 210. The erroneous thesis of the "Jewish neurosis" was very much in fashion at the time, largely owing to Charcot's teachings. See Élisabeth Roudinesco, *La bataille de cent ans: Histoire de la psychanalyse en France* (Paris: Éditions Ramsay, 1982), republished as *Histoire de la psychanalyse en France: La bataille de cent ans, 1885–39* along with a second volume, *Histoire de la psychanalyse en France, 2: La bataille de cent ans, 1925–1985* (Paris: Seuil, 1986); the two titles were combined in a single volume, *Histoire de la psychanalyse en France* followed by *Jacques Lacan: Esquisse d'une vie, histoire d'un système de pensée,* and a brief final section titled *Héritages* (Paris: Pochothèque, 2009; hereafter *HPF-JL*). [TN: Only the second volume of *Histoire* is available in English, as *Jacques Lacan and Co.: A History of Psychoanalysis in France, 1925–1985,* trans. Jeffrey Mehlman (Chicago: University of Chicago Press, 1990 [1982–1986]). The third section of *HPF-JL* is available in English as *Jacques Lacan,* trans. Barbara Bray (New York: Columbia University Press, 1997).]

8. Several commentators have imagined mistakenly that Jacob had remained very attached to the Orthodox rites.

9. I thank Michel Rotfus, who provided me with several sources on the evolution of the Jews of the four provinces of the Habsburg Empire.

10. Genealogical table in Sigmund Freud, *Lettres de famille de Sigmund Freud et des Freud de Manchester, 1911–1938* (Paris: Presses Universitaires de France, 1996), vi–vii. [TR: I have been unable to locate a copy of the English version on which the French translation is based, *The Family Letters of Sigmund Freud and the Freuds of*

Manchester, ed. Tom Johnson, unpublished dummy (Wivenhoe, UK: Mark Paterson, 1991).]

11. In 1979, seeking to Christianize Freud's destiny, Marie Balmary ferreted out a supposed "hidden fault" in Jacob's life, and made the baseless claim that Rebekka had committed suicide by jumping from a train. See Marie Balmary, *Psychoanalyzing Psychoanalysis: Freud and the Hidden Fault of the Father,* trans. Ned Lucacher (Baltimore: Johns Hopkins University Press, 1982 [1979]).

12. The birth certificate designates him by his Jewish first name, Schlomo (Shelomoh), born in Freiberg, on Tuesday, Rosh Chodesh Iyyar 5616 in the Jewish calendar, that is, May 6, 1856. The house where he was born was located at Schlossergasse 117. Balmary claimed that Amalia was pregnant before the wedding and that Freud was born on March 6, not May 6. These assertions are completely unfounded. The original document is now available on the Internet and the date of May 6 leaves no room for doubt.

13. Translated from the Hebrew by Yosef Hayim Yerushalmi, in *Freud's Moses: Judaism Terminable and Interminable* (New Haven, CT: Yale University Press, 1991), 71. Yerushalmi advances the hypothesis that Freud, contrary to what he always maintained, in fact knew Hebrew. To Abraham A. Roback, who had sent him a signed copy of his book in 1930, Freud wrote, "My education was so little Jewish that I am not even capable of reading your dedication, manifestly written in Hebrew. I later regretted this gap" (*Correspondance, 1873–1939* [Paris: Gallimard, 1967 (1960)], 223–224).

14. Sigmund Freud, *The Interpretation of Dreams* (1900), SE 4:192.

15. Sigmund Freud, "Obituary of Professor S. Hammerschlag" (1904), SE 9:255. Cf. Theo Pfrimmer, *Freud, lecteur de la Bible* (Paris: Presses Universitaires de France, 1984). See also Ernst Hammerschlag (Samuel's grandson), recollections, n.d. (1928–1929?), LoC, box 113, folder 20.

16. Some uncertainty surrounds the name given to this governess. Resi Wittek is the name given in an official document dated June 5, 1857. That of Monika Zajic appears on another document as a relative of the locksmith Zajic, who was the Freud family's landlord in Freiberg. The two women are certainly one and the same person. See Krüll, *Sigmund,* 335.

17. Freud to Fliess, October 4, 1897, in Sigmund Freud, *The Origins of Psychoanalysis: Letters, Drafts and Notes to Wilhelm Fliess, 1887–1902,* ed. Marie Bonaparte, Anna Freud, and Ernst Kris, trans. Eric Mosbacher and James Strachey (Garden City, NY: Doubleday, 1957), 223; cf. Sigmund Freud, *The Complete Letters of Sigmund Freud to Wilhelm Fliess, 1877–1904,* ed. and trans. Jeffrey Moussaieff Masson (Cambridge, MA: Belknap Press of Harvard University Press, 1985), 269. [TN: Translations from Freud's letters to Fliess will be cited from *Origins* except where the letter or passage cited is not included in that volume.]

18. Sigmund Freud, *Three Essays on Human Sexuality* (1905), SE 7:123–245.

19. Krüll (in *Sigmund*) proposes this hypothesis, as do many others after her.

20. Sigmund Freud, "Screen Memories" (1899), *SE* 3:311, 316. See also Siegfried Bernfeld, "An Unknown Autobiographical Fragment by Freud," *American Imago* 4, no. 1 (1946): 3–19; and Suzanne Cassirer-Bernfeld, "Freud's Early Childhood," *Bulletin of the Menninger Clinic* 8 (1944): 107–115. As I have already emphasized, I have carefully avoided reconstructing Freud's life on the basis of a reinterpretation of his dreams.

21. Freud to Fliess, October 4, 1897, in Freud, *Origins,* 222 ("cruelly," in *Complete Letters to Fliess,* 268).

22. Freud, *Interpretation of Dreams, SE* 5:483.

23. Fritz Wittels, *Sigmund Freud, His Personality, His Teaching, and His School* (Freeport, NY: Books for Libraries Press, 1971 [1924]), 60n2.

24. Other Galicians were to have prestigious destinies: Isidor Isaac Rabi, whose parents emigrated to the United States in 1899, won the Nobel Prize in physics in 1944; similarly, Roald Hoffmann, born in 1937, in exile in the United States, won the Nobel Prize in chemistry, and George Charpack, an émigré in France, won the Nobel Prize in physics. Freud dreamed of the prize, which he never received.

25. Freud, *Interpretation of Dreams, SE* 4:197.

26. Ibid., 196.

27. Ludwig Börne and Leland De La Durantaye, "How to Become an Original Writer in Three Days (First Published in 1823)," *Harvard Review,* no. 31 (2006): 76; see Sigmund Freud, "A Note on the Prehistory of the Technique of Analysis" (1920), *SE* 18:261–265; Akibah Ernst Simon, "Freud und Moses," in *Entscheidung zum Judentum: Essays und Vorträge* (Frankfurt: Suhrkamp, 1980), 196–211. Jones emphasizes that the gift was offered for Freud's fourteenth birthday.

28. Freud, *Interpretation of Dreams, SE* 4:138.

29. Alain de Mijolla, "Mein Onkel Josef à la une," *Études freudiennes* 15–16 (April 1979): 183–192; Nicholas Rand and Maria Torok, *Questions for Freud: The Secret History of Psychoanalysis* (Cambridge, MA Harvard University Press, 1997).

30. Sigmund Freud, *The Letters of Sigmund Freud to Eduard Silberstein, 1871–1881,* ed. Walter Boehlich, trans. Arnold J. Pomerans (Cambridge, MA: Belknap Press of Harvard University Press, 1990 [1989]). Freud later received Eduard's wife, Pauline Silberstein (1871–1891) for some consultations; she was suffering from psychotic melancholia. She committed suicide by jumping out of the top floor of her apartment building. See J. W. Hamilton, "Freud and the Suicide of Pauline Silberstein," *Psychoanalytic Review* 89, no. 6 (2002): 889–909.

31. Freud to Silberstein, February 27, 1875, in Freud, *Letters to Silberstein,* 92.

32. Freud, *Interpretation of Dreams, SE* 4:216.

33. The *Neue Freie Presse* followed in the wake of *Die Presse,* which had been created in March 1848, during the revolutionary springtime.

34. Freud to Silberstein, September 4, 1982, in Freud, *Letters to Silberstein,* 17. The anecdote is retold in a different form in "Screen Memories."

35. Freud to Emil Fluss, September 18, 1872, in Sigmund Freud, *Lettres de jeunesse* (Paris: Gallimard, 1990 [1989]), 228. Meseritsch (or Gross-Meseritsch) is a Moravian

city located between Freiberg and Vienna. Certain journalists have thought they discerned an anti-Semitic aspect in this discourse.

36. Ibid., 230.

37. Anna Freud Bernays, *Eine Wienerin in New York: die Erinnerungen der Schwester Sigmund Freuds,* ed. Christfried Tögel (Berlin: Aufbau Verlag, 2004).

38. Judith Heller-Bernays (1885–1977), Lucy Leah-Bernays (1886–1980), Hella Bernays (1893–1994), Martha Bernays (1894–1979). On the exceptional destiny of Edward Bernays (1891–1995), theorist of propaganda, see below. Martha Bernays, Eli's sister, married Sigmund Freud in 1886.

39. Hermann Graf (1897–1917); Cäcilie Graf (1899–1922).

40. Margarethe Freud-Magnus, known as Gretel (1887–1984), Lilly Freud-Marlé (1888–1970), Martha Gertrud, known as Tom Seidman-Freud (1892–1930), Theodor Freud (1904–1927), Georg Freud (1904; a twin was stillborn). See Christfried Tögel, "Freuds Berliner Schwester Maria (Mitzi) und ihre Familie," *Luzifer-Amor 33* (2004): 33–50; and Lilly Freud-Marlé, *Mein Onkel Sigmund Freud: Erinnerungen an eine grosse Familie,* letters collected by Christfried Tögel (Berlin: Aufbau, 2006).

41. Rose Winternitz-Waldinger (1896–1969). On the lives and testimonies of Freud's nieces and nephews, collected by Kurt Robert Eissler for the Library of Congress, see the Epilogue.

42. This decline, observed by all demographers, cannot be attributed simply to contraception, which was beginning to spread among the well-to-do classes with the use of condoms or coitus interruptus. I touch on this problem in Élisabeth Roudinesco, *La famille en désordre* (Paris: Fayard, 2002).

43. Marie Bonaparte, unpublished journal.

44. Jacques Le Rider, *Modernity and Crises of Identity: Culture and Society in Fin-de-Siècle Vienna,* trans. Rosemary Morris (New York: Continuum, 1993 [1944]); and see Gay, *Freud: A Life,* 14–21. In a scathing attack, Jacques Bénesteau asserted that there was no anti-Semitism in Vienna owing to the massive presence of Jews in the liberal and intellectual professions, and that Freud had invented the anti-Semitic persecutions directed toward himself: *Mensonges freudiens* (Hayen, Belgium: Mardaga, 2002), 190–191. On the contrary, it was that presence that contributed to a powerful increase in anti-Semitism in Vienna.

45. On the birth of the infernal couple, the Semite and the Aryan, see Maurice Olender, *The Languages of Paradise: Race, Religion, and Philology in the Nineteenth Century,* trans. Arthur Goldhammer (Cambridge, MA: Harvard University Press, 1992 [1989]).

46. André Bolzinger, *Portrait de Sigmund Freud: Trésors d'une correspondance* (Paris: Campagne Première, 2012), 132.

47. Sigmund Freud, *An Autobiographical Study* (1925), SE 20:8.

48. After Luise von Karpinski, a Polish psychologist, it is to Maria Dorer that we owe the first scholarly study on the place of Herbart's theses in the genesis of the Freudian theory of the unconscious: *Les bases historiques de la psychanalyse,* trans.

Marc Géraud (Paris: L'Harmatttan, 2012 [1932]). The Swedish historian and psycho-analyst Ola Andersson returned to this question in 1962: *Studies in the Prehistory of Psychoanalysis: The Etiology of Psychoneuroses and Some Related Themes in Sigmund Freud's Scientific Writings and Letters, 1886–1896* (Stockholm: Svenska Bokförlaget, 1962); in French as *Freud avant Freud: La préhistoire de la psychanalyse*, trans. Sylvette Gleize, preface by Per Magnus Johansson and Élisabeth Roudinesco, coll. Les Empêcheurs de penser en rond (Paris: Synthélabo, 1997); an appendix presents an exchange of letters between Andersson and Ellenberger.

49. Josef Paneth, too, later contributed to Freud's financial support. See the tes-timony of Marie Paneth (Josef's daughter-in-law) of March 7, 1940, recorded by Kurt Robert Eissler, LoC, box 114, folder 16.

50. Jones, *Life and Work*, 1:29. Freud thus never separated himself as much from philosophical speculation as he thought he had, as we shall see later on.

51. For the study of the anatomo-clinical method (Xavier Bichat), see Michel Fou-cault, *The Birth of the Clinic: An Archaeology of Medical Perception*, trans. A. M. Sheridan Smith (New York: Vintage Books, 1994 [1963]). On physiology and the experimental method, see Georges Canguilhem, "Claude Bernard," in *Études d'histoire et de phi-losophie des sciences* (Paris: Vrin, 1968), 127–171.

52. Freud to Silberstein, September 9, 1875, in Freud, *Letters to Silberstein*, 127.

53. A lovely description of life in this milieu can be found in Albrecht Hirsch-müller, *The Life and Work of Josef Breuer: Physiology and Psychoanalysis*, translation of *Physiologie und Psychoanalyse in Leben und Werke Josef Breuers* (New York: New York University Press, 1978), 31–49.

54. A good analysis of this period in Freud's life can be found in Frank J. Sulloway, *Freud, Biologist of the Mind: Beyond the Psychoanalytic Legend* (New York: Basic Books, 1979). In this book, Sulloway proposes the (questionable) hypothesis that throughout his life Freud remained a hidden biologist (a cryptobiologist) despite his orientation toward psychology. See also Gertrudis van de Vijver and Filip Geerardyn, eds., *The Pre-psychoanalytic Writings of Sigmund Freud* (London: Karnac, 2002).

55. Jacques Le Rider, *Les Juifs viennois à la Belle Époque* (Paris: Albin Michel, 2012), 142.

56. Elise Gomperz (1848–1929), Theodor Gomperz's wife, suffered from nervous ailments. She consulted Charcot, who referred her to Freud in 1892 so she could pursue a cathartic treatment. Freud used electroshock therapy and hypnosis. Nothing indicates that this treatment was a failure, as Mikkel Borch-Jacobsen sug-gests in his book *Les patients de Freud: Destins* (Auxerre, France: Éditions Sciences humaines, 2011). Elise remained what she had been, a "nervous" and melancholic woman, all her life, but her relations with Freud remained excellent to the end.

57. Fleischl-Marxow died prematurely in 1891, and Exner became Brücke's successor.

58. Johann Wolfgang von Goethe, *Faust*, part 1, trans. David Constantine (London: Penguin, 2005), 68.

2. Loves, Tempests, Ambitions

1. Sigmund Freud, *The Interpretation of Dreams* (1900), *SE* 5:483. The *Standard Edition* gives the German in italics in the text *(früh sich einst dem trüben Blick gezeigt)* and adds the quotation from Goethe's *Faust* (dedication) in English in a note.

2. Sigmund Freud, "Great Is Diana of the Ephesians" (1911), *SE* 12:343, after a poem by Goethe.

3. That is, born with thick black hair.

4. Monique Schneider, "Freud, lecteur et interprète de Goethe," in "Goethe cosmopolite," special issue, *Revue germanique internationale* 12 (1999): 243–256.

5. Goethe's *Die Leiden des Jungen Werthers* is an epistolary novel published in 1774.

6. An extensive description of Freud's "maladies" is found in Max Schur, *Freud: Living and Dying* (New York: International Universities Press, 1972). Moreover, in his correspondence, Freud speaks freely of his "maladies" in technical terms, as doctors are inclined to do.

7. See Schur, *Freud*, 61–62, citing a letter to Fliess of December 22, 1897 (in Sigmund Freud, *The Origins of Psychoanalysis: Letters, Drafts and Notes to Wilhelm Fliess, 1887–1902*, ed. Marie Bonaparte, Anna Freud, and Ernst Kris, trans. Eric Mosbacher and James Strachey [Garden City, NY: Doubleday, 1957], 241–243). In his letters, Freud sometimes indirectly evokes his own practice of masturbation.

8. Charles Darwin, "Notebook M," *Charles Darwin's Notebooks, 1836–1844: Geology, Transmutation of Species, Metaphysical Enquiries*, transcribed and edited by Paul H. Barrett et al. (London: British Museum, 1987), 128.

9. See Jean Bollack, *Jacob Bernays (1821–1881): Un homme entre deux mondes* (Villeneuve d'Ascq, France: Presses Universitaires du Septentrion, 1998). Freud was inspired by Bernays's theory of catharsis and recommended to Arnold Zweig that he read Bernays's correspondence; see Freud to Zweig, November 27, 1932, in Sigmund Freud, *Letters of Sigmund Freud and Arnold Zweig*, ed. Ernst L. Freud, trans. Elaine Robson-Scott and William Robson-Scott (New York: Harcourt, Brace and World, 1970), 48.

10. The correspondence between Sigmund and Martha during their engagement (1,500 letters between 1882 and 1886) is being published under the direction of Ilse Grubrich-Simitis and Albrecht Hirschmüller. The first two volumes, covering the period 1882–1883, have already appeared; three others are in preparation. See Sigmund Freud and Martha Bernays, *Die Brautbriefe*, vol. 1, *Sei mein, wie ich mir's denke* (Frankfurt: Fischer Verlag, 2011), and vol. 2, *Unser Roman in Fortsetzungen* (Frankfurt: Fischer Verlag, 2013). I also consulted the volume of Freud's *Correspondance* published in 1973, which includes eighty-three letters from Sigmund to Martha. Ernest Jones and Peter Gay have made abundant use of this correspondence, to which they had access at the Library of Congress, where it is housed. See also Katja Behling, *Martha Freud: A Biography*, foreword by Anton W. Freud (Cambridge, UK: Polity, 2005 [2003]), and Ilse Grubrich-Simitis, "L'affectif et la théorie: Sigmund et

Martha: prélude freudien—Germes et concepts psychanalytiques fondamentaux,"
Revue française de psychanalyse 3, no. 76 (2012): 779–795. This correspondence, still
unpublished in part, is an important source for understanding Freud's evolution.
In addition to the love letters, it contains numerous remarks on his work, his en-
counters, his tastes, his daily life, his anxieties, and his research; it also includes
some unforgettable portraits of his teachers and his contemporaries. See also
André Bolzinger, *Portrait de Sigmund Freud: Trésors d'une correspondance* (Paris:
Campagne Première, 2012). Hanns Lange's research on the family is included in
the catalog of the Freud Museum in London. Certain excerpts are cited in Em-
manuel Rice, *Freud and Moses: The Long Journey Home* (New York: State University
of New York Press, 1990).

11. Freud to Martha, June 30, 1884, in Sigmund Freud, *Letters of Sigmund Freud,
1873–1939*, ed. Ernst L. Freud, trans. Tania Stern and James Stern (London: Hogarth,
1970), 117.

12. Anna was Freud's sister. Eli repaid Martha the full amount.

13. Freud to Martha, December 12, 1883, unpublished, cited in Ernest Jones, *The
Life and Work of Sigmund Freud*, vol. 1, *The Formative Years and the Great Discoveries,
1856–1900* (New York: Basic Books, 1953–1957), 117.

14. The correspondence between Freud and his sister-in-law has recently been
published in French as Sigmund Freud and Minna Bernays, *Correspondance (1882–
1938): Sigmund Freud, Minna Bernays*, trans. Olivier Mannoni (Paris: Seuil, 2015). For
the original German, see Sigmund Freud and Minna Bernays, *Briefwechsel, 1882–1938*,
ed. Albrecht Hirschmüller (Tübingen, Germany: Diskord, 2005).

15. On the genesis of this extraordinary rumor, which still circulates, see
Chapter 9.

16. The best reference here is Sigmund Freud, *Cocaine Papers*, ed. Robert Byck
(New York: New American Library, 1974). This work brings together Freud's five
texts on the subject: "Über Coca" (1884), 47–73; "Contribution to the Knowledge of
the Effects of Cocaine" (1885), 95–104; "Addenda to 'Über Coca'" (1885), 105–109; "On
the General Effect of Cocaine" (1885), 111–118; and "Craving for and Fear of Cocaine"
(1887), 169–176; it includes commentary by a number of scholars. See also Jacques
Michel, "La cocaïne de Freud," in *La philosophie du remède*, ed. Jean-Claude Beaune
(Paris: Champ Vallon, 1993), 1–14; Françoise Coblence, "Freud et la cocaïne," *Revue
française de psychoanalyse* 2, no. 66 (2002): 371–383; and also Frank J. Sulloway, *Freud,
Biologist of the Mind: Beyond the Psychoanalytic Legend* (New York: Basic Books, 1979),
25–28.

17. Freud to Martha, June 2, 1994, cited in Freud, *Cocaine Papers*, 10.

18. Most notably, Freud was accused of having deliberately assassinated his friend
Fleischl-Marxow in order to eliminate a rival, then of having contributed to the rise
of the third scourge of humanity (after alcohol and morphine), and finally of having
written all of his works under the influence of cocaine. In reality, he stopped using
cocaine regularly in 1887, then definitively in 1892, when he became even more de-

pendent on tobacco. On the baseless accusations, see E. M. Thornton, *Freud and Cocaine: The Freudian Fallacy* (London: Blond and Briggs, 1983). For several years, the official historians, for their part, minimized the importance of the cocaine episode.

19. *Allotrion:* a Greek term signifying what is other, or foreign to oneself.

20. Freud to Bernays, October 5, 1882, in Freud and Bernays, *Brautbriefe,* 1:367.

21. See William Johnston, *The Austrian Mind: An Intellectual and Social History, 1848–1938* (Berkeley: University of California Press, 1972), 267–283.

22. Henri F. Ellenberger, *The Discovery of the Unconscious: The History and Evolution of Dynamic Psychiatry* (New York: Basic Books, 1970), 434, citing a depiction by Bernard Sachs, an American student of Meynert. See Albrecht Hirschmüller, *The Life and Work of Josef Breuer: Physiology and Psychoanalysis,* translation of *Physiologie und Psychoanalyse in Leben und Werke Josef Breuers* (New York: New York University Press, 1978), 89.

23. Sigmund Freud, *Project for a Scientific Psychology* (1897–1902), *SE* 1:281–391. See also Christine Lévy-Friesacher, *Meynert-Freud, "l'amentia"* (Paris: Presses Universitaires de France, 1983).

24. Patients afflicted with neuroses were also treated in psychiatric wards or by private psychiatrists. Moreover, the term "psychoneuroses" was often used to designate these pathologies, whose contours varied from one era to the next.

25. The best work on Josef Breuer is Hirschmüller's *Life and Work of Josef Breuer.* Let us note that Jones, for his part, paints a detestable, unjust, and erroneous picture of Breuer, presenting him as a timid therapist incapable of understanding anything at all about sexuality.

26. Hirschmüller, *Life and Work of Josef Breuer,* 34.

27. Ibid., 94.

28. [TN: *La maladie de Charcot,* often referred to as Lou Gehrig's disease or ALS in English.]

29. A term proposed in 1769 by the Scottish doctor William Cullen (1710–1790) to define the nervous ailments that led to personality disorders. See Élisabeth Roudinesco and Michel Plon, *Dictionnaire de la psychanalyse* (Paris: Fayard, 2006 [1997]).

30. This is the term used by Ellenberger (in *Discovery*), who remains the best historian of dynamic psychiatry, particularly concerning the historical development of magnetism and the shift from magnetic cures to psychotherapy. See also Jean Clair, ed., *L'âme au corps: Arts et sciences, 1793–1993,* exhibition catalog (Paris: Réunion des musées nationaux/Gallimard/Electra, 1993).

31. In Élisabeth Roudinesco, *Histoire de la psychanalyse en France* followed by *Jacques Lacan: Esquisse d'une vie, histoire d'un système de pensée* (Paris: Pochothèque, 2009), I describe Charcot's trajectory at length, along with the question of hysteria and its dismantling by Joseph Babinski, as well as the critiques of Charcot by Léon Daudet (his former student). See also Jean-Martin Charcot, *Charcot the Clinician, the Tuesday Lessons: Excerpts from Nine Case Presentations on General Neurology Delivered at the*

Salpêtrière Hospital in 1887–88, trans. Christopher G. Goetz (New York: Raven, 1987 [1892]); Paul Richer, *Les démoniaques dans l'art* (Paris: Macula, 1984 [1887]); Georges Didi-Huberman, *The Invention of Hysteria: Charcot and the Photographic Iconography of the Salpêtrière*, trans. from the French (Cambridge, MA: MIT Press, 2003 [1982]).

32. [TN: The doctrine held that each illness was associated with a specific location in the brain.]

33. He remained in Paris for four and a half months.

34. Hippolyte Taine, *The Origins of Contemporary France*, 6 vols., trans. John Durand (New York: Holt, 1876–1894 [1875–1893]). Publication of the work began in 1875. The theses of pathological crowds and the fear they inspire are found again in Gustave Le Bon, *The Crowd: A Study of the Popular Mind*, translation of *La psychologie des foules*, introduction by Robert K. Merton (New York: Macmillan, 1896 [1895]). We know that Freud came to rely on this work as he developed his collective psychology, although without completely embracing the "French-style" theme of inegalitarianism and the hereditary unconscious.

35. Drumont's *La France juive: Essai d'histoire contemporaine* appeared in 1886 (Paris: C. Marpon and E. Flammarion).

36. Freud to Martha, in Freud, *Letters, 1873–1939*, 186, 300.

37. Freud to Martha, in Freud, *Letters, 1873–1939*, 209. He translated Charcot's *Tuesday Lessons* into German, and when Charcot died in 1893, Freud wrote a beautiful obituary showing how important to him the master's teaching had been. See Sigmund Freud, "Charcot" (1893), *SE* 3:7–23.

38. See Chapter 3; and see Carlo Bonomi, "Pourquoi avons-nous ignoré Freud le 'pédiatre'? Le rapport entre la formation pédiatrique de Freud et les origines de la psychanalyse," in *La psychanalyse: 100 ans déjà . . . Contributions à l'histoire intellectuelle du XXe siècle*, ed. André Haynal (Geneva: Georg, 1996), pp. 87–153.

39. This fact was established by Hirschmüller, who consulted the register of the Jewish community in Vienna to find the birth records of Freud's three sons. See Emmanuel Rice, "The Jewish Heritage of Sigmund Freud," *Psychoanalytic Review* 2 (1994): 236–258. Bonomi, too, consulted that register. On Freud's resistance to conformity with religious traditions, see the biographical sketch of his son Martin, in Sigmund Freud, *Lettres à ses enfants* (Paris: Aubier, 2012 [2010]), 96.

40. Spinoza attributed the survival of the Jewish people to the hatred of other nations in the third chapter of his *Theological-Political Treatise*, Gebhardt edition, trans. Samuel Shirley, introduction by Seymour Feldman (Indianapolis: Hackett, 1998 [1670]).

41. Freud, *Lettres à ses enfants*. Freud's family circle is addressed in more detail in Part Three of this book.

42. Freud to Jung, September 19, 1907, and February 2, 1910 (after the trip to the United States), in Sigmund Freud and C. G. Jung, *The Freud/Jung Letters: The Correspondence between Sigmund Freud and C. G. Jung*, ed. William McGuire, trans. Ralph Manheim and R. F. C. Hull (Princeton, NJ: Princeton University Press, 1974), 89,

272. I thank John Forrester for sending me his manuscript essay on this topic: "The Minna Affair: Freud's Other Women?" See Lisa Appignanesi and John Forrester, *Freud's Women* (New York: Basic Books, 1992), 50–52, 143–145. Very early in his life, Freud had the impression of being old, precisely because of the extinction of his "libido." I shall come back to this point.

43. This is why he chose the tragedy of Oedipus as the model for kinship.

44. Freud, "Charcot," *SE* 3:132.

45. In 1864, Moriz Benedikt had argued that hysteria was a disease without uterine causes. He also asserted the existence of masculine hysteria. On the fate of this strange pioneer, see Henri F. Ellenberger, *Médecines de l'âme: Essais d'histoire de la folie et des guérisons psychiques* (Paris: Fayard, 1995).

46. Sigmund Freud, "Über männliche Hysterie" (1886). This talk was not published, nor was the second one he gave, on November 26. We are acquainted with its contents through review articles: *Anzahl Gesellschaft der Ärtze zu Wien* 25 (1886): 149–152; *München Medizinische Wochenschrift* 33 (1886): 768–885; *Wiener Medizinische Wochenschrift* 36 (1886): 1445–1447. Ellenberger was the first to report on the content of the debates that pitted Freud against his Viennese colleagues. See Henri F. Ellenberger, "Freud's Lecture on Masculine Hysteria (October 15, 1886): A Critical Study," ch. 3 in *Beyond the Unconscious: Essays of Henri F. Ellenberger in the History of Psychiatry*, ed. Mark S. Micale, trans. Françoise Dubor and Mark S. Micale (Princeton, NJ: Princeton University Press, 1993), 119–135. See also Sulloway, *Freud, Biologist*, 36–37.

47. In his autobiography, Freud emphasized the mediocre welcome his lecture had received, insisting that one of the participants denied the existence of male hysteria (*An Autobiographical Study* [1925], *SE* 20:15–16). Moreover, he asserted that Meynert had confided to him, just before he died, that he himself was a case of male hysteria. The confidence seems too lovely to be true.

48. Hippolyte Bernheim, *Hypnosis and Suggestion in Psychotherapy*, trans. from 2nd rev. ed. by Christian A. Herter (New Hyde Park, NY: University Books, 1964 [1891]). See also Roudinesco and Plon, *Dictionnaire*.

49. Transference was to become a major concept in Freudian theory.

50. Freud, *Autobiographical Study*, *SE* 20:27.

51. Sigmund Freud and Josef Breuer, *Studies on Hysteria* (1895), *SE* 2. Anna von Lieben appeared under the name of Frau Cäcilie.

52. Conversation of Kurt Robert Eissler with Henriette Motesiczky von Kesseleökeö (1882–1978), Anna von Lieben's daughter, LoC, box 116, 1973. And see Peter Swales, "Freud, His Teacher, and the Birth of Psychoanalysis," in *Freud: Appraisals and Reappraisals*, ed. Paul E. Stepansky (Hillsdale, NJ: Analytic Press, 1986), 3–82.

53. Otorhinolaryngology.

54. Freud wrote 287 letters to Fliess. The epistolary exchanges between the two continued from 1887 to 1904. See Sigmund Freud, *The Complete Letters of Sigmund*

Freud to Wilhelm Fliess, 1877–1904, ed. and trans. Jeffrey Moussaieff Masson (Cambridge, MA: Belknap Press of Harvard University Press, 1985); and Sigmund Freud, *The Origins of Psychoanalysis: Letters, Drafts and Notes to Wilhelm Fliess, 1887–1902,* ed. Marie Bonaparte, Anna Freud, and Ernst Kris, trans. Eric Mosbacher and James Strachey (Garden City, NY: Doubleday, 1957).

55. W. A. Hack (1851–1887), an otorhinolaryngologist in Fribourg-en-Brisgau, had already undertaken to describe the nasal reflex neurosis.

56. Wilhelm Fliess, *Die Beziehungen zwischen Nase und weiblichen Geschlectsorganen, in ihrer biologischen Bedeutung dargestellt* (Leipzig: Deuticke, 1897); in French as *Les relations entre le nez et les organes génitaux féminins, présentées selon leurs significations biologiques,* trans. Patrick Ach and Jean Guir (Paris: Seuil, 1977), in a collection titled "Le champ freudien" directed by Jacques Lacan. In an article from 1895 devoted to a monograph on migraines by Paul Julius Moebius (1853–1907), Freud praised Fliess as a remarkable researcher in Berlin. See Sigmund Freud, "Besprechung von P. J. Moebius: *Die Migräne*" (1895), in *Gesammelte Werke* (Frankfurt: S. Fischer Verlag, 1960– [hereafter *GW*]), *Nachtragsband* (1987), 364–369; in French as "La migraine de Moebius" (1895), in *Oeuvres complètes de Freud: Psychanalyse,* ed. and trans. Jean Laplanche, Pierre Cotet, André Bourguignon, François Robert, et al. (Paris: Presses Universitaires de France, 1989), 3:97–103.

57. Sigmund Freud, "Outline of a Scientific Psychology," first published in *The Birth of Psycho-analysis,* later, in *The Origins of Psycho-analysis,* as *Project for a Scientific Psychology.*

58. Max Schur was the first, in 1966, to reveal Eckstein's sufferings (her identity had been concealed by the psychoanalysts for a long time). Her history, amply developed in Freud's letters to Fliess, drew subsequent commentary on numerous occasions. See Mikkel Borch-Jacobsen, *Les patients de Freud: Destins* (Auxerre, France: Éditions Sciences humaines, 2011), 66–73. Bonomi hypothesizes that Eckstein experienced her operation as the repetition of the excision that she had undergone in childhood and that Freud describes in his correspondence with Fliess. See Carlo Bonomi, "Withstanding Trauma: The Significance of Emma Epstein's Circumcision to Freud's Irma Dream," *Psychoanalytic Quarterly* 82 (July 2013): 689–740.

59. Freud to Fliess, March 8, 1895, in Freud, *Complete Letters to Fliess,* 117.

60. Freud, *Project for a Scientific Psychology,* SE 1:353–355.

61. Freud to Fliess, January 17, 1897, in Freud, *Complete Letters to Fliess,* 224–225.

62. Albert Hirst (1887–1914), transcript of 1952 interviews with Eissler, LoC, box 115, folder 12. Born Albert Hirsch, he changed his surname when he emigrated to the United States. He was analyzed by Freud, who told him at the outset that his habit of masturbating was not harmful. Rather than having him lie on the couch, Freud had him sit on a chair and asked him to adopt the position he used for masturbation. Hirst also had problems with ejaculation. See David J. Lynn, "Sigmund Freud's Psychoanalysis of Albert Hirst," *Bulletin of History of Medicine* 1, no. 71 (Spring 1977): 69–93.

63. The transcripts of the 1952 interviews with Eissler are in the Library of Congress.

64. See Sulloway, *Freud, Biologist,* 141–147.

65. The best dossier on the relations between Freud and Fliess is the one compiled by Erik Porge, *Vol d'idées? Wilhelm Fliess, son plagiat et Freud,* followed by Wilhelm Fliess, *Pour ma propre cause* (Paris: Denoël, 1994). See also Schur, *Freud,* and of course Sulloway, *Freud, Biologist.*

66. Otto Weininger, *Sex and Character,* authorized translation from the 6th German ed. (London: W. Heinemann, 1906? [1903]). Translated into ten languages, Weininger's book was a best seller in its day, and was reprinted twenty-eight times up to 1947 before it fell into oblivion. See Jacques Le Rider, *Le cas Otto Weininger: Racines de l'antiféminisme et de l'antisémitisme* (Paris: Presses Universitaires de France, 1982).

67. Paul Julius Moebius (1853–1907): a German neurologist, the author of several pathographies, was convinced that women were mentally inferior to men. He supported the idea that hysterical manifestations were produced at the bodily level by psychological representations.

68. The complete set of texts concerning this episode can be found in Porge, *Vol d'idées?* Swales imagines, without offering the slightest proof for his claims, that during the encounter at Lake Achen Freud tried to kill Fliess: "Freud, Fliess, and Fratricide: The Role of Fliess in Freud's Conception of Paranoia," in *Sigmund Freud: Critical Assessments,* ed. Laurence Spurling, vol. 1 (London: Routledge, 1982).

69. Freud to Fritz Wittels, August 15, 1924, in Freud, *Letters, 1873–1939,* 350–352.

70. This episode has been recounted several times by Jones, Schur, Gay, and of course Marie Bonaparte herself.

71. Freud to Ferenczi, October 6, 1910, in Sigmund Freud and Sándor Ferenczi, *Correspondence of Sigmund Freud and Sándor Ferenczi,* ed. Eva Brabant, Ernst Falzeder, and Patrizia Giampieri-Deutsch, trans. Peter T. Hoffer, introduction by André Haynal, vol. 1, *1908–1914* (Cambridge, MA: The Belknap Press of Harvard University Press, 1993), 221.

72. Freud to Fliess, November 14, 1897, in Freud, *Origins,* 237–238; cf. Freud, *Complete Letters to Fliess,* 281. Freud ended up reducing his so-called self-analysis to a fragment, "a piece" (Freud to Fliess, January 3, 1899, in Freud, *Origins,* 274; cf. Freud, *Complete Letters to Fliess,* 338).

73. It took the work of scholarly historiography to challenge the psychoanalytic movement's gilded legend of a self-engendered Freud. Let us note that in 1967 Octave Mannoni replaced the term "self-analysis" with the term "original analysis," showing that the place occupied by Fliess's theories in Freud's doctrine was the expression of a complex distribution between knowledge and delirium. See Octave Mannoni, *Clefs pour l'imaginaire; ou, L'autre scène* (Paris: Seuil, 1969).

74. Freud, *Origins,* 320; cf. Freud, *Complete Letters to Fliess,* 412. See also Schur, *Freud,* 206–208.

75. Genesis 32:22–32.

76. Let us note in this connection that Freud felt great admiration for the Viennese writer Richard Beer-Hofmann and that he was particularly fond of one of his best-known plays, *Le rêve de Jacob,* published in 1918. The struggle with the angel was present throughout Freud's life. And he used it, too, in order to evoke the internal tyrant that never left him, and above all his cancer. Israel is also the name that would be given in 1948 to the Jewish State of which Theodor Herzl dreamed: a state condemned to perpetual combat against men and against itself, a thematics taken up again by Freud in 1930, and then in "Moses and Monotheism."

3. The Invention of Psychoanalysis

1. It was replaced by that of the "depressed subject," tired of himself. I evoke this problematic in Élisabeth Roudinesco, *Why Psychoanalysis?,* trans. Rachel Bowlby (New York: Columbia University Press, 2001 [1999]). The more emancipated women became during the twentieth century, the less they were regarded as hysterics. As a result, masculine hysteria was increasingly an object of study.

2. The historian Mark Micale has imagined that Freud chose not to present cases of masculine hysteria (in *Studies on Hysteria*) because this neurosis was too close to his own experience. And he advances the hypothesis, without the slightest proof, that Freud's own neurasthenia was a masked hysteria, and that Freud "theorized" it while concealing his own case behind his description of hysterical women. See *Hysterical Men: The Hidden History of Male Nervous Illness* (Cambridge, MA: Harvard University Press, 2008).

3. Sigmund Freud and Josef Breuer, *Studies on Hysteria* (1895), SE 2:55, 56, 58, 62.

4. Breuer credited Anna O. (Bertha Pappenheim), who spoke English, with the invention of two terms: "talking cure" and "chimney sweeping" (a clearing-away that allowed memories to be recovered).

5. Albrecht Hirschmüller has provided the best biographical reconstitution of Bertha Pappenheim's story.

6. As I have already indicated, I shall not address—or will barely touch on—the question of the implantation of psychoanalysis in France, on which I have written at length elsewhere. On the relations between Freud and Janet, see Élisabeth Roudinesco, *Histoire de la psychanalyse en France* followed by *Jacques Lacan: Esquisse d'une vie, histoire d'un système de pensée* (Paris: Pochothèque, 2009; hereafter *HPF-JL*).

7. Freud and Breuer, *Studies on Hysteria,* preface to the 1st ed., SE 2:xxix.

8. Ibid., 305.

9. Most notably by Jones, Ola Andersson, Henri F. Ellenberger, Peter Swales, Hirschmüller, and Mikkel Borch-Jacobsen.

10. Most of these patients are listed under their own names and with their real fates in Élisabeth Roudinesco and Michel Plon, *Dictionnaire de la psychanalyse* (Paris: Fayard, 2006).

11. See Dora Edinger, *Bertha Pappenheim* (Highland Park, IL: Congregation Solel, 1968 [1963]).

12. Sigmund Freud and Stefan Zweig, *Correspondance, 1908–1929,* trans. Gisella Hauer and Didier Plassard (Paris: Payot and Rivages poche, 1995 [1987]), 88–89.

13. Ernest Jones, *The Life and Work of Sigmund Freud,* vol. 1, *The Formative Years and the Great Discoveries, 1856–1900* (New York: Basic Books, 1953–1957), 226. On the revision of this legend, in addition to Henri F. Ellenberger, *Médecines de l'âme: Essais d'histoire de la folie et des guérisons psychiques* (Paris: Fayard, 1995), and Albrecht Hirschmüller, *The Life and Work of Josef Breuer: Physiology and Psychoanalysis,* translation of *Physiologie und Psychoanalyse in Leben und Werke Josef Breuers* (New York: New York University Press, 1978), see John Forrester, "The True Story of Anna O.," *Social Research* 53, no. 2 (Summer 1986): 327–347. I have shared with Borch-Jacobsen a very enlightening passage from an unpublished manuscript by Marie Bonaparte on Freud's confidences. See Mikkel Borch-Jacobsen, *Remembering Anna O.: A Century of Mystification,* trans. Kirby Olson with Xavière Callahan and the author (New York: Routledge, 1996 [1995]). Despite all these works, psychoanalysts continue to prefer the legend of Anna O. to the history of Bertha Pappenheim. See Roudinesco and Plon, *Dictionnaire,* 1127.

14. Sigmund Freud to Robert Breuer, June 26, 1925, cited in Hirschmüller, *Life and Work of Josef Breuer,* 192.

15. Sigmund Freud, "Heredity and the Etiology of the Neuroses" (1896), *SE* 3:141–156.

16. According to the testimony of Marie Bonaparte, whose information came from Freud himself.

17. The medieval church gave priority to devotion and pilgrimages, whereas the church that emerged from the Council of Trent (1545–1563) instituted confession in response to the Protestant offensive. Jacques Le Goff was always convinced, as were Michel Foucault and Michel de Certeau, that this practice was directly related to Freud's invention.

18. Freud to Fliess, October 15, 1897, in *Extracts from the Fliess Papers, SE* 1:262.

19. Freud, "Heredity," *SE* 3:156.

20. Freud to Fliess, April 16, 1896, cited in Sigmund Freud, "The Aetiology of Hysteria," *SE* 3:189, editor's note.

21. Freud to Fliess, November 2, 1896, in Sigmund Freud, *The Origins of Psychoanalysis: Letters, Drafts and Notes to Wilhelm Fliess, 1887–1902,* ed. Marie Bonaparte, Anna Freud, and Ernst Kris, trans. Eric Mosbacher and James Strachey (Garden City, NY: Doubleday, 1957), 173.

22. Freud to Fliess, February 8, 1897, in Sigmund Freud, *The Complete Letters of Sigmund Freud to Wilhelm Fliess, 1877–1904,* ed. and trans. Jeffrey Moussaieff Masson (Cambridge, MA: Belknap Press of Harvard University Press, 1985), 230–231.

23. Freud was an eager reader of Jacob Burckhardt's books. They occupied an important place in his library and he occasionally made notes in the margins.

24. Sigmund Freud, *Unser Herz zeigt nach dem Süden: Reisebriefe 1895–1923* (Berlin: Aufbau-Verlag, 2002); in French as *"Notre coeur tend vers le sud": Correspondance de voyage, 1895–1923,* ed. Christfried Tögel with Michale Molnar, trans. Jean-Claude Capèle, preface by Élisabeth Roudinesco (Paris: Fayard, 2003).

25. Freud to Fliess, September 6, 1897, in Freud, *Complete Letters to Fliess,* 263.

26. Freud to Fliess, September 21, 1897 (known as the equinox letter), in Freud, *Origins,* 218, 221; cf. Freud, *Complete Letters to Fliess,* 264, 266.

27. On this question, see Carlo Bonomi, *Sulla soglia della psicoanalisi: Freud e la follia infantile* (Turin: Bollati Boringhieri, 2007).

28. In 1977, the historian Katharina Rutschky gave the name *Schware Pädagogik* ("dark pedagogy") to these educational methods. The term was later taken up by the Swiss psychoanalyst Alice Miller. Michael Haneke illustrated the harmful effects of these methods in his film *The White Ribbon.*

29. Daniel Paul Schreber, *Memoirs of My Nervous Illness,* trans. Ida Macalpine and Richard A. Hunter (New York: New York Review of Books, 2000 [1903]); Sigmund Freud, "Psycho-analytic Notes on an Autobiographical Account of a Case of Paranoia (Dementia Paranoides)" (1911), *SE* 12:1–82.

30. Jean-Jacques Rousseau, *Émile; or, On Education,* ed. and trans. Allan Bloom (New York: Basic Books, 1979), 334.

31. Jean-Jacques Rousseau, *The Confessions and Correspondence, including the Letters to Malesherbes,* ed. Christopher Kelly, Roger D. Masters, and Peter G. Stillman, trans. Christopher Kelly, vol. 5 of *The Collected Writings of Rousseau* (Hanover, NH: University Press of New England, 1990), 91.

32. See Jacques Derrida, "'. . . That Dangerous Supplement . . . ,'" in *Of Grammatology,* trans. Gayatri Chakkravorty Spivak (Baltimore: Johns Hopkins University Press, 1976 [1967]), pp. 141–164. See also Thomas Laqueur, *Making Sex: Body and Gender from the Greeks to Freud* (Cambridge, MA: Harvard University Press, 1990).

33. Freud, *Origins,* 227; cf. Freud, *Complete Letters to Fliess,* 272.

34. Ibid.

35. Several versions exist.

36. The expression "family romance" was invented by Freud and Otto Rank in 1909 to designate the way subjects modify their genealogical ties by inventing families other than their own. See Otto Rank, *The Myth of the Birth of the Hero: A Psychological Exploration of Myth,* trans. Gregory C. Richer and E. James Lieberman (Baltimore: Johns Hopkins University Press, 2004 [1909]).

37. The term first appeared in 1910 in Sigmund Freud, "A Special Type of Choice of Object Made by Men (Contributions to the Psychology of Love I)" (1910), *SE* 11:170. I note that Freud is mistaken about the first occurrence of the famous "complex" in his work; he refers back to *The Interpretation of Dreams* (see *SE* 4:263n2).

38. Sigmund Freud, "Fragments of an Analysis of a Case of Hysteria" (1905 [1901]), *SE* 7:1–122. The best reconstitution of Dora's story is Patrick J. Mahony, *Freud's Dora: A Psychoanalytic, Historical, and Textual Study* (New Haven, CT: Yale University

Press, 1996). See also Arnold Rogow, "A Further Footnote to Freud's 'Fragment of an Analysis of a Case of Hysteria,'" *Journal of the American Psychoanalytical Association* 26 (1978): 311–330; Hélène Cixous, *Portrait of Dora*, in *Selected Plays of Hélène Cixous*, trans. Ann Liddle (New York: Routledge 2004), 35–59; Hannah S. Decker, *Freud, Dora and Vienna* (New York: Free Press, 1991). This last book offers a good description of the Jews of Bohemia in the late nineteenth century.

39. Mahony, *Freud's Dora*, 124.

40. Ménière's disease.

41. Like Felix Deutsch, Ida emigrated to the United States and escaped the Nazi persecutions. She died of cancer in 1945. Deutsch learned of her death ten years later, and, according to an informant, he asserted that she had been one of "the most off-putting hysterics that [he] had ever met." Kurt Robert Eissler noted his opposition to this testimony in a letter to Anna Freud on August 10, 1952. Moreover, it appears that Ida never actually expressed the pride in being a famous case that Deutsch had attributed to her in 1923.

42. Freud, *Interpretation of Dreams*, preface to the 2nd ed., *SE* 4:xxvi.

43. Jones, *Life and Work*, 1:350.

44. Karl Albert Scherner, *La vie du rêve* (Paris: Champ social, 2003 [1861]); Alfred Maury, *Le sommeil et les rêves: Études psychologiques sur ces phénomènes* (Paris: Didier, 1861); Léon Hervey de Saint-Denys, *Dreams and How to Guide Them*, trans. Morton Schatzman (London: Duckworth, 1982 [1867]); Joseph Delboeuf, *Le sommeil et les rêves et autres textes* (Paris: Fayard, 1993 [1885]). For a comprehensive study, see Jacqueline Carroy, *Nuits savants: Une histoire des rêves (1800–1945)* (Paris: EHESS, 2012). Freud had collected an impressive number of books on dreams for his personal library.

45. See Frank J. Sulloway, *Freud, Biologist of the Mind: Beyond the Psychoanalytic Legend* (New York: Basic Books, 1979), 323–324. In his *Discovery of the Unconscious: The History and Evolution of Dynamic Psychiatry* (New York: Basic Books, 1970), Ellenberger devoted some lovely pages to works on dreams in general and to Freud's work in particular. See also Roudinesco and Plon, *Dictionnaire*.

46. [TN: Vergil, *The Aeneid*, trans. Sarah Ruden (New Haven, CT: Yale University Press, 2008), 153 (book 7, line 312).]

47. Franz von Thun und Hohenstein (1847–1916), an aristocrat, a landowner, and a bureaucrat characteristic of the imperial monarchy. He served twice as governor of Bohemia before he held, briefly, the position of minister-president of Austria, from March 1898 to October 1899.

48. Carl E. Schorske, *Fin-de-Siècle Vienna: Politics and Culture* (New York: Vintage Books, 1981 [1961]), especially chapter 4, "Politics and Patricide in Freud's *Interpretation of Dreams*," 181–207. See also Jacques Le Rider, "Je mettrai en branle l'Achéron: Fortune et signification d'une citation de Virgile," *Europe*, no. 954 (October 2008): 113–122.

49. Freud to Werner Achelis, January 30, 1897, in Sigmund Freud, *Letters of Sigmund Freud, 1873–1939*, ed. Ernst L. Freud, trans. Tania Stern and James Stern (London: Hogarth, 1970), 375. Freud had announced his choice to Fliess in a letter on July 17,

1899 (Freud, *Origins*, 288–289; cf. Freud, *Complete Letters to Fliess*, 360–361). See Ferdinand Lassalle, *Der italienische Krieg und die Ausgabe Preußens* (1859), in *Fernand Lassalle's Politische Reden und Schriften* (Leipzig: Karl Fr. Pfau, 1892), 2:369–442.

50. Schorske, *Fin-de-Siècle Vienna*, 200–201.

51. Sigmund Freud, "On the History of the Psycho-analytic Movement" (1914), *SE* 14:22. The expression "splendid isolation" was frequently used to define British foreign policy at the end of the nineteenth century. Freud borrowed it for his own purposes in response to an injunction from Fliess, who was trying to console him.

52. Ibid.

53. Cited in Schorske, *Fin-de-Siècle Vienna*, 22. Freud spent almost his entire life in Vienna, a city to which he was all the more attached because he detested it.

54. See Didier Anzieu, *Freud's Self-Analysis*, trans. Peter Graham (Madison, CT: International Universities, 1986 [1959]); Max Schur, *Freud: Living and Dying* (New York: International Universities Press, 1972); Jacques Lacan, *The Ego in Freud's Theory and in the Technique of Psychoanalysis, 1954–1955*, seminar, book 2, trans. Sylvana Tomaselli (New York: W. W. Norton, 1988 [1977]), 146–171; Marthe Robert, *The Psychoanalytic Revolution: Sigmund Freud's Life and Achievement*, trans. Kenneth Morgan (New York: Harcourt, Brace and World, 1966 [1964]); Roudinesco and Plon, *Dictionnaire*.

55. See Alison Rose, *Jewish Women in Fin de siècle Vienna* (Austin: University of Texas Press, 2008).

56. Freud to Fliess, June 12, 1900, in Freud, *Origins*, 323; cf. Freud, *Complete Letters to Fliess*, 417.

57. Freud to Fliess, July 10, 1900, in Freud, *Origins*, 324; cf. Freud, *Complete Letters to Fliess*, 421. Not until May 6, 1977, was Freud's wish granted and a plaque placed on the Bellevue house. In 1988 Gerd Kimmerle and Ludger M. Hermanns gave the name *Luzifer-Amor* to a journal devoted to the history of psychoanalysis, which has been edited since 2004 by Michael Schröter. See Renate Sachse, "*Luzifer-Amor* 51," *Essaim* 32 (2014): 103–113.

58. See Norman Kiell, *Freud without Hindsight: Reviews of His Work, 1893–1939* (Madison, CT: International Universities Press, 1988), and Ellenberger, *Discovery*.

59. On Freud's relationships with the French surrealists, which I do not address in this book, see Roudinesco, *HPF-JL*.

60. The letter was signed by Emperor Franz Joseph on March 5, 1902. See Ellenberger, *Discovery*, 452–454.

4. The Belle Époque

1. Unpublished interview, Marie Bonaparte archives.

2. See Jean-Yves Tadié, *Le lac inconnu: Entre Proust et Freud* (Paris: Gallimard, 2012). On Freud's relations with French writers—André Gide, Romain Rolland, André Breton, and others—see Élisabeth Roudinesco, *Histoire de la psychanalyse en France*

followed by *Jacques Lacan: Esquisse d'une vie, histoire d'un système de pensée* (Paris: Pochothèque, 2009; hereafter *HPF-JL*).

3. Jacques Le Rider, *Les Juifs viennois à la Belle Époque* (Paris: Albin Michel, 2012).

4. Freud to Ferenczi, June 8, 1913, in Sigmund Freud and Sándor Ferenczi, *Correspondence of Sigmund Freud and Sándor Ferenczi*, ed. Eva Brabant, Ernst Falzeder, and Patrizia Giampieri-Deutsch, trans. Peter T. Hoffer, introduction by André Haynal, vol. 1, *1908–1914* (Cambridge, MA: The Belknap Press of Harvard University Press, 1993), 490–491.

5. Alfred Kubin, *Réflexion*, 1902. Peter Gay has astutely noted this detail.

6. Related by Judith Heller-Bernays, March 1953, LoC, box 120, folder 36.

7. Martin Freud, *Glory Reflected: Sigmund Freud—Man and Father* (London: Angus and Robertson, 1957), 46.

8. Sigmund Freud, *The Psychopathology of Everyday Life* (1901), *SE* 6.

9. This was the first of Freud's books I read myself, on my mother's recommendation, before I encountered his classic work on Leonardo da Vinci.

10. On Hans's son Otto Gross, see Chapter 5.

11. "Nun ist die Luft von solchem Spuk so voll, / Dass niemand weiss, wie er ihn meiden soll" (Goethe, *Faust*, part 2, act 5, scene 5) [Now fills the air so many a haunting shape, / That no one knows how best he may escape (Bayard Taylor's translation)]; epigraph to part 1 of Freud, *Psychopathology of Everyday Life*, *SE* 6:vii.

12. Freud to Fliess, May 8, 1901, in Sigmund Freud, *The Origins of Psychoanalysis: Letters, Drafts and Notes to Wilhelm Fliess, 1887–1902*, ed. Marie Bonaparte, Anna Freud, and Ernst Kris, trans. Eric Mosbacher and James Strachey (Garden City, NY: Doubleday, 1957), 331; also in Sigmund Freud, *The Complete Letters of Sigmund Freud to Wilhelm Fliess, 1877–1904*, ed. and trans. Jeffrey Moussaieff Masson (Cambridge, MA: Belknap Press of Harvard University Press, 1985), 441.

13. Ibid. This motto ("It is buffeted by the waves but does not sink") is inscribed on the Paris coat of arms.

14. Freud to Martha, September 1, 1900, in Sigmund Freud, *Unser Herz zeigt nach dem Süden: Reisebriefe 1895–1923* (Berlin: Aufbau-Verlag, 2002), 128 (in French as *"Notre coeur tend vers le sud": Correspondance de voyage, 1895–1923*, ed. Christfried Tögel with Michale Molnar, trans. Jean-Claude Capèle, preface by Élisabeth Roudinesco [Paris: Fayard, 2003], 132).

15. Postcards to Martha, September 2, 3, and 4, 1891, in Freud, *Unser Herz*, 135–137 (*"Notre coeur,"* preface, 15).

16. Carl E. Schorske, *Thinking with History: Explorations in the Passage to Modernism* (Princeton, NJ: Princeton University Press, 1998), 202.

17. Freud to Martha, postcard, September 4, 1904, in Freud, *Unser Herz*, 190 (*"Notre coeur,"* 181).

18. In 1936, in a letter to Romain Rolland, Freud described the disturbance he had felt that day on the Acropolis; see Sigmund Freud, "A Disturbance of Memory on the Acropolis" (1936), *SE* 22:237–248. This text has been commented on dozens

of times. Henri Rey-Flaud interprets the phenomenon of uncanniness as a "psychotic" point in Freud's psychic universe; see *Je ne comprends pas de quoi vous me parlez: Pourquoi refusons-nous parfois de reconnaître la réalité?* (Paris: Aubier, 2014). For my part, I would say that the text must also be read as a reflection on "Joseph" (the biblical character but also Napoleon Bonaparte's brother), on the status of Jewishness, and on the question of the life already lived, as Thomas Mann was to put it.

19. Sigmund Freud, *Jokes and Their Relation to the Unconscious* (1905), *SE* 8. Unlike the first two books in the sequence, this one was subject to very few changes by the author.

20. Theodor Lipps, *Komik und Humor: Eine psychologisch-ästhetische Untersuchung* (N.p.: Dogma, 2013 [1898]).

21. Freud, *Jokes, SE* 8:115.

22. Ibid., 236.

23. Sigmund Freud, *Three Essays on the Theory of Sexuality* (1905), *SE* 7:123–245.

24. Charles Baudelaire, "Moestra et errabunda," in *The Flowers of Evil,* trans. James McGowan, introduction by Jonathan Culler (New York: Oxford University Press, 1993), 131.

25. Used here for the first time.

26. I addressed this question in Roudinesco, *HPF-JL;* see also Élisabeth Roudinesco and Michel Plon, *Dictionnaire de la psychanalyse* (Paris: Fayard, 2006).

27. Adolf Albrecht Friedländer, "Hysteria and Modern Psychoanalysis" (1909), *Journal of Abnormal Psychology* 5, no. 6 (February–March 1911): 297–319.

28. The thesis of the *genius loci* and of pansexualism was taken up again by Janet during the famous congress in London in which he opposed Jones and Jung: see Pierre Janet, "La psychanalyse," report to the 17th Congress of Medicine in London, *Journal de psychologie normale et pathologique* 11 (March–April 1914): 97–130. See also Roudinesco, *HPF-JL.*

29. Bruno Goetz, "That Is All I Have to Say about Freud: Bruno Goetz's Reminiscences of Sigmund Freud," trans. Shirley E. Jones, *International Review of Psychoanalysis* 2 (1975): 141.

30. Ibid., 142.

31. Bruno Walter, *Theme and Variations: An Autobiography,* trans. James A. Galston (New York: Alfred A. Knopf, 1946), 164–168; André Haynal, "Freud psychothérapeute: Essai historique," *Psychothérapies* 4 (2007): 239–242. Mahler's "cure" has been recounted many times.

32. Ernest Jones, *The Life and Work of Sigmund Freud* (New York: Basic Books, 1953–1957), 2:80.

33. See Haynal, "Freud psychothérapeute"; see also Roudinesco and Plon, *Dictionnaire.*

34. Stefan Zweig, *The World of Yesterday: An Autobiography,* translation of *Die Welt von Gestern* (New York: Viking Press, 1943), 86.

5. Disciples and Dissidents

1. In 1923, ruined by the defeat of the Central powers, Kahane committed suicide by slashing his wrists.

2. The PMG met from October 1902 to September 1907. We have no photos and no transcriptions of the debates that took place in that context between 1902 and 1906. For the following period, see Herman Nunberg and Ernst Federn, eds., *Minutes of the Vienna Psychoanalytic Society,* trans. M. Nunberg, 4 vols. (New York: International Universities Press, 1962–1975). These volumes include transcriptions of 250 meetings. See also Elke Mühlleitner, *Biographisches Lexikon der Psychoanalyse: Die Mitglieder der Psychologische Mittwochs-Gesellschaft und der Wiener Psychoanalytischen Vereinigung, 1902–1938* (Tübingen, Germany: Diskord, 1992); Ernst Falzeder and Bernhard Handlbauer, "Freud, Adler et d'autres psychanalystes: Des débuts de la psychanalyse organisée à la fondation de l'Association psychanalytique internationale," *Psychothérapies* 12, no. 4 (1992): 219–232. In this chapter I am drawing on an unpublished seminar I gave on this subject at the Université de Paris VII-Diderot in 1998.

3. Between 1902 and 1907, the Wednesday Psychological Society included twenty-three original members of several nationalities, among whom, besides Freud, there were nine natives of Vienna, six other Austrians, three Romanians (from Bukovina), a Pole (Galicia), one Czech (Prague), and two Hungarians. Of the seventeen Jewish members, five were exterminated by the Nazis (Alfred Bass, Adolf Deutsch, Alfred Meisl, Isidor Isaak Sadger, and Guido Brecher). The eleven others who were still living in 1938 emigrated to Great Britain or the United States. In this first circle, doctors constituted a majority (seventeen). The suicide rate was slightly higher than among other population groups (two out of twenty-three). Women were represented starting in 1910, when the PMG became the Vienna Psychoanalytic Association (Wiener Psychoanalytische Vereinigung). Margarethe Hilferding, from Vienna, was killed by the Nazis, as was her husband, Rudolf.

4. Olga Hönig (1877–1961) had been sexually abused by two of her brothers. She refused Kurt Robert Eissler's request for testimony.

5. Sigmund Freud, "Analysis of a Phobia in a Five-Year-Old Boy" (1922), *SE* 10:5–14; Max Graf, "Reminiscences of Professor Sigmund Freud," *Psychoanalytic Quarterly* 11 (1942): 465–476; Max Graf, interview with Kurt Eissler (Geneva: Balint Archives); in French as "Entretien avec Kurt Eissler" (1952), *Bloc-notes de la psychanalyse* 14 (1995): 123–149. Eissler also recorded a conversation with Herbert Graf in 1959, available in the Library of Congress.

6. Wilhelm Stekel, *Autobiography: The Life Story of a Pioneer Psychoanalyst,* ed. Emil A. Gutheil (New York: Liveright, 1950); Vincent Brome, *Freud and His Early Circle: The Struggles of Psychoanalysis* (London: Heinemann, 1967); Paul Roazen, *Freud and His Followers* (New York: Knopf, 1975). Stekel committed suicide in exile in London on June 25, 1940.

7. The writer Manès Sperber devoted an admirable biography to Adler: *Masks of Loneliness: Alfred Adler in Perspective,* trans. Krishna Winston (New York: Macmillan, 1974 [1970]). See also Paul E. Stepansky, *In Freud's Shadow: Adler in Context* (Hillside, NJ: Analytic Press, distr. L. Erlbaum, 1983). The break between Freud and Adler was ferocious on both sides. Henri F. Ellenberger rightly attributes an important place to Adler and his teaching in the history of dynamic psychology and psychotherapies. Adler gave ten talks to the Wednesday Psychological Society.

8. Freud to Pfister, February 26, 1911, in Sigmund Freud and Oskar Pfister, *Psychoanalysis and Faith: The Letters of Sigmund Freud and Oscar Pfister,* ed. Heinrich Meng and Ernst L. Freud, trans. Eric Mosbacher (London: Hogarth Press and the Institute of Psychoanalysis, 1963), 48.

9. J. Keith Davies and Gerhard Fichtner, eds., *Freud's Library: A Comprehensive Catalogue,* bilingual German-English (London: Freud Museum, 2006), 20.

10. Freud to Jung, September 19, 1907, in Sigmund Freud and C. G. Jung, *The Freud/Jung Letters: The Correspondence between Sigmund Freud and C. G. Jung,* ed. William McGuire, trans. Ralph Manheim and R. F. C. Hull (Princeton, NJ: Princeton University Press, 1974), 88.

11. Alexander Grinstein, *Freud at the Crossroads* (Madison, CT: International Universities Press, 1990), 313.

12. Ibid.; chapter 13, "The 'Good Books'" (303–564), includes a lengthy analysis of the possible meaning of the books Freud chose. See also Sergio Paulo Rouanet, *Os dez amigos de Freud* (Rio de Janeiro: Companhia das Letras, 2003).

13. His real name was Otto Rosenfeld. See James Lieberman, *Acts of Will: The Life and Work of Otto Rank* (New York: Free Press, 1985).

14. That is, outsiders in relation to the original inner circle. The Viennese Hanns Sachs was not part of the initial circle either. He joined the WPV in 1909, then moved to Berlin so he could participate in the expansion of the Berliner Psychoanalytisches Institut. Theodor Reik, also from Vienna, joined in 1911. The pastor Pfister, a friend of Jung, visited Freud in 1909 and they became friends, engaging in a significant correspondence: see Freud and Pfister, *Psychoanalysis and Faith*. See also Élisabeth Roudinesco and Michel Plon, *Dictionnaire de la psychanalyse* (Paris: Fayard, 2006).

15. The three titles eventually merged and gave birth to the *Internationale Zeitschrift für Psychoanalyse und Imago (IZP-Imago);* the latter folded in 1941 and was replaced by the *International Journal of Psychoanalysis (IJP),* founded by Jones in 1920. See also Roudinesco and Plon, *Dictionnaire.*

16. "Very honored friend, the best among men." See André Bolzinger, *Portrait de Sigmund Freud: Trésors d'une correspondance* (Paris: Campagne Première, 2012).

17. Alain de Mijolla, "Images de Freud, au travers de sa correspondance," *Revue internationale d'histoire de la psychanalyse* 2 (1989): 9–50; Gerhard Fichtner, "Les lettres de Freud en tant que source historique," *Revue internationale d'histoire de la psychanalyse* 2 (1989): 51–80; Gerhard Fichtner, "Bibliographie des lettres de Freud," *Revue*

internationale d'histoire de la psychanalyse 2 (1989): 80–108; Élisabeth Roudinesco, unpublished seminar on Freud's correspondence, 1999.

18. Sigmund Freud, "On the History of the Psycho-analytic Movement" (1914), *SE* 14:7.

19. Sigmund Freud, *An Autobiographical Study* (1925), *SE* 20.

20. Sigmund Freud, "A Difficulty in the Path of Psycho-analysis" (1917), *SE* 17:135–144.

21. In 1936, the IPV became the International Psychoanalytic Association (IPA). Starting in 1910, all the existing groups, including the WPV, were brought together in this centralized organization.

22. Sándor Ferenczi, "On the Organization of the Psycho-analytical Movement" (1911), in *Final Contributions to the Problems and Methods of Psycho-analysis,* ed. Michael Balit, trans. Eric Mosbacher et al. (New York: Brunner/Mazel, 1955, repr. 1980), 302.

23. Magnus Hirschfeld (1868–1935) was a German psychiatrist who militated in favor of a better comprehension of "intermediate sexual states" (homosexuality, transvestism, hermaphroditism, transsexualism) and participated between 1908 and 1911 in the foundation of the Psychoanalytic Association of Berlin. In 1897, he founded the first equal rights organization: the Humanitarian Scientific Committee (Wissenschaftlich-humanitäres Komitee), which later became the Hirschfeld Institute. See Laure Murat, *Loi du genre: Une histoire culturelle du troisème sexe* (Paris: Fayard, 2006).

24. Sándor Ferenczi, *Les écrits de Budapest* (Paris: EPEL, 1994), 255. See also Sándor Ferenczi, *Oeuvres complètes: Psychanalyse,* 4 vols. (Paris: Payot, 1968–1982), and Sándor Ferenczi, *The Clinical Diary of Sándor Ferenczi,* ed. Judith Dupont, trans. Michael Balint and Nicola Zarday Jackson (Cambridge, MA: Harvard University Press, 1988); Sándor Ferenczi and Otto Rank, *The Development of Psychoanalysis,* trans. Caroline Newton (Madison, CT: International Universities Press, 1986 [1924]); Georg Groddeck, "Correspondence with Sigmund Freud (1917–1934)," in *The Meaning of Illness: Selected Psychoanalytic Writings,* ed. Lore Schacht, trans. Gertrud Mander (New York: International Universities Press, 1977), 31–108; and Sigmund Freud, *Correspondance,* 3 vols. (Paris: Calmann-Lévy, 1992–2000).

25. This theme is found again in Freud's *Totem and Taboo* (1913 [1912–1913]), *SE* 13:1–162.

26. Ferenczi to Freud, May 23, 1919, in Sigmund Freud and Sándor Ferenczi, *Correspondence of Sigmund Freud and Sándor Ferenczi,* ed. Eva Brabant, Ernst Falzeder, and Patrizia Giampieri-Deutsch, trans. Peter T. Hoffer, introduction by André Haynal (Cambridge, MA: Belknap Press of Harvard University Press, 1993), 2:356.

27. Karl Abraham, "Mental After-Effects Produced in a Nine-Year-Old Child by the Observation of Sexual Intercourse between Its Parents," in *Selected Papers of Karl Abraham, M.D.,* ed. Ernest Jones, trans. Douglas Bryan and Alix Strachey (London: Hogarth, 1927), 164–168; Sigmund Freud and Karl Abraham, *The Complete*

Correspondence of Sigmund Freud and Karl Abraham, 1907–1925, ed. Ernst Falzeder, trans. Caroline Schwarzacher et al. (London: Karnac, 2002 [1965]).

28. Freud and Eitingon exchanged 821 letters: see Sigmund Freud and Max Eitingon, *Correspondance, 1906–1939,* ed. Michael Schröter, trans. Olivier Mannoni (Paris: Hachette Littératures, 2009 [2004]). See also Guido Liebermann, *La psychanalyse en Palestine, 1918–1948: Aux origines du mouvement analytique israélien* (Paris: Campagne Première, 2012).

29. Berlin remained the nerve center of the international psychoanalytic movement until the advent of Nazism in the early 1930s.

30. "Policlinic": a clinic in the city *(polis);* not to be confused with a "polyclinic," a place where multiple pathologies are treated.

31. There is a good description of the clinic's activities in Henri F. Ellenberger, *Discovery of the Unconscious: The History and Evolution of Dynamic Psychiatry* (New York: Basic Books, 1970). See also Roudinesco and Plon, *Dictionnaire.*

32. Eugen Bleuler, *Dementia praecox; or, The Group of Schizophrenias,* trans. Joseph Zinkin (New York: International Universities Press, 1950 [1911]).

33. See C. G. Jung, *Collected Works of C. G. Jung,* 20 vols. (Princeton, NJ: Princeton University Press, 1960–1979), and Freud and Jung, *Freud/Jung Letters.* The best source for the story of Jung's personal life is Deirdre Bair, *Jung: A Biography* (Boston: Little, Brown, 2003). Bair had access in particular to the transcribed interview notes that had served as a first draft of Jung's autobiography; cf. C. G. Jung, *Memories, Dreams, Reflections,* recorded and edited by Aniela Jaffé, trans. Richard Winston and Clara Winston (New York: Pantheon Books, 1963 [1962]). The various biographers have offered several different versions of the relationship between Freud and Jung. Ellenberger (in *Discovery)* offers an excellent analysis of Jung's trajectory. A conversation held between Jung and Kurt Eissler on August 29, 1953, can be found in LoC, box 114, folder 4.

34. Freud to Karl Abraham, May 3, 1908, in Freud and Abraham, *Complete Correspondence,* 38.

35. "If I am Moses, then you are Joshua and will take possession of the promised land of psychiatry, which I shall only be able to glimpse from afar" (Freud to Jung, January 17, 1909, in Freud and Jung, *Freud/Jung Letters,* 194–197).

36. See Élisabeth Roudinesco, "Carl Gustav Jung: De l'archétype au nazisme: Dérives d'une psychologie de la différence," *L'Infini* 63 (Fall 1998): 74–94.

37. Freud to Karl Abraham, May 3, 1908, in Freud and Abraham, *Complete Correspondence,* 38. Freud used the word "race" as well as the terms "Semite" and "Aryan," which had been invented by nineteenth-century philologists. See Élisabeth Roudinesco, *Retour sur la question juive* (Paris: Albin Michel, 2009).

38. Jung had been strongly marked by Theodore Flournoy's *De l'Inde à la planète Mars;* translated as *From India to the Planet Mars: A Study of a Case of Somnambulism with Glossolalia,* trans. Daniel B. Vermilye (New York: Harper and Bros., 1900). Cf. Élisabeth Roudinesco, *Histoire de la psychanalyse en France* followed by *Jacques Lacan: Esquisse d'une vie, histoire d'un système de pensée* (Paris: Pochothèque, 2009).

39. Which Ellenberger calls a "creative neurosis."

40. Jung became the founder of a school of analytic psychology that did not avoid the pitfalls of secularism. His anti-Semitism became more and more manifest during the 1930s. Many books have been devoted to the break between Freud and Jung. Bair and Peter Gay offer markedly different versions, both nevertheless more objective than that of Jones. Linda Donn's account is the most interesting: *Freud and Jung: Years of Friendship, Years of Loss* (New York: Scribner, 1988).

41. Bair, *Jung*, 167.

42. Freud to Jung, October 28, 1907, in Freud and Jung, *Freud/Jung Letters*, 49; and see Bair, *Jung*, 71. Freud had been the first to formulate the hypothesis of the "self-preservation complex."

43. The scandal was revealed in 1975 by Stephanie Zumstein-Preiswerk, Hélène's niece, and it was examined by Ellenberger in *Médecines de l'âme: Essais d'histoire de la folie et des guérisons psychiques* (Paris: Fayard, 1995).

44. A psychiatrist inspired by the phenomenological tendency based on the work of Edmund Husserl and Martin Heidegger, Ludwig Binswanger (1881–1966) was also a lifelong admirer of Freud and his doctrine. See Sigmund Freud and Ludwig Binswanger, *The Sigmund Freud-Ludwig Binswanger Correspondence, 1908–1938*, ed. Gerhard Fichtner, trans. Arnold J. Pomerans (New York: Other Press, 2003).

45. There are several versions of this encounter, about which Freud says nothing at all—neither in his contribution to the history of the psychoanalytic movement nor in his self-presentation. I have thus combined the various sources: Jung, *Memories, Dreams, Reflections*, and the typed transcript of the August 29, 1953, conversation between Jung and Eissler (LoC). Bair gives a highly credible account of the meeting in *Jung*, 115–120. See also Ludwig Binswanger, who recounts the event in part in *Discours, parcours, et Freud* (Paris: Gallimard, 1970), 267–277; Martin Freud, *Glory Reflected: Sigmund Freud—Man and Father* (London: Angus and Robertson, 1957); Donn, *Freud and Jung*.

46. Followers of spiritism thought that a fluid emanating from a cataleptic subject could cause furniture to crack, footstools to rise, and objects to move about.

47. Ernest Jones, *The Life and Work of Sigmund Freud* (New York: Basic Books, 1953–1957), 2:33. We know that Freud was not particularly fond of his earliest disciples in the Wednesday gatherings, as he later confided to Binswanger: "So now you've seen that gang?" (Binswanger, *Discours*, 271).

48. Binswanger, *Discours*, 268–269.

49. Joë Bousquet, *Le passeur s'est endormi* (Paris: Denoël, 1939), 262.

50. Sigmund Freud, "Delusions and Dreams in Jensen's 'Gradiva,'" (1907 [1906]), *SE* 9:1–95. In English, see Wilhelm Jensen, *Gradiva*, followed by Sigmund Freud, *Delusion and Dream in Wilhelm Jensen's "Gradiva,"* trans. Helen M. Downey (Los Angeles: Sun and Moon, 1993).

51. Freud to Arthur Schnitzler, May 8, 1906, in Sigmund Freud, *Letters of Sigmund Freud, 1873–1939*, ed. Ernst L. Freud, trans. Tania Stern and James Stern (London: Hogarth, 1970), 123.

52. Otto Gross, *Psychanalyse et révolution: Essais,* trans. Jeanne Étoré (Paris: Éditions du Sandre, 2011), with a remarkable extensive preface by Jacques Le Rider, 7–86. Bair offers an interesting account of the relations between Jung and Gross, in *Jung,* 135–144.

53. Hans Gross's theories have to be viewed in the context of *pédagogie noire,* or "cruel parenting."

54. On this aspect of Gross's life, see Martin Green, *The Von Richthofen Sisters; The Triumphant and the Tragic Modes of Love: Else and Frieda von Richthofen, Otto Gross, Max Weber, and D. H. Lawrence, in the Years 1870–1970* (New York: Basic Books, 1974).

55. Jacques Le Rider, preface to Gross, *Psychanalyse,* p. 25.

56. Jones was working in the Burghölzli clinic at the time. See Freud to Jones, May 13, 1908, in Sigmund Freud, *The Complete Correspondence of Sigmund Freud and Ernest Jones, 1908–1939,* ed. R. Andrew Paskauskas (Cambridge, MA: Belknap Press of Harvard University Press, 1993), 1.

57. There were numerous others, among whom Viktor Tausk, Georg Groddeck, and Wilhelm Reich were the most famous and the most inventive.

58. Gross, *Psychanalyse,* 78.

59. Letter from Max Weber to Else Jaffé, September 13, 1907, cited in Le Rider, preface to Gross, *Psychanalyse,* 83–85.

60. Ernest Jones, *Free Associations: Memories of a Psychoanalyst* (New York: Basic Books, 1959). In addition to his biography of Freud, Jones wrote numerous articles that have been collected in several volumes, including *Hamlet and Oedipus* (Garden City, NY: Doubleday, 1954 [1949]), and *Essays in Applied Psycho-analysis,* 2 vols. (New York: International Universities Press, 1964 [1951?]). Between 1908 and 1939, Freud and Jones exchanged 671 letters.

61. Freud to Jung, May 3 and July 18, 1908, in Freud and Jung, *Freud/Jung Letters,* 145, 165.

62. Her real name was Louise Dorothea Kann.

63. Between the two wars, the APsaA became the most powerful force in the IPA, as it brought together all the American psychoanalytical societies, which were populated at the time by almost all the German-speaking émigrés who fled Europe starting with the advent of Nazism in 1933. From London, Jones maintained real power over the American association.

64. James Jackson Putnam was one of Freud's correspondents. See Sigmund Freud and James Jackson Putnam, *James Jackson Putnam and Psychoanalysis: Letters between Putnam and Sigmund Freud, Ernest Jones, William James, Sándor Ferenczi, and Morton Prince, 1877–1917,* ed. Nathan G. Hale Jr. (Cambridge, MA: Harvard University Press, 1971).

65. On the history of the implantation of psychoanalysis in Canada, see Roudinesco and Plon, *Dictionnaire.*

66. Lisa Appignanesi and John Forrester, *Freud's Women* (New York: Basic Books, 1992).

67. In 1910, aware of the harmful effects of this mania, Freud gave the name "wild" psychoanalysis to a technical error committed by a practitioner when he or she disclosed to the patient secrets that the practitioner had divined starting in the very first session.

68. The story of Spielrein has been the subject of several novels and films, especially David Cronenberg's highly successful *A Dangerous Method* (2011). It has been retold many times. See Aldo Carotenuto, *A Secret Symmetry: Sabina Spielrein between Jung and Freud*, trans. Arno Pomerans, John Shepley, and Krishna Winston (New York: Pantheon Books, 1982). The book includes a dossier discovered by Carotenuto and Carlo Trombetta: Spielrein's diary, her letters to Jung and Freud, and Freud's responses. See also Coline Covington and Barbara Wharton, eds., *Sabina Spielrein: Forgotten Pioneer of Psychoanalysis* (London: Routledge, Taylor and Francis, 2015), and Roudinesco and Plon, *Dictionnaire*. Bair tells the story of Spielrein's treatment and her relations with Jung and Bleuler in detail, contributing new information.

69. Report of C. G. Jung cited by Bair, based on the Burghölzli archives (Bair, *Jung*, 88).

70. Sabina Spielrein, "Über den psychologischen Inhalt eines Falles von Schizophrenie (Dementia praecox)" ("On the Psychological Content of a Case of Schizophrenia," 1911), *Jahrbuch für psychoanalytische und psychopathologische Forschungen* 3 (1912): 329–400. The text was discussed by Jung in *Symbols of Transformation: An Analysis of the Prelude to a Case of Schizophrenia*, 2nd ed., vol. 5 of *Collected Works of C. G. Jung*, trans. R. F. C. Hull (Princeton, NJ: Princeton University Press, 1956).

71. Sabina Spielrein, "Destruction as the Cause of Coming into Being" (1912), in Covington and Wharton, *Sabina Spielrein: Forgotten Pioneer*, 185–212.

72. Freud to Spielrein, August 28, 1913, in Carotenuto, *Secret Symmetry*, 120–121. Afterward, Freud never stopped reproaching Spielrein for remaining attached to Jung, to the point of offering "wild" interpretations of the fact that she had wanted to have a child by Jung, whom she idealized as a "Germanic knight," the better to express her revolt against a father by whom, in reality, she would have liked to have a child.

73. Élisabeth Roudinesco, "Les premières femmes psychanalystes," *Mil neuf cent: Revue d'histoire intellectuelle* 16 (1998): 27–41, repr. in *Topique* 71 (2000): 45–56; and an unpublished seminar (1998). See also Roudinesco and Plon, *Dictionnaire*. Among the forty-two women members of the WPV in 1938, the rates of suicide, mental illness, and violent death were somewhat higher than among the men (Roudinesco, unpublished seminar; Roudinesco and Plon, *Dictionnaire*).

74. Daniel Paul Schreber, *Memoirs of My Nervous Illness*, trans. Ida Macalpine and Richard A. Hunter (New York: New York Review of Books, 2000 [1903]); Sigmund Freud, "Psycho-analytic Notes on an Autobiographical Account of a Case of Paranoia (Dementia Paranoides)" (1911), *SE* 12.

75. Freud returned to this thesis in *Totem and Taboo* and elsewhere.

76. Martin Stingelin, "Les stratégies d'autolégitimation dans l'autobiographie de Schreber," in *Schreber revisité*, Cerisy conference (Leuven, Belgium: Presses Universitaires de Louvain, 1998), 115–227.

77. Luiz Eduardo Prado de Oliveira, ed. and trans., *Le cas Schreber: Contributions psychanalytiques de langue anglaise* (Paris: Presses Universitaires de France, 1979); Chawki Azouri, *"J'ai réussi où le paranoïaque échoue": la théorie a-t-elle un père?* (Paris: Denoël, 1990).

78. In English as Elias Canetti, *Crowds and Power*, trans. Carol Stewart (New York: Viking, 1962).

79. Rudolf von Urbantschitsch (1879–1964), a psychiatrist and psychoanalyst, emigrated to California in 1936.

80. We owe the reconstruction of this tragic history to Ulrike May. See Renate Sachse, "À propos de la recherche d'Ulrike May: Sur dix-neuf patients en analyse chez Freud (1910–1920)," *Essaim* 2 (2008): 187–194; Ulrike May, "Freuds Patientenkalender: Siebzehn Analytiker in Analyse bei Freud (1910–1920)," *LuziferAmor* 19, no. 37 (2006): 43–97; see also Mikkel Borch-Jacobsen, *Les patients de Freud: Destins* (Auxerre, France: Éditions Sciences humaines, 2011).

81. Jung discussed the case of "the man with the phallic sun" in *Psychology of the Unconscious: A Study of the Transformations and Symbolisms of the Libido*, trans. Beatrice M. Hinkle (Princeton, NJ: Princeton University Press, 1991 [1916]). Jung had entrusted the treatment of this patient to his student Johann Honneger, who was himself afflicted with manias; he committed suicide in March 1911 by taking a massive dose of morphine.

6. The Discovery of America

1. The best book on the introduction of psychoanalysis into the United States is Nathan G. Hale's *Freud and the Americans: The Beginnings of Psychoanalysis in the United States, 1876–1917* (New York: Oxford University Press, 1971). See also Eli Zaretsky, *Secrets of the Soul: A Social and Cultural History of Psychoanalysis* (New York: Alfred A. Knopf, 2004).

2. Hale, *Freud and the Americans*, 48.

3. Sigmund Freud, " 'Civilized' Sexual Morality and Modern Nervous Illness" (1908), *SE* 9:177–204.

4. There are numerous versions of the story of this trip. See especially those of Jones, Peter Gay, Donn, Deirdre Bair, Hale, and finally Vincent Brome, *Freud and His Early Circle: The Struggles of Psychoanalysis* (London: Heinemann, 1967), and Vincent Brome, *Jung* (New York: Athaneum, 1981), 247–271. The various exchanges of letters among Ferenczi, Jung, Freud, Putnam, and Hall contribute to the story as well. On this topic I have also consulted Saul Rosenzweig, *Freud, Jung, and Hall the King-Maker: The Historic Expedition to America (1909)* (Seattle: Hogrefe and Huber, 1992); and Anthony Ballenato, "Freud et la modernité américaine: L'introduction

de la psychanalyse à New York (1909–1917)," master's II thesis, University of Paris VII, 2007–2008, directed by Élisabeth Roudinesco. Ballenato was able to use unpublished archives.

5. Freud did not mention this episode in his travel journal, except to note that he had fallen victim to a sudden weakness owing to fatigue.

6. C. G. Jung, *Memories, Dreams, Reflections,* recorded and edited by Aniela Jaffé, trans. Richard Winston and Clara Winston (New York: Pantheon Books, 1963 [1962]), 161, 160. The theme of the archaic comes up repeatedly in the history of psychoanalysis, and it came back in other forms in subsequent debates between Freud and Rank, then between the Freudians and the Kleinians, and finally with the Lacanians. I addressed this in Élisabeth Roudinesco, *Histoire de la psychanalyse en France* followed by *Jacques Lacan: Esquisse d'une vie, histoire d'un système de pensée* (Paris: Pochothèque, 2009; hereafter *HPF-JL*). See also the positions of Nicolas Abraham and Maria Torok on the question of the crypt, *The Wolf Man's Magic Word: A Cryptonomy,* trans. Nicholas Rand, foreword by Jacques Derrida (Minneapolis: University of Minnesota Press, 1986), and see Henri Rey-Flaud, *Je ne comprends pas de quoi vous me parlez: Pourquoi refusons-nous parfois de reconnaître la réalité?* (Paris: Aubier, 2014).

7. Which allowed the anti-Freudians once again to assert that Freud was anti-Semitic, and the Jungians to assert that Jung was not, since he was friendly with a Jew and many of his disciples were Jews. William Stern (1871–1938) was invited to Worcester on the same basis as numerous other psychologists.

8. These are Freud's exact words, reported by Jung in his conversation at the Library of Congress with Kurt Eissler (cited in Brome, *Jung,* 117). On the genesis of the sentence invented by Lacan in 1955 and attributed to Freud, following his own encounter with Jung, see Roudinesco, *HPF-JL,* and Élisabeth Roudinesco, "Lacan, the Plague," *Psychoanalysis and History* 10 (2008): 225–235. Lacan claimed that Freud said, "They don't realize that we're bringing them the plague." We now know that Freud never uttered these words, but the legend is tenacious.

9. Freud to Ferenczi, January 10, 1909, in Sigmund Freud and Sándor Ferenczi, *Correspondence of Sigmund Freud and Sándor Ferenczi,* ed. Eva Brabant, Ernst Falzeder, and Patrizia Giampieri-Deutsch, trans. Peter T. Hoffer, introduction by André Haynal (Cambridge, MA: Belknap Press of Harvard University Press, 1993), 1:33.

10. Spread later on by Jung, over the years the rumor of an incestuous Freud became one of the major themes of psychoanalytic historiography in the English-speaking world, in particular after the publication in 1947 of Helen Walker Puner's book, *Sigmund Freud: His Life and Mind,* with a presentation by Paul Roazen and a preface by Erich Fromm (New Brunswick, NJ: Transaction, 1992 [1947]). No serious historian has ever offered the slightest proof of the existence of this "liaison" that gave rise to a large number of articles and several books. Cf. Élisabeth Roudinesco, *Mais pourquoi tant de haine?* (Paris: Seuil, 2010).

11. There are several versions of this story. See the conversation between C. G. Jung and Kurt Eissler, August 19, 1953, LoC, box 114, folder 4, drawn on by Bair; see also Jung, *Memories, Dreams, Reflections,* 158.

12. Deirdre Bair, *Jung: A Biography* (Boston: Little, Brown, 2003), 165.

13. The best narrative is in William W. Koelsch's report on the Fifth Annual Paul S. Clarkson Colloquium, in celebration of the seventy-fifth anniversary of the visit by Freud and Jung: *Incredible Day-Dream: Freud and Jung at Clark, 1909* (Worcester, MA: Clark University, Friends of the Goddard Library, 1984). Koelsch searched the university archives and supplied numerous details on the lecturers invited in 1909 who were present at Freud's talks between September 6 and September 10. This source is complemented by Bair's commentaries, which include details about Jung's reactions. We may note that Freud was convinced that blacks would become a majority population in the United States one day.

14. In one of his lectures, Jung presented the case of a little girl who was actually his daughter.

15. These five lectures were later written up by Freud and translated very quickly into several languages. See Sigmund Freud, "Five Lectures on Psycho-analysis" (1910 [1909]), *SE* 11:1–55; the citation regarding Bell is from 42–43.

16. Sigmund Freud, *An Autobiographical Study* (1925), *SE* 20:52.

17. Emma Goldman, *Living My Life* (New York: Knopf, 1970 [1931]), 1:455. And see Ballenato, master's thesis, 30.

18. Linda Donn, *Freud and Jung: Years of Friendship, Years of Loss* (New York: Scribner, 1988), 109.

19. Testimony of Judith Bernays Heller, LoC, box 121, folder 7, and Marion Ross, *Carnets:* Miscellaneous, 1914–1975, LoC, box 121, folder 7.

20. Freud takes up this idea in "Group Psychology and the Analysis of the Ego" (1921), *SE* 18:101, citing the parable from Schopenhauer, *Parerga und Paralipomena,* part 2, 31, "Gleichnisse und Parabeln."

21. Testimony of Barbara Low (1877–1955), undated, LoC, box 121, folder 5.

22. From which he recovered.

23. Freud to Jung, October 17, 1909, in Sigmund Freud and C. G. Jung, *The Freud/ Jung Letters: The Correspondence between Sigmund Freud and C. G. Jung,* ed. William McGuire, trans. Ralph Manheim and R. F. C. Hull (Princeton, NJ: Princeton University Press, 1974), 255; Sigmund Freud, *Leonard Da Vinci and a Memory of His Childhood* (1910), *SE* 11:57–138. In French as *Un souvenir d'enfance de Léonard de Vinci* (Paris: Gallimard, 1987 [1910]), with an excellent preface by Jean-Bertrand Pontalis and a thorough bibliography indicating the sources on which Freud drew. The essay was written between January and March 1910 and published in May.

24. Freud, *Leonardo, SE* 11:80, 67.

25. All these works can be consulted in Freud's library, with annotations in his own hand. In his essay, he sometimes cites the original Italian, even though he had the German translation as well. In English, see Eugène Müntz, *Leonardo da Vinci,*

Artist, Thinker and Man of Science, trans. from the French (London: W. Heinemann, 1898); Giorgio Vasari, *Lives of the Artists*, ed. and trans. Julia Conaway Bondanella and Peter Bondanella (Oxford: Oxford University Press, 1991 [1550]); Dmitry S. Merezhkovsky, *The Birth of the Gods*, trans. Natalie A. Duddington (New York: E. P. Dutton, 1926)—this is the central volume of a trilogy titled *Christ and Antichrist*. See also Smiraglia Scognamiglio, *Ricerche e documenti sulla giovinezza di Leonardo da Vinci* (Naples, 1900).

26. Marie Bonaparte was confronted by a cabal when her French translation of the novel was published.

27. Freud, *Leonardo*, *SE* 11:81.

28. See ibid., 81n1. The *Codex Atlanticus* is a collection of drawings and notes by da Vinci housed in the Biblioteca Ambrosiana in Milan.

29. Freud, *Leonardo*, *SE* 11:100; Freud used the term "narcissism" here for the first time.

30. The first painting was completed between 1503 and 1506, the second between 1508 and 1516.

31. In 1956, Meyer Schapiro reproached Freud not only for confusing a vulture with a kite, but especially for his lack of knowledge of art history. While the first error seems minor to me, the second has to be taken into account. It attests to the dangers that come with interpretation, even if we know that Freud was familiar with the sketches. He commented on them in notes added in 1919 and 1923. See Meyer Schapiro, "Freud and Leonardo: An Art Historical Study," in *Theory and Philosophy of Art: Style, Artist, and Society* (New York: George Braziller, 1994), 153–192. Kurt Robert Eissler responded to Schapiro in *Leonardo da Vinci: Psychoanalytic Notes on the Enigma* (New York: International Universities Press, 1961), as did Jacques Lacan in *The Object Relation, 1956–1957*, seminar, book 4, ed. Jacques-Alain Miller, trans. L. V. A. Roche, http://www.scribd.com/doc/143580546/The-Seminar-of -Jacques-Lacan-Book-4-The-Object-Relation#scribd. The anti-Freudians treated Freud as a con man and a falsifier. See Han Israëls, "Freud and the Vulture," *History of Psychiatry* 4 (1993): 577–586.

32. Freud, *Leonardo*, *SE* 11:120–121.

33. Freud to Andreas-Salomé, February 9, 1919, in Sigmund Freud and Lou Andreas-Salomé, *Letters*, ed. Ernst Pfeiffer, trans. William Robson-Scott and Elaine Robson-Scott (New York: Harcourt Brace Jovanovich, 1972), 90.

34. Most notably, as we have seen, by representing paranoia as a defense mechanism against homosexuality.

35. This game of infinite deciphering was highly profitable to Dan Brown when he was writing his *Da Vinci Code*. In another context, an anonymous caricaturist once drew Freud's face, putting in the place of his nose and forehead the body of a woman in ecstasy, accompanied by the legend "What's on a Man's Mind." Millions of copies were sold, and the caricature was later reproduced on clothing and trinkets almost as widely as the *Mona Lisa*.

36. The term first appeared in 1910 in Sigmund Freud, "A Special Type of Choice of Object Made by Men (Contributions to the Psychology of Love I)" (1910), *SE* 11:171. We should recall that Freud himself was mistaken about the point at which he introduced the complex in his work: he claimed that it first appeared in *The Interpretation of Dreams*.

37. Freud, "Special Type of Choice of Object," *SE* 11:171.

38. Sigmund Freud, *Totem and Taboo* (1913 [1912–1913]), *SE* 13:1–162.

39. In 1995, I devoted my seminar to the study of the relations between psychoanalysis and anthropology; I draw on several elements from the seminar here. See also my preface to the new French edition of Georges Devereux, *Psychothérapie d'un Indien des Plaines,* trans. Françoise de Gruson with Monique Novodorsqui (Paris: Fayard, 1998); for the original English, see Georges Devereux, *Reality and Dreams: Psychotherapy of a Plains Indian* (Garden City, NY: Anchor Books, 1969). See also Élisabeth Roudinesco and Michel Plon, *Dictionnaire de la psychanalyse* (Paris: Fayard, 2006); Claude Lévi-Strauss, *Totemism,* trans. Rodney Needham (London: Merlin, 1964 [1962]). Freud frequently cited the work of the French historian Salomon Reinach, *Cultes, mythes et religions* (Paris: Ernest Leroux, 1905).

40. Edward Burnett Tylor, *Primitive Culture,* 2 vols. (London: John Murray, 1871); William Robertson Smith, *Lectures on the Religion of the Semites: The Fundamental Institutions* (New York: Macmillan, 1927 [1889]); Edward Westermarck, *The History of Human Marriage,* 3 vols. (London: Macmillan, 1891); James Jasper Atkinson, "Primal Law," in Andrew Lang, *Social Origins* (London: Longmans, Green, 1903), 209–294; James George Frazer, *The Golden Bough: A Study in Magic and Religion,* 12 vols. (London: Macmillan, 1911–1915). The English edition of Frazer's book is in Freud's library.

41. See Roudinesco and Plon, *Dictionnaire;* see also Alfred L. Kroeber, "*Totem and Taboo:* An Ethnologic Psychoanalysis," *American Anthropologist* 22 (1920): 48–55; Bronislaw Malinowski, *Argonauts of the Western Pacific: An Account of Native Enterprise and Adventure in the Archipelagoes of Melanesian New Guinea* (London: G. Routledge and Sons, 1922); Bronislaw Malinowski, *Sex and Repression in Savage Society* (London: K. Paul, 1927); Ernest Jones, *Essays in Applied Psycho-analysis,* 2 vols. (New York: International Universities Press, 1964 [1951?]); Eugène Enriquez, *De la horde à l'État* (Paris: Gallimard, 1983).

42. Freud to his children, September 12, 1913, in Sigmund Freud, *Unser Herz zeigt nach dem Süden: Reisebriefe 1895–1923* (Berlin: Aufbau-Verlag, 2002), 373 (in French as *"Notre coeur tend vers le sud": Correspondance de voyage, 1895–1923,* ed. Christfried Tögel with Michale Molnar, trans. Jean-Claude Capèle, preface by Élisabeth Roudinesco [Paris: Fayard, 2003], 331).

43. Testimony of Jerome Alexander, October 21, 1951, LoC, box 120, folder 2.

44. Sigmund Freud, "The Moses of Michelangelo" (1914), *SE* 13:211–238.

45. See Ernest Jones, *The Life and Work of Sigmund Freud* (New York: Basic Books, 1953–1957), 2:363–367; see also Ilse Grubrich-Simitis, *Back to Freud's Texts: Making*

Silent Documents Speak, trans. Philip Slotkin (New Haven, CT: Yale University Press, 1996 [1993]), 174–175.

46. Sigmund Freud, "Group Psychology and the Analysis of the Ego" (1921), *SE* 18:65–144.

47. Phyllis Grosskurth, *The Secret Ring: Freud's Inner Circle and the Politics of Psychoanalysis* (Reading, MA: Addison-Wesley, 1991).

48. Gerhard Wittenberger and Christfried Tögel, eds., *Die Rundbriefe des "Geheimen Komitees,"* 4 vols. (Tübingen, Germany: Diskord, 1995–2003).

49. Sigmund Freud, letter to Mitzi, July 13, 1941, LoC, family papers.

50. See Peter Gay, *Freud: A Life for Our Time* (New York: W. W. Norton, 1988), 348. Grosskurth (in *Secret Ring*) gives a good description of the committee's activities during the war, and then between 1920 and 1927. For a more complete understanding of the prewar context, following the correspondence between Freud and his disciples is essential.

51. Sigmund Freud, "On Narcissism: An Introduction" (1914), *SE* 14:67–102.

7. The War of Nations

1. Freud to Abraham, July 26, 1914, in Sigmund Freud and Karl Abraham, *The Complete Correspondence of Sigmund Freud and Karl Abraham, 1907–1925,* ed. Ernst Falzeder, trans. Caroline Schwarzacher et al. (London: Karnac, 2002 [1965]), 264.

2. Mathilde, Freud's eldest daughter, married to Robert Hollitscher, and Sophie, who had married Max Halberstadt, both lived in Hamburg.

3. Freud to Andreas-Salomé, November 25, 1914, in Sigmund Freud and Lou Andreas-Salomé, *Letters,* ed. Ernst Pfeiffer, trans. William Robson-Scott and Elaine Robson-Scott (New York: Harcourt Brace Jovanovich, 1972), 21.

4. Freud to Ferenczi, August 23, 1914, in Sigmund Freud and Sándor Ferenczi, *Correspondence of Sigmund Freud and Sándor Ferenczi,* ed. Eva Brabant, Ernst Falzeder, and Patrizia Giampieri-Deutsch, trans. Peter T. Hoffer, introduction by André Haynal (Cambridge, MA: Belknap Press of Harvard University Press, 1993), 2:13.

5. Peter Gay devotes some fine pages to this Freudian moment of the war; see *Freud: A Life for Our Time* (New York: W. W. Norton, 1988), 342–357. See also Phyllis Grosskurth, *The Secret Ring: Freud's Inner Circle and the Politics of Psychoanalysis* (Reading, MA: Addison-Wesley, 1991), 68–95.

6. Sigmund Freud, "Thoughts for the Times on War and Death" (1915), *SE* 14:273–302.

7. Homer, *The Odyssey,* trans. Robert Fagles, introduction by Bernard Knox (New York: Penguin, 1996), book 11, lines 547–558.

8. Freud, "Thoughts for the Times," *SE* 14:300.

9. Freud to Ferenczi, March 11, 1914, in Freud and Ferenczi, *Correspondence,* 1:545.

10. André Bolzinger, *Portrait de Sigmund Freud: Trésors d'une correspondance* (Paris: Campagne Première, 2012), 80.

11. Freud to Ferenczi, November 6, 1917, in Freud and Ferenczi, *Correspondence,* 2:245.

12. And, starting in 1920, the ego, the id, and the superego.

13. These essays are found in *SE* 14:109–258. See also Sándor Ferenczi, "La métapsychologie de Freud," in *Oeuvres complètes: Psychanalyse* (Paris: Payot, 1968–1982), 4:253–265 (given as a lecture in Vienna in 1921, first published in Hungarian in 1922; see Ferenczi to Freud, December 26, 1921, in Freud and Ferenczi, *Correspondence,* 3:76n1). Freud's texts on metapsychology are among those most discussed by the international psychoanalytic community, though they have attracted little attention from researchers. See Élisabeth Roudinesco and Michel Plon, *Dictionnaire de la psychanalyse* (Paris: Fayard, 2006).

14. On December 30, 1914, Tausk gave a lecture on this subject to the WPV. Afterward, in 1915, Freud wrote a first draft of his text.

15. Letters from and to Karl Abraham, March 31–May 4, 1915, in Freud and Abraham, *Complete Correspondence,* 303–310.

16. Sigmund Freud, *Übersicht der Übertragungsneurosen* (Frankfurt: S. Fischer, 1985), in English as *A Phylogenetic Fantasy: Overview of the Transference Neuroses,* ed. Ilse Grubrich-Simitis, trans. Axel Hoffer and Peter T. Hoffer (Cambridge, MA: Belknap Press of Harvard University Press, 1987). This text was rediscovered in 1983 in Ferenczi's archives and published with commentary by Ilse Grubrich-Simitis.

17. Sándor Ferenczi, "Stages in the Development of the Sense of Reality" (1913), in *First Contributions to Psycho-analysis,* trans. Ernest Jones (New York: Brunner/ Mazel, 1952, repr. 1980), 213–239.

18. The theory of recapitulation holds that the individual development of an organism reproduces the stages in the evolution of its ancestors.

19. See Lucille B. Ritvo, *Darwin's Influence on Freud: A Tale of Two Sciences* (New Haven, CT: Yale University Press, 1990). Ritvo offers the best analysis of the Freudian theory of recapitulation, borrowed both from Darwin and from Lamarck. She contradicts, with good reason, Frank J. Sulloway's thesis according to which Freud was a cryptobiologist. She sees him rather as a biologist of the psyche, an heir to Romanticism who continued to work in the realm of philosophies of the subject.

20. Freud, *Phylogenetic Fantasy,* 20: "With these particulars we have basically done no more than save our scientific fantasies from being criticized as absurd"; Ferenczi to Freud, October 26, 1915, in Freud and Ferenczi, *Correspondence,* 2:84–85.

21. Jean-Baptiste Lamarck, *Zoological Philosophy: An Exposition with Regard to the Natural History of Animals,* trans. Hugh Elliot (New York: Hafner, 1914).

22. Contrary to a widespread view, we know that the two conceptions of the evolution of humanity were not opposed to one another. Like Lamarck, Darwin took into account the idea of the heredity of acquired characteristics. This thesis, supported by Freud and Ferenczi against Jones, had been invalidated by August Weismann.

23. Freud to Abraham, November 11, 1917, in Freud and Abraham, *Complete Correspondence*, 359–360.

24. Sigmund Freud, *Introductory Lectures on Psycho-analysis* (1916–1917), *SE* 15–16.

25. See Élisabeth Roudinesco, *Histoire de la psychanalyse en France* followed by *Jacques Lacan: Esquisse d'une vie, histoire d'un système de pensée* (Paris: Pochothèque, 2009; hereafter *HPF-JL*).

26. Freud to Abraham, December 10, 1917, in Freud and Abraham, *Complete Correspondence*, 364.

27. Phyllis Grosskurth, *Melanie Klein: Her World and Her Work* (New York: Knopf, 1986), 73; Sigmund Freud, "Lines of Advance in Psycho-analytic Therapy" (1918), *SE* 17:157–168.

28. Freud, "Lines of Advance," *SE* 17:162; author's italics.

29. Ibid., 167–168.

30. Sándor Ferenczi et al., *Psycho-analysis and the War Neuroses*, introduction by Sigmund Freud (London: International Psychoanalytical Press, 1921). Ernst Simmel (1882–1947) was a German psychiatrist and psychoanalyst who founded the sanatorium Schloss Tegel in 1925, modeled on the great clinics at Bellevue and Burghölzli. Arrested by the Gestapo in 1933, he managed to emigrate to the United States thanks to Brunswick, who paid a ransom to the Nazis. He settled in Los Angeles and for the rest of his life remained nostalgic for the old world in Europe. See later in this chapter for details about Viktor Tausk.

31. Stefan Zweig, *The World of Yesterday: An Autobiography*, translation of *Die Welt von Gestern* (New York: Viking Press, 1943), 305.

32. Sigmund Freud, "On the Teaching of Psycho-analysis in Universities" (1920), *SE* 17:171–173.

33. William Johnston, *The Austrian Mind: An Intellectual and Social History, 1848–1938* (Berkeley: University of California Press, 1972), 341.

34. Freud to Jones, April 18, 1919, in Sigmund Freud, *The Complete Correspondence of Sigmund Freud and Ernest Jones, 1908–1939*, ed. R. Andrew Paskauskas (Cambridge, MA: Belknap Press of Harvard University Press, 1983), 340.

35. Grosskurth, *Secret Ring*, 110. See also Gerhard Wittenberger and Christfried Tögel, eds., *Die Rundbriefe des "Geheimen Komitees"* (Tübingen, Germany: Diskord, 1995–2003), December 1 and 11, 1921, 2:297, 303, and January 11, 1922, 3:14–15. Jones had refused to include in the IPV a certain Dutch psychoanalyst who had been imprisoned for homosexuality, and he used this case as a pretext in defense of his position.

36. A great deal has been published on this subject, and I have dealt with it myself on several occasions. See Élisabeth Roudinesco, "Psychanalyse et homosexualité: Réflexions sur le désir pervers, l'injure et la function paternelle," conversation with François Pommier, *Cliniques méditerranéennes*, no. 65 (Spring 2002): 7–34.

37. Over the years, Hirschfeld's petition had been signed by six thousand people, including Alfred Einstein and Zweig. The article in question stipulated

that "unnatural fornication, whether between persons of the male sex or of humans with beasts, is to be punished by imprisonment" (paragraph 175, version of May 15, 1871, https://en.wikipedia.org/wiki/Paragraph_175).

38. On this process in France and on the role of Joseph Babinksi, one of Jean-Martin Charcot's disciples, see Roudinesco, *HPF-JL*.

39. In 1927, Wagner-Jauregg received the Nobel Prize for his work on the treatment of malaria. An admirer of German nationalism, he was sympathetic toward Nazism at the end of his life. See Clare Chapman, "Austrians Stunned by Nobel Prize-Winner's Nazi Ideology," *Scotland on Sunday,* January 24, 2004.

40. These treatments were known as "electrotherapy" or "faradization" at the time.

41. A dossier concerning this affair, including documents, testimony, and the investigation, was put together by Kurt Robert Eissler and published in German in 1979; in English as Kurt Robert Eissler, *Freud as an Expert Witness: The Discussion of War Neuroses between Freud and Wagner-Jauregg* (New York: International Universities Press, 1986). The text includes Freud's "Memorandum on the Electrical Treatment of War Neurotics" (20–28; see *SE* 17:211–215), transcripts of testimony by Freud (57–74) and other witnesses, and numerous other documents. See also Henri F. Ellenberger's account in *Discovery of the Unconscious: The History and Evolution of Dynamic Psychiatry* (New York: Basic Books, 1970), 837–839. Ellenberger did not have access to all the archives, so his account is different from Eissler's, but it nevertheless has the merit of correcting the errors made by Jones. The documents Eissler used are in the Library of Congress.

42. Eissler, *Freud as Expert Witness,* 15–16.

43. Ibid., 202–205 (excerpts from Kauders's testimony).

44. Ibid., 62.

45. Ibid., 241–242.

46. The Saborskys were a wealthy industrial family that had adopted Rosa.

47. Ernst Lanzer's identity was revealed for the first time by Patrick J. Mahony in *Freud and the Rat Man* (New Haven, CT: Yale University Press, 1986). In addition to presenting a detailed historical investigation, Mahony compares the version given by Freud in "Notes upon a Case of Obsessional Neurosis" (1909) (*SE* 10:151–250) with Freud's preliminary notes, "Original Record of the Case" (1955 [1907–1908]) (*SE* 17:251–318), which had not been integrated into Freud's initial published account.

48. Leonard Shengold was the first to show, in 1965, that this story was drawn from Octave Mirbeau's 1899 novel *Le jardin des supplices (The Torture Garden);* see Leonard Shengold, "More about Rats and Rat People," *International Journal of Psychoanalysis* 52, no. 3 (1971): 277–288.

49. Freud, "Notes," *SE* 10:167; author's italics.

50. Ibid., 213.

51. On this topic, I do not share the opinion expressed by Mikkel Borch-Jacobsen in *Les patients de Freud: Destins* (Auxerre, France: Éditions Sciences humaines, 2011),

111. The distortions between the notes and the case study, which have been brought to light by Mahony, show on the contrary that Freud found in Lanzer an exemplary patient for whom he felt real empathy.

52. It was published in the form of an "excerpt."

53. Mahony thinks, on the contrary, that what we have here is an Oedipal drama in which Lanzer occupies the role of a "Viennese Sphinx." And he offers a Kleinian interpretation: Lanzer identified with his mother in order to introject the penis of his father. Dozens of commentaries have been written about the story, with the result that the "Rat Man" "case" has eclipsed the patient's own story.

54. Even if he sometimes doubted this, as Freud reported in "Notes," SE 10:180, 185.

55. Freud, "Notes," SE 10:249.

56. In the Library of Congress there are several photographs showing Pankejeff, his sister, and his mother before a pile of animals. These have rarely been taken into account by commentators, even though Pankejeff mentions them in telling his life story. The real identity of the patient, nicknamed "the Wolf Man," was revealed in 1973. To reconstitute his story, several contradictory accounts have to be reconciled: see Muriel Gardiner, ed., *The Wolf-Man: With the Case of the Wolf-Man, by Sigmund Freud and a Supplement by Ruth Mack Brunswick* (New York: Basic Books, 1971); and Karin Obholzer, *The Wolf-Man: Conversations with Freud's Patient—Sixty Years Later*, trans. Michael Shaw (New York: Continuum, 1982). In these two books, produced at the end of his life, Pankejeff is often mistaken and gives conflicting versions of his analysis with Freud: one account, intended for psychoanalysts, was related to Gardiner, and the other, intended for a broad public, to Obholzer, an Austrian journalist. See also Patrick J. Mahony, *Cries of the Wolf Man* (New York: International University Press, 1984). Mahony's reconstitution is quite reliable. Cf. also Borch-Jacobsen, *Patients de Freud*, and Mikkel Borch-Jacobsen and Sonu Shamdasani, *The Freud Files: An Inquiry into the History of Psychoanalysis* (Cambridge: Cambridge University Press, 2012). These two texts are excessively weighted against Freud, even if the documents cited are indisputable. To these must be added the interviews carried out by Eissler, available in five files at the Library of Congress, 1954–1955, box 116.

57. Obholzer, *Wolf-Man*, 30.

58. Ibid., 39.

59. Ibid., 30.

60. Freud to Ferenczi, February 13, 1910, in Freud and Ferenczi, *Correspondence*, 1:138. Pankejeff did not describe this scene.

61. Sigmund Freud, "From the History of an Infantile Neurosis" (1918), SE 17:1–124.

62. Hence the differences between Pankejeff's testimony and the confidences received or reconstructed by Freud in the treatment narrative.

63. Freud, "Infantile Neurosis," SE 17:29.

64. He had used that expression in a letter to Fliess on May 2, 1897, with reference to acts of seduction (Sigmund Freud, *The Origins of Psychoanalysis: Letters, Drafts and Notes to Wilhelm Fliess, 1887–1902,* ed. Marie Bonaparte, Anna Freud, and Ernst Kris, trans. Eric Mosbacher and James Strachey [Garden City, NY: Doubleday, 1957], 199; cf. Sigmund Freud, *The Complete Letters of Sigmund Freud to Wilhelm Fliess, 1877–1904,* ed. and trans. Jeffrey Moussaieff Masson [Cambridge, MA: Belknap Press of Harvard University Press, 1985], 239).

65. Freud, "Infantile Neurosis," *SE* 17:37–38.

66. Ruth Mack Brunswick, "A Supplement to Freud's 'History of an Infantile Neurosis,'" in Gardiner, *Wolf-Man,* 263–307.

67. Otto Rank, *The Trauma of Birth* (London: Kegan Paul, Trench, Trubner, 1929 [1924]); Grosskurth, *Secret Ring,* 179–180.

68. Freud to Ferenczi (citing Dr. Pankejeff), June 8, 1926, in Freud and Ferenczi, *Correspondence,* 3:262–263.

69. See Part Three.

70. On the comments of Jacques Lacan, Serge Leclaire, Nicolas Abraham, Maria Torok, Jacques Derrida, and Gilles Deleuze, see Roudinesco, *HPF-JL.* Carlo Ginzburg notes that the dream may have been inspired by legends about werewolves: instead of becoming a werewolf, a path he might have taken three centuries earlier, Pankejeff became a neurotic on the verge of psychosis; see Carlo Ginzburg, "Freud, the Wolf-Man, and Werewolves," in *Clues, Myths, and the Historical Method,* trans. John Tedeschi and Anne C. Tedeschi (Baltimore: Johns Hopkins University Press, 1989), 146–155.

71. Gardiner, *Wolf-Man,* and Obholzer, *Wolf-Man.*

72. This is the case in particular of Borch-Jacobsen and of many others as well.

73. Quoted in Theodor Reik, *The Compulsion to Confess: On the Psychoanalysis of Crime and Punishment* (New York: Farrar, Straus, and Cudahy, 1959), 473–474.

74. I shall not take up the history of psychoanalysis in France here.

75. Freud to Eitingon, January 21, 1920, in Max Schur, *Freud: Living and Dying* (New York: International Universities Press, 1972), 317–318.

76. Freud to Pfister, January 27, 1920, in Sigmund Freud and Oskar Pfister, *Psychoanalysis and Faith: The Letters of Sigmund Freud and Oscar Pfister,* ed. Heinrich Meng and Ernst L. Freud, trans. Eric Mosbacher (London: Hogarth Press and the Institute of Psychoanalysis, 1963), 75.

77. Freud to Max Halberstadt, January 1, 1920, in Sigmund Freud, *Lettres à ses enfants* (Paris: Aubier, 2012 [2010]), 492.

78. Sigmund Freud, "Contributions to a Discussion on Suicide" (1910), *SE* 11:231–232.

79. Freud to Ferenczi, December 30, 1912, 1, 457–458, and May 14, 1920, in Freud and Ferenczi, *Correspondence,* 3:20. Twain sent the following telegram to a newspaper that had announced his death: "The reports of my death are greatly exaggerated."

80. Lou Andreas-Salomé, *The Freud Journal of Lou Andreas-Salomé*, trans. Stanley A. Leavy (New York: Basic Books, 1964), 168.

81. Sigmund Freud, "Viktor Tausk" (1919), *SE* 17:273–275; and Freud to Andreas-Salomé, August 1, 1919, in Freud and Andreas-Salomé, *Letters*, 98.

82. Sándor Ferenczi, "On the Technique of Psycho-analysis" (1919), in *Further Contributions to the Theory and Technique of Psycho-analysis*, ed. John Rickman, trans. Jane Isabel Suttie et al. (New York: Brunner/Mazel, 1950, repr. 1980), 177–189.

83. Jones gave his version of the committee's internal discord in the final volume of his biography, *The Life and Work of Sigmund Freud* (New York: Basic Books, 1953–1957), 3:44–77. Jones's account must be compared with those of the other committee members, available in the *Rundbriefe*. See also Grosskurth, *Secret Ring*.

84. Freud to Ferenczi, December 25, 1920, in Freud and Ferenczi, *Correspondence*, 3:42.

85. Freud to Georg Groddeck, June 5, 1917, in Georg Groddeck, "Correspondence with Sigmund Freud (1917–1934)," in *The Meaning of Illness: Selected Psychoanalytic Writings*, ed. Lore Schacht, trans. Gertrud Mander (New York: International Universities Press, 1977), 36–38. It is thanks to the work of Roger Lewinter that Groddeck's work is known in France; see also Catherine Clément, "La sauvagerie de l'amour même," *L'Arc* 78 (1980): 1–4.

86. Jacquy Chemouni, "Psychopathologie de la démocratie," *Frénésie* 10 (Spring 1992): 265–282.

87. "Nature cures, the doctor cares."

88. Georg Groddeck, *Nasamecu: La nature guérit*, trans. Pierre Villain, preface by Catherine Clément (Paris: Aubier-Montaigne, 1992).

89. Georg Groddeck, *Lebenserinnerunger* (1929), in *Der Mensch und sein Es* (Wiesbaden, Germany: Limes Verlag, 1970).

90. Let us recall that in 1911, along with Havelock Ellis, Hirschfeld, and Eduard Bernstein, Freud had signed an Appeal to the Men and Women of All the Civilized Countries for the purpose of promoting a hygienicist policy aimed at improving the physical and psychic health of the human "race." See Paul Weindling, *Health, Race, and German Politics between National Unification and Nazism, 1870–1945* (Cambridge: Cambridge University Press, 1989), 250. On the evolution of the eugenicist idea, see Roudinesco, *HPF-JL*.

91. Georg Groddeck, *Conférences psychanalytiques à l'usage des malades (1915–1916)*, 3 vols. (Paris: Champ libre-Roger Lewinter, 1982).

92. Georg Groddeck, *Der Seelensucher* (Frankfurt: Stroemfeld, 1998 [1921]); in French as *Le chercheur d'âme: Un roman psychanalytique* (Paris: Gallimard, 1982).

93. Georg Groddeck, *The Book of the It*, trans. V. M. E. Collins (London: Vision, 1950).

94. Freud to Groddeck, December 21, 1924, in Groddeck, "Correspondence," 90; see also Groddeck, *Book of the It*.

95. Thomas Mann, *The Magic Mountain*, trans. John E. Woods (New York: Knopf, 1995 [1924]), 61.

96. See Roudinesco and Plon, *Dictionnaire*.

97. Georg Groddeck, *Un problème de femme*, trans. Roger Lewinter (Paris: Mazarine, 1979 [1903]); Georg Groddeck, "Le double sexe de l'être humain" (1931), *Nouvelle revue de psychanalyse* 7 (Spring 1973): 193–199. And see Jacques Le Rider, *Modernity and Crises of Identity: Culture and Society in Fin-de-Siècle Vienna*, trans. Rosemary Morris (New York: Continuum, 1993 [1944]).

98. In 1965, two of Groddeck's biographers imagined that the doctor had exchanged letters with Hitler. The rumor was invalidated by Roger Lewinter in a letter to *Le Monde* published September 7, 1980.

8. Dark Enlightenment

1. The term was used by Theodor Adorno.

2. With the word *Unheimliche*, Freud designated a disturbing impression of strangeness emanating from some long-familiar thing, as exemplified by the fear of castration, the figure of the double, and the automaton. See Sigmund Freud, "The Uncanny" (1919), *SE* 17:217–256; see also Jean Clair, *Malinconia: Motifs saturniens dans l'art de l'entre-deux-guerres* (Paris: Gallimard, 1996), especially the chapter titled "De la métaphysique à l'inquiétante étrangeté" (From metaphysics to the uncanny), 59–85.

3. Sigmund Freud, "Beyond the Pleasure Principle" (1920), *SE* 18:59. On the genesis of the text and its variants, see Ilse Grubrich-Simitis, *Back to Freud's Texts: Making Silent Documents Speak*, trans. Philip Slotkin (New Haven, CT: Yale University Press, 1996 [1993]), 182–191. An extensive debate in which Michael Schröter and Ulrike May challenged Grubrich-Simitis's view on the genesis of "Beyond the Pleasure Principle" can be traced in the journal *Luzifer-Amor* 51 (2013), entirely devoted to "Beyond the Pleasure Principle"; see Michael Schröter and Ulrike May, eds., *S. Freud "Jenseits des Lustprinzips," Neu-Edition, Erstabdruck der Urfassung (1919)* [S. Freud, "Beyond the Pleasure Principle," new edition, first printing of the first edition (1919)], special edition, *Luzifer-Amor* 51 (2013); Ilse Grubrich-Simitis, "Die Neurepräsentation von 'Jenseits des Lustprinzips' ist ganz so neu nicht" [The new representation of "Beyond the Pleasure Principle" is not so new now], *Psyche* 67, no. 8 (August 2013): 679–688; and Michael Schröter, "Kommentare: Jenseits des Kanons: Eine Erwiderung auf Ilse Grubrich-Simitis' Kritik an der Neu-Ausgabe von 'Jenseits des Lustprinzips'" [Commentary: Beyond the canon: A reply to Ilse Grubrich-Simitis's critique of the new edition of "Beyond the Pleasure Principle"], *Psyche* 67, no. 8 (August 2013): 794–798.

4. According to a remark by Jacques Derrida, who wrote one of the most dazzling commentaries on "Beyond the Pleasure Principle" in *The Post Card: From Socrates to Freud and Beyond*, trans. Alan Bass (Chicago: University of Chicago Press, 1987 [1980]).

5. Sigmund Freud, *An Autobiographical Study* (1925), *SE* 20: 59–60.

6. Sigmund Freud to Ernst Freud, January 17, 1938, in Sigmund Freud, *Letters of Sigmund Freud, 1873–1939*, ed. Ernst L. Freud, trans. Tania Stern and James Stern (London: Hogarth, 1970), 294.

7. Jean de La Fontaine, "The Two Rats, the Fox, and the Egg," in *The Original Fables of La Fontaine*, trans. F. C. Tilney (London: J. M. Dent and Sons, 1913), 85.

8. See J. Keith Davies and Gerhard Fichtner, eds., *Freud's Library: A Comprehensive Catalogue*, bilingual German-English (London: Freud Museum, 2006). Freud was interested in Sade's life but not in his works. See Élisabeth Roudinesco, *Our Dark Side: A History of Perversion*, trans. David Macey (Cambridge, UK: Polity, 2009 [2007]).

9. Georges Bataille, *The Accursed Share: An Essay on General Economy*, trans. Robert Hurley, 3 vols. (New York: Zone Books, 1988–1993).

10. Gilles-Gaston Grangier, *L'irrationnel* (Paris: Odile Jacob, 1998). I have already drawn on this book in Élisabeth Roudinesco, *Why Psychoanalysis?*, trans. Rachel Bowlby (New York: Columbia University Press, 2001 [1999]).

11. George Sylvester Viereck, "Sigmund Freud Confronts the Sphinx," in *Glimpses of the Great* (New York: Macauley, 1930), 28. See also Emilio Rodrigué, *Le siècle de la psychanalyse*, 2 vols. (Paris: Payot, 2000 [1996]).

12. In a text dated January 21, 1919, he expressed his desire to have his body cremated when he died (interview with Eric Willis, director of the crematorium at Golders Green, April 24, 2014). See also Helen Fry, *Freud's War* (Stroud, UK: History Press, 2009).

13. Freud, "Beyond the Pleasure Principle," *SE* 18:21–22.

14. Sigmund Freud, "Instincts and Their Vicissitudes" (1915), *SE* 14:109–140. On the genesis of the notion of sadomasochism, see Élisabeth Roudinesco and Michel Plon, *Dictionnaire de la psychanalyse* (Paris: Fayard, 2006).

15. Freud, "Beyond the Pleasure Principle," *SE* 18:22.

16. In a note added later to "Beyond the Pleasure Principle," Freud made the following observation: "When this child was five and three-quarters, his mother died. Now that she was really 'gone' ('o-o-o'), the little boy showed no signs of grief. It is true that in the interval a second child had been born and had roused him to violent jealousy" (*SE* 18:15). The child in question was Heinz (Heinerle) Halberstadt (1918–1923), Sophie's second son, who died at age four.

17. Freud refers to the 1581 Italian edition, *La Gerusalemme liberata*, cantos 12–13 ("Beyond the Pleasure Principle," *SE* 18:22). The English citations are from Torquato Tasso, *Jerusalem Delivered: An English Prose Version*, trans. and ed. Ralph Nash (Detroit: Wayne State University Press, 1987).

18. The eunuch Arsetes informs her of this, fearing that when she changes her armor she will be mistaken for the warrior who killed Tancred's companion Arimon (Tasso, *Jerusalem Delivered*, canto 12, 259–260).

19. Ibid., 166–271.

20. Freud's terms: see "Beyond the Pleasure Principle," *SE* 18:22.

21. Ibid.

22. The thematics was not new; it had been developed in particular by the Romantics. See Henri F. Ellenberger's account in *Discovery of the Unconscious: The History and Evolution of Dynamic Psychiatry* (New York: Basic Books, 1970), 514–516.

23. August Weismann, *Essays upon Heredity and Kindred Biological Problems*, 2 vols., ed. Arthur B. Poulton et al. (Oxford: Clarendon, 1891–1892). Freud cites three articles from this volume in particular. Cf. Charles Lenay, "Les limites naturelles de la durée de vie et la question de l'hérédité de l'acquis," *Études sur la mort* (Le Bouscat, France: L'Esprit du temps, 2003).

24. Freud, "Beyond the Pleasure Principle," *SE* 18:50. Sulloway uses the term "biogenetic romance" to characterize the Freudian conception of the death drive: Frank J. Sulloway, *Freud, Biologist of the Mind: Beyond the Psychoanalytic Legend* (New York: Basic Books, 1979), 409.

25. He theorized this topography two years later: see Sigmund Freud, *The Ego and the Id* (1923), *SE* 19:1–66.

26. Sigmund Freud, "The Dissection of the Psychical Personality," in *New Introductory Lectures on Psycho-analysis* (1933), *SE* 22:80. On the various translations of this pronouncement, and especially Lacan's, see Jacques Lacan, "The Freudian Thing, or the Meaning of the Return to Freud in Psychoanalysis," in *Écrits: The First Complete Edition in English*, trans. Bruce Fink with Héloïse Fink and Russell Grigg (New York: W. W. Norton, 2006 [1966]), 334–363; see also Élisabeth Roudinesco, *Histoire de la psychanalyse en France* followed by *Jacques Lacan: Esquisse d'une vie, histoire d'un système de pensée* (Paris: Pochothèque, 2009; hereafter *HPF-JL*).

27. François Requet, "Nietzsche et Freud: Le rapport entre cruauté, culpabilité et civilisation," Master's thesis, Université de Franche-Comté, 2005–2006.

28. He noted moreover that he owed a debt to Heinrich Gomperz, the son of Theodor Gomperz and his wife, Else (Freud's former patient), for some useful observations. And he compared Aristophanes's proposition to an identical myth from the Upanishads. The German translation of the *Symposium* that is found in Freud's library dates from 1932.

29. Freud, "Beyond the Pleasure Principle," *SE* 18:64n1.

30. William McDougall, *Psycho-analysis and Social Psychology* (London: Methuen, 1936), 64.

31. Ernest Jones, *The Life and Work of Sigmund Freud* (New York: Basic Books, 1953–1957), 3:266–286. See also Sulloway, *Freud, Biologist*, 394.

32. Sigmund Freud to Fritz Wittels, December 18, 1923, cited by Jones, *Life and Work*, 3:40–41.

33. Freud to Eitingon, July 18, 1920, in Sigmund Freud and Max Eitingon, *Correspondance, 1906–1939*, ed. Michael Schröter, trans. Olivier Mannoni (Paris: Hachette Littératures, 2009 [2004]), 230.

34. Derrida, *Post Card*, 355.

35. See Yirmiyahu Yovel, *Spinoza and Other Heretics*, 2 vols. (Princeton, NJ: Princeton University Press, 1989).

36. In particular by Jacques Lacan, *The Four Fundamental Concepts of Psychoanalysis*, seminar, book 11, ed. Jacques-Alain Miller, trans. Alan Sheridan (New York: W. W. Norton, 1998 [1973]); see also Jean Laplanche, *Life and Death in Psychoanalysis*, trans. Jeffrey Mehlman (Baltimore: Johns Hopkins University Press, 1976 [1970]); and Roudinesco and Plon, *Dictionnaire*. The notion of death instinct was accepted very quickly in Japan upon the creation, in 1928, of the first institute of psychoanalysis in Tokyo. The psychologist Yaekichi Yabe, passing through Vienna in 1930, told Freud that for the Japanese, the idea that life tended toward death was part of the teaching of classical Buddhism. See Roudinesco and Plon, *Dictionnaire*.

37. Freud to Ferenczi, May 8, 1921, in Sigmund Freud and Sándor Ferenczi, *Correspondence of Sigmund Freud and Sándor Ferenczi*, ed. Eva Brabant, Ernst Falzeder, and Patrizia Giampieri-Deutsch, trans. Peter T. Hoffer, introduction by André Haynal (Cambridge, MA: Belknap Press of Harvard University Press, 1993), 3:55–56.

38. Sigmund Freud, "Group Psychology and the Analysis of the Ego" (1921), *SE* 18. Freud's comments on Le Bon's text refer to Rudolf Eisler's German translation, where *foule* ("crowd") is rendered as *Masse*. In Strachey's standard edition, Le Bon's *Psychologie des foules* is cited from *The Crowd: A Study of the Popular Mind* (New York: Macmillan, 1896 [1895]); in the French edition of Freud's complete works, the translators retranslate from the German edition used by Freud and give the original French in notes. For decades after Le Bon's book appeared, and well after the author's death, this work was one of the best-selling books of all time, admired as much by the anti-Enlightenment thinkers who were hostile to the French Revolution as by dictators, namely Mussolini and Hitler.

39. Le Bon, *The Crowd*, 10, 128–132.

40. On Le Bon's role in the history of psychoanalysis in France, see Roudinesco, *HPF-JL*. Marie Bonaparte greatly admired Le Bon, even comparing him with Freud.

41. William McDougall, *The Group Mind* (London: Ayer, 1973 [1920]). Freud cites the original English edition of this work.

42. Ibid., 136. McDougall is referring to three well-known American writers, militants in the cause of Negro rights: Frederick Douglass (1818–1895), Booker T. Washington (1856–1915), and W. E. B. DuBois (1868–1963).

43. In France, Bataille in particular relied heavily on this thesis when he founded, with René Allendy, Adrien Borel, Paul Schiff, and others, a Society of Collective Psychology. See Roudinesco, *HPF-JL*, 615–647 and 1653–1677. On Lacan's reformulation, see ibid., 1718–1719. It is noteworthy that Elias Canetti, who had also studied the question of the irruption of the irrational in mass phenomena, never cites Freud's work, although he knew it very well. Cf. Elias Canetti, *Crowds and Power*, trans. Carol Stewart (New York: Viking, 1962 [1960]).

44. Michel Plon, "Au-delà et en deça de la suggestion," *Frénésie* 8 (1969): 96.

45. Excerpts from these films as well as an interview with Edward Bernays recorded shortly before his death in 1995 are available on the Internet. Between 1922

and 1931, Freud corresponded several times with this nephew, who managed the rights to Freud's books in the United States. LoC, box 1, folders 1–5.

46. On the history of spiritism or spiritualism at the origin of psychoanalysis, see Ellenberger, *Discovery*. See also Arthur Conan Doyle's quite astonishing book, *The History of Spiritualism*, 2 vols. (New York: George H. Doran, 1926), and Roudinesco and Plon, *Dictionnaire*.

47. Freud to Carrington, July 24, 1921, in Freud, *Letters, 1873–1939*, 334.

48. Wladimir Granoff and Jean-Michel Rey, *L'occulte, objet de la pensée freudienne* (Paris: Presses Universitaires de France, 1983).

49. See Sigmund Freud, "Psycho-analysis and Telepathy" (1941 [1921]), *SE* 18:173–194; "Dreams and Telepathy" (1922), *SE* 18:195–220; "Dreams and Occultism" (1932), in "New Introductory Lectures on Psycho-analysis" (1932), *SE* 22: 31–56.

50. Jones, *Life and Work*, 3:395–396.

51. In *HPF-JL*, I show that this has also been a recurring symptom throughout the history of psychoanalysis.

52. Jacques Derrida, "Telepathy," trans. Nicholas Royle, in *Psyche: Inventions of the Other*, ed. Peggy Kamuf and Elizabeth Rottenberg (Stanford, CA: Stanford University Press, 2007 [1981]), 1:261.

9. Families, Dogs, Objects

1. In a forty-page text addressed to Kurt Robert Eissler dated October 28, 1952, Ernst Waldinger evoked Freud's daily life in Vienna in the period between the two wars. LoC, box 121, folder 33.

2. On the destinies of Freud's nieces and nephews, see later in this chapter.

3. So did Rudolf Halberstadt, Max's brother.

4. See Joseph Wortis, *Fragments of an Analysis with Freud* (New York: Simon and Schuster, 1984 [1954]), 144.

5. Ernstl Halberstadt, the toddler with the spool, was Freud's only grandchild who returned to live in Germany; he was also the only one who became a psychoanalyst. Freud's daughters Anna and Mathilde had no children. Eva Freud (1924–1944) died childless. Five of Freud's grandsons survived him (Anton Walter, Stefan, Lucian, Clemens, Ernstl) and one granddaughter (Sophie). On the fate of Freud's grandchildren, nephews, and nieces, see later in this chapter.

6. On the lives of Freud's children, see Sigmund Freud, *Lettres à ses enfants* (Paris: Aubier, 2012 [2010]); Elisabeth Young-Bruehl, *Anna Freud: A Biography*, 2nd ed. (New Haven, CT: Yale University Press, 2008 [1988]); Günter Gödde, *Mathilde Freud: Die älteste Tochter Sigmund Freuds in Briefen und Selbstzeugnissen* (Berlin: Psychosozial Verlag/Edition Kore, 2002). See also, despite its questionable interpretations, Eva Weissweiler's well-documented *Les Freud: Une famille viennoise* (Paris: Plon, 2006); also Paul Ferris, *Dr. Freud: A Life* (Washington, DC: Counterpoint, 1998); and Hans Lampf, interview with Kurt Eissler, 1953, LoC, box 114, folder 13.

7. Here are Jung's exact words, in an interview in German with Kurt Eissler on August 29, 1953: "Die jüngere Schwester hatte eine grosse Übertragung, und Freud, und Freud was not insensible." And to another of Eissler's questions on the "liaison," he replied, "Och, Bindung? Ich weiss nicht wieviel!? Ja! aber, Gott, man weiss ja, wie die Sachen sind, nicht war!?" Translation: "The youngest sister had a huge transference onto Freud, and he was not insensitive to this." Eissler then asked him to specify whether or not they were in a sexual relationship, and Jung replied: "Oh, a liaison!? I don't know to what point, but, my God, everybody knows how it is, no!?" LoC, box 114, folder 4. In 1957, Jung appears to have made another statement of the same sort to his friend John Billinsky, who made it public in 1969, after Jung's death. But Deirdre Bair asserts that Billinsky attributed to Jung statements that he had not made; see Deirdre Bair, *Jung: A Biography* (Boston: Little, Brown, 2003), 702.

8. Christfried Tögel, "Freud Diarium," http://www.freud-biographik.de/frdbio.htm, last accessed April 10, 2016.

9. Dozens of novels, articles, and essays have been devoted to this "liaison," which doubtless never happened and which has become, in any case, one of the commonplaces of the late twentieth-century anti-Freud movement, especially in the hands of Peter Swales, Franz Maciejewski, and Michel Onfray. The last goes so far as to assert that Freud obliged Minna to abort a child he had fathered in 1923, forgetting that in 1923 she was fifty-eight years old. See Michel Onfray, *Le crépuscule d'une idole: L'affabulation fabuleuse* (Paris: Grasset, 2010). On Freud's private life, see Ronald W. Clark, *Freud, the Man and the Cause: A Biography* (New York: Random House, 1980). On Freud's travels, see Sigmund Freud, *Unser Herz zeigt nach dem Süden: Reisebriefe 1895–1923* (Berlin: Aufbau-Verlag, 2002) (Sigmund Freud, *"Notre coeur tend vers le sud": Correspondance de voyage, 1895–1923,* ed. Christfried Tögel with Michale Molnar, trans. Jean-Claude Capèle, preface by Élisabeth Roudinesco [Paris: Fayard, 2003]). In my preface to that book, I listed all the sources associated with the rumor. See also Weissweiler, *Les Freud,* 124–125: Weissweiler adopts the hypothesis of the "liaison" and the "abortion" while emphasizing that this is indeed an interpretation and not an established fact. For my part, following Peter Gay and John Forrester, I have devoted a lengthy study to this extraordinary rumor in Élisabeth Roudinesco, *Mais pourquoi tant de haine?* (Paris: Seuil, 2010).

10. All these vociferous charges were echoed in numerous essays, novels, and imagined biographies after Freud's death, and especially after the publication of Jones's biography and subsequent scholarly and critical works (from Henri F. Ellenberger to Frank J. Sulloway).

11. This Germanophobic campaign came after a similar one waged against Albert Einstein. See Élisabeth Roudinesco, *Histoire de la psychanalyse en France* followed by *Jacques Lacan: Esquisse d'une vie, histoire d'un système de pensée* (Paris: Pochothèque, 2009), and Charles Blondel, *La psychanalyse* (Paris: Alcan, 1924). In 1910, the German psychiatrist Alfred Hoche (1864–1943), of the eugenicist school, had characterized psychoanalysis as an "epidemic" and its partisans as members of a "sect"; see Alfred

Hoche, "Eine psychische Epidemie unter Ärzten," *Medizinische Klinik* 6, no. 26 (1910): 1007–1010.

12. Roudinesco, *Histoire*, 367.

13. Éliane Kaufholz-Messmer, *Karl Kraus*, Cahiers de l'Herne 28 (Paris: Éditions de l'Herne, 1975); Karl Kraus, *Dicta and Contradicta*, trans. Jonathan McVity (Urbana: University of Illinois Press, 2001); and Fritz Wittels, "La névrose de *Fackel*," *Les premiers psychanalystes*, ed. Herman Nunberg, Ernst Federn, and Nina Schwab-Bakman (Paris: Gallimard, 1978), 2:373–378. During the session of January 1910, Freud had told Wittels he was wrong.

14. Elias Canetti, *The Torch in My Ear*, trans. Joachim Neugroschel (New York: Farrar, Straus and Giroux, 1982), 120.

15. A contraceptive ring or diaphragm.

16. Starting in the late nineteenth century, abortion was viewed as a crime against the individual, the race, and the nation. See Jean-Yves Le Naour and Catherine Valenti, *Histoire de l'avortement, XIXe–XXe siècle* (Paris: Seuil, 2003).

17. Freud to Lippman, February 15, 1920, in Freud, *Lettres à ses enfants*, 569. Freud said nothing about contraception outside marriage, nor about abortion. Let us note that the use of pessaries was already advocated in the early twentieth century in books on sexual hygiene, and in particular by the celebrated Anna Fischer-Dückelmann (1856–1917), a Viennese émigré in Switzerland who published a best seller on this subject. Freud himself announced Sophie's death to his mother, in a letter dated January 26, 1920 (Sigmund Freud, *Letters of Sigmund Freud, 1873–1939*, ed. Ernst L. Freud, trans. Tania Stern and James Stern [London: Hogarth, 1970], 326–327.

18. It was at the end of February 1923 that Freud first detected, on the right side of his jaw, what he called a "leucoplasia" but was in reality an epithelioma; this was confirmed on April 7, 1923. See Max Schur, *Freud: Living and Dying* (New York: International Universities Press, 1972), 347–366.

19. On November 20, 1923, Max married Bertha Katzenstein (1897–1982), with whom he had a daughter, Eva Spangenthal, Ernstl's half sister. See Freud to Max Halberstadt, December 3, 1923, in Freud, *Lettres à ses enfants*, 533–534.

20. Sigmund Freud to Sam Freud, December 31, 1930, cited in Sigmund Freud, *The Diary of Sigmund Freud, 1929–1939: A Record of the Final Decade* (New York: Scribner's, 1992), 55.

21. Anton Walter Freud (1921–2004) and Sophie Freud-Lowenstein (born in 1924). See Sophie Freud, *Living in the Shadow of the Freud Family* (Westport, CT: Praeger, 2007).

22. Lucie to Freud, December 3, 1923, in Freud, *Lettres à ses enfants*, 240.

23. Archives of the British Architectural Library (RIBA), https://www.architecture.com/RIBA/Visitus/Library/TheRIBALibrary.aspx. The project was never pursued.

24. Anna Freud to Sigmund Freud, August 6, 1915, in Sigmund Freud and Anna Freud, *Correspondence, 1904–1938*, ed. Ingeborg Meyer-Palmedo, trans. Nick Somers (Cambridge, UK: Polity, 2014), 113.

25. Freud to Binswanger, January 11, 1929, in Sigmund Freud and Ludwig Binswanger, *The Sigmund Freud-Ludwig Binswanger Correspondence, 1908–1938*, ed. Gerhard Fichtner, trans. Arnold J. Pomerans (New York: Other Press, 2003), 195.

26. Sigmund Freud to Anna Freud, April 12, 1914, in Freud and Freud, *Correspondence*, 80.

27. A psychoanalyst, Jean-Pierre Kamieniak, has imagined that for Freud dogs were substitutes that allowed him to mourn his daughter and his grandson; this is not accurate, even though Freud did insist that the presence of dogs consoled him for these losses, and that the death of a dog reminded him of that of human beings. In reality, Freud associated the indispensable presence of the canine race around him with that of women, but he never looked at the dogs as substitutes for anything whatsoever. See Jean-Pierre Kamieniak, "Citizen Canis, Freud et les chiens," *Le Coq-Héron* 215 (2013): 96–108. Freud's positions on the subject are found in his unpublished exchanges with Marie Bonaparte.

28. Marie Bonaparte, unpublished archives.

29. I showed this in Élisabeth Roudinesco, *Our Dark Side: A History of Perversion*, trans. David Macey (Cambridge, UK: Polity, 2009 [2007]). I do not share the opinion of Élisabeth de Fontenay, who, not having had access to Marie Bonaparte's unpublished archives, imagines wrongly that Freud credited animals with a symbolic capacity almost like that of humans. And she attributes to him the original paternity of a supposed "fourth narcissistic wound," which does not exist in his work.

30. Hilda Doolittle, *Tribute to Freud* (New York: Pantheon, 1956), 147, 166.

31. Zweig to Freud, February 1, 1937, in Sigmund Freud, *Letters of Sigmund Freud and Arnold Zweig*, ed. Ernst L. Freud, trans. Elaine Robson-Scott and William Robson-Scott (New York: Harcourt, Brace and World, 1970), 136.

32. Freud to Arnold Zweig, February 10, 1937, in Freud, *Correspondance, 1906–1939*, ed. Michael Schröter, trans. Olivier Mannoni (Paris: Hachette Littératures, 2009 [2004]), 909.

33. Lou Andreas-Salomé, *The Freud Journal of Lou Andreas-Salomé*, trans. Stanley A. Leavy (New York: Basic Books, 1964), 89.

34. Anna Freud to Sigmund Freud, January 7, 1913, in Freud and Freud, *Correspondence*, 63.

35. Sigmund Freud to Anna Freud, July 16, 1914, in ibid., 82.

36. Freud to Jones, July 22, 1914, in Sigmund Freud, *The Complete Correspondence of Sigmund Freud and Ernest Jones, 1908–1939*, ed. R. Andrew Paskauskas (Cambridge, MA: Belknap Press of Harvard University Press, 1993), 294.

37. Jones to Freud, July 27, 1914, in ibid., 295.

38. Sigmund Freud, "The Psychogenesis of a Case of Homosexuality in a Woman" (1920), *SE* 18:145–172. Margarethe Csonka's life (1900–1999) has given rise to a considerable literature, in particular the account presented by Ines Rieder and Diana Voigt, historians of lesbianism who met Margarethe before her death: *Die Geschichte der Sidonie C* (2000), published in French translation under the very questionable title *Sidonie Csillag, homosexuelle chez Freud, lesbienne dans le siècle* (Paris: EPEL, 2003).

In this work, which is a collection of personal testimonies, Margarethe appears under the pseudonym Sidonie Csillag. In the French translation, her "case" is reinterpreted in the "Lacanian" manner by Jean Allouch. Mikkel Borch-Jacobsen gives a less fanciful interpretation of the story, affirming—mistakenly, nonetheless—that Freud was fooled by Margarethe. See Mikkel Borch-Jacobsen in *Les patients de Freud: Destins* (Auxerre, France: Éditions Sciences humaines, 2011), 180–186. It should be noted that Eissler recorded testimony by Margarethe Csonka von Trautenegg, who confirmed that she had little appreciation for Freud and had not had much to tell him (LoC, box 2).

39. Statement reported by Rieder and Voigt, *Sidonie Csillag,* 66.

40. Ibid., 77.

41. Freud identified three sets of characteristics: (1) physical sexual characteristics; (2) mental sexual characteristics; (3) kind of object choice ("Psychogenesis," *SE* 18:170).

42. Ibid., 171. Eugen Steinach (1861–1944) was an Austrian physician, a pioneer in endocrinology and in the principles of sexual differentiation. He became famous for his invention of a vasoligature, an operation on the vas deferens that he believed would regenerate the hormonal cells and thus promote rejuvenation. Freud underwent this operation in 1923. As cancer was a disease of old age, it was thought that by stimulating the hormonal cells one could postpone a relapse.

43. The unification of Austria and Germany.

44. Her analysis took place between April 1 and July 14, 1921, with a one-hour session each day.

45. Anna Guggenbühl, *Wie benimmt sich der Prof. Freud eigentlich?* (Giessen, Germany: Psychosozial-Verlag, 2009); in French as *Mon analyse avec le professeur Freud,* ed. Anna Koellreuter, trans. Jean-Claude Capèle (Paris: Aubier, 2010).

46. Lou Andreas-Salomé and Anna Freud, *À l'ombre du père: Correspondance, 1919–1937,* trans. Stephane Michaud (Paris: Hachette Littérature, 2006), 43.

47. Sigmund Freud, "A Child Is Being Beaten: A Contribution to the Study of the Origin of Sexual Perversions" (1919), *SE* 17:175–204; Anna Freud, "Beating Fantasies and Daydreams" (1922), in *The Writings of Anna Freud* (New York: International Universities Press, 1966), 1:137–157.

48. The published correspondence between Freud and Andreas-Salomé has been expurgated; it includes no allusions to this analysis.

49. Anna Freud led the *Kinder-seminar,* an informal study group for Freud's younger disciples in Vienna.

50. Peter Heller, *A Child Analysis with Anna Freud,* trans. Salomé Burckhardt and Mary Weigand, rev. by the author (Madison, CT: International Universities Press, 1990), xxxi.

51. Freud to Binswanger, January 11, 1929, in Freud and Binswanger, *Correspondence,* 195. The correspondence between Anna Freud and Dorothy Burlingham is preserved in the Freud Museum in London; it is not yet available to researchers.

52. He owned some three thousand objects, of which two thousand were imported to England. See Richard H. Armstrong, *A Compulsion for Antiquity* (Ithaca, NY: Cornell University Press, 2005).

53. Peter Gay, "Introduction: Freud: For the Marble Tablet," in *Berggasse 19: Sigmund Freud's Home and Offices, Vienna, 1938: The Photographs of Edmund Engelman,* by Edmund Engelman (New York: Basic Books, 1976), 33.

54. Kiddush (sanctification) is the ceremony marking the beginning of the Sabbath. For information about and discussions of these objects, see Yosef Hayim Yerushalmi, in *Freud's Moses: Judaism Terminable and Interminable* (New Haven, CT: Yale University Press, 1991); see also Erica Davies, "Eine Welt wie im Traum, Freuds Antikensammllung," in *"Meine alten und dreckigen Götter," Aus Sigmund Freuds Sammlung,* ed. Lydia Marinelli, exhibition catalog (Frankfurt: Stroemfeld, 1998). On Freud's Mexican objects, see Rubén Gallo, *Freud's Mexico: Into the Wilds of Psychoanalysis* (Cambridge, MA: MIT Press, 2010).

55. Several dozen illustrated books attest to the fantastic organization that reigned over daily life at 19 Berggasse: see Ernst Freud, Lucie Freud, and Ilse Grubrich-Simitis, eds., *Sigmund Freud: His Life in Pictures and Words,* with a biographical sketch by Kurt R. Eissler, trans. Christine Trollope (New York: Harcourt Brace Jovanovich, 1978 [1976]); and Freud, *Diary.*

56. William Bayard Hale, *The Story of a Style* (New York: B. W. Huebsch, 1920).

57. A disorder of a mucous membrane characterized by white plaques.

58. Several books have been devoted to Freud's cancer. See in particular Schur, *Freud.* Jones and Gay have provided versions entirely in keeping with reality.

59. See Schur, *Freud,* 361. It was a warty carcinoma, which was described for the first time in 1948 by the American doctor Lauren V. Ackerman (1905–1993). In 1923, people talked about a "slow-moving cancer of the upper maxillary."

60. A few years later, in London, Jones told Freud about this discussion. Furious, Freud let his anger spill over: "Mit welchem Recht" ("With what right") had they decided to hide the truth from him? Freud could not bear being subjected to a "regime of protection." See Phyllis Grosskurth, *The Secret Ring: Freud's Inner Circle and the Politics of Psychoanalysis* (Reading, MA: Addison-Wesley, 1991), 131–132.

61. Postcard to the family, September 16, 1923, in Freud, *Unser Herz,* 384 (*"Notre coeur,"* 338).

62. See Sharon Romm and Edward Luce, "Hans Pichler: Oral Surgeon to Sigmund Freud," *Oral Surgery, Oral Medicine and Oral Pathology* 57, no. 1 (January 1984): 31–32; and Xavier Riaud, *Pionniers de la chirurgie maxillo-faciale (1914–1918)* (Paris: L'Harmattan, 2010). Certain commentators have asserted that Freud's maxillofacial cancer—described by several historians of medicine and attested by the archives—was not serious or was imaginary, that the main cause of its aggravation could be attributed to Hajek's failed operation, to radiation treatment, and to the inappropriate treatments administered by Schur, and that cocaine use was responsible for the appearance of the first lesion. See Jacques Bénesteau, *Mensonges freudiens* (Hayen,

Belgium: Mardaga, 2002), 162–163. In this book, based entirely on rumors, the names of Pichler and Kazanjian do not appear. In addition, the author confuses "papillomatosis" and "carcinoma," and he implies that Freud's cancer was invented by his idolaters in order to present him as a martyr. The alleged nonexistence of Freud's cancer is, like the hypothetical liaison with Minna, one of the favorite themes of the revisionist school.

63. André Bolzinger, *Portrait de Sigmund Freud: Trésors d'une correspondance* (Paris: Campagne Première, 2012), 71–72. All these citations have been drawn from Freud's correspondence and translated by the author.

64. Peter Gay, *Freud: A Life for Our Time* (New York: W. W. Norton, 1988), 442–443.

10. The Art of the Couch

1. At the end of the volume the reader will find a nonexhaustive list of Freud's patients established by Richard G. Klein and Ernst Falzeder, to which I have added some names. See also Ulrike May, "Neunzehn Patienten in Analyse bei Freud (1910–1920)—Teil I: Zur Dauer von Freuds Analysen; Teil II: Zur Frequenz von Freuds Analysen," *Psyche, Zeitschrift für Psychoanalyse und ihre Anwendungen* 6–7 (June–July 2007): 590–625. David J. Lynn and George E. Vaillant have analyzed and evaluated forty-three of Freud's cases, in "Anonymity, Neutrality and Confidentiality in the Actual Methods of Sigmund Freud: A Review of 43 Cases, 1907–1939," *American Journal of Psychiatry* 155, no. 2 (February 1998): 163–171. Mikkel Borch-Jacobsen has provided very interesting portraits of thirty-one patients, although he is overly critical of Freud. See also the already dated work by Paul Roazen, *Freud and His Followers* (New York: New American Library, 1971); Manfred Pohlen, *En analyse avec Freud* (Paris: Taillandier, 2010 [2006]); Élisabeth Roudinesco and Michel Plon, *Dictionnaire de la psychanalyse* (Paris: Fayard, 2006). Some of the archives on patients in the Library of Congress are accessible but not yet declassified.

2. I address this question in Élisabeth Roudinesco, *Histoire de la psychanalyse en France* followed by *Jacques Lacan: Esquisse d'une vie, histoire d'un système de pensée* (Paris: Pochothèque, 2009), as well as in the *Dictionnaire*, where a bibliography on the issue can be found.

3. It is in fact because psychoanalysts have not wanted to confront these treatments that were not recounted by Freud himself that they have never been able to produce an authentic evaluation of his practice. All tendencies taken together (Kleinian, Lacanian, post-Lacanian, Ferenczian, and so on), they have been content to comment, as on a canonized corpus, on the story of Anna O. and the "cases" related in *Studies on Hysteria*, along with the famous *Five Psychoanalyses*, of which only three can be counted as treatments. Thus they have left the field open to the anti-Freudians, who have taken advantage of this to transform Freud into a charlatan incapable of curing any patient whatsoever. The reality, as we have seen, is much more complex.

4. Among them were Ernst Blum, Marie Bonaparte, Maryse Choisy, Jakob Julius David, Viktor von Dirsztay, Hilda Doolittle, Henri Flournoy, Horace Westlake Frink, Bruno Goetz, Abram Kardiner, Carl Liebman, Gustav Mahler, Raymond de Saussure, James and Alix Strachey, Bruno Walter, Margaret Wittgenstein, and Joseph Wortis.

5. This notebook can be consulted in the Library of Congress.

6. Henri Roudier, a mathematician, assessed Freud's fortune for me at different stages of his life—in florins and in crowns before the First World War, in shillings and dollars starting in 1924 (Henri Roudier, "Freud et l'argent," unpublished). We should note that all the "conversions" that have been proposed for evaluating the price of Freud's sessions and converting them to twenty-first-century euros or dollars have no scientific foundation, and moreover the authors of these exercises contradict one another: 450 euros for some, 1,000 or even 1,300 for others. Such conversions can in no case be taken seriously; they are clearly intended to imply that Freud was a swindler or rapacious. One can only evaluate his fortune by comparing it to the fortunes of contemporaries who came from the same social class and practiced the same profession. Of course, Freud had become rich in relation to the relative poverty in which his father had lived at the same age. See Christfried Tögel, "Sigmund Freud's Practice: Visits and Consultation, Psychoanalyses, Remuneration," *Psychoanalytic Quarterly* 78, no. 4 (2009): 1033–1058.

7. Freud to Andreas-Salomé, October 20, 1921, in Sigmund Freud and Lou Andreas-Salomé, *Letters*, ed. Ernst Pfeiffer, trans. William Robson-Scott and Elaine Robson-Scott (New York: Harcourt Brace Jovanovich, 1972), 109. Freud was alluding to the fact that part of Andreas-Salomé's family had been ruined by the Bolshevik revolution.

8. In New York at the same time, the price per session was fifty dollars. Here is a note from the economist Thomas Piketty about Freud's revenues: "Freud was a well-to-do doctor, and there was nothing scandalous about this, considering the very high level of inequality that characterized the era. The average income at the time was 1,200 to 1,300 gold francs per year and per inhabitant. In France, in the period 1900–1910, as in Vienna too, no doubt, the average income was about 1,200–1,300 gold francs per year and per adult inhabitant. Today, the average income (before taxes) is about 25,000 euros per year and per adult inhabitant. To compare the amounts, the best method is thus to multiply the amounts in gold francs in 1900–1910 by a coefficient of about 20. I have not found the exchange rate for the florin, but it seems to me that it was exactly 1 florin=1 gold franc; or else 1 florin=2 gold francs? Sorry, I no longer have it. If my notes are accurate, Tögel credits Freud with an income of about 25,000 florins, which would correspond to an annual income of 500,000 euros today. This is a very high income, to be sure, but fairly representative of the top 1% at the time. Assuming constant inequality, this would correspond rather to around 250,000 euros in annual income today" (personal communication, July 10, 2014).

9. Freud to Ferenczi, August 27, 1925, in Sigmund Freud and Sándor Ferenczi, *Correspondence of Sigmund Freud and Sándor Ferenczi*, ed. Eva Brabant, Ernst Falzeder, and Patrizia Giampieri-Deutsch, trans. Peter T. Hoffer, introduction by André Haynal (Cambridge, MA: Belknap Press of Harvard University Press, 1993), 3:227.

10. Smiley Blanton, *Diary of My Analysis with Sigmund Freud* (New York: Hawthorn Books, 1971), 78. I do not share Patrick Mahony's opinion; he has interpreted Freud's anti-Americanism in the Kleinian manner by hypothesizing that Freud was using it defensively to protect the idealized image of his mother, and that for him America represented an "archaic mother" whose demoniacal power he had repressed. See Louise Grenier, *Penser Freud avec Patrick Mahony* (Quebec: Liber, 2004), 39.

11. Sigmund Freud, letter to Rado, September 30, 1925, LoC, Manuscript Division, Sigmund Freud collection.

12. Sigmund Freud to Istvan Hollos, October 4, 1928, in Istvan Hollos, *Mes adieux à la Maison jaune* (Paris: Éditions du Coq-Héron, 1986).

13. As an example, we can take the Viennese architect Karl Mayreder (1856–1935), who was treated by Freud for ten weeks in 1915 for chronic melancholia; Mayreder consulted a record number of doctors (fifty-nine) whose prescriptions and other therapies were totally ineffective. But Freud alone was subsequently accused of failing to cure him. This thesis of Freud's sole responsibility is taken up again by Mikkel Borch-Jacobsen in *Les Patients de Freud: Destins* (Auxerre, France: Éditions Sciences humaines, 2011). See also Frank Cioffi, *Freud and the Question of Pseudoscience* (Chicago: Open Court, 1999), and Bénesteau, *Mensonges*.

14. Edoardo Weiss interviewed by Kurt Eissler, December 13, 1953, LoC, box 121, folder 34, with various commentaries and reminiscences. See also Anna Maria Accerboni, "Sigmund Freud as Remembered by Edoardo Weiss, the Italian Pioneer of Psychoanalysis," *International Review of Psycho-analysis* 17, no. 3 (1990): 351–359.

15. Giorgio Voghera, *Gli anni della psicoanalisi* (Pordenone, Italy: Edizioni Studio Tesi, 1980).

16. See Maurizio Serra, *Italo Svevo ou l'Antivie* (Paris: Grasset, 2013), 258–259; Italo Svevo, *Zeno's Conscience*, trans. William Weaver (New York: Alfred A. Knopf, 2001).

17. The company business entailed painting ships' hulls.

18. Ettore Scola to Livia, June 6, 1920, cited in Serra, *Italo Svevo*, 131.

19. Serra, *Italo Svevo*, 261.

20. Freud to Abraham, October 31, 1914, and Abraham to Freud, October 28, 1914, in Sigmund Freud and Karl Abraham, *The Complete Correspondence of Sigmund Freud and Karl Abraham, 1907–1925*, ed. Ernst Falzeder, trans. Caroline Schwarzacher et al. (London: Karnac, 2002 [1965]), 282–284.

21. Quoted in Anna Maria Accerboni Pavanello, "La sfida di Svevo alla psicoanalisi," in *Guarire dalla cura: Italo Svevo e i medici* (Trieste: Museo Sveviano, 2008), 110–112. See also Serra, *Italo Svevo*, 249.

22. Serra, *Italo Svevo*, 264.

23. Svevo, *Zeno's Conscience*, 436–437.

24. Mario Lavagetto, *L'impiegato Schmitz e altri saggi su Svevo* (Turin, Italy: Einaudi, 1975); also mentioned by Serra.

25. Accerboni Pavanello, "Sfida."

26. On the relations between Freud and Oskar Pfister, see chapter 12.

27. Among Freud's 170 patients, there were about 20 Americans, almost all from New York. Monroe Meyer (1892–1939), a melancholic psychiatrist, committed suicide with an ice pick at age forty-seven. Freud was accused later by the anti-Freudians of having caused this intentional death, which occurred eighteen years after Meyer's stint in Vienna. Leonard Blumgart (1881–1959) remained faithful to Freudian orthodoxy.

28. Clarence Oberndorf (1882–1954) was an orthodox Freudian, hostile to lay analysis. He wrote the first official book on the history of psychoanalysis in the United States.

29. As he confided to Jones; see Peter Gay, *Freud: A Life for Our Time* (New York: W. W. Norton, 1988), 564.

30. Testimony of Clarence Oberndorf, December 12, 1952, LoC, box 115, folder 6.

31. Abram Kardiner, *My Analysis with Freud: Reminiscences* (New York: Norton, 1977), 97, 58.

32. Ibid., 53.

33. Ibid., 69.

34. Ibid., 67. Freud had received the photos in October 1921, just as Kardiner was beginning his analysis.

35. Ibid., 68.

36. Horace W. Frink, *Morbid Fears and Compulsions* (Boston: Moffat, Yard, 1918).

37. Thaddeus Ames (1885–1963) had met Freud in Vienna between 1911 and 1912.

38. Freud to Jones, July 27, 1921, in Sigmund Freud, *The Complete Correspondence of Sigmund Freud and Ernest Jones, 1908–1939*, ed. R. Andrew Paskauskas (Cambridge, MA: Belknap Press of Harvard University Press, 1983), 424. Frink's first treatment lasted five months, between March and July 1921; the analysis resumed between April and July 1922. Between November and December, he went through a third series of sessions. See Roazen, *Freud and His Followers*; L. Edmunds, "Freud's American Tragedy," *Johns Hopkins Magazine* 30 (1988): 40–49. See also Grenier, *Penser Freud*, 40–45; Borch-Jacobsen, *Patients de Freud*, 198–212. Frink's analysis has been ignored by the psychoanalytic community and by several of Freud's biographers, with the exception of Gay, who relates it correctly in *Freud: A Life* (565), emphasizing Freud's anti-Americanism. The affair is discussed in the Freud-Jones correspondence, and in Roudinesco and Plon, *Dictionnaire*.

39. Freud to Jones, November 6, 1921, in Freud, *Complete Correspondence of Freud and Jones*, 443. Abraham Bijur died in May 1922; his open letter had not been published.

40. Freud to Horace Frink, November 17, 1921, LoC, Manuscript Division, Sigmund Freud collection. Cited in part in Grenier, *Penser Freud*, 43.

41. Freud to Jones, September 25, 1924, in Freud, *Complete Correspondence of Freud and Jones,* 552.

42. Medical Archives of Johns Hopkins Medical Institution, the Frink Family Collection. And see Michael Specter, "Sigmund Freud Urged His Disciple to Divorce: Wanted Him to Marry Another Woman, Daughter Finds," *Los Angeles Times,* November 12, 1987.

43. Jones to Freud, September 29, 1924, in Freud, *Complete Correspondence of Freud and Jones,* 554.

44. Jeannine Hayat, "Lytton Strachey: L'historien intime de deux reines," *LISA* e-journal, January 2007. See Lytton Strachey, *Eminent Victorians: Cardinal Manning, Dr. Arnold, Florence Nightingale, General Gordon* (New York: Modern Library, 1933 [1918]); *Queen Victoria* (New York: Blue Ribbon Books, 1931 [1928]); *Elizabeth and Essex: A Tragic History* (New York: Harcourt, Brace, 1928). See also Florian Reviron, "De Lytton Strachey à Virginia Woolf," in *La biographie littéraire en Angleterre, XVII–XIXe: Configuration, reconfiguration du soi artistique* (Saint-Étienne, France: Publications de l'Université de Saint-Étienne, 1999), 117–139.

45. John Maynard Keynes, *The Economic Consequences of the Peace* (New York: Harcourt, Brace and Howe, 1920 [1919]); Jacques Bainville, *Les conséquences politiques de la paix* (Paris: Gallimard, 2002). Bainville was one of Keynes's most virulent critics. See Gilles Dostaler and Bernard Maris, *Capitalisme et pulsion de mort* (Paris: Albin Michel, 2009). These two authors compare Keynes's critique of the self-destructive capacity of capitalism to Freud's theorization of the death drive.

46. See the excellent book by Perry Meisel and Walter Kendrick, eds., *Bloomsbury/Freud: The Letters of James and Alix Strachey, 1924–1925* (New York: Basic Books, 1985).

47. Ibid., 29–30.

48. Kardiner, *My Analysis,* 78.

49. John Rickman, testimony of British psychiatrist Lionel S. Penrose, July 28, 1953, LoC, box 117. On Rickman's story (he was later analyzed by Ferenczi and Klein), see Roudineso and Plon, *Dictionnaire.*

50. Meisel and Kendrick, *Bloomsbury/Freud,* x.

51. James Strachey, "Bibliography: List of English Translations of Freud's Works," *International Journal of Psychoanalysis* 26, nos. 1–2 (1945): 67–76; James Strachey, "Editor's Note" (1962), *SE* 3:71–73; James Strachey, "General Preface" (1966), *SE* 1:xiii–xxii; Alan Tyson, "A Chronological Hand-List of Freud's Works," *International Journal of Psychoanalysis* 37, no. 1 (1956): 19–33; Bruno Bettelheim, *Freud and Man's Soul* (New York: Alfred A. Knopf, 1982).

52. In the words of Meisel and Kendrick, *Bloomsbury/Freud,* 3.

53. Melanie Klein, *The Psycho-analysis of Children,* trans. Alix Strachey (London: Hogarth, 1937 [1932]). Klein had three children: Hans, Erich (later Eric Cline), and Melitta, who later became her worst enemy.

54. On Klein's trajectory, which will be discussed in Chapter 11, see Phyllis Grosskurth, *Melanie Klein: Her World and Her Work* (New York: Knopf, 1986).

55. Klein settled definitively in London in September 1926.

56. See Ronald W. Clark, *Freud, the Man and the Cause: A Biography* (New York: Random House, 1980).

57. Patrick Lacoste, *L'étrange cas du professeur M* (Paris: Gallimard, 1990), 93–94.

58. Ernest Jones, *The Life and Work of Sigmund Freud* (New York: Basic Books, 1953–1957), 3:116.

59. Especially when John Huston wanted to make a film about Freud's life on the basis of a scenario by Jean-Paul Sartre. See Élisabeth Roudinesco, *Philosophy in Turbulent Times: Canguilhem, Sartre, Foucault, Althusser, Deleuze, Derrida*, trans. William McCuaig (New York: Columbia University Press, 2008 [2005]).

60. Francis Bacon (1561–1626), a philosopher and a man of science who served as lord chancellor.

61. Peter Gay, "Freud and the Man from Stratford," in *Reading Freud: Explorations and Entertainments* (New Haven, CT: Yale University Press, 1990), 17.

62. J. Thomas Looney, *"Shakespeare" Identified in Edward de Vere, the Seventeenth Earl of Oxford, and the Poems of Edward de Vere*, 2 vols. (Port Washington, NY: Kennikat Press for Minos, 1975 [1920]). Looney's thesis was taken up again in 2002 by Roland Emmerich in his film *Anonymus*.

63. Among the eighty-two alternative candidates for the paternity of Shakespeare's work, we find Christopher Marlow, Cervantes, John Donne, Robert Devereux (Essex), and Daniel Defoe. Two of Looney's disciples also imagined that Queen Elizabeth had had a child with de Vere.

64. Edward de Vere (1550–1604), seventeenth Count of Oxford, great chamberlain, peer, and courtesan of the Elizabethan period, had married Anne Cecil, Countess of Oxford (1556–1588), daughter of William Cecil (1520–1589), a state councillor to Elizabeth, and his wife, Mildred Cooke (1526–1589). He fell into disgrace and was sent to the Tower of London for seducing Anne Vavasour (1560–1650), maid of honor of Queen Elizabeth (1558–1603). Henry Wriothesley (1573–1624), third Count of Southampton, a friend of the second Count of Essex (1565–1601), was the alleged intended recipient of Shakespeare's sonnets and the poet's presumed lover. Many authors have attempted to prove that Shakespeare was homosexual. On the absurdity of the attribution of the authorship of Shakespeare's works to de Vere, see Alan H. Nelson, *Monstrous Adversary* (Liverpool: Liverpool University Press, 2003).

65. Freud to Lytton Strachey, December 25, 1928, in Meisel and Kendrick, *Bloomsbury/Freud*, 334. [TN: The editors point out in a footnote that "Freud's handwriting deteriorates markedly in the latter half of the letter."]

66. Many books have been written about the resemblance between Freud and the detective invented by Sir Arthur Conan Doyle, who was himself fascinated by spiritism.

67. The historian Carlo Ginzburg designated this phenomenon as the emergence, in the rational approach to signs, of a troubling and disturbing element that always

escaped science; see Carlo Ginzburg, *Clues, Myths, and the Historical Method*, trans. John Tedeschi and Anne C. Tedeschi (Baltimore: Johns Hopkins University Press, 1989).

11. Among Women

1. Otto Rank, *The Trauma of Birth* (London: Kegan Paul, Trench, Trubner, 1929 [1924]).

2. Freud to Ferenczi, March 26, 1924, in Sigmund Freud and Sándor Ferenczi, *Correspondence of Sigmund Freud and Sándor Ferenczi*, ed. Eva Brabant, Ernst Falzeder, and Patrizia Giampieri-Deutsch, trans. Peter T. Hoffer, introduction by André Haynal (Cambridge, MA: Belknap Press of Harvard University Press, 1993), 3:135.

3. Ninth IPV Congress, September 2–5, 1925.

4. Beata Rank (1896–1967), known as Tola, also became a psychoanalyst.

5. Rank, *Trauma;* Sándor Ferenczi, *Thalassa: A Theory of Genitality* (New York: W. W. Norton, 1968 [1963]).

6. Freud to Ferenczi, April 23, 1926, in Freud and Ferenczi, *Correspondence,* 3:257. And see Freud's letter to Otto Rank, August 4, 1922, in Sigmund Freud and Otto Rank, *The Letters of Sigmund Freud and Otto Rank,* ed. James Lieberman and Robert Kramer, trans. Gregory C. Richter (Baltimore: Johns Hopkins University Press, 2012), 134–136.

7. Sigmund Freud, "Inhibitions, Symptoms and Anxiety" (1926), *SE* 20:75–176.

8. Sándor Ferenczi, "Confusion of Tongues Between Adults and the Child" (1932), in *Final Contributions to the Problems and Methods of Psychoanalysis,* ed. Michael Balint, trans. Eric Mosbacher et al. (New York: Brunner/Mazel, 1955, repr. 1980), 156–167.

9. On Rank's stay in Paris, and on his relations with Anaïs Nin, see Élisabeth Roudinesco, *Histoire de la psychanalyse en France* followed by *Jacques Lacan: Esquisse d'une vie, histoire d'un système de pensée* (Paris: Pochothèque, 2009; hereafter *HPF-JL*), 451–454; and James Lieberman, *Acts of Will: The Life and Work of Otto Rank* (New York: Free Press, 1985). Rank ended up settling permanently in the United States.

10. Sándor Ferenczi, "The Little Rooster Man" (1913), in J. Borossa, ed., *Sándor Ferenczi: Selected Writings* (Harmondsworth, UK: Penguin, 1999), 84–91.

11. Anna Freud, *The Psycho-analytical Treatment of Children: Technical Lectures and Essays* (London: Imago, 1946).

12. Sigmund Freud, "Letters from Sigmund Freud to Joan Riviere (1921–1939)," ed. Athol Hughes, *International Review of Psycho-analysis* 19 (1992): 278.

13. Grete Lainer [Hermine von Hug-Hellmuth], *A Young Girl's Diary,* trans. Eden Paul and Cedar Paul (New York: Thomas Selzer, 1921), 7. This book was published as an authentic work by Grete Lainer with a preface by Freud; in French, see Hermine von Hug-Hellmuth, *Essais psychanalytiques: Destin et écrits d'une pionnière de la psychanalyse des enfants,* ed. and trans. Dominique Soubrenie, preface by Jacques Le Rider, postface by Yvette Tourne (Paris: Payot, 1991). When I wrote a review of the

book in 1991 for *Libération*, revealing the fraud, I received letters from psychoanalysts who accused me of "conspiring" against Freud. They still believed that the murder and the falsification were lies invented by the anti-Freudians.

14. Like many female psychoanalysts of that generation, with the exception of Karen Horney. See Élisabeth Roudinesco, "Les premières femmes psychanalystes," *Mil neuf cent: Revue d'histoire intellectuelle* 16 (1998): 27–41; repr. in *Topique* 71 (2000): 45–56.

15. Phyllis Grosskurth offers a good description of Klein's childhood and her relations with her parents, relying on Klein's unpublished "autobiography" and on the archives preserved in the Melanie Klein trust. I had the opportunity to speak with Grosskurth during one of her trips to Paris.

16. See Sigmund Freud, "On the Universal Tendency to Debasement in the Sphere of Love" (1912), *Contributions to the Psychology of Love* II, *SE* 11:177–190, and Sigmund Freud, "Femininity" (1933 [1932]), *SE* 22:112–135.

17. During a meeting with Goethe at Erfurt on October 2, 1808, the emperor evoked the tragedies of destiny of which he disapproved and which, according to him, belonged to a darker period than their own: "What does destiny matter to us today?" he had said. "Destiny is politics." I commented on this statement in Élisabeth Roudinesco, *La famille en désordre* (Paris: Fayard, 2002), in the chapter titled "Les femmes ont un sexe."

18. Freud, "Femininity," *SE* 22:124.

19. The texts of the historic debate between Vienna and London have been collected by Marie-Christine Hamon and published in French translation as *Féminité mascarade* (Paris: Seuil, 1994). See also Sigmund Freud, "Some Psychical Consequences of the Anatomical Distinction between the Sexes" (1925), *SE* 19:241–258, and Helene Deutsch, *The Psychology of Women: A Psychoanalytical Interpretation by Helene Deutsch,* 2 vols. (New York: Grune and Stratton, 1944–1945). The title of the 1994 book comes from a famous text by Joan Riviere, "Womanliness as a Masquerade," *International Journal of Psychoanalysis* 10 (1929): 303–313, in which Riviere shows that intellectual women who have fully succeeded in their social integration and in their married lives are condemned to display their femininity as a mask the better to conceal their anxiety.

20. Virginia Woolf, *Three Guineas* (London: Hogarth, 1938).

21. Freud to Jones, October 9, 1927, in Sigmund Freud, *The Complete Correspondence of Sigmund Freud and Ernest Jones, 1908–1939,* ed. R. Andrew Paskauskas (Cambridge, MA: Belknap Press of Harvard University Press, 1983), 633.

22. Numerous books have been devoted to the history of child psychoanalysis after 1945, especially in the English school, as represented by D. W. Winnicott and John Bowlby. See Élisabeth Roudinesco and Michel Plon, *Dictionnaire de la psychanalyse* (Paris: Fayard, 2006); and, for France, Roudinesco, *HPF-JL.*

23. Freud, "Femininity," *SE* 22:132.

24. Sigmund Freud, "The Theme of the Three Caskets" (1913), *SE* 12:301.

25. Freud, "Universal Tendency," *SE* 11:185.

26. Ibid., 183.

27. Freud, "Femininity," *SE* 22:133–134.

28. Nicole Loraux, *The Experiences of Tiresias: The Feminine and the Greek Man*, trans. Paula Wissing (Princeton, NJ: Princeton University Press, 1995).

29. Sigmund Freud, "The Question of Lay Analysis" (1926), *SE* 20:212.

30. Henry M. Stanley, *Through the Dark Continent*, 2 vols. (New York: Dover, 1988 [1878]). Also see Michel Lurdos, "Au coeur du continent noir: Henry Morton Stanley," in *Regards sur les littératures coloniales*, ed. Jean Sévry (Paris: L'Harmattan, 1999), 3:97–108.

31. See Georges Duby and Michelle Perrot, *Histoire des femmes*, vol. 4, *Le XIXe siècle* (Paris: Plon, 1991).

32. On later debates about female sexuality, and especially on the respective positions of Simone de Beauvoir, Jacques Lacan, and their successors, see Roudinesco, *HPF-JL;* Roudinesco and Plon, *Dictionnaire;* and Élisabeth Roudinesco, "Soudain, *Le Deuxième Sexe* . . . ," *Les temps modernes*, nos. 647–648 (January–March 2008): 192–213. Numerous works have been devoted to this question, especially regarding the distinction between sex and gender, as much within the psychoanalytic movement as elsewhere. See also Lisa Appignanesi and John Forrester, *Freud's Women* (New York: Basic Books, 1992).

33. See Célia Bertin, *La femme à Vienne au temps de Freud* (Paris: Stock/Laurence Pernoud, 1989), and Ursula Prokop, *Margaret Stonborough-Wittgenstein: Intellectuelle, mécène et bâtisseuse* (Paris: Noir sur Blanc, 2010 [2005]). Freud was close to Margaret, but he had no contact either with the Vienna Circle, founded by Moritz Shlick, or with Ludwig Wittgenstein, Margaret's brother, a friend of Karl Kraus, who criticized Freud's theory of dreams. See Ludwig Wittgenstein, "Conversations on Freud," in *Lectures and Conversations on Aesthetics, Psychology and Religious Beliefs*, compiled from notes taken by Yorick Smythies, Rush Rhees, and James Taylor, ed. Cyril Barrett (Berkeley: University of California Press, 2007), 41–52.

34. See Roudinesco and Plon, *Dictionnaire*.

35. Lou Andreas-Salomé, *Looking Back: Memoirs*, ed. Ernst Pfeiffer, trans. Breon Mitchell (New York: Paragon House, 1991 [1901]), 85.

36. Jacques Le Rider, *Modernity and Crises of Identity: Culture and Society in Fin-de-Siècle Vienna*, trans. Rosemary Morris (New York: Continuum, 1993 [1944]), and Lou Andreas-Salomé, *L'amour du narcissisme*, trans. Isabelle Hildenbrand (Paris: Gallimard, 1980 [1977]).

37. Heinz Frederick Peters, *My Sister, My Spouse: A Biography of Lou Andreas-Salomé* (New York: Norton, 1962), 255.

38. Freud to Andreas-Salomé, November 10, 1912, in Sigmund Freud and Lou Andreas-Salomé, *Letters*, ed. Ernst Pfeiffer, trans. William Robson-Scott and Elaine Robson-Scott (New York: Harcourt Brace Jovanovich, 1972), 11.

39. Quoted in Peters, *My Sister*, 282.

40. The main character in Tolstoy's *War and Peace*.

41. Freud to Andreas-Salomé, February 17, 1918, in Freud and Andreas-Salomé, *Letters*, 75.

42. Lou Andreas-Salomé, *My Thanks to Freud (Mein Dank an Freud): Open Letter to Professor Sigmund Freud for His 75th Birthday* (1931), trans. William Needham, https://ia601009.us.archive.org/6/items/MeinDank/Mein%20Dank.pdf. In French as *Lettre ouverte à Freud,* trans. Dominique Miermont (Paris: Seuil, 1994).

43. Marie Bonaparte, "Cahier biographique en huit cahiers" (October 1951), unpublished. See also Célia Bertin, *Marie Bonaparte: A Life* (New York: Harcourt Brace Jovanovich, 1982). The first edition of this book was titled *La dernière Bonaparte* (The last Bonaparte). On Marie Bonaparte's career and her role in the history of psychoanalysis in France, see Roudinesco, *HPF-JL,* and Roudinesco and Plon, *Dictionnaire.*

44. Marie Bonaparte, *Sommaire de mon analyse et de ma correspondance avec Freud, avec Agenda (Cahiers noirs),* December 14, 1925, unpublished. Marie Bonaparte's archives, deposited in the Library of Congress, cannot be consulted until 2020. Thanks to Célia Bertin, I possess a copy. In addition to the *Sommaire,* the archives include 126 letters (1926–1938), 15 of which were published by Ernest Jones and Max Schur, and a long interview on various subjects. See also Marie Bonaparte, *Cinq cahiers écrits par une petite fille entre sept ans et demi et dix ans avec leurs commentaires* (1939–1951), 4 vols., privately printed for the author; Marie Bonaparte, "Extraits du Cahier 1," *L'Infini* 2 (Spring 1983): 76–89. In the same issue, see Élisabeth Roudinesco, "Histoire de la psychanalyse en France," conversation with Philippe Sollers, 62–75. An exchange of letters between Marie Bonaparte and Anne Berman can be consulted at the Bibliothèque Nationale de France; it deals primarily with the situation of psychoanalysis in France.

45. René Laforgue (1894–1962), a psychiatrist and a psychoanalyst, the founder of the French psychoanalytic movement and of the Société psychanalytique de Paris (SPP, 1926) alongside Édouard Pichon, Eugénie Sokolnicka, Bonaparte, Rudolph Loewenstein, and Raymond de Saussure. See Roudinesco, *HPF-JL,* especially the chapter titled "Histoire des douze."

46. A. E. Narjani [Marie Bonaparte], "Considérations sur les causes anatomiques de la frigidité chez la femme," *Bruxelles médical* (1924): 768–778.

47. Especially with Professor Halban. This procedure, which is actually nothing but an excision, is called the "Halban-Narjani" operation.

48. Marie Bonaparte, *Female Sexuality* (New York: International Universities Press, 1953).

12. Between Fetish Medicine and Religion

1. See Henri F. Ellenberger, *Discovery of the Unconscious: The History and Evolution of Dynamic Psychiatry* (New York: Basic Books, 1970), especially the very fine passages devoted to the history of dynamic psychiatry from Mesmer to Freud.

2. See Georges Bataille, *The Accursed Share: An Essay on General Economy,* trans. Robert Hurley, 3 vols. (New York: Zone Books, 1988–1993). I address this issue in Élisabeth Roudinesco, *Le patient, le thérapeute et l'État* (Paris: Fayard, 2004).

3. Let us recall that, in Sophocles's tragedy, after his crime Oedipus went from the status of sage and tyrant to that of stain and scapegoat.

4. *Laienanalyse,* conventionally rendered in English by the cognate term "lay analysis," has to be translated into French as *analyse profane,* or "secular analysis." While in German, *laien* means at once "lay," "amateur," and "secular" as opposed to "sacred," in French, the term *laïc* refers to the republican ideal of *laïcité,* "secularity," which does not apply to the struggle waged during this period in favor of allowing psychoanalysis to be practiced by analysts who did not have medical degrees.

5. Let us recall that Stekel committed suicide in London in 1940.

6. Peter Gay gives a good account of the Wagner-Jauregg affair, in *Freud: A Life for Our Time* (New York: W. W. Norton, 1988). See also Harald Leupold-Löwenthal, "Le procès de Theodor Reik," *Revue internationale d'histoire de la psychanalyse* 3 (1990): 57–69, and Susann Heenen-Wolff, "La discussion sur l' 'analyse profane' dans l'*Internationale Zeitschrift für Psychoanalyse* de l'année 1927," *Revue internationale d'histoire de la psychanalsye* 3 (1990): 71–88; see also the discussions of lay analysis in the *International Journal of Psychoanalysis,* 1927. For the French debate, see Élisabeth Roudinesco, *Histoire de la psychanalyse en France* followed by *Jacques Lacan: Esquisse d'une vie, histoire d'un système de pensée* (Paris: Pochothèque, 2009; hereafter *HPF-JL*).

7. See Richard Sterba, *Reminiscences of a Viennese Psychoanalyst* (Detroit: Wayne State University Press, 1982), 82–83, and Theodor Reik, *Surprise and the Psychoanalyst: On the Conjecture and Comprehension of Unconscious Processes,* trans. Margaret M. Green (London: K. Paul, Trench, Trübner, 1936 [1935]). I am borrowing certain elements from my preface to the French re-edition of Reik's book.

8. Jacques Palaci, "Remembering Reik," preface [in French] to *Le psychologue surpris,* by Theodor Reik, trans. Denise Berger (Paris: Denoël, 1976), 30.

9. See Pascal Hachet, *Les psychanalystes et Goethe* (Paris: L'Harmattan, 1995). Kurt Robert Eissler produced the most masterful study of Goethe, devoting two thousand pages to the elucidation of a ten-year period in the life of the poet, a span of time recognized as inaugurating a new period of creativity: *Goethe: A Psychoanalytic Interpretation of a Decade in His Life (1776–1786),* 2 vols. (Detroit: Wayne State University Press, 1963).

10. Tandler emigrated in 1938 and joined Max Eitingon.

11. Freud to Tandler, March 8, 1925, in Sigmund Freud, *Letters of Sigmund Freud, 1873–1939,* ed. Ernst L. Freud, trans. Tania Stern and James Stern (London: Hogarth, 1970), 359–360.

12. Sigmund Freud, "The Question of Lay Analysis" (1926), *SE* 20. The French translation, *La question de l'analyse profane,* has an excellent preface by Jean-Bertrand Pontalis and an appendix by Michel Schneider on the controversies.

13. Siegfried Bernfeld, "Letter to Anna Freud, November 23, 1937," *Revue internationale d'histoire de la psychanalyse* 3 (1990): 335.

14. On the major controversies in France, see Roudinesco, *HPF-JL*.

15. It should be noted that the third monotheism, Islam, is almost absent from Freud's work, even if he does refer to it occasionally. See Fethi Benslama, *La psychanalyse à l'épreuve de l'islam* (Paris: Aubier, 2002).

16. Henry Institoris and Jacques Sprenger, *Le marteau des sorcières* (Paris: Jérôme Milton, 2005 [186 or 1487]). Freud consulted the book in Latin, but he owned a copy in German.

17. Sigmund Freud, "Obsessive Actions and Religious Practices" (1907), *SE* 9:115–127; Sigmund Freud, "A Seventeenth-Century Demonological Neurosis" (1923), *SE* 19: 67–109.

18. The best commentary on this approach is by Michel de Certeau, *The Writing of History,* trans. Tom Conley (New York: Columbia University Press, 1988 [1975]), in a chapter titled "What Freud Makes of History," 287–307.

19. Sigmund Freud, *The Future of an Illusion* (1927), *SE* 21:1–56.

20. Freud to Ferenczi, January 26, 1927, in Sigmund Freud and Sándor Ferenczi, *Correspondence of Sigmund Freud and Sándor Ferenczi,* ed. Eva Brabant, Ernst Falzeder, and Patrizia Giampieri-Deutsch, trans. Peter T. Hoffer, introduction by André Haynal (Cambridge, MA: Belknap Press of Harvard University Press, 1993), 3:298.

21. The French translation of the correspondence between Freud and Pfister, published by Gallimard in 1966, is incomplete and not very reliable. A new edition is forthcoming. In English, see Sigmund Freud and Oskar Pfister, *Psychoanalysis and Faith: The Letters of Sigmund Freud and Oscar Pfister,* ed. Heinrich Meng and Ernst L. Freud, trans. Eric Mosbacher (London: Hogarth Press and the Institute of Psychoanalysis, 1963).

22. See Danielle Milhaud-Cappe, *Freud et le mouvement de pédagogie psychanalytique, 1908–1937: A. Aichhorn, H. Zulliger, O. Pfister* (Paris: Vrin, 2007).

23. See Élisabeth Roudinesco and Michel Plon, *Dictionnaire de la psychanalyse* (Paris: Fayard, 2006).

24. Oskar Pfister, "A Friendly Disagreement with Prof. Sigmund Freud: The Illusion of a Future," ed. Paul Roazen, trans. Susan Abrams with Tom Taylor, *International Journal of Psychoanalysis* 74 (1993): 557–579.

25. Freud to Romain Rolland, July 20, 1929, regarding the "oceanic" feeling, in Freud, *Letters of Sigmund Freud, 1873–1939,* 389; see Roudinesco, *HPF-JL*. Nevertheless, Freud was fond of Mozart.

26. See Michel de Certeau, *The Mystic Fable: The Sixteenth and Seventeenth Centuries,* ed. Luce Giard, trans. Michael B. Smith, vol. 2 (Chicago: University of Chicago Press, 1992–2015), 36.

27. These undergarments were designed to protect or support men's genital organs during athletic events. They could be worn as bathing suits, and they symbolized male pride; in America they came to be called "jockstraps."

28. I have reconstructed Liebman's story on the basis of stories he himself confided to his psychiatrists after 1935, when he was a patient in the psychiatric clinic at Harvard's McLean Hospital; these narratives appear in the medical records. In addition, I had access to some of the letters Freud exchanged with Julius and Marie Liebman, and to observations by Leopold Stieglitz, the Liebman family doctor. I consulted Freud's letters to Pfister and Ferenczi; the latter gave his own version of the case. See David J. Lynn, "Freud's Analysis of A. B., a Psychotic Man, 1925–1930," *Journal of the American Academy of Psychoanalysis* 21, no. 1 (Spring 1993): 63–78; Alex Beam, *Gracefully Insane: The Rise and Fall of America's Premier Mental Hospital* (New York: Public Affairs, 2003), ch. 6, 93–117. See also Kurt Robert Eissler's interview with Julius Liebman, February 6, 1954, LoC, box 114, folder 16. Carl (or Karl) Liebman is often referred to as "A. B., the psychotic youth." I note that Mikkel Borch-Jacobsen gives a version that overly minimizes Freud's lucidity about the tragic nature of this treatment: *Les patients de Freud: Destins* (Auxerre, France: Éditions Sciences humaines, 2011).

29. Freud to Oskar Pfister, December 21, 1924–January 3, 1926, in Freud and Pfister, *Psychoanalysis and Faith*, 96–102.

30. Sigmund Freud, "The Infantile Genital Organization: An Interpolation into the Theory of Sexuality" (1923), *SE* 19:139–145. The term had been used for the first time in 1914, in Sigmund Freud, "On Narcissism: An Introduction," *SE* 14:67–102.

31. Sigmund Freud, "Negation" (1925), *SE* 19:233–239. For *Verneinung,* I have opted for the translation proposed by Jean Hyppolite in 1956 and picked up by Olivier Mannoni: "denegation." On the very lengthy debate that led to Lacan's creation of the concept of forclusion, see Roudinesco, *HPF-JL.*

32. The first description of fetishism was produced by the French magistrate Charles de Brosses (1709–1777), and the term was conceptualized by Alfred Binet (1847–1911).

33. In particular Élisabeth Bathory (1560–1614), a famous Hungarian countess convinced that by bathing in the blood of other women she would preserve her youth. See Élisabeth Roudinesco, *Our Dark Side: A History of Perversion,* trans. David Macey (Cambridge, UK: Polity, 2009 [2007]). Certain women take the bodies of their children, or parts of their bodies, as fetishes.

34. Freud did not make a distinction between the two terms, saying "penis" or "phallus" indiscriminately.

35. Freud to Pfister, April 11, 1927, in Freud and Pfister, *Psychoanalysis and Faith,* 108.

36. Sigmund Freud, "Fetishism" (1927), *SE* 21:152–153.

37. Freud to Jung, November 21, 1909, in Sigmund Freud and C. G. Jung, *The Freud/Jung Letters: The Correspondence between Sigmund Freud and C. G. Jung,* ed. William McGuire, trans. Ralph Manheim and R. F. C. Hull (Princeton, NJ: Princeton University Press, 1974), 266.

38. Freud, "Fetishism," *SE* 21:156.

39. *Schamgürtel* has been translated into French as *gaine pubienne,* "pubic girdle," or *cache-sexe,* "posing pouch." Only Mannoni has noted that the word referred to the *sublicaculum* worn by the Romans, whereas in our day it designates a sadomasochistic garment made of straps with an opening for the genitals. In the *Standard Edition,* James Strachey and Joan Riviere chose to translate *Schamgürtel* as the equivalent of the French *suspensoir:* "athletic support-belt" and "suspensory belt," terms that have nothing to do with a belt of shame or a pubic girdle.

40. Emy I. Moebius, letter to Kurt Eissler, September 11, 1952, LoC, box 21, folder 8.

41. Detlef Berthelsen, *La famille Freud au jour le jour: Souvenirs de Paula Fichtl,* trans. Lucien-Marie Robin (Paris: Presses Universitaires de France, 1991 [1987]). Before the First World War, when his children were young and still living at home, Freud had four people in domestic service.

42. They first met in 1908; see Stefan Zweig, *Appels aux Européens,* trans. Jacques Le Rider (Paris: Bartillat, 2014 [1932–1934]). For the original German of the two essays included in *Appels,* see Stefan Zweig, "Die moralische Entgiftung Europas: Ein Vortrag für die Europatagung der Accademia die Roma" (1932), in *Zeiten und Schicksale: Aufsätze und Vorträge aus den Jahren 1902–1942,* ed. Knut Beck (Frankfurt: S. Fischer, 1990), 40–56.

43. Freud to Stefan Zweig, February 17, 1931, in *Letters of Sigmund Freud, 1873–1939,* 402; Stefan Zweig, *Mental Healers: Franz Anton Mesmer, Mary Baker Eddy, Sigmund Freud,* trans. Eden Paul and Cedar Paul (London: Cassell, 1933).

44. Zweig, *Mental Healers,* 272.

45. Stefan Zweig, *Twenty-Four Hours in the Life of a Woman,* trans. Anthea Bell (London: Pushkin, 2003 [1927]).

46. Freud to Stefan Zweig, September 4, 1926, in Sigmund Freud and Stefan Zweig, *Correspondance, 1908–1929,* trans. Gisella Hauer and Didier Plassard (Paris: Payot and Rivages poche, 1995 [1987]), 48. Freud later commented on several of Zweig's novellas.

47. Thomas Mann, *Freud's Position in the History of Modern Thought* (London: Burns Oates and Washbourne, 1933 [1929]).

48. Freud to Andreas-Salomé, July 28, 1929, in Sigmund Freud and Lou Andreas-Salomé, *Letters,* ed. Ernst Pfeiffer, trans. William Robson-Scott and Elaine Robson-Scott (New York: Harcourt Brace Jovanovich, 1972), 181–182.

49. Freud to Andreas-Salomé, May 9, 1928, in ibid., 174.

50. These notes were unearthed in 1985 by Karl Sablik: "Freud et Julius Tandler: Une mystérieuse relation," *Revue internationale d'histoire de la psychanalyse 3* (1990): 96.

51. Sigmund Freud, *The Diary of Sigmund Freud, 1929–1939: A Record of the Final Decade* (New York: Scribner's, 1992), 45.

13. Facing Hitler

1. Mark Edmundson, *The Death of Sigmund Freud: The Legacy of His Last Days* (New York: Bloomsbury, 2007), 1.

2. Ibid., 8.

3. See Thomas Mann, "A Brother," trans. H. T. Lowe-Porter, in *Order of the Day: Political Essays and Speeches of Two Decades* (Freeport, NY: Books for Libraries Press, 1969), 153–161. The first English-language version, published in April 1938, was titled *That Man Is My Brother*. See also Jean Finck, *Thomas Mann et la psychanalyse* (Paris: Les Belles Lettres, 1982).

4. Thomas Mann, "Allemagne ma souffrance" (1933), in *Les exigences du jour*, trans. Louise Servicen and Jeanne Najac (Paris: Grasset, 2003 [1976]), 186.

5. Mann, "Brother," 160.

6. Mann drew on this thematics of a double Germany later on, in *Doctor Faustus: The Life of the German Composer Adrian Leverkühn as Told by a Friend*, trans. John E. Woods (New York: Alfred A. Knopf, 1997). Ian Kershaw does likewise when he asserts, at the end of his biography of Hitler, "The Germany which had produced Adolf Hitler, which had seen its future in his vision, had so readily served him, and had shared in his *hubris*, had also had to share his nemesis" (*Hitler, 1936–45: Nemesis* [New York: W. W. Norton, 2000], 841).

7. Mann, *Les exigences du jour*, 308.

8. This secondary residence, nicknamed "the Berghof," was acquired by Hitler in 1933 thanks to the royalties from *Mein Kampf*. It was destroyed in 1945.

9. In German, Freud used the word *Kultur* to designate both civilization *(Zivilisation)* and the spirit of the Enlightenment, in the French and German senses *(Lumières, Aufklärung)*. He thus refused to distinguish the culture that covers a set of traditions, modes of thought, representations, and beliefs, from civilization, a broader term that presupposes the idea of a universal reason proper to humanity, contrasting the "savage," the "barbarian," or the "uneducated" with the civilized subject. Thus *Kultur* in the Freudian sense can be translated by "civilization" as well as by "culture." In France, there were intense debates between the partisans of the word "culture" and the supporters of the term "civilization." I retrace this story in Élisabeth Roudinesco, *Histoire de la psychanalyse en France* followed by *Jacques Lacan: Esquisse d'une vie, histoire d'un système de pensée* (Paris: Pochothèque, 2009; hereafter *HPF-JL*), especially with regard to Édouard Pichon's highlighting of "French civilization" to the detriment of the German culture. See also Jacques Le Rider, Michel Plon, Gérard Raulet, and Henri Rey-Flaud, *Autour du "Malaise dans la culture" de Freud* (Paris: Presses Universitaires de France, 1998); and Pierre Pellegrin, in Sigmund Freud, *Malaise dans la culture* (Paris: Garnier-Flammarion, 2010), introduction, 7–67, notes, 177–210. The two best translations of the book in French are by Bernard Lortholary (Paris: Seuil, 2010), and Marc Crépon and Marc B. de Launay, in *Sigmund Freud: Anthropologie de la guerre* (bilingual edition). These three translators

opted for *Malaise dans la civilisation*. For the standard English translation, see Sigmund Freud, *Civilization and Its Discontents* (1929), *SE* 21:57–145.

10. Displacement of the instinctual drive toward a nonsexual goal.

11. Freud, *Civilization*, *SE* 21:111.

12. Sigmund Freud, "On the Psychical Mechanism of Hysterical Phenomena: A Lecture" (1893), *SE* 3:36. Freud was apparently alluding to a phrase by John Hughlings-Jackson, who for his part was clearly paraphrasing Rousseau: "It has been said that he who was the first to abuse his fellow-man instead of knocking out his brains without a word, laid thereby the basis of civilization."

13. Ibid., 90.

14. Jean-Jacques Rousseau, *Discourse on the Origins of Inequality (Second Discourse): Polemics; and Political Economy*, ed. Roger D. Masters and Christopher Kelly, trans. Judith R. Bush (Hanover, NH: University Press of New England, 1992), 41.

15. On this term see later in this chapter.

16. Freud, *Civilization*, *SE* 21:145.

17. Richard Nikolaus von Coudenhove-Kalergi (1894–1972), an Austrian diplomat, was the first to think of adopting Beethoven's "Ode to Joy" as a European anthem. After the Anschluss, he went into exile in France, then in Switzerland and in the United States. He became a Gaullist after becoming a French citizen. He published a book on anti-Semitism that Freud knew well: *Das Wesen des Antisemitismus* (in English, *Anti-Semitism throughout the Ages*, by H. J. M. Coudenhove-Kalergi, R. N. Coudenhove-Kalergi, and A. S. Rappoport, trans. Angelo Solomon [London: Hutchinson, 1935]).

18. He had made his last trip there with his daughter Anna in 1923.

19. Freud, *Civilization*, *SE* 21:69–70.

20. Einstein to Freud, July 30, 1932, in "Why War?," *SE* 22:201, 199.

21. "Why War?," *SE* 22:195–215.

22. In French translations, this term is sometimes left in German, sometimes translated as *vision du monde* ("worldview"). In the *Standard Edition*, it is not translated. See Sigmund Freud, "The Question of a *Weltanschauung*" (1933), *SE* 22:158–182. Literally, the word is composed of *Welt*, "world," and *Anschauung*, "contemplation, vision, experience." It has multiple meanings: ideology, political conception of the world, worldview, and even philosophical discourse.

23. Freud, "Question of a *Weltanschauung*," *SE* 22:158.

24. Ibid., 160–161.

25. Ibid., 177.

26. On this point, see Bernd Nitzschke's fine article, "La psychanalyse considérée comme une science 'a'-politique," trans. Sabine Bollack, *Revue internationale d'histoire de la psychanalyse* 5 (1992): 170–182.

27. The history of psychoanalysis in Russia has yet to be written. On this topic, Alexander Etkind's book *Eros of the Impossible: The History of Psychoanalysis in Russia*, trans. Noah Rubins and Maria Rubins (Boulder, CO: Westview, 1997), is insufficient.

See Jean Marti, "La psychanalyse en Russie (1909–1930)," *Critique* 346 (March 1976): 199–237, and Alberto Angelini, *La psicoanalisi in Russia: Dai precursori agli anni trenta* (Naples: Liguori, 1988). I myself retraced part of this history for the period 1930–1950 (see Roudinesco, *HPF-JL*). The Russian psychoanalytic movement was gradually eradicated starting in 1930. The label "bourgeois science" came into use only in 1949, in the context of the Stalinist crusade against the sciences and the arts orchestrated by Trofim Lysenko and Andrei Zhdanov.

28. Keren Hayesod was an organization founded in 1920 for the purpose of settling immigrants in Palestine.

29. On this topic, see Guido Liebermann, *La psychanalyse en Palestine, 1918–1948: Aux origines du mouvement analytique israélien* (Paris: Campagne Première, 2012). David Montague Eder (1866–1936) was a psychiatrist and a psychoanalyst, cofounder with Jones of the English psychoanalytic movement; he was a cousin of the militant Zionist and Socialist Israel Zangwill (1864–1926).

30. The original manuscript of Freud's letter, dated February 26, 1930, and the copy prepared by an unknown typist are preserved in the Hebrew University of Jerusalem in the Abraham Schadron collection. I have already published this letter and commented on its content in Élisabeth Roudinesco, "À propos d'une lettre inédite de Freud sur le sionisme et la question des lieux saints," *Cliniques méditerranéennes* 70 (2004): 5–17. See also Élisabeth Roudinesco, *Retour sur la question juive* (Paris: Albin Michel, 2009). The English translation is by Ivan Ward, revised by an unnamed critic who found Ward's translation "tendentious and lending itself to 'Palestinian propaganda'": Sigmund Freud to Chaim Koffler, Freud Museum website, September 11, 2000, http://www.freud.org.uk/education/blog/40083/a-new-translation/.

31. Sigmund Freud to Albert Einstein, February 26, 1930, cited by Peter Gay in *Freud: A Life for Our Time* (New York: W. W. Norton, 1988), 598n.

32. On the impossible resolution of the issue of sacred sites, see Charles Enderlin, *Shattered Dreams: The Failure of the Peace Process in the Middle East, 1995–2002* (New York: Other Press, 2003 [2002]), and Charles Enderlin, *Au nom du Temple: Israël et l'irrésistible ascension du messianisme juif (1967–2003)* (Paris: Seuil, 2013).

33. Among the best sources on the collaboration of psychoanalysts with the Nazis, see Jean-Luc Évard, ed. and trans., *Les années brunes: la psychanalyse sous le IIIe Reich* (Paris: Éditions Confrontation, 1984); Hans-Martin Lohmann, ed., *Psychoanalyse und Nationalsozialismus: Beiträge zur Bearbeitung eines unbewältigten Traumas* (Frankfurt: Fischer, 1984); Geoffrey Cocks, *Psychotherapy in the Third Reich: The Göring Institute,* 2nd ed. (New Brunswick, NJ: Transaction, 1997); Regine Lockot, *Erinnern und Durcharbeiten* (Frankfurt: Fischer, 1985); Jennifer Curio, "Ce qui est arrivé à la psychanalyse en Allemagne," DEA thesis, Université Paris-Nord, 1997. Jones and Gay made no mention of this episode.

34. Freud to Ferenczi, April 2, 1933, in Sigmund Freud and Sándor Ferenczi, *Correspondence of Sigmund Freud and Sándor Ferenczi,* ed. Eva Brabant, Ernst Falzeder,

and Patrizia Giampieri-Deutsch, trans. Peter T. Hoffer, introduction by André Haynal (Cambridge, MA: Belknap Press of Harvard University Press, 1993), 3:449.

35. Historians use the term "Austrofascism" to characterize this episode in Austrian history, which lasted from March 1933 to July 1934, the date of Dollfuss's assassination by Austrian Nazis.

36. Freud to Hilda Doolittle, March 5, 1934, in Hilda Doolittle, *Tribute to Freud* (New York: Pantheon, 1956), 167.

37. Freud used the term *Hitlerei* ("Hitlerite") to designate Hitlerian politics. The German suffix *-ei* generally marks the place where a profession is exercised.

38. Letter from Maurizio Serra to Élisabeth Roudinesco, March 5, 2014. See Roberto Zapperi, *Freud e Mussolini* (Milan: Franco Angeli, 2013).

39. Benito Mussolini and Giovacchino Forzano, *Napoleon: The Hundred Days* (London: Sidgwick and Jackson, 1932). In 1934, Forzano made a film based on this play in three acts and thirteen tableaux, following the canon of the Fascist aesthetic.

40. The German copy of Forzano's book is included in the catalog of Freud's library (2583), with the dedication in Italian.

41. The handwritten dedication is dated April 26, 1933. See Anna Maria Accerboni, "Psychanalyse et fascisme: Deux approches incompatibles. Le rôle difficile d'Edoardo Weiss," *Revue internationale d'histoire de la psychanalyse* 1 (1988): 225–245; Paul Roazen, "Questions d'éthique psychanalytique: Edoardo Weiss, Freud et Mussolini," *Revue internationale d'histoire de la psychanalyse* 1 (1988): 150–167; Glauco Carloni, "Freud and Mussolini: A Minor Drama in Two Acts, One Interlude and Five Characters," exhibition catalog, *L'Italia nella psicoanalisi* (Rome, 1989), 51–60. The comments sent by Weiss to Kurt Eissler, dated December 13, 1953, are in the Library of Congress, box 121, folder 34.

42. One would have to be seriously ignorant of history to think that Freud could have been a Fascist, a charge Michel Onfray does not fail to make in his polemical tract *Le crépuscule d'une idole: L'affabulation fabuleuse* (Paris: Grasset, 2010), 524–533, 590–591. Onfray consulted neither the archives of the Library of Congress nor the correspondence on this topic between Freud and Weiss. He does not take into account the reliable sources, cites Cocks's work incorrectly, and lashes out at Paul-Laurent Assoun, the author of the *Dictionnaire des oeuvres psychanalytiques* (Paris: Presses Universitaires de France, 2009); he proceeds to assert that the history of Freud's dedication has gone unmentioned by the psychoanalytic community, forgetting that the dedication has been discussed many times by most historians of Freudianism and by most of Freud's biographers.

43. Accerboni, "Psychanalyse et fascisme," 229n5.

44. Weiss always denied that a meeting with Ciano had taken place, as he said later to Roazen. Accerboni asserts, to the contrary, that the meeting did occur. It is possible that there was an indirect contact between Weiss and Ciano.

45. In 1935, Camillo Berneri sent Freud his book *Le Juif antisémite* (Paris: Vita, 1935) with the dedication "In respectful homage." He had also written an article about

Freud's book on Leonardo da Vinci; see Freud's library, no. 217, Freud Museum, London.

46. "Enquête sur Sigmund Freud et sur la WPV effectuée par la diplomatie fasciste italienne en 1935," document, *Revue internationale d'histoire de la psychanalyse 5* (1992): 143–150.

47. Elena Mancini, *Magnus Hirschfeld and the Quest for Sexual Freedom: A History of the First International Sexual Freedom Movement* (New York: Palgrave Macmillan, 2010).

48. The Schutzstaffel (SS) and the Sturmabteilung were major Nazi paramilitay organizations.

49. An amalgam of the slogans chanted by the SS at the book burning. See https://www.stormfront.org/forum/t158874/.

50. Ernest Jones, *The Life and Work of Sigmund Freud* (New York: Basic Books, 1953–1957), 3:182.

51. Karen Brecht, Hella Ehlers, and Christine Trollope. *"Here Life Goes On in a Most Peculiar Way . . .": Psychoanalysis before and after 1933*, trans. from the German (Hamburg: Kellner, 1992), 100–101. The article was published in *Deutsche Volksgesundheit aus Blut und Boden*.

52. Brecht et al., *"Here Life Goes On,"* 112. In his inflammatory tract, Onfray asserts that Eitingon shared Jones's opinion about "rescuing" psychoanalysis (*Crépuscule*, 549).

53. Freud to Jones, May 29, 1933, in Sigmund Freud, *The Complete Correspondence of Sigmund Freud and Ernest Jones, 1908–1939*, ed. R. Andrew Paskauskas (Cambridge, MA: Belknap Press of Harvard University Press, 1983), 721. The "American," Elizabeth Severn, later participated in an experiment in mutual analysis. Ferenczi mentions her in his clinical diary under the initials R. N.

54. Sándor Ferenczi, *The Clinical Diary of Sándor Ferenczi*, ed. Judith Dupont, trans. Michael Balint and Nicola Zarday Jackson (Cambridge, MA: Harvard University Press, 1988). This diary was published long after Ferenczi's death. Freud was unaware of its existence.

55. Ferenczi to Freud, April 9, 1933, in Freud and Ferenczi, *Correspondence*, 3:450.

56. Sigmund Freud, "Sándor Ferenczi" (1933), SE 22:225–229.

57. Wilhelm Reich, *The Mass Psychology of Fascism*, trans. Vincent R. Carfagno (New York: Farrar, Straus and Giroux, 1970 [1933]); see also Wilhelm Reich, *Reich Speaks of Freud*, ed. Mary Higgins and Chester M. Raphael, trans. Therese Pol (New York: Farrar, Straus and Giroux, 1967), and Russell Jacoby, *The Repression of Psychoanalysis: Otto Fenichel and the Political Freudians* (New York: Basic Books, 1983).

58. Brecht et al., *"Here Life Goes On,"* 119. Boehm's account is in perfect harmony with Freud's position, as evidenced by Freud's letter to Eitingon of April 17, 1933, in Sigmund Freud and Max Eitingon. *Correspondance, 1906–1939*, ed. Michael Schröter, trans. Olivier Mannoni (Paris: Hachette Littératures, 2009 [2004]), 789.

59. Accused of fraud owing to his commercialization of "orgone accumulators," Reich died in the Lewisburg Federal Penitentiary in Pennsylvania in 1957. Some of

his archives, in particular those having to do with his relations with Freud, are in the Library of Congress.

60. See Doolittle, *Tribute*. I wrote a preface for the French re-edition of the book.

61. Joseph Wortis, *Fragments of an Analysis with Freud* (New York: Simon and Schuster, 1984 [1954]). Wortis (1906–1995) introduced insulin therapy as a treatment for schizophrenia in the United States. He supported the Republicans during the Spanish Civil War; he later participated in the anti-Freud campaign orchestrated by the Communist Party, denounced psychoanalysis as a "bourgeois science," and in 1950 wrote the first serious study on "Soviet" psychiatry.

62. Ernst Kretschmer, opening address, 6th Allgemeine ärztliche Kongress für Psychotherapie, Dresden, in honor of Freud's 75th birthday, May 14–17, 1931, *Archiv für Psychiatrie* 96 (1932): 219.

63. Jung to Rudolf Allers, November 23, 1933, in C. G. Jung, *Letters 1: 1906–1950*, ed. Gerhard Adler with Aniela Jaffé (Princeton, NJ: Princeton University Press, 1973), 132.

64. C. G. Jung, "Geleitwort," *Zentralblatt für Psychotherapie* 6, no. 1 (1933): 10–11, repr. in C. G. Jung, *Gesammelte Werke* (Olten, Switzerland: Walter Verlag, 1974), 10:581–583; in English, see C. G. Jung, "Editorial" (1933), in *Collected Works of C. G. Jung*, trans. R. F. C. Hull, vol. 10, *Civilization in Transition* (Princeton, NJ: Princeton University Press, 1967), 533–534.

65. C. G. Jung, "An Interview on Radio Berlin: Conducted by Adolf Weizsäcker, June 26, 1933," in *C. G. Jung Speaking: Interviews and Encounters* (Princeton, NJ: Princeton University Press, 1977), 65. The original version of the text became available in 1987 and was analyzed by M. von der Tann in "A Jungian Perspective on the Berlin Institute for Psychotherapy: A Basis for Mourning," *San Francisco Jung Institute Library Journal* 8, no. 4 (1989): 43–73.

66. He explained his policy in two letters dated January 22, 1934, one to Paul Bjerre, the other to Alfonse Maeder, in Jung, *Letters*, 135–138.

67. C. G. Jung, "Zur gegenwärtigen Lage der Psychotherapie," *Zentralblatt für Psychotherapie* 7 (1934): 1–16; repr. in Jung, *Gesammelte Werke* 10:181–201; in English as "The State of Psychotherapy Today" (1934) in Jung, *Collected Works* 10:165–166. An excerpt is found in Yosef Hayim Yerushalmi, *Freud's Moses: Judaism Terminable and Interminable* (New Haven, CT: Yale University Press, 1991), 48–49; see also Roudinesco, *Retour*, 153, where I cite the text in Le Rider's translation. I do not share the opinion of Deirdre Bair, who exonerates Jung from all anti-Semitism and believes that his collaboration with Göring was attributable to Cimbal's influence (see *Jung: A Biography* [Boston: Little, Brown, 2003], 440), nor that of Richard Noll (*The Aryan Christ: The Secret Life of Carl Jung* [New York: Random House, 1997]), who reduces the whole of Jung's work to a Nazi doctrine. On Jung's anti-Semitism, see also Andrew Samuels, "National Psychology, National Socialism, and Analytical Psychology: Reflections on Jung and Anti-Semitism," *Journal of Analytical Psychology* 37 (1992): 3–28, 127–148. I organized the sixteenth colloquium of the Société

internationale d'histoire de la psychiatrie et de la psychanalyse (SIHPP) on this topic: "Carl Gustav Jung, l'oeuvre, la clinique, la politique," with the participation of Deirdre Bair, Mireille Cifali, Christian Jambet, Michel Plon, and Andrew Samuels, Hôpital Sainte-Anne, Paris, November 24, 2001.

68. Jung to James Kirsch, May 26, 1934, in Jung, *Letters*, 161–162.

69. Jung to Gerhard Adler, June 9, 1934, in ibid., 164.

70. Jung to Erich Neumann, December 22, 1935, in ibid., 206–207.

71. Victor Klemperer, *The Language of the Third Reich: LTI, Lingua Tertii Imperii: A Philologist's Notebook*, trans. Martin Brady (New Brunswick, NJ: Athlone, 2000).

72. "Man sollte sich nicht allzulaut über die Psychoanalyse des Juden 'Freud' empören, wenn man und solange man *überhaupt* nicht anders über Alles und Jedes 'denken' kann als so, daß Alles als 'Ausdruck' 'des Lebens' animal und auf 'Instinkte' und 'Instinktschwund zurückführt.' Diese 'Denk'-weise, die überhaupt im voraus kein 'Sein' zuläßt, ist der reine Nihilismus." Martin Heidegger, "Cahier XIV" [Überlegungen XIV, 1940–1941], in *Gesamtausgabe*, vol. 96, ed. Peter Trawny (Frankfurt: Klostermann, 2014), 218. See also Peter Trawny and Andrew J. Mitchell, *Heidegger and the Myth of a Jewish World Conspiracy* (Chicago: University of Chicago Press, 2015).

73. On the relations between Heidegger and the Swiss German psychiatrist Medard Bossa (1903–1990), trained at the Burghölzli clinic, see Martin Heidegger, *Séminaires de Zurich* (Paris: Gallimard, 2010 [1987]). On the relations between Lacan and Heidegger, see Roudinesco, *HPF-JL.*

74. Quoted in Sigmund Freud, *The Diary of Sigmund Freud, 1929–1939: A Record of the Final Decade* (New York: Scribner's, 1992), 200.

75. Lilly Freud-Marlé, *Mein Onkel Sigmund Freud: Erinnerungen an eine grosse Familie*, letters collected by Christfried Tögel (Berlin: Aufbau, 2006).

76. A well-known vacation spot northwest of Vienna with restaurants and summer homes. Starting in 1934, Freud rented a fine house with a garden where he settled with his family in the spring or summer.

77. Thomas Mann, "Freud and the Future" (1936), in *Freud, Goethe, Wagner* (New York: Alfred A. Knopf, 1937), 23.

78. Sigmund Freud, "A Disturbance of Memory on the Acropolis" (1936), *SE* 22.

79. The three volumes were in his library (no. 2345), all first published by S. Fischer Verlag (Frankfurt): *The Tales of Jacob* (1933), *The Young Joseph*, and *Joseph in Egypt*. The final volume, *Joseph the Provider*, would appear in 1943. A first English translation was done by H. T. Lowe-Porter (New York: Alfred A. Knopf, 1948), and a new translation by John E. Woods was published, also by Knopf, in 2005. See Freud's letter to Thomas Mann, November 29, 1936, in Sigmund Freud, *Letters of Sigmund Freud, 1873–1939*, ed. Ernst L. Freud, trans. Tania Stern and James Stern (London: Hogarth, 1970), 432–434.

80. Napoléon François Charles Joseph Bonaparte (1811–1832), known as "l'Aiglon," king of Rome and duke of Reichstadt, son of Napoléon and Marie-Louise of Austria.

81. Freud learned about Napoleon's life from Bergler and from the work of Albert Vandal, *L'avènement de Bonaparte* (2 vols., Paris: Plon-Nourrit, 1903–1907; the French edition of 1910 was in Freud's library, no. 3497). See also Jones, *Life and Work,* 3:190–191. Freud had also read Adolphe Thiers's volumes on the consulate and the empire.

82. Jacques Lacan, "Beyond the 'Reality Principle,' " in *Écrits: The First Complete Edition in English,* trans. Bruce Fink with Héloïse Fink and Russell Grigg (New York: W. W. Norton, 2006 [1966]), 58–74.

83. Freud and Andreas-Salomé, *Letters,* 11.

84. Richard Sterba, *Reminiscences of a Viennese Psychoanalyst* (Detroit: Wayne State University Press, 1982), 156.

85. Abraham H. Maslow, "Was Adler a Disciple of Freud? A Note," *Journal of Individual Psychology* 18 (1962): 125.

86. Sigmund Freud to Arnold Zweig, June 22, 1937, cited for the first time by Jones (Freud, *Complete Correspondence of Freud and Jones,* 208); not included in the published Freud-Zweig correspondence; cited by Paul E. Stepanski in his biography of Adler, *In Freud's Shadow: Adler in Context* (Hillside, NJ: Analytic Press, distr. L. Erlbaum, 1983), 262.

87. Freud to Andreas-Salomé, January 6, 1935, in Sigmund Freud and Lou Andreas-Salomé, *Letters,* ed. Ernst Pfeiffer, trans. William Robson-Scott and Elaine Robson-Scott (New York: Harcourt Brace Jovanovich, 1972), 204.

88. Lou Andreas-Salomé, "Mein Bekenntnis zum heutigen Deutschland" (1934), unpublished, located in the archives of Lou Andreas-Salomé, Göttingen. In 2008, Dorian Astor claimed that this text, which is not accessible to researchers, was Nazi inspired and contained anti-Semitic passages. See Dorian Astor, *Lou Andreas-Salomé* (Paris: Gallimard, 2008), 348–353. This thesis was invalidated with solid arguments by Isabelle Mons, in *Lou Andreas-Salomé* (Paris: Perrin, 2012). I have not consulted that archive, but Mons sent me the notes that she took after examining it.

89. Sigmund Freud, "Lou Andreas-Salomé" (1937), *SE* 23:297.

90. See Sigmund Freud, "Analysis Terminable and Interminable" (1937), *SE* 23:209–253, and Sigmund Freud, "Constructions in Analysis" (1937), *SE* 23:255–269; see also Sigmund Freud, "New Introductory Lectures on Psycho-analysis" (1932), *SE* 22.

91. Freud, "Analysis Terminable and Interminable," *SE* 23:216.

92. He thus included analysis in the category of impossible tasks like governing or educating.

93. Freud, "Analysis Terminable and Interminable," *SE* 23:249.

94. James Lieberman, *Acts of Will: The Life and Work of Otto Rank* (New York: Free Press, 1985), 321. And see Joseph Wortis, *Fragments of an Analysis with Freud* (New York: Simon and Schuster, 1984 [1954]), 121. The thesis of Rank's "madness," like that of Ferenczi's, was taken up again by Jones.

95. Freud to Jones, March 2, 1937, in Freud, *Complete Correspondence of Freud and Jones,* 757.

96. Stefan Zweig to Freud, November 15, 1937, in Sigmund Freud and Stefan Zweig, *Correspondance, 1908–1929*, trans. Gisella Hauer and Didier Plassard (Paris: Payot and Rivages poche, 1995 [1987]), 113.

14. Death at Work

1. See Mary V. Dearborn, *Queen of Bohemia: The Life of Louise Bryant* (Boston: Houghton Mifflin, 1996). Dercum's disease, or adiposis dolorosa, is accompanied by mental disorders.

2. Edward Mandell House (1858–1938) was a diplomat and politician who advised Wilson on the drafting of the "fourteen points." He was sidelined in 1919.

3. Sigmund Freud and William Bullitt, *Woodrow Wilson: A Psychological Study* (New Brunswick, NJ: Transaction, 1998 [1966]). For the interpretation of the text, see Élisabeth Roudinesco and Michel Plon, *Dictionnaire de la psychanalyse* (Paris: Fayard, 2006). The money Bullitt sent served to replenish the coffers of the publishing house. See also Peter Gay's discussion in his *Freud: A Life for Our Time* (New York: W. W. Norton, 1988), 553–558.

4. Hence the severe judgment of Erik Erikson, who emphasized that the text seemed to have been written by an untalented student who understood neither the language nor the thought of his master; see Erik H. Erikson, review of Sigmund Freud and William C. Bullitt, *Thomas Woodrow Wilson: Twenty-Eighth President of the United States: A Psychological Study*, in *International Journal of Psychoanalysis* 48 (1967): 463.

5. Wilson drafted the speech without consulting his European counterparts. In it, he claimed to be redrawing the boundaries of the former Central European empires and governing international relations by creating a League of Nations.

6. On this topic, see Catherine Clément, *Pour Sigmund Freud* (Paris: Mengès, 2005), 127–143.

7. Sigmund Freud, *Moses and Monotheism* (1939), SE 23:1–137.

8. The German word *Geistigkeit* can be rendered in English as "spirituality," "intellectuality," or "the life of the mind." The word "spiritualism" does not fit the Freudian hypothesis. Among the several French translations of the work, I have chosen that of Cornélius Heim, *L'homme Moïse et la religion monothéiste* (Paris: Gallimard, 1986 [1939]). Among the best commentators—beyond Yosef Hayim Yerushalmi, whose *Freud's Moses* was a veritable event—let us recall Jacques Le Rider, *Freud, de l'Acropole au Sinaï* (Paris: Presses Universitaires de France, 2002); Edward Said, *Freud and the Non-European* (London: Verso, 2003); and Henri Rey-Flaud, *"Et Moïse créa les Juifs . . .": Le testament de Freud* (Paris: Aubier, 2006). I comment on most of these works as well as on that of Freud in Élisabeth Roudinesco, *Retour sur la question juive* (Paris: Albin Michel, 2009). See also Ilse Grubrich-Simitis, "Freud's Study of Moses as Daydream: A Biographical Essay," in *Early Freud and Late Freud: Reading Anew "Studies on Hysteria" and "Moses and Monotheism,"* trans. Philip Slotkin (London:

Routledge, 1997), pp. 53–89. With René Major, I organized the colloquium of the SIHPP in London in 1994, during which Jacques Derrida responded to Yerushalmi with a text published the following year as *Mal d'archive,* in English as *Archive Fever: A Freudian Impression?,* trans. Eric Prenowitz (Chicago: University of Chicago Press, 1996 [1995]). This event was the object of a malevolent commentary full of errors during a colloquium in honor of Yerushalmi organized in Paris by Sylvie-Anne Goldberg at the Musée d'art et d'histoire du judaïsme on April 11, 2011. See Sylvie-Anne Goldberg, ed., *L'histoire et la mémoire de l'histoire: Hommage à Y. H. Yerushalmi* (Paris: Albin Michel, 2012). I published a response on this topic addressed to Goldberg and Michael Molnar in the *Bulletin de la SIHPP* (August 3, 2012).

9. Spinoza's name and works do not appear in the catalog of Freud's library. He apparently was not familiar with the famous passage in the third chapter of the *Theological-Political Treatise* on the survival of the Jews.

10. The best work since the late seventeenth century on the genesis of the myth of Moses as an Egyptian is Jan Assmann's *Moses the Egyptian: The Memory of Egypt in Western Monotheism* (Cambridge, MA: Harvard University Press, 1997). See also Jacques Le Rider, "Moïse l'Égyptien," in "Sigmund Freud, de *L'Interprétation des rêves* à *L'Homme Moïse,*" special issue, *Revue germanique internationale* 14 (2000):127–150. The holdings in Freud's library include an impressive number of books by Egyptologists and biblical exegetes. In this area, Freud's erudition was immense.

11. Otto Rank, *The Myth of the Birth of the Hero: A Psychological Exploration of Myth,* trans. Gregory C. Richer and E. James Lieberman (Baltimore: Johns Hopkins University Press, 2004 [1909]).

12. In the biblical story, the pharaoh's daughter finds the child in a basket; she adopts him and takes on his birth mother as his wet nurse.

13. In 1912, Karl Abraham had published an article on the subject: "Amenhotep IV: A Psycho-analytical Contribution towards the Understanding of His Personality and of the Monotheistic Cult of Aton" (1912), *Clinical Papers and Essays on Psychoanalysis,* preface by Ernest Jones (London: Hogarth, 1955), 262–290.

14. Ernst Sellin, *Mose und seine Bedeutung für die Israelitisch-jüdische Religionsgeschichte* (Leipzig: A. Deichertsche Verlagsbuchhandlung, 1922). Sellin's thesis on the murder of Moses had already been invalidated, at that point, by Abraham Shalom Yahuda (1877–1951). Freud had learned of Sellin's work through Arnold Zweig.

15. In the biblical version, Moses breaks the tablets of the law when he sees the Hebrews worshipping the golden calf. He goes back into the Sinai to seek new tablets from Yahweh and dies at age 120 without having reached the Promised Land. Joshua is his successor. The Hebrews wandered in the desert for forty years.

16. Edward Meyer, *Die Israeliten und ihre Nachbarstämme: Alttestamentliche Untersuchungen* (Halle: Max Niemeyer, 1906).

17. Midian was a son of Abraham; his descendants are called Midianites. Freud evokes other historians and exegetes, whose works, along with Meyer's, figure in the catalog of his library. Sellin's 1922 book is not included.

18. In the biblical narrative, the two stories are linked. As an adult, Moses kills an Egyptian and flees toward Midianite territory, where he discovers his vocation: from inside a bush, Yahweh calls him to return to Egypt and liberate the enslaved Hebrews.

19. Jacques Lacan perfectly captured this Freudian dualism in *The Ethics of Psychoanalysis, 1959–1960,* seminar, book 7, trans. Dennis Porter (New York: W. W. Norton, 1992 [1986], 172–178.

20. Freud, *Moses and Monotheism, SE* 23:55.

21. Ibid., 57.

22. Ibid., 88.

23. Ibid., 91–92.

24. This is brought out very clearly by Peter Gay in *A Godless Jew: Freud, Atheism, and the Making of Psychoanalysis* (New Haven, CT: Yale University Press, 1987). I develop this thesis in Roudinesco, *Retour sur la question juive.*

25. This is what led Yerushalmi to say that Freud made psychoanalysis an extension of Judaism without God: an interminable Judaism. Or rather, I would say, an interminable Jewishness. I develop this thesis in Roudinesco, *Retour sur la question juive.*

26. In 1655, at the request of Rabbi Menasseh ben Israel, Cromwell put an end to the banishment of Jews and authorized freedom of worship.

27. Mark Edmundson, *The Death of Sigmund Freud: The Legacy of His Last Days* (New York: Bloomsbury, 2007), 130.

28. David Bakan, *Sigmund Freud and the Jewish Mystical Tradition* (Princeton, NJ: Van Nostrand, 1958).

29. Carl E. Schorske, *Fin-de-Siècle Vienna: Politics and Culture* (New York: Vintage Books, 1981 [1961]); Yirmiyahu Yovel, *Spinoza and Other Heretics,* 2 vols (Princeton, NJ: Princeton University Press, 1989); Gay, *Godless Jew;* Yosef Hayim Yerushalmi, *Freud's Moses: Judaism Terminable and Interminable* (New Haven, CT: Yale University Press, 1991).

30. Martin Buber, *Moses,* translation of *Mosheh* (Oxford: East and West Library, 1946).

31. Freud to Marie Bonaparte, January 27, 1938, unpublished archives, cited in Max Schur, *Freud: Living and Dying* (New York: International Universities Press, 1972), 493–494.

32. Ian Kershaw, *Hitler, 1936–45: Nemesis* (New York: W. W. Norton, 2000), 65–66.

33. Ibid., 75.

34. Ibid., 410.

35. On March 15, he sent a telegram to this effect to the State Department; a facsimile can be found in Sigmund Freud, *The Diary of Sigmund Freud, 1929–1939: A Record of the Final Decade* (New York: Scribner's, 1992), 231.

36. Quoted in Richard Sterba, *Reminiscences of a Viennese Psychoanalyst* (Detroit: Wayne State University Press, 1982), 160. Freud was referring to Sterba.

37. Quoted in Kershaw, *Hitler,* 85. Gay gives an excellent description of the furor that was unleashed in Austria in March 1938.

38. On April 2, 1938, France, Great Britain, and the United States recognized the legality of the Anschluss.

39. Giovacchino Forzano, "Letter to Mussolini, March 14, 1938," in Paul Roazen, "Psychoanalytic Ethics: Edoardo Weiss, Freud, and Mussolini," *Journal of the History of the Behavioral Sciences* 27, no. 4 (1991): 372. Notwithstanding the assertions of Concetta Forzano on the subject, Mussolini seems not to have responded to this request from her father. I asked Maurizio Serra to carry out research on this topic, and he found nothing in the archives. In the testimony he deposited in the Library of Congress, Weiss said that he never had the slightest proof that Mussolini had the favorable intentions that Forzano believed he had toward Freud.

40. On Freud's emigration, in addition to the archives in the Library of Congress and those of Bonaparte, one can consult the works already cited by Ernest Jones, Max Schur, Martin Freud, Eva Weissweiler, Richard Sterba, Mark Edmundson, Detlef Berthelsen (on Paula Fichtl), and Elisabeth Young-Bruehl. It is also important to read Freud's correspondence along with that of Ernest Jones, Max Eitingon, Arnold Zweig, Minna Bernays, Anna Freud, and Freud's other children. See also Freud, *Diary:* "Here life goes on in a most peculiar way"; and Sophie Freud, *Living in the Shadow of the Freud Family* (Westport, CT: Praeger, 2007). Consulting all these sources makes it possible to follow in day-by-day detail all the financial, legal, and administrative negotiations that led to Freud's emigration and that of his family members, as well as the evacuation of his archives and collections to England. A rumor spread by Barbara Hannah claims that Franz Riklin Jr. was sent to Vienna by Jung to give Freud a significant sum of money to help him go into exile. Freud is said to have responded that he wanted to owe nothing to his enemies. This rumor has been invalidated by Deirdre Bair in *Jung: A Biography* (Boston: Little, Brown, 2003), 457–458. See also Robert McCully's testimony, recorded by Kurt Robert Eissler, LoC, n.d., box 121, folder 17.

41. Testimony of Emy Moebius, who later emigrated to Florida. Letter from Emy Moebius to Kurt Eissler, September 11, 1952, LoC box 21, folder 8.

42. A year later they were acquired by Jacob Schatsky, librarian of the Psychiatric Institute of New York.

43. The document was published as "Protocol of Agreement, March 20, 1938," *International Journal of Psychoanalysis* 5, no. 3 (1938): 374–375.

44. "Shabbes Goy" is the term for a non-Jew charged with helping Jews carry out certain tasks on the Sabbath *(Shabbat).*

45. Carl Müller-Braunschweig to Richard Sterba, May 5, 1938, ending in the ritual formula "Heil Hitler," in Sterba, *Reminiscences,* 164–165.

46. On Indra's role, see Alexander Waugh, *The House of Wittgenstein: A Family at War* (New York: Doubleday, 2008). On the details of the anti-Jewish laws applied to Freud's family and his sisters, see Harald Leupold-Löwenthal, "The Emigration of

Freud's Family," trans. Edith Kurzweil, *Partisan Review* 56, no. 1 (1989): 57–64; see also Alfred Gottwaldt, "Les soeurs de Sigmund Freud et la mort: Remarques concernant leur destin de déportation et de meurtre de masse," *Revue française de psychanalyse* 68, no. 4 (2004): 1307–1316.

47. It was on the site of this sumptuous hotel, destroyed in 1945, that Simon Wiesenthal installed his Documentation Center of the Association of Jewish Victims of the Nazi Regime. In 1985, a monument was erected there in memory of the victims.

48. Detlef Berthelsen, *La famille Freud au jour le jour: Souvenirs de Paula Fichtl,* trans. Lucien-Marie Robin (Paris: Presses Universitaires de France, 1991 [1987]), 81.

49. Eva Freud (1924–1944) died in Marseille from an infection following an abortion. See Roudinesco and Plon, *Dictionnaire.*

50. W. Ernst Freud, "Souvenirs personnels à propos de l'Anschluss," *Revue internationale d'histoire de la psychanalyse* 3 (1990): 409–414.

51. David J. Lynn, "Freud's Psychoanalysis of A. B., a Psychotic Man, 1925–1930," *Journal of the American Academy of Psychoanalysis* 21, no. 1 (Spring 1993): 63–78. See also "Obituary," *Insurance Advocate* 85 (1974): 9. Hirst's testimony is found in the Library of Congress, box 115, folder 12.

52. Lilly adopted Angela, her orphaned niece, the daughter of Tom Seidmann-Freud, who had committed suicide in 1930, as had her husband a little before she did. In a letter to his sister Mitzi dated December 28, 1930, Freud explained that he could not take responsibility for Angela in Vienna. LoC, box 3, folder 11.

53. She was born in the United States, where her mother had immigrated before returning to Vienna. See Ernst Waldinger, "My Uncle Sigmund Freud," *Books Abroad* 15, no. 1 (January 1941): 1–9. A lengthy account by Waldinger is found in the Library of Congress, box 121, folder 33.

54. Freud insisted in vain that Maximilien Steiner, a member of the WPV since 1908, be included in the group.

55. Sophie Freud, *Living in the Shadow,* 137. Born in 1924, living in the United States, Sophie Freud married Paul Loewenstein, a German immigrant who had escaped from a transit camp in France. A psychosociologist, Sophie specialized in the protection of children.

56. August Aichhorn (1878–1949) remained in Vienna, while his son was arrested by the Nazis and deported to Dachau as a political prisoner. After the war and his son's liberation, August participated in the rebuilding of the WPV. Ernst Federn (1914–2007), the son of Paul Federn, was deported to Buchenwald, and he escaped, as did Bruno Bettelheim (1903–1990). Ernst Federn returned to live in Vienna in 1972, after an American interlude. Bettelheim settled in Chicago.

57. Edmund Engelman, *Berggasse 19: Sigmund Freud's Home and Offices, Vienna, 1938: The Photographs of Edmund Engelman* (New York: Basic Books, 1976), 143. Engelman's photos were sold to buyers around the world. They bore living witness to forty-seven years of life devoted to science, art, and culture.

58. "Erklärung. Ich bestätige gerne, dass bis heute den 4. Juni 1938, keinerlei Behelligung meiner Person oder meiner Hausgenossenvorgekommen ist. Behöden und Funktionäre der Partei sind mir und meinen Hausgenossen ständig korrekt und rücksichtsvoll entgegen getreten. Wien, den 4. Juni 1938. Prof. Dr. Sigm. Freud"; cited in English in Edmundson, *Death*, 121–122. This document, signed by Freud, was included in the Nebehay catalog of May 11, 1989. It was purchased by the Austrian National Library (Österreichische Nationalbibliothek), where it can be consulted.

59. Jones, Gay, Edmundson, and many others have commented extensively on this sentence. Alain de Mijolla was one of the first, in France, to cast doubt on its veracity. See Alain de Mijolla, ed., *International Dictionary of Psychoanalysis = Dictionnaire international de la psychanalyse* (Paris: Calmann-Lévy, 2002), 1:683.

60. The best account of Freud's journey is that of Paula Fichtl, recorded by Berthelsen in *Famille Freud*. She described in detail the reactions of the travelers, how they were dressed, and how they ate.

61. Sigmund Freud, letter to Alexander, July 17, 1938, LoC, family papers.

62. Schur, *Freud*, 498–499n3. There are several versions of Sauerwald's attitude. See also Waldinger's account, LoC, box 121, folder 33.

63. Sigmund Freud, "A Short Account of Psycho-analysis" (1924 [1923]), *SE* 19:189–209.

64. Arthur Koestler, *The Invisible Writing*, vol. 2 of *Arrow in the Blue: An Autobiography*, 2 vols. (London: Collins, with H. Hamilton, 1952–1954), 409. Jones stresses that Koestler published two different accounts, each including errors regarding his visit to Freud. See Ernest Jones, *The Life and Work of Sigmund Freud* (New York: Basic Books, 1953–1957), 3:236.

65. Adele Jeiteles (1871–1970), who lived to be nearly one hundred, was from an important Jewish family of the Austro-Hungarian Empire. Her uncle, suffering from a melancholic psychosis, had consulted Freud in 1900 before committing suicide.

66. Eissler interviewed Koestler and someone else with his mother in 1953, producing an account that was later used by Koestler's biographer, who produced a terrible portrait of the writer. See Michael Scammell, *Koestler: The Literary and Political Odyssey of a Twentieth-Century Skeptic* (New York: Random House, 2009); and Koestler, *Invisible Writing*.

67. Melitta Schmideberg, "Contribution à l'histoire du mouvement psychanalytique en Angleterre" (1971), *Confrontation* 3 (Spring 1980): 11–22.

68. Ernest Jones, "Bulletin of IPA," *International Journal of Psychoanalysis* 20 (1939): 116–127. See also Élisabeth Roudinesco, *Histoire de la psychanalyse en France* followed by *Jacques Lacan: Esquisse d'une vie, histoire d'un système de pensée* (Paris: Pochothèque, 2009; hereafter *HPF-JL*), 1606–1607.

69. Alexandre Etkind took up this thesis in his *Eros of the Impossible: The History of Psychoanalysis in Russia,* trans. Noah Rubins and Maria Rubins (Boulder, CO: Westview, 1997), as did many others after him. However, the thesis has been invalidated on the basis of archives consulted by Guido Liebermann in *La psychanalyse en*

Palestine, 1918–1948: Aux origines du mouvement analytique israélien (Paris: Campagne Première, 2012).

70. Freud to Marie Bonaparte, October 4, 1938, in Sigmund Freud, *Correspondance, 1927–1939* (Paris: Gallimard, 1973 [1968]), 493. In the London *Times* of November 7, 1938, Winston Churchill was quoted as saying, "Britain and France had to choose between dishonour and war. They chose dishonour. They will have war."

71. Sigmund Freud, "A Comment on Anti-Semitism" (1938), *SE* 23:287–293.

72. Arthur Freud was ultimately released, and he left a written account cited by Martin Gilbert in *Kristallnacht: Prelude to Destruction* (New York: HarperCollins, 2006), 54–55.

73. Edmundson, *Death*, 187.

74. Freud to Marie Bonaparte, November 12, 1938, in Freud, *Correspondance 1927–1939*, 497. Freud was mistaken: he had left his sisters 160,000 schillings.

75. Célia Bertin, *Marie Bonaparte: A Life*, translation of *La dernière Bonaparte* (New York: Harcourt Brace Jovanovich, 1982), 204.

76. See Roudinesco, *HPF-JL*.

77. This text appears in facsimile in Ruth Sheppard, *Explorer of the Mind: The Illustrated Biography of Sigmund Freud* (London: André Deutsch, 2012).

78. See *Sigmund Freud: L'invention de la psychanalyse*, a documentary made in 1997 by Élisabeth Kapnist and Élisabeth Roudinesco, produced by Françoise Castro.

79. Freud to Zweig, March 5, 1939, in Sigmund Freud, *The Letters of Sigmund Freud and Arnold Zweig*, ed. Ernst L. Freud, trans. Elaine Robson-Scott and William Robson-Scott (New York: Harcourt, Brace and World, 1970), 178. See also Marie Bonaparte's unpublished archives; and Denis Toutenu, "Freud, une photo inédite: La consultation du Pr Lacassagne à Londres, le 26 février 1939," *Revue française de psychanalyse* 4, no 66 (2002): 1325–1334. The medical report can be found in LoC, box 120, folder 53.

80. Freud to Jones, March 7, 1939, in Sigmund Freud, *The Complete Correspondence of Sigmund Freud and Ernest Jones, 1908–1939*, ed. R. Andrew Paskauskas (Cambridge, MA: Belknap Press of Harvard University Press, 1993), 769.

81. Freud, *Diary*, 308.

82. Jones to Freud, September 3, 1939, in Freud, *Complete Correspondence of Freud and Jones*, 770. On September 2, 1939, the Nazis had invaded Poland.

83. According to the words of Jean-Paul Sartre, cited as the epigraph in this book (Jean-Paul Sartre, "The Republic of Silence," in *The Aftermath of War (Situations III)*, trans. Chris Turner [London: Seagull Books, 2008], 5).

84. Freud, *Diary*, 264.

85. Gay, *Freud: A Life*, 651. Max Schur's notes are in the Library of Congress Manuscript Division, Sigmund Freud collection; their content differs from the version he gave in *Freud: Living and Dying*. Gay relied substantially on the notes; he made it clear that there were three injections and not just two. See also Edmundson, *Death*,

224–226. In her account, Paula Fichtl asserted that Schur was not present when Freud died and that it was Stross who administered the lethal dose. While it is true that Schur had to leave as quickly as possible, before his visa expired, nothing proves that he was not present at Freud's bedside. Fichtl was also mistaken about the dosage, the day, and the number of injections. Her version was taken up by Roy B. Lacoursière in "Freud's Death: Historical Truth and Biographical Fictions," *American Imago* 65, no. 1 (2008): 107–128. In this article, Lacoursière asserts that Stross left archives on the topic, but he does not say what they contain and he himself did not consult them. Freud read Balzac's novel in French in a 1920 edition that belonged to Anna (reference LDFRD 5680). For more on this matter, we shall have to await the opening of Stross's correspondence, archived in the Freud Museum.

86. And not at 2:45 P.M., as Bonaparte says in her diary.

87. Raul Hilberg, *La destruction des Juifs d'Europe* (Paris: Fayard, 1988), 190.

88. Jones, *Life and Work*, 3:248.

89. Stefan Zweig, "Eulogy for Sigmund Freud Delivered by Stefan Zweig on September 26, 1939, Golders Green Crematorium, London, England," in *Freud by Zweig*, trans. Eden Paul and Cedar Paul (Lexington, MA: Plunkett Lake Press, 2012).

Epilogue

1. Harry Freud, letter to Dolfi, Paula, Rosa, and Mitzi, September 25, 1939, LoC, box 3, folder 7ff.

2. The *Judenvermägenabgabe,* or JUVA, is known in English as the Atonement Tax or the Jewish Wealth Tax.

3. Harald Leupold-Löwenthal, "The Emigration of Freud's Family," trans. Edith Kurzweil, *Partisan Review* 56, no. 1 (1989): 63.

4. Forty-seven thousand Viennese Jews were deported and assassinated. The name of Adolfine does not appear on the list of those who died in Theresienstadt on that date. Owing to a confusion of names, the date of her death is often given as February 5, 1943. In a chaotic novel, the Macedonian writer Goce Smilevski accused Freud of being responsible for his sisters' deportation—of having refused to add their names to his list of "postulants" for emigration. With such reasoning, one could hold all the Viennese Jews who managed to reach exile in 1938 responsible for the extermination of their relatives. See Goce Smilevski, *La liste de Freud* (Paris: Belfond, 2013), and see Michel Rotfus's commentary in his blog, "Poétiser à Auschwitz," *Médiapart,* October 7, 2013, https://blogs.mediapart.fr/michelrotfus/blog/071013/goce-smilevski-la-liste-de-freud-poetiser-auschwitz-dit-il.

5. *"The Trial of German Major War Criminals,* Part 8, 27-Feb-1946, testimony of Samuel Rajzman of Treblinka, p. 18," xoxol.org, January 24, 2010, http://www.xoxol.org/nuremberg/nuremberg01.html, cited by Leupold-Löwenthal, "Emigration," and Alfred Gottwaldt, "Les soeurs de Sigmund Freud et la mort: Remarques

concernant leur destin de déportation et de meurtre de masse," *Revue française de psychanalyse* 68, no. 4 (2004): 1307–1316. It has been established that Samuel Rajzman's account concerned Rosa Graf. Christfried Tögel thinks that Rosa was transported on March 1, 1943: see "Bahnstation Treblinka: Zum Schicksal von Sigmund Freuds Schwester Rosa Graf," *Psyche. Zeitschrift für Psychoanalyse und ihre Anwendungen* 44 (1990): 1019–1024. As for Gottwaldt, he insists that the other two sisters may also have been exterminated in Treblinka, and that Rosa had arrived on September 29, 1942, on the Bs 800 transport. Several rumors have circulated about the deportation of Freud's sisters. Michel Onfray goes so far as to affirm that Rosa, Mitzi, and Paula crossed paths with Rudolf Höss at Auschwitz, and he imagines that they saw Höss as a substitute for their brother, since Freud, an executioner himself and a Fascist fan of Mussolini, was incapable of telling the difference between an executioner and a victim: see *Le crépuscule d'une idole: L'affabulation fabuleuse* (Paris: Grasset, 2010), 566.

6. At the beginning of the war, in England, they were considered "enemy aliens" and lived in internment camps.

7. Clement Freud, *Freud Ego* (London: BBC Worldwide, 2001).

8. Esther Freud, *Marrakech Express* (Paris: Livre de poche, 1999); Esther Freud, *Nuits d'été en Toscane* (Paris: Albin Michel, 2009).

9. See Geordie Greig, *Breakfast with Lucian: The Astounding Life and Outrageous Times of Britain's Great Modern Painter* (New York: Farrar, Straus and Giroux, 2013), 44.

10. Ibid., 47–48.

11. Sigmund Freud, *The Diary of Sigmund Freud, 1929–1939: A Record of the Final Decade* (New York: Scribner's, 1992), 306. David Cohen devoted a book to this affair, which gave rise to many different interpretations: *The Escape of Sigmund Freud* (London: Overlook Press, 2012).

12. Burlingham initially moved into a house on Maresfield Gardens.

13. Kata Levy (1883–1969) was a Hungarian psychoanalyst who had been analyzed by Freud. She emigrated to London with her husband in 1956. She had been informed of the extermination of Freud's sisters by the Red Cross.

14. Anna Freud, "An Experiment in Group Upbringing" (1951), in *The Writings of Anna Freud* (New York: International Universities Press, 1968), 4:163–229. Jenny Aubry was inspired by this thesis to undertake her own experiment with abandoned children; see *Psychanalyse des enfants séparés* (Paris: Denoël, 2003). See also the unpublished presentation by Maria Landau during the third day-long conference of the Association Jenny Aubry, devoted to separation (April 18, 2003); reviewed by Michel Rotfus, *Médiapart*, April 26, 2003, https://blogs.mediapart.fr/michelrotfus/blog/260413/les-enfants-et-la-psychanalyse-3eme-journee-de-l-association-jenny-aubry-les-maladies-de-la-separation.

15. An expurgated version of these letters appeared in French in 1950 under the title *La naissance de la psychanalyse;* in English, see Sigmund Freud, *The Origins of Psychoanalysis: Letters, Drafts and Notes to Wilhelm Fliess, 1887–1902*, ed. Marie Bonaparte,

Anna Freud, and Ernst Kris, trans. Eric Mosbacher and James Strachey (Garden City, NY: Doubleday, 1957).

16. On the genesis of the work and the difficulties Jones encountered, see Mikkel Borch-Jacobsen and Sonu Shamdasani, *The Freud Files: An Inquiry into the History of Psychoanalysis* (Cambridge: Cambridge University Press, 2012), 235–286.

17. Anna Freud, *The Psycho-analytical Treatment of Children: Technical Lectures and Essays* (London: Imago, 1946).

18. After Lucie attempted suicide following Ernst's death, Lucian made some fifteen portraits of her, starting in 1972.

19. Eva Weissweiler, *Les Freud: Une famille viennoise* (Paris: Plon, 2006), 374. It was in the national park at Dartmoor that Arthur Conan Doyle's story "The Hound of the Baskervilles" was set.

20. I do not share the opinion of Borch-Jacobsen, who asserts that Eissler deceived—even swindled—the American people in using the Library of Congress as a lockbox to confiscate the archives for his own benefit and to hide them from researchers. See Borch-Jacobsen and Shamdasani, *Freud Files*, 424.

21. Henri F. Ellenberger, *The Discovery of the Unconscious: The History and Evolution of Dynamic Psychiatry* (New York: Basic Books, 1970). Initially published in French as *À la découverte de l'inconscient: Histoire de la psychiatrie dynamique*, trans. J. Feisthauer (Paris: SIMEP-éditions, 1974), the volume was republished two decades later, at the initiative of Olivier Bétourné, in keeping with Ellenberger's own wishes, as *Histoire de la découverte de l'inconscient* (Paris: Fayard, 1994). Ellenberger then turned the handling of his archives over to the SIHPP; I am looking after them today, with the help of his son Michel Ellenberger.

22. See Jeffrey Moussaieff Masson, "Freud and the Seduction Theory: A Challenge to the Foundations of Psychoanalysis," *Atlantic Monthly* 253, no. 2 (February 1984): 23–30.

23. Jeffrey Moussaieff Masson, *The Assault on Truth: Freud's Suppression of the Seduction Theory* (New York: Farrar, Straus and Giroux, 1984).

24. Janet Malcolm, *In the Freud Archives* (New York: Knopf, 1984).

25. I had the opportunity to meet Masson when the French translation of his book came out. He was really convinced that all children were victims of sexual abuse on the part of adults. Born in 1941, the author of numerous books, he is now a vegan and a militant for animal rights; he lives in Auckland surrounded by his family and his many dogs. I had a brief exchange of letters with Eissler between December 1994 and January 1995 about Ellenberger when I was working on the publication of *Médecines de l'âme*.

26. See Elisabeth Young-Bruehl, *Anna Freud: A Biography*, 2nd ed. (New Haven, CT: Yale University Press, 2008 [1988]), 436–438.

27. See Adolf Grünbaum, *The Foundations of Psychoanalysis: A Philosophical Critique* (Berkeley: University of California Press, 1984). In this book, Grünbaum lashes out fiercely against three philosophers—Karl Popper, Jürgen Habermas, and Paul

Ricoeur—and reproaches them for not having been critical enough of psychoanalysis. I analyze Grünbaum's book in Élisabeth Roudinesco, *Why Psychoanalysis?* trans. Rachel Bowlby (New York: Columbia University Press, 2001 [1999]).

28. As I have already pointed out, in 1994, under the aegis of the SIHPP, René Major and I organized a colloquium on the archives.

29. A typed document dated July 31, 1995. I exchanged several messages on the subject with Schorske, Gay, Yosef Yerushalmi, Mahoney, Ilse Grubrich-Simitis, John Forrester, and many others. In a letter he sent on this occasion, Schorske pointed out that he saw the return of a certain McCarthyism in this offensive.

30. Nicolas Weill and Raphaëlle Rérolle, conversation with Élisabeth Roudinesco, and Nicolas Weill, conversation with with Mikkel Borch-Jacobsen, *Le Monde*, June 14, 1996.

31. Patrick Sabatier, conversation with Michael S. Roth, *Libération*, October 26, 1998; Michael S. Roth, ed., *Freud: Conflict and Culture: Essays on His Life, Work, and Legacy* (New York: Knopf, 1998).

32. I coordinated two collective works in response to these best sellers, with Sylvain Courage, Pierre Delion, Christian Godin, Roland Gori, Franck Lelièvre, Guillaume Mazea, Jack Ralite, and Jean-Pierre Sueur, *Pourquoi tant de haine? Anatomie du "Livre noir de la psychanalyse"* (Paris: Navarin, 2005), and Élisabeth Roudinesco, *Mais pourquoi tant de haine?* (Paris: Seuil, 2010).

33. The break-in took place during the night of December 31, 2013–January 1, 2014.

Works Cited

Abraham, Karl. "Amenhotep IV: A Psycho-analytical Contribution towards the Understanding of His Personality and of the Monotheistic Cult of Aton" (1912). In *Clinical Papers and Essays on Psycho-analysis*, preface by Ernest Jones, 262–290. London: Hogarth, 1955.

————. "Mental After-Effects Produced in a Nine-Year-Old Child by the Observation of Sexual Intercourse between Its Parents." In *Selected Papers of Karl Abraham, M.D.*, ed. Ernest Jones, trans. Douglas Bryan and Alix Strachey, 164–168. London: Hogarth, 1927.

Abraham, Nicolas, and Maria Torok. *The Wolf Man's Magic Word: A Cryptonomy.* Trans. Nicholas Rand. Foreword by Jacques Derrida. Minneapolis: University of Minnesota Press, 1986.

Accerboni, Anna Maria. "Psychanalyse et fascisme: Deux approches incompatibles. Le rôle difficile d'Edoardo Weiss." *Revue internationale d'histoire de la psychanalyse* 1 (1988): 225–245.

————. "Sigmund Freud as Remembered by Edoardo Weiss, the Italian Pioneer of Psychoanalysis." *International Review of Psycho-analysis* 17, no. 3 (1990): 351–359.

Accerboni Pavanello, Anna Maria. "La sfida di Svevo alla psicoanalisi." In *Guarire dalla cura: Italo Svevo e i medici*, 85–131. Trieste: Museo Sveviano, 2008.

Alexander, Jerome. Testimony, October 21, 1951. LoC, box 120, folder 2.

Andersson, Ola. *Studies in the Prehistory of Psychoanalysis: The Etiology of Psychoneuroses and Some Related Themes in Sigmund Freud's Scientific Writings and Letters, 1886–1896.* Stockholm: Svenska Bokförlaget, 1962. In French as *Freud avant Freud: La préhistoire de la psychanalyse*, trans. Sylvette Gleize, preface by Per Magnus Johansson and Élisabeth Roudinesco, coll. Les Empêcheurs de penser en rond. Paris: Synthélabo, 1997.

Andreas-Salomé, Lou. *L'amour du narcissisme.* Trans. Isabelle Hildenbrand. Paris: Gallimard, 1980 (1977).

————. *The Freud Journal of Lou Andreas-Salomé.* Trans. Stanley A. Leavy. New York: Basic Books, 1964.

———. *Looking Back: Memoirs.* Ed. Ernst Pfeiffer. Trans. Breon Mitchell. New York: Paragon House, 1991 (1901).

———. "Mein Bekenntnis zum heutigen Deutschland" (1934). Unpublished, located in the archives of Lou Andreas-Salomé, Göttingen.

———. *My Thanks to Freud (Mein Dank an Freud): Open Letter to Professor Sigmund Freud for His 75th Birthday* (1931). Trans. William Needham. https://ia601009.us .archive.org/6/items/MeinDank/Mein%20Dank.pdf. In French as *Lettre ouverte à Freud*, trans. Dominique Miermont. Paris: Seuil, 1994.

Andreas-Salomé, Lou, and Anna Freud. *À l'ombre du père: Correspondance, 1919–1937.* Trans. Stephane Michaud. Paris: Hachette Littérature, 2006.

Angelini, Alberto. *La psicoanalisi in Russia: Dai precursori agli anni trenta.* Naples: Liguori, 1988.

Anzahl Gesellschaft der Ärtze zu Wien. Unsigned review of "Über männliche Hysterie" (1886), by Sigmund Freud. Vol. 25 (1886): 149–152.

Anzieu, Didier. *Freud's Self-Analysis.* Trans. Peter Graham. Madison, CT: International Universities, 1986 (1959).

Appignanesi, Lisa, and John Forrester. *Freud's Women.* New York: Basic Books, 1992.

Armstrong, Richard H. *A Compulsion for Antiquity.* Ithaca, NY: Cornell University Press, 2005.

Assmann, Jan. *Moses the Egyptian: The Memory of Egypt in Western Monotheism.* Cambridge, MA: Harvard University Press, 1997.

Assoun, Paul-Laurent. *Dictionnaire des oeuvres psychanalytiques.* Paris: Presses Universitaires de France, 2009.

Astor, Dorian. *Lou Andreas-Salomé.* Paris: Gallimard, 2008.

Atkinson, James Jasper. "Primal Law." In Andrew Lang, *Social Origins,* 209–294. London: Longmans, Green, 1903.

Aubry, Jenny. *Psychanalyse des enfants séparés.* Paris: Denoël, 2003.

Azouri, Chawki. *"J'ai réussi où le paranoïaque échoue": La théorie a-t-elle un père?* Paris: Denoël, 1990.

Bainville, Jacques. *Les conséquences politiques de la paix.* Paris: Gallimard, 2002.

Bair, Deirdre. *Jung: A Biography.* Boston: Little, Brown, 2003.

Bakan, David. *Sigmund Freud and the Jewish Mystical Tradition.* Princeton, NJ: Van Nostrand, 1958.

Ballenato, Anthony. "Freud et la modernité américaine: L'introduction de la psychanalyse à New York (1909–1917)." Master's II thesis, University of Paris VII, 2007–2008.

Balmary, Marie. *Psychoanalyzing Psychoanalysis: Freud and the Hidden Fault of the Father.* Trans. Ned Lucacher. Baltimore: Johns Hopkins University Press, 1982 (1979).

Bataille, Georges. *The Accursed Share: An Essay on General Economy.* Trans. Robert Hurley. 3 vols. New York: Zone Books, 1988–1993.

Baudelaire, Charles. *The Flowers of Evil.* Trans. James McGowan. Introduction by Jonathan Culler. New York: Oxford University Press, 1993.

Beam, Alex. *Gracefully Insane: The Rise and Fall of America's Premier Mental Hospital.* New York: Public Affairs, 2003.

Behling, Katja. *Martha Freud: A Biography.* Foreword by Anton W. Freud. Cambridge, UK: Polity, 2005 (2003).

Bénesteau, Jacques. *Mensonges freudiens.* Hayen, Belgium: Mardaga, 2002.

Benslama, Fethi. *La psychanalyse à l'épreuve de l'islam.* Paris: Aubier, 2002.

Bernays, Anna Freud. *Eine Wienerin in New York: Die Erinnerungen der Schwester Sigmund Freuds.* Ed. Christfried Tögel. Berlin: Aufbau Verlag, 2004.

Berneri, Camillo. Article about Freud's book on Leonardo. Bibliothèque Freud no. 217; London: Freud Museum.

———. *Le Juif antisémite.* Paris: Vita, 1935.

Bernfeld, Siegfried. "Letter to Anna Freud, November 23, 1937." *Revue internationale d'histoire de la psychanalyse* 3 (1990): 335.

———. "An Unknown Autobiographical Fragment by Freud." *American Imago* 4, no. 1 (1946): 3–19.

Bernheim, Hippolyte. *Hypnosis and Suggestion in Psychotherapy.* Trans. from 2nd rev. ed. by Christian A. Herter. New Hyde Park, NY: University Books, 1964 (1891).

Berthelsen, Detlef. *La famille Freud au jour le jour: Souvenirs de Paula Fichtl.* Trans. Lucien-Marie Robin. Paris: Presses Universitaires de France, 1991 (1987).

Bertin, Célia. *La femme à Vienne au temps de Freud.* Paris: Stock/Laurence Pernoud, 1989.

———. *Marie Bonaparte: A Life.* Translation of *La dernière Bonaparte.* New York: Harcourt Brace Jovanovich, 1982.

Bettelheim, Bruno. *Freud and Man's Soul.* New York: Alfred A. Knopf, 1982.

Binswanger, Ludwig. *Discours, parcours, et Freud.* Paris: Gallimard, 1970.

Blanton, Smiley. *Diary of My Analysis with Sigmund Freud.* New York: Hawthorn Books, 1971.

Bleuler, Eugen. *Dementia praecox; or, The Group of Schizophrenias.* Trans. Joseph Zinkin. New York: International Universities Press, 1950 (1911).

Blondel, Charles. *La psychanalyse.* Paris: Alcan, 1924.

Bollack, Jean. *Jacob Bernays (1821–1881): Un homme entre deux mondes.* Villeneuved'Ascq, France: Presses Universitaires du Septentrion, 1998.

Bolzinger, André. *Portrait de Sigmund Freud: Trésors d'une correspondance.* Paris: Campagne Première, 2012.

Bonaparte, Marie. "Cahier biographique en huit cahiers" (October 1951). Unpublished.

———. *Cinq cahiers écrits par une petite fille entre sept ans et demi et dix ans avec leurs commentaires* (1939–1951). 4 vols. Privately printed for the author.

———. "Extraits du Cahier 1." *L'Infini* 2 (Spring 1983): 76–89.

————. *Female Sexuality.* New York: International Universities Press, 1953.

————. *Sommaire de mon analyse et de ma correspondance avec Freud, avec Agenda (Cahiers noirs).* December 14, 1925. Unpublished.

Bonaparte, Marie, and Anne Berman. Exchange of letters. Bibliothèque nationale de France.

Bonomi, Carlo. "Pourquoi avons-nous ignoré Freud le 'pédiatre'? Le rapport entre la formation pédiatrique de Freud et les origines de la psychanalyse." In *La psychanalyse: 100 ans déjà . . . Contributions à l'histoire intellectuelle du XXe siècle,* ed. André Haynal, 87–153. Geneva: Georg, 1996.

————. *Sulla soglia della psicoanalisi: Freud e la follia infantile.* Turin: Bollati Boringhieri, 2007.

————. "Withstanding Trauma: The Significance of Emma Epstein's Circumcision to Freud's Irma Dream." *Psychoanalytic Quarterly* 82 (July 2013): 689–740.

Borch-Jacobsen, Mikkel. *Les patients de Freud: Destins.* Auxerre, France: Éditions Sciences humaines, 2011.

————. *Remembering Anna O.: A Century of Mystification.* Trans. Kirby Olson with Xavière Callahan and the author. New York: Routledge, 1996 (1995).

Borch-Jacobsen, Mikkel, and Sonu Shamdasani. *The Freud Files: An Inquiry into the History of Psychoanalysis.* Cambridge: Cambridge University Press, 2012.

Börne, Ludwig, and Leland De La Durantaye. "How to Become an Original Writer in Three Days (First Published in 1823)." *Harvard Review,* no. 31 (2006): 75–76.

Bousquet, Joë. *Le passeur s'est endormi.* Paris: Denoël, 1939.

Brecht, Karen, Hella Ehlers, and Christine Trollope. *"Here Life Goes On in a Most Peculiar Way . . .": Psychoanalysis before and after 1933.* Trans. from the German. Hamburg: Kellner, 1992.

Brome, Vincent. *Freud and His Early Circle: The Struggles of Psychoanalysis.* London: Heinemann, 1967.

————. *Jung.* New York: Athaneum, 1981.

Brunswick, Ruth Mack. "A Supplement to Freud's 'History of an Infantile Neurosis.'" In *The Wolf-Man: With the Case of the Wolf-Man, by Sigmund Freud and a Supplement by Ruth Mack Brunswick,* ed. Muriel Gardiner, 263–307. New York: Basic Books, 1971.

Buber, Martin. *Moses.* Translation of *Mosheh.* Oxford: East and West Library, 1946.

Canetti, Elias. *Crowds and Power.* Trans. Carol Stewart. New York: Viking, 1962 (1960).

————. *The Torch in My Ear.* Trans. Joachim Neugroschel. New York: Farrar, Straus and Giroux, 1982.

Canguilhem, Georges. "Claude Bernard." In *Études d'histoire et de philosophie des sciences,* 127–171. Paris: Vrin, 1968.

Carloni, Glauco. "Freud and Mussolini: A Minor Drama in Two Acts, One Interlude and Five Characters." Exhibition catalog, *L'Italia nella psicoanalisi,* 51–60. Rome, 1989.

Carotenuto, Aldo. *A Secret Symmetry: Sabina Spielrein between Jung and Freud.* Trans. Arno Pomerans, John Shepley, and Krishna Winston. New York: Pantheon Books, 1982.

Carroy, Jacqueline. *Nuits savants: Une histoire des rêves (1800–1945).* Paris: EHESS, 2012.

Cassirer-Bernfeld, Suzanne. "Freud's Early Childhood." *Bulletin of the Menninger Clinic* 8 (1944): 107–115.

Certeau, Michel de. *The Mystic Fable: The Sixteenth and Seventeenth Centuries.* Ed. Luce Giard. Trans. Michael B. Smith. 2 vols. Chicago: University of Chicago Press, 1992–2015.

———. *The Writing of History.* Trans. Tom Conley. New York: Columbia University Press, 1988 (1975).

Chapman, Clare. "Austrians Stunned by Nobel Prize-Winner's Nazi Ideology." *Scotland on Sunday,* January 24, 2004.

Charcot, Jean-Martin. *Charcot the Clinician, the Tuesday Lessons: Excerpts from Nine Case Presentations on General Neurology Delivered at the Salpêtrière Hospital in 1887–88.* Trans. Christopher G. Goetz. New York: Raven, 1987 (1892).

Chemouni, Jacquy. "Psychopathologie de la démocratie." *Frénésie* 10 (Spring 1992): 265–282.

Cioffi, Frank. *Freud and the Question of Pseudoscience.* Chicago: Open Court, 1999.

Cixous, Hélène. *Portrait of Dora.* In *Selected Plays of Hélène Cixous,* trans. Ann Liddle, 35–59. New York: Routledge, 2004.

Clair, Jean, ed. *L'âme au corps: Arts et sciences, 1793–1993.* Exhibition catalog. Paris: Réunion des musées nationaux/Gallimard/Electra, 1993.

———. *Malinconia: Motifs saturniens dans l'art de l'entre-deux-guerres.* Paris: Gallimard, 1996.

———. *Vienne: L'apocalypse joyeuse.* Exhibition catalog. Paris: Centre Georges-Pompidou, 1986.

Clark, Ronald W. *Freud, the Man and the Cause: A Biography.* New York: Random House, 1980.

Clément, Catherine. *Pour Sigmund Freud.* Paris: Mengès, 2005.

———. "La sauvagerie de l'amour même." *L'Arc* 78 (1980): 1–4.

Coblence, Françoise. "Freud et la cocaïne." *Revue française de psychoanalyse* 2, no. 66 (2002): 371–383.

Cocks, Geoffrey. *Psychotherapy in the Third Reich: The Göring Institute.* 2nd ed. New Brunswick, NJ: Transaction, 1997.

Cohen, David. *The Escape of Sigmund Freud.* London: Overlook, 2012.

Coudenhove-Kalergi, H. J. M., R. N. Coudenhove-Kalergi, and A. S. Rappoport. *Anti-Semitism throughout the Ages.* Trans. Angelo Solomon. London: Hutchinson, 1935.

Covington, Coline, and Barbara Wharton, eds. *Sabina Spielrein: Forgotten Pioneer of Psychoanalysis.* London: Routledge, Taylor and Francis, 2015.

Curio, Jennifer. "Ce qui est arrivé à la psychanalyse en Allemagne." DEA thesis, Université Paris-Nord, 1997.

Darwin, Charles. *Charles Darwin's Notebooks, 1836–1844: Geology, Transmutation of Species, Metaphysical Enquiries.* Transcribed and edited by Paul H. Barrett et al. London: British Museum, 1987.

Davies, Erica. "Eine Welt wie im Traum, Freuds Antikensammllung." In *"Meine alten und dreckigen Götter," Aus Sigmund Freuds Sammlung,* ed. Lydia Marinelli. Exhibition catalog. Frankfurt: Stroemfeld, 1998.

Davies, J. Keith, and Gerhard Fichtner, eds. *Freud's Library: A Comprehensive Catalogue.* Bilingual German-English. London: Freud Museum, 2006.

Dearborn, Mary V. *Queen of Bohemia: The Life of Louise Bryant.* Boston: Houghton Mifflin, 1996.

Decker, Hannah S. *Freud, Dora and Vienna.* New York: Free Press, 1991.

Delboeuf, Joseph. *Le sommeil et les rêves et autres textes.* Paris: Fayard, 1993 (1885).

Derrida, Jacques. *Archive Fever: A Freudian Impression?* Trans. Eric Prenowitz. Chicago: University of Chicago Press, 1996.

———. *The Post Card: From Socrates to Freud and Beyond.* Trans. Alan Bass. Chicago: University of Chicago Press, 1987 (1980).

———. "Telepathy." Trans. Nicholas Royle. In *Psyche: Inventions of the Other,* ed. Peggy Kamuf and Elizabeth Rottenberg, 1:226–261. Stanford, CA: Stanford University Press, 2007 (1981).

———. "'. . . That Dangerous Supplement . . .'" In *Of Grammatology,* trans. Gayatri Chakkravorty Spivak, 141–164. Baltimore: Johns Hopkins University Press, 1976 (1967).

Deutsch, Helene. *The Psychology of Women: A Psychoanalytical Interpretation by Helene Deutsch.* 2 vols. New York: Grune and Stratton, 1944–1945.

Devereux, Georges. *Reality and Dream: Psychotherapy of a Plains Indian.* Garden City, NY: Anchor Books, 1969. In French as *Psychothérapie d'un Indien des Plaines,* trans. Françoise de Gruson with Monique Novodorsqui, preface by Élisabeth Roudinesco (Paris: Fayard, 1998).

Didi-Huberman, Georges. *The Invention of Hysteria: Charcot and the Photographic Iconography of the Salpêtrière.* Trans. from the French. Cambridge, MA: MIT Press, 2003 (1982).

Donn, Linda. *Freud and Jung: Years of Friendship, Years of Loss.* New York: Scribner, 1988.

Doolittle, Hilda. *Tribute to Freud.* New York: Pantheon, 1956.

Dorer, Maria. *Les bases historiques de la psychanalyse.* Trans. Marc Géraud. Paris: L'Harmattan, 2012 (1932).

Dostaler, Gilles, and Bernard Maris. *Capitalisme et pulsion de mort.* Paris: Albin Michel, 2009.

Doyle, Arthur Conan. *The History of Spiritualism.* 2 vols. New York: George H. Doran, 1926.

Drumont, Édouard. *La France juive: Essai d'histoire contemporaine.* Paris: C. Marpon and E. Flammarion, 1886.

Duby, Georges, and Michelle Perrot. *Histoire des femmes*. Vol. 4, *Le XIXe siècle*. Paris: Plon, 1991.

Edinger, Dora. *Bertha Pappenheim*. Highland Park, IL: Congregation Solel, 1968 (1963).

Edmunds, L. "Freud's American Tragedy." *Johns Hopkins Magazine* 30 (1988): 40–49.

Edmundson, Mark. *The Death of Sigmund Freud: The Legacy of His Last Days*. New York: Bloomsbury, 2007.

Eissler, Kurt Robert. *Freud as an Expert Witness: The Discussion of War Neuroses between Freud and Wagner-Jauregg*. New York: International Universities Press, 1986.

———. *Goethe: A Psychoanalytic Interpretation of a Decade in His Life (1776–1786)*. 2 vols. Detroit: Wayne State University Press, 1963.

———. Interviews, 1954–1955. LoC, box 116.

———. Interview with Julius Liebman. February 6, 1954. LoC, box 114, folder 16.

———. *Leonardo da Vinci: Psychoanalytic Notes on the Enigma*. New York: International Universities Press, 1961.

———. Testimony of Robert McCully. N.d. LoC, box 121, folder 17.

Ellenberger, Henri F. *The Discovery of the Unconscious: The History and Evolution of Dynamic Psychiatry*. New York: Basic Books, 1970.

———. "Freud's Lecture on Masculine Hysteria (October 15, 1886): A Critical Study." In *Beyond the Unconscious: Essays of Henri F. Ellenberger in the History of Psychiatry*, ed. Mark S. Micale, trans. Françoise Dubor and Mark S. Micale, 119–135. Princeton, NJ: Princeton University Press, 1993.

———. *Médecines de l'âme: Essais d'histoire de la folie et des guérisons psychiques*. Paris: Fayard, 1995.

Enderlin, Charles. *Au nom du Temple: Israël et l'irrésistible ascension du messianisme juif (1967–2003)*. Paris: Seuil, 2013.

———. *Shattered Dreams: The Failure of the Peace Process in the Middle East, 1995–2002*. New York: Other Press, 2003 (2002).

Engelman, Edmund. *Berggasse 19: Sigmund Freud's Home and Offices, Vienna, 1938: The Photographs of Edmund Engelman*. New York: Basic Books, 1976.

"Enquête sur Sigmund Freud et sur la WPV effectuée par la diplomatie fasciste italienne en 1935." Document. *Revue internationale d'histoire de la psychanalyse* 5 (1992): 143–150.

Enriquez, Eugène. *De la horde à l'État*. Paris: Gallimard, 1983.

Erikson, Erik H. Review of Sigmund Freud and William C. Bullitt, *Thomas Woodrow Wilson: Twenty-Eighth President of the United States: A Psychological Study*. *International Journal of Psychoanalysis* 48 (1967): 462–468.

Etkind, Alexander. *Eros of the Impossible: The History of Psychoanalysis in Russia*. Trans. Noah Rubins and Maria Rubins. Boulder, CO: Westview, 1997.

Évard, Jean-Luc, ed. and trans. *Les années brunes: La psychanalyse sous le IIIe Reich*. Paris: Éditions Confrontation, 1984.

Falzeder, Ernst. "Existe-t-il encore un Freud inconnu?" *Psychothérapies* 27, no. 3 (2007): 175–195.

Falzeder, Ernst, and Bernhard Handlbauer. "Freud, Adler et d'autres psychanalystes: Des débuts de la psychanalyse organisée à la fondation de l'Association psychanalytique internationale." *Psychothérapies* 12, no. 4 (1992): 219–232.

Ferenczi, Sándor. *The Clinical Diary of Sándor Ferenczi.* Ed. Judith Dupont. Trans. Michael Balint and Nicola Zarday Jackson. Cambridge, MA: Harvard University Press, 1988.

———. "Confusion of Tongues between Adults and the Child" (1932). In *Final Contributions to the Problems and Methods of Psychoanalysis,* ed. Michael Balint, trans. Eric Mosbacher et al., 156–167. New York: Brunner/Mazel, 1955, repr. 1980.

———. *Les écrits de Budapest.* Paris: EPEL, 1994.

———. "The Little Rooster Man" (1913). In J. Borossa, ed., *Sándor Ferenczi: Selected Writings,* 84–91. Harmondsworth, UK: Penguin, 1999.

———. *Oeuvres complètes: Psychanalyse.* 4 vols. Paris: Payot, 1968–1982.

———. "On the Organization of the Psycho-analytical Movement" (1911). In *Final Contributions to the Problems and Methods of Psycho-analysis,* ed. Michael Balit, trans. Eric Mosbacher et al., 299–307. New York: Brunner/Mazel, 1955, repr. 1980.

———. "On the Technique of Psycho-analysis" (1919). In *Further Contributions to the Theory and Technique of Psycho-analysis,* ed. John Rickman, trans. Jane Isabel Suttie et al., 177–189. New York: Brunner/Mazel, 1950, repr. 1980.

———. "Stages in the Development of the Sense of Reality" (1913). In *First Contributions to Psycho-analysis,* trans. Ernest Jones, 213–239. New York: Brunner/Mazel, 1952, repr. 1980.

———. *Thalassa: A Theory of Genitality.* New York: W. W. Norton, 1968 (1963).

Ferenczi, Sándor, Karl Abraham, Ernst Simmel, and Ernest Jones. *Psycho-analysis and the War Neuroses.* Introduction by Sigmund Freud. London: International Psychoanalytical Press, 1921.

Ferenczi, Sándor, and Otto Rank. *The Development of Psychoanalysis.* Trans. Caroline Newton. Madison, CT: International Universities Press, 1986 (1924).

Ferris, Paul. *Dr. Freud: A Life.* Washington, DC: Counterpoint, 1998.

Ferrone, Vincenzo, and Daniel Roche, eds. *Le monde des Lumières.* Paris: Fayard, 1999.

Fichtner, Gerhard. "Bibliographie des lettres de Freud." *Revue internationale d'histoire de la psychanalyse* 2 (1989): 80–108.

———. "Les lettres de Freud en tant que source historique." *Revue internationale d'histoire de la psychanalyse* 2 (1989): 51–80.

Finck, Jean. *Thomas Mann et la psychanalyse.* Paris: Les Belles Lettres, 1982.

Fliess, Wilhelm. *Die Beziehungen zwischen Nase und weiblichen Geschlectsorganen, in ihrer biologischen Bedeutung dargestellt.* Leipzig: Deuticke, 1897. In French as *Les relations entre le nez et les organes génitaux féminins, présentées selon leurs significations biologiques,* trans. Patrick Ach and Jean Guir. Paris: Seuil, 1977.

Flournoy, Theodore. *From India to the Planet Mars: A Study of a Case of Somnambulism with Glossolalia*. Trans. Daniel B. Vermilye. New York: Harper and Bros., 1900.

Forrester, John. "The True Story of Anna O." *Social Research* 53, no. 2 (Summer 1986): 327–347.

Forzano, Giovacchino. "Letter to Mussolini, March 14, 1938." In Paul Roazen, "Psychoanalytic Ethics: Edoardo Weiss, Freud, and Mussolini," *Journal of the History of the Behavioral Sciences* 27, no. 4 (1991): 366–374.

Foucault, Michel. *The Birth of the Clinic: An Archaeology of Medical Perception*. Trans. A. M. Sheridan Smith. New York: Vintage Books, 1994 (1963).

Frazer, James George. *The Golden Bough: A Study in Magic and Religion*. 12 vols. London: Macmillan, 1911–1915.

Freud, Anna. "Beating Fantasies and Daydreams" (1922). In *The Writings of Anna Freud*, 1:137–157. New York: International Universities Press, 1966.

———. "An Experiment in Group Upbringing" (1951). In *The Writings of Anna Freud*, 4:163–229. New York: International Universities Press, 1968.

———. *The Psycho-analytical Treatment of Children: Technical Lectures and Essays*. London: Imago, 1946.

Freud, Clement. *Freud Ego*. London: BBC Worldwide, 2001.

Freud, Ernst, Lucie Freud, and Ilse Grubrich-Simitis, eds. *Sigmund Freud: His Life in Pictures and Words*, with a biographical sketch by Kurt R. Eissler. Trans. Christine Trollope. New York: Harcourt Brace Jovanovich, 1978 (1976).

Freud, Esther. *Marrakech Express*. Paris: Livre de poche, 1999.

———. *Nuits d'été en Toscane*. Paris: Albin Michel, 2009.

Freud, Harry. Letter to Dolfi, Paula, Rosa, and Mitzi, September 25, 1939. LoC, box 3, folder 7ff.

Freud, Martin. *Glory Reflected: Sigmund Freud—Man and Father*. London: Angus and Robertson, 1957.

Freud, Sigmund. "Besprechung von P. J. Moebius: *Die Migräne*" (1895). In *Gesammelte Werke*. Frankfurt: S. Fischer Verlag, 1960– . *Nachtragsband* (1987), 364–369.

———. *Cocaine Papers*. Ed. Robert Byck. New York: New American Library, 1974.

———. *The Complete Correspondence of Sigmund Freud and Ernest Jones, 1908–1939*. Ed. R. Andrew Paskauskas. Cambridge, MA: Belknap Press of Harvard University Press, 1993.

———. *The Complete Letters of Sigmund Freud to Wilhelm Fliess, 1877–1904*. Ed. and trans. Jeffrey Moussaieff Masson. Cambridge, MA: Belknap Press of Harvard University Press, 1985.

———. *Correspondance*. 3 vols. Paris: Calmann-Lévy, 1992–2000.

———. *The Diary of Sigmund Freud, 1929–1939: A Record of the Final Decade*. New York: Scribner's, 1992.

———. Document, June 4, 1938. Austrian National Library.

———. *L'homme Moïse et la religion monothéiste*. Trans. Cornélius Heim. Paris: Gallimard, 1986 (1939).

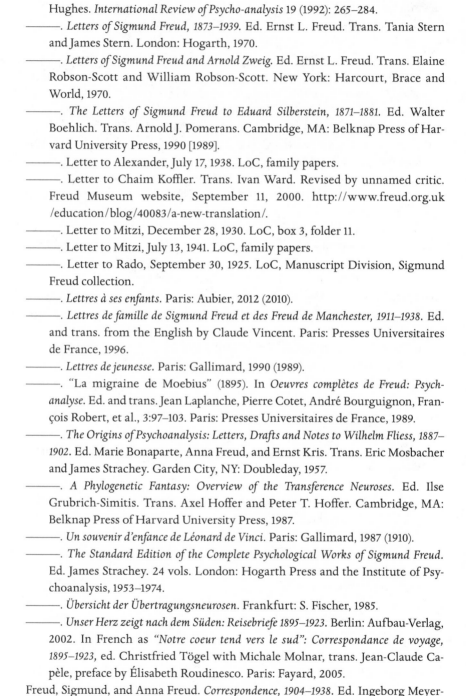

———. "Letters from Sigmund Freud to Joan Riviere (1921–1939)." Ed. Athol Hughes. *International Review of Psycho-analysis* 19 (1992): 265–284.

———. *Letters of Sigmund Freud, 1873–1939.* Ed. Ernst L. Freud. Trans. Tania Stern and James Stern. London: Hogarth, 1970.

———. *Letters of Sigmund Freud and Arnold Zweig.* Ed. Ernst L. Freud. Trans. Elaine Robson-Scott and William Robson-Scott. New York: Harcourt, Brace and World, 1970.

———. *The Letters of Sigmund Freud to Eduard Silberstein, 1871–1881.* Ed. Walter Boehlich. Trans. Arnold J. Pomerans. Cambridge, MA: Belknap Press of Harvard University Press, 1990 [1989].

———. Letter to Alexander, July 17, 1938. LoC, family papers.

———. Letter to Chaim Koffler. Trans. Ivan Ward. Revised by unnamed critic. Freud Museum website, September 11, 2000. http://www.freud.org.uk /education/blog/40083/a-new-translation/.

———. Letter to Mitzi, December 28, 1930. LoC, box 3, folder 11.

———. Letter to Mitzi, July 13, 1941. LoC, family papers.

———. Letter to Rado, September 30, 1925. LoC, Manuscript Division, Sigmund Freud collection.

———. *Lettres à ses enfants.* Paris: Aubier, 2012 (2010).

———. *Lettres de famille de Sigmund Freud et des Freud de Manchester, 1911–1938.* Ed. and trans. from the English by Claude Vincent. Paris: Presses Universitaires de France, 1996.

———. *Lettres de jeunesse.* Paris: Gallimard, 1990 (1989).

———. "La migraine de Moebius" (1895). In *Oeuvres complètes de Freud: Psychanalyse.* Ed. and trans. Jean Laplanche, Pierre Cotet, André Bourguignon, François Robert, et al., 3:97–103. Paris: Presses Universitaires de France, 1989.

———. *The Origins of Psychoanalysis: Letters, Drafts and Notes to Wilhelm Fliess, 1887–1902.* Ed. Marie Bonaparte, Anna Freud, and Ernst Kris. Trans. Eric Mosbacher and James Strachey. Garden City, NY: Doubleday, 1957.

———. *A Phylogenetic Fantasy: Overview of the Transference Neuroses.* Ed. Ilse Grubrich-Simitis. Trans. Axel Hoffer and Peter T. Hoffer. Cambridge, MA: Belknap Press of Harvard University Press, 1987.

———. *Un souvenir d'enfance de Léonard de Vinci.* Paris: Gallimard, 1987 (1910).

———. *The Standard Edition of the Complete Psychological Works of Sigmund Freud.* Ed. James Strachey. 24 vols. London: Hogarth Press and the Institute of Psychoanalysis, 1953–1974.

———. *Übersicht der Übertragungsneurosen.* Frankfurt: S. Fischer, 1985.

———. *Unser Herz zeigt nach dem Süden: Reisebriefe 1895–1923.* Berlin: Aufbau-Verlag, 2002. In French as *"Notre coeur tend vers le sud": Correspondance de voyage, 1895–1923,* ed. Christfried Tögel with Michale Molnar, trans. Jean-Claude Capèle, preface by Élisabeth Roudinesco. Paris: Fayard, 2005.

Freud, Sigmund, and Anna Freud. *Correspondence, 1904–1938.* Ed. Ingeborg Meyer-Palmedo. Trans. Nick Somers. Cambridge, UK: Polity, 2014.

Freud, Sigmund, and Arnold Zweig. *Correspondance, 1927–1939.* Paris: Gallimard, 1973 (1968).

———. *The Letters of Sigmund Freud and Arnold Zweig.* Ed. Ernst L. Freud. Trans. Elaine Robson-Scott and William Robson-Scott. New York: Harcourt, Brace and World, 1970.

Freud, Sigmund, and C. G. Jung. *Freud / Jung Letters: The Correspondence between Sigmund Freud and C. G. Jung.* Ed. William McGuire. Trans. Ralph Manheim and R. F. C. Hull. Princeton, NJ: Princeton University Press, 1974.

Freud, Sigmund, and James Jackson Putnam. *James Jackson Putnam and Psychoanalysis: Letters between Putnam and Sigmund Freud, Ernest Jones, William James, Sándor Ferenczi, and Morton Prince, 1877–1917.* Ed. Nathan G. Hale Jr. Cambridge, MA: Harvard University Press, 1971.

Freud, Sigmund, and Karl Abraham. *The Complete Correspondence of Sigmund Freud and Karl Abraham, 1907–1925.* Transcribed and edited by Ernst Falzeder. Trans. Caroline Schwarzacher et al. London: Karnac, 2002 (1965).

Freud, Sigmund, and Lou Andreas-Salomé. *Letters.* Ed. Ernst Pfeiffer. Trans. William Robson-Scott and Elaine Robson-Scott. New York: Harcourt Brace Jovanovich, 1972.

Freud, Sigmund, and Martha Bernays. *Die Brautbriefe.* Ed. Ilse Grubrich and Albrecht Hirschmüller. Vol. 1, *Sei mein, wie ich mir's denke,* 2011; vol. 2, *Unser Roman in Fortsetzungen,* 2013. Frankfurt: Fischer Verlag.

Freud, Sigmund, and Minna Bernays. *Correspondance (1882–1938): Sigmund Freud, Minna Bernays.* Trans. Olivier Mannoni. Paris: Seuil, 2015. Originally published as *Briefwechsel, 1882–1938,* ed. Albrecht Hirschmüller. Tübingen, Germany: Diskord, 2005.

Freud, Sigmund, and Ludwig Binswanger. *The Sigmund Freud-Ludwig Binswanger Correspondence, 1908–1938.* Ed. Gerhard Fichtner. Trans. Arnold J. Pomerans. New York: Other Press, 2003.

Freud, Sigmund, and William Bullitt. *Woodrow Wilson: A Psychological Study.* New Brunswick, NJ: Transaction, 1998 (1966).

Freud, Sigmund, and Max Eitingon. *Correspondance, 1906–1939.* Ed. Michael Schröter. Trans. Olivier Mannoni. Paris: Hachette Littératures, 2009 (2004).

Freud, Sigmund, and Sándor Ferenczi. *Correspondence of Sigmund Freud and Sándor Ferenczi.* 3 vols. Ed. Eva Brabant, Ernst Falzeder, and Patrizia Giampieri-Deutsch. Trans. Peter T. Hoffer. Introduction by André Haynal. Cambridge, MA: Belknap Press of Harvard University Press, 1993.

Freud, Sigmund, and Oskar Pfisler. *Psychoanalysis and Faith: The Letters of Sigmund Freud and Oskar Pfister.* Ed. Heinrich Meng and Ernst L. Freud. Trans. Eric Mosbacher. London: Hogarth Press and the Institute of Psychoanalysis, 1963.

Freud, Sigmund, and Otto Rank. *The Letters of Sigmund Freud and Otto Rank.* Ed. James Lieberman and Robert Kramer. Trans. Gregory C. Richter. Baltimore: Johns Hopkins University Press, 2012.

Freud, Sigmund, and Stefan Zweig. *Correspondance, 1908–1929.* Trans. Gisella Hauer and Didier Plassard. Paris: Payot and Rivages poche, 1995 (1987).

Freud, Sophie. *Living in the Shadow of the Freud Family.* Westport, CT: Praeger, 2007.

Freud, W. Ernst. "Souvenirs personnels à propos de l'Anschluss." *Revue internationale d'histoire de la psychanalyse* 3 (1990): 409–414.

Freud-Marlé, Lilly. *Mein Onkel Sigmund Freud: Erinnerungen an eine grosse Familie.* Letters collected by Christfried Tögel. Berlin: Aufbau, 2006.

Friedländer, Adolf Albrecht. "Hysteria and Modern Psychoanalysis" (1909), *Journal of Abnormal Psychology* 5, no. 6 (February–March 1911): 297–319.

Frink, Horace W. *Morbid Fears and Compulsions.* Boston: Moffat, Yard, 1918.

Fry, Helen. *Freud's War.* Stroud, UK: History Press, 2009.

Gallo, Rubén. *Freud's Mexico: Into the Wilds of Psychoanalysis.* Cambridge, MA: MIT Press, 2010.

Gardiner, Muriel, ed. *The Wolf-Man: With the Case of the Wolf-Man, by Sigmund Freud and a Supplement by Ruth Mack Brunswick.* New York: Basic Books, 1971.

Gay, Peter. *Freud: A Life for Our Time.* New York: W. W. Norton, 1988.

———. "Freud and the Man from Stratford." In *Reading Freud: Explorations and Entertainments,* 5–53. New Haven, CT: Yale University Press, 1990.

———. *A Godless Jew: Freud, Atheism, and the Making of Psychoanalysis.* New Haven, CT: Yale University Press, 1987.

———. "Introduction: Freud: For the Marble Tablet." In *Berggasse 19: Sigmund Freud's Home and Offices, Vienna, 1938: The Photographs of Edmund Engelman,* by Edmund Engelman, 13–54. New York: Basic Books, 1976.

Gicklhorn, Renée. "La famille Freud à Freiberg" (1969). *Études freudiennes* 11–12 (January 1976): 231–238.

Gilbert, Martin. *Kristallnacht: Prelude to Destruction.* New York: HarperCollins, 2006.

Ginzburg, Carlo. *Clues, Myths, and the Historical Method.* Trans. John Tedeschi and Anne C. Tedeschi. Baltimore: Johns Hopkins University Press, 1989.

———. "Freud, the Wolf-Man, and Werewolves." In *Clues, Myths, and the Historical Method,* trans. John Tedeschi and Anne C. Tedeschi, 146–155. Baltimore: Johns Hopkins University Press, 1989.

Gödde, Günter. *Mathilde Freud: Die älteste Tochter Sigmund Freuds in Briefen und Selbstzeugnissen.* Berlin: Psychosozial Verlag/Edition Kore, 2002.

Goethe, Johann Wolfgang von. *Faust.* Part 1. Trans. David Constantine. London: Penguin, 2005.

Goetz, Bruno. "That Is All I Have to Say about Freud: Bruno Goetz's Reminiscences of Sigmund Freud." Trans. Shirley E. Jones. *International Review of Psychoanalysis* 2 (1975): 139–143.

Goldberg, Sylvie-Anne, ed. *L'histoire et la mémoire de l'histoire: Hommage à Y. H. Yerushalmi.* Paris: Albin Michel, 2012.

Goldman, Emma. *Living My Life.* 2 vols. New York: Knopf, 1970 (1931).

Gottwaldt, Alfred. "Les soeurs de Sigmund Freud et la mort: Remarques concernant leur destin de déportation et de meurtre de masse." *Revue française de psychanalyse* 68, no. 4 (2004): 1307–1316.

Graf, Max. Interview with Kurt Eissler, December 1952. Geneva: Balint Archives. In French as "Entretien avec Kurt Eissler" (1952), *Bloc-notes de la psychanalyse* 14 (1995): 123–149.

———. "Reminiscences of Professor Sigmund Freud." *Psychoanalytic Quarterly* 11 (1942): 465–476.

Grangier, Gilles-Gaston. *L'irrationnel.* Paris: Odile Jacob, 1998.

Granoff, Wladimir, and Jean-Michel Rey. *L'occulte, objet de la pensée freudienne.* Paris: Presses Universitaires de France, 1983.

Green, Martin. *The Von Richthofen Sisters; The Triumphant and the Tragic Modes of Love: Else and Frieda von Richthofen, Otto Gross, Max Weber, and D. H. Lawrence, in the Years 1870–1970.* New York: Basic Books, 1974.

Greig, Geordie. *Breakfast with Lucian: The Astounding Life and Outrageous Times of Britain's Great Modern Painter.* New York: Farrar, Straus and Giroux, 2013.

Grenier, Louise. *Penser Freud avec Patrick Mahony.* Quebec: Liber, 2004.

Grinstein, Alexander. *Freud at the Crossroads.* Madison, CT: International Universities Press, 1990.

Groddeck, Georg. *The Book of the It.* Trans. V. M. E. Collins. London: Vision, 1950.

———. *Conférences psychanalytiques à l'usage des malades (1915–1916).* 3 vols. Paris: Champ libre-Roger Lewinter, 1982.

———. "Correspondence with Sigmund Freud (1917–1934)." In *The Meaning of Illness: Selected Psychoanalytic Writings,* ed. Lore Schacht, trans. Gertrud Mander, 31–208. New York: International Universities Press, 1977.

———. "Le double sexe de l'être humain" (1931). *Nouvelle revue de psychanalyse* 7 (Spring 1973): 193–199.

———. *Lebenserinnerunger* (1929). In *Der Mensch und sein Es,* 267–399. Wiesbaden, Germany: Limes Verlag, 1970.

———. *Nasamecu: Der gesunde und kranke Mensch Gemeinverständlich dargestellt.* Ed. Michael Giefer. Frankfurt: Stroemfeld, 2014 (1913). In French as *Nasamecu: La nature guérit,* trans. Pierre Villain, preface by Catherine Clément (Paris: Aubier-Montaigne, 1992).

———. *Un problème de femme.* Trans. Roger Lewinter. Paris: Mazarine, 1979 (1903).

———. *Der Seelensucher.* Frankfurt: Stroemfeld, 1998 (1921). In French as *Le chercheur d'âme: Un roman psychanalytique* (Paris: Gallimard, 1982).

Gross, Otto. *Psychanalyse et révolution: Essais.* Trans. Jeanne Étoré. Preface by Jacques Le Rider. Paris: Éditions du Sandre, 2011.

Grosskurth, Phyllis. *Melanie Klein: Her World and Her Work.* New York: Knopf, 1986.

———. *The Secret Ring: Freud's Inner Circle and the Politics of Psychoanalysis.* Reading, MA: Addison-Wesley, 1991.

Grubrich-Simitis, Ilse. "L'affectif et la théorie: Sigmund et Martha: prélude freudien—Germes et concepts psychanalytiques fondamentaux." *Revue française de psychanalyse* 3, no. 76 (2012): 779–795.

———. *Back to Freud's Texts: Making Silent Documents Speak.* Trans. Philip Slotkin. New Haven, CT: Yale University Press, 1996 (1993).

———. "Freud's Study of Moses as Daydream: A Biographical Essay." In *Early Freud and Late Freud: Reading Anew "Studies on Hysteria" and "Moses and Monotheism,"* trans. Philip Slotkin, 53–89. London: Routledge, 1997.

———. "Die Neurepräsentation von 'Jenseits des Lustprinzips' ist ganz so neu nicht." *Psyche* 67, no. 8 (August 2013): 679–688.

Grünbaum, Adolf. *The Foundations of Psychoanalysis: A Philosophical Critique.* Berkeley: University of California Press, 1984.

Guggenbühl, Anna. *Wie benimmt sich der Prof. Freud eigentlich?* Giessen, Germany: Psychosozial-Verlag, 2009. In French as *Mon analyse avec le professeur Freud,* ed. Anna Koellreuter, trans. Jean-Claude Capèle (Paris: Aubier, 2010).

Hachet, Pascal. *Les psychanalystes et Goethe.* Paris: L'Harmattan, 1995.

Hale, Nathan G. *Freud and the Americans: The Beginnings of Psychoanalysis in the United States, 1876–1917.* New York: Oxford University Press, 1971.

Hale, William Bayard. *The Story of a Style.* New York: B. W. Huebsch, 1920.

Hamilton, J. W. "Freud and the Suicide of Pauline Silberstein." *Psychoanalytic Review* 89, no. 6 (2002): 889–909.

Hamon, Marie-Christine, ed. and trans. *Féminité mascarade.* Paris: Seuil, 1994.

Hayat, Jeannine. "Lytton Strachey: L'historien intime de deux reines." *LISA* e-journal, January 2007.

Haynal, André. "Freud psychothérapeute: Essai historique." *Psychothérapies* 4 (2007): 239–242.

Heenen-Wolff, Susann. "La discussion sur l' 'analyse profane' dans l'*Internationale Zeitschrift für Psychoanalyse* de l'année 1927." *Revue internationale d'histoire de la psychanalyse* 3 (1990): 71–88.

Heidegger, Martin. "Cahier XIV." In *Gesamtausgabe,* vol. 96, ed. Peter Trawny. Frankfurt: Klostermann, 2014.

———. *Séminaires de Zurich.* Paris: Gallimard, 2010 (1987).

Heller, Judith Bernays. Testimony. LoC, box 121, folder 7.

Heller, Peter. *A Child Analysis with Anna Freud.* Trans. Salomé Burckhardt and Mary Weigand. Revised by the author. Madison, CT: International Universities Press, 1990.

Hervey de Saint-Denis, Léon. *Dreams and How to Guide Them.* Trans. Morton Schatzman. London: Duckworth, 1982 (1867).

Hilberg, Raul. *The Destruction of the European Jews.* Chicago: Quadrangle Books, 1961.

Hirschmüller, Albrecht. *The Life and Work of Josef Breuer: Physiology and Psychoanalysis.* Translation of *Physiologie und Psychoanalyse in Leben und Werke Josef Breuers.* New York: New York University Press, 1978.

Hoche, Alfred. "Eine psychische Epidemie unter Ärzten." *Medizinische Klinik* 6, no. 26 (1910): 1007–1010.

Hollos, Istvan. *Mes adieux à la Maison jaune.* Paris: Éditions du Coq-Héron, 1986.

Homer. *The Odyssey.* Trans. Robert Fagles. Introduction by Bernard Knox. New York: Penguin, 1996.

Hug-Hellmuth, Hermine von. *Essais psychanalytiques: Destin et écrits d'une pionnière de la psychanalyse des enfants.* Ed. and trans. Dominique Soubrenie. Paris: Payot, 1991.

Institoris, Henry, and Jacques Sprenger. *Le marteau des sorcières.* Paris: Jérôme Milton, 2005 (1486 or 1487).

Israëls, Han. "Freud and the Vulture." *History of Psychiatry* 4 (1993): 577–586.

Jacoby, Russell. *The Repression of Psychoanalysis: Otto Fenichel and the Political Freudians.* New York: Basic Books, 1983.

Janet, Pierre. "La psychanalyse." Report to the 17th Congress of Medicine, London. *Journal de psychologie normale et pathologique* 11 (March–April 1914): 97–130.

Jensen, Wilhelm. *Gradiva*, followed by Sigmund Freud, *Delusion and Dream in Wilhelm Jensen's "Gradiva."* Trans. Helen M. Downey. Los Angeles: Sun and Moon, 1993.

Johnston, William. *The Austrian Mind: An Intellectual and Social History, 1848–1938.* Berkeley: University of California Press, 1972.

Jones, Ernest. "Bulletin of IPA." *International Journal of Psychoanalysis* 20 (1939): 116–127.

———. *Essays in Applied Psycho-analysis.* 2 vols. New York: International Universities Press, 1964 (1951?).

———. *Free Associations: Memories of a Psychoanalyst.* New York: Basic Books, 1959.

———. *Hamlet and Oedipus.* Garden City, NY: Doubleday, 1954 (1949).

———. *The Life and Work of Sigmund Freud.* 3 vols. New York: Basic Books, 1953–1957.

Jung, C. G. *Collected Works of C. G. Jung.* 20 vols. Princeton, NJ: Princeton University Press, 1960–1979.

———. Conversation with Kurt Eissler, August 29, 1953. LoC, box 114, folder 4.

———. "Editorial" (1933). In *Collected Works of C. G. Jung*, trans. R. F. C. Hull, vol. 10, *Civilization in Transition*, 533–534. Princeton, NJ: Princeton University Press, 1967.

———. "Geleitwort." *Zentralblatt für Psychotherapie* 6, no. 1 (1933): 10–11, repr. in C. G. Jung, *Gesammelte Werke.* Olten, Switzerland: Walter Verlag, 1974. Vol. 10, 581–583.

———. "An Interview on Radio Berlin: Conducted by Adolf Weizäcker, June 26, 1933." In *C. G. Jung Speaking: Interviews and Encounters*, 59–66. Princeton, NJ: Princeton University Press, 1977.

———. *Letters 1: 1906–1950.* Ed. Gerhard Adler with Aniela Jaffé. Princeton, NJ: Princeton University Press, 1973.

————. *Memories, Dreams, Reflections.* Recorded and edited by Aniela Jaffé. Trans. Richard Winston and Clara Winston. New York: Pantheon Books, 1963 (1962).

————. *Psychology of the Unconscious: A Study of the Transformations and Symbolisms of the Libido.* Trans. Beatrice M. Hinkle. Princeton, NJ: Princeton University Press, 1991 (1916).

————. "The State of Psychotherapy Today" (1934). In *Collected Works of C. G. Jung*, trans. R. F. C. Hull, vol. 10, *Civilization in Transition*, 157–173. Princeton, NJ: Princeton University Press, 1967.

————. *Symbols of Transformation: An Analysis of the Prelude to a Case of Schizophrenia.* 2nd ed. Vol. 5 of *Collected Works of C. G. Jung*, trans. R. F. C. Hull. Princeton, NJ: Princeton University Press, 1956.

Kamieniak, Jean-Pierre. "Citizen Canis, Freud et les chiens." *Le Coq-Héron* 215 (2013): 96–108.

Kardiner, Abram. *My Analysis with Freud: Reminiscences.* New York: Norton, 1977.

Kaufholz-Messmer, Éliane. *Karl Kraus.* Cahiers de l'Herne 28. Paris: Éditions de l'Herne, 1975.

Kershaw, Ian. *Hitler, 1936–45: Nemesis.* New York: W. W. Norton, 2000.

Keynes, John Maynard. *The Economic Consequences of the Peace.* New York: Harcourt, Brace and Howe, 1920 (1919).

Kiell, Norman. *Freud without Hindsight: Reviews of His Work, 1893–1939.* Madison, CT: International Universities Press, 1988.

Klein, Melanie. *The Psycho-analysis of Children.* Trans. Alix Strachey. London: Hogarth, 1937 (1932).

Klemperer, Victor. *The Language of the Third Reich: LTI, Lingua Tertii Imperii: A Philologist's Notebook.* Trans. Martin Brady. New Brunswick, NJ: Athlone, 2000.

Koelsch, William W. *Incredible Day-Dream: Freud and Jung at Clark, 1909.* Worcester, MA: Clark University, Friends of the Goddard Library, 1984.

Koestler, Arthur. *The Invisible Writing.* Vol. 2 of *Arrow in the Blue: An Autobiography.* 2 vols. London: Collins, with H. Hamilton, 1952–1954.

Kraus, Karl. *Dicta and Contradicta.* Trans. Jonathan McVity. Urbana: University of Illinois Press, 2001.

Kretschmer, Ernst. Opening address, 6th Allgemeine ärztliche Kongress für Psychotherapie, Dresden, in honor of Freud's 75th birthday, May 14–17, 1931. *Archiv für Psychiatrie* 96 (1932): 219.

Kroeber, Alfred L. "*Totem and Taboo*: An Ethnologic Psychoanalysis." *American Anthropologist* 22 (1920): 48–55.

Krüll, Marianne. *Sigmund, fils de Jakob: Un lien non dénoué.* Paris: Gallimard, 1983 (1979).

Lacan, Jacques. "Beyond the 'Reality Principle.'" In *Écrits: The First Complete Edition in English*, trans. Bruce Fink with Héloïse Fink and Russell Grigg, 58–74. New York: W. W. Norton, 2006 (1966).

———. *The Ego in Freud's Theory and in the Technique of Psychoanalysis, 1954–1955.* Seminar, book 2. Trans. Sylvana Tomaselli. New York: W. W. Norton, 1988 (1977).

———. *The Ethics of Psychoanalysis, 1959–1960.* Seminar, book 7. Trans. Dennis Porter. New York: W. W. Norton, 1992 (1986).

———. *The Four Fundamental Concepts of Psycho-analysis.* Seminar, book 11. Ed. Jacques-Alain Miller. Trans. Alan Sheridan. New York: W. W. Norton, 1998 (1973).

———. "The Freudian Thing, or the Meaning of the Return to Freud in Psychoanalysis." In *Écrits: The First Complete Edition in English,* trans. Bruce Fink with Héloïse Fink and Russell Grigg, 334–363. New York: W. W. Norton, 2006 (1966).

———. *The Object Relation, 1956–1957.* Seminar, book 4. Ed. Jacques-Alain Miller. Trans. L. V. A. Roche. http://www.scribd.com/doc/143580546/The-Seminar-of -Jacques-Lacan-Book-4-The-Object-Relation#scribd.

Lacoste, Patrick. *L'étrange cas du professeur M.* Paris: Gallimard, 1990.

Lacoursière, Roy B. "Freud's Death: Historical Truth and Biographical Fictions." *American Imago* 65, no. 1 (2008): 107–128.

La Fontaine, Jean de. *The Original Fables of La Fontaine.* Trans. F. C. Tilney. London: J. M. Dent and Sons, 1913.

Lainer, Grete [Hermine von Hug-Hellmuth]. *A Young Girl's Diary.* Preface by Sigmund Freud. Trans. Eden Paul and Cedar Paul. New York: Thomas Selzer, 1921.

Lamarck, Jean-Baptiste. *Zoological Philosophy: An Exposition with Regard to the Natural History of Animals.* Trans. Hugh Elliot. New York: Hafner, 1914.

Lampf, Hans. Interview with Kurt Eissler, 1953. LoC, box 114, folder 13.

Laplanche, Jean. *Life and Death in Psychoanalysis.* Trans. Jeffrey Mehlman. Baltimore: Johns Hopkins University Press, 1976 (1970).

Laqueur, Thomas. *Making Sex: Body and Gender from the Greeks to Freud.* Cambridge, MA: Harvard University Press, 1990.

Lassalle, Ferdinand. *Der italienische Krieg und die Ausgabe Preußens* (1859). In *Fernand Lassalle's Politische Reden und Schriften,* 2:369–442. Leipzig: Karl Fr. Pfau, 1892.

Lavagetto, Mario. *L'impiegato Schmitz e altri saggi su Svevo.* Turin, Italy: Einaudi, 1975.

Le Bon, Gustave. *The Crowd: A Study of the Popular Mind.* Translation of *La psychologie des foules.* Introduction by Robert K. Merton. New York: Macmillan, 1896 (1895).

Le Naour, Jean-Yves, and Catherine Valenti. *Histoire de l'avortement, XIXe–XXe siècle.* Paris: Seuil, 2003.

Lenay, Charles. "Les limites naturelles de la durée de vie et la question de l'hérédité de l'acquis." *Études sur la mort.* Le Bouscat, France: L'Esprit du temps, 2003.

Le Rider, Jacques. *Le cas Otto Weininger: Racines de l'antiféminisme et de l'antisémitisme.* Paris: Presses Universitaires de France, 1982.

———. *Freud, de l'Acropole au Sinaï.* Paris: Presses Universitaires de France, 2002.

————. "Je mettrai en branle l'Achéron: Fortune et signification d'une citation de Virgile." *Europe*, no. 954 (October 2008): 113–122.

————. *Les Juifs viennois à la Belle Époque.* Paris: Albin Michel, 2012.

————. *Modernity and Crises of Identity: Culture and Society in Fin-de-Siècle Vienna.* Trans. Rosemary Morris. New York: Continuum, 1993 (1944).

————. "Moïse l'Égyptien." In "Sigmund Freud, de *L'Interprétation des rêves* à *L'Homme Moïse.*" Special issue, *Revue germanique internationale* 14 (2000): 127–150.

Le Rider, Jacques, Michel Plon, Gérard Raulet, and Henri Rey-Flaud. *Autour du "Malaise dans la culture" de Freud.* Paris: Presses Universitaires de France, 1998.

Leupold-Löwenthal, Harald. "The Emigration of Freud's Family." Trans. Edith Kurzweil. *Partisan Review* 56, no. 1 (1989): 57–64.

————. "Le procès de Theodor Reik." *Revue internationale d'histoire de la psychanalyse* 3 (1990): 57–69.

Lévi-Strauss, Claude. *Totemism.* Trans. Rodney Needham. London: Merlin, 1964 (1962).

Lévy-Friesacher, Christine. *Meynert-Freud, "l'amentia."* Paris: Presses Universitaires de France, 1983.

Lewinter, Roger. *Le Monde.* September 7, 1980.

Lieberman, James. *Acts of Will: The Life and Work of Otto Rank.* New York: Free Press, 1985.

Liebermann, Guido. *La psychanalyse en Palestine, 1918–1948: Aux origines du mouvement analytique israélien.* Paris: Campagne Première, 2012.

Lipps, Theodor. *Komik und Humor: Eine psychologisch-ästhetische Untersuchung.* N.p.: Dogma, 2013 (1898).

Lockot, Regine. *Erinnern und Durcharbeiten.* Frankfurt: Fischer, 1985.

Lohmann, Hans-Martin, ed. *Psychoanalyse und Nationalsozialismus: Beiträge zur Bearbeitung eines unbewältigten Traumas.* Frankfurt: Fischer, 1984.

Looney, J. Thomas. *"Shakespeare" Identified in Edward de Vere, the Seventeenth Earl of Oxford, and the Poems of Edward de Vere.* 2 vols. Port Washington, NY: Kennikat Press for Minos, 1975 (1920).

Loraux, Nicole. *The Experiences of Tiresias: The Feminine and the Greek Man.* Trans. Paula Wissing. Princeton, NJ: Princeton University Press, 1995.

Low, Barbara. Testimony. N.d. LoC, box 121, folder 5.

Lurdos, Michel. "Au coeur du continent noir: Henry Morton Stanley." In *Regards sur les littératures coloniales,* ed. Jean Sévry, 3:97–108. Paris: L'Harmattan, 1999.

Lynn, David J. "Freud's Analysis of A. B., a Psychotic Man, 1925–1930." *Journal of the American Academy of Psychoanalysis* 21, no. 1 (Spring 1993): 63–78.

————. "Sigmund Freud's Psychoanalysis of Albert Hirst." *Bulletin of History of Medicine* 1, no. 71 (Spring 1977): 69–93.

Lynn, David J., and George E. Vaillant. "Anonymity, Neutrality and Confidentiality in the Actual Methods of Sigmund Freud: A Review of 43 Cases, 1907–1939." *American Journal of Psychiatry* 155, no. 2 (February 1998): 163–170.

Mahony, Patrick J. *Cries of the Wolf Man*. New York: International University Press, 1984.

———. *Freud and the Rat Man*. New Haven, CT: Yale University Press, 1986.

———. *Freud's Dora: A Psychoanalytic, Historical, and Textual Study*. New Haven, CT: Yale University Press, 1996.

Malcolm, Janet. *In the Freud Archives*. New York: Knopf, 1984.

Malinowski, Bronislaw. *Argonauts of the Western Pacific: An Account of Native Enterprise and Adventure in the Archipelagoes of Melanesian New Guinea*. London: G. Routledge and Sons, 1922.

———. *Sex and Repression in Savage Society*. London: K. Paul, 1927.

Mancini, Elena. *Magnus Hirschfeld and the Quest for Sexual Freedom: A History of the First International Sexual Freedom Movement*. New York: Palgrave Macmillan, 2010.

Mann, Thomas. "Allemagne ma souffrance" (1933). In *Les exigences du jour*, trans. Louise Servicen and Jeanne Najac, 180–262. Paris: Grasset, 2003 (1976).

———. "A Brother." Trans. H. T. Lowe-Porter. In *Order of the Day: Political Essays and Speeches of Two Decades*, 153–161. Freeport, NY: Books for Libraries Press, 1969.

———. *Les exigences du jour*. Trans. Louise Servicen and Jeanne Najac. Paris: Grasset, 2003 (1976).

———. *Doctor Faustus: The Life of the German Composer Adrian Leverkühn as Told by a Friend*. Trans. John E. Woods. New York: Alfred A. Knopf, 1997.

———. "Freud and the Future" (1936). In *Freud, Goethe, Wagner*, 1–45. New York: Alfred A. Knopf, 1937.

———. *Freud's Position in the History of Modern Thought*. London: Burns Oates and Washbourne, 1933 (1929).

———. *Joseph and His Brothers: The Stories of Jacob, Young Joseph, Joseph in Egypt, Joseph the Provider*. Trans. H. T. Lowe-Porter. New York: Alfred A. Knopf, 1948. New translation by John E. Woods (New York: Knopf, 2005 [1933–1943]).

———. *The Magic Mountain*. Trans. John E. Woods. New York: Knopf, 1995 (1924).

Mannoni, Octave. *Clefs pour l'imaginaire; ou, L'autre scène*. Paris: Seuil, 1969.

Marti, Jean. "La psychanalyse en Russie (1909–1930)." *Critique* 346 (March 1976): 199–237.

Marx, Karl, and Friedrich Engels. *The Communist Manifesto*. Trans. Samuel Moore with Friedrich Engels. Introduction by David Harvey. London: Pluto, 2008.

Maslow, Abraham H. "Was Adler a Disciple of Freud? A Note." *Journal of Individual Psychology* 18 (1962): 125.

Masson, Jeffrey Moussaieff. *The Assault on Truth: Freud's Suppression of the Seduction Theory*. New York: Farrar, Straus and Giroux, 1984.

————. "Freud and the Seduction Theory: A Challenge to the Foundations of Psychoanalysis." *Atlantic Monthly* 253, no. 2 (February 1984): 23–30.

Maury, Alfred. *Le sommeil et les rêves: Études psychologiques sur ces phénomènes.* Paris: Didier, 1861.

May, Ulrike. "Freuds Patientenkalender: Siebzehn Analytiker in Analyse bei Freud (1910–1920)." *LuziferAmor* 19, no. 37 (2006): 43–97.

————. "Neunzehn Patienten in Analyse bei Freud (1910–1920)—Teil I: Zur Dauer von Freuds Analysen; Teil II: Zur Frequenz von Freuds Analysen." *Psyche, Zeitschrift für Psychoanalyse und ihre Anwendungen* 6–7 (June–July 2007): 590–625.

McDougall, William. *The Group Mind.* London: Ayer, 1973 (1920).

————. *Psycho-analysis and Social Psychology.* London: Methuen, 1936.

Meisel, Perry, and Walter Kendrick, eds. *Bloomsbury/Freud: The Letters of James and Alix Strachey, 1924–1925.* New York: Basic Books, 1985.

Merezhkovsky, Dmitri S. *The Birth of the Gods.* Trans. Natalie A. Duddington. New York: E. P. Dutton, 1926.

Meyer, Edward. *Die Israeliten und ihre Nachbarstämme: Alttestamentliche Untersuchungen.* Halle: Max Niemeyer, 1906.

Micale, Mark. *Hysterical Men: The Hidden History of Male Nervous Illness.* Cambridge, MA: Harvard University Press, 2008.

Michel, Jacques. "La cocaïne de Freud." In *La philosophie du remède,* ed. Jean-Claude Beaune, 1–14. Paris: Champ Vallon, 1993.

Mijolla, Alain de. "Images de Freud, au travers de sa correspondance." *Revue internationale d'histoire de la psychanalyse* 2 (1989): 9–50.

————, ed. *International Dictionary of Psychoanalysis = Dictionnaire international de la psychanalyse.* 3 vols. Paris: Calmann-Lévy, 2002.

————. "Mein Onkel Josef à la une." *Études freudiennes* 15–16 (April 1979): 183–192.

Milhaud-Cappe, Danielle. *Freud et le mouvement de pédagogie psychanalytique, 1908–1937: A. Aichhorn, H. Zulliger, O. Pfister.* Paris: Vrin, 2007.

Moebius, Emy I. Letter to Kurt Eissler, September 11, 1952. LoC, box 21, folder 8.

Mons, Isabelle. *Lou Andreas-Salomé.* Paris: Perrin, 2012.

Mühlleitner, Elke. *Biographisches Lexikon der Psychoanalyse: Die Mitglieder der Psychologische Mittwoch-Gesellschaft und der Wiener Psychoanalytischen Vereinigung, 1902–1938.* Tübingen, Germany: Diskord, 1992.

München Medizinische Wochenschrift. Unsigned review of "Über männliche Hysterie" (1886), by Sigmund Freud. Vol. 33 (1886): 768–885.

Müntz, Eugène. *Leonardo da Vinci, Artist, Thinker and Man of Science.* Trans. from the French. London: W. Heinemann, 1898.

Murat, Laure. *Loi du genre: Une histoire culturelle du troisème sexe.* Paris: Fayard, 2006.

Mussolini, Benito, and Giovacchino Forzano. *Napoleon: The Hundred Days.* London: Sidgwick and Jackson, 1932.

Narjani, A. E. [Marie Bonaparte]. "Considérations sur les causes anatomiques de la frigidité chez la femme." *Bruxelles médical* (1924): 768–778.

Nelson, Alan H. *Monstrous Adversary*. Liverpool: Liverpool University Press, 2003.

Nitzschke, Bernd. "La psychanalyse considerée comme une science 'a'-politique." Trans. Sabine Bollack. *Revue internationale d'histoire de la psychanalyse* 5 (1992): 170–182.

Noll, Richard. *The Aryan Christ: The Secret Life of Carl Jung*. New York: Random House, 1997.

Nunberg, Herman, and Ernst Federn, eds. *Minutes of the Vienna Psychoanalytic Society*. Trans M. Nunberg. 4 vols. New York: International Universities Press, 1962–1975.

Obholzer, Karin. *The Wolf-Man: Conversations with Freud's Patient—Sixty Years Later*. Trans. Michael Shaw. New York: Continuum, 1982.

"Obituary." *Insurance Advocate* 85 (1974): 9.

Olender, Maurice. *The Languages of Paradise: Race, Religion, and Philology in the Nineteenth Century*. Trans. Arthur Goldhammer. Cambridge, MA: Harvard University Press, 1992 (1989).

Onfray, Michel. *Le crépuscule d'une idole: L'affabulation fabuleuse*. Paris: Grasset, 2010.

Palaci, Jacques. "Remembering Reik." Preface to *Le psychologue surpris*, by Theodor Reik, trans. Denise Berger, 9–31. Paris: Denoël, 1976.

Pellegrin, Pierre. Introduction and notes. In Sigmund Freud, *Malaise dans la culture*, 7–67, 177–210. Paris: Garnier-Flammarion, 2010.

Peters, Heinz Frederick. *My Sister, My Spouse: A Biography of Lou Andreas-Salomé*. New York: Norton, 1962.

Pfister, Oskar. "A Friendly Disagreement with Prof. Sigmund Freud: The Illusion of a Future." Ed. Paul Roazen. Trans. Susan Abrams with Tom Taylor. *International Journal of Psychoanalysis* 74 (1993): 557–579.

Pfrimmer, Theo. *Freud, lecteur de la Bible*. Paris: Presses Universitaires de France, 1984.

Plon, Michel. "Au-delà et en deça de la suggestion." *Frénésie* 8 (1969): 89–114.

Pohlen, Manfred. *En analyse avec Freud*. Paris: Taillandier, 2010 (2006).

Porge, Erik. *Vol d'idées? Wilhelm Fliess, son plagiat et Freud*, followed by Wilhelm Fliess, *Pour ma propre cause*. Paris: Denoël, 1994.

Prado de Oliveira, Luiz Eduardo, ed. and trans. *Le cas Schreber: Contributions psychanalytiques de langue anglaise*. Paris: Presses Universitaires de France, 1979.

Prokop, Ursula. *Margaret Stonborough-Wittgenstein: Intellectuelle, mécène et bâtisseuse*. Trans. Françoise Stonborough. Paris: Noir sur Blanc, 2010 (2005).

"Protocol of Agreement, March 20, 1938." Document. *International Journal of Psychoanalysis* 5, no. 3 (1938): 374–375.

Puner, Helen Walker. *Sigmund Freud: His Life and Mind*. New Brunswick, NJ: Transaction, 1992 (1947).

Rand, Nicholas, and Maria Torok. *Questions for Freud: The Secret History of Psychoanalysis*. Cambridge, MA: Harvard University Press, 1997.

Rank, Otto. *The Myth of the Birth of the Hero: A Psychological Exploration of Myth.* Trans. Gregory C. Richer and E. James Lieberman. Baltimore: Johns Hopkins University Press, 2004 (1909).

———. *The Trauma of Birth.* London: Kegan Paul, Trench, Trubner, 1929 (1924).

Reich, Wilhelm. *The Mass Psychology of Fascism.* Trans. Vincent R. Carfagno. New York: Farrar, Straus and Giroux, 1970 (1933).

———. *Reich Speaks of Freud.* Ed. Mary Higgins and Chester M. Raphael. Trans. Therese Pol. New York: Farrar, Straus and Giroux, 1967.

Reik, Theodor. *The Compulsion to Confess: On the Psychoanalysis of Crime and Punishment.* New York: Farrar, Straus, and Cudahy, 1959.

———. *Surprise and the Psycho-analyst: On the Conjecture and Comprehension of Unconscious Processes.* Trans. Margaret M. Green. London: K. Paul, Trench, Trübner, 1936 (1935). In French as *Le psychologue surpris,* trans. Denise Berger, preface by Élisabeth Roudinesco (Paris: Denoël, 2011).

Reinach, Salomon. *Cultes, mythes et religions.* Paris: Ernest Leroux, 1905.

Requet, François. "Nietzsche et Freud: Le rapport entre cruauté, culpabilité et civilisation." Master's thesis, Université de Franche-Comté, philosophy section, 2005–2006.

Reviron, Florian. "De Lytton Strachey à Virginia Woolf." In *La biographie littéraire en Angleterre, XVII–XIXe: Configuration, reconfiguration du soi artistique,* 117–139. Saint-Étienne, France: Publications de l'Université de Saint-Étienne, 1999.

Rey-Flaud, Henri. *"Et Moïse créa les Juifs . . .": Le testament de Freud.* Paris: Aubier, 2006.

———. *Je ne comprends pas de quoi vous me parlez: Pourquoi refusons-nous parfois de reconnaître la réalité?* Paris: Aubier, 2014.

Riaud, Xavier. *Pionniers de la chirurgie maxillo-faciale (1914–1918).* Paris: L'Harmattan, 2010.

Rice, Emmanuel. *Freud and Moses: The Long Journey Home.* New York: State University of New York Press, 1990.

———. "The Jewish Heritage of Sigmund Freud." *Psychoanalytic Review* 2 (1994): 236–258.

Richer, Paul. *Les démoniaques dans l'art.* Paris: Macula, 1984 (1887).

Rickman, John. Testimony of Lionel S. Penrose, July 28, 1953. LoC, box 117.

Rieder, Ines, and Diana Voigt. *Sidonie Csillag, homosexuelle chez Freud, lesbienne dans le siècle.* Paris: EPEL, 2003 (2000).

Ritvo, Lucille B. *Darwin's Influence on Freud: A Tale of Two Sciences.* New Haven, CT: Yale University Press, 1990.

Riviere, Joan. "Womanliness as a Masquerade." *International Journal of Psychoanalysis* 10 (1929): 303–313.

Roazen, Paul. *Freud and His Followers.* New York: Knofp, 1975.

———. "Questions d'éthique psychanalytique: Edoardo Weiss, Freud et Mussolini." *Revue internationale d'histoire de la psychanalyse* 1 (1988): 150–167.

Robert, Marthe. *The Psychoanalytic Revolution: Sigmund Freud's Life and Achievement.* Trans. Kenneth Morgan. New York: Harcourt, Brace and World, 1966 (1964).

Rodrigué, Emilio. *Le siècle de la psychanalyse.* 2 vols. Paris: Payot, 2000 (1996).

Rogow, Arnold. "A Further Footnote to Freud's 'Fragment of an Analysis of a Case of Hysteria.'" *Journal of the American Psychoanalytical Association* 26 (1978): 311–330.

Romm, Sharon, and Edward Luce. "Hans Pichler: Oral Surgeon to Sigmund Freud." *Oral Surgery, Oral Medicine and Oral Pathology* 57, no. 1 (January 1984): 31–32.

Rose, Alison. *Jewish Women in Fin de Siècle Vienna.* Austin: University of Texas Press, 2008.

Rosenzweig, Saul. *Freud, Jung, and Hall the King-Maker: The Historic Expedition to America (1909).* Seattle: Hogrefe and Huber, 1992.

Ross, Marion. *Carnets:* Miscellaneous, 1914–1975. LoC, box 121, folder 7.

Rotfus, Michel. "Poétiser à Auschwitz." *Médiapart,* October 7, 2013.

——. Review of talk by Maria Landau. *Médiapart,* April 26, 2003.

Roth, Michael S., ed. *Freud: Conflict and Culture: Essays on His Life, Work, and Legacy.* New York: Knopf, 1998.

Rouanet, Sergio Paulo. *Os dez amigos de Freud.* Rio de Janeiro: Companhia das Letras, 2003.

Roudinesco, Élisabeth. "À propos d'une lettre inédite de Freud sur le sionisme et la question des lieux saints." *Cliniques méditerranéennes* 70 (2004): 5–17.

——. "Carl Gustav Jung: De l'archétype au nazisme: Dérives d'une psychologie de la différence." *L'Infini* 63 (Fall 1998): 74–94.

——. *La famille en désordre.* Paris: Fayard, 2002.

——. *Histoire de la psychanalyse en France,* followed by *Jacques Lacan: Esquisse d'une vie, histoire d'un système de pensée.* Paris: Pochothèque, 2009.

——. "Histoire de la psychanalyse en France." Conversation with Philippe Sollers. *L'Infini* 2 (Spring 1983): 62–75.

——. *Jacques Lacan.* Trans. Barbara Bray. New York: Columbia University Press, 1997.

——. *Jacques Lacan and Co.: A History of Psychoanalysis in France.* Trans. Jeffrey Mehlman. Chicago: University of Chicago Press, 1990 (1986).

——. "Lacan, the Plague." *Psychoanalysis and History* 10, no. 2 (2008): 225–235.

——. *Mais pourquoi tant de haine?* Paris: Seuil, 2010.

——. *Our Dark Side: A History of Perversion.* Trans. David Macey. Cambridge, UK: Polity, 2009 (2007).

——. *Le patient, le thérapeute et l'État.* Paris: Fayard, 2004.

——. *Philosophy in Turbulent Times: Canguilhem, Sartre, Foucault, Althusser, Deleuze, Derrida.* Trans. William McCuaig. New York: Columbia University Press, 2008 (2005).

——. "Les premières femmes psychanalystes." *Mil neuf cent: Revue d'histoire intellectuelle* 16 (1998): 27–41. Repr. in *Topique* 71 (2000): 45–56.

———. "Psychanalyse et homosexualité: Réflexions sur le désir pervers, l'injure et la function paternelle." Conversation with François Pommier. *Cliniques méditerranéennes*, no. 65 (Spring 2002): 7–34.

———. Response to Sylvie-Anne Goldberg and Michael Molnar. *Bulletin de la SIHPP*, August 3, 2012.

———. *Retour sur la question juive*. Paris: Albin Michel, 2009.

———. Review of *Essais psychanalytiques: Destin et écrits d'une pionnière de la psychanalyse des enfants*, by Hermine von Hug-Hellmuth. *Libération* (December 12, 1991).

———. "Soudain, *Le Deuxième Sexe . . .* " *Les temps modernes*, nos. 647–648 (January–March 2008): 192–213.

———. *Why Psychoanalysis?* Trans. Rachel Bowlby. New York: Columbia University Press, 2001 (1999).

Roudinesco, Élisabeth, and Michel Plon. *Dictionnaire de la psychanalyse*. Paris: Fayard, 2006.

Roudinesco, Élisabeth, Sylvain Courage, Pierre Delion, Christian Godin, Roland Gori, Franck Lelièvre, Guillaume Mazea, Jack Ralite, and Jean-Pierre Sueur. *Pourquoi tant de haine? Anatomie du "Livre noir de la psychanalyse."* Paris: Navarin, 2005.

Rousseau, Jean-Jacques. *The Confessions and Correspondence, including the Letters to Malesherbes*. Ed. Christopher Kelly, Roger D. Masters, and Peter G. Stillman. Trans. Christopher Kelly. Vol. 5 of *The Collected Writings of Rousseau*. Hanover, NH: University Press of New England, 1990.

———. *Discourse on the Origins of Inequality (Second Discourse): Polemics; and Political Economy*. Ed. Roger D. Masters and Christopher Kelly. Trans. Judith R. Bush. Hanover, NH: University Press of New England, 1992.

———. *Emile; or, On Education*. Ed. and trans. Allan Bloom. New York: Basic Books, 1979.

Sabatier, Patrick. Conversation with Michael Roth. *Libération*, October 26, 1998.

Sablik, Karl. "Freud et Julius Tandler: Une mystérieuse relation." *Revue internationale d'histoire de la psychanalyse* 3 (1990): 89–103.

Sachse, Renate. "À propos de la recherche d'Ulrike May: Sur dix-neuf patients en analyse chez Freud (1910–1920)." *Essaim* 2 (2008): 187–194.

———. "Luzifer-Amor 51." *Essaim* 32 (2014): 103–113.

Said, Edward. *Freud and the Non-European*. London: Verso, 2003. Saint-Just, Louis Antoine de. *Rapport sur le mode d'exécution du décret contre les ennemis de la Révolution, fait au nom du Comité de salut public par St.-Just, le 13 ventôse, l'an 2 de la République*. Paris: Imprimerie nationale, 1794.

Samuels, Andrew. "National Psychology, National Socialism, and Analytical Psychology: Reflections on Jung and Anti-Semitism." *Journal of Analytical Psychology* 37 (1992): 3–28, 127–148.

Sartre, Jean-Paul. "The Republic of Silence." In *The Aftermath of War (Situations III)*. trans. Chris Turner, 3–7. London: Seagull Books, 2008.

Scammell, Michael. *Koestler: The Literary and Political Odyssey of a Twentieth-Century Skeptic*. New York: Random House, 2009.

Schapiro, Meyer. "Freud and Leonardo: An Art Historical Study" (1956). In *Theory and Philosophy of Art: Style, Artist, and Society*, 153–192. New York: George Braziller, 1994.

Scherner, Karl Albert. *La vie du rêve*. Paris: Champ social, 2003 (1861).

Schmideberg, Melitta. "Contribution à l'histoire du mouvement psychanalytique en Angleterre" (1971). *Confrontation* 3 (Spring 1980): 11–22.

Schneider, Monique. "Freud, lecteur et interprète de Goethe." In "Goethe cosmopolite." Special issue, *Revue germanique internationale* 12 (1999): 243–256.

Schorske, Carl E. *Fin-de-Siècle Vienna: Politics and Culture*. New York: Vintage Books, 1981 (1961).

———. *Thinking with History: Explorations in the Passage to Modernism*. Princeton, NJ: Princeton University Press, 1998.

Schreber, Daniel Paul. *Memoirs of My Nervous Illness*. Trans. Ida Macalpine and Richard A. Hunter. New York: New York Review of Books, 2000 (1903).

Schröter, Michael. "Kommentare: Jenseits des Kanons: Eine Erwiderung auf Ilse Grubrich-Simitis' Kritik an der Neu-Ausgabe von 'Jenseits des Lustprinzips.'" *Psyche* 67, no. 8 (August 2013): 794–798.

Schröter, Michael, and Ulrike May, eds. *S. Freud "Jenseits des Lustprinzips," Neu-Edition, Erstabdruck der Urfassung (1919)*. Special edition, *Luzifer-Amor* 51 (2013).

Schur, Max. *Freud: Living and Dying*. New York: International Universities Press, 1972.

———. Notes. LoC, Manuscript Division, Sigmund Freud collection.

Scognamiglio, Smiraglia. *Ricerche e documenti sulla giovinezza di Leonardo da Vinci*. Naples, 1900.

Sellin, Ernst. *Mose und seine Bedeutung für die Israelitisch-jüdische Religionsgeschichte*. Leipzig: A. Deichertsche Verlagsbuchhandlung, 1922.

Serra, Maurizio. *Italo Svevo ou l'Antivie*. Paris: Grasset, 2013.

Shengold, Leonard. "More about Rats and Rat People." *International Journal of Psychoanalysis* 52, no. 3 (1971): 277–288.

Sheppard, Ruth. *Explorer of the Mind: The Illustrated Biography of Sigmund Freud*. London: André Deutsch, 2012.

Simon, Akibah Ernst. "Freud und Moses." In *Entscheidung zum Judentum: Essays und Vorträge*, 196–211. Frankfurt: Suhrkamp, 1980.

Smilevski, Goce. *La liste de Freud*. Paris: Belfond, 2013.

Smith, William Robertson. *Lectures on the Religion of the Semites: The Fundamental Institutions*. New York: Macmillan, 1927 (1889).

Specter, Michael. "Sigmund Freud Urged His Disciple to Divorce: Wanted Him to Marry Another Woman, Daughter Finds." *Los Angeles Times*, November 12, 1987.

Sperber, Manès. *Masks of Loneliness: Alfred Adler in Perspective.* Trans. Krishna Winston. New York: Macmillan, 1974 (1970).

Spielrein, Sabina. "Über den psychologischen Inhalt eines Falles von Schizophrenie (Dementia praecox)" ("On the Psychological Content of a Case of Schizophrenia," 1911). *Jahrbuch für psychoanalytische und psychopathologische Forschungen* 3 (1912): 329–400.

Spinoza, Baruch. *Theological-Political Treatise.* Gebhardt edition. Trans. Samuel Shirley. Introduction by Seymour Feldman. Indianapolis: Hackett, 1998 (1670).

Stanley, Henry M. *Through the Dark Continent.* 2 vols. New York: Dover, 1988 (1878).

Stekel, Wilhelm. *Autobiography: The Life Story of a Pioneer Psychoanalyst.* Ed. Emil A. Gutheil. New York: Liveright, 1950.

Stepansky, Paul E. *In Freud's Shadow: Adler in Context.* Hillside, NJ: Analytic Press, distr. L. Erlbaum, 1983.

Sterba, Richard. *Reminiscences of a Viennese Psychoanalyst.* Detroit: Wayne State University Press, 1982.

Stingelin, Martin. "Les stratégies d'autolégitimation dans l'autobiographie de Schreber." In *Schreber revisité* (Cerisy conference), 115–227. Leuven, Belgium: Presses Universitaires de Louvain, 1998.

Strachey, James. "Bibliography: List of English Translations of Freud's Works." *International Journal of Psychoanalysis* 26, nos. 1–2 (1945): 67–76.

———. "Editor's Note." In *The Standard Edition of the Complete Psychological Works of Sigmund Freud,* ed. James Strachey, 3:71–73. London: Hogarth Press and the Institute of Psychoanalysis, 1962.

———. "General Preface." In *The Standard Edition of the Complete Psychological Works of Sigmund Freud,* ed. James Strachey, 1:xiii–xxii. London: Hogarth Press and the Institute of Psychoanalysis, 1966.

Strachey, Lytton. *Elizabeth and Essex: A Tragic History.* New York: Harcourt, Brace, 1928.

———. *Eminent Victorians: Cardinal Manning, Dr. Arnold, Florence Nightingale, General Gordon.* New York: Modern Library, 1933 (1918).

———. *Queen Victoria.* New York: Blue Ribbon Books, 1931 (1928).

Sulloway, Frank J. *Freud, Biologist of the Mind: Beyond the Psychoanalytic Legend.* New York: Basic Books, 1979.

Svevo, Italo. *Zeno's Conscience.* Trans. William Weaver. New York: Alfred A. Knopf, 2001.

Swales, Peter. "Freud, Fliess, and Fratricide: The Role of Fliess in Freud's Conception of Paranoia." In *Sigmund Freud: Critical Assessments,* ed. Laurence Spurling, 1:302–330 London: Routledge, 1982.

———. "Freud, His Teacher, and the Birth of Psychoanalysis." In *Freud: Appraisals and Reappraisals,* ed. Paul E. Stepansky, 3–82. Hillsdale, NJ: Analytic Press, 1986.

Tadié, Jean-Yves. *Le lac inconnu: Entre Proust et Freud.* Paris: Gallimard, 2012.

Taine, Hippolyte. *The Origins of Contemporary France.* 6 vols. Trans. John Durand. New York: Holt, 1876–1894 (1875–1893).

Tann, M. von der. "A Jungian Perspective on the Berlin Institute for Psychotherapy: A Basis for Mourning." *San Francisco Jung Institute Library Journal* 8, no. 4 (1989): 43–73.

Tasso, Torquato. *Jerusalem Delivered: An English Prose Version.* Trans. and ed. Ralph Nash. Detroit: Wayne State University Press, 1987.

Thornton, E. M. *Freud and Cocaine: The Freudian Fallacy.* London: Blond and Briggs, 1983.

Tögel, Christfried. "Bahnstation Treblinka: Zum Schicksal von Sigmund Freuds Schwester Rosa Graf." *Psyche: Zeitschrift für Psychoanalyse und ihre Anwendungen* 44 (1990): 1019–1024.

———. "Freud Diarium." http://www.freud-biographik.de/frdbio.htm. Last accessed April 28, 2016.

———. "Freuds Berliner Schwester Maria (Mitzi) und ihre Familie." *Luzifer-Amor* 33 (2004): 33–50.

———. "Sigmund Freud's Practice: Visits and Consultation, Psychoanalyses, Remuneration." *Psychoanalytic Quarterly* 78, no. 4 (2009): 1033–1058.

Toutenu, Denis. "Freud, une photo inédite: La consultation du Pr Lacassagne à Londres, le 26 février 1939." *Revue française de psychanalyse* 4, no. 66 (2002): 1325–1334.

Trawny, Peter, and Andrew J. Mitchell. *Heidegger and the Myth of a Jewish World Conspiracy.* Chicago: University of Chicago Press, 2015.

Tylor, Edward Burnett. *Primitive Culture.* 2 vols. London: John Murray, 1871.

Tyson, Alan. "A Chronological Hand-List of Freud's Works." *International Journal of Psychoanalysis* 37, no. 1 (1956): 19–33.

Vandal, Albert. *L'avènement de Bonaparte.* 2 vols. Paris: Plon-Nourrit, 1903–1907.

Vasari, Giorgio. *Lives of the Artists.* Ed. and trans. Julia Conaway Bondanella and Peter Bondanella. Oxford: Oxford University Press, 1991 (1550).

Vergil. *The Aeneid.* Trans. Sarah Ruden. New Haven, CT: Yale University Press, 2008.

Viereck, George Sylvester. "An Interview with Freud" (1926). In *Glimpses of the Great,* 23–38. New York: Macauley, 1930.

Vijver, Gertrudis van de, and Filip Geerardyn, eds. *The Pre-psychoanalytic Writings of Sigmund Freud.* London: Karnac, 2002.

Voghera, Giorgio. *Gli anni della psicoanalisi.* Pordenone, Italy: Edizioni Studio Tesi, 1980.

Waldinger, Ernst. "My Uncle Sigmund Freud." *Books Abroad* 15, no. 1 (January 1941): 1–9.

Walter, Bruno. *Theme and Variations: An Autobiography.* Trans. James A. Galston. New York: Alfred A. Knopf, 1946.

Waugh, Alexander. *The House of Wittgenstein: A Family at War.* New York: Doubleday, 2008.

Weill, Nicolas. Conversation with Mikkel Borch-Jacobsen. *Le Monde,* June 14, 1996.

Weill, Nicolas, and Raphaëlle Rérolle. Conversation with Élisabeth Roudinesco. *Le Monde,* June 14, 1996.

Weindling, Paul. *Health, Race, and German Politics between National Unification and Nazism, 1870–1945.* Cambridge: Cambridge University Press, 1989.

Weininger, Otto. *Sex and Character.* Authorized translation from the 6th German ed. London: W. Heinemann, 1906? (1903).

Weismann, August. *Essays upon Heredity and Kindred Biological Problems.* 2 vols. Ed. Arthur B. Poulton et al. Oxford: Clarendon, 1891–1892.

Weiss, Edoardo. Comments sent to Kurt Eissler about Freud and Mussolini. December 13, 1953. LoC, box 121, folder 34.

Weissweiler, Eva. *Les Freud: Une famille viennoise.* Paris: Plon, 2006.

Westermarck, Edward. *The History of Human Marriage.* 3 vols. London: Macmillan, 1891.

Wiener Medizinische Wochenschrift. Unsigned review of "Über männliche Hysterie" (1886), by Sigmund Freud. Vol. 36 (1886): 1445–1447.

Wittels, Fritz. "La névrose de *Fackel.*" In *Les premiers psychanalystes,* ed. Herman Nunberg, Ernst Federn, and Nina Schwab-Bakman, 2:373–378. Paris: Gallimard, 1978.

———. *Sigmund Freud, His Personality, His Teaching, and His School.* Freeport, NY: Books for Libraries Press, 1971 (1924).

Wittenberger, Gerhard, and Christfried Tögel, eds. *Die Rundbriefe des "Geheimen Komitees."* 4 vols. Tübingen, Germany: Diskord, 1995–2003.

Wittgenstein, Ludwig. "Conversations on Freud." In *Lectures and Conversations on Aesthetics, Psychology and Religious Beliefs,* ed. Cyril Barrett, 41–52. Berkeley: University of California Press, 2007.

Woolf, Virginia. *Three Guineas.* London: Hogarth, 1938.

Wortis, Joseph. *Fragments of an Analysis with Freud.* New York: Simon and Schuster, 1984 (1954).

Yerushalmi, Yosef Hayim. *Freud's Moses: Judaism Terminable and Interminable.* New Haven, CT: Yale University Press, 1991.

Young-Bruehl, Elisabeth. *Anna Freud: A Biography.* 2nd ed. New Haven, CT: Yale University Press, 2008 (1988).

Yovel, Yirmiyahu. *Spinoza and Other Heretics.* 2 vols. Princeton, NJ: Princeton University Press, 1989.

Zapperi, Roberto. *Freud e Mussolini.* Milan: Franco Angeli, 2013.

Zaretsky, Eli. *Secrets of the Soul: A Social and Cultural History of Psychoanalysis.* New York: Alfred A. Knopf, 2004.

Zweig, Stefan. *Appels aux Européens.* Trans. Jacques Le Rider. Paris: Bartillat, 2014 (1932–1934).

———. "Eulogy for Sigmund Freud Delivered by Stefan Zweig on September 26, 1939, Golders Green Crematorium, London, England." In *Freud by Zweig,*

translated by Eden Paul and Cedar Paul. Lexington, MA: Plunkett Lake Press, 2012.

———. *Mental Healers: Franz Anton Mesmer, Mary Baker Eddy, Sigmund Freud.* Trans. Eden Paul and Cedar Paul. London: Cassell, 1933.

———. "Die moralische Entgiftung Europas: Ein Vortrag für die Europatagung der Accademia die Roma" (1932). In *Zeiten und Schicksale: Aufsätze und Vorträge aus den Jahren 1902–1942,* ed. Knut Beck, 40–56. Frankfurt: S. Fischer, 1990.

———. *Twenty-Four Hours in the Life of a Woman.* Trans. Anthea Bell. London: Pushkin, 2003 (1927).

———. *The World of Yesterday: An Autobiography.* Translation of *Die Welt von Gestern.* New York: Viking Press, 1943.

Bibliography: Freud in French

To write this book, I consulted a large number of archives, which I list here. I have used various complete editions of Freud's work in German and in English, as well as several other reference works that provide indispensable information about Freud's life and work. The most extensive chronology of Freud's life to date is available in German; I refer to that as well. It should be noted that editions of Freud's pre-psychoanalytic works are in preparation.

Where France is concerned, I have chosen to mention different translations depending on the context:

1. Some of the earliest translations produced for Gallimard, Presses Universitaires de France (PUF), and Payot, by Samuel Jankélévitch, Yves Le Lay, Ignace Meyerson, Blanche Reverchon-Jouve, Marie Bonaparte, and Anne Berman.
2. Later translations produced by Fernand Cambon, Cornelius Heim, Philippe Koeppel, Patrick Lacost, Denis Messier, Marielène Weber, and Rose-Marie Zeitlin under the direction of Jean-Bertrand Pontalis (1924–2013) for Gallimard.
3. *Oeuvres complètes de Freud: Psychanalyse (OCF.P)*, an edition begun in 1988 and not yet completed, by a team including Jean Laplanche (1924–2012), Pierre Cotet, André Bourguignon (1920–1996), François Robert, and some twenty other authors, for PUF. The artisans of this very controversial undertaking seek to return to an "original Germanity" of the Freudian text. Thus they call themselves "Freudologists," convinced that the Freudian language is not German but "Freudian," that is, an "idiom of German that is not German but a language invented by Freud." Translated this way, Freud's work includes numerous neologisms, including *souhait* or *désirance* for *désir* (German *Wunsch,* English "desire"), *animique* for *âme* (*Seele,* "soul") or *psyché* ("psyche"), *fantaisie* for *fantasme* (*Fantasie,* "fantasy" or "phantasm").
4. Translations carried out under the direction of Jean-Pierre Lefebvre for the Éditions du Seuil, in the "Points Essais" collection.

5. Translations by Olivier Mannoni published by Payot, in the "Petite Bibliothèque Payot" collection.
6. Some additional translations.

1. Manuscript Sources

1. The Library of Congress (LoC), Washington, DC, Manuscript Division, Sigmund Freud Collection, Papers of Sigmund Freud: projects, handwritten and typewritten correspondence regarding Freud's writings, family documents, patients' files, legal and testamentary documents, military and school records, certificates, notebooks, genealogical data, interviews carried out by Kurt Eissler, testimonies, photographs and drawings, press clippings and other printed material. Enough to nourish study of the many facets of Freud's life: not only his writings but also his relations with family, friends, and colleagues.
2. Archives, works, and documents in the Freud Museum of London and the Freud Museum of Vienna.
3. Archives of Marie Bonaparte (source: Célia Bertin).
4. Archives of Élisabeth Roudinesco (letters, documents, notes, seminars).
5. Archives of Henri F. Ellenberger, Société internationale d'histoire de la psychiatrie et de la psychanalyse (SIHPP), Henry-Ey Library, Sainte-Anne Psychiatric Hospital, Paris.

2. Print Sources

Complete Works of Freud in German and in English
Gesammelte Schriften (GS). 12 volumes. Vienna, 1924–1934.
Gesammelte Werke (GW). 18 volumes and 1 complementary volume, unnumbered. Volumes 1–17: London, 1940–1952. Volume 18: Frankfurt, 1968. Complementary volume: Frankfurt, 1987. The entire edition from 1960 on: Frankfurt: S. Fischer Verlag.
Studienausgabe. 10 volumes and 1 complementary volume, unnumbered. Frankfurt: S. Fischer Verlag, 1969–1975.
The Standard Edition of the Complete Psychological Works of Sigmund Freud (SE). 24 volumes. Texts edited by James Strachey, in collaboration with Anna Freud, Alix Strachey, and Alan Tyson. London: Hogarth Press and the Institute of Psychoanalysis, 1953–1974.

Freud's Principal Psychoanalytic Works and Correspondence in French
Oeuvres complètes de Freud: Psychanalyse (OCF.P), 1886–1939. 21 volumes (unfinished edition, lacking volumes 1 and 21). Paris: PUF, 1988–. With a glossary, an index, and a presentation volume: *Traduire Freud,* by André Bourguignon, Pierre Cotet,

Jean Laplanche, and François Robert. Volume 1, forthcoming, contains articles and lectures on hysteria, phobias, defensive psychoneuroses, J.-M. Charcot, H. Bernheim, hypnosis, suggestion, and other clinical problems. Most of these texts have been translated for publication in various journals. Volume 21, forthcoming, contains an index and a glossary.

Principal Works and Articles

1884–1887 *De la cocaïne,* five articles on cocaine, edited by Robert Byck, translated by E. Sznycer, Brussels: Complexe, 1971; retranslated as *Un peu de cocaïne pour me délier la langue,* by M. Roffi, Paris: Max Milo, 2005.

1891 *Contribution à la conception des aphasies: Une étude critique,* translated by C. Van Reeth, Paris: PUF, 1983; retranslated as *Pour concevoir les aphasies: Une étude critique,* by F. Cambon Paris: EPEL, 2010.

1893 "Charcot," translated by J. Altounian, A. Bourguignon, and A. Rauzy, in *Résultats, idéees, problèmes,* volume 1, Paris: PUF, 1984.

1895 "Études sur l'hystérie," preface by M. Bonaparte, translated by A. Berman, Paris: PUF, 1967; retranslated by J. Altounian, P. Cotel, P. Haller, C. Jouanlanne, F. Kahn, R. Lainé, M.-T. Schmidt, A. Rauzy, and F. Robert, *OCF.P* 2, 2009.

"Deux comptes rendus contemporains à propos de la conference 'De l'hystérie,'" translated by F. Kahn and F. Robert, Paris: PUF, 2006; *OCF.P* 2, 2009.

"Obsessions et phobies," published in French, *OCF.P* 3, 1989.

1896 "L'hérédité et l'étiologie des névroses," published in French, *OCF.P* 3, 1989.

"L'étiologie de l'hystérie," in *Névrose, psychose et perversion,* translated by J. Bissery and J. Laplanche, Paris: PUF, 1973; retranslated as "Sur l'étiologie de l'hystérie" by J. Altounian and A. Bourguignon, *OCF.P* 3, 1989.

1899 "Sur les souvenirs-écrans," translated by D. Berger, P. Bruno, D. Guérineau, and F. Oppenot, in *Névrose, psychose et perversion,* Paris: PUF, 1973; retranslated as "Des souvenirs-couverture" by J. Doron, *OCF.P* 3, 1989; retranslated as "Sur les souvenirs-écrans" by D. Messier, in *Huit études sur la mémoire et ses troubles,* Paris: Gallimard, 2010.

1900 *L'interprétation des rêves,* translated by I. Meyerson, Paris: PUF, 1926; retranslated as *L'interprétation du rêve* by J. Altounian, P. Cotet, R. Lainé, A. Rauzy, and F. Robert, *OCF.P* 4, 2003; retranslated by J.-P. Lefebvre, Seuil, 2010.

1901 *Psychopathologie de la vie quotidienne,* translated by S. Jankélévitch, Paris: Payot, 1969; retranslated as *La psychopathologie de la vie quotidienne* by D. Messier, Paris: Gallimard, 1988; retranslated as *Sur la psychopathologie de la vie quotidienne* by J. Altounian and P. Cotet, *OCF.P* 5, 2012.

Le rêve et son interprétation, translated by H. Legros, Paris: Gallimard, 1925; retranslated as *Sur le rêve* by C. Heim, Paris: Gallimard, 1988; retranslated as *Sur le rêve* by J.-P. Lefebvre, Paris: Seuil, 2011; retranslated as *Du rêve* by P. Cotet and A. Rauzy, *OCF.P* 5, 2012.

1903 "La méthode psychanalytique de Freud," in *La technique psychanalytique*, translated by A. Berman, Paris: PUF, 1953; retranslated by J. Altounian, P. Cotet, J. Laplanche, and F. Robert, *OCF.P* 6, 2006.

1904 "De la psychothérapie," in *La technique psychanalytique*, translated by A. Berman, Paris: PUF, 1953; retranslated by P. Cotet and F. Lainé, *OCF.P* 6, 2006.

1905 "Fragment d'une analyse d'hystérie" (Dora), in *Cinq psychanalyses*, translated by M. Bonaparte and R. M. Loewenstein, Paris: PUF, 1966; retranslated by F. Kahn and F. Robert, *OCF.P* 6, 2006.

Le mot d'esprit et ses rapports avec l'inconscient, translated by M. Bonaparte and M. Nathan, Paris: Gallimard, 1930; retranslated as *Le mot d'esprit et sa relation à l'inconscient* by D. Messier, Paris: Gallimard, 1988; retranslated as *Le trait d'esprit et sa relation à l'inconscient* by J. Altounian, P. Haller, D. Hartmann, C. Jouanlanne, F. Kahn, R. Lainé, A. Rauzy, and F. Robert, *OCF.P* 7, 2014.

Trois essais sur la théorie sexuelle, translated by B. Reverchon-Jouve, Paris: Gallimard, 1923; retranslated as *Trois essais sur la théorie sexuelle* by P. Koeppel, Paris: Gallimard, 1987; retranslated by P. Cotet and F. Rexand-Galais, *OCF.P* 6, 2006; retranslated by M. Géraud, Paris: Seuil, 2012; retranslated by C. Cohen-Skalli, O. Mannoni, and A. Weill, Paris: Payot, 2014.

1906 "L'établissement des faits par voie diagnostique et la psychanalyse," in *L'inquiétante étrangeté et autres essais*, translated by A. Rauzy, Paris: Gallimrd, 1985; retranslated as "Diagnostic de l'état des faits et psychanalyse" by A. Rauzy, *OCF.P* 8, 2007; retranslated by O. Mannoni in *L'inquiétant familier*, Paris: Payot, 2011.

1907 *Délire et rêves dans un ouvrage littéraire; la "Gradiva" de Jensen*, translated by M. Bonaparte, Paris: Gallimard, 1931; retranslated as *Le délire et les rêves dans la "Gradiva"de W. Jensen* by P. Arhex and R.-M. Zeitlin, Paris: Gallimard, 1991; retranslated by J. Altounian, P. Haller, D. Hartmann, and C. Jouanlanne, *OCF.P* 8, 2007; retranslated by D. Tassel, preface by Henry Rey-Flaud, Paris: Seuil, 2013.

"Les explications sexuelles données aux enfants: Lettre ouverte au Dr. M. Fürst," in *La vie sexuelle*, translated by D. Berger, Paris: PUF, 1969; retranslated as "Sur les éclaircissements sexuels apportés aux enfants: Lettre ouverte au Dr. M. Fürst" by P. Cotet and F. Rexand-Galais, *OCF.P* 8, 2007.

"Actes obsédants et exercices religieux," translated by M. Bonaparte, in *L'avenir d'une illusion*, Paris: PUF, 1971; retranslated as "Actions de contrainte et exercices religieux" by F. Kahn and F. Robert, *OCF.P* 8, 2007; retranslated as "Actes compulsionnels et exercices religieux" by D. Messier in *Religion*, Paris: Gallimard, 2012.

1908 "Le créateur littéraire et la fantaisie," in *L'inquiétante étrangeté et autres essais*, translated by B. Féron, Paris: Gallimard, 1985; retranslated as "Le poète et l'activité de fantaisie" by P. Cotet, R. Lainé, and M.-T. Schmidt, *OCF.P* 8, 2007; retranslated by O. Mannoni in *L'inquiétant familier*, Paris: Payot, 2011.

"La morale sexuelle 'civilisée' et la maladie nerveuse des temps modernes," in *La vie sexuelle*, translated by D. Berger, Paris: PUF, 1969; retranslated as "La mo-

rale sexuelle 'culturelle,'" by P. Cotet, R. Lainé, and M.-T. Schmidt, *OCF.P* 8, 2007; retranslated by O. Mannoni in *L'inquiétant familier,* Paris: Payot, 2011.

"Les theories sexuelles infantiles," in *La vie sexuelle,* translated by J.-B. Pontalis, Paris: PUF, 1969; retranslated by R. Lainé and A. Rauzy, *OCF.P* 8, 2007.

"Le roman familial des névrosés," translated by J. Laplanche, in *Névrose, psychose et perversion,* Paris: PUF, 1973; reprinted in *OCF.P* 8, 2007.

1909 "Analyse d'une phobie chez un petit garcon de cinq ans" (Little Hans), in *Cinq psychanalyses,* translated by M. Bonaparte and R. M. Loewenstein, Paris: Gallimard, 1935; retranslated by R. Lainé and J. Stute-Cadiot, *OCF.P* 9, 1998.

"Remarques sur un cas de névrose obsessionnelle" (Rat Man), in *Cinq psychanalyses,* translated by M. Bonaparte and R. M. Loewenstein, Paris: Denoël and Steele, 1954; retranslated as "Remarques sur un cas de névrose de contrainte" by P. Cotet and F. Robert, *OCF.P* 9, 1998.

1910 *Cinq leçons sur la psychanalyse,* translated by Y. Lelay, Geneva: Payot, 1921; reprinted as *La Psychanalyse,* Paris: Payot, 1923; retranslated as *Sur la psychanalyse: Cinq conférences* by C. Heim, Paris: Gallimard, 1991; retranslated as *De la psychanalyse* by R. Lainé and J. Stute-Cadiot, *OCF.P* 10, 1993; retranslated as *Cinq conférences sur la psychanalyse* by B. Lortholary, Paris: Seuil, 2012.

"Les perspectives d'avenir de la thérapeutique analytique," in *La technique psychanalytique,* translated by A. Berman, Paris: PUF, 1953; retranslated by F. Cambon, Paris: Gallimard, 1985; retranslated as "Les chances d'avenir de la thérapie psychanalytique" by R. Lainé and J. Stute-Cadiot, *OCF.P* 10, 1993.

"À propos de la psychanalyse dite 'sauvage,'" in *La technique psychanalytique,* translated by A. Berman, Paris: PUF, 1953; retranslated as "De la psychanalyse 'sauvage'" by J. Altounian, A. Balseinte, and E. Wolff, *OCF.P* 10, 1993.

"Des sens opposés dans les mots primitifs," *L'inquiétante étrangeté et autres essais,* translated by M. Bonaparte and E. Marty, Paris: Gallimard, 1933; retranslated by F. Cambon, Paris: Gallimard, 1985; retranslated as "Du sens opposé des mots originaires" by J. Altounian, A. Bourgignon, and P. Cotet, *OCF.P* 10, 1993.

Un souvenir d'enfance de Léonard de Vinci, translated by M. Bonaparte, Paris: Gallimard, 1927; retranslated by J. Altounian, A. Bourguignon, P. Cotet, and R. Lainé, preface by J.-B. Pontalis, Paris: Gallimard, 1987; retranslated by J. Altounian, A. Bourguignon, P. Cotet, R. Lainé, and A. Rauzy, *OCF.P* 10, 1993; retranslated by D. Tassel, Paris: Seuil, 2011.

1911 "Le maniement de l'interprétation du rêve en psychanalyse," in *La technique psychanalytique,* translated by A. Berman, Paris: PUF, 1953; retranslated by P. Cotet, R. Lainé, A. Rauzy, F. Robert, and J. Stute-Cadiot, *OCF.P* 11, 1998.

"Remarques psychanalytiques sur l'autobiographie d'un cas de paranoïa" (President Schreber), in *Cinq psychanalyses,* translated by M. Bonaparte and R. M. Loewenstein, Paris: Gallimard, 1935; retranslated as "Remarques psychanalytiques sur un cas de paranoïa *(Dementia paranoides)* décrit sous forme autobiographique"

by P. Cotet and R. Lainé, *OCF.P* 10, 1993; retranslated by O. Mannoni, Paris: Payot, 2011.

"Grande est la Diane des Éphésiens," translated by J. Altounian, A. Bourguignon, P. Cotet, and A. Rauzy, in *Résultats, idées, problèmes*, volume 1, Paris: PUF, 1984; reprinted in *OCF.P* 11, 1998; retranslated by D. Messier in *Religion*, Paris: Gallimard, 2013.

1912 "Conseils au médecin dans le traitement psychanalytique," in *La technique psychanalytique*, translated by A. Berman, Paris: PUF, 1953; retranslated by J. Altounian, F. Baillet, A. Bourguignon, E. Carstanjen, P. Cotet, R. Lainé, C. von Petersdoff, A. Rauzy, F. Robert, and J. Stute-Cadiot, *OCF.P* 11, 1998.

"La dynamique du transfert," in *La technique psychanalytique*, translated by A. Berman, Paris: PUF, 1953; retranslated as "Sur la dynamique du transfert" by A. Rauzy, *OCF.P* 11, 1998.

"Contributions à la psychologie de la vie amoureuse," three texts (1910–1918): (1) "Un type particulier de choix d'objet chez l'homme"; (2) "Sur le plus général des rabaissements de la vie amoureuse"; (3) "Le tabou de la virginité," in *La vie sexuelle*, translated by J. Laplanche, Paris: PUF, 1969; retranslated by J. Altounian, F. Baillet, A. Bourgignon, P. Cotet, and A. Rauzy, *OCF.P* 10, 11, and 15, 1993, 1998, and 1996.

Totem et tabou, translated by S. Jankélévitch, Paris: Payot, 1923; retranslated by M. Weber, Paris: Gallimard, 1993; retranslated by J. Altounian, F. Bailet, A. Bourguignon, E. Carstanjen, P. Cotet, and A. Rauzy, *OCF.P* 11, 1998; retranslated by M. Crépon and M. de Launey, in *Anthropologie de la guerre*, Paris: Fayard, 2010; retranslated by D. Tassel, Paris: Seuil, 2011.

1914 "Le *Moïse* de Michel-Ange," in *L'inquiétante étrangeté et autres essais*, translated by P. Cotet and R. Lainé, Paris: Gallimard, 1985; retranslated by J. Altounian, A. Bourguignon, P. Cotet, P. Haller, D. Hartmann, R. Lainé, J. Laplanche, A. Rauzy, and F. Robert, *OCF.P* 12, 2005.

"Le début du traitement," in *La technique psychanalytique*, translated by A. Berman, Paris: PUF, 1981; retranslated as "Sur l'engagement du traitement" by J. Altounian, P. Haller, and D. Hartmann, *OCF.P* 12, 2005; retranslated by O. Mannoni in *L'inquiétant familier*, Paris: Payot, 2011.

"Remémoration, répétition et perlaboration," in *La technique psychanalytique*, translated by A. Berman, Paris: PUF, 1981; retranslated by J. Altounian, A. Bourguignon, P. Cotet, P. Haller, G. Hartmann, R. Lainé, J. Laplanche, A. Rauzy, and F. Robert, *OCF.P* 12, 2005.

"Observations sur l'amour de transfert," in *La technique psychanalytique*, translated by A. Berman, Paris: PUF, 1953; retranslated as "Remarques sur l'amour du transfert" by J. Altounian, A. Bourguignon, P. Cotet, P. Haller, D. Hartmann, R. Lainé, J. Laplanche, A. Rauzy, and F. Robert, *OCF.P* 12, 2005.

"Pour introduire le narcissisme," in *La vie sexuelle*, translated by J. Laplanche, Paris: PUF, 1969; retranslated by J. Laplanche, *OCF.P* 12, 2005; retranslated by O. Mannoni, Paris: Payot, 2012.

Sur l'histoire du mouvement psychanalytique, translated by C. Heim, Paris: Gallimard, 1911; retranslated as "Contribution à l'histoire du mouvement psychanalytique" by A. Berman in *La technique psychanalytique,* Paris: PUF, 1981; retranslated by P. Cotet and R. Lainé, *OCF.P* 12, 2005.

"De la fausse reconnaissance ('déjà raconté') au cours du traitement psychanalytique," in *La technique psychanalytique,* translated by A. Berman, Paris: PUF, 1981; retranslated by P. Cotet and R. Lainé, *OCF.P* 12, 2005.

"Extrait de l'histoire d'une névrose infantile" (Wolf Man), written in 1914, published in 1918, translated by M. Bonaparte and R. M. Loewenstein, in *Cinq psychanalyses,* Paris: PUF, 1954; retranslated as "À partir d'une névrose infantile" by J. Altounian and P. Cotet, *OCF.P* 13, 1988.

1915 "Considérations actuelles sur la guerre et sur la mort," in *Essais de psychanalyse,* translated by S. Jankélévitch, Paris: Payot, 1927; retranslated by A. Bourguignon, A. Cherki, and P. Cotet, Paris: Payot, 1981; retranslated as "Considération actuelle sur la vie et la mort" by M. Crépon and M. de Launey in *Anthropologie de la guerre,* Paris: Fayard, 2012.

"Un cas de paranoïa en contradiction avec la théorie psychanalytique," translated by D. Guérineau, in *Névrose, psychose et perversion,* Paris: PUF, 1973; retranslated as "Commuication d'un cas de paranoïa contredisant la théorie psychanalytique" by J. Altounian, A. Bourguignon, P. Cotet, J.-G. Delarbre, and D. Hartmann, *OCF.P* 13, 1988.

1915–1917 A set of texts on metapsychology: "Pulsions et destin des pulsions," "Le refoulement," "L'inconscient," "Complément métapsychologique à la doctrine du rêve," "Deuil et mélancolie," translated by A. Berman and M. Bonaparte, in *Métapsychologie,* Paris: Gallimard, 1952; retranslated by J. Laplanche, J.-B. Pontalis, J.-P. Briand, J.-P. Grossein, and M. Tort, Paris: Gallimard, 1968; retranslated by J. Altounian, A. Balseinte, A. Bourguignon, A. Cherki, P. Cotet, J.-G. Delarbre, D. Hartmann, J.-R. Ladmiral, J. Laplanche, J.-L. Martin, A. Rauzy, and P. Soulez, *OCF.P* 13, 1988; "Pulsions et destin des pulsions" retranslated by O. Mannoni, Paris: Payot, 2012. *Vue d'ensemble des névroses du transfert: Un essai métapsychologique,* translated by P. Lacoste, Paris: Gallimard, 1986; retranslated by J. Laplanche, *OCF.P* 13, 1988.

1916–1917 "Fugivité," translated by M. Bonaparte, in *Revue française de psychanalyse,* 1956; retranslated as "Passagèreté" by J. Altounian, A. Bourguignon, P. Cotet, and A. Rauzy, *OCF.P* 13, 1988; retranslated by D. Messier in *Huit études sur la mémoire et ses troubles,* Paris: Gallimard, 2010.

Introduction à la psychanalyse, translated by S. Jankélévitch, Paris: Payot, 1922; retranslated as *Conférences d'introduction à la psychanalyse* by F. Cambon, Paris: Gallimard, 1999; retranslated as *Leçons d'introduction à la psychanalyse* by A. Bourguignon, J.-G. Delarbre, D. Hartmann, and F. Robert, *OCF.P* 14, 2000. Twenty-eight lectures.

"Parallèle mythologique à une représentation obsessionnelle plastique," in *L'inquiétante étrangeté et autres essais,* translated by B. Ferron, Paris: Gallimard,

1985; retranslated by J. Altounian, A. Bourguigonon, P. Cotet, J. G. Delarbre, J. Doron, R. Doron, J. Dupont, D. Hartmann, R. Lainé, J. Laplanche, C. von Petersforff, A. Rauzy, F. Robert, J. Stute-Cadiot, C. Vincent, and A. Zäh-Gratiaux, *OCF.P* 15, 2002.

1917 "Une difficulté de la psychanalyse," translated by M. Bonaparte and E. Marty, in *Essais de psychanalyse appliquée*, 1933; retranslated by B. Féron in *L'inquiétante étrangeté et autres essais*, Paris: Gallimard, 1985; retranslated by J. Altounian, A. Bourguignon, P. Cotet, and A. Rauzy, *OCF.P* 15, 2002.

"Sur les transpositions des pulsions, plus particulièrement dans l'érotisme anal," in *La vie sexuelle*, Paris: PUF, 1969; retranslated by J. Altounian, A. Bourguignon, P. Cotet, and J. Stute-Cadiot, *OCF.P* 15, 1996.

"Un souvenir d'enfance dans *Fiction et vérité* de Goethe," translated by M. Bonaparte and E. Marty; retranslated as "Un souvenir d'enfance de *Poésie et vérité* de Goethe" by B. Féron in *L'inquiétante étrangeté et autres essais*, Paris: Gallimard, 1985; retranslated by J. Altounian, A. Bourguignon, P. Cotet, and R. Lainé, *OCF.P* 15, 1996.

1919 "Les voies nouvelles de la thérapeutique psychanalytique," in *La technique psychanalytique*, translated by A. Berman, Paris: PUF, 1981; retranslated as "Les voiles de la thérapeutique psychanalytique" by J. Altounian and P. Cotet, *OCF.P* 15, 1996.

"Doit-on enseigner la psychanalyse à l'Université?," translated by J. Dor, in *Résultats, idées, problèmes*, volume 1, Paris: PUF, 1984; retranslated as "Faut-il enseigner la psychanalyse à l'Université?" by J. Dupont, *OCF.P* 15, 1996.

"On bat un enfant: Contribution à l'étude de la genèse des perversions textuelles," translated by H. Hoesli, in *Revue française de psychanalyse* 6, 1933; retranslated as "Un enfant est battu: Contribution à la connaissance de la genèse des perversions sexuelles" by D. Guérineau in *Névrose, psychose et perversion*, Paris: PUF, 1973; retranslated by J. Altounian and P. Cotet, *OCF.P* 15, 1996.

"L'inquiétante étrangeté," translated by M. Bonaparte and E. Marty, in *Essais de psychanalyse appliquée*, Paris: Gallimard, 1952; retranslated as "L'inquiétant" by J. Altounian, A. Bourguignon, P. Cotet, and J. Laplanche, *OCF.P* 15, 1996; retranslated as *L'inquiétant familier* by O. Mannoni, Paris: Payot, 2011.

"Introduction à *La psychanalyse des névroses de guerre*," translated by J. Altounian, in *Résultats, idées, problèmes*, volume 1, Paris: PUF, 1984; retranslated by A. Bourguignon and C. von Petersdorff, *OCF.P* 15, 1996; retranslated as "De la psychanalyse des névroses de guerre" by O. Mannoni in *Sur les névroses de guerre*, Paris: Payot, 2010.

1920 "Sur la psychogenèse d'un cas d'homosexualité féminine," translated by D. Guérineau, in *Névrose, psychose et perversion*, Paris: PUF, 1973; retranslated as "De la psychogenèse d'un cas d'homosexualité féminine" by J. Altounian, P. Cotet, C. Vincent, and A. Zäh-Gratiaux, *OCF.P* 15, 1996.

Au-delà du principe de Plaisir, in *Essais de psychanalyse,* translated by J. Laplanche and J.-B. Pontalis, Paris: Payot, 1981; retranslated by J. Altounian, A. Bourguignon, P. Cotet, and A. Rauzy, *OCF.P* 15, 1996; retranslated by J.-P. Lefebvre, Paris: Seuil, 2014.

1921 "Psychanalyse et télépathie," translated by J. Altounian, O. Bourguignon, J. Laplanche, and A. Rauzy, in *Résultats, idées, problèmes,* volume 2, Paris: PUF, 1995; retranslated by J. Altounian, O. Bourguignon, J. Laplanche, A. Rauzy, B. Chabot, and J. Stute-Cadiot, *OCF.P* 16, 1991.

Psychologie collective et analyse du moi, translated by S. Jankélévitch, Paris: Payot, 1924; retranslated by J. Laplanche and J.-B. Pontalis in *Essais de psychanalyse,* Paris: Payot, 1972; retranslated as *Psychologie des foules et analyse du moi* by J. Altounian, O. Bourguignon, and A. Rauzy, Paris: Payot, 1981; retranslated as *Psychologie des masses et analyse du moi* by J. Altounian, A. Bourguignon, P. Cotet, and A. Rauzy, *OCF.P* 16, 1991; retranslated by D. Tassel, Paris: Seuil, 2014.

1922 "De quelques mécanismes névrotiques dans la jalousie, la paranoïa et l'homosexualité," translated by J. Lacan, in *Revue française de psychanalyse* 5, 1932; retranslated by D. Guérineau in *Névrose, psychose et perversion,* Paris: PUF, 1973; retranslated by J. Altounian and F. M. Gathelier, *OCF.P* 16, 1991.

"Psychanalyse et télépathie," translated by B. Chabot, in *Résultats, idées, problèmes,* volume 2, Paris: PUF, 1985; retranslated by J. Altounian, A. Bourguignon, P. Cotet, and J. Stute-Cadiot, *OCF.P* 16, 1991.

"Rêve et télépathie," translated by J. Altounian, O. Bourguignon, J. Laplanche, and A. Rauzy, in *Résultats, idées, problèmes,* volume 2, Paris: PUF, 1985; retranslated by J. Altounian, O. Bourguignon, J. Laplanche, A. Rauzy, B. Chabot, F.-M. Gathelier, and J. Stute-Cadiot, *OCF.P* 16, 1991.

"Une névrose démoniaque au XVIIe siècle," translated by M. Bonaparte and E. Marty, in *Essais de psychologie appliquée,* Paris: Gallimard, 1952; retranslated as "Une névrose diabolique au XVIIe siècle" by B. Féron in *L'inquiétante étrangeté et autres essais,* Paris: Gallimard, 1985; retranslated by O. Mannoni in *L'inquiétant familier,* Paris: Payot, 2011.

1923 *Le moi et le ça,* in *Essais de psychanalyse,* translated by J. Laplanche, Paris: Payot, 1982; retranslated by C. Baliteau, A. Bloch, J.-M. Rondeau, and J. Stute-Cadiot, *OCF.P* 16, 1991.

1924 "Le déclin du complexe d'Oedipe," in *La vie sexuelle,* translated by D. Berger, Paris: PUF, 1969; retranslated as "L'organisation génitale infantile" by J. Doron and R. Doron, *OCF.P,* 16, 1991.

1925 *Ma vie et la psychanalyse,* translated by M. Bonaparte, Paris: Gallimard, 1925; retranslated as *Sigmund Freud présenté par lui-même* by F. Cambon, Paris: Gallimard, 1984; retranslated as *Autoprésentation* by J. Altounian, C. Avignon, A. Balseinte, A. Bourguignon, M. Candelier, C. Chiland, P. Cotet, J.-G. Delarbre, J. Doron, R. Doron, M. Hanus, D. Hartmann, H. Hildebrand, R. Lainé, J.

Laplanche, A. Lindenberg, C. von Petersdorff, M. Pollack-Cornillot, A. Rauzy, and M. Strauss, *OCF.P* 17, 1992.

"Résistances à la psychanalyse," written in French by Freud, *La Revue juive* 1 (1925); reprinted in *Résultats, idées, problèmes*, volume 2, Paris: PUF, 1985; translated from the German version as "Les résistances contre la psychanalyse" by J. Altounian and P. Cotet, *OCF.P* 17, 1992.

"Notes sur le 'Bloc-notes magique,'" translated by J. Laplanche and J.-B. Pontalis, in *Résultats, idées, problèmes*, volume 2, Paris: PUF, 1985; retranslated as "Note sur le 'Bloc magique'" by J. Altounian and P. Cotet, *OCF.P* 17, 1992; retranslated under the first title by D. Messier in *Huit études sur la mémoire et ses troubles*, Paris: Gallimard, 2010.

"La négation," translated by J. Laplanche, in *Résultats, idées, problèmes*, volume 2, Paris: PUF, 1985; reprinted, *OCF.P* 17, 1992; retranslated as "La dénégation" by O. Mannoni in *Trois mécanismes de défense*, Paris: Payot, 2012. This essay has been translated some ten times. It was Jean Hippolyte, in 1956, who proposed to use the term *dénégation* rather than *négation*.

"Quelques conséquences psychologiques de la différence anatomique entre les sexes," in *La vie sexuelle*, translated by D. Berger, Paris: PUF, 1969; retranslated as "Quelques conséquences psychiques de la différence des sexes au niveau anatomique" by M. Candelier, C. Chiland, and M. Pollack-Cornillot, *OCF.P* 17, 1992.

1926 *Inhibition, symptôme et angoisse*, translated by M. Tort, Paris: PUF, 1965; retranslated by J. Doron and R. Doron, *OCF.P* 18, 1994; retranslated by O. Mannoni, Paris: Payot, 2014.

Psychanalyse et médecine, translated by M. Bonaparte, Paris: Gallimard, 1928; retranslated as *La question de l'analyse profane* by J. Altounian, A. Bourguignon, O. Bourguignon, P. Cotet, and A. Rauzy, Paris: Gallimard, 1985; retranslated by J. Altounian, A. Bourguignon, O. Bourguignon, P. Cotet, and A. Rauzy, *OCF.P* 18, 1994.

1927 "Le fétichisme," in *La vie sexuelle*, translated by D. Berger, Paris: PUF, 1969; retranslated by R. Lainé, *OCF.P* 18, 1994; retranslated by O. Mannoni in *Trois mécanismes de défense*, Paris: Payot, 2012.

L'avenir d'une illusion, translated by M. Bonaparte, Paris: PUF, 1971; retranslated by J. Altounian, A. Balseinte, A. Bourgignon, P. Cotet, J.-G. Delarbre, and D. Hartmann, *OCF.P* 18, 1994; retranslated by B. Lortholary, Paris: Seuil, 2011; retranslated by D. Messier in *Religion*, Paris: Gallimard, 2012; retranslated by Claire Gillie, preface by Paul-Laurent Assoun, Paris: Cerf, 2012.

1929 "Un événement de la vie religieuse," in *L'avenir d'une illusion*, translated by M. Bonaparte, Paris: PUF, 1971; retranslated as "Une expérience vécue religieuse" by A. Balseinte and E. Wolff, *OCF.P* 18, 1994; retranslated as "Une expérience vécue à caractère religieuse" by D. Messier in *Religion*, Paris: Gallimard, 2012.

"Dostoïevski et le parricide," translated by J.-B. Pontalis and C. Heim, in *Résultats, idées, problèmes,* volume 2, Paris: PUF, 1985; retranslated as "Dostoïevski et la mise à mort du père" by J. Altounian, A. Bourguignon, E. Carstanjen, and P. Cotet, *OCF.P* 18, 1994.

1930 *Malaise dans la civilisation,* translated by C. Odier (1934), Paris: PUF, 1971; retranslated as *Le malaise dans la culture* by P. Cotet, R. Lainé, J. Stute-Cadio, and J. André, Paris: PUF, 1995; retranslated by P. Cotet, R. Lainé, and J. Stute-Cadiot, *OCF.P* 18, 1994; retranslated as *Malaise dans la civilisation* by B. Lortholary, Paris: Seuil, 2010; retranslated under the same title by M. Crépon and M. de Launay in *Anthropologie de la guerre,* Paris: Fayard, 2010.

1931 "Des types libidinaux," translated by D. Berger, in *La vie sexuelle,* Paris: PUF, 1969; retranslated by M. Candelier, C. Chiland, and M. Pollack-Cornillot, *OCF.P* 19, 1995.

"Sur la sexualité feminine," translated by D. Berger, in *La vie sexuelle,* Paris: PUF, 1969; retranslated by M. Candelier, C. Chiland, and M. Pollack-Cornillot, *OCF.P* 19, 1995.

1933 *Nouvelles conférences d'introduction à la psychanalyse,* translated by A. Berman, Paris: Gallimard, 1926; retranslated as *Nouvelle suite des leçons d'introduction à la psychanalyse* by M. R. Zeitlin, Paris: Gallimard, 1984 (seven lectures: "Révision de la théorie du rêve," "Le rêve et l'occultisme," "La décomposition de la personnalité psychique," "Angoisse et vie pulsionnelle," "La féminité," "Éclaircissements, applications, orientations," "Sur une *Weltanschauung*"); retranslated by J. Altounian, A. Bourguignon, P. Cotet, A. Rauzy, and M. R. Zeitlin, *OCF.P* 19, 1995.

Pourquoi la guerre?, Institut international de coopération intellectuelle, Société des Nations, 1933; retranslated by J. Altounian, A. Bourguignon, P. Cotet, and A. Rauzy, *OCF.P* 19, 1995; retranslated by M. Crépon and M. de Launey in *Anthropologie de la guerre,* Paris: Fayard, 2010.

1936 "Un trouble de mémoire sur l'Acropole," translated by M. Robert, in *Résultats, idées, problèmes,* volume 2, Paris: PUF, 1985; retranslated as "Un trouble du souvenir sur l'Acropole: Lettre à Romain Rolland" by P. Cotet and R. Lainé, *OCF.P* 19, 1995; retranslated by D. Messier in *Huit études sur la mémoire et ses troubles,* Paris: Gallimard, 2010.

1937 "Analyse terminée et analyse interminable," translated by A. Berman, in *Revue française de psychanalyse* 11, 1939; retranslated as "L'analyse avec fin et l'analyse sans fin" by J. Altounian, A. Bourguignon, P. Cotet, J. Laplanche, and F. Robert in *Résultats, idées, problèmes,* volume 2, Paris: PUF, 1985; retranslated by J. Altounian, A. Bourguignon, P. Cotet, J. Laplanche, and F. Robert, *OCF.P* 20, 2010.

"Constructions dans l'analyse," translated by E. R. Hawelka, U. Huber, and J. Laplanche, in *Résultats, idées, problèmes,* volume 2, Paris: PUF, 1985; retranslated by J. Altounian, P. Cotet, J. Laplanche, and F. Robert, *OCF.P* 20, 2010.

1938 "Un mot sur l'antisémitisme," translated by P. Cotet and R. Lainé, *OCF.P* 20, 2010.

1939 *Moïse et le monothéisme*, translated by A. Berman, Paris: PUF, 1948; retranslated as *L'homme Moïse et la religion monothéiste* by C. Heim, Paris: Gallimard 1986; retranslated under the same title by J. Altounian, P. Cotet, P. Haller, C. Jouanlanne, R. Lainé, and A. Rauzy, *OCF.P* 20, 2010; retranslated under the same title by J.-P. Lefebvre, Paris: Seuil, 2012; retranslated under the same title by O. Mannoni, Paris: Payot, 2014.

1940 *Abrégé de psychanalyse*, translated by A. Berman, Paris: PUF, 1951; revised by J. Laplanche, Paris: PUF, 1985; retranslated by F. Kahn and F. Robert, *OCF.P* 20, 2010.

Collections of Freud's Letters

La naissance de la psychanalyse: Lettres à Wilhelm Fliess, incomplete edition prepared by M. Bonaparte, A. Freud, and E. Kris, translated by A. Berman, Paris: PUF, 1956. Contains "Esquisse d'une psychologie scientifique" (1895).

Lettres à Wilhelm Fliess, 1897–1904, transcribed by G. Fichtner, complete edition prepared by J. M. Masson, revised and augmented by M. Schröter, translated by F. Kahn and F. Robert, Paris: PUF, 2006. Contains "Esquisse d'une psychologie scientifique" (1895). Masson's presentation is not included in the French edition.

Correspondance, 1873–1939, translated by A. Berman and J.-P. Grossein, Paris: Gallimard, 1960.

"Notre coeur tend vers le sud": Correspondance de voyage, 1895–1923, translated by J.-C. Capèle, edited and presented by C. Tögel with M. Molnar, preface by É. Roudinesco, Paris: Fayard, 2005.

Lettres à ses enfants, edited by M. Schröter, with I. Meyer-Palmedo and E. Falzeder, translated by F. Cambon, Paris: Aubier, 2012.

Freud's Correspondence

Karl Abraham—*Correspondance complète, 1907–1926*, translated, presented, and annotated by F. Cambon, Paris: Gallimard, 1926.

Lou Andreas-Salomé—*Correspondance avec Sigmund Freud, 1912–1938*, followed by *Journal d'une année, 1912–1913*, translated by L. Jumel, Paris: Gallimard, 1970.

Ludwig Binswanger—*Correspondance, 1908–1938*, edited and introduced by G. Fichtner, translated by R. Menahem and M. Strauss, preface by J. Gillibert, Paris: Calmann-Lévy, 1995.

Hilda Doolittle—*Visage de Freud*, translated by F. de Gruson, Paris: Denoël, 1977; retranslated as *Pour l'amour de Freud*, by N. Canova and E. Ochs, preface by É. Roudinesco, Paris: Éditions des femmes-Antoinette Fouque, 2010.

Max Eitingon—*Correspondance, 1906–1939*, edited by M. Schröter, translated by O. Mannoni, Paris: Hachette Littératures, 2009.

Sándor Ferenczi—*Correspondance, 1906–1933,* 3 volumes, edited under the direction of A. Haynal, translated by the Groupe de traduction du *Coq-héron,* Paris: Calmann-Lévy, 1992–2000.

Anna Freud—*Correspondance, 1904–1938,* edited by I. Meyer-Palmedo, translated by O. Mannoni, preface by É. Roudinesco, Paris: Fayard, 2012.

Freud Family—*Lettres de famille de Sigmund Freud et des Freud de Manchester, 1911–1938,* presented and translated from English by C. Vincent, Paris: PUF, 1996.

Ernest Jones—*Correspondance complète, 1908–1939,* edited by R. Andrews Paskauskas, translated from English and German by P.-E. Dauzat, with M. Weber and J.-P. Lefebvre, introduction by R. Steiner, Paris: PUF, 1998.

Carl Gustav Jung—*Correspondance, 1906–1914,* 2 volumes, edited by W. McGuire, translated from German and English by R. Fivaz-Silbermann, Paris: Gallimard, 1975.

Oskar Pfister—*Correspondance, 1923–1936,* published through the efforts of E. L. Freud and H. Meng, translated by L. Jumel, preface by D. Widlöcher, Paris: Gallimard, 1991. Incomplete version.

Romain Rolland—*Correspondance. 1923–1936,* edited and translated by H. Vermorel and M. Vermorel, preface by A. Bourguignon, Paris: PUF, 1993.

Eduard Silberstein—*Lettres de jeunesse, 1882–1939,* translated by C. Heim, Paris: Gallimard, 1990.

Sabina Spielrein—*Sabina Spielrein entre Freud et Jung,* documents discovered by A. Carotenuto and C. Trombetta, French edition by M. Guibal and J. Nobécourt, translated from Italian by M. Armand and from German by M. de Launay and P. Rusch, Paris: Aubier-Montaigne, 1981.

Edoardo Weiss—*Lettres sur la pratique psychoanalytique,* preceded by *Souvenirs d'un pionnier de la psychanalyse,* translated by J. Etoré, introduction by J. Chazaud and M. Grotjahn, Toulouse: Privat, 1975.

Arnold Zweig—*Correspondance, 1908–1939,* published through the efforts of E. and L. Freud, translated by L. Weibel with J.-C. Gehrig, preface by M. Robert, Paris: Gallimard, 1973.

Stefan Zweig—*Correspondance, 1908–1929,* translated by G. Hauer and D. Plassard, text and notes by H.-U. Lindken, preface by R. Jaccard, Paris: Payot and Rivages poche, 1995.

Collections of Texts in French and in English

Les premiers psychanalystes: Minutes de la Société psychanalytique de Vienne, 1906–1978, 4 volumes, Paris: Gallimard, 1976–1983.

Revue internationale d'histoire de la psychanalyse, 6 issues, edited under the direction of Alain de Mijolla, Paris: PUF, 1988–1993.

Freud's Library: A Comprehensive Catalogue, bilingual German-English, edited by Michael Schröter with Keith Davies and Gerhard Fichtner, London: Freud Museum, 2006. With a CD containing the titles of the volumes in Freud's library.

Résumé des oeuvres complètes de Freud, 4 volumes, under the direction of L. Joseph and C. Masson, Paris: Hermann, 2009.

Forthcoming, under the direction of Mark Solms, publication of two hundred articles, texts, and brief papers by Freud dating from 1877 to 1900. See F. Geeradyn and G. Van de Vijver, editors, *Aux sources de la psychanalyse,* Paris: L'Harmattan, 2006.

3. Reference Works

Jean Laplanche and Jean-Bertrand Pontalis, *Vocabulaire de la psychanalyse,* Paris: PUF, 1967.

Élisabeth Roudinesco and Michel Plon, *Dictionnaire de la psychanalyse* (1997), Paris: Livre de poche, "La Pochothèque," 2011.

Alain Delrieu, *Index thématique, raisonné, alphabétique, chronologique, commenté,* Paris: Anthropos, 2001.

Paul-Laurent Assoun, *Dictionnaire des oeuvres psychanalytiques,* Paris: PUF, 2009.

4. Comprehensive Chronology of Freud's Life and Work

See Christfried Tögel, "Freud Diarium," 470 pages in German: http://www.freud -biographik.de. Accessed April 28, 2016.

Freud's Patients

Altman, Rosa: 1898
Ames, Thaddeus H.: 1921
Banfield Jackson, Edith: 1930–1938
Bauer, Ida ("Dora" case): 1900
Beddow, David: 1933–1934
Bernfeld, Suzanne Paret (née Cassirer): 1932–1934
Blanton, Smiley: 1929, 1930, and, intermittently, 1935, 1937, 1938
Blum, Ernst: 1922
Blumgart, Leonard: 1921
Bonaparte, Eugénie: a few sessions after 1925
Bonaparte, Marie: 1925–1938
Boss, Médard: a few sessions around 1925
Brunswick, David: 1927–1931
Brunswick, Mark: 1924–1928
Brunswick, Ruth Mack: 1922
Bryant, Louise: 1930
Bullitt, William C.: 1930
Burlingham, Dorothy: 1927–1939
Burrow, Trigant: 1924
Cherniakova, Sascha: 1905
Choisy, Maryse: 1924, three sessions
Csonka, Margarethe: 1920
David, Jakob Julius
Deutsch, Helene: 1918–1919
Dirsztay, Viktor von: 1909, 1917–1920
Doolittle, Hilda: 1933–1934
Dorsey, John: 1935–1936
Dubovitz, Margit: 1920
Eckstein, Emma: 1895–1904

Eder, David: 1913
Eim, Gustav: 1893
Eitingon, Max: 1909
Fellner, Oscar: 1895–1900
Ferenczi, Sándor: 1914–1916
Ferstel, Baronne Marie von (née Thorsch): 1899–1903
Fischer-Colbrie, Arthur: 1915–1916
Flournoy, Henri: 1922
Forsyth, David: 1920
Forzano, Concetta: 1933, consultation
Freud, Anna: 1918–1921, 1924–1929
Freund, Anton von: 1918–1919
Freund, Rózsi von (née Brody): 1915–1916
Frink, Horace W.: 1920–1921
Gattel, Felix: 1897–1898
Goetz, Bruno: 1905
Grinker, Roy: 1935–1936
Guggenbühl, Anna: 1921
Haller, Maggie: 1901–1912
Hartmann, Dora (née Karplus): 1920
Hartmann, Heinz: 1925
Hering, Julius: 1919
Hinkle-Moses, Beatrice: 1909
Hirschfeld, Elfriede: 1908
Hirst, Ada (née Hirsch): 1908
Hirst, Albert (né Hirsch): 1909
Hitschman, Eduard: 1907
Hoesch-Ernst, Lucy: 1913–1914
Hönig, Olga: 1897
Jeiteles, Adele: 1890
Jekels, Ludwig: 1905
Jokl, Robert Hans: 1919
Kann, Loe: 1912–1914
Kardiner, Abram: 1921
Karpas, Morris J.: 1909, a few sessions
Kosawa, Heisaku: 1932
Kremzir, Margit (née Weiss de Szurda): 1900, fourteen sessions
Kriser, Rudolf: 1916, 1917–1919
Lampl-De Groot, Jeanne (née De Groot): 1922–1925, 1931
Landauer, Karl: 1912
Lanzer, Ernst ("Rat Man" case): 1907–1908
Lehrman, Phillip: 1928–1929

Levy, Kata (née Toszegh): 1918
Lieben, Baronne Anna von: 1887
Liebman, Carl: 1925–1930
Mahler, Gustav: 1908, four hours
McCord, Clinton: 1929
Meyer, Monroe: 1921
Money-Kyrie, Roger: 1922–1924
Moser, Fanny (née Sulzer-Wart) ("Emmy von N." case): 1889–1890
Myreder, Karl: 1915, ten weeks
Nunberg, Margarethe (née Rie): 1918–1919
Oberhozer, Emil: 1913
Oberndorf, Clarence: 1921
Öhm, Aurelia (née Kronich) ("Khatarina" case): 1893
Palmstierna, Vera (née Herzog): 1934
Palos, Elma: 1912
Pankejeff, Sergius (or Sergei) Constantinovitch ("Wolf Man" case): 1910–1914
Polon, Albert: 1921
Powers, Lillian Delger: 1924–1926
Putnam, James J.: 1911, six hours
Rank, Otto: 1924
Reik, Theodor: 1930
Revesz-Rado, Erszebet: 1918
Rickman, John: 1920–1922
Riviere, Joan: 1922–1926
Rosanes, Flora: 1896
Rosenfeld, Eva: 1929–1932
Sarasin, Philippe: 1923, two hours
Saussure, Raymond de: 1920
Schmideberg, Walter: 1935–1937
Schwarcz, Aranka: 1916, 1917, 1918
Silberstein, Pauline: 1891, consultation
Sokolnicka, Eugenie: 1913
Spitz, René A.: 1910–1911
Stekel, Wilhelm: 1900, a few weeks
Stern, Adolf: 1919
Strachey, Alix: 1920
Strachey, James: 1920
Swoboda, Hermann: 1900
Tansley, Arthur: 1922, 1923, 1924
Taylor, Scofield: 1921
Van der Leeuw, Jan: 1934
Van Emden, Jan: 1912

Family Tree

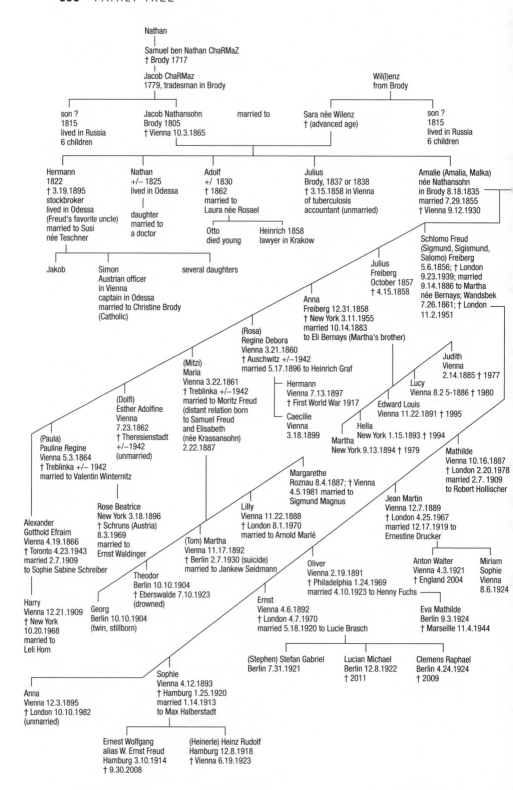

Nathan

Samuel ben Nathan ChaRMaZ
† Brody 1717

Jacob ChaRMaz
1779, tradesman in Brody

Wil(l)enz
from Brody

son ?
1815
lived in Russia
6 children

Jacob Nathansohn
Brody 1805
† Vienna 10.3.1865

married to

Sara née Wilenz
† (advanced age)

son ?
1815
lived in Russia
6 children

Hermann
1822
† 3.19.1895
stockbroker
lived in Odessa
(Freud's favorite uncle)
married to Susi
née Teschner

Nathan
+/− 1825
lived in Odessa

daughter
married to
a doctor

Adolf
+/ 1830
† 1862
married to
Laura née Rosael

Otto
died young

Heinrich 1858
lawyer in Krakow

Julius
Brody, 1837 or 1838
† 3.15.1858 in Vienna
of tuberculosis
accountant (unmarried)

Amalie (Amalia, Malka)
née Nathansohn
in Brody 8.18.1835
married 7.29.1855
† Vienna 9.12.1930

Jakob

Simon
Austrian officer
in Vienna
captain in Odessa
married to Christine Brody
(Catholic)

several daughters

Schlomo Freud
(Sigmund, Sigismund,
Salomo) Freiberg
5.6.1856; † London
9.23.1939; married
9.14.1886 to Martha
née Bernays; Wandsbek
7.26.1861; † London
11.2.1951

Julius
Freiberg
October 1857
† 4.15.1858

Anna
Freiberg 12.31.1858
† New York 3.11.1955
married 10.14.1883
to Eli Bernays (Martha's brother)

(Rosa)
Regine Debora
Vienna 3.21.1860
† Auschwitz +/−1942
married 5.17.1896 to Heinrich Graf

Judith
Vienna
2.14.1885 † 1977

Lucy
Vienna 8.2 5−1886 † 1980

Edward Louis
Vienna 11.22.1891 † 1995

(Mitzi)
Maria
Vienna 3.22.1861
† Treblinka +/−1942
married to Moritz Freud
(distant relation born
to Samuel Freud
and Elisabeth
(née Krassansohn)
2.22.1887

Hermann
Vienna 7.13.1897
† First World War 1917

Caecilie
Vienna
3.18.1899

Hella
New York 1.15.1893 † 1994

Martha
New York 9.13.1894 † 1979

Mathilde
Vienna 10.16.1887
† London 2.20.1978
married 2.7. 1909
to Robert Hollischer

(Dolfi)
Esther Adolfine
Vienna
7.23.1862
† Theresienstadt
+/−1942
(unmarried)

(Paula)
Pauline Regine
Vienna 5.3.1864
† Treblinka +/− 1942
married to Valentin Winternitz

Margarethe
Roznau 8.4.1887; † Vienna
4.5.1981 married to
Sigmund Magnus

Lilly
Vienna 11.22.1888
† London 8.1.1970
married to Arnold Marlé

Jean Martin
Vienna 12.7.1889
† London 4.25.1967
married 12.17.1919 to
Ernestine Drucker

Alexander
Gotthold Efraim
Vienna 4.19.1866
† Toronto 4.23.1943
married 2.7.1909
to Sophie Sabine Schreiber

Rose Beatrice
New York 3.18.1896
† Schruns (Austria)
8.3.1969
married to
Ernst Waldinger

(Tom) Martha
Vienna 11.17.1892
† Berlin 2.7.1930 (suicide)
married to Jankew Seidmann

Oliver
Vienna 2.19.1891
† Philadelphia 1.24.1969
married 4.10.1923 to Henny Fuchs

Anton Walter
Vienna 4.3.1921
† England 2004

Miriam
Sophie
Vienna
8.6.1924

Harry
Vienna 12.21.1909
† New York
10.20.1968
married to
Leli Horn

Theodor
Berlin 10.10.1904
† Eberswalde 7.10.1923
(drowned)

Georg
Berlin 10.10.1904
(twin, stillborn)

Ernst
Vienna 4.6.1892
† London 4.7.1970
married 5.18.1920 to Lucie Brasch

Eva Mathilde
Berlin 9.3.1924
† Marseille 11.4.1944

(Stephen) Stefan Gabriel
Berlin 7.31.1921

Lucian Michael
Berlin 12.8.1922
† 2011

Clemens Raphael
Berlin 4.24.1924
† 2009

Anna
Vienna 12.3.1895
† London 10.10.1982
(unmarried)

Sophie
Vienna 4.12.1893
† Hamburg 1.25.1920
married 1.14.1913
to Max Halberstadt

Ernest Wolfgang
alias W. Ernst Freud
Hamburg 3.10.1914
† 9.30.2008

(Heinerle) Heinz Rudolf
Hamburg 12.8.1918
† Vienna 6.19.1923

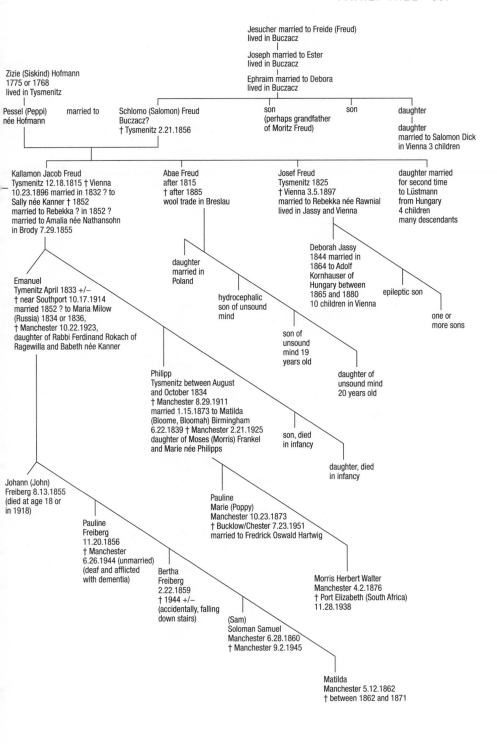

Jesucher married to Freide (Freud)
lived in Buczacz

Joseph married to Ester
lived in Buczacz

Ephraim married to Debora
lived in Buczacz

Zizie (Siskind) Hofmann
1775 or 1768
lived in Tysmenitz

Pessel (Peppi)
née Hofmann

married to

Schlomo (Salomon) Freud
Buczacz?
† Tysmenitz 2.21.1856

son
(perhaps grandfather
of Moritz Freud)

son

daughter

daughter
married to Salomon Dick
in Vienna 3 children

Kallamon Jacob Freud
Tysmenitz 12.18.1815 † Vienna
10.23.1896 married in 1832 ? to
Sally née Kanner † 1852
married to Rebekka ? in 1852 ?
married to Amalia née Nathansohn
in Brody 7.29.1855

Abae Freud
after 1815
† after 1885
wool trade in Breslau

Josef Freud
Tysmenitz 1825
† Vienna 3.5.1897
married to Rebekka née Rawnial
lived in Jassy and Vienna

daughter married
for second time
to Lüstmann
from Hungary
4 children
many descendants

Emanuel
Tymenitz April 1833 +/−
† near Southport 10.17.1914
married 1852 ? to Maria Milow
(Russia) 1834 or 1836,
† Manchester 10.22.1923,
daughter of Rabbi Ferdinand Rokach of
Ragewilla and Babeth née Kanner

daughter
married in
Poland

hydrocephalic
son of unsound
mind

Deborah Jassy
1844 married in
1864 to Adolf
Kornhauser of
Hungary between
1865 and 1880
10 children in Vienna

epileptic son

one or
more sons

son of
unsound
mind 19
years old

daughter of
unsound mind
20 years old

Philipp
Tysmenitz between August
and October 1834
† Manchester 8.29.1911
married 1.15.1873 to Matilda
(Bloome, Bloomah) Birmingham
6.22.1839 † Manchester 2.21.1925
daughter of Moses (Morris) Frankel
and Marie née Philipps

son, died
in infancy

daughter, died
in infancy

Johann (John)
Freiberg 8.13.1855
(died at age 18 or
in 1918)

Pauline
Freiberg
11.20.1856
† Manchester
6.26.1944 (unmarried)
(deaf and afflicted
with dementia)

Bertha
Freiberg
2.22.1859
† 1944 +/−
(accidentally, falling
down stairs)

Pauline
Marie (Poppy)
Manchester 10.23.1873
† Bucklow/Chester 7.23.1951
married to Fredrick Oswald Hartwig

Morris Herbert Walter
Manchester 4.2.1876
† Port Elizabeth (South Africa)
11.28.1938

(Sam)
Soloman Samuel
Manchester 6.28.1860
† Manchester 9.2.1945

Matilda
Manchester 5.12.1862
† between 1862 and 1871

Acknowledgments

I thank Anthony Ballenato, who did a great deal of research in English on the Internet for this book, and who accompanied me to London and to the Library of Congress in Washington, DC.

Thanks to Olivier Mannoni, a translator of Freud's works, who enlightened me on many occasions. I thank Isabelle Mons, a Germanist and a biographer of Lou Andreas-Salomé, for her help. And also Christian Sommet, who helped me analyze a text by Martin Heidegger on Freud and psychoanalysis.

Thanks to Lisa Appignanesi, Dany Nobus, and the whole team at the Freud Museum of London, who welcomed me warmly; to John Forrester, a professor of history and philosophy at Cambridge, a distinguished connoisseur of Freud's works and of the relations between Freud and Minna Bernays; to Julia Borossa, the director of the program in psychoanalysis at Middlesex University; and to Eric Willis, who received me at the Golders Green crematorium in London.

Thanks to Inge Scholz-Strasser and Daniela Finzi for welcoming me at the Freud Museum in Vienna.

I thank Margaret McAleer, the head curator of the Manuscript Department at the Library of Congress; she was of great help in my research. I also thank Anton O. Kris, director of the Sigmund Freud Archives (SFA), who evoked his memories for me, and François Delattre, ambassador of France to the United States, who received me warmly. I owe a debt of gratitude to Catherine Albertini, cultural attaché at the French embassy in the United States, for her support and her enthusiasm. And I am not forgetting the help provided by Jean-Louis Desmeure.

I thank Maurizio Serra, a diplomat and biographer of Italo Svevo, who through a lengthy and fascinating exchange of letters helped me gain a good understanding of the relations between Edoardo Weiss, Giovacchino Forzano, and Bruno Veneziani.

I also thank Carlo Bonomi for his knowledge of Freud's relation to pediatrics and for all that he contributed on the question of early childhood trauma. Guido Liebermann, a historian of psychoanalysis in Palestine, brought me decisive testimony on Max Eitingon's life. I owe a great deal to Patrick Mahony and to our exchanges over two decades. I thank Henri Rey-Flaud, who was present throughout the drafting of this book. I shall not forget my debt toward Carl Schorske and Jacques Le Rider.

Thanks to Gilles Pecout, who welcomed my seminar on the history of psychoanalysis into the History Department of the École normale supérieure. And thanks to all the faithful attendees who have followed this seminar for more than twenty years. Thanks to Luc Fachetti for his patience, and to Jean-Claude Baillieul for the scrupulousness of his corrections. I am not forgetting the support I have had for so many years from André Gueslin in the History Department of the University of Paris VII-Diderot.

Warm thanks go to Olivier Bétourné, who edited and corrected this book as it was originally published in France with talent and enthusiasm.

Finally, for making this English-language edition possible, I thank acquiring editor Sharmila Sen and the production team at Harvard University Press, and most especially Catherine Porter for her elegant translation.

Index